ATHLONE
1900-1923
POLITICS,
REVOLUTION &
CIVIL WAR
JOHN BURKE

The History Press Ireland

First published 2015

The History Press Ireland
50 City Quay
Dublin 2
Ireland
www.thehistorypress.ie

British Library Cataloguing in Publication Data.
A catalogue record for this book is available from the British Library.

ISBN 978 1 84588 859 6

Typesetting and origination by The History Press

Contents

Acknowledgments

Detailed studies such as this always require an author to enlist the help of others. In the first instance I would like to thank Dr Mary Harris (NUIG) for her professionalism and knowledge during the Ph.D process that inspired this publication. Thanks also to Tadhg Carey, editor of the *Westmeath Independent*, for allowing me access to the newspaper's unique records. Dr Harman Murtagh selflessly agreed to read an early draft of the text; his encouraging words helped with the push towards publication. Gearoid O'Brien, Executive Librarian at the AHL, was, as ever, exceptionally generous with his time, sources and knowledge – I doubt I'll ever be able to repay him. I am similarly indebted in so many ways to my long-time mentor and friend, Dr Patrick Murray. To have a scholar of his stature on your side is a gift that not many people are lucky enough to experience. This book would not be what it is without his considered critiques and suggestions, all of which improved the text immeasurably.

Penultimate thanks have to go to my family, who supported my efforts every step of the way, not just in this project, but in all my endeavours. Finally, to my darling wife Clair, my inspiration in so many ways, this is dedicated to you.

List of Abbreviations

AC: Anglo Celt

ACS: *An Claidheamh Soluis*

AP (S.ed.): *An Phoblacht* (Scottish edition)

AFIL: All for Ireland League

AG: Adjutant General

AHL: Aidan Heavey Library

AtÓ: *An tÓglách*

AOF: Ancient Order of Foresters

AOH: Ancient Order of Hibernians

APW: Athlone Printing Works

AT: *Athlone Times*

ATC: Athlone Trades Council

AWM: Athlone Woollen Mills

BMHWS: Bureau of Military History Witness Statement

CI: County Inspector

CDB: Congested Districts Board

CMA: Competent Military Authority

CT: *Connacht Tribune*

DÉ: Dáil Éireann

DI: District Inspector

DELG: Department of Environment and Local Government

DORA: Defence of the Realm Act

FÉ: Fianna Éireann

FJ: *Freeman's Journal*

GAA: Gaelic Athletic Association

GL: Gaelic League

GSWR: Great South Western Railway

HC: Head Constable

HJ: *Hibernian Journal*

IA: *Iris an Airm*

IB: *Irish Bulletin*

ICA: Irish Citizen Army

IF: *Irish Freedom*

IG: Inspector General

II: *Irish Independent*

IN: *Irish Nation*

INF: Irish National Foresters

INL: Irish National League

INV: Irish National Volunteers

IP: *Irish People*

IPP: Irish Parliamentary Party

IRA: Irish Republican Army

IRB: Irish Republican Brotherhood

IT: *The Irish Times*

ITGWU: Irish Transport and General Workers' Union

IV: Irish Volunteers

JP: Justice of the Peace

LGB: Local Government Board

LO: *Leitrim Observer*

MC: *Meath Chronicle*

MG: *Manchester Guardian*

MGWR: Midland Great Western Railway

MOR: Military Operations Report

MP: Member of Parliament

MRWN: *Midland Reporter and Westmeath Nationalist*

MVF: Midland Volunteer Force

NAI: National Archives of Ireland

NG: *Nenagh Guardian*

NLI: National Library of Ireland

NUR: National Union of Railwaymen

NYT: *The New York Times*

OO: Orange Order

OC: Officer in Command

PhÉWN: *Poblacht na hÉireann – War News*

PLG: Poor Law Guardians

PRONI: Public Records Office of Northern Ireland

RWB: Republican War Bulletin

RDC: Rural District Council

RH: *Roscommon Herald*

RIC: Royal Irish Constabulary

RJ: *Roscommon Journal*

RM: Resident Magistrate

RM: *Roscommon Messenger*

ROIA: Restoration of Order in Ireland Act

SF: Sinn Féin

SF: *Sinn Féin* newspaper

TD: Teachta Dála

TF: *The Fenian*

TIP: *The Irish Peasant*

TIW: *The Irish Worker*

TI: *The Irishman*

TL: *The Leader*

TLA: Trade and Labour Association

TP: *The Peasant*

TVL: *The Voice of Labour*

TTL: Town Tenants' League

TW: *The Watchword*

UCDA: University College Dublin Archives

UDC: Urban District Council

UI: *United Irishman*

UIL: United Irish League

USA: United States of America

UVF: Ulster Volunteer Force

WE: *Westmeath Examiner*

WG: *Westmeath Guardian*

WI: *Westmeath Independent*

Introduction

Athlone, 1900-23:
Politics, Revolution and Civil War

It is probable that the political realities that confronted the people of Athlone in the autumn of 1923 were far removed from those they would have envisaged, or perhaps hoped for, in 1900. Relatively comfortable resting within the British Empire at the start of the century, most locals certainly saw the appeal of Home Rule but appeared content to direct their political grievances at Irish MPs who, in turn, engaged with the British parliament in London. Just over twenty years later, Athlone's citizens were instead looking to Irish TDs for assistance with their difficulties, representatives who answered to an Irish parliament in Dublin. The intervening two decades had seen a remarkable ideological realignment in Irish politics, realignment that was itself influenced by a concatenation of events at local, national and international levels. While Athlone's experience of the events that precipitated the redefinition in Ireland's political status reflected much of what was seen across the country, the townspeople undoubtedly witnessed unique occurrences and encountered distinctive personalities that ensured a singular experience of the period.

To provide a more comprehensive and representative account of the complicated transition, I decided at an early stage that a thorough investigation of the often neglected first decade of the twentieth century had to be completed. Understandably, many historians begin their studies with the impressive Irish Parliamentary Party (IPP) election results in 1910, or the move towards a Home Rule Bill in 1912, points in history at which Irish constitutional nationalism was perhaps at its zenith. By engaging in a study of the ensuing decade they can then chart the fall of the IPP after the 1916 Easter Rising to its nadir in the 1918 general election, while concomitantly assessing the rise to supremacy of advanced nationalism, most prominently through a study of Sinn Féin (SF) and the Irish

Volunteers (IV)/Irish Republican Army (IRA). This shorter time frame, though attractive to both historians and publishers, can however mislead the casual history reader; too often generalisations creep in, important facts are omitted and history and historiography come into conflict. A study encompassing a longer time span allows for a more reliable graph of political evolution to be drawn up, one that can assist the reader to achieve a better understanding of the background to Irish nationalism in the early twentieth century. In covering the longer time span, this book is also intended to provide a comprehensive account of the evolution of the various forms of nationalism in Athlone: constitutional, advanced and cultural.

A comprehensive study of a border town such as Athlone will always require the author to stray outside the urban boundaries. This study not only provides a representative assessment of the development of nationalism in the town, but also that of the surrounding regions of south Westmeath and south Roscommon, two areas which, in common with much of the midlands (Longford excluded), have received little academic attention during the period under study. Professional historians have generally viewed the midlands as 'inactive' during this period, less interesting for a historiographical work than more volatile regions like Cork or Dublin. However, inactivity, while seldom drawing the eye of the controversy-hungry researcher or those in search of a gripping story, is quite often more representative of political developments in many regions as it characterises the experience of the majority, people whose life experiences should never be deemed less valid due to the absence of political controversy or gunshots. Unfortunately, providing the impression that an area was inactive can also dissuade researchers from engaging in the work necessary to test that assertion; as this study will show, an in-depth exploration of an 'inactive' region can unearth quite a few surprises.

During the ten years from 2012 to 2022, the 'Decade of Centenaries', it is certain that many new studies will emerge on this period in Irish history. Undoubtedly numbered among these will be numerous revisionist works, yet again reanalysing the topics that constitute much of the 'popular history' encountered so regularly. It is to be hoped that amongst them too will be numerous comprehensively researched academic works on the experience of the period in regions hitherto neglected. Such studies would allow for the reliable identification of regional contrasts and provide better context for the manifestation of national history at local level. The aggregation of many such works would greatly influence some commonly held and often misleading generalisations by identifying undue extrapolation, allowing for the introduc- tion of localised idiosyncrasies into the national story and ensuring that local experiences find greater purchase in the historiography of the nation.

For the purposes of this study on Athlone, a chronological approach was adopted, one that was further refined thematically over seven chapters. The first two chapters deal ostensibly with the same time period, 1900-1912, with chapter 2 straying briefly into 1913. Chapter 1 discusses the development of constitutional nationalism in Athlone by looking at the efforts and travails of the town's constitutional Nationalist bodies, most important among them the United Irish League (UIL). It also assesses the work of the region's parliamentary representatives, as well as support for, and reaction to, bills and acts formulated and passed at Westminster. The second chapter analyses the work and success of Athlone's cultural nationalists in the Gaelic League (GL), advanced nationalists in Athlone's early SF branch, with the Ancient Order of Hibernians (AOH), the IPP-linked Roman Catholic benefit society, concluding the chapter. Chapter 3 looks at developments in connection with the quest for Home Rule legislation from 1912 to 1914, detailing the support for the measure in Athlone, the opposition to it from unionists and the formation of the Midland Volunteer Force (MVF), a precursor to the IV and the local answer to the creation of a militant unionist anti-Home Rule volunteer force. After a discussion of the early stages of IV development in Athlone, the effect that the commencement of the Great War had on the Athlone's volunteer corps is discussed. The fourth of the seven chapters first examines the consequences that the start of the Great War had on support for British Army recruitment, the local economy and Athlone's social and political life. It then moves towards the 1916 Easter Rising, assessing what happened in the Athlone region during the rebellion, discussing the effect that the British reaction had in changing locals' perception of the rebels, and finishes by analysing their coincident reassessment of the IPP as the party best positioned to represent their views.

The remaining three chapters then recount and analyse the politics and military conflict that eventually led to the creation of the Irish Free State. Chapter 5 embarks upon a study of the move of the Athlone electorate to SF during the period 1917 to 1918 with a brief exploration of the by-elections in the constituencies of North Roscommon and South Longford, as well as an analysis of SF's efforts to implement a land policy. A detailed discussion of the consequences of British attempts to introduce conscription into Ireland is then presented, using the endeavours of local MPs, political parties and activists to flesh out the reaction of the local electorate, before embarking on a detailed analysis of the 1918 general election. The penultimate chapter details the local experience of the War of Independence during the period 1919-21, and assesses the contribution to the republican cause made by militants in the Athlone region, as well as the reaction of the British Crown forces. It also measures the success of the republican court system, along with the electoral fortunes of the various parties during the 1920 local authority elections. The chapter concludes with the implementation of the truce between republicans and the British Government in the summer of 1921, from where chapter 7 takes over the analysis of the post-truce period before embarking upon a detailed assessment of the move towards civil war in the locality, the war itself, the general elections that were staged and the eventual declaration of a cessation by the defeated republicans in the summer of 1923.

The political history of Athlone prior to the study period has already been summarised in the author's previous publication, *Athlone in the Victorian Era* (2007).[1] However, a restatement of some of the facts contained therein, allied with a degree of political scene-setting, will assist in ensuring that the political situation as it pertained in 1900 is placed in context.

By any standard in Irish political history, the changes witnessed in the country during the late nineteenth-century were momentous. The successful efforts of the IPP, under Charles Stewart Parnell, to force a number of concessions from the British on the issue of land ownership provided the party with much of the confidence needed to move its focus to the far larger issue of Irish Home Rule. The defeat of the two separate Home Rule Bills in 1886 and 1893 were serious blows to Irish political aspirations, yet it was not their failure alone that led Irish constitutional nationalism into a political mire. The period between the two bills had seen the emergence of controversial revelations about Parnell's affair with Katherine O'Shea, revelations that greatly compromised both his political authority and physical health. Parnell's death in 1891 saw the IPP fragment into a number of competing factions whose obsession with jostling for position within their own party was to ensure that the party's approach to the pursuance of Irish autonomy was undermined by disunity.

In Athlone it was certain, both before and after his death, that the bulk of the townspeople supported Parnell and his drive for Home Rule, yet the political controversy that surrounded his affair, his death and the consequent fragmentation of the IPP ensured that nationalist grass-roots activity in the locality fell precipitously. The town's branch of the Parnellite Irish National League (INL), though never particularly active, became moribund, while the competing Irish National Federation (INF) branch never achieved the foothold its organisers would have desired. The polarisation of constitutional nationalist debate in the country fed into the selection of Irish MPs, with the results for the two local constituencies of South Westmeath and South

Roscommon in the 1892 general election illustrating how the infighting was seriously disrupting Irish nationalist unity. A split in the Parnellite Nationalist vote in South Westmeath ensured that the anti-Parnellite MP Donal Sullivan won the contest and remained as incumbent in 1900. The constituency of South Roscommon remained loyal to Parnell, electing Luke Hayden in 1892 and subsequently replacing him with his brother John Patrick in 1897, after Luke's premature death.

The fact that the east and west sides of Athlone were located in different parliamentary constituencies also assisted little in promoting nationalist unity in the town, the MPs' own allegiances notwithstanding. The implementation of the 1898 Local Government Act had ensured that all of 'Athlone Urban' was located in County Westmeath, yet it was to be seen repeatedly that the Act itself did little to change the age-old perception of the River Shannon marking a definitive boundary between the town's two sides. This lack of electoral consistency was to confuse many on the newly expanded register, and, as will be seen, presented additional difficulties in organising Athlone's politically minded individuals into a cohesive group.

Such obvious disunity and confusion was detrimental to the causes of promoting Irish political unity and seeking Irish political autonomy. It was in this uncertain atmosphere that Athlone's inhabitants were to move forward into the new century.

Athlone, the United Irish League and Parliamentary Politics

After the reunification of the Irish Parliamentary Party under John Redmond, Ireland's constitutional nationalists focused their efforts on concerns outside the party. Though Home Rule was its overriding goal, the issue of land distribution and property ownership, the 'surrogate for nationalism',[1] preoccupied the IPP for the first decade of the twentieth-century. In the case of Athlone, and other provincial Irish towns, there were both urban and rural aspects to the issue. The substantial number of lease-holding urbanites wanted fairer tenancy arrangements, while land purchase preoccupied most rural tenant farmers whose acres bordered the town, and whose produce supplied its markets. Both groups relied primarily on the IPP's grass-roots organisation, the United Irish League (UIL), to progress their claims, yet, in Athlone, tensions were to arise as both the league and IPP concentrated on rural issues. Such tensions could not but impact on the support for constitutional nationalism in the town, with factors such as the efforts of individual activists, local MPs and the effect of new legislative changes all influencing the relationship between Athlone's populace and constitutional nationalist organisations.

As already noted, the issue of property ownership in Ireland had both urban and rural resonances. In towns such as Athlone, urban tenants' rights were greatly attenuated by existing legislation, which provided landlords with much freedom in rental agreements. Tenants had no guarantee of tenure, no say in rent increases or power of compulsion over landlords with regard to maintenance or upgrading of properties and, given their fiscal situation, no real hope of purchasing their dwellings. The issue of providing suitable housing for local labourers was a contentious topic in the late nineteenth and early twentieth centuries and while there had been an improvement in the quality of some dwellings, it was still recognised that the deficiencies were such that they handicapped the economic development of the town and its people.[2] The nineteenth-century Land League's aversion to dealing with disaffected urban dwellers had really set the tone; politicians concentrated on the pursuit of rural land redistribution as it offered greater political benefits.[3]

Outside Athlone's urban boundary, rural dwellers were dealing with a different basic problem: a minority of people, landlords and graziers, controlled the majority of the land. Tenant farmers in south Westmeath and south Roscommon were expected to eke out a living on plots whose economic viability was at best uncertain. The region around the town had not seen an appreciable fall in the proportion of large farms since the end of the Famine, when depopulation allowed landowners and large farmers to retain or consolidate their land holdings.[4] Small farmers were also frustrated in their efforts to enlarge their holdings by the existence of numerous part-time farmers. Census returns show that among the latter were auctioneers, grocers, magistrates, merchants, publicans, shopkeepers, blacksmiths and carpenters.[5] These men often leased lands from men such as Lord Castlemaine and Charles O'Donoghue, neither of whom appeared interested in selling any portion of their estates.[6] There was also a minority of small established landholders around Athlone who had, over a protracted period, purchased small tracts of land, thus becoming more extensive landowners. These men were considered even less likely to sell.[7] Existing land legislation brought in after the Land War of 1879-82 was deficient, Home Rule and internal conflict had preoccupied the IPP since then, and it was not until the establishment of the UIL in 1898 that an influential political body again made the land issue its main focus.

Formed in Mayo mainly through the work of former Irish Party member William O'Brien, the UIL provided much of the motivation that led to IPP reunification. While its work has often been, as Roy Foster puts it, 'written out' of history,[8] it is apparent that the league was to provide a forum for the nationalist grass roots in Athlone, as O'Brien sought to re-establish a direct link between the IPP and its supporters. The exceptional growth of the organisation was a cause of some concern for the IPP which initiated, as Patrick Maume has noted, 'a process of reunification among MPs, led from above, to counter the UIL threat … from below'.[9] By June 1900 the IPP had agreed to adopt the UIL as its official grass roots organisation, and set about re-establishing a large, unified nationalist political force in Ireland.[10]

However, unsurprisingly, the adoption of the UIL was not a smooth process, even after the official endorsement. The success of the newly unified group in Athlone was to hinge on number of factors, one of the most important being the support provided by the two local MPs. Both were IPP members, though they worked for different factions during the IPP split and had contrasting opinions on the league. The South Roscommon MP was Parnellite John Patrick Hayden, who had gained the seat after the death of his brother Luke in 1897.[11] His South Westmeath counterpart was anti-Parnellite Donal Sullivan, IPP joint secretary, who had first gained his seat in 1885, retaining it in 1892 running on an INF ticket.[12] Like his brothers, A.M. and T.D. Sullivan (both also former MPs), he was a religious man whose election victories were often ascribed to support he gained from the Roman Catholic clergy.[13]

Hayden was supportive of the league from the start. Roscommon had forty-seven branches[14] by the time of the June 1900 adoption, with the land problems in the county (primarily in the densely populated north, where the Congested Districts Board (CBD) operated) ensuring that the UIL found ample support.[15] Hayden met with O'Brien early to convey his support and his backing ensured that other prominent local nationalists followed suit.[16]

In south Westmeath the situation was somewhat different. It was noted by the Royal Irish Constabulary (RIC) County Inspector (CI) in March 1900 that most 'held aloof in a very marked way from the league' with the number of branches bearing testament to that; just ten.[17] UIL organiser James Lynam attempted to establish branches in the region after unification, with Moate, Ballinahown, Drumraney and Mountemple targeted in July and the possibility of an Athlone branch first mentioned in August.[18] Lynam's efforts, and those of local league enthusiasts, saw the number of branches grow to twenty-six by the end of 1900,[19] with the vast majority founded in November and December after a divisive debate on the selection of the South Westmeath IPP general election candidate had been resolved.

The main source of the division amongst south Westmeath nationalists centred on the loyalties of Donal Sullivan. Sullivan's association with the INF, whose founder, Timothy Healy, was a harsh critic of the UIL,[20] was highlighted as an indication of antipathy towards the new nationalist movement. Additionally, Healy's marriage to Sullivan's niece was used against the South Westmeath MP, a man the O'Brienite *Irish People* described as 'faithful to monopoly'.[21] Admittedly, Sullivan's response to the league had not been positive; he had avoided the National Convention and stated that his involvement with the league required the direction of 'the priests and people of South Westmeath',[22] who, in the case of the clergy at any rate, had not provided much support either locally or nationally by this point.[23] Lynam disliked Sullivan's standpoint and publicly questioned the MP's suitability. However, momentum behind a drive to pressurise Sullivan was dealt a blow when influential local landowner and UIL supporter Charles O'Donoghue (who had contested the South Westmeath seat in 1892 against Sullivan[24]) stated that he would ensure no one was hounded out of his position on the basis of inferences drawn from familial ties.[25]

John Redmond, the IPP leader, was also drawn into the controversy. The Mullingar Rural District Council (RDC) had complained to him about Sullivan (despite not being in his constituency), and Redmond, in reply to a letter written by O'Donoghue to the *Freeman's Journal*,[26] stated that he was not a party to any efforts to oust Sullivan; indeed, he rebutted the charge that a meeting had been held to plan for doing just that. He admitted that Sullivan had been a critic of his for nearly a decade but stated that it would be almost 'criminal' if the IPP orchestrated attempts to get 'between him and his constituents with the object of getting him deprived of his Parliamentary seat'. Redmond additionally noted that the UIL did not engage the services of paid organisers for the purpose of 'fomenting trouble and disorder, organising opposition to harmless and useful Irish members'.[27] O'Donoghue, for his part, thanked Redmond for the clarification, though he iterated that he and others in the constituency were still not convinced that 'wire-pulling' was entirely absent.[28]

O'Donoghue's support did not arrest efforts to oust Sullivan. Both he and William Smith (managing director of the Athlone Woollen Mills (AWM), Athlone's largest private employer) were proposed as alternatives, but upon being informed of the proposition, O'Donoghue reiterated that he would not

Donal Sullivan MP. (*WI*, 9 March 1907)   J.P. Hayden MP. (Leo Daly, *Titles*)

contribute to a split in the party ranks and would neither stand, nor encourage others to do so.[29] The *Westmeath Independent* noted how the situation appeared to bear out one of the problems the UIL encountered nationally: 'The apprehension … is that the league may be worked for unworthy motives, and as a means of wreaking vengeance on those who do not see eye-to-eye with its founder.'[30]

The south Westmeath convention in Moate in the first week in October saw Lynam propose that Sullivan be replaced. The ensuing debate heard the incumbent restate his faith in the people and clergy of his constituency, who were even less inclined to support the UIL when their candidate was being victimised. In an attempt to dispel the notion that he was anti-UIL, Sullivan stated that he did not attend the National Convention due to his 'honest poverty'.[31] Support from a number of Athlone men, such as the prominent Protestant businessman Thomas Chapman (Dublin-born managing director of the Athlone Printing Works and *Westmeath Independent* owner), the Roman Catholic Administrator of St Mary's parish, Revd Dr D. Langan, and William Smith, assisted in seeing him returned, more aware now that a closer relationship with the UIL was a necessity for a man in his position.[32] The 'former apathy and indecision borne of internecine strife' was dispelled, according to the local press.[33] Nationalist energies were now free to focus on the creation of new league branches.

With the Sullivan debate resolved, nationalists in Athlone looked to establish a local UIL branch, assured that they would not be working against one of the local representatives. A foundation meeting was held on 12 November with J.P. Hayden and E. Haviland Burke MPs in attendance, along with UIL organiser R.A. Corr. Charles O'Donoghue chaired and was elected president with, significantly, given the local clergy's hitherto poor support, the Roman Catholic Dean of Elphin, J.J. Kelly, elected as vice-president.[34] Other committee positions were occupied by Thomas Chapman, as well as a number of former, current and future urban district councillors.[35] The *Irish People* spoke optimistically of the foundation, stating that the meeting was redolent of 'the days when Athlone stood to a man under the banner of the Land League'.[36] The organisers emphasised that the establishment of a branch would feed into national moves to reunite Irish nationalists, and though they highlighted the needs of labourers and urban tenants, nationalist duty, rather than social or economic issues, was the most compelling argument presented to would-be members.[37]

Despite the auspicious start, the branch quickly withered away. Just two meetings,[38] which discussed urban grumbles (such as fixity of tenure, fair rents and reasonable complaint mechanisms) and party unity (some were still unsure of Sullivan's loyalties) were held after that of 12 November and while Dean Kelly promoted the league in neighbouring districts and four members travelled to the inaugural meeting of the South Westmeath UIL Executive in December,[39] the inability of John Redmond to attend a rally in Athlone in January 1901 impeded promotional efforts.[40] By April, a meeting of the local executive noted general apathy in the region and heard that '... the Athlone people seem to have done nothing at all ... and have displayed no interest ... in the National Movement'.[41] The local press offered a similar, if more qualified remark: '... as far as the *general* [my italics] body of nationalists [in Athlone] are concerned ... it seems next to impossible [to] make them recognise their obligations'.[42]

Local apathy with regard to the UIL was not to be lifted in the short term as reports on the 'desolate county of Westmeath['s] ... fertile wasted acres' did little to motivate the urban members.[43] RIC reports cited factors such as good crop prices locally, a lack of support from the clergy – Dean Kelly excepted – emigration and numerous 'worries other than politics', as contributing to the indifference to the league.[44] Other problems encountered included the perception that the UIL (whose relationship with the IPP was still not well defined), like the earlier Land League, appeared dedicated to the land struggle; that it was a rural organisation, uninterested in urban complaints, despite UIL protestations and some historiographical evidence to the contrary.[45] Additionally, reports from Roscommon detailing volatile encounters between members and landowners may have dissuaded timid nationalists from engaging with the organisation,[46] even though it was known that its leadership espoused passive resistance or 'moral force'.[47]

The latter half of 1901 saw the apathy begin to lift around Athlone, if not in the town itself. Charles O'Donoghue in his numerous chairmanships[48] espoused the idea that land was for the people, even though this stance required that he would have to divide up his own extensive landholdings.[49] The *Westmeath Independent* spoke favourably of the move towards 'national agitation' and noted that 'Westmeath is waking up'.[50] Donal Sullivan joined the Ballinahown branch of the UIL, the presence of Canon Columb on the committee easing his fears on the lack of clerical involvement.[51] Nationally the organisation was described as 'decidedly active' in providing a more structured approach to the land issue.[52] Both Westmeath and Roscommon gained additional branches and witnessed concerted efforts by politicians to motivate people to adopt a virile approach to achieving land redistribution.[53] At a meeting in Mullingar in October, Athlone nationalists heard John Redmond speak of the aims of the IPP and, mindful of the poor urban participation, he also spelt out what the UIL intended to do for urban labourers and town tenants.[54] However, it appears that despite reports of much interest locally in

what Redmond had to say, there was no effort to hold a follow-up meeting in
Athlone to promote the cause, unlike other towns and villages in the region.[55]

Athlone's apathy aside, calls for an escalation in agitation were heeded in
neighbouring districts, and greater pressure was put on landowners to sell.
Practices such as boycotting and physical intimidation were introduced, as
were United Irish League Courts, giving the UIL, as Heather Laird has
put it, a 'de facto governmental role'.[56] Alarmed at the increase in agitation,
Conservative Irish Chief Secretary George Wyndham applied the 1887
Coercion Act (or Jubilee Coercion Act; it was introduced in the fiftieth year
of Queen Victoria's reign) to parts of the country in December. Despite this,
the Inspector General (IG) of the RIC, Neville Chamberlain, believed the
league in January 1902 to be 'stronger than it has ever been … and steadily
increasing its influence'.[57] Research has shown the IG's opinion was well
founded, as UIL branch numbers increased by 18 per cent from July 1901
to March 1902, boycotting rose by over one third in the six months to
March 1902 and the number of meetings held more than tripled.[58]

Despite growth in support in both Roscommon and Westmeath generally,[59]
the UIL continued to encounter indifference in Athlone. The local newspaper
editor, Limerick man Michael McDermott-Hayes, decried this, and, not for
the first or indeed last time, suggested that Athlone was just apathetic rather
than uninterested:

> The committee of the local branch ought to be called together … and
> the necessary arrangements made. Athlone is not out of harmony with
> the national movement, but it … suffers from an apathy which should
> be shaken off.[60]

Movement on reorganisation in local UIL circles did not, however, occur.
Even the arrest of J.P. Hayden for unlawful assembly amongst other charges,[61]
though apparently of great annoyance to local nationalists, elicited just tacit
support for a banquet to be held upon his release.[62]

Often it requires an event with more obvious local resonance to arouse
people's interest and the 1902 local authority elections appeared to do just
that. The elections were the first that the UIL targeted in an attempt to place
members in positions of authority, positions that would allow the UIL to not
only exert a direct influence on policies, but also reassert itself in the wake
of its adoption by the Irish Party.[63] The run up to polling day saw the UIL
expand its influence in Westmeath where, for local authority purposes, Athlone
was located in its entirety.[64] League candidates and their supporters canvassed

vigorously for their interests while actively opposing those from outside UIL ranks.[65] Chief Secretary Wyndham's first steps towards creating a new Irish land bill ensured additional interest in the elections, for if league members secured representation on County and District Councils, they could assist supporters when the time for applying Wyndham's scheme came.[66]

Despite reports of UIL infighting (in four cases both candidates for a seat were UIL members[67]) the league was successful in Westmeath. Members ousted Lord Greville[68] and Sir Walter Nugent (from a landed Catholic family[69]) from the council and elected Charles O'Donoghue as chairman.[70] Nationally, the UIL dominated many local government bodies; in Leinster the organisation took 57 per cent of the county council seats, while Connacht saw a return of 83 per cent.[71] The league could now use its representatives to strengthen the links between local government and Irish nationalism as a step towards '… vindication of its claim to be the national authority to which the Irish people owed allegiance'.[72]

In both Roscommon and Westmeath, the league became more active in land affairs, with the De Freyne estate in north Roscommon leading the way.[73] The dominance of the UIL on the Westmeath County Council meant that virtually all new appointments went to a 'Leaguer', who then favoured fellow members in the allocation of duties.[74] More frequently the CI's reports noted how a 'terrorising influence' or 'covert intimidation' had become widespread, with league meetings providing additional drive.[75] Both counties, along with fourteen others, were proclaimed under the Crimes Act: Roscommon in March 1902 and, seven months later, Westmeath. Additional RIC men were allocated, angering the ratepayers who had to cover half the cost of supporting them.[76] The South Westmeath UIL Executive complained about the coercive tactics and passed a resolution asking Donal Sullivan to leave Parliament as a protest and divert his energies into 'perfecting the popular organisation in this constituency'.[77]

Late 1902 and early 1903 saw much debate on the proposed land bill published in the pages of the *Westmeath Independent*.[78] The rejection by the IPP of Wyndham's first draft saw the local newspaper describe the Chief Secretary as 'the most incompetent of English officials',[79] with the rejection leading Wyndham to establish a conciliatory Land Conference to deal with the problems more efficiently.[80] Generally well-received locally, the conference's report gained the support of the Athlone Urban District Council (UDC) and South Westmeath UIL Executive, while also drawing the ire of Donal Sullivan.[81] Out of the country at the time of its convening,[82] he condemned the conference, 'amazed' at some of its provisions, while being resigned '[to]

try and make the best out of a bad bargain'.[83] William O'Brien lambasted
Sullivan for promoting misconceptions about the report, stating that he
should be '… carefully distinguished from those … of high intelligence and
patriotic sincerity who are disappointed that the recommendations … are
not more sweeping'.[84] J.P. Hayden was also unsure about the report, though
observably more sanguine than Sullivan.[85]

The report was to inform rather than dictate the shape of the bill that
followed. Provisions for a better system of land purchase by small farmers were
proposed, yet still no compulsory purchases, the 'catchcry' of the UIL, and a
deal-breaker for landlords.[86] It was intended to use English capital to fund
purchases and guarantee farmers that future annuities would be between 10
and 40 per cent lower than existing rents. Landlords were given the incentive
of a 12 per cent bonus upon completion of a deal, as well as retention of their
own 'demesne farms', mortgaged to the Land Commission at an attractive
rate. The bill also targeted congested areas where agricultural viability was a
problem and the Land Commission was provided with additional powers to
improve and modernise farms in such districts.[87] Publication of the bill led to
additional IPP members airing their qualms, including the party's second in
command, John Dillon,[88] who saw much of this sort of 'constructive Unionism'
as 'a plot to weaken Home Rule sentiment'.[89] William O'Brien spent much
time clarifying aspects of the proposed legislation to ensure that misinformation (which did inform some downbeat early *Westmeath Independent* articles),
was countered.[90] As more information was released, McDermott-Hayes eventually stated that the Wyndham Bill 'embodies the essential provisions towards
the fashioning of a great Act'.[91] Soon after the IPP convention in April backed
the bill, the *Westmeath Independent* stated that rejection would make it appear
'we had practically taken leave of our senses'.[92]

The wave of support that was building led the UIL to send another
organiser to south Westmeath in June; J.A. O'Sullivan. He, along with
some local councillors, organised a branch foundation meeting in Athlone
at which Dean Kelly noted 'we are very much behind [in Athlone]'.
The meeting ended without agreement after hearing numerous speakers
offer their opinions on the UIL, with one of the more interesting queries
aired relating to whether Athlone's first branch had ever really existed.[93]
A lot of pushing from Thomas Chapman saw the establishment of a
Parliamentary Fund to support the unwaged Irish MPs at a subsequent
meeting during the same week, while the payment of the affiliation
fee of £6 saw the yet-to-be-established branch join the ranks of the
UIL Directory.[94]

O'Sullivan had a similar lack of success elsewhere in Westmeath. The CI equated the mood of the people to that experienced before the Land League agitation. They were biding their time, keeping their own counsel and assessing changes as they came without undue interference.[95] O'Sullivan repeatedly tried to organise an Athlone UIL branch and while there was support and indications of increased nationalist sentiment in the town,[96] the situation remained the same.[97] The *Irish People* decried the lack of urban organisation, unwisely using the very poorly received Town Tenants (Ireland) Bill as refutation to the 'silly shibboleth that the Irish Party's only … concern was for farmers'. It additionally highlighted the preponderance of 'flunkeys' (in this context, those loyal to the crown) in urban areas and noted it was difficult to get 'public opinion in a large town … into a cohesive movement'.[98] The *Westmeath Independent* highlighted the main factor behind O'Sullivan's failure; the Land Bill had very poor provisions for labourers and town tenants and it was manifestly obvious that the UIL was still not fighting for the needs of urbanites.[99]

The eventual passing of the 1903 Land Act (Wyndham Act), described by F.S.L. Lyons as 'probably the most momentous piece of social legislation since the Union' in August initially elicited mainly positive reviews, with some prominent exceptions.[100] The act was 'of a scale to match the needs of the situation it was designed to meet',[101] and a vast improvement on earlier acts.[102] Wyndham's efforts saw 'a truly massive transfer of property'[103] and assisted in the 'achievement of peasant proprietorship for over two-thirds of Irish tenants'[104] over the following decade.

With the act secured, Donal Sullivan, aware of nationalist complacency that might have followed as a consequence, wrote to Canon Columb of the Ballinahown UIL outlining the next objectives:

> … we have … just captured the breastworks of the enemy's citadel … We have the labourers' question, the town tenants' question, and the … education question … before we marshal our forces for the restoration of our national rights.[105]

Sullivan's fighting talk did little to stir local nationalists. In Athlone the continued inactivity greatly annoyed local clergyman Fr Michael Keane, whose letter to the *Westmeath Independent*, dated 15 October 1903, asked:

> Is it not the business of the UIL to look to the tenants' interests and show a little more proof of life than that given by an annual spurt,

followed by a collection, with no further signs of activity until the next annual wake up?[106]

His sentiments were echoed in the editorial, with McDermott-Hayes indicating that the recent Parliamentary Fund collection in Athlone which had received over £70 in just one week,[107] provided evidence of local support for the league. However, it appears that paying into the fund was seen by some as an offset against engaging in more demonstrative acts of nationalist support; the fee was paid so active participation was not necessary. Indeed, apart from seven men designated erroneously as 'St. Peters' branch representatives' at a UIL meeting at Curraghboy, situated to the north-west of the town, towards the end of October, there was no indication of life in the UIL in Athlone.[108] It is certain that the Land Act dealt the UIL a serious blow in the wider Athlone district, as the league's raison d'être of land redistribution, was largely addressed and its ability to find a new focus appeared in doubt.[109] Perhaps most indicative of the move away from the league was the collapse of the Moate and Tang UIL branches soon after the Land Act was enacted.[110] Both branches had been dominated by farmers, a group whose reason for political engagement was largely addressed by the provisions of the Act.

The malaise in Athlone nationalist political life continued and, indeed, was exacerbated by the perfunctory efforts of the IPP, which continued to ignore the difficulties experienced by townspeople. A proposed Labourers' Bill of 1904 was extremely poor, 'treacherous' according to the local press, and hardly a rallying call for UIL enrolment.[111] Even when the local UDC attempted to make use of the Wyndham Act to provide a small number of labourers' houses in Athlone, their misinterpretation of the provisions of the act led them to cancel the scheme, a move which so incensed William Smith of the AWM that he threatened to move his massive factory out of the town altogether.[112] Laurence Ginnell, UIL secretary, pointed out to John Redmond that urban tenants and labourers were being ignored by the party and that nothing was being done to show them, '… that the UIL is a National Organisation of which they can avail'.[113] Measures to address their difficulties were needed, a compelling reason to join the league had to be presented, and while some labourers did join, as Paul Bew has noted, they showed little 'passion or … enthusiasm'.[114]

Recognition of the continued problems in urban tenancy arrangements in Athlone did see some interested locals attempt a more proactive approach. Late 1903 and early 1904 saw efforts made to establish a Town Tenants' Association, yet, again, they were frustrated by local indifference.[115] The uninspiring Donal Sullivan held a number of unsuccessful meetings

Thomas Chapman. (AHL)

Michael McDermott-Hayes. (*WI*, 18 March 1966)

towards the end of September 1904 in an attempt to 'arouse' the nationalist spirit of the local populace[116] and head off the spread of an increasingly bitter North Westmeath dispute between J.P. Hayden and Laurence Ginnell, the neighbouring example of nationalist disagreement over the efficacy of the Wyndham Act.[117] Other proposals to rouse Athlone nationalists were made; most prominent among them was McDermott-Hayes' October call for the establishment of a UIL branch in the town, a call that again went unheeded.[118] The foundation of the Town Tenants' League (TTL), initially a subset of the UIL,[119] led to appeals for a local branch of that organisation to be established; however, this too made little headway. Eventually in November a Town Tenants' Committee was formed as a sub-committee of the local Trade and Labour Association (TLA), which was founded in March 1904.[120] It achieved so little that the local press questioned whether Athlone's tenants actually had any grievances.[121] It was apparent that Athlone's nationalists were in a rut of inactivity, with the spectacular failure of a rally in October highlighting not only local apathy, but also lack of interest among some IPP representatives; neither J.P. Hayden nor Michael Reddy (MP for King's County) showed up, despite being scheduled to so do. The small number of local UIL enthusiasts present passed resolutions in support of self-government, the Irish Party, John Redmond and, yet again, the formation of a local UIL branch.[122] Surprisingly however, after such a long line of false starts, this time the call to establish a branch was actually heeded.

Two weeks after the meeting, a UIL stand was set up outside St Peter's Roman Catholic church. Subscriptions were collected and members enrolled. The need for 'earnest and determined' men was highlighted in the *Westmeath Independent*; one 'phantom' branch was enough.[123] An editorial noted in a hopeful tone:

> Once the people of Athlone are aroused from the insipidity which somehow possessed them ... they will more than make up for lost time by taking their rightful place in the National struggle with all the force of renewed strength.[124]

The collection and membership drive were followed in late November by the establishment of a branch of the UIL for St Peter's Parish and district.[125] The committee saw Dean Kelly occupy the presidency, with UDC members taking committee positions. Due to parliamentary constituency boundaries, the branch did not cover the whole of the town, while the parochial mindset of those at the meeting made it obvious that many saw a definite division in Athlone: not only two parishes, but two dioceses, two counties and two provinces. Speakers such as Fr Michael Keane made it clear that they did not know how the UIL was to develop in Athlone as a whole and were unconcerned; their parish had a branch, so their duty was discharged.[126] McDermott-Hayes tried to impress on the members the role the UIL could play in helping local urban tenants, and the branch adopted resolutions demanding better terms for lessees along with a better labourers' bill, Home Rule and equality of education.[127]

The energy behind the St Peter's UIL branch fed into a second attempt to open a TTL branch in Athlone in January 1905.[128] Auspiciously, the general secretary of the TTL, J.M. Briscoe, visited the town and his efforts assisted in the creation of a committee. Familiar names, such as Michael McDermott-Hayes and Thomas Chapman, assumed positions alongside UDC members J.J. Coen and Denis Connell, neither of whom was an active supporter of local nationalist organisations. Their inclusion appeared to show their faith in the non-sectarian ethos of the TTL, and appeared to pave the way for tenants' problems to be resolved by a representative body that did not have the UIL's political baggage.[129] However, as with the first UIL branch, the auspicious start meant little and the Athlone TTL branch disappeared just five weeks later.[130] Whether the '... tension between the circumstances of its foundation ... and the ... desires of the organisation's leadership to represent all ... irrespective of their political allegiances',[131] was partially to blame in Athlone is unclear; what is apparent is that, yet again, apathy set in and interest waned. Indeed, such was

Athlone's lack of interest in the organisation that even when towns such as Sligo and Mullingar exhibited a less than enthusiastic approach, at least they were able to maintain a branch of the TTL for a protracted period.[132]

While the failure of the TTL appeared to reinforce Athlone's well-established inability to provide support for branches of nationalist organisations, the continued existence of St Peter's UIL gave some hope to those who hoped to reverse the trend. Additional optimism was fostered by the creation of a second UIL branch in Athlone in May 1905, as parishioners in St Mary's, not to be outdone by their western counterparts, formed their own committee. The move was prompted not only by the presence of the branch across the river but by both the ignominy of low Parliamentary Fund donations in the parish and a successful rally in April attended by TTL president William Field MP and J.P. Hayden.[133] The branch had the backing of local priests, as well as that of Thomas Chapman and urban and county councillors. The *Westmeath Independent* provided good coverage, promoted enrolment and, in an attempt to dispel the rural reputation of the league, highlighted how the branch 'embraces ... multiple interests'.[134] Discussions at branch meetings covered topics such as fundraising initiatives and inter-branch co-operation in Athlone, a matter on which there was no consensus.[135] The lack of unity was deplored in the local press, which noted that when funds were sent to Dublin after the 1905 collection, 'the largest ... since the memorable days of the Parnell split', both branches sent the cheques separately.[136]

Locally the UIL was finally taking hold, albeit not in an ideal fashion, while nationally it was restoring some of its post-Wyndham Act losses, as manipulation of the legislation and the slow progress of land purchase assisted in promoting the league's message.[137] Both Athlone branches raised funds and met frequently, but separately; indeed, in the case of St Peter's, the branch met fortnightly towards the end of the year.[138] St Mary's provided the first official Athlone UIL representation in four years at the quarterly South Westmeath UIL Executive meeting in July while St Peter's, tellingly, dealt with local rural land issues, most prominently the sale of the Mount William estate, a large holding on the western fringes of the town.[139]

The increased support for Irish nationalism in Athlone was also bolstered by developments in Westminster. The IPP emerged from the elections of December 1905 with eighty MPs, in a parliament that for the first time in twenty years had a Liberal majority.[140] That position led to greater optimism amongst nationalists, who believed that Irish political influence was strongest when Liberals were in power; the *Westmeath Independent* described the party as 'more or less our allies'.[141] Sullivan and Hayden were returned unopposed with the

Sir Walter Nugent MP. (NLI, *Irish Life*, 1 December 1916)

Laurence Ginnell MP. (NLI, *IL*, 14 March 1913)

increasingly prominent 53-year-old Laurence Ginnell elected MP after defeating Sir Walter Nugent for the North Westmeath IPP endorsement. The incumbent, Kennedy, had become 'a party in himself', and received little support.[142]

While the energy behind local nationalism appeared to be growing, 1906 was to prove that Athlone's apathy, while somewhat less obvious, was still present, albeit in an augmented form. St Peter's UIL continued to meet, successfully reorganised, but was stymied by both the refusal of the South Roscommon UIL Executive to meet in the town[143] and parochial rivalries, or what the press referred to as, '[issues of] a personal or self-interested type'.[144] The direction in which the branch was heading led one member, local merchant M.J. Lennon UDC, to highlight some policies of the emerging SF party,[145] though he did not advocate a move away from the IPP, which was yet to show what could be achieved with a stronger parliamentary position.[146] St Mary's UIL branch appeared dormant for the greater part of the year and reorganisation efforts failed miserably. 'It is a pity that the little political activity … should have oozed out', wrote McDermott-Hayes in the *Westmeath Independent*, criticising both branches.[147] The lack of activity and the absence of a funding drive had to be tackled and to this end a massive demonstration was jointly organised by both branches for early October with John Redmond as the main speaker.[148]

Held one day after the anniversary of the death of C.S. Parnell, the Magnificent Muster of the men of the Midlands saw 6,000 people gather at the Fairgreen on the east side of the town. Dean Kelly opened proceedings by demanding a Home Rule measure akin to that enjoyed by Australia and Canada, ridiculed SF and criticised 'conciliation' politics which, he believed, led to increased land costs, something the *Irish People* forcefully rebutted in its analysis of the meeting.[149] Redmond spoke of Parnell, the need for unity and the 'duty' that Irish nationalists owed to the Liberal Party, which had initiated moves towards creating a scheme for Irish self-government. He stated that if the Liberal plan was unworkable, the IPP would reject it regardless of the discomfort it might cause in Westminster.[150] The crowd, described as attentive, heard him state that any government measure in relation to Irish governance could not be 'cramped, crippled [or] impractical'.[151] He was issuing a warning; while he was agreeable to devolution (or, as the liberal British newspaper the *Manchester Guardian* put it in its appraisal of the Athlone meeting, 'anything that can be fairly regarded as an instalment'[152]) on the road to Home Rule, neither he, nor the Irish people, should be given a perfunctory gesture.[153]

The chances of a workable scheme being drawn up by the government may have been seen as a long shot by some urban dwellers given the provisions of the Town Tenants (Ireland) Act, which was passed in December 1906. Its clauses, more influenced by unionists than by the TTL,[154] were inadequate to the task of addressing urban tenants' issues, which were, despite IPP rhetoric to the contrary, relegated yet again.[155] Such poor legislation may have contributed to the absence of UIL activity in Athlone in the months after the Redmond rally. No funding drive was inaugurated (the *Irish People* argued that raising money was the UIL's only function now[156]) and meetings, though held, were poorly attended and achieved little.[157] A *Westmeath Independent* editorial from February 1907 was heavy with criticism:

> It is a poor tribute to the public spirit … that not more than half a dozen members can be together at any time to attend a meeting … nor hardly subscriptions enough to affiliate with the central executive.[158]

Trying to raise the hackles of local nationalists, it continued by stating that Athlone was never a 'hot bed' of nationalism and that its consistently apathetic approach was at least that; consistent. One of the attendees at a St Peter's branch meeting complained how there were always 'Nationalists enough' at election time,[159] highlighting the local indifference that David Fitzpatrick has identified as 'the recurrent cancer' of Irish nationalism in the early twentieth-century.[160] Indifference, while seen by some contemporaries as virtually unforgivable, was really to be expected. Ireland had lurched from one political crisis to another for decades; people did not become excited at every new development, and experience had taught them that such developments often brought disappointment. Local interest in political matters was to be aroused sooner rather than later, however. The death of Donal Sullivan at the age of 67 (he suffered a heart attack while in the House of Commons) in early March 1907[161] triggered a by-election, which took place in early April.[162]

The election of a new candidate from a pool of three to the South Westmeath seat was an opportunity for the IPP to install someone more energetic than Sullivan, a man described by T.M. Healy as a 'modest Nationalist … who never spoke and rarely appeared in public'.[163] Though popular, Sullivan was an uninspiring figure, whose exemplary attendance record at Westminster ensured he was an infrequent visitor to his constituency.[164] The candidate of most interest to Athlone voters was local solicitor, 32-year-old Henry J. Walker. He occupied committee positions in both the local Gaelic League and St Mary's UIL,[165] with the latter proposing his candidacy, despite his own uncertainty about his suitability.[166] Walker's doubts may have addled his chances from the start, as some league members stated that they would not go to the convention in Moate 'pledged' to him; they wished to assess each candidate on his merits.[167]

The second aspirant was 42-year-old baronet, Sir Walter Nugent. He had lost his Westmeath County Council seat to a UIL candidate in May 1902 and withdrew from the local elections of 1905, recognising that his political affiliations were unattractive to voters. Nugent pragmatically re-emerged as a UIL member in May the same year to unsuccessfully contest the North Westmeath seat in opposition to Laurence Ginnell, followed by moves towards the seat for North Meath.[168] Again he failed but maintained a high profile and active participation in the league in Westmeath, selling lands to tenants under the Wyndham Act.[169] Reports in the *Westmeath Independent* noted that Nugent was popular in rural regions and had been co-opted to the county council just weeks before the election.[170]

The third candidate, dismissed as an also-ran in the local press, was Longford nationalist William Ganly, who had spent most of the previous two-and-a-half decades in Argentina. *The Irish Times*, for example, did not mention his candidacy until the day of the convention, singling out Nugent and 'a prominent league organiser and barrister'.[171]

In a constituency where Sullivan had always relied on clerical support, appealing to the clergy was essential. In this, Nugent was undoubtedly the most successful. Early on he gained the support of the Revd Dr Hoare, Bishop of Ardagh and Clonmacnoise and Revd Dr Clancy, Bishop of Elphin, and while later clarifications showed that neither bishop was actively opposed to Walker, it was clear that clerical support went with the baronet.[172] Nugent courted the rural electorate in places such as Kilbeggan and Ballinagore, as did Ganly, while Walker was less conspicuous outside of Athlone. His chances of gaining extra votes from the town were dealt a blow when neither the Athlone Poor Law Guardians (PLG) nor TLA were invited to the convention.[173]

The winner of the election, with almost three times more votes than his nearest rival, was Walter Nugent.[174] In his letter of defeat Walker, who came in last, stated that his lack of fame (when compared to Nugent) and the absence of the TLA were his main handicaps. It is more probable that his absence from rural rallies, excess reliance on the restricted Athlone electorate (only those in St Mary's ward were eligible to vote), and the early endorsement of Nugent by Bishop Hoare were to blame. Walker received only two of thirty-two clerical votes cast; the rest went to Nugent and accounted for around a quarter of his total.[175] The Athlone electorate had backed Walker strongly, but rurally he faired poorly. Some Athlone UIL members complained in vain after the convention, even handling some priests 'roughly' and shouting: 'A priests' convention … Nugent is not elected by the people, but the priests'. Some of Ganly's supporters counselled that he should ignore the poll, given the clergy's excessive influence over the result, while Nugent's magnanimous acceptance speech was interrupted by shouts of 'you have not the voice of the people … The priests have usurped … the people'.[176] The advanced nationalist publication the *Peasant* took some interest in the convention, implying electoral impropriety and questioning why, for a Westmeath election, so many King's County priests were present.[177] The complaints came to nothing however, and the local press counselled that Nugent, who later took the parliamentary seat unopposed, should be accepted 'on trial'.[178]

In Westminster the new South Westmeath MP had to help the IPP deal with the fallout from the failed Irish Council Bill. This was a Liberal stop-gap measure intended to placate the Irish Party. Redmond initially supported it, believing that it would pave the way for Home Rule.[179] J.P. Hayden criticised it, though he believed it was possible to 'amend it into something useful', while Laurence Ginnell just condemned it, stating that it would be 'passed to the flames'.[180] Most commentators, not focussed on the long-term goal of Home Rule, complained about its weaknesses and many in the IPP questioned the relevance of attending Westminster if such 'insulting' legislation was the result.[181] Leaving Westminster was one of the more prominent SF policies and for IPP members to suggest it set alarm bells ringing. Upon hearing them John Redmond quickly condemned the bill, fearing yet another split in the party.[182] The IG noted that soon after the rejection, 'dissatisfaction and disunion' had pervaded IPP ranks, with the *Westmeath Independent* gaining the agreement of the *Irish People* in stating that 'we now find ourselves almost back … to the point at which Mr. Parnell started'.[183]

In Athlone the bill was described as 'political buffoonery' and 'less than half' what the Tories would have given a few years previously.[184] The UDC wanted to send delegates to the national convention at which the bill was to be discussed, though M.J. Lennon, an increasingly vocal SF advocate, pointed out that the certainty of its being rejected made the trip pointless. St Mary's UIL also discussed the bill, though appeared quite uninformed.[185] They sent Thomas Chapman, Town Clerk P.V.C. Murtagh and branch secretary M.J. Hughes to the convention that saw the bill rejected.[186]

Some nationalists saw the bill as proof that the government was not sufficiently motivated to solve Irish problems and a more direct approach had to be adopted. Others, possibly certain of the outcome or set on implementing their own ideas regardless, had already taken the issue of further land redistribution into their own hands and had initiated what became known as the Ranch War. Initially started in the as yet 'grazier-made wilderness'[187] of north Westmeath in October 1906,[188] it soon spread to Roscommon and was the most serious agrarian agitation seen since the 1880s.[189] Driven by the 'uncontrollable' Laurence Ginnell, a man with first-hand experience of the desperate struggle of Irish tenants farmers in the late nineteenth-century, the agitation was concentrated in midland and western counties where aggrieved farmers continued to be more numerous and inequity was more noticeable with large graziers and smallholders existing side-by-side.[190]

In 1903, before the Wyndham Act would have had an appreciable effect, government statistics for the Athlone Poor Law Union, a region comprised mainly of the southern parts of both Roscommon and Westmeath, showed that of the almost 5,000 individual holdings, more than half were less than 15 acres in extent, with 40 per cent of that figure accounting for holdings of less than 5 acres.[191] The majority of the land in the Union was leased out to tenants or untenanted,[192] with ownership of the properties resting with a large minority. In 1904, after the act had been passed, there was no real change, though the pace of purchases was slow, so this may not have been surprising.[193] By 1906 it is probable that a general maintenance of the status quo led Ginnell to push for a more radical approach inspired by reports such as that in *The Leader* of 10 February 1906, which continued to refer to 'Westmeath's broad acres'.[194]

The promoters of the 'war' intended to solve two main problems. The first was that of convincing landowners to sell, while the second was ensuring that nobody leased lands from landowners who were uncooperative.[195] Ginnell, in common with other radical political figures, wished to mobilise 'supra-local and local popular support … [by] organising campaigns of direct action, with a view to influencing state policy and local conditions'.[196] His efforts were initially aided by calls from the IPP hierarchy for an increase in agitation after the failure of the Irish Council Bill,[197] yet support for Ginnell's actions was not comprehensive, especially in areas where landlords, graziers and tenants had cosy commercial arrangements or maintained civil relations.[198]

Towards the end of 1907, more frequent acts of agitation were seen in the Athlone region, where untenanted 'premium quality grasslands' were common.[199] Around the town, an intimidatory atmosphere began to manifest as unsympathetic farmers saw their farms raided and their livestock driven away by men using hazel switches. Court proceedings involving large numbers of local men were instituted and, fearful of inviting reprisals from agitators, car owners refused to rent their vehicles to the RIC, who wished to investigate reports of unrest. At a UIL meeting in Mount Temple, Walter Nugent's inter-vention was required to ensure the safety of one police note-taker against whom the assembled crowd turned.[200] The *Westmeath Independent*, with support from the *Irish People*, called for greater direction to be provided by Redmond, taking the form of 'an intelligible policy sufficiently direct and well-defined', to unite efforts for change.[201] The O'Brienite paper often found itself in agreement with the Athlone editor, who stated that the problems faced by Irish nationalism came about as a result of giving 'too much confidence … to the English parties … we have been made feel the want of reliance on ourselves'.[202] The police blamed the 'exaggerated tone of the press and the wild speeches of Mr Ginnell' for the continued angry scenes,[203] while the *Westmeath Independent* took a different line, believing Ginnell to be 'all cry and little wool [sic][wolf]'[204] Opinions aside, Ginnell's agitation was widespread and led Westmeath to a very high level of cattle driving when viewed in a national context between 1907 and 1909,[205] and the highest level over the period 1907-1911 of five counties (grouped by Michael Wheatley with Roscommon, Sligo, Longford, and Leitrim) in the midlands and north west.[206]

In Westmeath, the main political effect of the Ranch War was the enliv-ening of the feud between Hayden and Ginnell,[207] and the creation of an obvious contrast between radical and pragmatic elements in local nationalism. Hayden, often mistakenly cited as the North Westmeath MP due to his efforts in the constituency,[208] refused to speak at a rally in the county at Moyvore in December due to Ginnell's presence. Walter Nugent, who blamed the legislators rather than the agitators, made it clear in his speech at the same rally that while he admired Ginnell's dedication, repeated transgressions were counterproductive and would lead Irish Chief Secretary Augustine Birrell to impose the Coercion Act.[209] Hayden and Nugent were, like other IPP members, 'disquieted by the excesses of the unrest',[210] while Ginnell, who had a low opinion of Birrell, saw few other options.[211] He believed if people '[laid] down the hazel, they might lay down their hope', and continued his push, criticising the UIL for not fighting for the rights of those it purported to represent.[212] Ginnell's direct action tactics saw him arrested and imprisoned in December, with the *Westmeath Independent* criticising partisan judges and a conniving Tory press for the increased problems.[213] McDermott-Hayes also noted – in agreement with the *Irish Independent*, which described Nugent's speech as a 'counterblast' – that the Moyvore meeting highlighted, despite IPP proclamations of party unity, that 'diametrically opposite' political doctrines were being voiced by members of the same party.[214] Nugent and Hayden were agitation averse (many party members and supporters were graziers), while Ginnell appeared to be looking for a rebirth of the Land League, whose activities the UIL was never going to mimic.[215]

The energy that was put into agitation could not continue indefinitely however, and by February 1908 tranquillity began to manifest in most areas.[216] Of the areas that saw little diminution in agrarian agitation, Westmeath was perhaps most prominent,[217] with boycotting and cattle driving continuing to keep the police occupied.[218] The continued volatility even motivated St Peter's UIL, which was singled out by the CI in February (the first and last time this was to happen), such was its level of activity.[219] The *Westmeath Independent* did not compliment the branch for its work however, given that just four people from the thirty in attendance at a meeting in late January were from 'urban' Athlone. The branch was dominated by rural interests, despite having more urban traders and local businessmen on the committee than farmers, and had failed, like the UIL generally, to show people its lobbying potential on the behalf of town-dwellers, even during such fractious times: 'The "cui bono" – what good is it argument, is used in reply to … well-deserved criticism', wrote McDermott-Hayes in an editorial which rated Athlone's sense of nationalist duty as 'zero'.[220]

Local press criticism allied with the first successful attempt to have the South Roscommon UIL Executive meeting held in Athlone soon led St Peter's branch to enjoy a period of greater urban participation.[221] A code was established for members of the committee, the most important provision being the expulsion of those who missed three meetings in succession without a reasonable excuse.[222] St Mary's UIL also began to reorganise and it was decided by committee members such as Thomas Chapman and

H.J. Walker that locals should be made feel the guilt of their absence, though exactly how that was to happen was not laid out.[223] It appeared that organisers were growing weary of fruitlessly requesting locals to join the league and were considering resorting to coercion.

Hopes that local nationalists would be able to stimulate interest in the UIL were, however, dealt a blow by further evidence of IPP weakness in Westminster. Statements from the Liberal leadership showed, according to the local press, that Home Rule was 'no longer even a matter of moment' and that the Irish people had been 'duped'.[224] This view was reportedly widely held in Athlone, as news that numerous Liberal members complained about the party concentrating too much on Irish affairs made the headlines.[225] What appears to have annoyed many nationalists even more than the Liberals' position was the IPP's reaction. They lobbied little and for the second time in the space of a year, questions were asked about the efficacy of parliamentary arrangements. In what was probably their most politically mature session to date, St Peter's UIL condemned the government, stating that the IPP should reassess their political alliance.[226] McDermott-Hayes' editorials during April included numerous pessimistic references to the situation:

> Truly the Irish cause has fallen on evil days. From a republic and an Independent Parliament … the National claims are now reduced to little better than local, almost parochial necessities, and Ireland … is recognised by Nationalists as a mere appendage of Britain.[227]

Activity in UIL circles in Westmeath, now showing signs of a more distinct schism thanks to Ginnell, who was released from prison in April,[228] continued to be high and the county was once more subjected to a greater and more costly RIC presence.[229] Walter Nugent's vote against William O'Brien's reassembling of the Land Conference drew the ire of the *Irish People*, which stated that even though Nugent published a letter of apology to address his constituents' annoyance at his ballot, 'afterthoughts never suffice to explain away … actions which are inimical to the best interests of the country'.[230] Nugent, who believed that little new would come from such a conference, stated that he had instead backed a John Dillon-led committee; incorrectly believing that it was to address, rather than just assess, financial difficulties that arose from the land question.[231] The *Westmeath Independent* stated that the 'worse policy was decided upon', and continued to promote a 'working arrangement' between landlords and the IPP that would solve the land issue.[232] Nationally, the absence of strong leadership saw UIL branches and courts provide most of the direction at local level,[233] and incidences of cattle driving increased to the highest frequency yet seen.[234] The South Westmeath UIL Executive, in opposition to the Standing Committee of the UIL, refused to suspend the Rochfortbridge UIL branch for suggesting that the IPP were acting more in the interests of English Liberalism than Irish Nationalism. The *Irish People* claimed that the incident showed that the 'whole movement had gone to seed'.[235]

The continued growth in dissatisfaction with the IPP was more apparent both nationally and locally by autumn 1908.[236] In early September the chairman of the Athlone UDC, M.J. Lennon, ruled that no member was to attend a meeting in Clara to be addressed by John Dillon, 'one of the most formidable opponents of the land settlement'. The majority of those present agreed with Lennon that the IPP lacked focus and were inactive on issues that concerned their supporters.[237] Party members spent more time airing opinions than acting, with the weak Housing of the Working Classes (Ireland) Bill singled out by the press as an example of how little influence they had in Parliament, despite their assertion of a Liberal 'alliance'.[238] The *Irish People* (always happy to criticise John Dillon) relayed news of Lennon's decree under the headline 'The Midlands in Revolt', stating that it hoped that the 'lesson of an important centre like Athlone will not be ignored or underestimated'.[239] The belief of most present at the meeting (just six men in total – two dissenters) was that while Athlone had traditionally backed the IPP, recent internal bickering had led to the party becoming impotent, navel-gazing and disconnected.[240]

Lennon's action led the St Peter's UIL to issue a statement that the council 'did not represent the Nationalist opinion of Athlone'.[241] Dean Kelly decried the 'false and unfair' attack on the Irish Party, singling out the 'gross calumny' that the IPP was opposed to land purchase.[242] A letter of complaint from the branch, which was represented at Dillon's Clara meeting,[243] was ridiculed by some UDC members who joked that a letter from a dogs' home or vegetarian society would have carried more weight![244] Just one week after the UDC insult, it was decided that both UIL branches would jointly organise a Nationalist meeting, where news of Chief Secretary Birrell's move towards a new land bill would be discussed.[245] News of the bill did lead to a diminution in the level of cattle driving locally, though most were counselled to keep 'the hazel up the chimney'[246] in case Birrell did not deliver.[247] In the more peaceful atmosphere it was hoped that a large meeting might have been better able to inform people of IPP efforts in relation to the bill, as well as stimulate interest in the league in Athlone. The speeches at the meeting were of a sort already quite familiar to those assembled. Hayden and Nugent spoke of having confidence in Redmond and the Irish Party's ability to deliver

Home Rule, as did Dean Kelly and H.J. Walker. Local UIL arrangements were criticised, especially those in St Mary's parish, and J.P. Hayden proposed that the town should really look towards establishing a single branch unless some sort of positive rivalry could be brought about.[248]

The meeting appeared to have the desired effect. St Peter's Parliamentary Fund was established the following week,[249] and St Mary's UIL held a meeting four weeks later where a large attendance showed a greater level of support. Indeed, 'a more healthy tone' had been given to the branch by the local parish administrator, Fr McCabe, who garnered enough funds to affiliate.[250] The efforts made by St Mary's UIL led the local press to describe it as 'a model' for how branches should be formed. A meeting to sign up new members featured entertainment provided by the Athlone Brass Band. The branch was trying to expand its membership by showing that its meetings could also be enjoyable social occasions where a variety of activities could take place, not just purely austere political get-togethers or, as David Fitzpatrick put it, 'forums for political harangues'.[251] St Mary's also welcomed its first female member and actively sought out representatives to visit nearby rural areas such as Clonbrusk, Cornamagh and Coosan with a view to boosting numbers.[252]

The activity of the local branches was reflected elsewhere in Westmeath. Of the forty-two branches established in the county, eleven were described by RIC sources as active, one of the highest ever estimates. The district's UIL courts continued to meet, adjudicate, and issue decrees, which were still 'enforceable in the traditional fashion',[253] i.e. through boycotting and other forms of intimidation. The RIC had attempted to curb the reporting of such court rulings, which were making magistrates all over the country that bit more reluctant to sentence members of the public.[254] To this end they had begun to visit newspaper offices and in Athlone, the *Westmeath Independent* was the main target. Their visit to Thomas Chapman elicited a poor reception.[255]

Unsurprisingly, given what had been witnessed when the 1903 Land Act was being drafted, the 1909 Land Bill caused much IPP infighting. Approval for the bill was forthcoming at the IPP Convention in February (a positive move, according to the *Westmeath Independent*), though William O'Brien opposed it and soon resigned again, with Ginnell 'howled down' for his opposition to the measure, at what Paul Bew has described as 'probably the stormiest meeting ever held by constitutional nationalists'.[256] Dean Kelly, who was also in attendance, forwarded a resolution on unity, while Redmond decried 'Our own mad and wicked discord', seeing it as one of the main obstacles to the search for Home Rule.[257]

Around Athlone, anticipation of the bill promoted a reduction in agitation, with the number of cattle drives and related problems decreasing in both Westmeath and Roscommon.[258] Both Athlone UIL branches held numerous meetings during the year, dealing mainly with mundane topics, but apart from a brief escalation in activity during July in response to the local SF branch becoming more vocal, they did little else.[259] Indeed, St Mary's UIL actually cancelled one scheduled meeting as it was believed that the local land situation was that much more tranquil and positive.[260] There was some activity in regions further from the town. RIC reports revealed that some UIL branches were spearheading cattle drives and ensuring that an 'obnoxious presence is brought to bear' in land disputes.[261] However, the CI for Roscommon did admit that while many league branches were active, 'members are slower in inflicting sharp penalties … , there are fewer acts of intimidation … [and] people are venturing … to place their stocks on … large farms'.[262]

Even though Walter Nugent believed that Westmeath's UIL was the best in the country with, according to his information, 'more lands … bought by the Estates Commissioners … more ranches split up … proportionately … than anywhere else in Ireland',[263] coercion was still needed to convince some landowners, such as Lord Castlemaine, to sell.[264] Others certainly sold land willingly, as statistics for 1908 and 1909 show that the number of plots owned in the Athlone Poor Law Union rose by over 600 or almost 25 per cent, while those tenanted fell by a similar number, signifying an obvious shift. Large land holdings were reduced by just a small margin and subdivision was not wide-spread by any means; what was being redistributed were holdings of less than 30 acres.[265] Birrell's Bill was eagerly awaited in Westmeath, for it appeared that some degree of compulsion, for which the Bill provided, would have to be introduced to deal with intransigent landowners of larger plots. On the whole, however, UIL activity continued to fall, due 'to the desire of the leaders … not to impede … the … Land Bill by any overt acts of hostility'.[266]

However, the final version of the 1909 Land Act was to disappoint. It introduced an element of compulsion to land deals where intransigence was the main obstacle, while limiting the amount of money the British Exchequer had to allocate. The act expanded the CDB's geographical remit to include all of Roscommon and most of the counties on the west and south-western seaboard, areas where purchase was especially difficult.[267] It gained unenthusiastic support from the IPP and John Redmond, while the *Westmeath Independent* termed it 'emasculated'.[268] The act would see more land in Athlone Union come under the ownership of former tenants, but the shift was quite small; just seventy-five plots changed hands over the next two years.[269] With such a disappointment, it would have appeared likely that extra-parliamentary agitation would again begin to increase, yet it quickly became apparent that activities at Westminster in relation to the 1909 budget were to provide hope for Irish nationalists.

When the government's plans for a budget began to surface in the summer of 1909, it was obvious that much of what they were proposing was going to cause difficulties. In an Irish context, plans to tax spirits and tobacco were quite unpopular, most certainly in Athlone, where vocal opposition came quickly.[270] IPP efforts to address the concerns were rather anaemic, and the party began to witness a fall in support.[271] Some organisations, St Mary's UIL included, stated that they understood the balancing act that Redmond was attempting to maintain,[272] and when the IPP eventually resolved to abstain from a vote on the budget, they gained the support of the Athlone PLG and UDC for so doing.[273] It was apparent that Irish concerns were of little importance in the wider debate on the fiscal plan, however, with the idea of taxing profits from land ownership in Britain seeing the proposal thrown out by the House of Lords, and the calling of an early general election.[274]

As occurred in many constituencies, South Westmeath and South Roscommon saw the return of the incumbents without much ado.[275] North Westmeath, however, hosted one of the most fractious contests as the rivalry between Laurence Ginnell and J.P. Hayden intensified. Ginnell had ignored the IPP convention in Mullingar, which he claimed was 'rigged', stating that the local UIL was run by a Masonic clique of 'self-appointed conspirators'. He defeated the league candidate, Director of the South Westmeath UIL Executive Patrick McKenna, by 1,996 votes to 1,379. McKenna failed despite support from Hayden, Walter Nugent and most of the clergy.[276] Ginnell was promptly expelled from the IPP and remained excluded, as unenthusiastic efforts made by Nugent and John Redmond to have him readmitted came to nothing.[277]

The result of the general election placed the IPP in a strong position. It transpired that an almost even split had resulted between the Liberals, who secured 275 seats, and the Conservatives, who increased their representation to 273. The Irish nationalist total of eighty-two seats[278] meant that they held the balance of power. Redmond was in a position 'of leverage undreamt of since Parnell's day and potentially even more powerful than that achieved by Parnell himself';[279] the question posed by commentators was whether Redmond could use the result to push for Home Rule.[280] However, Redmond's ability to do so was hampered by one serious problem: the House of Lords veto. The veto had brought down the government, and with it the Lords would block any attempt to introduce Home Rule for Ireland. To facilitate the passage of any Home

John Dillon MP in Athlone, April 1910. Individuals of note: J.P. Hayden MP (back row, second left). Seated (l-r): John Dillon MP, Dean J.J. Kelly and Sir Walter Nugent MP. (AHL)

Rule measure, the veto would have to be abolished or subjected to a time limit, though some commentators were unsure of Liberal willingness to take on the Upper House in such a confrontational manner.[281] This obstacle was highlighted in the *Westmeath Independent*, which editorialised that the Prime Minister's cowardice would lead to another election, sooner rather than later.[282]

Regardless of the probable use of the veto by the Lords in the event of a Home Rule bill, the strategy to be pursued by the IPP had to be explained to the electorate. It was announced that John Redmond was to speak in Tipperary, while John Dillon was to visit Athlone to make a 'historic pronouncement', a weighty description for the proposed speech from which Dillon distanced himself.[283] The guaranteed attendance of the IPP second in command led to a rare example of co-operation between Athlone's UIL branches, who decided that St Mary's Square would be the venue.[284]

On Sunday, 3 April 1910, a crowd estimated at 2,500 gathered for the address. The *Westmeath Independent* stated the meeting showed that there was 'no ripple of faction' in the hearts of Nationalists of the midlands and west, even after William O'Brien's acrimonious split from the IPP,[285] adding that:

> … in the Midlands, the great demonstration in Athlone on Sunday last is ample proof … [that] the popular voice and sentiments are in thorough accord with … the Irish Parliamentary Party under John Redmond.[286]

Dillon, an effigy of whom had been burned in Athlone around the time of the IPP schism, was warmly welcomed.[287] His speech dealt with the supposed 'historic announcement', the budget, Birrell's Land Act and William O'Brien.[288] Dillon adopted a rather ambivalent approach to the budget, stating that it was not as bad as many believed, an initial step towards softening up the electorate for the possibility of the IPP supporting the measure. Obviously there was a quid pro quo involved; Irish MPs' support, now so precious to the Liberals, hinged upon the reintroduction of a Home Rule bill, something far more important to the IPP than an annual budget.[289] The CI for Westmeath was unimpressed by Dillon's oratory, stating it was 'really … an appeal for funds'.[290] Certainly, for many who attended, it must have been disappointing, containing nothing really new. It appeared that the inspector may have been correct in his assertion, for the two Athlone UIL branches initiated fundraising drives soon after, but did little else.[291]

Since the January election, the British Government had been unable to resolve the quandary of the House of Lords' veto.[292] After months of negotiation and the convening of a constitutional congress as well as 'more subterranean manoeuvres', McDermott-Hayes was proved right and another general election was called.[293] As in previous elections, factionalism within the UIL registered prominently before polling day,[294] while news of an interview John Redmond gave to the *Daily Express* in which he supposedly called for Ireland to be granted political autonomy similar to that of a Canadian province or American state caused the party additional problems. Most nationalist MPs dealt with the interview as a fabrication, though Walter Nugent came out in its defence, stating that it provided clarity on the demands of an IPP too often accused of being vague. McDermott-Hayes promoted the more popular belief and doubted whether the report of the interview was an accurate reflection of what was said, arguing that Redmond did not support such a diluted version of self-government.[295]

In Athlone the election passed off without incident. Attempts by William O'Brien's AFIL to establish in the region in the months before the election had been unsuccessful, with opposition to the main nationalist party almost non-existent around Athlone.[296] The fact that the UIL's 'machinery' was in good working order (both of the town's branches had affiliated the same month[297]) and a quick visit from John Dillon[298] assisted in ensuring that the two IPP candidates with influence on Athlone affairs, Walter Nugent and J.P. Hayden, regained their seats with even less ado.[299] The fact that no conventions were held given the short timeframe saw Laurence Ginnell (still promoting 'a hurricane of cattle driving'), returned unopposed in North Westmeath.[300]

The result placed Irish MPs in an even stronger position, providing them with eighty-four seats.[301] The problem of the House of Lords veto was soon

dealt with through the threat of instating numerous Liberal Lords to the House
to counteract the Conservative majority. Consequently the Lords accepted
the Parliament Act of 1911, which limited their veto to that of a suspensory
power only.[302] The removal of the veto and the strength of the IPP meant that a
concerted push for Home Rule could now be made, something which caused
great concern among Irish unionists, who believed that the Roman Catholic
domination of an Irish Home Rule Parliament would greatly undermine
their social, economic and political position. They initiated a campaign to
thwart moves towards Irish political autonomy, something that Walter Nugent,
speaking at the South Westmeath UIL Executive in January 1911, saw as little
threat. He asked that people to be patient and tolerant; his belief was that giving
unionists enough rope would elicit the usual result.[303]

To assist in the push for Home Rule, it was important that the IPP and UIL
could rely upon their grass roots supporters in and around Athlone. However,
this reliance was handicapped by Laurence Ginnell, who had created a
separate 'independent' UIL in North Westmeath,[304] and post-election indifference which saw the number of affiliated UIL branches in Westmeath fall
sharply; thirty-five in 1909/10 to twenty-five in 1910/11, a much greater
decline than witnessed in some neighbouring counties.[305] Despite the fall,
the police believed the League in both Westmeath and Roscommon to be
'quiet … but nevertheless quite alive', and it appeared that UIL members,
as with the 1903 and 1909 Land Acts, were adopting a wait and see approach
to parliamentary manoeuvres.[306] The *Westmeath Independent* started to devote
more editorial column inches to the pursuit of Home Rule than any other
topic promoting it as '… the inevitable outcome of the political situation'.[307]

In May, Walter Nugent, the most prominent proponent of Redmondite
policy in the county, called for unity and consolidation in the British Empire
and for Ireland to be treated as an equal amongst the 'colonies'.[308] He, along with
other IPP MPs, spent much time in Britain giving speeches on Home Rule,[309]
to what the *Westmeath Independent* described as 'well-intentioned, but ignorant
Englishmen'.[310] Criticism of Irish MPs did surface, however, as each began to
receive a stipend of £400 from the government. The IPP had raised objections
to the money; they did not want to be paid until an Irish Parliament had been
established. The government ignored them.[311] Others, SF primarily, argued that
the IPP was compromised by accepting the money and likened it to a bribe.[312]

The political scene remained quiet around Athlone for the reminder of the
year, though the establishment of a local Ancient Order of Hibernians (Board
of Erin) division in May did evince additional support for the IPP in town.[313]
A visit of the 'Eighty Club' (Liberal supporters who had backed earlier Home

Rule Bills) to Athlone awakened St Peter's UIL from its nine-month slumber during September, with St Mary's' shorter hibernation of about six months broken similarly by the same visit.[314] An 'abundant harvest' and other interests outside of politics kept most occupied.[315]

Perhaps fearful that complacency was entering local nationalist circles, moves were initiated in October to inform people of their role in the pursuit of Home Rule. An exercised McDermott-Hayes asked why there was 'apathy of organisation [amongst Nationalists] all over the county [when] there are so many interests at stake'.[316] The period of inactivity, replicated in many parts of the country,[317] did however see the establishment of another Athlone TTL branch, this time somewhat more successfully.[318] Soon after, as the Home Rule bill moved closer to completion, Athlone's nationalists finally decided to consolidate the local league branches, gaining the support of the press:

> Because of Athlone being ... in ... South Westmeath and South Roscommon, two branches of the ... league have been maintained ... the arrangement is not ... good or useful ... it has not induced that attendance which is necessary.[319]

It was pointed out that one branch dealing with two different executives could be quite awkward, and at the establishment meeting for the new branch both Walter Nugent and J.P. Hayden stated that an Athlone representative could attend either, or both, of the executive meetings in Westmeath and Roscommon.[320] The new branch was to coordinate local support for the IPP's Home Rule efforts; Hayden explicitly stated that there would be no lobbying for additional legislation for urban tenants.[321] The formation meeting saw Dean Kelly gain the presidency with Fr McCabe, former president of St Mary's UIL, as vice-president. Representatives from both parishes took committee positions and a hyperbolic piece of prose announced the new venture in the local press: 'Let it not be said of the men of Athlone that they ... failed in their patriotism, or did not, by every means in their power, sustain that sacred cause for which our forefathers died'.[322]

By the end of the third week in January 1912, a new all-town branch of the UIL was established. Called the Athlone Young Ireland[323] Branch of the United Irish League, the institution was dismissed by the RIC as nothing more than 'making a show of keeping the league alive there [Athlone]'.[324] Its foundation was greeted with greater optimism by the town's nationalists who, for the first time in almost two decades, were looking to ensure that local support for achieving Home Rule was as well organised as possible.

2

Supplementing the Nationalist Debate

Athlone, in common with many other towns in Ireland, was not reliant solely on the UIL and IPP to inform its citizens' nationalist agenda. Other organisations influenced the content and direction of the nationalist debate during the early years of the twentieth century, with three of the most prominent – the Gaelic League, SF and the Ancient Order of Hibernians (AOH) – each establishing a presence in Athlone. These groups, while not gaining the same degree of influence as the UIL, supplemented local political discourse from their different ideological platforms and provided evidence of diverse avenues of thought, which impacted on constitutional nationalist activities. Occurrences such as the Boer War in South Africa, IPP successes and failures, legislative and governmental changes as well as unique local situations all exerted an influence, informing the organisations' political philosophies, stratagems for expansion and level of success in Athlone.

THE GAELIC LEAGUE

By the beginning of the twentieth century, Athlone's centuries-long association with Britain had shaped much of the town's cultural landscape. Sports promoted by the local British Army garrison, such as soccer, cricket, rugby and rowing were the most popular athletic pursuits, while the staging of English plays, recitals or band performances (usually aping British Army bands) was typical of the more sedate cultural experiences of many locals.[1] However, by the end of the nineteenth century, Athlone's cultural activities were taking on a Celtic tinge. Irish music concerts began to be organised, local children were enrolled in newly founded clubs specialising in Irish sports and a different dynamic developed as the townspeople began to reacquaint themselves with their Celtic past. This cultural nationalism was an important influence when it came to defining how Ireland's nationalists saw themselves in the early twentieth century and was driven primarily by the Gaelic League (*Conradh na Gaeilge*) and the Gaelic Athletic Association (GAA or *Cumann Lúthcleas Gael*). Unlike the GAA, the formation, membership and progress of the GL in Athlone were traced in a detailed fashion in contemporary sources; consequently it will be the focus of the study.

The arrival of the GL in Athlone in 1901 came about eight years after the league itself was first established by Douglas Hyde and Eoin MacNeill as a non-political promoter of Irish language, music, dance, literature and industry.[2] The organisation gained initial success in Westmeath in the late nineteenth century, and rumours were heard of moves towards a local branch in 1899 when the Coiste Gnótha (executive committee) was established to regulate the growing network of *craobhacha* (branches).[3] In keeping with the tradition of local consistency when it came to establishing organisations, the first attempt came to nothing and it was not until September 1901 that local enthusiasm, partially inspired by the Boer War in South Africa, which was depicted largely as a cultural battle between Britain and the Boers,[4] led to branch formation.[5] The local *craobh* (branch) provided the GL with a boost in the midlands, where counties such as Longford and Queen's County exhibited the lowest levels of participation in Ireland.[6]

The need for a branch in Athlone is evident from the census returns of 1901. Irish had been the language of commerce at local markets up to the Famine of 1845–51, but death, emigration and the increased use of English in trading and religious contexts in the second half of the century precipitated a decline.[7] In Athlone 'Urban' in 1901, 231 people (155 females and 76 males) spoke Irish and English, with no Irish monoglots recorded in the total population of over 6,600. Of those who claimed to speak Irish, more than half were over 30, while the largest single proportion comprised girls between 3 and 10 years of age, who outnumbered their Irish-speaking male counterparts by a factor of forty-two to one.[8] Few Irish speakers lived in regions east of the town, while outside the western boundaries almost 800 people (evenly split between males and females) spoke the language. However, almost half of those were over 60 years of age, an indication of people born pre-Famine, possibly native speakers, learning Irish before its decline.[9] The GL had to tackle the obviously poor participation by males in Athlone's schools, as well as ignorance of Irish amongst most adults.

Given that knowledge of the poor state of Irish would have been readily apparent, the local enthusiasts who came together in September 1901 to form a local branch did so cautiously. Local solicitor J.J. Walsh organised a meeting to gauge interest, holding it in the Fr Mathew Temperance Hall, the perfect venue for GL organisers, who desired that members be abstemious.[10] Those assembled heard of plans for an Irish class and local branch, but were also informed that support had to be given or efforts would be abandoned.[11] The reaction of the crowd disappointed organisers, something alluded to in the *Westmeath Independent*:

> The residents of Athlone ... act on the principle of making haste slowly. Devoid, to some extent, of that enthusiasm and precipitancy attributed to us as national characteristics, the people of Athlone are seldom the first to associate ... with a new movement but they do not ... remain behind to be the last to throw their lot in ... [12]

In the days after the meeting, the Roman Catholic tinge with which the GL became increasingly identified came to the fore as Dean Kelly, Revd Dr Thomas Langan and curate Fr Patrick Forde, who by this time was a figure of some prominence in the League,[13] assisted Walsh in securing greater support.[14] By the third week in October, 120 people had joined the classes, a committee was formed and the affiliation fee was subscribed. Dean Kelly was elected president and Langan vice-president,[15] while Fr Forde and Walsh were joint Secretaries.[16] Athlone's level of clerical involvement was high, a factor that was considered essential to league success.[17] Priests advertised the GL from the pulpit and, using their senior position in school management structures, ensured that Irish was placed on schools' curricula. The local branch gained the plaudits of the bilingual GL organ, *An Claidheamh Soluis agus Fáinne an Lae*, which pointed out that Irish was being taught in the Bower and Mercy Convent schools, the Marist Brothers school and Deerpark National School. The newspaper also related that the *Westmeath Independent* was 'honestly sympathetic and helpful', while stating hyperbolically that 'Irish Ireland had captured the gate of Connacht, and will soon, please God, rule supreme in the West'.[18]

Other committee positions in St Ciarán's branch, named after the founder of the nearby monastic settlement of Clonmacnoise, were occupied by professionals such as solicitor H.J. Walker and urban councillors Denis O'Connell and Patrick Quinn.[19] The composition of the committee conformed to that of others all over Ireland which, according to Tom Garvin, consisted mainly

Athlone GL members, 1920. The image presents what appears to be a typical composition of the town's GL branch membership. (AHL)

of the middle class and clergy.[20] Arthur E. Clery, writing in 1919, similarly described a middle-class roster; however, as Peter Murray argues, the league was not quite the 'elite socialisation agency'[21] such analyses would lead the reader to believe. As argued cogently by Timothy McMahon, GL membership was more varied, and this was reflected in Athlone in a subscription list published in November 1901.[22] While the league encountered difficulties in attracting working-class members given its scholarly reputation,[23] in Athlone, donations from local industrial workers outnumbered those from solicitors, other professionals or the clergy. As in most branches, the majority of members were young men, with a small number of women – who signed up on equal terms – also on the roster.[24]

To imbue the populace with a love for their Gaelic past and assist the inchoate branch, Douglas Hyde visited Athlone in January 1902. The well-attended meeting saw 'practically all classes' represented and, according to a local reporter, gave evidence of no 'sectarian tinge', something that would have pleased Hyde.[25] Hyde pressed home the belief of the GL that the Irish language was not in immutable decline and hoped that 'Athlone will … cry "halt" as the country approaches the … precipice of Anglicisation'.[26] He declared that moving closer to the English culturally would lead an Irishman to 'become a good Englishman in sentiment and approve of the Boer War!'[27] He promoted embracing the Celtic past and made it clear that the aims of the GL were cultural, not political, an assertion with which many contemporaries and most historians disagree.[28] He wanted the Irish to be like 'the Jews, who had their own language for family and community … while relegating English to [the status of being] the … language of commerce'.[29] Additionally, he warned against reading 'penny dreadfuls, shilling shockers, police intelligence, garbage and snippets'.[30]

Hyde's visit inspired a proactive approach to the GL in Athlone. Successful Gaelic concerts, 'so different from the performances we have been accustomed to in this embattled garrison town',[31] were staged to provide alternatives to the hitherto better patronised and more regularly held 'British' entertainments. The advanced nationalist weekly the *United Irishman* congratulated Walsh and Forde on their efforts in organising the concerts in Athlone where 'for a long time the West Briton … held sway'.[32] The *Westmeath Independent* also contributed, beginning what became a regular practice of publishing articles on the Gaelic Revival.

However, the momentum gained in cultural nationalist circles was ephemeral. Critical reports on poor attendances at Irish classes, even when they were boosted by local teachers attending during the summer, and the use of pictorial metaphor as in a picture of Éire fighting an English language snake, did little to inspire.[33] The branch appeared disorganised and while both Walsh and Forde attended the league's *Ard Fheis* (national convention) in 1902, they did not bring back any ideas which invigorated the branch.[34] The local newspaper surmised that people associated the GL with language only and not music or dance, which, when brought to the fore, as on St Stephen's Night 1902, promoted a more exciting image.[35] It was probable that few recognised or cared about the ideological importance of the league's aims, despite Hyde's references. Local organisers, the 'few, but brave Gaels of Athlone',[36] were unable to make the necessary impact. Perhaps, as one correspondent to the local press put it, Athlone was immutably anglicised:

> … to the progress Gaelwards in Athlone 'tis pretty much the old story … A few earnest men who work and say nothing; more who are full of sympathy; but that Irish is too hard, whereby they confess their own … stupidity or laziness; but by far the bigger crowd consists of those who hourly tremble less Tommy Atkins and Co. should detect anything distinctly Irish about them.[37]

Indications were that this may have been the case. The local branch withered during 1903 after suffering the handicaps of J.J. Walsh's death and Fr Langan's departure.[38] McDermott-Hayes suggested, unfairly, that the anti-GL phenomenon was localised, and hoped that league news from other regions would help Athlone's 'lethargic inhabitants ... see something of the National fire which is kindling all over Ireland, but without our radius'.[39] The revival of the Irish language was unable to maintain high-level support and a correspondent to the local press commented:

> 'Nothing Irish will ever succeed in Athlone.' These are not the words of hostile strangers but rather of intelligent, though somewhat hasty, natives of this old Irish town, who would sorely resent such language from a stranger.[40]

The GL all over Ireland, like the UIL, saw many branches fail to maintain viable levels of support. The reasons posited by Timothy McMahon include sectarian tensions (more prevalent in the north) and class differences, which saw some avoid the GL, given their unwillingness to rub shoulders with those of a different social standing. Most prominently he cites indifference and boredom: 'When branch activities shifted from ... lectures or dances to classroom work, numbers dwindled ... most were drawn into the league for the craic'.[41]

From the gradual expiration of the Athlone GL branch during 1903 to St Patrick's Day 1904, Irish language enthusiasts made accusations, such as that 'Athlone ... sulks when Ireland wants her help',[42] to highlight how they believed the town was being remiss. To expose locals to efforts being made in other regions, it was decided that Athlone would host a *feis* (festival), a GL-linked event which became common in Ireland from 1900.[43] Preparations, spearheaded by Fr Forde, began in March and the local press assured its readers that Athlone was, at last, becoming receptive to the GL message:

> Is Athlone awaking? ... For years ... a veritable Sleepy Hollow, while all the country around it was stirred ... This is ... pleasing news for it reassures us that the spirit of the old border town was only sleeping, and is now ... to fall in with the work in hand all over the country.[44]

Local organisers reminded the townspeople of the sacrifice made for Ireland by Athlone people in 1691,[45] and while the *feis* did not gain central GL approval until just weeks before it was staged, enthusiasm was high:[46]

> A few months ago the belief could hardly be entertained that Athlone would shake itself free of the apathy into which [it] ... had fallen ...

while no doubt the sympathies of the people are national ... there was no virility.[47]

The flow of comment on the need to rouse Athlone from its lethargy increased in the run-up to the event.[48] The words 'apathy', 'indifference', 'un-national' and 'dormant', all used to describe Athlone's past relations with the GL, were replaced by the words 'ambition', 'pride' and 'awakening'. The summation of the event's fortunes after its conclusion presented hope: 'A great work, well begun, zealously presented, and magnificently successful is the sum of the Feis that was held'.[49] Local children enjoyed competition success and it was suggested that their victories may have belied some of the established notions on Athlone's relationship with the Irish language:

> Analysis ... leaves the impression that the Feis was even more important and of wider interest than we locally supposed. It brought home to us that so far from Athlone occupying a backward position in the Irish Ireland movement, as everyone believed, noble effort was quietly at work in our schools, where unquestionably the ultimate achievement must be laid.[50]

An Claidheamh Soluis was also impressed and wished that Feis Chiaráin 'affords hope that the slow-moving Midlands are about to realise that the language movement is for them too'. It congratulated Fr Forde for his efforts, going as far as to question whether 'there [would] have been a Feis Chiaráin without an tAthair Pádraig MacConshnámha?'[51] The *United Irishman* spoke of Athlone's long-standing association with the Saxon, describing the *feis* as 'a triumphant opening for better days'.[52] *The Leader* was similarly effusive, with Thomas Murray's anti-Anglicisation entries being of most interest to the editor. One depiction of a 'Shoneen'[53] he considered worthy of publication.[54] The success saw Irish classes planned for the autumn to occupy enthusiasts for the 'quiet' or 'indoor' season.[55]

Despite the success of the *feis*, the task of inspiring the locals was going to be more difficult, as highlighted by the *Westmeath Independent*:

> Alas ... Feis Áth Luain has come and gone ... with its passing we relaxed ... into ... old ways. A branch of the ... league was to be established, an Irish class was to be put on foot ... none of these things have been done ... plain talk is required ... it is anything but creditable that a town like Athlone cannot keep a branch ... alive. It does not speak very well for our nationality.[56]

The problem with *feiseanna* was that while they generated interest in the locality in which they were staged, they did so only for a short period, once a year. They inadvertently promoted the idea that preparation for a *feis* was the main use for Irish in areas where the language was not spoken habitually.[57] Perhaps the ideological significance of Irish was neither appreciated nor understood locally or, more worryingly for the GL, the anglicisation of Athlone was too embedded; learning Irish was unattractive and unimportant.

Despite the slump in interest, GL supporters announced plans to put local structures on 'a more solid footing' during September, though Fr Forde could not assist as he had been redeployed.[58] The *United Irishman* saw his loss as serious, but struck a sanguine note, stating that news of a search for an Irish teacher for Athlone provided evidence that local language enthusiasts were using Forde's instruction as a basis for further expansion.[59] An advertisement for the post was placed in *An Claidheamh Soluis* and weekly meetings were held, which discussed how best to deploy the successful applicant.[60] Hitherto teaching had been undertaken by local enthusiasts, whose level of Irish was often poor, with supplemental assistance from *timirí* (travelling GL organisers), and *muinteorí taistil* (travelling teachers).[61] A trained professional was obviously preferable, and it was agreed that whoever was chosen would primarily work with two national schools, Our Lady's Bower for girls and the Marist Brothers for boys. Instating Irish teachers in schools was designed to secure 'a central position for the Irish language' within the education system, which had hitherto, due to 'state bias'[62] and indifference amongst the Roman Catholic hierarchy,[63] fostered ignorance of the tongue. The introduction of teachers in single-sex schools was preferred by the clergy; classes held in local halls were often mixed, which, most famously in Portarlington, could lead to divisive disagreements.[64]

To ensure the harmonious coordination of local Irish Ireland activities, it was decided, in the winter of 1904, to establish a new GL branch. Moves were made in the second week of October, at the same time, perhaps coincidentally, as the formation of a UIL branch for St Peter's parish was being discussed. The audience at the foundation meeting was small; workingmen, labourers and local clerics mainly, with a few female enthusiasts.[65] Dean Kelly chaired and assured the crowd that the branch would be more successful than the first, though, as was noted in the local newspaper: 'Enthusiasm is easily manifested, cheers come freely ... but substantial work is what is wanted.' McDermott-Hayes also noted that while the organisers' 'determination was evident to everybody', he queried the trepidation amongst the audience, 'why ... those empty places among the front seats ...

the crowding among the lower benches?' William Smith, temperance advocate and manager of the AWM attended in support, as did Thomas Chapman[66] of the APW and H.J. Walker.[67] GAA players, by now becoming increasingly numerous, were targeted for attendance at classes, which were run by trained teacher and native speaker Tadhg O'Shea, whose exposure to more modern educational systems in the Munster Training College at Ballingeary would have enabled him to communicate the language in a more structured fashion.[68] His appointment was welcomed by the *United Irishman*, which singled out local curate Fr Michael Keane for his efforts, efforts which showed that, 'the Athlone Gaelic League do not intend to weakly abandon the work because Father Forde ... is no longer with them'.[69] Classes ran for the rest of the year in the town hall, with concerts staged to raise interest and funds.[70]

The success of the previous year's *feis* saw planning for 1905's event in January, soon after the branch's AGM.[71] Again, the inspirational quality of the *feis* was required. Class attendance was down, a drop attributed in a letter in the local newspaper to indolence, decadent pursuits and a persistent lack of interest in Ireland and her past:

> People, who have plenty of time for walking the streets, yet cannot find time to devote an hour ... to attend the classes ... as for knowing anything about their country's history they are ready to discuss the merits of the latest novel or coming horse race, but that is all they seem to care about.[72]

Many initiatives to break the cycle of fluctuating class attendance were seen all over Ireland, as organisers recognised that Irish was difficult to master. Many would not engage with classes in the first instance, assured that the language was beyond them. Of those that did attend, many did so for just a few sessions, with 'new beginners' providing an unreliable attendance gauge over the class term.[73] People were more likely to engage with the more entertaining aspects of league activity, rather than the ideological drive to reintroduce Irish as the primary spoken language.

The St Patrick's Day parade in 1905 saw much for Athlone's Gaelic enthusiast to celebrate. Large crowds attended, many businesses having closed upon the request of the GL,[74] and the local press described it as 'one of the most glorious ... public events witnessed within the old border town in our generation'.[75] The showcasing of a distinctly Irish parade counterbalanced the celebrations often held by the garrison to commemorate a monarch's birthday or other State event. The colour and pomp of such occasions had often brought out large crowds in Athlone,[76] whose inhabitants were happy to punctuate their generally banal existence with something more exciting, virtually regardless of its purpose. The St Patrick's Day success saw class numbers rise in the weeks before the *feis* and a rare written endorsement from Donal Sullivan MP provided extra publicity, as did better exposure in *An Claidheamh Soluis* and the *United Irishman*; the latter noting the remarkable change in the formerly 'hopeless' Athlone.[77]

The *feis* saw a 'vast assemblage' gathered, according to the *Westmeath Independent*, for the 'physical expression of the resources at command to build up an Irish Ireland'.[78] *An Claidheamh Soluis* highlighted greater participation from Athlone, Tullamore, Mullingar, Castlerea and Athleague,[79] stating, in agreement with the *United Irishman*, that 'Athlone again showed advance'.[80] The *feis* inspired a sustained interest in the Irish Ireland movement and a regular 'Gan Teanga, Gan Tír' ('Without a Language, Without a Country') piece in the *Westmeath Independent*. 'The league has progressed exceedingly [well]', noted the *Westmeath Independent*, 'in addition to the work it has done for … the language it has given … impetus to the Industrial Revival movement in the town', a point raised by Cardinal Logue upon his visit in September.[81]

Positivity permeated the GL and the annual report for 1905 noted good activity levels, despite the encumbrance of Athlone being a 'garrison town … [with] West-British' propensities.[82] The *United Irishman* and *Irish Peasant* congratulated Dean Kelly for his efforts, with the latter describing him as 'an earnest student of the language, which he turned to at an advanced age … an excellent example to the rising generation'.[83] However, as in years past, there was to be a lull in enthusiasm, as the months rolled by. This annual occurrence led a contributor to the local paper to state that local support for the GL was disingenuous and that British pursuits gained better support:

> We have still our cricket clubs, manned by 'Nationalists', we have our homes hung with prints from various London illustrated periodicals – 'Little Bobs', red coated huntsmen, etc.[84]

One instance that may have shown in microcosm the approach some Athlone people took to the Irish Ireland movement was highlighted in *The Leader* in February 1906. D.P. Moran drew attention to a presentation in the Marist Brothers' school for teacher Fr M.J. Kennedy, who was provided with an award for his efforts in promoting the Irish language. Despite resolving to make the presentation as 'thoroughly Irish in character as possible', Kennedy received 'Anglo Irish books, Belleek pottery' and, most heinously, an address from pupils in French![85] Moran highlighted the incongruities and appeared shocked and annoyed in equal measure that the irony was lost on those present. In contrast, the *Irish Peasant*, while noting the French address, cited the efforts of Athlone's priests, teachers and school managers (with the exception of the Protestant schools) for the example they set in teaching the native tongue: 'Our hand to you, Athlone.'[86] *The Nationalist* was similarly complimentary, noting Fr Michael Keane's efforts as the 'life and soul of the movement'.[87] Despite the positive endorsements, it does appear that there were fundamental flaws in the understanding some had of the GL's purpose.

The familiar cycle recommenced in March 1906 and while the *feis* was the 'Greatest Irish Ireland gathering yet held in Athlone', the *Irish Peasant* was critical of the low standards in some competitions.[88] The visit of Dublin's Cúchulainn Gaelic Society to Athlone before the event saw an insulting brochure circulated, which stated that the garrison town had 'an extra virulent type of shoneen and … several Nationalist Yeomen'.[89] However, such insults did not motivate the GL, although many of its members may have agreed. Like their counterparts all over Ireland, Athlone's members may have been tiring of seeking new ways to inspire interest in the language.[90] Classes closed after the *feis* and a proposed *aeridheacht* (grand festival), usually an adjunct of a *feis* programme, never materialised.[91]

While the promotion of the Irish language was the Athlone GL's over-riding concern, more banal matters often occupied the committee. By the end of April 1907, consistently poor financial support meant that the branch was running up debts. The league 'may languish and die', wrote McDermott-Hayes, upon hearing that local members were discussing the viability of the town's branch.[92] The *Peasant* highlighted that it was always the same men who subscribed to the GL fund – other sources had to be tapped[93] – and it was agreed that instead of a *feis*, an *aeridheacht* would be staged in conjunction with a GAA match. The abandonment of the *feis* annoyed the more staunch language promoters, but, as was noted in the *Westmeath Independent*, 'the aeridheacht … is more popular with the general crowd',[94] and it would provide competition for army dances, support for which was previously highlighted as an impediment to the Irish Ireland movement in Athlone.[95] It was hoped that the event would bring people to the town, generate interest in the movement and, most importantly at this juncture, raise money.[96] The event certainly achieved the latter objective, as the branch saw out the year on the best 'financial footing' in its history.[97]

Peculiarly, what followed the improved fiscal situation was not growth, but decline. Classes catered for small numbers; ladies were conspicuous by their absence,[98] while the return of Fr Forde did nothing to tackle the recurrent somnolence.[99] No *feis* was proposed, the *aeridheacht* was perfunctorily organised and the viability of running Irish classes was debated.[100] Teachers were dependent on them, and due to this they were maintained, albeit unenthusiastically.[101] Failure appeared inevitable, yet, as often happened, a national issue was to greatly influence local efforts.

The familiar cycle of the Athlone GL was radically shaken during 1909/10, as what became known as the 'University Controversy' raged. The first years of the twentieth century had seen the GL lobby for a more prominent role for Irish in educational establishments, mainly at primary and secondary level.[102] Much of the lobbying had proved successful. However, the GL campaign to make Irish a compulsory subject for entry to the National University proved both controversial and divisive. Opposition from many Roman Catholic bishops, who believed that such a move would force students to apply to the Protestant Trinity College Dublin, led the league into direct conflict with the Church, a conflict that had both national and local repercussions for the organisation.

To present the GL argument, Douglas Hyde, '*An Craoibhín Aoibhinn*' (The Pleasant Little Branch),[103] came to Athlone in January 1909 and addressed a packed town hall.[104] M.J. Lennon presided as Hyde outlined how he saw the provision of Irish in universities as a unifying cultural force amongst Irish people.[105] Lennon spoke expressively, demanding that the hands of 'Castle Catholics' and 'West Britons' be kept off the Irish University, and hyperbolically cited the example of the Jacobites defending Athlone in 1691; 'victory or death'.[106] A letter from Revd Dr O'Hickey, Professor of Irish at the seminary in Maynooth, in response to a telegram from Fr Forde,[107] was read out. It detailed the disappointment O'Hickey felt at the decision of the Standing Committee of the Bishops not to support the league. O'Hickey declared that: 'But with or without the help of the lordships "on the cause must go"'.[108] The bishops, while disagreeing with the League, had, at least on paper, allowed for 'fair argument' from the clergy;[109] a resolution passed at the Athlone meeting noted satisfaction with their open-mindedness.[110] Both *The Leader* and *Irish Nation* covered the meeting, writing that while the GL organised it, a far wider cross-section of local society was attracted; the issue was greater than either the league or clergy.[111] McDermott-Hayes, quoted in *An Claidheamh Soluis*, stated that the heights to which the controversy was heading showed Ireland was 'deeply suffering from an intellectual grievance'.[112]

The controversy radically altered the local league. Despite supposedly allowing for fair argument, many bishops instead censured clerics who opposed the Episcopate's view. In Athlone, Fr Forde, a figure of minor but well-publicised prominence in the affair,[113] was reprimanded by Dr Clancy, Bishop of Elphin,[114] for the public reading of the letter he received from O'Hickey.[115] The bishop's reproach led Forde to distance himself from the league.[116] As O'Hickey later reported: 'In the interests, doubtless of ecclesiastical discipline … Fr Forde … and sundry other priests, were obliged to abandon the public advocacy of essential Irish.'[117] O'Hickey was dismissed from his professorship for his stance and while he gained support from numerous newspapers, the *Westmeath Independent* included ('the Gaelic League is mighty and shall prevail'[118]), it was obvious that a serious schism had been created. Indeed, it was noted that in Elphin specifically from early 1909, numerous priests had 'found it necessary to retire from the league'[119] to preserve their clerical integrity.[120] The consequent local difficulties led to a marked decline in the activity of the local league branch.[121] Perhaps the only positive step was the establishment of a Pipers' Club, which was intended to work with the league in organising events. Opened in the first week of October, it was the venue for Irish classes which had, by November, lost their teacher as well as their local branch.[122]

Despite the poor participation by locals in the GL, a void was created by the absence of a town branch.[123] However, it did not persist long. The Clan Uisneach (named after the mythologically important Hill of Uisneach in Westmeath) *Coiste Ceanntair* (area executive) was founded in July 1909 at Ballymore,[124] north-east of Athlone, and oversaw many Irish Ireland organisations and activities in south Westmeath, especially from the summer of 1910 onwards. The Clan joined forces with the Athlone Pipers' Club, a newly constituted Athlone GL committee and numerous other interested parties in the region.[125] The changes in the town's GL committee occurred around August 1909, but reports citing the names of the new members in Athlone are scarce.[126] This probably reflects the uncertainty and upheaval in local GL circles, and it is not until 1911 that reports on the membership of the committee become common.

When the reports did emerge, they showed that big changes had occurred. The Athlone GL president was 24-year-old Hugh Hanley, with 22-year-old Patrick Farrell as vice president and 23-year-old Kieran Begadon as secretary.[127] None of the three were formerly prominent in Athlone's nationalist life, be it in political or cultural circles, and reflected a radical change in the age profile of the branch's committee. Involvement from Athlone-based priests was now greatly diminished, with only Fr Peter Conefry of

St Mary's parish, part of the Diocese of Ardagh and Clonmacnoise, appearing to have an obvious association with the committee.[128] From summer 1910, Clan Uisneach (still clerically dominated by priests from rural south Westmeath, outside of the Diocese of Elphin) started a vigorous promotion of Irish culture. Perhaps fittingly, its first major task in Athlone was staging a 3,000-person-strong parade to celebrate the addition of Irish to the syllabus for university entry, a victory ascribed not only to the GL but to many local councils who threatened to withhold scholarships to the university in the absence of the measure.[129]

Clan Uisneach met regularly, organised an *aeridheacht* and classes, assisted the Athlone GL with the Manchester Martyrs[130] parade, and made headlines by censuring UDC member Robert English for refusing to deal with a pledge at the local Sessions, due to it being submitted in Irish.[131] By January 1911 the Clan's energy was unabated and Athlone was earmarked to hold its first *feis* since 1906: '*Feis Uisneach*'.[132] It appeared that the local GL was enjoying a period of sustained support; however, it soon became clear that not all Irish enthusiasts in the region were pleased with the activities of Clan Uisneach.

One of the first signs of conflict arose with the establishment of a collection for the *feis*. Reports emerged that Dean Kelly provided permission for fundraising, something the Dean stringently denied in the *Freeman's Journal*: 'I distinctly required, on more than one occasion that my name … not be mentioned in connection with the Feis of the "Clan Uisneagh [*sic*] … Gaelic League."'[133] Such a strong disassociation, even taking the diocesan boundary and the estrangement of the Elphin clergy into account, appears to indicate a greater antipathy to Clan Uisneach's efforts than perhaps should have existed. Similarly, soon after the Dean's comments, it was related that 'despite … attempts at opposition', a Clan Uisneach *aeridheacht* held at Ballymore was carried off successfully.[134]

It is certain from reading correspondence in the local press that differing opinions were held on how the GL in south Westmeath was developing. One correspondent, '*Fear Liath*' (Grey Man), questioned the reported success of the GL and noted that friction had entered local league circles: 'Is it not a sorry sight to witness men and women in South Westmeath … who were with the Gaelic League in the days of stress and storm, now standing with arms folded outside the ranks?'[135] He noted how some had to defend themselves against accusations of opposition to the GL and that the league in the region was dominated by 'those to whom the social aspect only – song and dance – appeals. The primary object … is forgotten'.[136] He contended that the GL was being subverted by a number of individuals who excluded others or, through their dominance, dissuaded people from either joining in the first instance, or remaining once enrolled. The Coiste Ceanntair he accused of being undemocratic, secretive, exclusive and unwelcoming.

The following week the 'In Gaeldom' column, the weekly GL news and debate section of the *Westmeath Independent*, congratulated *Fear Liath* on his letter and noted that it was the first of many received on the same topic. The writer stated that the dominance of the social aspect of the league's work was a fact in the region, and the exclusivity of committees or 'ornamental officer system … has been an expensive luxury … and has done harm … dampened enthusiasm and killed initiative'.[137] Another contributor bemoaned the division and questioned whether 'the cause must suffer while we thrash out our differences?'[138] A letter from '*Fear Dubh*' (Black Man), backed up the allegation of exclusive committees, comparing them to a 'Star Chamber'[139] and stated that notices in the press about the Coiste Ceanntair holding 'the usual quarterly meeting … etc, will deceive nobody':

> It is a … fact that this body does not meet quarterly and that the last meeting … was called for a purpose which those connected with it well understand. The meeting before that, to which certain members were not invited … lest they ask injudicious questions, was also a meeting for a similar purpose.[140]

He asked that the Athlone GL take the lead in tackling the problem, for he believed that the town's branch (perhaps due to its size) was the only one not beset by the difficulties that were handicapping others in south Westmeath.[141]

Other evidence of antagonism involving Clan Uisneach came to light somewhat later. Reports noted that the departure of the Irish teacher after the University Controversy was not as clear cut as it first appeared. Clan Uisneach found it difficult to hire a replacement as no applications were received, except from travelling teachers with restricted availability. In the *Irish Independent*, a letter stated that the teacher was hounded out and 'put upon the spit by a junta of individuals posturing as the Uisneach Coisde [*sic*] Ceanntair'. In the same edition, the secretary of Clan Uisneach stated that the teacher was not rehired due to his intention to remain independent of Clan Uisneach. The secretary noted that: 'Our Coisde [*sic*] Ceanntair has had a hard uphill fight, and … had to face a great amount of … opposition'.[142]

Despite the hostility, many prominent townspeople happily associated with Clan Uisneach. Thomas Chapman and councillors M.J. Hughes and

M.J. Lennon helped organise the *Uisneach Feis*, promoting the wearing of Irish clothes only, while some local clergymen subscribed funds.[143] In a comment directed at most towns, *An Claidheamh Soluis* stated that rural league members, presumably culturally purer given their less frequent contact with garrison staff and other urban impurities, could assist in the de-anglicisation of Athlone.[144] Despite receiving the plaudits of *An Claidheamh Soluis* and SF, the event was generally considered a failure.[145] The crowds were large, between 10,000 and 15,000, but, as was noted by the press, the occasion was unimpressive. Few houses were decorated and the number of schools that participated was disappointing.[146] The antipathy of Dean Kelly and bad press may have been to blame, in addition to inclement weather, for the poor turnout, which appeared to confirm that Clan Uisneach was not as widely supported as its members might have wished.

The foundation of a branch of the advanced nationalist scout troop Fianna Éireann (FÉ)[147] in the Pipers' Club was the only notable occurrence for the rest of 1911 as Clan Uisneach organised the usual classes and made a request of the UDC to place street nameplates in Irish, while devoting most energy to concerts and excursions.[148] Their efforts were lauded in the *Westmeath Independent*: 'It is true to say that the Gaelic movement took no substantial hold in Athlone until the advent of the Pipers' Band and ... the Uisneach Club.'[149] It appeared that the accusations made against Clan Uisneach with regard to ignoring the language had some foundation, though perhaps those involved believed the local indifference to the Irish language too difficult to tackle, and that they needed to work with what was popular.

By the end of 1911, the Gaelic League had been operating in Athlone for a decade. The success of Irish language promotion by the GL over that period can be gauged, at least to some extent, by comparing statistics from the 1911 census returns with those of 1901. By 1911 over 600 people (roughly two-and-a-half times the 1901 figure) within the urban boundary claimed to speak both Irish and English, with a more equal split between the sexes of the population, now numbering 7,472.[150] Unlike 1901, the majority was less than 18 years of age, with the greatest number, almost 180, in the 10–15 year range. The east side of the town had the greater number of Irish speakers, due to the presence of the largest schools, though the west now claimed more Irish speakers than all of Athlone in 1901. It is obvious that the introduction of the language into schools was boosting the figures: between 1899 and 1911, the number of children being taught Irish in the country rose from 1,825 to 180,000,[151] though adults were still shying away; figures indicate an increase of just fifty new Irish speakers in the adult demographic.[152] Outside of the urban boundaries, little had changed with small increases in those claiming to speak both languages.[153] Obviously, teaching Irish in schools was more common and impacting on local bilingualism amongst children, although to what standard is unknown. What is also obvious is that league efforts to entice adults to learn the language were failing. While a number had used their Irish names when completing the census form, a sign perhaps more indicative of their nationalism than their linguistic prowess, they were in the minority, with perhaps the starkest evidence of the GL's failure to render Irish an accessible subject being the attestation of Dean Kelly to his continued inability to speak the language.

Whatever the statistics tell us, it was certain, at least in the opinion of 'Fírín' who penned the 'In Gaeldom' column for the *Westmeath Independent*, that by January 1912 the vitality of the local GL was putting other areas to shame.[154] A profit of £40 had been realised in 1911, with a larger profit envisaged for 1912.[155] The *Uisneach Feis* was again organised for Athlone this year, with an industrial exhibition on the fringes.[156] Unlike in previous years, the *feis* was entirely organised by the Athlone GL, which appears to have been imbued with a degree of vitality through osmosis. While the move appeared to presage a reassertion of GL control in Athlone to town-based members, it was reasoned that such members could deal with the day-to-day organisation better than Clan Uisneach, whose committee was mainly rurally-based. However, it is certain that there was some move towards change as Dean Kelly was happy to associate with the *feis* as patron after much of the antagonism caused by the University Controversy had abated; not as president however. That was a position eventually awarded to Clan Uisneach's Fr Casey from Ballymore.[157]

One sizable problem was encountered however, a problem which highlighted, despite Hyde's assertion to the contrary, that the GL was undoubtedly a political as well as a cultural force. To stage the *feis* a large plot of land was required, and that year the Athlone PLG were petitioned for the use of lands at the workhouse. Permission was refused, not by the Guardians but by the Local Government Board (LGB), the government's local authority overseer. GL organisers quickly set about trying to overturn what was described as 'merely a manifesto of the English Garrison to everything Irish'.[158] The PLG, after receiving the LGB's letter of refusal, stated that they would not stop the league; indeed, the chairman stated: 'We will storm the place.'[159] McDermott-Hayes described the LGB's actions as 'too bigoted and contemptible for editorial comment', though, unsurprisingly, he made quite a stern comment: '[The LGB] ... are so impregnated with hatred of anything Irish, they will sacrifice every pretence to consistency of administration to defeat [Irish initiatives].'[160] The LGB stated that a High Court injunction would be sought, if necessary; they had used injunctions before, citing one incident in Cork.[161]

The actions of the LGB were predicated on the 'Gaelic' nature of the event. Over the previous decade no problem had been encountered when the grounds were used for the 'Midland Counties Horticultural and Home Industries Association', despite part of the LGB's reasoning behind the *feis* refusal being that no 'bazaars, fetes, public or political meetings in workhouses' were permissible.[162] The PLG eventually had to acquiesce to LGB demands, though they made it clear that they saw the refusal as 'bigoted' and 'spiteful'.[163] Eventually, the *feis* was held in the grounds of Our Lady's Bower school and convent.[164]

The new year of 1913 saw the Athlone GL and Pipers' Club meet in January to discuss unspecified 'important reforms'; the reintroduction of Dean Kelly and other Elphin clergymen after the death of Bishop Clancy the previous October had altered the Athlone GL equation.[165] Reports of the GL experiencing a sustained positive spell were made and it appeared, with the reintroduction of Kelly, that relations began to normalise.[166] A reconciliation period was in play during the spring of 1913 as the pre-controversy and post-controversy committees assessed how best to advance the local league.

However, it was unlikely that the groups would be able to reconcile their approaches to the cultural reinvention of the local populace. At a large nationalist rally after the 1913 St Patrick's Day parade, Dean Kelly emphasised the importance of the Irish language over all other aspects of GL activity. At the same meeting, Fr Michael McCabe, possibly directing his comments at Clan Uisneach, stated that the 'fanaticism' of some GL members was alienating others.[167] Member of the new guard, Hugh Hanley, contrary to GL rules, set about trying to organise a political rally for Athlone during April, a move that was problematic for Dean Kelly, who always had a clear view of the GL's non-political brief.[168] Hanley, in line with others around Ireland, obviously backed the move towards politicising the GL, as the push for Home Rule gained momentum.[169] His efforts and those of like-minded activists all over Ireland would eventually contribute to moving the GL away from Hyde's ideal and towards becoming 'narrower in its conception of Irishness and increasingly nationalist in politics'.[170] McDermott-Hayes wrote that the GL's recidivist tendency (no doubt informed by local occurrences), towards internal strife could lead to a split, which would threaten the league's very existence.[171]

By September, the familiarisation period was over and moves were made to establish a new branch and search for a permanent home.[172] The latest *craobh* saw Dean Kelly reclaim his position at the top of the Athlone GL after an absence of over three years, while the name Clan Uisneach, and indeed many of its local associates, was conspicuously absent during the formation of the branch.[173] Perhaps due to its increasing political stance and the promotion of Irish entertainments instead of the language, Clan Uisneach's role in Athlone's GL activity was restricted to assisting in organising the 1914 *feis*.[174] An optimistic article was printed in relation to this latest branch which, tellingly, appeared to gloss over the efforts of Clan Uisneach during the previous four years:

> Athlone can justly boast ... of what we may expect in future for the Gaelic Revival, a vigorous assurance that Athlone is intent to take up again the prominent place it occupied in the early days of the Gaelic League.[175]

Politics were to be left to the UIL and IPP; under Dean Kelly the local GL was constituted to assist the aim of an Irish Ireland from a cultural platform.

SINN FÉIN

The establishment of an Athlone branch of SF was one of the later political developments in the town, coming in the spring of 1909. SF entry into Athlone, a town which had known little of political nationalism outside of the constitutional, appeared to herald a change in the local political discourse. The foundation of the local branch had been preceded by quite a lengthy period of discussion on the merits of advanced nationalist ideology in Athlone, a discussion that had begun in earnest with the December 1904 review by Michael McDermott-Hayes of *The Resurrection of Hungary – A parallel for Ireland* (1904). Written by Dublin journalist Arthur Griffith, the book outlined what Griffith believed to be a template for working towards Irish independence. In it he recounted, using a 'rather questionable, if interesting account of Hungarian history',[176] and 'misapplied historical parallels',[177] how nineteenth-century Hungarian separatists had won their freedom. Most prominently, he promoted the policies of parliamentary abstentionism and dual monarchy,[178] believing that a return to the 1782 Irish constitution[179] could be the basis for the desired political reform.[180] In a generally positive review, McDermott-Hayes promoted Griffith's desire that the Irish language be revitalised and indigenous industries promoted: both, Griffith believed, were essential in creating a comprehensive cultural and economic break between Britain and Ireland.[181] However, the editor was not impressed at Griffith's call for Irish MPs to abandon Westminster.[182]

Others outside Athlone were less averse to the idea of parliamentary abstentionism and the popularity of *The Resurrection of Hungary* brought Griffith into contact with a number of advanced nationalist individuals and organisations. That contact led to negotiations, which eventually saw the creation of the 'Sinn Féin Policy' in late 1905, and the unofficial adoption of the name Sinn Féin to describe the as yet loose alliance that had been created.[183] In Athlone, the SF policy quickly began to gain promoters, with the *Midland Tribune*, printed in Mullingar and available in Athlone, singled out by the RIC for its pro-Griffith stance.[184] It may have been through this publication or Griffith's *United Irishman*, which was recommended by the local GL, that UDC, UIL and GL member, M.J. Lennon, became familiar with SF policies, policies that, as already noted, he highlighted at a St Peter's UIL meeting in February 1906. He stated he was 'a believer in the newer policy of Sinn Féin', but, following the lead given by Griffith at the time, was willing to see what the IPP achieved in the short term with the Liberal government.[185] Lennon again noted his support for SF at a meeting to organise the St Patrick's Day parade a week later[186] and his position as the de facto local promoter of SF indicated his belief in the rising stock of Griffith's ideas.

Despite the fact that late 1906 saw much ideological wrangling between Griffith and other advanced nationalists in Dublin, it is apparent that provincially, Athlone included, SF policies were growing in influence.[187] The Manchester Martyrs parade in the town in November 1906 showed, at least in the eyes of McDermott-Hayes, that 'Hungarian' ideas were having a noticeable effect:

> The growth of ... the Gaelic League ... and the extension of the Sinn Féin or 'Rely on Ourselves' policy ... has brought to the front ... ardent ... young men who hold in deep veneration the memory of ... [those] who died for Ireland.[188]

While the parade report stated that it was disorganised, it also noted that there 'could be no truer indication of the deep-spread patriotism of the people'.[189] Disorganisation aside, there was additional evidence that SF policies were spreading in Westmeath, as recognised by the CI, who believed that real headway had yet to be made.[190] The *Westmeath Independent* gave SF coverage, providing reports on meetings and lectures given by its members,[191] while

M.J. Lennon. (NLI, *IL*, 8 October
1915)

McDermott-Hayes continued to comment on its policy, contrasting the
Hungarian situation with that of Ireland.[192]

Additional commentary on the possible efficacy of SF policies came in
the wake of the IPP's embarrassingly impotent efforts with regard to the
Irish Council Bill. As already noted, M.J. Lennon tried to dissuade the UDC
from sending delegates to the IPP conference that was to consider the bill,
believing it too poor to gain support.[193] The Dungannon Clubs, part of the
still nebulous SF alliance, sent a request to the UDC asking that they pass a
resolution on the necessity of repudiating parliamentary agitation. Although
the resolution did not pass, Lennon was in favour, as was GAA activist Patrick
Norton, with an editorial in the *Westmeath Independent* stating that the resolution was 'worthy in its own way', and something that would appeal to the
younger generation who favoured direct action.[194]

Nationally the failure of the bill saw the resignation of a small number of
IPP MPs, with the most prominent, C.J. Dolan in North Leitrim, proving
to be instrumental in uniting those under the SF umbrella into a more
cohesive movement.[195] Dolan's subsequent move to contest the constituency's by-election from a SF platform coincided with the visit of SF
promoter and Irish Republican Brotherhood (IRB) member Major John
MacBride to Athlone. He made enquiries as to the level of SF support in
the town, visiting a Dr Sheridan in Kiltoom, north-west of Athlone, as well
as M.J. Lennon.[196] The RIC kept a close eye on MacBride and the information presented to the CI led him to express the view that it was likely

'the Sinn Féin movement will soon be started [however,] it is not likely to take hold'.[197]

SF ideology and support was certainly growing, though McDermott-Hayes questioned the need for an antagonistic relationship between the IPP and SF; he, taking the Griffith line, believed the two were not poles apart in their political aspirations.[198] A massive meeting at Finea to commemorate Myles 'The Slasher' O'Reilly[199] in Westmeath in August 1907 saw advanced nationalist Bulmer Hobson explain SF policy, as he saw it, to the assembled crowd of 7,000, which included IPP quasi-member Laurence Ginnell.[200] The same meeting saw the defection to SF of prominent Longford UIL member William Ganly, who had lost the recent by-election in South Westmeath to Walter Nugent.[201] Changes in political allegiance were also witnessed in County Roscommon, where some UIL members were flirting with SF as local animosity over county council jobs was directed at J.P. Hayden, amongst other IPP supporters.[202] At the same time, SF became more conspicuous in King's County, and, while not on a large scale,[203] it was noted by the IG that nationally it appeared that 'the energy of its [Sinn Féin's] adherents, in a measure, makes up for [the small numbers]'.[204]

One member of the energetic minority, Major MacBride, who spent much time travelling Ireland promoting advanced nationalist ideology, returned to Athlone in November 1907. At the annual Manchester Martyrs parade MacBride delivered a speech, apparently while drunk, on the Fenian virtue that was coming to the fore due to the IRB and local INF,[205] despite the latter being generally termed a 'non-sectarian … friendly society'.[206] M.J. Lennon and local publican O.J. Dolan spoke on a similar theme. The meeting saw 2,000 people gather and the RIC noted that observations were made that 'Fenianism was in the air … and would never die out until Ireland was free'.[207] MacBride remained in Athlone for a few weeks, spending time with the 'more advanced element' of the INF, making speeches and presenting lectures on fighting with the Boers.[208]

Given the opposition he was encountering in Roscommon, and recognising SF moves in Athlone, J.P. Hayden wrote to the local press, stating that 'the signs … indicate … that in a very short time nothing will be heard of … Sinn Féin'.[209] His assertion that SF was a ephemeral organisation was not widely held amongst the IPP, especially in Leitrim, where the by-election campaign was becoming increasingly rough.[210] The IG of the RIC noted: 'The strength and importance of this movement [SF] is shown by the anxiety of the Irish Parliamentary Party to crush it.'[211] Some IPP members ridiculed SF, a practice criticised in the *Westmeath Independent*: 'Sinn Féin will not be silenced or made to appear a ridiculous policy by the intemperate speeches of … less conspicuous members of the Irish Party.'[212] While still an IPP supporter, McDermott-Hayes believed that the party was neither operating well, nor as vocal as SF on certain issues; consequently, support for the latter on aspects of their program was justified.[213]

SF gained a boost in Athlone with the municipal elections of 1908, which saw M.J. Lennon elected as UDC chairman.[214] His instatement caused disquiet at a St Peter's UIL meeting where a speaker noted the inability of the UIL to make consistent gains. 'Even Sinn Féin has made progress', noted one attendee, half joking, wholly in earnest, who then declared, lest he was misinterpreted; 'not one of the so-called Sinn Féiners … [has] any sincerity'.[215] The chairman, Fr Flynn, compounded this sentiment by stating that those 'who said they were Sinn Féiners have handed in their guns on being elected to offices of trust or emolument'. Clearly directed at M.J. Lennon, the statement was informed by news that Lennon was being considered for a Justice of the Peace commission. The meeting heard that the UIL was willing to take back any SF men, though, surprisingly, it appeared that the most prominent, Lennon, had never left.[216]

Indeed, it appears that M.J. Lennon continued to espouse SF policies while still a member of the UIL and he was appointed, just two weeks later, as a representative for the St Peter's branch at the South Roscommon Executive meeting in Athlone.[217] He actually took the chair and while it is difficult to tease out the man's loyalties, it should be noted that he used his speech to promote local industry, rather than readily identifiable IPP policies.[218]

In early April, SF moves to establish in the town were again highlighted by local police reports. The party was putting in additional work following its surprisingly good showing in the North Leitrim by-election, which made the headlines in both the local and national press.[219] Though SF had offered 'a significant, but not in any way decisive challenge to the IPP machine',[220] it had proven itself more than just a fringe faction. The *Peasant* wrote of the 'triumph in the failure of Leitrim' and the party made small gains in a number of local authority areas in the aftermath.[221] The move by the Liberal government to suspend efforts to introduce Home Rule legislation made the IPP appear even more impotent, and gave SF additional impetus. In the aftermath of the election and Liberal Party actions, the *Irish Independent* related that: 'Athlone Sinn Féiners believe that the attitude of the government … supplies an unanswerable case for the adoption of their policy.'[222] Efforts were made yet again by SF activists to capitalise and Athlone soon had Major MacBride visit for what was to be one of at least three failed attempts to open a branch during 1908.[223]

Lennon too must have believed SF's star to be in the ascendant. He continued to ruffle local UIL feathers, never more so than when he, as already related, attempted to prevent UDC members from going to Clara for a John Dillon speech. One St Peter's UIL member held that it 'was a great mistake to appoint a Sinn Féiner to the chairmanship'.[224] Lennon's views on Dillon caused him to be challenged at a UDC meeting, with *The Peasant* reporting that Lennon rather unconvincingly rebutted allegations that he was a Sinn Féiner; he stated that he was not a 'good enough Irishman' to be one.[225] Along with querying the incongruity of Lennon being a JP while holding the views he did, the newspaper also asked why he was just 'talking much of Sinn Féin … why does he not … establish a branch?'[226]

January 1909 saw no local elections held for positions on the UDC; the number of candidates equalled the number of available seats. Lennon did, however, in his last few days as chairman, want to ensure a lively political atmosphere. At a meeting called to consider the selection of delegates for the upcoming IPP National Convention, Lennon demanded a resolution 'that the Act of Union was illegal, that all Irish reps [sic] should withdraw from the British constitution and call into existence the Irish Constitution; the King, Lords and Commons of Ireland', references to the 1782 constitution and the 1783 Renunciation Act.[227] Unsurprisingly, the escalation in his rhetoric, also seen during the same week in connection with the University Controversy,[228] caused disquiet; some councillors stated that they would attend as representatives of other organisations out of fear of being tarnished by their chairman's speeches.[229] Lennon laid his cards on the table, stating that he did not want delegates to travel and that the IPP was moving towards an Imperial Home Rule Parliament: 'If that's the definition of Irish Independence, I say it is not right.'[230]

Lennon continued to increase his promotion of SF during the spring of 1909, supporting the fundraising drive for a daily edition of the *Sinn Féin*.[231] Enough money was collected in Athlone to purchase fifty shares, a fair success, which indicated increased local interest in what the newspaper would have to impart.[232] Another indicator of growing interest in SF was a report from February 1909, which noted that local SF enthusiasts were actively pursuing the formation of a branch.[233] The initial foundation meeting was postponed when Arthur Griffith could not attend,[234] though this did not delay them long, and on 21 March a meeting was convened, at which the Athlone SF branch was formed.

The meeting heard from Andrew O'Byrne (Aindrias Ó Broin), SF general secretary, and James Deakin from the National Executive Council. The latter, expanding on the content of a letter sent to the *Westmeath Independent*, counselled against an armed struggle given the 'might of England', while both asked those assembled to boycott English goods and support indigenous industries. They spoke at length on Ireland's industry, language and literature, the deficient land acts, SF policy in regard to Westminster and external governance.[235] Of local interest was news that some within SF were not averse to the idea of establishing a National Assembly in Athlone after independence. Unsurprisingly, Lennon was appointed president and he aired his views, contrary as these were to those heard already, on the necessity for, at the very least, gun training in schools and the establishment of rifle clubs.[236] Additionally, in a fine example of cognitive dissonance, he noted the need for religious tolerance before singling out two prominent Protestants, Lord Castlemaine and a Mr Smyth, whom he believed were unfairly occupying places on the Athlone PLG board. He questioned why the IPP was in Westminster and asked that all Irish people join with SF and 'build up the country politically and industrially'. A resolution was passed: 'That the people of Ireland are a free people, and that no law made without their authority or consent is, or ever can be, binding on their conscience.'[237]

The number of people at the meeting is uncertain. The RIC, in two separate reports, put the number at eighty, with few enrolling on the night. The *Westmeath Independent* stated that the numbers were small at first, but reached about 300 by the end.[238] Locals in attendance included urban councillors Patrick Norton and Michael Hogan as well as former UIL collector and local GAA vice-chairman Owen Sweeney.[239] Whatever the numbers, those at the next meeting to elect officers were fewer. The RIC noted that just fourteen people saw Lennon installed as president and Thomas Murray (Athlone GL secretary) elected as secretary.[240] The local newspaper quantified membership numbers at forty-three in total after the meeting. Of that, three were unnamed women, SF being perhaps the only prominent local political organisation that admitted women, outside of the GL, with reports of St Mary's UIL enrolling ladies difficult to substantiate.[241]

The branch was unable to elect a vice-president; for reasons not stated, the three who were proposed demurred, something not mentioned by *Sinn Féin*, which constructed a most positive account of the meeting.[242] A committee was formed to reflect both rural and urban Athlone, with the three lady members co-opted. Interestingly, Lennon noted his disappointment at not being allowed to enter the local British Army barracks for boxing matches due to party rules.[243]

A *Westmeath Independent* editorial after the meeting noted: 'The more we get at the inside of the Sinn Féin propaganda, the more reasonable it appears', though McDermott-Hayes was applying the statement to the industrial elements rather than the political. A letter to the newspaper in the same issue from a SF member stated that the new Athlone branch would allow for 'misconceptions' to be addressed vis á vis 'this newer national movement', which intended to adopt a direct approach, rather than the 'kid-glove tactics' of the Irish Party.[244]

The branch was affiliated by late April and, according to the RIC, confined 'its attention to furthering the sale of Irish manufactured goods', a trait that led to SF clubs in Leinster being concentrated mainly in urban areas.[245] The police observation was well-founded. Most of the meetings held dealt almost exclusively with the issue of Irish industry, while also referring to asides such as co-operation with the UIL on the issue of industrial development.[246] Lennon advocated 'People's Banks', which could provide credit for the landless, emigration-prone small farmers and excoriated the 'shopkeepers and gombeen men jobbing in land' for exacerbating land ownership inequality.[247] Members complained about the 1909 budget and decided that their political views would not impact on their job security, therefore negating the need for insurance as recommended by the party leadership. The branch discussed its support for cattle driving and organised a number of meetings in connection with promoting Irish industry, one of which saw numerous political organisations (INF, TLA, St Mary's UIL and UDC) in attendance, as well as prominent Protestant businessmen such as John Burgess.[248] Some instances of poor planning and scheduling were witnessed, and while the branch maintained a nucleus of loyal members, it did not make gains.[249] Budget proposals submitted to the UDC in September were basically ignored, and little interest was taken in the branch's involvement with the Manchester Martyr's procession.[250] The party was having difficulty making an impact in Athlone and by mid-November the branch suffered a death blow when M.J. Lennon resigned after 'he had regained confidence in the Irish Party'.[251]

The meeting that heard of the resignation saw much debate before his announcement, which may have highlighted some of the issues that were troubling many SF branches. The parent organisation's debit balance of £200 was highlighted and contrasted with the £1,000 bill that would be realised if all of the work demanded by the SF congress was carried out. The debt was partially due to the fact that more than half the branches had not sent on affiliation fees, individual membership fees or sums gained from collections, a situation that SF's poor provincial framework had allowed to develop and persist.[252] The meeting also heard members condemn the IPP for choosing inadequate men to occupy parliamentary seats, and criticised it for abstaining on the budget vote. Walter Nugent's pragmatic approach to gaining political office rankled some members, as did the infighting seen between neighbouring MPs.[253] The SF credentials of Athlone people were called into question, while, tellingly, one member wondered what actually made a person a Sinn Féiner.

Throughout the debate, the branch's most politicised yet, Lennon gave a series of short opinions which, it became apparent, were leading up to a confirmation of a shift in his political ideology. He spoke on how counter-productive the rivalry between the IPP and SF was, and noted how many Irish Party supporters in Athlone were 'better Nationalists than I am'. When questioned by Patrick Norton on the incongruity of holding such a view while occupying the branch presidency, Lennon stated that he could not support parliamentary abstentionism if the IPP could again find a level of independence similar to that enjoyed during the days of Parnell.[254] In reply, Thomas Murray stated that anyone against abstention was not a Sinn Féiner.

Lennon chose the placing of a resolution on the IPP abstention from the budget vote as his opportunity to resign, stating that he hoped 'the gentleman you put in my position may be able to fill it better'. His resignation, he averred falsely, was not just from SF, but from politics altogether, a decision he had made a month previously, obviously soon after he had stated that he 'did not believe in the United Irish League'.[255] Some requested he stay on, while others believed his decision was due to personality conflicts with other members. Lennon rejected this kind of reason for his departure, other than to say it was a personal decision.[256] D.P. Moran of *The Leader* believed that the resignation in Athlone highlighted:

> … the sham and hollowness of the Sinn Féiners. Real Sinn Féiners would … rejoice at the muddles of the Irish Party, and … aim at its destruction … Sinn Féin is merely a game of humbug from first to last.[257]

Lennon may have decided that he had misinterpreted the political currents. SF had not made sustained gains since the Irish Council Bill fallout, despite continued IPP weakness, and he may have been jumping ship in what might flatteringly be termed political pragmatism. After his resignation it was rumoured that Westmeath's only SF branch was to close, though this was, at least initially, untrue. Lennon's replacement was Joseph Byrne, 'a carpenter of no previous note in politics', who, by his own admission, 'didn't carry enough weight' to further the branch.[258] The resolution that led to Lennon announcing his retirement was sent to the UDC and, tellingly, it was dealt with contemptuously. One councillor stated: 'Put it in the waste paper basket. They have no defender left.'[259]

Lennon's re-defection in late 1909 came when SF was, for all intents and purposes, non-existent outside of Dublin.[260] The Athlone branch joined the ranks of defunct provincial SF clubs, with virtually no activity outside of a St Patrick's Day organisational meeting the following March.[261] Similarly moribund branches were seen in Leitrim, after the post-election fervour had fizzled out, and Longford, as poor provincial structures left branches isolated. An indication of indifference to the Athlone branch on Griffith's part may be inferred from the almost total absence of coverage of its work after its foundation. Just one meeting in April was mentioned, and the branch's activities did not make the pages of either the weekly or daily editions of *Sinn Féin* from then onwards. SF members such as Bulmer Hobson wanted administrative decentralisation, though Griffith appeared uncommitted to the effort required and consequently SF conventions never drew up the structures for managing a provincial presence.[262] 'Branches were never an essential feature, and the organisation did not collapse after 1910 when most provincial branches became dormant', writes Richard Davis, noting the party's Dublin-centred nature.[263]

After the 1910 general elections, SF allowed the IPP breathing space as the latter attempted to use its improved parliamentary position to achieve Home Rule.[264] The SF convention of 1910, a turning point in the decline of the organisation, saw disillusioned IRB members leave the party.[265] The IPP had gained the crucial balance of power in Westminster and Griffith, 'like so many other separatists, began to reconcile himself to the Redmondite agenda'.[266] SF moved away from the day-to-day political arena, restricting itself to protesting against a loyalty address to King George V in 1911, promoting Irish industry and anti-enlistment drives.[267] The local RIC believed the Athlone branch to exist 'only in name' by the end of the same year, though given the inactivity of the previous eighteen months, even this may have been an exaggeration.[268] Opportunities had not yet arisen for SF to convince either the people of Ireland or the people of Athlone of the merits of its policies.

THE ANCIENT ORDER OF HIBERNIANS

By the time the AOH established an Athlone division in the early summer of 1911, it was considered to be one of the most powerful nationalist organisations in Ireland. Nominally professing to a raison d'etre of promoting the interests and values of Roman Catholics, the Order was viewed as a counterbalance to the Protestant Orange Order and, as a corollary, initially found its greatest support in northern areas where Orange lodges were most common.[269] The desire to establish a nationwide presence forced the AOH to undergo a protracted process of redefinition that saw it create alliances and adopt additional roles and responsibilities, each of which softened its sectarian façade and expanded its appeal. Its entry into Athlone came towards the end of that process, and undoubtedly relied upon it, as the midland town exhibited little in the way of sectarian tensions, which had been essential to the Order's early growth.

The first step towards becoming more widely accepted came in 1900 when the IPP, in a move designed to increase their influence in the north, granted AOH members, known as brethren, permission to attend the National Convention.[270] The mutually beneficial arrangement saw the AOH increase its influence in the south, forced out many radicals and assisted in ensuring the AOH was approved as a benefit society in 1903.[271] Initially, Catholic Church authorities considered the AOH too secretive, and imposed a ban on Catholic membership. This ban was lifted in 1904[272] and the Hibernians slowly began to spread towards Athlone from the west, via County Roscommon. Even with the ban lifted, the Order received little support from Roscommon priests,[273] requiring the additional assistance of official registration as a friendly society in February 1905 to precipitate division establishments in the county.[274] After this additional approval, the *Westmeath Independent*, which was consulted extensively in Roscommon, welcomed the AOH, describing it as a benefit society from the USA, one of the many origins ascribed to the organisation.[275] The greatest boost to the Order came in 1905 with the election of Joe Devlin, a protégé of John Redmond, as president. He 'proceeded to remould the character of the organisation',[276] moving 'the Catholic content of Irish nationalism to lay leadership'.[277] The Order committed itself to the policy of the IPP, while somewhat unconvincingly underplaying its political attributes, and adopted the subtitle 'Board of Erin' to distinguish itself from smaller, more radical factions.[278] The effort paid off, and the Order began to experience growth in many western counties.[279]

Despite evidence of earlier AOH groups in Westmeath,[280] it appears that definitive moves toward founding an Athlone division came with the official introduction of the Board of Erin into the county during the spring of 1909.[281] The Order was welcomed at the South Westmeath UIL Executive quarterly meeting in April, which heard that the AOH would be 'working in harmony with the National organisation to advance the interests of our country'.[282] A letter published in the *Westmeath Independent* provided further clarity on the

Ancient Order of Hibernians, Athlone Division 680. (AHL)

Order's guiding principles, detailing how the Hibernians' pursuit of Irish freedom was based on the power of not only Irishness, but Roman Catholicism; 'the faith that supplied the vitality to a dying nation is its bulwark'.[283] The correspondence further noted that accusations of sectarianism should not have been allowed to obscure the fact that the Order was 'prepared to do [the] utmost to advance the interests of the Society in every possible way'. The writer, South Westmeath UIL Executive member Patrick McKenna, highlighted the renewed vigour of the Order and drew attention to links with its American sister organisation.[284] In conclusion, he noted that the Order could 'surely stand the tongue of Tim Healy', one of the AOH's most outspoken critics, and quite starkly noted that 'when the Order is launched in Westmeath … it will try … to make Ireland a nation … a Catholic nation'.[285]

By September 1909, in a move that had been seen in northern regions, AOH members in Roscommon were encouraged to join the UIL, probably in an attempt to assuage the opposition to the Order from Bishop Clancy of Elphin.[286] The bishop had initially backed the AOH,[287] but the Order's efforts to become more secretive and exclude certain clergymen led him to change his stance during 1907.[288] Growth continued in Roscommon regardless,[289] in part because 'there was demand for AOH divisions in areas where the UIL had atrophied'.[290] Indeed, many in the league promoted the Order's spread, as they recognised that it 'provided a new dynamism to replace the fading issue of land tenure'.[291] By January 1910, the IG believed the AOH and UIL to be in a symbiotic relationship,[292] while the IPP's success in the same year's general elections assured the Orders' leaders that their ideology would exert an influence at Westminster.[293]

After a period of over two years since its welcome to Westmeath, the AOH formed its first official division in the county at Athlone. Westmeath had, up to this point, been one of only six counties, the other five being Kilkenny, King's County, Queen's County, Kildare and Carlow, without an organised Hibernian presence.[294] These areas appeared not to require a powerful Roman Catholic lobby per se, yet the increasing influence being wielded by the AOH in politics, and moves by the Order to become eminent in the field of insurance meant that they ran the risk of being under serviced in its absence.

The foundation meeting on 28 May 1911 saw a small number of people attend to hear J.J. Bergin, John Nolan and Joseph Nolan of the Order's Central Executive speak on the AOH's role and aims. After taking his cue from UIL, RDC and former UDC member J.H. Rafferty, Bergin outlined the origins of the AOH:[295] their purpose was to be like YMCAs, which gave practical assistance to Protestants, as well as to be involved with the Irish Party. He explained that the Order was looking for the equitable treatment of Catholics in civil service appointments, but was not engaging in an anti-Protestant crusade. Indeed, the charge of sectarianism was rebutted by Bergin, who stated that Protestant IPP MPs, including Stephen Gwynn of Galway and Hugh Law of Donegal, gained their seats with AOH assistance; 'honest, conscientious Protestants' had nothing to fear from the Order. Bergin, like J.D. Nugent MP, secretary of the AOH and the most regular defender of the Order against accusations of sectarianism, was trying to dispel the notion that the Hibernians were trying to 'establish a new ascendancy', something of which the Order can be fairly accused.[296]

Bergin concluded his oration by alluding to the virtual absence of AOH divisions in the centre of Ireland. He stated that the midlands had to 'form the missing link needed to connect the whole of Ireland under the banner of Hibernianism'. Those who wished to join did so in a private session; between thirty and fifty enrolled, while the majority who attended departed.[297] The newly formed Athlone division, no. 680, was geographically well located to assist the Order in its expansion into both Westmeath and King's County, where it was weak, despite opening a Tullamore division in December 1908.[298] The *Hibernian Journal* carried a short piece on the creation of the Athlone division ('Athlone to the Front') and noted that it augured 'well for the future of the Order in the Midlands'.[299] Little activity was seen in the local division during its first month; the RIC believed it had made no progress by the end of June, but newspaper reports did note a rise of fifteen members.[300] The local brethren met and advertisements carrying times and venues were published, though no reports were given; the press were neither admitted nor provided with the minutes of meetings, something for which other organisations allowed.[301]

It transpired that Westmeath was to be harder to gain a foothold in than some other counties. In July, when the RIC reported substantial gains for the Order nationally, Athlone's division was still the only one in the county.[302] It was reportedly fully organised by 1 July and began to show activity in local politics, meeting with Walter Nugent to discuss the State Insurance Bill, the provisions of which were to assist greatly in the Order's growth.[303] The names of members were guarded and membership numbers were usually estimates made by local reporters; forty-five in July up to eighty in October.[304] The most significant action and indication that the division was gaining financial support was news that a premises on Abbey Lane was renovated and used as a meeting hall. The property was near St Peter's Roman Catholic church on the west side of the town and the ability of the Order to find a home so quickly appears indicative of better financial support and a focused view on how division 680 was to develop.[305]

As was inevitable, the names of the local brethren did surface. At the Manchester Martyrs parade organisation meeting in November 1911, W. Waterston and M.J. O'Meara UDC (UIL and PLG member) represented the local division.[306] Additional names came to light with the division's call to establish a vigilance committee to deal with imported low-grade literature from Britain.[307] When a committee meeting to progress the proposal was held, it became apparent that local publican and farmer, Bogginfin's J.H. Rafferty, was the division president and Waterston was vice-president.[308]

The vigilance committee itself ran for a short period, showing good cross-denominational support with Roman Catholic, Church of Ireland, Presbyterian and Methodist representatives involved.[309] Convened to deal with the 'indecent literature and morally unhealthy English Sunday newspapers'[310] circulating in Athlone, similar committees spread across Ireland during 1911.[311] The Order promoted the creation of a 'Catholic Press' and while these committees were not a direct attempt to achieve this (a multi-denominational committee would have been an incongruous step towards such a goal), they were an attempt to create a purer press.[312] It was hoped that bringing pressure to bear would dissuade people from buying 'penny' or 'ha'penny dreadfuls', whose existence was often lamented by men such as Douglas Hyde, Arthur Griffith and D.P. Moran, all of whom saw them as intellectually and culturally damaging. The fervour with which some committees went about their work was criticised by contemporaries in *An Claidheamh Soluis*, some of whom believed that such obsession was in and of itself immoral.[313] Others believed that the committees did not take into account the different grades of English literature; Shakespeare and the pages of a Sunday newspaper were not comparable.[314]

By the time of the official opening of the AOH hall in December, it was certain that the local AOH and UIL were working closely together.[315] Walter Nugent and J.P. Hayden officiated, with numerous UIL members present for the occasion. Hayden remarked that the passing of the Insurance Act ensured that the AOH had a bright future and that members would be 'free men in their own land' by the end of 1912, a reference to Home Rule.[316] The now 120-strong division 680 also welcomed Dean Kelly to the opening, and he appeared entirely supportive, chairing a celebratory buffet in the Prince of Wales Hotel.[317] The AOH was bedding in quite well in Athlone, but interestingly was not noted in the December 1911 report of the Order's activities, which recorded no Westmeath divisions.[318]

The Athlone division backed the establishment of the single UIL branch in early 1912 and brethren accompanied a UIL delegation to a Home Rule rally in Dublin on 31 May.[319] Westmeath gained a second division in the same month at Mullingar (by this time Roscommon had twenty-five[320]), as well as its first Auxiliary AOH Ladies' Division in Athlone[321] who, like their male counterparts, were little publicised, generally making the press only when they attended 'General Communion' with the men.[322] The inclusion of women in the AOH assisted the Order in ensuring that the rapid rise in female suffragist sentiment was somewhat curtailed,[323] something that would have pleased both Walter Nugent and the Irish Party.[324]

The stuttering progress of the AOH in Westmeath appears unusual when taken in the national context. The IG's report for June 1912 noted that the UIL and AOH were 'the most influential political associations throughout the country', the first time he singled out any group other than the UIL for that particular accolade since 1900.[325] There were 830 male and twenty-five female divisions of the Order, yet, even by the end of July, Westmeath accounted for just five of the 855 total; Athlone's two divisions, Mullingar, Moate and Streamstown.[326] The moves to have the AOH listed as an approved society under the National Insurance Act 1911 did provide greater impetus,[327] as the new law allowed groups and local societies to act as agents in the provision of State health insurance for less well-off members of the workforce. This 'distribution of the boons of "new liberalism"'[328] saw the AOH become the main administrator of the scheme in Athlone, along with the TLA, which dealt with the requirements of many of its 400 members.[329] The AOH hall maintained office hours so that Catholic workers could have their insurance forms processed – Protestants used the Union Friendly Society, which had been established in April 1912 by Ranelagh School headmaster and UDC member Robert Baile in co-operation with the Protestant clergy.[330]

Division 680 reported a healthy credit balance, organised excursions and continued to meet quite regularly for the next year, with numerous reports appearing in the local press.[331] Indeed, such was its perceived success that the National Convention had an unsuccessful proposal placed before it in August 1912, requesting that Athlone be given a District Board.[332] By May 1913 the division had a president (Rafferty), vice-president (M.J. O'Meara), honorary treasurer (J.O'Brien), recording secretary (Jos Harney), financial secretary (J.J. O'Brien) and an insurance secretary (P.J. Kelly).[333] The close ties to the UIL were maintained, with J.H. Rafferty chosen as a representative for the Roscommon section of Athlone Young Ireland UIL division at the National Executive.[334] Athlone's brethren were numbered amongst the 655 registered in Westmeath in mid-1913, a figure higher than those seen in Kilkenny, King's County, Queen's County, Kildare or Carlow, though still there was a 'wide field' for organising in the county.[335] Roscommon showed a membership of 1,386, but was part of what was surprisingly considered, given the Order's longer tenure there, the least organised province.[336] The Athlone division did not appear by 1913, as David Fitzpatrick has generalised, to be 'a direct competitor of the UIL's as principal launching pad for political office'.[337] It operated in an adjunctive, supportive role to the town's unified league branch, which like most of Athlone's political bodies, had its sights firmly set on the IPP fight for Home Rule.

3

The Search for Home Rule and the Development of Militancy

With the creation of a single UIL branch for Athlone and the apparent inexorable movement towards a Home Rule bill, the town's constitutional nationalists were enjoying their most positive phase yet seen in the twentieth century. Support for the new bill seemed close to total, with influential organisations such as the GL and AOH rowing in behind the cause. Advanced nationalist opposition, if any, had lost its only forum for debate with the de facto extinction of the SF branch, whose former members were either reconverted to the Home Rule cause or silent. However, the excited expectation of the bill was tempered by unionist moves to derail the Home Rule project, which they saw as inimical to their best interests. As the months passed, their opposition grew increasingly confrontational, with the creation and arming of a militant force influencing Athlone nationalists to create a counterforce to ensure that the threat of violent opposition would not snuff out hopes for a Dublin-based legislature. The evolution of the nationalist force and the continued growth of the unionist equivalent during 1914 appeared to presage a collision between the two, with commentators in Athlone and across Ireland warning of civil war. As tensions grew and politicians failed in their efforts to allay them, it was to be international circumstances, namely the declaration of war by Britain on Germany in August 1914, that ensured a clash was averted. Instead, in Ireland, a different conflict emerged, one rooted in the ideological differences between constitutional and advanced nationalists. Their divergent views on the role the nation should play in the war created a schism that was to rend asunder the façade of political unity, and permanently alter nationalist allegiances and ideology in Athlone.

After the creation of a unified UIL branch in January 1912, Athlone's constitutional nationalists concentrated on the push for Home Rule. Most league meetings held in the early months of the year discussed little other than that issue and the necessity for regular expressions of public support.[1] Locals donated generously to the parliamentary fund, and while the advent of the MPs' £400 salary led some to question its use, Dean Kelly made it clear that the fund was needed to combat unionist 'vilification' of the bill, and promote the establishment of an Irish parliament.[2] The *Westmeath Independent*, buoyed up by the single branch's establishment and the editor's committee position, stated that the towns of Ireland could be relied upon to support the IPP, whose move away from an agrarian-centred mandate had led to a fall-off in rural support.[3]

As the bill took shape, John Redmond tried to promote an inclusive policy to show that, despite differences, accommodations could be reached.[4] However, unionists became increasingly intransigent, averring that the bill would facilitate their subjugation. Walter Nugent, who like many of his colleagues donated £50 of his stipend to help counterbalance 'the lavish expenditure on the campaign of the enemies of Ireland against Home Rule',[5] believed that unionists were manipulating the facts to represent the bill in the most negative fashion. He specifically criticised the use of the Ne Temere decree[6] to 'twist' the Home Rule push, describing it as an 'illustration of the desperate straits to which our opponents are reduced'.[7] He spoke of Ulster Unionist leader Edward Carson's efforts to foment militancy in Belfast amongst a 'minority' and the boost it provided to the moral position of the IPP:

> It was not to drive cattle they were inciting them ... but to break heads ... it was not the ordinary workingmen ... who were in sympathy with this, but the same old minority set. The workingmen of the North sent Joe Devlin to Parliament.[8]

Though the increased militancy to which Nugent referred had been noticed as early as 1910,[9] it was more frequently observed the following year as Home Rule became a more likely proposition. The RIC recorded that Orange Lodges began producing drill books, with individual members attempting to procure weapons.[10] By January 1912, the Ulster Unionist Clubs began military training and a Colonel R.H. Wallace took a decisive step towards the creation of an organised force by securing a license.[11] The numbers drilling grew quickly, with reportedly 10,000 members enrolled in a loose alliance by February.[12] The previous two attempts to pass a Home Rule bill in 1886 and

1893 had seen no such body emerge;[13] it appeared that the nineteenth-century unionist tactic of rhetoric-based opposition was to be 'replaced, or perhaps reinforced, by deeds'.[14]

With unionist opposition to Home Rule still quite disorganised, Athlone's nationalists greeted the introduction of the third Home Rule Bill (Government of Ireland Bill) at parliament on 11 April 1912[15] with optimism. Redmond had attracted 'conditional support' from the majority of nationalists, locally, nationally and internationally, most of whom set about studying the bill's provisions.[16] It proposed a separate parliament with responsibility for internal affairs excluding, most prominently, the areas of defence, relations with the crown and customs and excise. Restricted tax powers were to be granted, though Ireland was only to have control over revenues when they were equal to expenditure for three years in a row.[17] Control of the judiciary and post office was to be transferred immediately, while responsibility for policing and banking would be held over for six and ten years respectively.[18] The new parliament was to have an equivalent to the House of Commons as well as a nominated Senate or upper house.[19]

In Athlone it appears that most inhabitants were supportive of the bill, albeit with qualification. The *Westmeath Independent* went with Redmond's description of the bill as 'adequate and generous'.[20] Local political organisations' were generally well disposed but some reservations, such as H.J. Walker's opposition to the nominated senate, were aired.[21] M.J. Lennon was optimistic but, as was commonly heard, demanded full control of customs, a call echoed by local JP, P.J. Egan, who believed that without customs control the bill was 'like so much skimmed milk'.[22] Lennon additionally questioned Ulster's position, a vital query that the bill had not actually addressed in any comprehensive way, and which was to become the most contentious issue.[23]

Unsurprisingly, unionist opposition did come, most prominently from Bonar Law, the recently elected leader of the Tories, who called the bill 'a corrupt parliamentary bargain', i.e. IPP support for the Liberals in exchange for Home Rule. In Athlone the most vocal unionist opposition came from Robert Baile UDC, who was against even the idea of Home Rule. Athlone's other pro-Union councillor, John Burgess, stated that he did not fear Irish self-government, a sentiment echoed by the Protestant labour councillor John Smith.[24] Burgess' and Smith's views were not reflecting a dramatic new approach by Athlone's Protestants to Home Rule, many of whom had been active in the local branch of the Irish Protestant Home Rule Association from 1886-1893.[25] Baile's opposition was perhaps representative of a tiny, not particularly vocal, minority in Athlone, with the only other prominent criticism from similar quarters, that of

Presbyterian minister Robert Watson, concentrating solely on the certainty of widespread squabbling as result of the bill's introduction.[26] Despite unionists energetically expostulating against the bill on the grounds of its probable post-enactment evolution, religious discrimination and the injurious effect of having non-industrialists such as John Redmond governing the economy, the bill began to move towards the statute books.[27]

In Athlone, the growing conviction amongst nationalists was that the bill was in an unassailable position, despite the increase in unionist fulmination. J.P. Hayden averred that it would become law by May 1914, provided there was an absence of 'an extraordinary political earthquake'.[28] Positivity permeated *Westmeath Independent* editorials, with the reception afforded to Prime Minister Asquith in Dublin in July 1912 hailed as evidence of the 'spirit of justice which permeates the British democracy'.[29] Athlone's inhabitants were assured by Walter Nugent that the bill was home and dry, and the town's UIL branches adopted a state of dormant expectation.[30]

Indeed, of the local MPs, it was Nugent who was most conspicuous in promoting the bill. His speeches painted a picture of the English Royals opening the Irish Parliament, cementing Ireland's equal role in the 'Great British Empire'.[31] Nugent's imperialist ideology (omnipresent in his rhetoric), though somewhat camouflaged previously under his 'Irish Nationalist' mantle, really began to come to the fore. It is certain that he saw Ireland's political existence only in imperialist terms and he called for the country to become a true part of the Empire.[32] Nugent, like his party leader, backed a federal system for the Empire whereby Ireland could operate as did Canada and Australia – local parliaments with a large degree of autonomy, while still part of the imperial network.[33] As noted by Gearóid Ó Tuathaigh, it was almost certain that IPP MPs, and their grass-roots followers, were 'comfortable with an Irish identity which could find institutional expression … in the larger family of the British Empire'.[34]

While most nationalists in Athlone viewed Home Rule imposition as a certainty, unionists in the north believed it could be derailed. During the summer of 1912, a large number of Catholic workers, as well as pro-Home Rule Protestants, were expelled from northern shipyards and there were riots in Belfast.[35] A propaganda campaign promoted an intensely negative interpretation of the financial and religious implications of the bill, while Bonar Law outraged many nationalist MPs by stating that even if Home Rule was passed, 'there were things stronger than Parliamentary majorities'.[36] The 'fallacious' economic arguments and the push for a 'violent refusal' of Home Rule evidenced in the Belfast riots were roundly criticised in the *Westmeath*

Independent, and qualified as blackguardism.[37] The newspaper wrote dismissively of Law's 'bluster' and Edward Carson's September creation, the Solemn League and Covenant.[38] The Covenant, which was couched in religious terms, declared the loyalty of unionists to the Crown while also asserting that any attempt to impose Home Rule would be stoutly resisted, even if such resistance ran contrary to the king's edict.[39] The signatories contended that the actual level of hostility to Home Rule had to be made clear; religious, loyal, law-abiding, peaceful people were, by the tens of thousands, threatening to resort to violence. To unionists the proposed legislation was 'extra-constitutional, to be resisted by every means'.[40]

As the intensity of unionist opposition increased, so too did the amount of time Athlone nationalists spent assessing the implications. The Covenant led McDermott-Hayes to refer to Edward Carson contemptuously as 'King Carson' or 'General Carson', the manufacturer of 'an exploded squib',[41] which had nonetheless gained over 200,000 signatures, a figure that was to grow.[42] Ineffective attempts to instigate a boycott of Belfast-produced goods were made in Athlone as elsewhere, and the town formed a committee, chaired by M.J. Lennon, to oversee the collection of a fund for expelled Belfast workers. The inaugural meeting heard H.J. Walker and Dean Kelly criticise Carson, ever more the personification of unionist opposition, for his role in promoting dissent.[43]

The issue of the nationalist response to the unionist threat also arose. McDermott-Hayes called for the establishment of rifle clubs in the southern provinces: 'If aggression is threatened in one end of the country ... to resist and suppress it must be at the command of the rest.'[44] Walter Nugent hypothesised, displaying some impressive presentiment, that militant unionists who wanted 'the government of Ireland entrusted to Carson' would inspire nationalists to take up arms against them. He believed that such a move could lead to the IPP being 'swept away to make room for a party of more irreconcilable men'.[45] He criticised the 'organised bogey of religious oppression', and stated that the 'absurd masquerade of wooden guns ... would be killed by ridicule within two years', an opinion that was widely held.[46] Indeed, it appears certain that unionist efforts to derail Home Rule were not seen as a serious threat in Athlone, with the *Manchester Guardian* highlighting how the UDC actually saw William O'Brien as the bill's 'greatest living enemy'.[47] Unionist attempts in the Commons to change the proposed legislation were ineffective and many maintained that the Ulster Covenant was merely bluster. In fact, Home Rule was seen as such a certainty locally that it was suggested that even the pretence of maintaining the Athlone UIL branch was a redundant act.[48]

By January 1913, the inability of Ulster unionists to gain concessions, including the proposal to exclude the nine Ulster counties from the bill's remit, led their leadership to concentrate on extra-parliamentary activities.[49] The Ulster Unionist Council officially adopted the Ulster Volunteer Force on 13 January and by so doing signalled that their threat of armed conflict was perhaps more than hyperbole.[50] Despite this move towards increasing belligerency, Athlone's nationalists continued to disregard 'the dangerous potentialities of Ulster Unionism'.[51] The first passing of the Home Rule Bill through the Commons on 16 January saw the obligatory celebratory meeting in Athlone and the press reported that the occasion proved to those who 'were possessed with the idea that the National movement was ... a mere agrarian struggle' that Irish autonomy had always been the IPP's ultimate goal.[52] The PLG congratulated both local MPs, as well as Athlone-born T.P. O'Connor MP, leader of the UIL of Great Britain, and the 'Great British Democracy'[53] for their role in securing the bill's passage. J.P. Hayden, perhaps no longer fearful of seismic activity, communicated that the position of Home Rule was now 'impregnable'.[54]

Locals painted the passing as a great IPP victory and to ensure that the eventual celebrations for the Home Rule Act were well directed, Athlone's UIL branch reorganised.[55] Indeed, managing a celebration was probably all the league would have on its agenda. Reports stated that the UIL in south Westmeath was waning, as Home Rule's imminent application led the clergy to move their efforts into non-political avenues.[56] Dean Kelly flirted with retiring from the organisation, but was convinced to remain by M.J. Lennon. The Dean decided that if the branch was to remain, it had to tackle its sectarian appearance; there were just two Protestants on the books. He promoted engaging with local Church of Ireland ministers; small-scale acts of inclusion would bode well for similar gestures on a grander scale.[57]

The excitement of the passing was short lived, however. The bill was rejected by the House of Lords on 30 January, a vote decried by Irish nationalists.[58] The more politically aware expected the setback, but in Athlone outrage was widespread, with words and terms such as 'insolent' and 'unchanged hatred' making the columns of the *Westmeath Independent*.[59] McDermott-Hayes had assured readers that the Lords would reject the bill three times until it was passed over their heads in 1914, but that did not mollify them.[60] The PLG excoriated local landowner Lord Castlemaine for his negative vote; 'not one per cent of the ratepayers' in Athlone agreed with him.[61] They passed a resolution condemning both him and another local 'No' voter, Lord Greville, former chairman of Westmeath County Council.[62] Dean Kelly led the charge as the UIL censured the Lords,[63] and, as ever, meetings were planned to show

Home Rule support. None were held, however, as 'meeting fatigue', identified by Town Clerk P.V.C. Murtagh, and a dearth of prominent speakers
conspired against organisers.[64]

During the early summer, local rhetoric on the certainty of Home Rule
was maintained, and the *Westmeath Independent* reiterated J.P. Hayden's
forecast of a May 1914 Home Rule Act.[65] If this assertion was correct,
unionists had just over twelve months to make decisive moves against
the legislation. Bonar Law's speeches remained strident, so much so that
McDermott-Hayes stated that the man was flirting with treason.[66] Edward
Carson called for additional funding,[67] directing much of what was collected
into a propaganda campaign against the financial implications of the bill.[68]
Opinions garnered by reporters showed that fiscal issues were of concern
to Athlone residents too, while editorials in the *Westmeath Independent*
reminded people that such provisions could be revisited when the act came
into effect,[69] a popular reading of the situation as 'nationalists placed their
faith in the dynamics of the legislation, rather than in its immediate prosaic
reality'.[70] As D.G. Boyce has written, one of the bill's most important aspects
was 'its lack of definition … the new parliament could make laws for the
peace, order and good government of Ireland. This left … large … scope for
the parliament to enhance its powers'.[71]

Unionist attempts to derail Home Rule provided McDermott-Hayes
with much to talk about in his editorials, though items of local interest
still dominated. Home Rule was delayed; unionist activities were an aside,
nothing more significant. He criticised Bonar Law for 'living on strategy',
and other unionists who had 'rubbishy' ideas on compromise.[72] He questioned 'the corner boy characteristics' of the marching season, asking if
such activity was to be expected of Orangemen in Home Rule Ireland.[73]
Unionists had, he maintained, merely substituted their 'usual blackguardism'
with 'mock grimness and determination', and he questioned their willingness
to act on their threats.[74] Riots in Derry during August assured him that some
unionists were, but even then, he questioned the worth of their manoeuvres:

> The Derry riots supply us with a foretaste of the 'revolution' we are
> to have up North … The drill clubs, about which Sir Edward Carson
> was so particular, seem to have performed their duties with singular
> inefficiency.[75]

The newspaper detailed how just two nationalists were injured by the
'Orangemen': 'That record tells very badly for the drill clubs … worse for

the revolution.' The fact that one unionist was fatally wounded was lamented, but accusations that the RIC man who shot him was a member of the AOH were discounted, and McDermott-Hayes stated that it was about time that unionists realised that they too had to obey the law.[76]

Whatever the uses for the UVF in Ireland, Edward Carson was certain that Home Rule could be won or lost in England. He called for a great unionist campaign, with a circular of support signed by many noted Irish unionists, including Lord Castlemaine. The local press described Carson's preaching of a civil war in Ireland to English audiences as a 'blunder'; threats were counterproductive. Additionally, it noted that attempts to foster religious hatred between Irish Catholics and English Protestants using 'the scruff of Belfast' were similarly unlikely to succeed.[77] Anti-Home Rule propaganda continued to grow as the bill passed its second reading in the Commons on 7 July,[78] with religious fears additionally stoked as prominent Church of Ireland clergymen entered the fray. A well-publicised letter from August 1913 by the Protestant Bishop of Tuam, Dr Plunkett, contained an appeal to Irish Protestants not to be taken in by Ulster Unionist propaganda.[79] Just weeks later his Kilmore, Elphin and Ardagh counterpart, Dr Elliott, spoke in counterpoint, emphasising the sectarian consequences of 'fearful Home Rule'.[80]

The ability of the UVF to inspire apprehension amongst nationalists (and the government) was boosted during the autumn when Carson stated that he aimed to have rifles on the shoulders of volunteers sooner rather than later. The use of wooden sticks had left the UVF open to ridicule from nationalists; something more threatening was essential.[81] The IPP, which had initially seen the UVF as just sabre rattlers, began to reassess the implications of the militancy, as did others, unsure as they were of Carson's actual intentions.[82] David Fitzpatrick has noted that responses to the UVF varied, though most frequently took the form of 'outrage, admiration and envy, culminating in imitation'.[83] Increasingly vocal individuals, such as Pádraig Pearse, a contributor to *An Claidheamh Soluis*, approved of Carson's attempt to arm; 'an Orangeman with a rifle [is] a much less ridiculous figure than a nationalist without one'.[84] Prominent IRB man Bulmer Hobson started drilling small numbers of men in imitation during the summer of 1913,[85] not to protect the bill, of which he was not an advocate, but to force the English into an '… aggressive posture, whereupon the military, as well as the moral advantage would pass to the Irish'.[86] However, as F.S.L. Lyons states, '[he] needed an open movement on a much larger scale'.[87] The Ulster Unionist leadership 'revelled in their impunity', and declared their intention to establish a Provisional Government in Ulster. Carson mocked the British cabinet, claiming that they 'dare not interfere' with the UVF or proposed legislature, despite the fact that both bodies were, or would be, considered illegal.[88]

With unionist efforts to force their agenda becoming more threatening as autumn progressed, local commentary moved away from ridicule and adopted a more serious line. Walter Nugent criticised the suggestion that the IPP wished to triumph over its opponents, the 'bluster of the Ulster minority', and stated that Carson had been implicitly 'rebuked' in Britain.[89] Local opinion, as relayed to *The Irish Times*, on the possibility of religious intolerance in Athlone post-Home Rule was 'nothing but idle nonsense';[90] long-standing trading relationships would not be jeopardised. As the partition of Ireland was more frequently promoted, southern unionists sensed impending abandonment,[91] with the *Westmeath Independent* targeting the 'traitorous' suggestion as the worst aspect of the circulating 'vile political traffic'.[92] Allowing unionists to dictate policy through the threat of violence was not to be countenanced. That threat had to be negated, and it was for this purpose that the Midland Volunteer Force (MVF) was formed in Athlone.

Pinpointing exactly when and by whom the idea for the MVF was first suggested is difficult, with no definitive account in existence. Flawed though it is, perhaps the most reliable guide, a retrospective from the *Westmeath Independent* of 25 August 1917, dates the idea to August/September 1913.[93] The article notes how, at a SF rally[94] on 12 August 1913, a 'few amongst the vast throng gave a thought to … out-Carsoning Carson and laid the foundations'.[95] A later correspondence from founder-member Seán O'Mullany noted that the MVF was 'launched' on the third Sunday in August, one week after this event.[96]

The first official meeting of the MVF occurred under the branches of a tree,[97] a prominent local landmark, in the Fairgreen, Athlone. Committee positions were allocated and McDermott-Hayes occupied the position of Chief of Staff; his press links making him the natural choice. The 40-year-old UIL member and APW worker J.R. Keating was elected president, his 19-year-old colleague, FÉ[98] instructor Seán O'Mullany, was declared honorary secretary and 38-year-old Athlone Woollen Mills employee James Gough was instated as treasurer. Army Reserve members 38-year-old labourer Patrick Croghan, 30-year-old fellow labourer Michael Curley, 26-year-old woollen mills operative Alfred Warby and his 39-year-old co-worker Patrick Downey were also given committee positions, as was a second FÉ instructor, 21-year-old Peter O'Brien.[99]

Plans for drilling, parades and recruiting were discussed, and a half crown started the treasury. Ex-servicemen with Boer War experience were to train the volunteers, with advertising of the first parade accomplished through the medium of flyers:

Midland Volunteer Force committee members, September 1913, (l-r): O'Brien, Warby, O'Mullany and Downey. Front (l-r): Curley, Gough, Croghan. (AHL)

Midland Volunteers – General Parade –
G.S.W.R. road on Wednesday night next.
Assembly for Company Drill 8 o'clock sharp.
Route March 8:30

We seek no quarrel with any man,
Whate'er his creed may be,
We welcome all to join us,
From the Bann down to the Lee;
We want a land united
To right the wrongs of years!
Then rally round the standard of the Midland Volunteers.

It is intended to add a cavalry brigade to the infantry force. All wishing to join either of the brigades can hand in names to the company officers on the Parade Ground, or they will be received at the Trades Hall, Northgate Street, any Friday evening from eight o'clock. Route march every Wednesday until countermanded. By order of the Executive. God Save Ireland![100]

James Gough presenting Seán O'Mullany with the first payment for the Force treasury under the landmark tree at the Fairgreen. (AHL)

Held during the second week in October, the first parade reportedly saw serried ranks of volunteers march through the town's main thoroughfares. The local newspaper used the occasion to both emphasise and ridicule the UVF threat,[101] stating that the number of Ulster Volunteers was 'going downwards, like a cow's tail'. The editor believed that a second review of the 'Ulster Volunteer Army' would show willing unionists to be 'as few in number as Slattery's Mounted "Fut" – Four and twenty fighting men, a couple of stout gossons!' Additionally, he questioned the use for the UVF, believing that it would more likely be deployed to quell the Labour movement in Belfast. Northern employers, 'who suck the life blood from the workers' were, McDermott-Hayes contended, 'the UVF "officers", [along] with a few crack-brained peers'.[102] In contrast, he painted a positive picture of the Athlone parade:

> Athlone, as in old days, is the standard bearer of the new activity, and how
> far matters have advanced was shown … when there was a formidable
> gathering of the new force and the first general parade held.[103]

The majority of recruits were said to be farm labourers, factory workers and 'journeymen'. Farmers were to form the cavalry; those remaining would comprise the foot infantry. Perhaps in answer to the repeated statements of unionists concerning the sectarian implications of Home Rule, the establishment of the MVF was partially justified on the basis of the perception of Catholic persecution in Ulster:

> The roasting of Catholic girl workers in Belfast last year and the brutalities of the shipyards has more than justified the Catholic population of Ireland taking precautionary measures for the future.[104]

The force was created to show the Belfast 'rowdies', who the MVF 'looked upon more with contempt than apprehension', that they would not be allowed to act with impunity. When Home Rule was passed, it was believed that 'the present noisy ones will speedily take leave of their blackguardism',[105] and the force would be surplus to requirements.

The planning for the second parade was quickly completed,[106] and despite differing local attitudes, the 1917 retrospective noting that 'the movement was sneered at by the unthinking and supercilious, and avoided by the timid',[107] the parade was reportedly more successful than the first. Described as a 'Brave Muster' of Midland Volunteers, the *Westmeath Independent* of 25 October 1913 spoke of twenty companies of 5,000 men marching through the streets, some in uniform: 'Practically the entire town population and many country visitors lined the footpaths to watch.' The newspaper stated that additional RIC men had been drafted in, but were either confined to barracks or dressed plainly to ensure tensions were not heightened.[108] The march ended with references to 'His Gracious Majesty the King', and a rather ambiguous and somewhat sectarian manifesto was issued:

> As loyal Irishmen to our King and country, the objects of the Midland Volunteers Force must enlist your sympathy and approval. We stand for an undivided Ireland and for equal laws and legislation for every citizen of this country, where needs be to lend physical assistance against the Protestant persecution of our Catholic fellow countrymen and to emancipate every citizen from political and religious intolerance, practised as we are aware against other than Catholics also, who have declared for a United Ireland, governed by a National Parliament, subject to the laws of the realm, assented to by his Gracious Majesty the King. We believe there is a great future for our country, but the essentials are the fullest liberty of conscience for all men, a country governed by all, by a Parliament and Executive answerable to the people of Ireland.[109]

Organisers stated that arms were to be acquired, but not through Dublin, and that the MVF would be highly mobile. They apparently set in motion the creation of outlying branches,[110] requested the use of the town hall for future meetings, the Athlone Castle for a headquarters and stated, somewhat prematurely:

> Since the formation of the Midland Volunteers Force … there is less talk in certain directions of Rebellion against the laws of the constitution, and less declarations of threatened hostility to the National Parliament of Ireland.[111]

The MVF parades are the most contentious aspect of its history. Huge numbers of marching volunteers were noted in the local press, numbers contradicted in other contemporary sources. The Westmeath CI noted in his report for October 1913:

> No public meetings or demonstrations were held during the month save the so-called parades of the Midland Volunteers which take place in Athlone and which are generally regarded as a farce in the locality.[112]

RIC Special Branch notes for the same month went into more detail, stating that, at most, fifty-four men marched on 22 October, the second parade, and that the first was a non-event. There was no mention of additional police in Athlone on either occasion. The RIC pinpointed McDermott-Hayes as the ring-leader, opining that he was misleading his readers, a point also made by local man Diarmuid Murtagh in his submission to the Bureau of Military History.[113]

Murtagh, who was 11 years old in 1913, stated that his father, P.V.C. Murtagh, confirmed that there was no first parade and that the second was a rushed ex post facto effort organised by MacDermott-Hayes to give 'barren verisimilitude to an otherwise bald and unconvincing narrative' and safeguard the editor's post as a Press Association correspondent. Interestingly, Murtagh believes that MacDermott-Hayes had no hand in the initial spreading of the rumour of a first parade, but did run a story on it and later organised the distribution of handbills for the second parade, as well as a barrel of porter for soldiers who agreed to assist him.[114] Murtagh, whose house was situated adjacent to the Fair Green, remembers perhaps 200 men marching around the Green and through the streets of the town, though he was unsure of the time of year, believing it to probably be September.[115] Murtagh's short submission adds yet another layer of confusion to the MVF story, yet obviously childhood recollections are often unreliable, especially when augmented with additional information from other parties and jotted down decades later.

What is certain is that false accounts were presented in the *Westmeath Independent*. The journalist who wrote the article from August 1917 noted that there were 2,000 men at the second parade (McDermott-Hayes was still editor), a fall of 3,000, while Seán O'Mullany, writing in 1963, put the numbers at 'about fifteen hundred'.[116] Undoubtedly many spectators would have amassed for the parade(s), with the inflation in the number of direct participants possibly indicating the Chief of Staff's efforts to represent the organisation in the most flattering light. By October 1913 the UVF was allegedly drilling up to 12,000 men,[117] and McDermott-Hayes may have believed that a nationalist equivalent had to have large numbers to be taken seriously. Establishing the idea that the MVF was on a large scale could have led to an influx of recruits who might otherwise have been unlikely to join the inchoate organisation. Though local cynicism may have been high given the factual disparities, he may also have been looking to inspire those further afield. His newspaper had the widest circulation in the midlands of any provincial title, covering Westmeath, Roscommon, Longford, Meath, King's County, Queen's County, Galway, Mayo, Sligo and Leitrim. The editor may have hoped that news of Athlone's efforts, if promulgated widely, might have inspired similar efforts elsewhere.

Regardless of the detail of the parades, news of the MVF spread. The *Evening Herald* of 14 October, and the *Freeman's Journal* and *The Irish Times* of 15 October all carried small pieces, the latter referring to an 'Alleged Parade'.[118] The second parade made the pages of the *Irish Independent*, which noted the singing of patriotic songs amongst the assembled 5,000, and described the MVF as created to oppose the Ulster Volunteers. A similar sentiment was published in the *Freeman's Journal* of 25 October, which gave a detailed description of the second parade under the headline; 'To Repel Carson's "Army"'.[119] Later the same month, D.P. Moran, editorialising in *The Leader*, stated that the force was not being awarded enough exposure:

> We do not think that enough attention has been given to the formation of a Volunteer Force in Athlone. It is all very well to look with contempt on the wooden guns of the Carsonite force … but Nationalist Ireland might do worse than take the opportunity to raise Volunteer forces throughout the country … Historic Athlone has given … a lead and … held its first parade.[120]

An enthusiastic *Derry Journal* provided the MVF with two-thirds of a column, describing the venture as 'the formation of drilled Irish Volunteer corps in the Midlands'.[121] Additional, albeit unsupportive, exposure was gained in the small-circulation advanced nationalist newspaper *Irish Freedom*, whose editor was unimpressed by the force's loyalties:

> The Athlone Midland Volunteers held a parade a few days ago ... cheers were given for "the King and Constitution, and the men of '98, '48 and '67. This is not so surprising ... When official 'Nationalism' (Redmondite brand) professes ... enthusiasm for the ... Empire it is little wonder if some ... followers ... doubt which side to cheer for ... in Athlone ... to be on the safe side they cheered both.[122]

As news was disseminated, other parties expressed their views. Laurence Ginnell was supposedly very excited by the emergence of the group and met with his followers just days after the first parade, issuing what amounted to a call to arms.[123] Similarly impressed was J.P. Farrell, MP for Longford, who asked that Athlone's example be followed.[124] News of the force also reached individuals in Dublin, most prominently the GL's Eoin MacNeill, who believed it to be a positive step.[125]

Perhaps coincidentally, what has been identified as the most inspirational piece written on the theme of Irish nationalist volunteers in the twentieth century came from MacNeill less than two weeks after reports of the second MVF parade. His article 'The North Began' in the 1 November issue of *An Claidheamh Soluis* could be described as an attempt to reassess the UVF and its implications from the nationalist perspective.[126] Writing that 'The Ulster Volunteer Movement is essentially and obviously a Home Rule movement', MacNeill cited historical precedent, as interpreted by him, noting that Irishmen, of whatever creed or ideology, should be the ones defending Ireland 'for the Empire'. He emphasised that: 'What matters is by whom Ireland is to be held.' There was nothing, he wrote, to stop people 'calling into existence citizen forces to hold Ireland', and stated that Carson's threat to march the UVF to Cork would see 'the greetings of ten times their number of National Volunteers'. The article is conciliatory towards unionists, and it is apparent that MacNeill was not promoting a force for the defence of the south against the north, as had MVF organisers.[127] Charles Townshend describes MacNeill's thesis as 'probably too subtle to convince most nationalists', though his argument is cited as the inspiration for the creation of the Irish Volunteers (IV), both by his contemporary acquaintances and in modern historiography.[128] Such an assertion may, however, have had more to do with the ideologies of competing groups rather than with a full and honest representation of the actual events of late 1913.

Hitherto, the historiography of the MVF has been informed mostly by the work of two historians, Padraig Ó Snodaigh (Oliver Snoddy), and F.X. Martin. Ó Snodaigh's works on the subject,[129] have described the MVF as a short-lived organisation, with an embellished reputation, which was nevertheless an important step in the creation of the Irish Volunteers. Martin's argument, which has been more influential, is that the MVF never existed at all, a point he makes in a book to which contributed and co-edited; *The Revolutionary Scholar, Eoin MacNeill 1867-1945, and the Making of the New Ireland* (1973). Martin begins his piece on the MVF using the qualification 'a Successful Hoax', which was, he wrote, still finding 'victims, even in our own times'.[130] He embarks on a tautological treatment of the issue and attempts to refute claims about the existence of the MVF made by Ó Snodaigh. Using partisan quotations from advanced nationalists[131] such as The O'Rahilly, Martin contends that the prevailing contemporary view was one of incredulity:

> Previous to this [the foundation of the Irish Volunteers in Dublin], a journalist in Westmeath, who is said to have conceived the possibility of a 'Midland Volunteer Force', had published a report of the inception of such a body in Athlone. Whether the Midland Volunteers had any real existence except in the columns is much debated, and seems open to doubt.[132]

Peculiarly and inadvisably given his unfamiliarity with O'Rahilly, Martin uses his own view on the man's personality to bolster the worth of the above quote: 'O'Rahilly, who was generous by nature … would not have withheld recognition and praise for the Midland Volunteers had they merited it.'[133] Such a statement, as will be suggested, highlights either Martin's naivety, or, as is more likely, a predetermined bias in his explorations.

Other historians have dealt with similar statements from equally partisan sources, but, unlike Martin, they have not been convinced by the claims of the sources' authors. A vitriolic diary entry on the bona fides of the MVF delivered by prominent Cork republican Liam de Róiste heaped abuse on Athlone's efforts:

It has recently been claimed … that the movement [Irish Volunteers] started in Athlone … there was a small paragraph in the papers … that a Volunteer corps of over 1000 men were drilling in Athlone as a counter blast to … Carson's Volunteers. I heard all about the matter at the Civic Exhibition in Dublin from a … teacher of Athlone. The whole affair existed in the mind of a journalist of the town on a 'booze'. The whole thing was discussed in a public house. It captured the imagination of the journalist. He sent the 'par' to the papers … That was Athlone's contribution to the idea.[134]

Historian Christopher Kennedy, who has studied de Róiste's diary, states that: 'The first conception of an Irish nationalist force has its roots in the midlands', and was not dissuaded from taking that opinion by de Róiste, whose view of the matter he qualifies as 'a little harsh on Athlone's contribution'.[135]

Martin, de Róiste and others call into question the bona fides of Michael McDermott-Hayes, at whom accusations of fantasist, liar and drink-dependant are levelled. Such assertions may be unfair given biographical information available on the *Westmeath Independent* editor, though, it must be noted that there is quite a degree of conflict in the sources.[136] Though it is likely that O'Rahilly, De Róiste or indeed Bulmer Hobson[137] were not seeking to assassinate the career of any particular journalist, it should be noted that any concession made by them with regard to the MVF would lead to some diminution in their role as pioneers of the IV movement. O'Rahilly stated at a gathering in Kildare in June 1914 that it was he who had organised the first meeting that had brought Irish Volunteers together,[138] while Bulmer Hobson claimed that it was his idea.[139] While it is possible to accommodate both claims – with qualifications – in the story of the IV's evolution, they indicate that O'Rahilly and Hobson were indeed quite concerned with establishing their legacies. What should also be noted, though its reliability is questionable due to O'Rahilly's death in 1916, is a note from the 1917 retrospective:

The late O'Rahilly in his 'The Secret History of the Irish Volunteers' referred with a certain amount of incredulity to … the Midland Volunteers … however, on being enlightened by a 'Midland' member, he announced his intention of correcting in a revised edition, the erroneous opinion he expressed.[140]

Ó Snodaigh has written that 'O'Rahilly's pamphlet had a political cause behind it and political arguments to be made in it',[141] namely tracing the IV genesis back to himself and like-minded men, rather than the MVF, which looked to Home Rule and had cheered for the king.[142] Martin appears to ignore this rather obvious point and even Ó Snodaigh, though recognising it, appeared unaware as to the significance and protracted nature of the debate both for and against the MVF, which will be explored later in more detail. It will become apparent that Athlone's contribution to the nationalist volunteer debate in the twentieth century has been understated.

The opposing views held by Ó Snodaigh and Martin have led to a distorted and, at times, confused representation of the force in modern historiography.[143] This is perhaps best evidenced in Michael Wheatley's *Nationalism and the Irish Party, Provincial Ireland 1910–1916* (2005), where the author in one instance describes the parade reports as 'wildly bogus' and the force itself a 'phantom' and 'fantasy'.[144] Not unreasonably, he highlights McDermott-Hayes'[145] embellishments, while also then contradictorily ascribing to the supposed phantom the award of the 'first modern, nationalist volunteer formation in Ireland'.[146] While a later article by the same author presents a more coherent picture of the MVF, his work is indicative of how Martin's flawed representation has muddied the historiographical waters.[147]

Regardless of what happened in Athlone in October, it is certain that the MVF was feeding the debate on the idea of a nationalist volunteer force. Frank Necy, a Dundalk IV member, though unsure as to the veracity of the reports on the MVF, was certain that 'whether imaginary or not, [they] attracted wide attention', while his Cork counterpart Michael Ó Cuill similarly cites Athlone's efforts as a step along the road towards the eventual creation of the Irish Volunteers.[148] *The Leader* revisited the force's significance on 8 November, without tying it to MacNeill's article:

> A few weeks ago we commented on the … Volunteer Force in Athlone. We have reason to believe that many young men in Dublin are now full of the idea … When the wooden musketeers of Carson's awkward squads meet with the connivance of the Government … the opportunity should not be lost in Dublin, Limerick, Wexford and other places to organise the young manhood of Nationalist Ireland … Athlone had led the way, who will follow suit?[149]

Athlone's activity may also have influenced Dublin unionists to move towards joining with the UVF during early November, and certainly influenced three letters to the *Irish Independent*, which emphasised the positive implications of the MVF and noted how a similar, more widespread force would have been useful in assisting England if Germany's increasing belligerence turned violent:[150]

'Athlone has given the watchword to the South and West', wrote a correspondent, 'and I am sure it will not be lost on them'.[151] A letter also came to Athlone from Tralee, where IRB members Éamon O'Connor and Austin Stack were turning their thoughts to the creation of a nationalist volunteer force.[152]

It is apparent that Eoin MacNeill was, despite his article pulling its punches somewhat, intent on forming a nationalist militia. Upon sending a copy of 'The North Began' to O'Rahilly, an accompanying note stated: 'We should follow the example they have given in Athlone and set up a force immediately.'[153] The first meeting to achieve this aim was held on 11 November at Wynn's Hotel in Dublin, where those present agreed that if a nationalist volunteer force was established, it had to include 'representatives of established nationalist bodies', i.e. the UIL, AOH, GAA, INF and Irish Party.[154] To this end, members of these organisations were courted and soon IPP supporters, such as L.J. Kettle and John Gore, assisted in organising a foundation meeting.[155] News of MacNeill's efforts was covered in the *East Galway Democrat*, which noted that the 'only place that has announced definite action is Athlone, where a strong force of Midland volunteers has been formed'. The Ballinasloe newspaper also highlighted one of the weaknesses of the MVF by stating that the 'Dublin movement is a bigger and more startling project for it is proposed to make it national in character'.[156] As news of the proposed meeting spread, the *Manchester Guardian* laid out the chronology of the evolution of the volunteer movement in southern Ireland:

> ... about six weeks ago we heard that Hibernians in and about Athlone were drilling ... to cope with the Ulstermen ... next ... presented the unionists of Dublin in a military aspect. Then ... [a promise] to drill the locked-out workers. Finally, a public meeting ... for the 25 November in order to begin enrolment of Irish volunteers.[157]

On the last Tuesday in November 1913, the Irish Volunteers were inaugurated at the Rotunda in Dublin. The provisional committee, which reflected the involvement of the various groups, was confirmed and the aims of the organisation were addressed.[158] Though the inclusive nature of the committee was to be commended, its diversity, and the absence of a strong figurehead, ensured that the IV's purpose was ill-defined.[159] The Rotunda meeting heard aggressive rhetoric on how Tory policy in Ulster had determined that 'violence [was to be] the determining factor in relations between Britain and Ireland', while MacNeill's oratory and a later speech by Pádraig Pearse, though strong, were not nearly as strident.[160] MacNeill outlined the duty of

safeguarding the rights of the Irish through IV corps who would engage
in defensive, not aggressive, actions and again made conciliatory statements
about the UVF: 'it is the Ulster Volunteers who have opened the way for
the Irish Volunteers.'[161] He was, as he had done in his article, preaching
about common Irish interests;[162] it was unsurprising therefore that Athlone's
contribution was not mentioned. Regardless, the *Westmeath Independent* was
certain as to what inspired the meeting, noting Athlone's role in making
'up-to-date-history'.[163]

While possibly inspiring those further afield, it appears certain that the
MVF was leading to the reinvigoration of at least one organisation closer
to home. Athlone's FÉ, whose inactivity had previously been lamented,
re-emerged in controversial fashion and came in for much praise from *Irish
Freedom* for their parading prowess:

> There were close on thirty members … and as they marched … they
> looked a fine body of young fellows, each of whom had on full costume.
> A short distance outside the town some drilling lessons were given.
> Large numbers are handing in their names for membership.[164]

While unaware or pointedly ignoring the roster overlap between the MVF
and FÉ instructors, the report detailed that the local troop had 'been enjoying
active service as of late', and highlighted news of an incident where members
of the Leinster Regiment moved out of the way of a scout march, fearful of
creating an unflattering incident. The advanced nationalist publication made
much of the episode, believing that it 'put a substantial check on recruiting
tactics in [Athlone]', while other press reports led to the occurrence making
the news in both Britain and America.[165] A coincidental assassination attempt
on Lord Castlemaine may have led some to assert that an anti-British mindset
was becoming locally pervasive. However, the RIC believed the attempt to
be more personal than political.[166]

By the time of the Rotunda meeting and during the period when the
Athlone FÉ were making headlines, the MVF appears to have done little.
The press reported no activity throughout November, but the force still
occupied column inches. An Irish member of the British Army posted in
India offered his services in a letter to the editor of the *Westmeath Independent*,
stating that '90% of the Irish Regiments in India would join' the MVF in
order to combat the 'Rabid Orangeism in the North East'.[167] D.P. Moran
highlighted the letter's contents and suggested 'there are two sides to the
army question in relation to Ireland'.[168]

Indeed, there were already two sides to the volunteer question in Athlone. Debates amongst MVF committee members concerning the motivation, philosophy and effect of the movement saw no consensus reached, resignations submitted and the committee becoming dormant. McDermott-Hayes targeted his fellow members with a plea in early December for them not to be 'pioneers only';[169] however, it appeared that the problems which arose were quite divisive. Some may have been fearful after the significance of what they were trying to achieve set in. Others probably questioned its legality, regardless of the fact that the UVF had not been targeted by the police.[170] The imposition of a proclamation against the importation of arms on 3 December[171] may have fuelled this belief, and led to an explicit statement a week later that the MVF was doing 'nothing illegal'.[172] The complex nature of Irish politics may have weighed on their minds; they were not practiced politicians and may have felt out of their depth. What is certain is that the disagreement caused Seán O'Mullany and James Gough to resign.[173] The manifesto called for loyalty to the king, Home Rule and Redmond; O'Mullany (who was to be arrested after the 1916 Rising[174]) and Gough were more advanced in their nationalism than their counterparts, at least six of whom – Keating, Downey, Warby, Curley, Croghan and O'Brien – were to fight for the British Army in the First World War and who, at this point, saw Ireland as part of the Empire, as did McDermott-Hayes.[175] Also, the manifesto had a problematic and confusing message with regard to religious persecutions. While it was stated that the Force 'discriminate[d] between Protestants and Orangemen',[176] this was a later clarification that tried to address the problem after it had arisen.

The period of MVF quietude continued until late December 1913, when reorganisation of the force began. The Athlone committee gained support from the local division of the AOH, the INF and TLA, while it appears that many of those present under the tree in September were absent. Others who attended, such as Dubliner Peter (Peadar) Malynn (a local GL and IRB member), were later to became prominent in the Athlone branch of the Irish Volunteers.[177] The inclusion of a comprehensive report in the *Westmeath Independent* belied McDermott-Hayes' apparent non-attendance and he queried; 'if the '[English] have Territorials, why not Volunteers in Ireland'.[178] Seamus McSweeney, local FÉ instructor, took the chair at the meeting, where it was heard that the force was to regroup and invite the 'assistance of the National Volunteers, Dublin, in holding a public meeting in the town'.[179] Soon after the meeting, Liam Mellows, a member of the IV committee who regularly interacted with the Athlone FÉ,[180] communicated with the MVF, asking them to submit to a merger.[181] Described by Michael Kenny as part of the evolution of the IV in Ireland,[182] the merger would have addressed MacNeill's desire to avoid competitive factionalism, provided, at least in theory, better direction and assisted in the promotion of a unified nationalist force in the region. It was agreed that Athlone's volunteers would merge, and during January 1914 a local IV corps was established,[183] with men such as Curley and Croghan re-emerging to drill local volunteers.[184]

The formation of the IV created a new organisation for Ireland's nationalists that quickly began to alter the political dynamic of the country. For some nationalists, both advanced and constitutional, its existence was an engaging development which helped re-energise the politics surrounding the Home Rule drive and provided them with an active organisation with which they could engage. In Athlone, the IV corps may have been a natural harbour for active nationalists looking for a new berth, certainly younger men who would have been unlikely to engage with the UIL branch even if it were not moribund. Increasingly identified as solely a fundraising body, Dean Kelly's attempts to reorganise the local league and stock it with young blood was seen as a redundant move, and failed comprehensively.[185] Issues surrounding land ownership, urban tenancy and other politically sensitive causes were seen as something that could be dealt with after Home Rule was enacted.[186] Joining a deflated UIL was not a productive move for nationalists. However, joining the IV was seen as a useful way of evincing support for the bigger issue, showing the UVF that it would not be allowed to direct the Home Rule process.

While nationalists listened attentively as IPP members J.P. Hayden and Walter Nugent espoused the virtues of Home Rule at rallies during the spring of 1914,[187] it was apparent that assuaging unionist fears was proving exceptionally difficult. Redmond's willingness to 'pay a big price for a settlement by consent'[188] was causing concern, as many commentators believed that the unionist minority was exercising too great an influence in negotiations.[189] Proposals for partitioning the country were discussed so frequently by early 1914 that 'reality [dictated that] the name of the game ... was how to manage an acceptable "'exclusion zone"'.[190] The Athlone PLG had little interest in dividing the country, with its minute book reflecting that 'you may be sure that you will only have one Ireland under Home Rule',[191] while the UDC[192] and Westmeath County Council both passed resolutions of confidence in the IPP leader's ability to ensure a single state.[193] The emotive political atmosphere began to feed into the GL with Dean Kelly again reminding members that the restoration of the Irish language was 'the great object ... all other[s] ... were subsidiary'.[194] O.J. Dolan argued that the large sums collected for the Parliamentary Fund proved that 'the slanders of the

Northern press that we don't want Home Rule' were false,[195] while in a letter
to H.J.Walker, J.P. Hayden repeated the need for sustained support in the face
of the 'concentration of ... the enemies of Ireland ... [to] prevent Irishmen
of all creeds and classes coming on terms of equality for the first time'.[196]
In what Paul Bew has described as a 'particularly able speech' delivered in
March, Walter Nugent maintained his previously heard arguments for Ireland
as part of the Empire, while highlighting incongruities in Carson's polemics
and condemning talk of civil war. Nugent believed Ireland would be as much
part of the British Empire after Home Rule as before; indeed, as Bew has
noted, Nugent 'almost seemed to be describing the strengthening of the
union rather than its weakening'.[197]

   The possibility of civil strife in Athlone if Home Rule was introduced
was raised by a journalist from *The Irish Times*. He believed that local
nationalists 'move as little as possible' in political circles and were loathe
to foment ill-feeling. Many 'thriving Catholic shopkeeper[s]', he stated,
along with Protestant businessmen, were 'unionist at heart' and would
rather lose Home Rule than have violence, motivated as they were more
by business than politics. 'Athlone', he stated, appeared 'to be particularly
fortunate' in that regard.[198] McDermott-Hayes reviewed the piece and, out
of keeping with most of his editorials that referenced *Irish Times* articles,
it was not condemned.[199]

   While political efforts to find a solution to the Ulster question were
continuing, the possibility of recourse to military action still loomed large.
The increased militarisation and its probable end result concerned many, especially in the case of the UVF, even though Carson had stated that force was
to be used against those who wished to impose Home Rule, i.e the British
Government. Needless to say, actually having to take on the government
(in this context, the British Army), would have been a major difficulty and
on 20 March the possibility of such an encounter was almost entirely negated
when what became known as the Curragh 'Mutiny' occurred. The incident
itself arose out of a misunderstanding with regard to the duties troops in Ulster
were to undertake. The government intended for them to protect military
stores in the region. However, subtle manipulation by unionist interests[200] in
the Curragh garrison, allied with 'monumental official bungling'[201] led to an
interpretation that the order called for the suppression of militant northern
unionists, something seventy officers in the Curragh made it clear they would
not be a party to.[202] The distortion of the command was disseminated widely,
with even *The New York Times* stating that Athlone's artillery had to 'hold itself
in readiness to proceed to Ulster at a moment's notice'.[203]

The incident shifted some initiative to the side of the unionists, who promoted the idea that there was an anti-Ulster unionist government stratagem at play.[204] McDermott-Hayes believed that the incident was nothing more than 'part of the Tory game that has been played all along the line'.[205] Those in cabinet who had wanted decisive action taken against the UVF, most prominently Winston Churchill, were now frustrated.[206] The incident ensured that Asquith's government recognised that it was limited as to the range of activities in which it could direct the army to engage. The episode led to a perception developing that 'unionist interests mandated government practice'.[207]

The Curragh debacle exerted quite an influence on the political environment, as an increasing number of nationalists began to view the IV in much the same light as unionists saw the UVF; a 'symbol of political earnestness and determination'.[208] The IV was not, however, spreading as rapidly as organisers hoped, and in Athlone the force was having difficulty expanding its roster. The main reasons for the weak growth appeared to be the clerical unease at the potential of the group, and the unwillingness of the IPP to lend its support.[209] Though a small number of enthusiasts drilled regularly in Athlone, the Westmeath CI observed that 'little interest appears to have been taken'.[210] The indoor venue for the exercises allied with the small membership of between forty and seventy lent credence to this opinion,[211] as infrequent co-operative marches with FÉ did little to change his mind.[212] Athlone's situation apparently contrasted with that of other regions. Locally there were army men willing to train the volunteers, but few volunteers. In places such as Dublin and Kerry there was a paucity of soldiers to train but greater numbers willing to be trained.[213] The local press highlighted the lack of interest, while continuing to warn of the Ulster threat.[214] As so often occurred, locals were informed that Athlone was being 'outstripped' by other districts.[215] The Mullingar IV boasted 230 members, while that of Castlepollard had sixty-nine.[216] A branch established in Boyle in April had 300 enrolled and the organisation was said to have the support of 'all sections of Nationalists' in Roscommon.[217] Both proportionately and numerically, Athlone was faring poorly. The activities in the Curragh provided some impetus for Athlone's organisers, who began to look to adjacent regions, especially those with GAA teams.[218] Players were drilled after games had finished on Sundays, and those interested were informed that MVF co-founder Michael Curley was also training volunteers in Athlone on Fridays.[219]

The slow increase in the level of activity in the IV in Athlone was additionally surprising given developments, both locally and further north. Reports emerged of increased military activity around Athlone during April, activity attributed to Ulster militancy. The RIC engaged in special drilling near the town, though they denied, not particularly convincingly, that it had anything to do with unionist activity.[220] Such a claim was harder to believe during the final days of April, when unionists landed over 24,000 rifles and millions of rounds of ammunition at Larne, County Antrim.[221] The landing, carried out in a subversive, yet assertive manner,[222] with unofficial assistance from members of the RIC and customs,[223] showed unionists were preparing to make a more definite move towards the violence they so often threatened.[224] With so much activity going on around them, Athlone's volunteers were surely not working under the misapprehension that all augured well for the painless introduction of Home Rule.

As 10,000 people gathered in Athlone to celebrate the successful third reading of the Home Rule Bill,[225] John Redmond made a direct move to ensure the IV was under IPP control. A number of factors convinced Redmond that he must assume control.[226] These included increased Ulster militancy, the massive growth in IV numbers from 14,000 to 69,000,[227] and even rumours that 500 guns had been handed out in the Athlone area.[228] His ability to ensure that his overtures were successful was bolstered by his party's position at Westminster; the IPP was as powerful as it had ever been. Resisting Redmond's proposition, a demand in reality, would have been inadvisable.[229]

The take-over happened quite rapidly. Redmond presented an ultimatum: his party either controlled the IV or he would take 'steps which might split the movement'.[230] The idea of a schism was anathema to Eoin MacNeill, who believed it would be 'a certain sign of weakness' in the Irish cause.[231] With MacNeill's agreement, Redmond appointed numerous Irish Party supporters to the IV committee, men described by Alvin Jackson as 'middle-aged and uninterested'.[232] Some existing members, IRB men mainly, felt aggrieved and disenfranchised; however, their lack of political clout, relative anonymity, and marginal influence over the larger body of volunteers ensured they could do little and they remained on as a minority.[233]

Redmond's endorsement, while changing the makeup of the IV committee, also facilitated changes at grass-roots level as clerical concerns were assuaged. From only seven in May, Westmeath's IV corps grew to twenty in June.[234] The IV in Roscommon also made rapid gains, with an additional endorsement from Archbishop Healy of Tuam, leading to an almost four-fold increase in volunteer numbers; 660 in May to almost 2,300 by July.[235] More ex-servicemen offered their skills as drill instructors and training benefited greatly as a result.[236] Nationally enrolments reached 132,000, considerably more than the reported 85,000 UVF members.[237]

In and around Athlone, there was additional evidence of change. Some reports stated that the membership of the local corps had risen to 500 and that army reservists were ignoring directions from the military to avoid IV association.[238] Local political figures such as O.J. Dolan became more readily identified with the IV and greater energy permeated a gathering at Streamstown in south Westmeath, where Athlone's founding role was highlighted; 'there, [Athlone] if occasion demanded it, would be men to resist another siege or two'.[239] Organised Labour's opposition to the volunteers did little to dissuade local men from enrolling,[240] with the UDC adopting a resolution criticising the actions of the army in the face of the 'Ulster question', and proposing the rapid organisation of the IV under Redmond and their deployment to 'protect our fellow Nationalists in Ulster from … attack'.[241] The *Westmeath Independent* wrote hubristically of Athlone's influence: 'The good sense … of Athlone pervades the National Forces from the Hills of Donegal to the Cove of Cork.'[242]

It became apparent, however, that the discontent felt by advanced nationalist members of the IV committee in Dublin was replicated in corps all over the country, including Athlone. A meeting was planned to discuss Redmond's endorsement, a meeting which, according to the *Westmeath Independent*, over 700 people attended. One of the most interesting developments at the meeting was the appearance of a Con Ua Frighil,[243] representing SF. He stated that between fifty and sixty Athlone SF members[244] were in attendance to highlight the 'non-political character' of the IV, the deficiencies in the Home Rule Bill and the Redmond's unjust appropriation of the Volunteers.[245] His speech was greeted mostly by jeers, but the fact that SF appeared to be reorganising in Athlone was of interest, especially considering that just two months earlier the CI believed that the SF branch 'may now be considered as extinct'.[246]

Other speakers included Owen Sweeney, who highlighted his belief that Irishmen should be allowed to bear arms, McDermott-Hayes, who proposed a vote of confidence in the IPP (which, after some SF resistance, was passed), and P.V.C. Murtagh, who believed that Eoin MacNeill's views would split the organisation.[247] The corps also received Protestant support in the form of a letter from St Peter's parish vicar, the Revd James F. Anderson. *The Irish Times* reported that the meeting was a fractious affair that looked as if 'recourse to physical violence' was likely at times, while the *Irish Independent* described the 'considerable disagreement' that manifested.[248] Con Ua Frighil wrote a letter to the latter newspaper the following day to chastise it for misspelling his name and stated his support for the idea of Home Rule, while clarifying his position on Redmond's endorsement.[249] The following Wednesday, the Athlone IV committee was formed with McDermott-Hayes, O.J. Dolan and Murtagh in positions of prominence.[250] Brother Bonaventure of the Marist Brothers praised the IPP for their efforts to ensure unity in the IV ranks, and he stated that 'it would have been a dire misfortune if anything happened to check the onward march of National progress'.[251]

The annoyance in some quarters at Redmond's annexation of the IV precipitated much debate on his right to do so. Throughout June, the genesis and intentions of the nationalist volunteer movement were debated by both sides, each seeking to establish their bona fides in relation to ownership of the group. For the purposes of forwarding the IPP argument, Athlone's MVF was quite convenient proof of a constitutional nationalist origin, and numerous articles from a variety of publications espoused this viewpoint. An editorial from the *Connacht Tribune* of 6 June noted that the movement 'began some months ago in Athlone. It was then taken up in Dublin, where a meeting was held in the Rotunda.'[252] The same text was employed by the *Southern Star* of 6 June and in the 13 June edition it detailed, on the basis of a letter provided by John Redmond, that 'It began in Athlone, where it was started by warm-hearted supporters of the Irish Party … in answer to the threats of mutiny and rebellion organised by the Tory clubs.'[253]

Ironically, it was the IPP newspaper the *Freeman's Journal* that was to bolster the argument of advanced nationalists with an article in its 8 June edition. In a hyperbolic piece, it reported that the movement was 'Begun in Athlone … as an answer to the mutiny in the Curragh Camp'.[254] This chronological absurdity was seized upon by SF a week later; Arthur Griffith noted its illogic and declared that the *Freeman's Journal* 'lies with an object';[255] i.e. falsely tracing the IV back to IPP-loyal founders. The *Freeman's Journal* editor had in the interim revisited the question to address the error, reiterating the constitutional origins of the movement. Athlone's organisers were men:

> … who believed that such a movement in answer to … threats of mutiny and rebellion organised by the Tory clubs would be a tower of strength behind the Party evidencing the hold of … Home Rule … on the manhood of Ireland, and the determination of … people not to be filched out of their rights.[256]

The 16 June edition hit out at the assertions of MacNeill and his colleagues:

> Athlone's Volunteers sprang up without any platform incentives and began their drilling before any provisional committee came into existence. They have ranged themselves under the Irish Leader's banner.[257]

A less partisan assessment came from D.P. Moran of *The Leader*. The 20 June edition questioned the claims made by the Rotunda attendees that it was they who pioneered the IV and they who should have controlled the committee. Moran pointed out that if such reason was to be used to decide committee positions, 'why not go back to ... Athlone?'[258] Asking, 'Who is "the father" of the Irish Volunteers?', Moran gave a rather abstract genesis for the movement as an organic growth that spontaneously combusted, while also tackling the factual details:

> The first sign of the combustion ... manifested at Athlone ... Athlone started the Volunteers in a more or less local way ... Then several gentlemen in Dublin decided to do something ... Mr John Gore, Mr John McNeill, The O'Rahilly and Mr. L.J. Kettle ... we [*The Leader*] did all we could to help ... Athlone, ourselves, and those ... in Dublin fade away before the ... fact that Ireland rose ... to the Irish Volunteers. Athlone deserves ... credit, those ... in Dublin deserve ... credit, we deserve ... credit ourselves.[259]

The debate slackened after Moran's article, though the *Freeman's Journal* continued to publish on Athlone's pioneering role during July, mainly from speeches delivered at rallies such as one from Tyrone during the second week of the month,[260] and the midlands, one week later: 'It was Athlone that sent out the Volunteer cry which had been so splendidly heard all over Ireland, and had given them [the IPP] an army ready for any emergency.'[261] A constitutional origin for the IV was without doubt the most popular reading of the organisation's genesis, despite that fact that the constitutional party had given no support to the MVF upon its inception.

The debate, and Athlone's prominent role, assisted in stimulating improvements in the town's corps. Local nationalists had not been occupied by the UIL for some time and while David Fitzpatrick has noted that unlike the league, the IV 'never became a power in local politics',[262] the organisation certainly provided a focus for those interested in Ireland's political future. The first 'general mobilisation' in Athlone in July 1914 saw 300 men march in parade formation through the streets, and locals generously supplied funds 'to equip' the IV, with Major Gerald Dease, one of Westmeath's Deputy Lieutenants,[263] assigned the task of organising Athlone as part of the Westmeath IV division.[264] T.P. O'Connor and Walter Nugent both donated money to the Athlone corps, which organised drilling exercises four nights a week in the Fairgreen for both urban and rural volunteers.[265] The *Freeman's Journal* stated that in Athlone 'a large number of young businessmen joined … and new members are coming in almost nightly'. By the end of July, Athlone's IV corps was 'nearly battalion strength'.[266] Rural regions received donations of 'new colours' (uniforms) blessed by parish priests, while PLG and UDC support was reiterated,[267] as members hoped that the IV could influence negotiations at Buckingham Palace, where proposals for excluding parts of Ulster were being debated.[268]

While the creation of the IV was seen as going part way towards addressing the imbalance between nationalists and unionists, the latter's better arsenal also had to be addressed. This was recognised in the Athlone corps, where the majority of members voted that a proposal to purchase bandoliers, haversacks and putties was considerably less practical than one to purchase rifles.[269] IV corps all over Ireland made their intentions clear as they passed resolutions 'demanding the non-enforcement of the Proclamation to prohibit the impor-tation of arms',[270] with the exhibition of 5,000 armed UVF men marching unhindered in the Belfast on 25 July providing additional impetus.[271] To address the imbalance and without John Redmond's knowledge, Roger Casement assisted in landing a small shipment of weapons, just 900 guns and 25,000 rounds of ammunition,[272] at Howth, County Dublin on 26 July. After these were unloaded by IV members, a short scuffle with soldiers from the King's Own Scottish Borders regiment ensued. The IV men quickly dispersed, while the soldiers made for their barracks under the watchful eyes of a taunting civilian crowd.[273] At Bachelor's Walk the situation turned violent when some spectators hurled stones at the soldiers, who then fired their weapons in retaliation, killing three and wounding three dozen more.[274]

Nationalists were outraged. Many observers stated that the govern-ment tolerated unionist gun-running but not a nationalist equivalent, or as McDermott-Hayes put it, 'suppress in Dublin what is tolerated in Belfast'.[275] John Redmond, in one of his 'most belligerent speeches', outlined a similar viewpoint and called for an enquiry.[276] J.P. Hayden seconded Redmond's call for an enquiry, demanded the removal of the offending regiment, the repeal of the Arms Proclamation and the administration of the laws of justice on an impartial basis.[277] Despite the fact that there were marked differences in the approach of the two volunteer organisations to the landing of armaments with the unionists being more clandestine, and the nationalists more provocative,[278] a sense of discrimination pervaded, and nationalist anger led to additional IV enrolments.

With political negotiations in stalemate, the possibility of civil war increased.[279] The government promised to strictly enforce the Arms Proclamation, a move the Athlone UDC described as 'interference … with the rights of every Irish citizen' and the *Irish Volunteer* claimed 'removed the parent of liberty, [the rifle]', from the hands of Irishmen, and gifted Englishmen the 'right to murder Irish people'.[280] In Athlone, the Bachelor's Walk shootings led to an additional forty joining the IV, with instruction under Alfred Warby and Michael Curley continuing apace. In Westmeath and Roscommon, membership continued to increase; the former now had forty-three branches of almost 4,200 men, with Roscommon presenting fifty-six branches of almost 5,600.[281] In two separate marches, 400 IV paraded through Athlone calling for justice over the 'Dublin murders', support for Redmond and, if necessary, militant pursuit of Home Rule. In what the *Manchester Guardian* referred to as a 'remarkable scene', the Athlone-based Dublin Military Reserve's show of support for the march received an enthusiastic response from locals. The *Westmeath Independent* stated that it showed that ill will was not directed at the army as a whole.[282]

Growing IV numbers, allied with increasingly common calls from national-ists to provide more forceful examples of their will, appeared to augur for the commencement of an internecine conflict. A.T.Q. Stewart has described unionists as ready for action: 'In Ulster the UVF was completely ready ... and waited only for Carson to telegraph "Go ahead" or "Hold back in the meantime".'[283] The RIC admitted that poor intelligence and insufficient strength would have rendered the police unable to deal with the two groups if they came to blows.[284] However, the move towards conflict was soon curtailed, as domestic concerns were overshadowed by international affairs. On 3 August 1914, Britain declared war on Germany and a continental war commenced. The *Freeman's Journal* stated that Ireland was to have its 'fate decided' by external events.[285]

The most immediate effect of the war on Irish politics was the relegation in importance of Home Rule. The government now had a far larger and more pressing situation to deal with and, as Prime Minister Asquith stated, problems in Ireland were 'put in the shade'.[286] This essential shift in priorities was something to which John Redmond reconciled himself. Home Rule, his highest priority, now hinged on showing the cabinet that Ireland was willing to support Britain in her time of need. On 3 August, after consulting perhaps no more than two MPs, J.P. Hayden and T.P. O'Connor, both with Athlone links,[287] Redmond pledged Ireland's support for the war, a move instrumental in persuading thousands of Irishmen, many of them IV, to enlist in the British Army.[288] His motivations were obvious, but some argued that such support should have been conditional on Home Rule already being implemented, not the reverse.[289] Edward Carson followed suit the next day, when he called on the UVF to go to the colours.[290]

Redmond's supportive speech was lauded in Athlone's local press.[291] 'Brave England' was the headline of an issue of the *Westmeath Independent*, which noted that Athlone was 'besieged by reservists', as all those under the 'Irish Command' filed in to receive their orders. Support for the effort was promoted by McDermott-Hayes, who counselled against using the war as an excuse to stage revolution in Ireland.[292] Those who may have been most likely to use the war as a cover for rebellion were not entirely discommoded by Redmond's speech, which outlined how nationalist volunteers would defend Ireland, thus freeing up British soldiers. However, they were not at all supportive of the promotion of closer ties with Britain, with the *Irish Volunteer* stating that if the IV were to arm, they should do so for 'Ireland alone'.[293]

As was to be expected, the Athlone IV corps lost many instructors to 'the colours' almost immediately. However, their loss, at least in terms of support if not training, was offset, somewhat unexpectedly, by local Protestants and unionists. At a meeting two days after Redmond's declaration, John Burgess, Thomas Chapman and other prominent Protestants who wanted Athlone 'to have the first body of unionists that had moved in joining the National Volunteers', applied to join the local corps. The previous day had seen the Athlone IV make friendly overtures to the British Army when O.J. Dolan announced that Britain could, 'if Home Rule were speedily given', have the service of 'any volunteers in Ireland'.[294] Burgess and his associates appeared to be reciprocating. He stated that Redmond, 'No matter how much they differed from him', had made an inspiring call and that Athlone would not only have the distinction of 'being the first town to move in the National Volunteer movement', but also that of having the first 'organised body of unionists' to join the Irish Volunteers.[295] Financial and practical support was promised; it was stated that the move would lead to all in the town 'being better friends in the future'.[296] The meeting was covered in detail in the *Irish Independent* and *The Irish Times*; the latter wrote of the cheers for, unsurprisingly, the king, and, considerably less common amongst unionists, John Redmond and the 'National Volunteers'.[297] Welcomed by O.J. Dolan, almost 100 'unionists' (not all unionists obviously, as Thomas Chapman's presence testifies), later mixed with hundreds of IV at the Fairgreen.[298] Dolan thanked them, stating they had given a lead to the rest of the country.[299]

A similar type of co-operation was seen in Mullingar later in the month when reportedly 3,000 IV put on a show of strength for an audience of prominent nationalist and unionist figures.[300] Clare and Sligo too saw moves towards greater co-operation between the IV and Protestants, but nothing on the scale of what occurred in Athlone, at least not so soon after the declaration of war.[301] The IV enrolment of prominent unionist and former MP Captain Bryan Cooper soon after, along with his call for other unionists to follow suit, led Asquith to assert that the Home Rule question had been altered; lines had been rubbed away by the scuffing of army boots.[302] In a symbolic act, a march held in Athlone towards the end of August saw 150 members of the Royal Field Artillery, mostly Irish, though some Scottish, joining the IV corps in marching around the town 'four deep'.[303] It was the last large-scale march for some time, as the negation of the unionist threat saw IV activity fall precipitously.

The war did not completely overshadow Redmond's victory in the final passing of the Home Rule Bill and receipt of royal assent on 18 September.[304] Small-scale celebrations in Athlone reflected the general situation across the country;[305] most were preoccupied with the war, including local SF members, who, as the Westmeath CI noted, had begun anti-recruitment efforts.[306] Unionists reacted angrily, albeit in measured fashion, after the king signed the bill into law. They recognised that continuing to threaten civil war or worse, act upon the threat, would have been an unpatriotic deed of immense proportions.[307] Bonar Law led the Conservatives out of the Commons when Asquith pushed forward with the bill. The prime minister made it clear, however, that forcing the Ulster Unionists to accept Irish Home Rule was still not countenanced.[308]

Importantly, the application of the Home Rule Act was suspended for one year, or the period of the war, if longer (a protracted conflict was not envisaged), with the question of the Amending Bill for Ulster left for consideration when hostilities ended.[309] The *Westmeath Independent* reflected Redmond's equanimity at the suspension: a short war could foster greater understanding between nationalists and unionists on the battlefronts, possibly making post-war negotiations more cordial.[310] However, such a view was to be proven unrealistically sanguine, as the reality of the post-war relationship between the two sides was to be influenced by circumstances which Redmond could not have forseen.

While the general response to Redmond's speech of 3 August was one of support, his next was to create a different dynamic. On 20 September at a rally in Woodenbridge, County Wicklow, he gave an unscheduled speech calling for the IV to fight 'wherever they were needed', a shift from his position of using them in Ireland alone.[311] Tellingly, this call came two days after royal assent had been given, and it has been argued by Joseph Finnan that it showed Redmond's commitment to Ireland rather than to the Empire; full support was not given until Home Rule was passed.[312] D.G. Boyce believes the call was 'probably unavoidable' in the circumstances, and led to a situation where 'Redmond and recruitment would stand or fall together'.[313] The speech was supported by McDermott-Hayes who, like Redmond, believed that Irish nationalists, fighting internationally, was an additional surety in the search for all-island Home Rule.[314] Unionists, while quite capable of articulating many reasons for partition regardless of nationalist overtures, had to be shown that both sides had common interests that could be accommodated in a Home Rule Ireland. Unionist enlistment exemplified their Britishness; Irish nationalists had to address this, for not to do so would have rendered starker the contrast between the two sides.[315]

It was obvious that Redmond saw the development of the war, and the role of Irish nationalists, differently to both Ireland's 'advanced' nationalists and the British. He envisaged the creation of an Irish army corps,[316] based around the two volunteer groups, which would eventually be 'in effect a national army for the new Ireland'. He was obviously aware of pre-existing Irish regiments, such as the Connaught Rangers and the Leinster Regiment, though was also quite conscious of the hierarchy within them, and their 'dilution' through British drafts.[317] He wanted an Irish corps that was not merely a sop or titular concession.[318] Though his Woodenbridge speech is often depicted as a miscalculation, it appears, as J.J. Lee suggests, that 'no one genuinely committed to Irish unity could have acted differently from Redmond'.[319]

The consequences of the speech at Woodenbridge were not slow in coming. Despite his aversion to splitting the IV, Eoin MacNeill made it known that he, and other advanced nationalist committee members, could no longer engage with the IPP leader; 'Redmond has announced a totally different policy and duty', wrote MacNeill.[320] Two separate organisations were created; the Irish National Volunteers (INV) or pro-Redmond side with 190,000 members and the IV, or MacNeill's Volunteers, with at most 12,000.[321] Redmond believed that control of the Volunteers had to rest with elected representatives, and described MacNeill and his associates as 'well-known cranks and mischief makers', an opinion that was echoed in the *Westmeath Independent*.[322] The IRB quickly took to dominating the smaller faction, and while J.J. Lee has described MacNeill's instigation of a schism as 'more visceral than cerebral',[323] it was much to the liking of the more advanced section, which took advantage of the lifting of the Arms Proclamation on 5 August and began sourcing weapons.[324] Having previously described the IPP and IV as 'England's recruiting Jackals', the hardline socialist *Irish Worker* was quite happy with the split, believing that it could allow the smaller faction to find some direction.[325]

Nationally, the split reignited the dispute over the origins and purpose of the IV, and again Athlone played a prominent role. McDermott-Hayes initiated the process in a letter to the *Freeman's Journal*, in which he poured scorn on the 'ridiculous pretensions of the Dublin "Unknowns"' in splitting the Volunteers. He provided an extract from the MVF manifesto of 22 October 1913, issued 'before there was a single corps in the City of Dublin, or before the "Unknowns" grabbed the movement'. The MVF was set up to deal with 'aggression daily threatened from the North, and to lend whatever assistance was possible to Mr. Redmond and the Irish Party'.[326] A week later, the vehemently anti-enlistment D.P. Moran consulted with members of the smaller faction and published a re-evaluation of his earlier opinion of the MVF:

> Some … force was started in Athlone – we understand it was more or less of a hoax … an Athlone … paper, of which a Mr. Hayes is editor … wrote the matter up as … fact; we understand that it was … farcical … we read the accounts, and it … occurred to us that the time was ripe for suggesting Volunteers to Ireland … the idea … seized on the imagination of many men in Dublin.[327]

Moran's article was reprinted in the *Irish Volunteer* (now solely promoting the IV) a week later and M.J. Judge, a regular contributor, supplemented it with his own views:

> Without desiring to deprecate Athlone I must say … that the Athlone Volunteers … had no existence save in the wild fancies of a journalist who had … indulged too freely in the 'glowing cup'. Irish journalists … are … very sober, steady and respectable people, who judge everybody by their own standard[s] … Therefore we can all understand how … easy it must be to … befool them, [this] explains the reference to the imaginary Athlone corps … in … the *Freeman's Journal* and … *Evening Telegraph* last week.[328]

The game of journalistic tennis continued as the *National Volunteer*, the INV paper, reproduced McDermott-Hayes' *Freeman's Journal* letter in its 17 October issue. On the front page ran the headline: 'Genesis of the "Originals".' The article stated that 'from Athlone the organisation spread … At length Dublin joined in'.[329] To balance the *Irish Worker*'s editorialising in opposition to a constitutional origin for the IV, the anti-Larkinite Labour publication *The Toiler* stated in its 17 October issue that: 'When the volunteers were first raised, they were Home Rulers to a man.'[330] Three weeks later, the *National Volunteer* wrote, as Moran had previously, of the spontaneous nature of the movement, and the original allegiance to Redmond. It claimed there were those:

> … who had worked the Sinn Féin red herring for all it was worth and tried to nobble the Gaelic League … One only has to read the names

of the self-constituted committee who appropriated the … movement to see how clever was the intrigue that was … hatched. Mr. Redmond decided to act … [331]

As with the first manifestation of the origin debate, it is certain that the most popularly consulted and widely circulated newspaper sources were promoting Athlone's MVF as the authentic genesis of the nationalist volunteer movement. The most declarative piece, which appeared to close the debate (at least in the contemporary press), came from the *Freeman's Journal*:

It originated in Athlone … before anyone in Dublin expressed the idea … Some people who like to pose as founders … are careful to observe that … The founders of the … movement [supported] the Irish Party, and it started … [due to] the menace of … resistance from a minority in one corner of Ireland. [332]

In Athlone, news of the schism spread quickly. Allegiance to the IPP and the war effort was promoted in the local press and McDermott-Hayes' efforts to denounce the 'factionalist clique' of MacNeill continued; Ireland had 'no frame of mind to tolerate the antics of a handful of cranks who arrogated an authority they do not possess'. [333] Reaction to the split led to an IV corps reorganisation meeting during the third week in October, and from the outset, the 'invite only' gathering was a fractious affair. A number of SF members gate-crashed in an effort to thwart organisers' attempts to perpetrate a fait accompli and of the 150 people in attendance, 100 voted for Redmond, a result that led to a disruptive ending as the minority registered their displeasure. A report in the *Westmeath Independent* stated: 'There was a show of hands in which irresponsible people took part. Had a ballot been taken not two dozen would be found to support the "Originals".' Subsequent to the vote, some of the anti-Redmond side shouted 'Cheers for the Kaiser', and 'Cheers for Germany'. [334] The *Irish Independent* related the fall-out and noted: 'The more reasonable of those on both sides averted a collision, which at one time appeared possible.' [335] Reported GL association with the minority was repudiated by the local league committee, which was not promoting SF and was not a 'chapel of ease for disturbing factions'. [336] McDermott-Hayes stated that the anti-Redmondites had, for all intents and purposes, been defeated by the overwhelming amount of support for the INV, who now had a 'great chance to be a national force'. [337] Redmond and his supporters had control of a comprehensively loyal volunteer organisation, which they soon set about reorganising. A series of aims and plans were drawn up to ensure the efficacy and efficiency of the INV, with Athlone designated as a winter camp (along with Cork, Galway and Wexford) for the training of officers and non-commissioned officers under the guidance of Col. Maurice Moore. A manifesto was issued calling for financial and numerical support from the Irish people.[338]

Five days after the initial IV meeting, another was held in Athlone, which confirmed the numerical dominance of Redmond's followers. A newly constituted INV committee was formed, from which all local advanced nationalists were excluded.[339] Consequently, it was necessary for such men to establish a branch of the IV in Athlone, and they gained some support from nearby rural areas such as Drumraney and Ballykeeran in Westmeath.[340] Nationally, the reorganisation of the smaller faction saw a number of new names come to the fore. Unsurprisingly, MacNeill, Hobson, and O'Rahilly retained their prominent positions, as Pádraig Pearse, Joseph Plunkett and Thomas McDonagh also assumed roles on the new IV committee.[341] The realigning of the committee was finalised at the 1st Annual Convention of the IV, which saw local men Peter Malynn (Athlone), Seamus O'Brien (Ballykeeran) and Seán McCormack (Drumraney) in attendance.[342] The IG noted that 11,000 men had enlisted as members, with the committee making serious efforts to boost that number significantly.[343]

Athlone readers of *Sinn Féin* and the *Irish Volunteer*[344] more frequently encountered articles detailing how England had brought Ireland years of misery, while the Germans were without any culpability in that regard. Fighting for the British against the Kaiser meant that you were fighting the wrong fight, against an 'enemy' without the tarnished record of Ireland's ally.[345] Supplementary to such publications were the speeches of Laurence Ginnell who presented a similar, darker and perhaps more realistic, if somewhat more cynical, view of the consequences of Irish involvement in the war:

> Now, when the Empire is in danger and … Volunteers may be very useful to stop German bullets and fill … ditches with Irish corpses, thus enabling the English to stay at home at the more profitable business of capturing German trade … to keep cowardly English soldiers … protecting the bridge of Drogheda … the Bridge of Athlone and bringing Irish girls to ruin.[346]

The lines between unionists and nationalists that some believed the war could erase were now being redrawn, albeit temporarily, to separate different nationalist ideologies in Ireland.

4

The Opportunities
of War

The declaration of war in August 1914 ensured that great change was witnessed in the political, economic and social life of Athlone's inhabitants. Local men were targeted for enlistment, while businesses turned their attention to supplying the needs of the thousands of recruits who entered the town for training. The move of many Athlone INV members to the front in the early stages of the war appeared to evince good support for the conflict, yet as it dragged on, casualties mounted and circumstances changed. Redmond's call to enlist became increasingly unpopular and constitutional nationalist organisations began to lose support in Athlone and across Ireland, with a concurrent, if not equal, rise in support for advanced nationalist bodies such as the IV and SF. The latter capitalised on the IPP's war preoccupation, as many began to wonder whether Irish MPs had now come to regard the cause of the British Empire as taking precedence over that of Ireland. Other hard-line nationalists saw the conflict as an opportune time to exercise a more direct influence on Ireland's political destiny and staged an ill-fated rebellion at Easter 1916. Initial widespread condemnation of the insurrection in Athlone was swiftly followed by massive sympathy for its instigators as the draconian British reaction impacted savagely on the day-to-day lives of the townspeople. The currency of the rhetoric employed by the rebellion's leaders increased in value, while that of the aging IPP began to appear stale, hollow and unsatisfactory in comparison. In Athlone SF support swelled, support for the IPP and the war fell, and for the first time in its existence, it appeared that the Irish Party was to have a political opponent in Ireland who not only aspired to usurp its place, but was in the early stages of achieving that aspiration.

SUPPORT FOR THE EFFORT?
RECRUITMENT AND THE WAR ECONOMY

Recruitment for the British war effort was a drama that played out across a multitude of stages in Ireland, and in Athlone the drive to find enlistees in the first eighteen months of hostilities was strongly supported. Before the outbreak, numerous local men were already part of the 20,780-strong Irish representation[1] in the army's regular forces, with many others, such as MVF co-founders Patrick Croghan and Michael Curley, part of the army reserve, which was almost 30,000 strong.[2] More men were needed and John Redmond's promotion of enlistment left Athlone's eligible constitutional nationalist men under no illusions as to their duty.

However, from the outset, it was apparent that the War Office, which maintained a 'dismal story of … obtuseness in handling Irish recruitment', was to frustrate the efforts of pro-war nationalists in Athlone.[3] In November 1914 it issued an appeal to local authorities that they induce employees with military experience to join the army. Athlone UDC, always supportive of the army (especially the economic benefits it brought to the town), pre-empted the request, promising half-pay for men who re-enlisted.[4] The War Office acknowledged receipt of the news, but returned the original note from the UDC replete with inter-office chatter. One unidentified official noted of the council's actions; 'if this is true, this is satisfactory for a Nationalist portion of Ireland'. However, a different script, denoting a second official, read: 'I doubt if you will consider it quite so satisfactory.' The councillors were incensed at the perceived (though not fully understood) slight and requested that Walter Nugent investigate.[5] The *Freeman's Journal* reprinted a piece from the *Westminster Gazette* on the controversy and recommended that:

> officials in the War Office … if they wish to exercise their wit or to show their political opinions [they should] not … return papers upon which they do to the original senders. Irishmen, like others, are apt to resent such things.[6]

Nugent's investigation elicited two letters of apology.[7]

The minor but widely reported controversy provided one example of the War Office's disregard for Irish nationalists' efforts. The eventual creation of the 16th (Irish) Division only came about after much cajoling by John Redmond,[8] and while new Protestant and UVF recruits did outnumber new Catholic and INV recruits,[9] there was still a large pool of eligible Catholic men that the War Office should have sought proactively. In reaction to the controversy, UDC member J.J. Coen described War Office officials as those 'who occupy snug berths … [and] not give half an hour to the service of the country', while M.J. Lennon was annoyed by their lack of faith, understandably so if it was the case, as he claimed it was, that 'practically every man available in Athlone has gone to the army'.[10]

While the early period of the war was certainly that of highest recruitment,[11] Lennon's assertion appears to be an overstatement. Early statistics presented in the *Irish Independent* provide the impression that Athlone men were not enthusiastic about soldiering. From the commencement of hostilities on 4 August to 28 November, just 120 had enlisted. Towns of a similar size, Tralee and Carlow, registered 336 and 264 respectively.[12] In explanation it was noted that Athlone was not an official recruiting centre; most who enlisted did so at the Connaught Rangers' depot in Galway or that of the Leinster Regiment in Birr.[13] Athlone had a recruiting officer, but he had no permanent office, was reportedly difficult to track down and enlisted few directly;[14] perhaps a good example of the 'notoriously inefficient voluntary recruiting system'[15] that the army maintained in Ireland in the early stages of the war.

Whatever the actual figures, the majority of newspaper reports from the early months of the conflict claimed good support for enlistment in Athlone. The emigration-prone farming community excepted,[16] the *Westmeath Independent* wrote proudly of locals' commitment; for example, two of Thomas Chapman's sons were at the front. The Midland Great Western Railway (MGWR), a substantial local employer, reportedly had 300 of its employees in training,[17] while *The Irish Times* and *Freeman's Journal* related that twenty-six Athlone Woollen Mills workers had also joined the army.[18] The fact that they had done so when 'slackness of work cannot be ascribed to their enlistment'[19] implied support for the aims of the army, rather than the stipend.[20] While historians have differed as to the motivations for enlistment, it does appear that influences such as patriotism, peer pressure, or even the desire for adventure outweighed the attraction of an army wage, given the conditions a soldier had to endure to secure it.[21]

The creation of a separate recruitment board for Ireland in early 1915, the Central Council for the Organisation of Recruiting in Ireland,[22] led to large numbers enlisting during the spring, roughly 1,100 per week.[23] Stories of Athlone men receiving the Distinguished Conduct Medal (DCM)[24] were used to promote the valorous nature of soldiering, but were overshadowed by reports of local fatalities at Gallipoli, the site of massive losses for the Entente.[25] The entry of dozens of wounded soldiers into Athlone's garrison infirmary was similarly a poor advertisement, as were the frequent funerals; indeed, such was the sense of pathos engendered by some wounded soldiers that even the local GAA donated funds, a move that surprised *The Irish Times*, which believed it unusual that money 'from such a source [would be] devoted to patriotic purposes'.[26] Numbers enlisting began to fall in the early summer, and, to combat this, a recruitment committee was established in Athlone in July. The committee was chaired by M.J. Lennon, with the questionable choice (given his familial ties to Lord Castlemaine) of Capt. Henry Handcock as army liaison.[27] The committee met fortnightly and asked local authorities to do their bit to promote recruitment; most did, albeit not unanimously.[28]

By midsummer estimates on the number of local recruits had reached the round figure of 1,000,[29] with J.P. Hayden's *Westmeath Examiner* averring that the county, despite the efforts of Laurence Ginnell,[30] had performed proportionately better than any other.[31] The *Westmeath Independent* promoted acceptance of the figure:

> Local experience shows there is scarcely a working class family in the town that has not one or more of its members at the front, and we know cases where there are as many as four sons ... serving.[32]

Information supplied to the newspaper led it to state that: 'Athlone holds the record of any town in Ireland in proportion to population for the number ... given to the army.'[33] The evidence for the claim came from local Post Office returns, which showed that 407 women, many concentrated in Irishtown, were collecting 'separation allowances',[34] in some cases for more than one man. The weakness in the arithmetic was recognised by the *Westmeath Independent*, though the lack of official figures did not weaken the a priori evidence; 'official knowledge [is] not needed'.[35] Local observations were the best indicator. By August, a figure of 1,200 was being promulgated.[36]

Such statements on the number of recruits were common in the pro-war provincial press in Ireland. Pressmen had little information to go on for the first eighteen months of the war and their ideology often coloured their reports, which at times conflicted with 'official' observations.[37] Requests by Irish MPs for information on the numbers enlisted were rebuffed; supplying such information was seen by the government as 'neither expedient nor desirable'.[38] While recruitment figures held by Irish Command were confidential, it does appear, given Ireland's unique situation, that some Irish representatives gained information, 'on a limited scale', which other MPs were denied.[39] Walter Nugent may have benefited from such information, for at a public function where he presented 'Certificates of Honour' to local army families in December 1915, he spoke of Athlone's contribution, clarifying earlier estimates.[40] He stated that Athlone Union[41] had produced 1,200 recruits since the war began (an important distinction[42]) and the urban area 700 (58 per cent of 1,200[43]), still a high figure for a town with a population less than 7,500 and an eligibility roll of perhaps at most 1,500.[44]

To assess whether such claims were credible, statistics compiled by the British Army later in the conflict are most useful, especially those contained in the *Statement Giving Particulars of Men of Military Age in Ireland* (1916). Between 15 August 1915 (when a National Register was set up[45]) and 15 October 1916, Westmeath furnished 350 recruits and Roscommon 256. From the start of the war to October 1916, Westmeath provided 1,064 recruits and Roscommon 860.[46] Subtracting the figures for the two periods shows that, by August 1915 when the 1,200 figure first surfaced, Westmeath had presented 714 new recruits to the army and Roscommon 604. Logically, if Walter Nugent was correct in saying that the figures he quoted corresponded only with those who enlisted since the war commenced, Athlone Union would have supplied 91 per cent of the new recruits for both counties and Athlone over 53 per cent. This would mean that towns like Mullingar and Boyle, outside the Union, had contributed just 118 men between them, something which is highly improbable. It would be more reasonable to suggest that the figure corresponded to all local men serving in the army, both pre and post-war recruits; however, a dearth of pre-war statistical data from the Athlone region makes assessing such a hypothesis problematic.

Some rough estimate systems have been used to provide figures for recruitment. David Fitzpatrick has asserted that 14 per cent casualties was the norm for Irish participants during the war.[47] If this is accurate then the fifty Athlone dead noted in the *Westmeath Independent* in October 1915 would, if the town followed this trend, have accounted for a total strength of perhaps 360 to 370, considerably lower than the figure often quoted.[48] Though a specious method to assess the town's contribution, the figure does coincidentally equal the number of Certificates of Honour handed out, 370,[49] a figure the *Westmeath Independent* believed to be artificially small.[50] From the spring of 1916 the provision of estimates for Athlone's contribution appeared to stop; if the figure increased further, it would have appeared entirely incredible.[51]

However many from Athlone enlisted during the first year of the war, it is certain that by late autumn 1915 the pool of volunteers had shrunk considerably. A moratorium on RIC enlistment and retirement did little to promote enlistment, and by October 1915, M.J. Lennon questioned why recruitment meetings were held at all.[52] The region, especially west of the Shannon, had apparently reached a point where 'the supply of volunteering recruits is practically exhausted'.[53] Recognition of the fall-off saw a new recruiting body, the 'Department for Recruiting in Ireland',[54] established the same month with new structures created, and 'the machinery for attestation … expanded and strengthened'.[55] A new enlistment campaign which used 'ever more sophisticated propaganda, methodical planning and effective deployment of public figures'[56] to entice men into serving abroad was also devised. The department's head, Lord Lieutenant Wimborne, believed that Irish recruitment could make '… good the waste of war', a belief which, despite early tabulations providing hope, appeared unrealistic.[57]

As Wimborne's scheme was rolled out, its effect in many places, including Athlone, was the opposite of that intended. Large numbers of farmers' sons, especially from Roscommon,[58] left the region, with Athlone's emigration agents recording seventy-six separate applications in just one day in early November after the drive commenced.[59] The fear of meeting the same fate as the passengers of the Lusitania, which was sunk in May, appeared not to dissuade them; agents were informed that the number seeking berths had led to full schedules for two weeks.[60] The mass emigration was condemned at a recruiting drive in Athlone by a LGB inspector, who argued that the 'runaways' should never be allowed back.[61] The Westmeath Independent, doing its bit to dissuade emigration, told would-be emigrants that they would have to run a gauntlet of 'Liverpool hooligans' before they could set sail for America.[62] To stem the flow, the government issued regulations that all 'British subjects' of nineteen years or more had to apply for passports to travel abroad or produce salient documents from a JP and the Foreign Office.[63] The regulations were adhered to by most companies, albeit unenthusiastically.[64] The measure led to a 'virtual stoppage of emigration to America',[65] something borne out by the statistics.[66]

The imposition of restrictive travel conditions meant that unless men were willing to emigrate illegally, they were still available to join the army. The government targeted their homes with postal enlistment requests,[67] often in ignorance of an individual's circumstances. Franciscan Friars, whose 'persecution' at the hands of the LGB, which demanded rates from the mendicants, hampered local recruiting,[68] Marist Brothers and profoundly disabled locals were all asked to fight for the Empire.[69] Few of those targeted answered the call, and the Westmeath CI noted that the recruiting levels seen twelve months previously were not reached.[70] Athlone, despite it being 'a first rate place to recruit',[71] had few willing volunteers.[72] The Irish population became increasingly apprehensive as rumours, promoted by SF, circulated regarding the imposition of conscription,[73] and while the *Hibernian Journal*, amongst other publications, stated that 'no heed should be paid to those who are seeking to raise the conscription scare',[74] it is certain that the measure was being considered.[75] Despite the fact that it was generally accepted that imposing conscription on Ireland would lead to an end of Irish support for the war, the winter of 1915 saw a Military Service Bill drafted.

The exigency of additional Irish troops did not, however, lead to conscription in Ireland. John Redmond secured the country's exclusion from the Military Service Act of January 1916, much to the annoyance of unionists,[76] maintaining the system of voluntary recruitment.[77] The Lord Lieutenant estimated that Ireland still had 100,000 eligible men and in the absence of conscription, he suggested transplanting female labour in certain professions.[78] Suggested mainly for the benefit of recruiting in towns, it was recognised that with the prevalent labour conditions, urban centres were 'not in a position to provide an additional large contingent'.[79] Rural men were still the most numerous amongst those available, but they maintained their unwillingness to enlist, especially in Connacht.[80] Accusations of pro-Germanism were levelled at farmers, who argued that their food production was essential to support soldiers. Their sons were needed to harvest; sending them overseas to be killed or maimed would have serious repercussions for farm labour.[81] As noted by Tom Garvin: 'To avoid enlistment was not regarded as particularly cowardly in rural Ireland, but as evidence of good sense.'[82]

Attempts to combat local farmers' maintenance of good sense were seen in the *Westmeath Independent* as weekly 'Galleries of Heroes', pictures of locals at the front, appeared alongside editorials on the malevolence of the Kaiser.[83] Despite the efforts of McDermott-Hayes and like-minded individuals, it was mounting Irish casualties, on a scale 'beyond anything in contemporary Irish experience',[84] that had the greatest influence. By April 1916 the desired 1,100 recruits per week had fallen to less than 500,[85] a figure that was to drop further in the aftermath of the travails of Easter.

Regardless of the locals' opinions of enlisting, it is certain that their views on the economic benefits of the war were generally positive. Athlone was earmarked to accommodate up to 5,000 troops in total, with 2,700 of that number entering the town's garrison during the winter and spring of 1914/15.[86] The *Westmeath Independent* stated: 'Scarcely a day passes but a dozen or two men arrive in Athlone and the vast majority … are Irish'.[87] To deal with the influx, plans were put in place to create makeshift huts in the grounds of Ranelagh Endowed School for almost 1,000 recruits and by the end of April 1915, it was reported that there were 4,000 troops in the town.[88] Small-scale initiatives such as the local 'Sewing Society', which repaired soldiers' uniforms, were established to help the many army men who were billeted in buildings such as Longworth Hall and the Masonic Lodge on Northgate Street, as well as the former IV drilling venue, Ferrier's Stores at Garden Vale.[89] A review of the effects of the first year of the war on Athlone presented a picture of change:

> Prior to the … war Athlone … was little more than a military town in name, there being only a couple of hundred R.F.A. men stationed there … war brought a drastic change … thousands of recruits … poured in … every available inch of room … was taken … camps sprung up.[90]

The arrival of so many men led to much money being spent in the public houses, though drunkenness was reportedly uncommon, as soldiers' leisure time was curtailed by the demands of training.[91] The local UDC, quite happy with the increased economic activity, congratulated the soldiers on their orderly behaviour and friendly attitude.[92] The memoir of a local man, Vergil Mannion, stated that many enjoyed the presence of the recruits, 'all … gentlemen',[93] while an allegation put by an English gunner[94] that soldiers were subject to hostility was rebutted by councillors. The headlines 'A Libel on Athlone' and 'Lies Spread in London' appeared in the pro-war *Freeman's Journal*,[95] while the *National Volunteer* dealt with the story similarly, describing it as 'unionist blackguardism'.[96]

Trades other than that of publicans also benefited. Large orders were placed with merchants for boots and other provisions,[97] as the 'thousands … attracted to the colours [and accommodated] in miles and miles of tents',[98] brought with them 'a golden stream'.[99] It was reported that many traders 'who formerly found it as much as they could to keep afloat [were] within the space of a few short months … comparatively well off'.[100] The Athlone Woollen Mills rehired men it had let go before the war, boosting its workforce to over 600.[101] A shortage of trained hands and fuel scarcity did cause problems, not only for the mills, it must be said, but all in all, the concern prospered.[102] Less well placed to benefit was the APW, which suffered as a result of paper shortages, and cabinet makers whose businesses failed as discretionary expenditure was cut.[103] Ireland did not benefit greatly from the upsurge in munitions work, seen in Athlone as a possible cure for local unemployment,[104] as the government had valid security and logistical concerns for not establishing many such factories in Ireland.[105] However, it was certain that workers generally had 'brighter job prospects than in peacetime, provided they had the versatility to adapt to the radically changed conditions'.[106]

Some appeared to view the new customers and concomitant increased

demand as ample excuse to engage in avaricious activities. Farmers, as soon
as war was declared, increased prices, precipitating food hoarding. The price
of basic staples such as sugar and flour achieved 'a ridiculous figure'[107] at
the Athlone markets in the first week of the conflict, while the price of hay,
potatoes, oats and milk ballooned during the year as army orders increased
inflation. 'Farmers had a record year', wrote local lady Cecilia H. Daniels in
a letter to a friend in Australia, 'there was [sic] such big prices for all kinds
of stock'.[108] War bonuses awarded by some local businesses to their workers
exacerbated inflation still further, and protests materialised all over Ireland
as the less well-off felt the pinch of rapacious commercial practices.[109] Roy
Foster has noted that the war 'created a spectacular boom in agricultural
prices, and high profits in agriculturally derived industries, though urban
workers were less advantaged'.[110] Because the war facilitated 'destruction on
an industrial scale' to meet demand for goods and services, 'an equivalent
production of the materials of war … not to mention an agricultural effort'
had to be improvised. However, such schemes created their 'own social and
political tensions',[111] as farmers benefited greatly while, at least according to
some observers, having sacrificed very little.[112] Those who relied on their
produce were to encounter increasing hardship as the conflict dragged on.

THE VOLUNTEERS

After the local instalment of the national schism in the volunteers, it was
apparent that of the two groups it was the Athlone IV that was in the greatest
need of organisation. Reportedly co-ordinated by the local SF branch, efforts
to do so in the town encountered difficulties due to what the RIC saw as
'very strong feeling against the party on the part … of the people of Athlone
and neighbourhood'.[113] James Gough and Seán O'Mullany confirmed their
ideological differences with their fellow MVF co-founders by being amongst
the twenty-five men who constituted the nucleus of the new group[114] which,
despite not being formally established, had received fourteen rifles.

The opposition they encountered is unsurprising given the greater number of
Redmondite volunteers, Athlone's relationship with the British Army and the
prevailing political environment. The town had a long tradition of recruitment;
local families with men at the front or those reaping the economic rewards of
the conflict were unlikely to take to the anti-recruitment message, something
noted by Patrick Shea, the son of a RIC officer stationed in the town:

> Athlone had long been a garrison town; the young men ... had gone to
> the war in ... numbers and the big army training camp ... brought new
> business ... and new diversions ... For most ... the appeal to participate
> in a hazardous form of extreme patriotism met with little response.[115]

Politically, as evidenced in local press articles, Home Rule was seen as a
post-war certainty, and enlisting was promoted as evidence of Irish gratitude.
It became more common, if not widespread, for the war to be seen as 'our'
war; Britain and Ireland's together.[116] The ability of anti-war groups to spread
their message in Athlone was additionally hampered by the suppression of
newspapers such as *Sinn Féin* and *Irish Freedom* in late 1914.[117] Such suppressions under the Defence of the Realm Act (DORA),[118] allied with the weight
of pro-war sentiment, meant that the efforts of advanced nationalists did not
have much effect on early recruitment levels, or support for the war. John
Dillon, often presented as an astute interpreter of the political trends, felt
that SF was making no headway, a belief maintained by the IPP during most
of 1915,[119] and while the IG noted that the party had 'greater influence than
is warranted by their numbers and position',[120] Dublin Castle 'felt that the
threat of sedition in the press had all but disappeared'.[121]

   Regardless of impediments and perceived poor success, Athlone's advanced
nationalists forged ahead. The IV corps was formally established in December 1914,
by which time an additional six rifles had been procured and drilling of two dozen
men was undertaken in the confines of the Pipers' Club.[122] The small numbers
involved reflected a similarly small roster in Westmeath generally, where between

Autumn 1914 muster of Athlone Irish Volunteers corp at the Fairgreen. (AHL)

Athlone (Drumraney, the only other Westmeath SF branch)[123] and Tang, the IV numbered just fifty-seven.[124] Optimistically, Liam Mellows, who had assisted in forming the corps, reported 'cheerily on Westmeath as a whole',[125] a rather misleading assessment, given that the three corps were all in south Westmeath. Reports of an inability to establish in other areas in the county were alluded to in the *Irish Volunteer*: 'In a few places they have got cold feet.'[126]

However small the membership of the IV, at least its members were active. Triumphant meetings of the Athlone INV in October were replaced by less impressive affairs in November; the interested parties were so few that they were able to conduct their business in P.V.C. Murtagh's office.[127] Perhaps the events of October were less a statement of intent for the local INV and more, as Michael Farry has said of the organisation in Sligo, 'a cosmetic exercise to show that Redmond had the support of the majority of … Volunteers'.[128] In contrast with the fortunes of the IV, the end of 1914 saw not optimistic predictions, informed though were by propagandist aspirations, for the INV but confirmation of the effect the war had on Redmond's putative Irish army. Between August and December the INV had shed roughly 1,000 members in Westmeath, representing approximately a 25 per cent drop.[129] County Roscommon witnessed a similar fall over the same period, proportionately around 20 per cent.[130] The *Westmeath Independent* reported that the move of INV instructors to war had handicapped the force greatly.[131] Only sixty members of the local pre-war hundreds could be mustered to attend a Redmond speech at Tuam in December.[132]

Despite the rather obvious trend downwards, Athlone's INV did attempt to maintain a façade of organisation and vitality. An impressive 'volunteer inspection' by Colonel Moore in December was followed by a rather more anaemic effort directed by Walter Nugent in January. The *Freeman's Journal* presented a canard about 'a numerous body' of armed men, while the *Westmeath Independent* stated that just forty were in attendance due to low interest and long working days at the local woollen factory.[133] Claims that the INV possessed a supply of 'up to date' Martini-Henri rifles were counterbalanced by reports that of the 106 rifles in their possession, fifty were borrowed, undoubtedly to lend the occasion a positive, albeit misleading, appearance.[134] Even then, the vast majority of the rifles were considered of poor quality, and were probably later recirculated to help another corps elsewhere.

The Athlone INV's slide towards obsolescence was recognised by prominent local nationalists. Dean Kelly, H.J. Walker, Thomas Chapman, O.J. Dolan and M.J. O'Meara (now AOH division president), assessed the local corps upon reaffiliating the UIL branch,[135] but appeared unable to provide invigoration.[136]

In reality both organisations were purposeless; McDermott-Hayes believed INV membership, possibly due to the virtual absence of a UVF threat, to be 'an aimless existence'.[137] The Athlone committee tried to imbue members with purpose through holding small parades for men as they went off to war, but this only strengthened the increasing belief that INV involvement sooner or later led to enlistment.[138] Athlone's INV numbers dwindled and only a small delegation could be mustered to attend the volunteer review in Dublin on Easter Sunday.[139] The event saw John Redmond inspect the largest ever body of volunteers, some 20,000. However, this too was more a theatrical display than an actual show of strength.[140]

The energy of the Athlone IV had not elicited much in the way of gains for that organisation either. Westmeath's IV corps had not added extra recruits by spring 1915 and the CI observed that 'the enthusiasm noticed at [the] commencement of [the] movement appears to be dying out'.[141] Athlone's strategic position ensured that IV and SF organisers, Patrick Erin Maguire being perhaps the most prominent, continued to target the town, but met with little success.[142] Locally, it appeared there was little appetite for nationalist volunteers of either hue.

Attempts to address Athlone's political malaise came in the summer of 1915. The creation of a wartime coalition government, intended to streamline decision making, in May led the IPP to instigate efforts to reorganise. In Ireland the new cabinet was received with uneasiness, as was Redmond's tacit support.[143] Edward Carson was made Attorney General, while Redmond, it was erroneously believed, was not offered a position.[144] IPP policy precluded Redmond from taking any post in government, and while T.P. O'Connor lobbied him to accept a portfolio, it appears that Redmond recognised how such a move would alienate so many of his supporters.[145] However, as noted by Paul Bew: 'Redmond got the worst of both worlds – responsibility for a British war policy that imposed heavy burdens on Ireland without the ability to influence it.'[146] John Dillon saw the coalition as detrimental to the IPP noting, in a letter to O'Connor:

> ... since the formation of the coalition ... we have been ... rapidly losing our hold on the people ... our loyal supporters ... believe our party has acted in a timorous ... manner and that Carson proved himself more than a match for Redmond.[147]

Redmond's recognition of unease and falling support amongst Irish nationalists led him to call for UIL and INV reorganisation in June.[148] Recognition of UIL disorganisation was widespread, with the *Westmeath Independent* stating that it evoked memories of the Parnell split and gave the appearance that nationalists were merely 'puppets' in a game which appeared to doom them to failure.[149] A meeting was held to assess the INV and UIL in Athlone during July and the 500 people in attendance heard speeches from the usual local speakers as well as Nugent and Hayden. Billed as a meeting for 'National Unity', there were discussions on the role of Redmond and the IPP; both had the usual 'unabated confidence' of the crowd. Nugent, one of the party's strongest advocates for the war,[150] was criticised by D.P. Moran for yet another imperialist speech: 'What brand or description of a nominal Nationalist is Sir Walter Nugent?'[151] J. Creed Meredith of the INV National Executive, flanked by local volunteers in military attire, stated that the Executive; 'were all well aware that it was Athlone that took the lead in the Volunteer Movement', and promoted reinvigorating the local corps, as did Dean Kelly, who also wanted the UIL to be reorganised as both were 'two wings of the same army'.[152]

The myriad reorganisation meetings nationally mirrored that of Athlone: no substantive changes were effected.[153] Two additional branches of the UIL (bringing the total to six) were affiliated in Westmeath, but the county was still second worst in Leinster.[154] Better gains were seen elsewhere, and while only Connacht had fewer branches by the end of 1915 than it had in 1912,[155] activity remained low. Athlone's INV branch engaged in some marching, but the regional and national decline continued.[156] J.P. Hayden's November rallying call that 'The duty of those who cannot join our countrymen on the battlefields of the continent is to keep the flag of Irish liberty flying until our comrades return' was widely ignored.[157] The corps became moribund before the turn of the year and never re-emerged. As in other regions, the RIC continued to enumerate INV corps numbers and strength, describing the group's existence as nominal, when the truth was it was entirely defunct. Government authorities believed that by the end of 1915 the 'Redmondite Volunteers had sunk into almost complete stagnation ... the largest actual and drilled force were the Irish Volunteers'.[158] Similarly Athlone's UIL branch exhibited no activity that made it into the local press during autumn; nationally, the organisation saw no progress.[159] The Athlone AOH continued to meet privately, making no public impact, while it took Douglas Hyde's resignation from the position of Gaelic League president to exercise members of the local branch, which maintained moderate levels of activity.[160]

The IPP really only had itself to blame for the poor support in towns like Athlone. The party had concentrated too much time on the war, was complacent about its supporters in the absence of elections and had largely ignored Ireland's younger generation.[161] Many farmers, hitherto the IPP's most active supporters, had gained title to their land and were working hard for the war effort; politics were of little interest to them; the IPP's inactivity had no longer had any material effect on their fortunes.[162] The absence of a truly competitive alternative party meant that resolutions of support continued to be directed towards Redmond, as authorities such as the Athlone PLG kept faith with what appeared to be Ireland's only option.[163] There was a political void in Ireland, a void that during the last months of 1915 advanced nationalists made moves to fill.

In Athlone a quiet summer for the IV, partially inspired by the arrest of some of the more prominent national figures, gave way to a more active autumn.[164] Coosan, on the town's north-eastern fringes, hosted one of three national IV training camps in September, where local volunteers mingled with others from all over Ireland.[165] Terence MacSwiney, who would later become a prominent figure in the movement, wrote of his experiences there in a propagandist two-part submission to the *Irish Volunteer*. The camp was established to ensure that officer-grade volunteers became familiar with 'the normal conditions of active service', so that they could disseminate the knowledge to subordinates in their area of operation. Discipline, fostering an esprit de corps, empowerment, the acquisition of military knowledge and increasing IV numbers were the main objectives of the organisers.[166] Though it had been stated by the RIC that locals were antipathetic to the IV, MacSwiney experienced things differently:

Some of the participants in the Coosan IV training camp. Most relevant are local organiser Peter Malynn (back row, first left) and Terence MacSwiney (back row, second right). (AHL)

... not an unfriendly eye received us, and how could it be otherwise, when our strapping boys in their jackets green came in perfect order ... into Mass ... even our critics get ... satisfaction from seeing the discipline ... and confidence of the Irish Volunteers; for they at least are a sure line of defence.[167]

Richard Mulcahy, another who would later gain prominence,[168] wrote of the freedom with which the uniformed volunteers walked around the district, stating that RIC interest never manifested as interference.[169] A picture of considerable activity is painted by MacSwiney and while it is probable that his report provides an unrealistically sanguine account, it is certain that the presence of the camp, allied with the Lord Lieutenant's recruitment drive and the threat of conscription, led the Athlone IV to rediscover the enthusiasm seen a year earlier.[170]

The local corps began weapon-free drilling in November under IRB man Peter Malynn, whose letters had come under the watch of the postal censor,[171] and while numbers were small – around twenty – their efforts were supplemented by the foundation of a Cumann na mBan branch in Athlone.[172] The female adjunct of the IV had a number of local GL enthusiasts on its roster and quickly set about engaging in 'Drill and Signalling Practice', raising money and learning first aid.[173] All the members, reportedly twenty, wore a Cumann na mBan badge to distinguish them, a practice that would allow the 1,700 members from the five dozen or so other branches to identify comrades more easily.[174] The *Irish Volunteer* stated that the branch quickly gained 'considerable membership'[175] and that the ladies maintained a non-militant approach to assisting the local volunteers.[176] By February 1916, the local IV corps' success was such that it was said to be an example to follow:

The Athlone corps has been growing steadily stronger ... and many new recruits have come ... This corps is becoming ... proficient in both drill and field work, and the progress that has been made within the last few months is satisfactory. Something more, however, might be done towards the surrounding country.[177]

The criticism levelled at neighbouring regions had some basis. Longford had no IV activity to speak of during 1915 and early 1916, and Roscommon had but a small group of men trying to keep the IV afloat there.[178] Ireland's exclusion from the Military Service Act in January 1916 gave the RIC hope that the rise in IV activity would not spread, but moves towards yet another

Military Service Bill in March ensured that the threat of conscription remained, and advanced national sentiment continued to grow.[179] As spring progressed, it was widely recognised in government circles that anti-British feeling was spreading in Ireland.[180]

The activities and growth of SF on the back of IV invigoration were greeted in the *Westmeath Independent* with generally supportive editorials. While this may appear peculiar given the publication's support for recruitment and McDermott-Hayes' ability to take personal umbrage at Ulster Unionist slights on perceived poor nationalist support for the war, it is probably indicative of a more mature view of Irish nationalism. For example, when a policeman was wounded in a confrontation with SF members in Tullamore, the consequent 'attempted murder' charges were heavily criticised in the newspaper. McDermott-Hayes believed that both sides had acted foolishly and tellingly stated that whatever the motivations ascribed to SF activities during the war, it was clear that they were 'the product of patriotic inspiration'.[181]

The more reasoned views of the *Westmeath Independent* editor were in contrast to those of 'extreme newspapers' or 'mosquito press',[182] such as *Irish Volunteer, Hibernian, Spark, Honesty, New Ireland* and *Irishman* which circulated in Athlone more frequently in the early months of 1916, albeit in small numbers.[183] Published to ensure that IV and SF members had the most up-to-date propaganda and could maintain their 'injurious effect on voluntary recruiting',[184] these titles took the topical Anglophobia sometimes seen in mainstream titles to the extreme, describing specific difficulties in the context of the overarching problem of British rule. The influence of such titles had grown since the late nineteenth century as literacy levels increased and the politically uninformed became fewer.[185] However, as of early 1916, the reading of such titles was restricted to a minority, as to be seen consulting one 'set oneself in a class apart, [something few were] prepared to do'.[186]

The impression of IPP inactivity on behalf of Ireland was also promoted in more influential sections of the press, with Laurence Ginnell's parliamentary activities coming in for much praise. *The Leader* referred to the IPP as the 'Flabby Party' and agitated for support for Ginnell from 'even a dozen or so independent men not afraid to ask questions, demand replies and otherwise stand up for the Irish end'.[187] Arthur Griffith's *Nationality* virtually adopted Ginnell as its political mascot, repeatedly contrasting the Westmeath MP's actions with those of the Irish Party.[188] More direct action to refocus the British on the demands of the Irish people was demanded with greater frequency from increasingly numerous quarters. Advanced nationalists were growing ever more convinced that the IPP's concentration on the war had left the door open for them 'to take initiatives, and ... exercise an influence on events'.[189] Direct action was to be their chosen path and its form was to alter the Irish political landscape utterly.

THE EASTER RISING

Since the outbreak of the war, the *Westmeath Independent* had dedicated many editorial column inches to the social, economic and political consequences of the international conflict. The events of Easter 1916 were to shift its focus back to Irish soil as the portents signalling of direct, extra-parliamentary activity recognised by the IG of the RIC in March were confirmed in bloody fashion.[190] Republicans had traditionally painted 'England's difficulty as Ireland's opportunity',[191] and the war provided the opening required. IRB men, partially informed by misleading recruitment propaganda that foretold of the war's imminent end, believed 'it was necessary to strike ... before the Irish heroes returned [from Europe] ... and claimed their justified place in the affection of the people'.[192] Easter 1916 was chosen as the time to do just that.

Though Dublin was the theatre in which most Easter Rising activity took place, the events that transpired there were but part of a wider plan to bring about a nationwide rebellion. A role for Athlone to play had been proposed, and witness statements from the Bureau of Military History, amongst other similarly constituted sources, provide some of the information (albeit at times contradictory) required to attempt a reconstruction of the plan local IV members were intended to enact. Drawn up by Liam Mellows and Pádraig Pearse, the stratagem called for IV from Athlone and surrounding areas such as Ballykeeran, Drumraney, Tyrellspass and Tang to rendezvous with others from King's County and Tipperary at Shannonbridge on the King's County/ Roscommon border on Easter Sunday.[193] These men would then take the military barracks in Athlone and raid surrounding RIC barracks for weaponry. 'A successful uprising in Athlone', stated Cumann na mBan member Nora Connolly O'Brien, 'would have brought out the entire west of Ireland on our side'.[194] Indeed, the capture of the Athlone garrison would have been a coup of tremendous proportions, given that its mid-war complement of soldiers regularly numbered over 1,000. While evidence from British Army officer Capt. Edward Gerrard states that the large stationary guns used by the army to defend the Athlone garrison would have taken two days to be made operational,[195] a surprise attack in the absence of quality assistance would have been foolhardy. Recognising this, the planners proposed to bolster the local IV with German prisoners emancipated from the British military camp at Oldcastle, County Meath, who would use their experience to operate artillery captured in Athlone, create a safe zone for IV who retreated from Dublin and, when ready, march on Mullingar.[196] Sensibly this plan was revised due to the small number of local volunteers willing to engage in military action; action many had joined the IV specifically to avoid.

What came of the efforts of this minority is very hard to discover.[197] The most comprehensive account of local efforts for the Rising was written by IRB man Michael McCormack, a member of the Drumraney Volunteers. He stated that the district's IRB men, including Cork man Seán O'Hurley and Peter Malynn, were informed of the intention to implement Mellows' plan by dispatch delivered by Cumann na mBan member Eileen Walsh.[198] The unspecified number of men spent Easter Saturday preparing for a march to Shannonbridge which was never undertaken, as a communiqué delivered by another Cumann na mBan member made it clear that no offensive actions were permitted. The men were instead ordered to return home and await further instructions.[199] Anthony McCormack of the Tang IV stated that 'The whole affair seemed to be a mass of confusion',[200] as members tried to come to terms with the conflicting orders and the surprise of having been asked to mobilise in the first instance. Many were probably relieved that they did not have to act. Richard Mulcahy has noted that many IV men were unnerved by the call to fight, for in the Athlone camp during the previous September, most approached the training as if they were 'learning Irish … [there was no] … gossip or … expectation that a rising was in the air'.[201] Indeed, it took many Volunteers by surprise, and similarly confused scenes were witnessed all over provincial Ireland.[202]

Reasons for the confusion are generally cited as being the promulgation of the 'Castle Document',[203] the general, if not total, failure of Roger Casement's weapon-sourcing expedition[204] and the countermand of Eoin MacNeill,[205] which saw the original date of Easter Sunday changed to Easter Monday as staunch nationalists forced their agenda past MacNeill. Indeed, it appears that a very small IV turnout in Tyrellspass, east of Athlone, was the only evidence of offensive Volunteer activity between Dublin and Galway.[206] Westmeath, 'the hinge of Pearse's grand strategy', was an empty theatre.[207]

Athlone's contribution to the Rising had more to do with suppressing than complementing the rebellion.[208] The soldiers in the barracks' artillery were called upon to supplement the armoury of the British forces in Dublin and Galway,[209] forces that gained the surrender of the rebel leaders in less than a week.[210] During the fighting, the disruption to rail services and the publication of daily newspapers meant that information related in the provincial press was often incomplete and presented against a backdrop of 'profound shock and confusion'.[211] In Athlone, much of what the townspeople learned during the week of hostilities was augmented by government propaganda. One poster, printed on the Wednesday, noted that 10,000 English troops had entered Dublin and were rapidly suppressing the insurgency. The poster's designers intended it to 'rally loyalist sentiment, reassure the quiescent and discourage would-be rebels from belatedly joining the ranks of their brothers at war'.[212]

In Athlone, opinions on the Rising in the immediate aftermath were entirely negative. The *Westmeath Independent* took serious issue with the 'Dublin riots', targeting Roger Casement and his 'irreconcilable associates', James Larkin, who was not even in Ireland, and James Connolly, for most of the blame.[213] McDermott-Hayes reinvigorated his polemics against the latter two, whom he had previously censured two-and-a-half years earlier, for putting 'an indelible mark of disgrace on our people', as their strike action forced many Dublin families to endure severe privations during August 1913.[214] Describing the Easter actions of the IV quite moderately as 'misplaced patriotism', the local paper pilloried the Irish Citizen Army (ICA) for its acts of 'scoundrelism', namely shop looting and vandalism.[215] McDermott-Hayes stated that the 'ridiculously designated "Irish Rebellion"' made the Irish look ungrateful for the Home Rule Act, and compromised its implementation: 'It is maddening to think the action of a handful of irreconcilables has jeopardised the work of so many years.'[216] His assessment followed that of John Redmond, who saw the event as a German-aided attack on Home Rule and the Irish Party.[217] Local opinion reflected the dominant feeling across Ireland, with authorities such as Westmeath County Council making a commitment to assist the government in bringing those responsible to book.[218]

A virtually united front of condemnation appeared as unionists registered their disgust,[219] and the *Irish Independent* recommended Irish enlistment in the army as expiation for the violence.[220] Recruitment efforts, so often hampered by the efforts of the IV, received a short-lived boost.[221] Poor government intelligence led to responsibility for the Rising being laid at the feet of SF instead of the IRB, but, as noted in *The Leader*: 'It is one of the ironies of history that the rebellion is known by the name Sinn Féin … the name has got its new significance.'[222] The speed with which people associated the rebellion with SF had much to do with Griffith's seemingly unending production of advanced nationalist journalism, which had, by 1916, created 'an almost exclusive association' between his party and the actions of those involved in the Rising.[223] As noted by Joseph Lee, the misapplication of blame by the British 'succeeded in investing … Sinn Féin with a degree of authority it never managed to achieve on its own'.[224]

With the surrender of the rebel leaders, the British Government set about making an example of them. It became quickly apparent, however, that a gross miscalculation on the part of the military authorities was to squander the support they gained from the Irish with their rapid suppression of the insurrection. Execution of the ringleaders, heavily publicised by Laurence Ginnell, who 'played the man's part' in the Commons,[225] began on 3 May and over a ten-day period, during which Irish people became increasingly horrified, fourteen men were shot by firing squad. The way in which they were tried was seen as extremely harsh (secret courts-martial with virtually no notice given to relatives of their executions), and fed a growing distaste for the methods of the government. Cabinet members themselves found the rapidity of the executions shocking and impressed on General Sir John Maxwell, Commander in Chief of British forces in Ireland, the need for a less draconian approach.[226] The imposition of martial law on 26 April,[227] despite the fact that most of the country had shown no signs of rebellion, affected so much of Irish life that resentment at the military was additionally bolstered. At the front, initial condemnation of the events in Dublin battled with a mounting sense of anger amongst the Irish troops at the 'punitive executions in their homeland'.[228]

By the time the *Westmeath Independent* had released its 6 May edition, eight of the leaders of the Rising had already been shot. The editor noted:

> [The] crime against the Government – against Ireland – has been a terrible one … the poor dreamers who, deluded by German intrigue, have been guilty of the maddest attempt at Revolution ever essayed in any country in the world.

However, he continued: 'It is the duty of Ireland to plead for mercy for the misguided young fellows dragged into this movement.' He still decried their acts but, maintaining his established ability to distinguish between arguments, he could not condemn the men themselves; their motivations were unselfish, redolent of other Irishmen who took up arms to fight for their beliefs:

> They are the class from whom has been drawn the Irish soldier who has made the world ring with his valour … Mercy for the men; punishment if it must be for the leaders – but not the punishment of death.[229]

The softening of his views on the leaders of the Rising grew, along with those
of many others around Ireland, as government policies became more oppressive. Athlone, along with Longford, Kilkenny and Castlebar, hosted a British
Army mobile column which scoured the region for dissidents.[230] The deployment of the Sherwood Foresters in the town was simply a 'show of force
designed to encourage loyal subjects and overawe disaffected nationalists'.[231]
Athlone was grouped with areas such as Limerick, Cork and Kilkenny for
rebel 'pacification', due to its inhabitants showing much discontent during
the week of the Rising.[232] The vast majority of searches were carried out in
the town itself, which was thought to harbour most of the district's activists.[233]
The CI noted that there had been a change in the local sympathies between
his report from April and that of May:

> There has ... undoubtedly been ... sympathy with the rebels ... chiefly
> confined to ... shop assistants, clerks and the labouring class. Among
> these ... there was noticeable unrest ... while the rebellion lasted ...
> principally in Athlone.[234]

The RIC believed that fifteen members of the SF branch had met before the
Rising in the Pipers' Club and that five or six were not at home on Easter
Monday. They believed that four had travelled to Galway for the rebellion there,
while the other member(s) may have travelled to Dublin.[235] Prime amongst
the suspects were Seán O'Mullany, who had led a small number of men out
prior to the countermand,[236] and Peter Malynn, whose houses were searched
on Wednesday 3 May, along with that of Seán O'Hurley, but no arrests were
made.[237] By 6 May arrests were seen: twenty-four in total locally, and between
3,200 and 3,400 nationally.[238] The three whose houses had been raided were
joined by members of Athlone's original SF branch, Owen Sweeney, Peter
Murray and Seamus O'Brien, as well as a number of other 'upright young
men', all of whom were removed to Athlone Castle.[239] Fifteen were soon
released after a military tribunal established their innocence, while those who
remained were sent to Richmond Barracks in Dublin.[240] The Athlone RIC
made it known that they were pursuing four other 'reputed Sinn Féin men' and
raids continued.[241] Upon the intervention of a local Franciscan friar, Fr Fidelius,
the four presented themselves and they too were sent to Dublin.[242]

Local anger quickly manifested. The *Westmeath Independent*, along with
dozens of other titles, printed excerpts from John Dillon's celebrated parliamentary speech, which told of the 'river of blood that was being made to flow
between the two races',[243] supplementing them with a detailed 'Toll of Blood'

list outlining the names of men executed, along with the sentences passed on those still in custody.[244] 'An image of bloody militarism was widely projected in Ireland', writes Charles Townshend, which drew much of its colour 'from the ill-judged military policy of wholesale arrests'.[245] McDermott-Hayes, in common with other pressmen,[246] shifted the blame for the Rising from nationalists to Ulster Unionists, stating that it had been 'born in Belfast'.[247] Members of the PLG sent a strongly-worded letter to Nugent, Hayden, and General Joseph Byrne in Richmond Barracks, outlining their opposition to the imprisonments:

> We ... strongly protest against the imprisonment ... without trial of thousands of young Irish men ... arrested on the grounds of mere suspicion. We believe it is useless to discuss a settlement to the Irish question so long as the bitter feeling of resentment against these arrests remains unappeased.[248]

The board called on both MPs to secure the release of the Athlone men who 'surrendered and delivered up their rifles when called to do so', and visit Wakefield prison to investigate both the conditions there and rumours that some men were held in solitary confinement.[249] Neither representative acted on the request. Their support for the war effort was strong and they may have been aware that the 'few Irish Party MPs [that] expressed fellow feeling with the rebels ... received little thanks'.[250]

Indeed, it was starting to become readily apparent that the IPP's actions in the aftermath of the Rising were leading to a serious increase in disaffection with the party, whose grass-roots support, it must be remembered, was anything but vibrant. While post-Rising annoyance certainly fuelled much of the invective that was directed at the IPP, Michael Wheatley contends that the change in opinion seen in the *Westmeath Independent* in the 6 May edition 'reflected pre-Rising sentiments as much as post-Rising repression'.[251] Paul Bew believes similarly, citing the results of pre-Rising by-elections which saw unconvincing IPP victories.[252] Tom Garvin states that the Rising provided a 'push to an edifice that was already on the verge of collapse',[253] while David Fitzpatrick believes that: 'In the months before the Rising provincial Nationalists did not dramatically repudiate party or cause ... [but] they did begin to examine their leaders critically ... their minds filled with dangerous notions.'[254] It is apparent that in Athlone such dangerous notions began to become more widespread as 1916 wore on.

Government policies continued to stoke anti-British sentiment, with efforts by the authorities to dehumanise those who fought on Easter

Monday doing little to turn the tide of opinion back in their favour. One of
the reasons behind this failure was the extensively published testimony of
an Athlone army colonel who was stationed in Dublin during the hostilities. R.K. Brereton lauded the civility of the rebels for the treatment they
afforded both him and those under his command who were captured during
the fighting. He described how the IV, 'alas, misguided and fed up with
lies and false expectations', fought honourably, and were sober, educated
men; 'incapable of acts of brutality'.[255] Such evidence may have influenced
Westmeath County Council in their resolution condemning the government, whose brutal executions were, they believed, beyond anything seen in
the Boer War.[256] Those arrested, imprisoned and executed, 'poets, dreamers,
Irishmen all', had been treated abominably.[257] Local feeling became stridently
anti-government, with the continuance of military raids doing nothing to
decrease such sentiment.[258] The CI in County Roscommon recognised, with
some bitterness, the posthumous growth in stature of men such as Pearse,
whose final letter to his mother was published in the *Westmeath Independent*,[259]
and Connolly: 'There is a sentimental sympathy for the rebels who were
executed … but none for the RIC or military who were killed.'[260]

Annoyance at the arrest of the local men was soon channelled into efforts
to gain their release. Fr Fidelius again stepped forward and was instrumental
in co-ordinating efforts to liberate them, as were Thomas Chapman and other
'prominent nationalists'.[261] The friar interviewed officials in both Athlone and
Dublin and compiled a petition protesting against their unlawful treatment.
His efforts saw seven released during the last week in May and a fund established to support those still interned.[262] The sale of SF badges, now frequently
worn by Athlone people, added to the takings.[263]

The UDC and PLG passed resolutions, not without controversy,[264]
complaining about the continued imprisonments and the scapegoating of GL
and GAA members, as well as the victimisation of certain Roman Catholic
priests.[265] Attempts by the British authorities to implicate the clergy incensed
the church hierarchy, many of whom communicated in no uncertain terms
their distaste for the actions of the government. Dermot Keogh writes that
by June: 'Episcopal opinion had been very significantly radicalised', and the
already low levels of support for the IPP amongst the most powerful
clergymen in Ireland dropped even further.[266]

Unsurprisingly, the Irish nationalist press did little to slow the growth in
anti-government sentiment, despite threats of DORA measures being
enacted.[267] In Athlone, the *Westmeath Independent*'s coverage of the local arrests
was so damning of the military authorities that both McDermott-Hayes and

THE OPPORTUNITIES OF WAR 135

Chapman were called to account for the editorial line. Eventually both men met with the head of the British forces in Ireland, General Maxwell, in Dublin and conducted a short meeting in which they put forth the case for the release of the Athlone detainees. They assured the general that freeing the men would have been of great assistance in normalising relationships in the town:

> [if we] … were in the position to carry back to Athlone the encouraging message of the prisoner's release it would do more to allay the … nervous excitement … prevailing about the midlands than any [other] action.[268]

Maxwell was quite aware of the anger generated by the arrests and the imposition of draconian laws and, as stated by David Fitzpatrick, after the 'initial frenzy of executions, raids, arrests and internments … [he] proved sparing in his use of coercion'.[269] McDermott-Hayes wrote that, 'while withholding an immediate compliance' in regard to the release of Edward Martin, Seán O'Hurley, Peter Malynn, Seamus O' Brien, Michael McCormack and George Amos, Maxwell's response 'raised cheery and confident hope'.[270]

It soon became clear that the confidence was somewhat misplaced. All six men were moved to Wakefield, and while the latter three were soon released, they had to endure quite uncomfortable conditions.[271] Malynn (whose brother Joseph had been arrested in Tralee) remained there while O'Hurley and Martin[272] were transferred from the harsh conditions in Wakefield to ones even more distasteful in Frongoch,[273] a specially emptied military camp in Wales.[274] Counterproductively, from the British point of view, Frongoch internees got to know each other quite well, with the camp developing into something of a republican think tank. Ideologies became hardened as the poor conditions did little to ingratiate the British to the prisoners, or indeed their supporters.[275] Information on the state of the penitentiaries was smuggled out by, amongst others, Laurence Ginnell, whose visiting privileges were eventually rescinded. True to form he ignored the proscription, using his Irish name to gain admission on one occasion.[276] Ironically, Ginnell's efforts for the prisoners while a free man made him 'the most disruptive influence in the prisons', but his actions eventually saw him join those he wished to assist.[277]

The plight of the three remaining prisoners never left the columns of the *Westmeath Independent*, which continued to draw parallels between those who died on Easter Monday and those dying on the battlefields of Europe. A picture of an Athlone native, Sean Costello, who died near Boland's Mill while fighting with the IV in Dublin, was prominently displayed in the publication,

Sean Costello memorial
montage showing his
funeral, Costello in IV
uniform and his birthplace.
(AHL)

as were others of local men who fell at the front.[278] The 'keenly felt' absence
of the prisoners was heightened at a requiem mass held for Costello, a former
employee of Malynn's.[279] The local RIC saw the mass as a good event at which
to assess local support for the IV and SF, and they monitored the interaction
of the congregation. Many were greatly annoyed by the suspicious inspections
as they attended to their religious obligations, something recognised by the
celebrant, who counselled that people take no action against the police upon
leaving the church. The *Westmeath Independent* reported:

> The feelings of the congregation were not at all soothed by the
> attention … received from the police. In addition to some men in
> uniform, there were a number … in plain clothes … it was … regarded
> as indicative of an atmosphere of suspicion in official circles … not
> calculated to create or foster good feeling.[280]

The political tension that was developing had soon reached levels last seen two
years previously. McDermott-Hayes' anger at the continued detention of the
prisoners and the government response to the Rising reinvigorated his polemics

on the unequal treatment meted out to nationalists and unionists. He decried the evolution of the partition-based 'bastard Home Rule' scheme, questioning how the treasonable efforts of 'high-placed lawyers' such as Edward Carson and James Campbell had gained them elevated government positions and allowed them to set the agenda on Irish administration; '... Mr. Lloyd George's scheme for the dismemberment of the nation'.[281] The editor was reflecting a growing belief that the government's recourse to brute force after the Rising, allied with its abortive attempts to find a political solution for the Irish problem, was weakening the desire for reconciliation on the island.[282] Local representative J.P. Hayden, in contrast, promoted the pursuit by the IPP of the agreement during the summer, providing unrealistic assessments of Redmond's efforts, not only in that pursuit but many others, such as securing the release of the internees and maintaining the vitality of the constitutional movement. As Michael Wheatley has written, Hayden's approach 'looked more ... barren and ineffective as the year progressed'.[283] Demonstrably, the IPP was not achieving redress for the Irish people, or even providing hope that it was on the horizon.

The Athlone UDC was perhaps the first local authority body in the region to show definite signs of disaffection with Redmond's party. Understandably anxious to have the Athlone internees return home, one member, Michael Burke, recommended that Laurence Ginnell, whose activities in Parliament were related more frequently in the local press,[284] be petitioned on the men's behalf. The request caused quite a bit of discussion amongst members, for going to Ginnell would have signalled that the council was repudiating the IPP; 'it would be a slap in the face', stated one member. Eventually it was to the Irish Party that approaches were made, but the debate was certainly indicative of a changing mood. Just one week later, notice was served in the council room that a vote was to be held on rescinding an earlier vote of confidence in the IPP;[285] a similar move was made by the PLG board.[286] No counter resolutions came from the local UIL, for though moribund before the Rising, like many other branches of the organisation, the events of Easter Monday killed it off completely.[287]

As anger with the IPP grew, so too did the stature of SF, a party that for the first time in over three decades was gaining enough support to perhaps challenge the constitutionalists' hold on the Irish electorate. By July the Westmeath CI described SF support in Athlone as 'undoubtedly strong',[288] and local shops did their bit to promote the 'rapidly developing cult of the dead leaders'[289] by displaying pictures of the executed men beside the lyrics of rebel songs.[290] The release of Peter Malynn in the first week of the month and Edward Martin two weeks later provided relief, while the continued detention of Seán O'Hurley and the impending execution of Roger Casement tempered celebrations.[291] Calls were made for a reprieve for Casement by virtually all local authorities, and the local press again outlined the honour of the man's motivations: 'His conduct, whatever may be thought of it, was political and inspired by the purpose of serving Ireland.' The *Westmeath Independent* dwelt on the rather obvious foolhardiness of creating yet another martyr: 'Casement dead at the hands of an English hangman is a greater living force for dissension between England and Ireland than a thousand Casements reprieved and alive.'[292] The generality of Athlone people were set against the execution, believing it to be a vengeful indulgence. A well-supported petition was circulated:

> … whilst we are in no way associated with the actions of Roger Casement, as Irishmen and his compatriots we hereby petition you on his behalf to stay the sentence of death … passed upon him. We feel the death penalty has already been enacted upon too many of our countrymen, and if carried out in his case, will create a very deep feeling of distrust and unrest, not only in Ireland, but amongst Irishmen all over the world.[293]

However, their efforts, those of the Roman Catholic hierarchy and people all over Ireland were to be in vain.[294] On 3 August, Casement was hanged in Pentonville Prison. 'Every consideration for Irish opinion was trampled on', ran an editorial in the *Westmeath Independent*.[295] His death led to 'rebel airs and seditious songs' being more frequently heard in Athlone, especially in connection with GAA matches, occasions which saw the display of many more SF badges.[296]

The release of Athlone's last internee, Seán O'Hurley,[297] counterbalanced the sadness felt at Casement's death and meant that all of those who were arrested in the town were now free to pursue their interests which, according to the RIC, consisted of them returning to active SF duty: 'Athlone continues to be the danger zone for Sinn Féin … The prominent Sinn Féiners who were arrested … and afterwards released, appear to be as active as ever.'[298] Most of the men, like many political prisoners, probably came out more committed to the cause;[299] injustice had radicalised them, 'made soldiers of nationalists [formerly] armed solely with enthusiasm'.[300] There was almost constant surveillance on the men who were seen, often in each others' company, at the train stations in the town. Tickets were purchased and embarkations for destinations such as Moate by figures such as Seán O'Mullany were made, though often without the expected disembarkation. It was inferred that the men were jumping off between stops to avoid detection.[301] The ability of the men to dodge the police was helped by the change in attitude of many people, especially in rural areas, who formerly might not have assisted them. The armed actions of a few during a week in April had perhaps achieved more for the Irish cause than three decades of parliamentary activity. Any move that the government may have seen as a concession, such as the release of prisoners, appeared to 'stimulate resentment', and move people more towards the SF way of thinking.[302] In Athlone, there was a definite shift occurring. Local lady, Cecilia H. Daniels, recognised this and outlined how the support of the Catholic clergy was strengthening the movement, predicting that: 'The Sin [sic] Fin [sic] rising will I fear have long consequences … the country [has] years of discomfort before it'.[303]

It cannot be gainsaid that there was a growing belief in the political ossification of the IPP in Athlone during the summer, autumn and winter of 1916. Throughout its time critiquing the policies and actions of SF, it is quite certain that the local press had never seen the party as a real alternative to Redmond's. Even with the death of Roger Casement, acknowledgement of the efforts of SF was couched in the context of what effect they would have on the Irish representatives at Westminster:

> No matter what else we owe Sinn Féin – we owe to it the awakening of the country and of the Irish Party to the … danger we exposed ourselves when we surrendered the … weapon of independent opposition to all British Parties.[304]

However, as the year moved towards closure, belief in the viability of SF as an alternative to the IPP grew. The June 1916 description of 'bastard Home Rule', something that needed to be addressed,[305] was repeated in September, but augmented by a demand that the Act 'be given to the flames'.[306] The financial aspects were forcefully repudiated, while the IPP's invertebrate stance on partition raised the hackles further. Redmond and his party felt 'tricked and betrayed'[307] by the British Government, with Lloyd George's failure to enact Home Rule leading Redmond to shun the Welshman, whom he held personally responsible.[308] Regardless, some IPP stalwarts (at least hitherto) like the *Westmeath Independent* editor saw little merit in Redmond's blaming the government; it was up to them to force the Irish agenda; the 'reverent and loyal rather than critical' tone of the pre-war provincial press was being displaced.[309] McDermott-Hayes' conversion appeared to have reached a critical juncture by September, when he backed the sentiment of a speech from the Bishop of Limerick that 'the true spirit of the country, and the complement of our demand based on it, [can be found] in the principle of Sinn Féin'.[310] McDermott-Hayes believed that SF had 'called back to the people the old National spirit of Ireland', and that IPP calls on internment, conscription and the dismissal of General Maxwell were all carbon copies of pre-existing

SF policies.[311] The position of Redmond's party 'at the end of the summer was … dire … its declared constitutional, parliamentary role was discredited'.[312] While articles in the *Westmeath Independent* highlighted the editor's and contributors' ignorance of the disarray in which SF found itself after the Rising, the 'label' became descriptive of more than the organisation itself, taking on a life independent of events orchestrated by the party.[313] McDermott-Hayes articles influenced increasingly fractious meetings of the PLG, where the topic of whether or not to support Redmond was discussed in unusually animated sessions.[314]

The continuance of oppressive government measures ensured that towards the end of 1916, the political unrest in Ireland was considered by Dublin Castle to be 'more extensive … than at the time of the rebellion'.[315] The anger gifted SF 'a rhetorical power … to organise a new political machine to coordinate action',[316] with the most simple and apparently unimportant events highlighting growing local animosity towards politicians at Westminster. The inability of Athlone's local MPs to ensure a relatively unhindered All-Ireland football semi-final in the town annoyed locals greatly; it was not only in more tradi-tional political issues that the IPP was seen as impotent. The game's protagonists, Cork and Mayo, along with enthusiastic locals, shouted 'up the Sinn Féiners' and 'Up the Rebels' after the game had ended.[317] The forced cancellation of special trains had ensured a serious loss to the local economy; the 15,000 spectators predicted to attend ended up being just 1,000. One councillor stated that such 'inconsiderate, unnecessary and provocative actions … can have but one effect – a feeling of bitterness towards English administration in this country.'[318] The local press termed the action provocative and counter-productive coming from a government which needed more troops to fight the war against Germany, especially given the prevalence of 'English slackers', 3.5 million in the editor's estimation.[319] Maintaining his support for the Entente, McDermott-Hayes reminded readers that the 'Hun Master' was dangerous and that while Easter 1916 would live on in the memory for decades, the threat from the continent could not be ignored.[320]

The Easter Rising and the consequent 'existence, or rather illusion, of martial law'[321] had, however, irreversibly exacerbated the decline in Irish recruitment. The *Westmeath Independent* stated that England's continuing 'colossal' stupidity when it came to dealing with Ireland stemmed from its people's inability to understand the feelings of Irish nationalists:

> If they [the English] want to learn the real feeling of the country let them stand outside an Irish convict prison when an English-made Irish convict is released. Let them attend a Franciscan Requiem Mass for

the Patriot Dead of Dublin. Let them look at the kneeling thousands outside Kilmainham Shambles.[322]

Indeed, the fall off in troop numbers and exceptionally poor levels of Irish volunteering during the summer months of 1916 had ensured the threat of conscription again became prominent, especially from September.[323] It may have mattered little in the region if Cecilia H. Daniels' statement that farm labourers were virtually non-existent were true. Most, she believed, were working in war-related employment, at the front, or had emigrated.[324] Eager to show its opposition whatever the labour situation, Athlone UDC adopted a Kerry County Council resolution to the effect that there would be 'grave consequences' if the government were to attempt to impose the measure; 'to demand equality of sacrifice when there is not, and cannot be, equality of benefit'.[325] Despite the high level of support for SF, a midlands-based intelligence officer noted that threats, such as that of grave consequences, were unlikely to be acted upon. The 'extremists' knew that the military presence, allied with the 'dispersal of all armed bodies in the past rebellion', ensured, he believed, that an armed approach would not work.[326]

The winter months saw much change in the administration of Ireland. A new Chief Secretary, H.E. Duke,[327] was installed, General Maxwell was recalled to Britain and a new government under David Lloyd George was instated.[328] The prime minister's speech to the Commons on December 19 placed the 'removal of the misunderstanding between Great Britain and Ireland' high on his agenda, and blamed the 'quagmire of distrust' that surrounded Irish politics for the lack of progress. A call to release the prisoners shouted out during the speech elicited a rather neutral response, but may have assisted Lloyd George in signing off on their liberation soon after.[329] The 569 remaining Irish internees were allowed out before Christmas and received a rapturous welcome all over Ireland, their political capital and radicalisation having reached new heights.[330] Their reintroduction to Irish society 'began a hesitant revival of separatist activity and a historic reorientation of Sinn Féin',[331] a reorientation in which Athlone was to play its part.

5

Confirmation of Change: The Move to Sinn Féin

The course charted by nationalist politics in Athlone after the Easter Rising can lead historical observers to few conclusions other than that there was a political sea-change in the offing. SF sentiment was growing at an exponential rate while, conversely, support for the IPP was in freefall. However, by 1917 the move away from the established political party was still evidenced mainly in anecdotal terms in Athlone, be it through reports of rhetoric at meetings, local authority debates or editorial commentary in the local press. More certain evidence of change and realignment came as SF contested by-elections, reorganised and consolidated its support base, while the IV too looked towards strengthening their organisation. The efforts of Athlone's nationalists on behalf of both groups were conducted against the backdrop of continued government labours to limit the spread of the new political movement, labours that would ultimately prove counterproductive. With the passage of time, the claim of the local Irish Parliamentary Party MPs that they continued to best represent their constituents' views became less and less credible as their influence waned and the policies and activities of SF began to win over the electorate. The ultimate confirmation of this trend was provided by the 1918 general election.

While it appears that SF was accruing much of the support needed to eventually replace the IPP as the dominant party in Athlone, the party's ability to defeat the IPP in an electoral contest so early in its development was far from certain. The death of J.J. O'Kelly, MP for the constituency of North Roscommon in January 1917, was to ensure that the electoral value of the currency of SF policy was to be tested sooner rather than later. The by-election that was called to fill the vacancy saw concerted efforts made to bolster SF support in Roscommon, efforts supplemented by an influx of activists from Athlone, where the party's popularity was more pronounced.[1] Using methods similar to those previously employed by the UIL, SF canvassers instituted a comprehensive and energetic campaign on behalf of George Noble Count Plunkett, father of the executed Easter Rising leader and signatory of the Proclamation, Joseph Plunkett.[2] Strictly speaking the Count was not a SF candidate (he ran as an independent), but his adherence to party policies was to develop with individual flair after the election.[3] *The Leader* looked forward to the contest, expecting that it would 'throw some interesting light on present day political Ireland'.[4]

Clerical support for a candidate, always of great importance, came most prominently for Plunkett in the person of Fr Michael O'Flanagan, a Roscommon-based curate with links to SF's most senior figures. At a meeting in Boyle chaired by J.P. Hayden, O'Flanagan had asked members of the UIL and AOH to permit Plunkett to run unopposed, thus, at least in his somewhat naive opinion, ensuring a united nationalist base in the county.[5] Unsurprisingly Hayden ruled the request out of order and O'Flanagan instead had to look to Hayden's nemesis Laurence Ginnell, amongst others, for political support.[6] The efforts of O'Flanagan, Ginnell and local SF activists, including a number of priests, ensured Plunkett's victory with an almost two-to-one margin, a result which shocked many observers.[7] The Count, who arrived in Roscommon just two days before the polls opened,[8] defeated Redmondite Hibernian, Thomas J. Devine, referred to in *The Leader* as an: '"I say ditto" automaton' and a 'cypher',[9] and Independent Nationalist, Jasper Tully, a former IPP member and erstwhile ally of Ginnell's.[10] Fr O'Flanagan believed that non-voters, women and older children, were instrumental in ensuring the victory. They exerted a special influence on their voting relatives, with the younger men both literally and figuratively carrying the older men upon their backs on a polling day that saw exceptionally heavy snow.[11] After the election Plunkett agreed to SF demands that he not take his seat at Westminster. The result led the Roscommon CI to observe that many AOH branches, especially in north Roscommon, had 'now … become Sinn Féin'.[12]

Athlone's growing SF support network celebrated their own efforts and Plunkett's victory with a procession through the town.[13] The movement of younger voters to SF was a massive factor in securing the post for Plunkett, even though the 3½-year-old electoral register meant that many who could have voted, having reached the requisite age, were unable to so do.[14] Many such men seem instead to have used their influence over those with voting rights.[15] Plunkett's election gave an important boost to the efforts of SF to establish itself as a viable alternative to the IPP, and allowed the party to attract 'several elements hitherto unsympathetic'.[16] Jasper Tully quickly recognised the strength of the movement and magnanimously stated that the few votes he secured 'should be added to Plunkett's'.[17] His newspaper, the *Roscommon Herald*,[18] began to promote SF,[18] aiding it in later successful electoral contests, for which the result in North Roscommon laid the groundwork.

Reaction in south Westmeath to Plunkett's election, apart from that of Athlone's SF members, was registered most prominently by the region's UIL executive, by this point a virtually redundant body. The chairman Eugene J. Robbins backed a resolution that congratulated the Roscommon voters on their 'patriotic action' and the Count on his victory, but did not support his parliamentary abstention, which most believed temporary. Robbins believed 'there were no … longer Irish representatives', and that Plunkett should go to Parliament if only 'to keep others in their place'.[19] The *Westmeath Independent* made the obvious observation that the resolution was 'an indication of the change of political opinion in South Westmeath, which has been so long a stronghold of the National Party'.[20]

The defeat of the IPP in the by-election (they had not taken Plunkett's candidacy seriously[21]) caused John Redmond much anxiety and he had to be restrained by party colleagues from issuing a memorandum evincing his own 'fatalistic despair'.[22] *The Leader* noted that the election was a 'rap on the knuckles' for the IPP, making it clear that the fact the party 'got one in the eye' should have been used by them as motivation to reinvigorate.[23] However, the *Westmeath Independent* appears to have discounted the IPP as an effective political force for Ireland: 'We do not suppose a party who could not win Home Rule when the road was clear will do better when it is bestrewn with difficulties.'[24] An editorial in the newspaper stated that the move to SF was on such a scale that the IPP was fighting a losing battle, though McDermott-Hayes was still not championing parliamentary abstentionism; the policy was 'foolish'.[25]

In the aftermath of the Roscommon victory, punitive government actions both locally and nationally continued to stoke the SF fire, providing party officials with specific targets, which were used to generate support.[26] The next focal point with national repercussions that prompted a concentration of SF minds in Athlone was the South Longford by-election in May. British policy ensured that the party's reluctant candidate, Roscommon man Joe McGuinness, was unable to canvass since he was in prison.[27] In his absence, it was up to supporters to promote his case and take advantage of the increasingly positive attitude to SF identified by the IG:

> Many circumstances … promote sympathy with the movement … the Sinn
> Féin rebellion forced … Home Rule … to the front; resentment at the
> failure of settlement proposals; dread of conscription, and … [the feeling]

that Ireland has not been equitably dealt with [in] the establishment of War Industries, and that ... people are at a disadvantage compared with the people of Great Britain in meeting the ... cost of living.[28]

The canvassing carried out by SF was comprehensive; it had to be, as in Longford the party was considered weak. Many of those involved in North Roscommon assisted, along with Laurence Ginnell and Arthur Griffith.[29] Athlone's SF and IV concentrated their efforts in Ballymahon,[30] helping to distribute a large amount of literature with the catchy slogan 'Put him in to get him out'.[31] Also circulated was a copy of an *Evening Herald* article by the Archbishop of Dublin, Dr Walsh, which outlined how IPP policies were ruining the country.[32] The printing of the excerpted article took place in the APW, where Thomas Chapman produced 6,000 copies free of charge.[33] This type of support, allied with positive coverage in the *Westmeath Independent*, which made its support of McGuinness quite clear,[34] greatly assisted SF.

The ability of SF to win the votes of the young men of the county, which led to familial disputes over voting allegiances,[35] the support of younger Roman Catholic clergymen and members of the AOH[36] ensured that McGuinness emerged victorious.[37] The influence of the archbishop's letter was such that *The Leader* claimed that 'to a certain extent, [it may] be put down as the Archbishop of Dublin's election'.[38] The win over the IPP man, and 'very strong candidate'[39] Patrick McKenna, who was chosen by Redmond after another instalment of IPP infighting,[40] was even more surprising given that most contemporary observers believed South Longford to be a strong IPP area, with twenty-five years of uncontested elections to prove the claim. North Roscommon had a history of agrarian unrest in the first decade of the twentieth century and always provided the sense of a more volatile electorate; loss of a 'sure' seat such as South Longford was more of a body blow to the Irish Party. The win for McGuinness, by just thirty-seven votes after three counts and accusations of intimidation and personation, showed that Plunkett's victory was not an aberration and appeared to pave the way for additional SF gains all over Ireland.[41]

The election result also highlighted how out of touch the IPP had become with its grass-roots organisation in Athlone. John Dillon believed that Longford's proximity to the town would ensure an IPP win: 'Irish Party support centred on Athlone ... a garrison town with a long recruiting tradition.'[42] Greater familiarity with the vitality of constitutional nationalism in Athlone would have led him to reassess his opinion. Dean Kelly, the IPP's strongest supporter and Dillon's local contact, was no longer present; his fifty-one year career had taken its toll and he had retired to Cork, where he died in mid-June.[43] His pre-eminent role in

Athlone's constitutional political life, spanning almost thirty years, ensured that a replacement of equal stature would have been difficult to find. It appears that nobody took up the reins; the Athlone UIL maintained the moribund state it had entered almost two years previously. There was intervention from a small number of the party faithful from Athlone, sometimes violent, though ultimately ineffective. Support for the IPP in the town was less overt than opposition to SF, as 'separation women' threw rocks while others, 'people associated with military affairs', raised Union flags and sang 'God Save the King' on the fringes of parades celebrating McGuinness' victory. In contrast, it was reported that in 'working class areas', republican flags were raised and rebel songs heard.[44]

The election in Longford provided an additional boost for SF in the midlands, and confirmed the relevance of the party in the political environment of the time. The *Westmeath Independent* noted that:

> On a new register, which embraces the young manhood of Ireland ... nothing is surer than the ... prophecy ... that with few exceptions, the Members of the Irish Party would be defeated at the next general election.[45]

A new branch of SF was established in Mullingar in the same month as the election, and with that, the two largest towns in the region had an easily recognised SF presence. Three SF clubs were also recorded in Roscommon in May, the first time any SF club had been officially acknowledged by the police.[46] Cecilia H. Daniels noted that the growth in SF was easily discerned, if their policies somewhat less so:

> We are having stirring times ... The Sinn Féin are going strong, the Catholic clergy, especially the young ones have joined in ... they have no definite object at present ... only to oust the Nationalists with their 400 a year.[47]

Advanced nationalism was gaining currency, and to drive home the advantages this brought, organisational moves were made and increasing pressure was placed on IPP MPs. A national appeal from the Volunteer Executive in Dublin saw IV corps all over the country reorganise, with Seán O'Hurley assuming leadership of the organisation in Athlone.[48] Articles in connection with SF meetings across Westmeath noted that calls were more frequently heard for the resignation of Walter Nugent, even from previously supportive clergymen.[49] The baronet continued to make pro-war, pro-Home Rule imperialist speeches, on one occasion stating: 'There was no sacrifice in order to win the war that

Westmeath would not make.'[50] He even expressed the highly unpopular idea of granting unionists disproportionate representation in the new Irish legislature, something he thought may have eased their trepidation.[51] It was apparent that men such as Nugent were unwittingly assisting SF through their rhetoric and actions, something which led the *Westmeath Independent* editor to highlight SF's evermore likely usurpation of the Irish Party. McDermott-Hayes was, however, somewhat ambiguous about where he believed the growing movement was heading: 'Sinn Féin, whatever it may ultimately end in, has caught the fancy of the country.'[52] He espoused the belief that the party was tending towards constitutionalism, not extremism, a view which supplemented his earlier notions on parliamentary abstention. His opinions probably indicated the evident difficulty newer SF converts had when it came to comprehending the full extent of the political paradigm shift for which the party was aiming.

Trends in SF support seen in Athlone were reflected in neighbouring regions and districts further afield.[53] Such was SF growth that the IPP appeared in a state of indecisive panic by June 1917, something recognised by Dublin Castle officials, who stated: 'it is manifest that the … Party has lost its dominating power in the country and is making no serious effort to regain it.'[54] The overwhelming victory of Éamon de Valera in the East Clare by-election with 71 per cent of the vote owed much to the widespread support of the Catholic clergy, including the local bishop, as well as his own heroic stature as the most prominent survivor of the Rising. His campaign was assisted by funds from many parts of the country, including Athlone.[55] The town staged celebratory processions, with an escalation in attacks from the separation women of Irishtown, who resorted to deploying hatpins, penknives and 'nightsoil'.[56] Similar scenes manifested elsewhere as disgruntled army supporters registered their annoyance at de Valera's win, which saw him replace the recently deceased William Redmond, brother of John. Redmond died at Messines, the first battle in which the Ulster 36th and Irish 16th Divisions had fought side-by-side, a battle described by Charles Townshend as 'a poignant image of the war that might have been'.[57] Following on from the losses in North Roscommon and South Longford, the East Clare by-election appeared to mark 'a significant milestone on the road along which the constitutional movement was reeling to destruction'.[58]

SF's recourse to highlighting the threat of conscription was not only effective at assisting the party win by-elections, but also in ensuring growth in its branch network and sister organisation, the Irish Volunteers. The ranks of most IV corps swelled during the summer of 1917, with the exception of some northern counties, as repeated reminders of the personnel implications of the continuing war were made.[59] One statement by Patrick Lennon to the Bureau of Military History recalled that the local growth happened over a period of a few days, with speeches by figures such as Harry Boland, described by David Fitzpatrick as 'surely the most versatile of Irish revolutionaries',[60] and Laurence Ginnell, now a parliamentary abstentionist and full SF member,[61] pushing people towards the IV; sure protection from forced enlistment.[62] In Athlone the IV established a football team, 'The Sean Costellos', named after the local man who died in the Rising, and used it as a front for assessing the bona fides of prospective volunteers.[63] The influx of men did not bring with it a concomitant rise in armaments however, with local companies resorting to using pikeheads – recommended by de Valera in the absence of other weaponry[64] – supplied by local blacksmith William J. Byrne of Connacht Street.[65]

The growth in SF clubs continued apace, and in Athlone the party's activity levels were high. Significantly, numerous SF meetings were held in the town hall.[66] Nationally, the party began to advertise its main objectives; abstention from Westminster, representation at the Peace Conference – designated to deal with the fallout from the war – and complete independence; at each of the many meetings held in the midlands, these were stated explicitly.[67] The number of SF clubs in Westmeath rose to seven, but Roscommon was really setting a blistering pace, mostly arising from short-lived infighting between Count Plunkett and Arthur Griffith;[68] twenty-two clubs formed in the space of two months.[69] Roscommon's changing political landscape saw some AOH divisions suspended due to the issuing 'of resolutions in the press calculated to injure the Order'. SF attracted many of the former brethren.[70]

The death of Dean Kelly and the absence of a realistic, or perhaps interested, successor to the role of de facto constitutional nationalist leader in Athlone appeared to show that organisationally, such nationalism in the town was probably at best restricted to a significant minority. To have any chance of re-establishing the IPP's political relevance and reverse the trend of decline and fracture in places like Athlone, Redmond had to make productive efforts to address the demands of Irish nationalists for greater autonomy. The entry of America into the First World War in April 1917 may have strengthened the IPP's hand in negotiations for, as noted in the *Freeman's Journal*, 'the request of an ally' such as America could influence the British.[71] To mollify the Americans, Lloyd George, more interested at this point in political expediency, established the Irish Convention,[72] a forum intended to give the impression that the responsibility for Ireland's future was now in the hands of Irishmen.[73]

It appears that the convention was largely ignored locally. J.J. Coen attended on behalf of Westmeath County Council, and the *Westmeath Independent*, while not completely dismissive, was more hopeful than expectant.[74] The restrictive terms of reference saw SF officially ignore the proceedings,[75] but the party did have some 'independent' observers present. The increasingly strong Labour Party also refused to engage, 'signalling how far it was now within the Nationalist camp'.[76] The two local MPs were supportive of the enterprise, as were many of their colleagues, with the prominent exception of John Dillon. Northern and southern unionists also attended, but were not unified in their approach.[77] Despite the fact that the convention 'comprised the most representative gathering of Irish elites ever to assemble',[78] the omission of SF was too important; anything decided would be non-representative and impossible to enact. Laurence Ginnell stated that if the 'men of Lewes', the prison in which many activists had been interned, were not represented, the convention was nothing more than a 'fraud and deception'.[79] As Roy Foster has put it, the convention was 'condemned to impotence'.[80]

If proof were needed that local political opinion was unaltered by the inception of the Irish Convention, the official reorganisation of the Athlone SF branch should have been adequate. Formerly, when Home Rule negotiations were ongoing, Athlone's political life became quiet; expectant. On this occasion SF was able to maintain a high level of activity, as the majority of Athlone's politically active nationalists had recognised the IPP as no longer an entity of political consequence. The reorganisation meeting was undertaken prior to a SF rally in the town in August where Arthur Griffith and Joe McGuinness addressed the local branches of SF, the IV and Cumann na mBan.[81] The meeting heard the UIL described as a memory and the AOH 'a skeleton stalking the land'.[82] Walter Nugent and J.P. Hayden were called upon to resign; they were no longer representing the political desires of their electorate.[83]

The constitution of the reorganised Athlone SF branch provides the best evidence of the acceptance of the party by a wide cross-section of the local populace. A recurring accusation levelled at the SF movement by the IG of the RIC, as well as many CIs, was that it was not attracting men with significant land or business interests.[84] Athlone's newly constituted branch appears to have gone against this general trend with 54-year-old Thomas Chapman instated as club chairman. The branch represented the often-seen duplication between those heading SF and the IV at local level, as Seán O'Hurley was installed as Chapman's second in command. O'Hurley, without doubt the most radical committee member, stated in a speech, which fell foul of the Press Censor, that:

> ... if this opportunity at the Peace Conference was lost there would be more Easter weeks ... they would always be ready ... to demand their freedom with their blood, and that would be on the shoulders of those who neglected their duty now.[85]

His inclusion, along with the SF membership of a small number of other IV members, highlighted how the relationship between the two groups 'was often blurred … sometimes the creation of two distinct and separate bodies seemed redundant'.[86] As noted by Michael McCormack, around Athlone the 'demarcation line between the Volunteers and Sinn Féin was never very rigid … most of the Volunteers was also members of the Sinn Féin organisation'.[87] Forty-six-year-old McDermott-Hayes' addition to the committee confirmed what his readers had become increasingly aware of, namely that the largest newspaper in the region was officially an SF promoter. Other committee positions were occupied by the most consistent local SF supporter, farmer Owen Sweeney,[88] as well as urban councillors. Others associated included former councillors, PLG members and local factory workers, with a strong representation from those engaged in agriculture in districts bordering the town.[89]

   David Fitzpatrick has contended that SF committee members in Clare were often former supporters of constitutional nationalism, be they members of one or more of the UIL, AOH or Redmondite Volunteers.[90] His argument extends to describing the move from such bodies to SF as one of continuity rather than change in provincial Ireland. The idea of a 'terminological revolution' during the years 1916–1922 espoused by Fitzpatrick has been tested, at least to some extent, in Longford and Sligo where similar, if somewhat less pronounced consistency, has been highlighted.[91] Fergus Campbell has highlighted that in Galway the majority of SF officials were young men with no former link to the Irish Party.[92] Athlone's experience tends to reflect Fitzpatrick's hypothesis rather more than Campbell's, though the theses advanced by both men can be accommodated in the makeup of the wider Athlone SF membership. From the names supplied in the local press, it can be inferred with a reasonable level of assuredness that the Athlone SF branch committee was constituted to a large extent by older men who were previously members or supporters of constitutional nationalist bodies. It is apparent that the majority of those who could be identified (twenty-five in total), outside of the committee itself (seventeen), were younger men who had not previously engaged with political movements in Athlone. The wider branch roster, while including men such as Seán O'Mullany (still only twenty-three) and Peter Malynn, reflected a newer, politically active cadre incorporating younger local farmers, shop assistants, labourers and at least one artisan.[93]

   SF's supremacy in Athlone's local political life was confirmed, while the party's growth in Westmeath continued, with nineteen branches accounting for almost 800 members, and 2,000 members aligned with thirty-seven Roscommon branches.[94] Nationally, the party encountered less and less resistance from the UIL and INV; both were doomed to extinction, according to *The Leader*, dating the demise to when Redmond 'put his two feet in it at Woodenbridge'.[95] The number of SF clubs in Ireland had grown to an estimated 690 with 44,000 members, roughly 10,000 of whom had joined in September,[96] after the passing of Thomas Ashe. Ashe's grizzly death as a result of being force-fed in prison while on hunger strike proved to many who were undecided the sense of SF arguments on the malignancy of British rule.[97]

In Athlone, Ashe's death was greeted with disbelief. Athlone UDC passed a resolution of sympathy with Ashe's family and registered their disgust at the 'pernicious system by which this man met his death'.[98] The *Westmeath Independent* noted that his spirit was now 'roaming the hills and valleys, cities and towns'; his sacrifice was inspirational.[99] A requiem mass was held in the friary[100] and over 450 people marched from the church behind a large SF flag which bore the letters IRA, an acronym for Irish Republican Army, the more frequently seen appellation for the Irish Volunteers.[101] Ashe's death, and an obvious sense that staunch nationalists were somewhat less fearful of British forces, saw Seán O'Hurley address the crowd (wearing an IV uniform) and condemn his 'murder'. O'Hurley promoted the IRA and, most provocatively, called on those assembled to avenge Ashe's death.[102] The manner of Ashe's passing dealt a further blow to British attempts to stem the growth of republican organisations; indeed it 'energised a whole cohort of Volunteers'.[103] The IV grew noticeably in the aftermath, coordinating the activities of a growing number of Irish militants, while also becoming a more distinct entity as a result.[104]

The influence of Ashe's death also reinvigorated Athlone's FÉ, whose re-emergence and proclivity for marching through Irishtown singing 'The Soldiers' Song' led to confrontations with separation women. As incidents increased, legal proceedings were initiated, and on at least one occasion the courtroom was invaded by sympathisers, who unfurled SF flags.[105] It was stated that the RIC had begun to assault scouts heard singing the song and the absence of censure from the presiding RM led McDermott-Hayes to state that it 'clearly implies a licence to the police to take the law into their own hands'.[106]

The increasing anti-British sentiment led the RIC to raid a small number of local shops that illegally stocked Ashe memorabilia, and officially warn Thomas Chapman, who printed some of the offending products.[107] Counterproductively, from a government point of view, these and other 'petty prosecutions' pushed more and more Athlone people in the direction of 'the policy of Sinn Féin ... [the] only effective weapon to save the Irish Nation'.[108] Local tensions were also heightened by threats arising from a dispute over the letting of the local sports ground, partially owned by the GL, to the army. The military officer in charge of the acquisition, Major Ball, had stated that the War Office would be informed of all 'patriotic or non-patriotic actions'.[109] While the land was let, the major was censured by the Chairman of the War Losses Commission, who stated that 'reference to the political opinions of a claimant, which had nothing whatever to do with the claim … could only have been introduced for prejudice'.[110] On the back of Ball's actions, the UDC adopted a resolution calling for the freedom to speak their minds and protection against 'the Prussianising of our country by Military and Civil Officials hostile to every ideal of the Irish people'.[111]

McDermott-Hayes continued to show his growing distaste for the IPP and introduced distinctions between an MIP and MEP, (Member of the Irish Parliament and Member of the English Parliament); the former 'scorn to touch the English bribe' of £400.[112] SF momentum continued to build, with the largest crowd in some years seen at the Manchester Martyrs parade in November.[113] Greater organisation amongst those gathered was recognised by observers, with a local intelligence officer observing that SF was working hard to ensure this was maintained:

> The whole … movement is peculiarly well disciplined, having regard to similar organisations in the past. The results of its indoor meetings are very hard to obtain. Drunkenness is almost unknown amongst those deeply implicated … [114]

As support for SF, grew its leadership recognised that clarification had to be given to both the aims of the party and its leadership structure. To this end, an *Ard Fheis* was held in October. At the meeting Éamon de Valera was elected president, and it was confirmed that SF wanted 'the international recognition of Ireland as an independent Irish republic'.[115] De Valera's election as president of SF was quickly followed by his assuming the equivalent role in the Volunteers, a move which helped limit the growth of a developing rift between advanced nationalist supporters of moral force, those who wished to pursue a political path, and the promoters of physical force.[116] The investing of the presidency of both organisations in de Valera 'effectively created a single movement',[117] 'a well-organised party with a military wing'.[118] His election may also have provided some clarity to the dual role adopted by men such as Seán O'Hurley in Athlone, confirming the compatibility of the two organisations. Francis Costello noted that from this time onwards the more radical element in the IV 'would be seen to drive the conduct' of SF.[119]

What was agreed on by all sides in SF and the IV was the necessity of having a larger, better armed and geographically more comprehensive volunteer movement.[120] Efforts to reorganise nationally had been under-taken in earnest in August 1917[121] and around Athlone the evidence suggests that expansion proceeded at pace. By the end of 1917 the Athlone IV was supplemented by perhaps a dozen other corps outside the town boundaries, some of whom had acquired weapons, mostly shotguns 'more ornamental, than of use'.[122] Seán O'Hurley had been instrumental in promoting the IV in both Athlone and nearby villages such as Knockcroghery and Lecarrow in south Roscommon.[123] At a meeting in the latter village, and in justification for his call for those assembled to source weapons, he stated, 'there is always something required behind our words to back them up'.[124]

Colonel Maurice Moore's move to integrate the remaining INV[125] companies into the IV in October 1917 led to even greater growth in November, which was also when some internees were released to re-engage with promotional efforts.[126] The IV leadership reorganised branches all over the country, promoting a code of secrecy and staging surreptitious drilling exercises, which were still outlawed under DORA.[127] The RIC estimated that by January 1918 there were over 13,000 men in the IV, in almost 190 branches.[128] Though the drilling was considered quite rudimentary and 'of little military value', it was recognised that it 'nevertheless ... serves the purpose of infusing a spirit of discipline, and will undoubtedly facilitate the leaders in mobilising a force if and when they require it'.[129] Illegal drilling and marching occurred in both Westmeath and Roscommon, but the RIC were low on intelligence about the republicans' intentions: the nature of their activities meant that 'it is not easy to learn what they discuss'.[130]

The poor police intelligence reflected an increased distrust of the RIC amongst many Irish nationalists. Promoted by republicans, the move to ostracise constabulary members was intended to weaken the force, and some success on that score was achieved.[131] The social exclusion of such men not only made their jobs more difficult but their lives increasingly uncomfortable and incentives, such as the granting of pension rights and preferential treatment in local authority job appointments, were drawn up by the increasingly high-profile Michael Collins for such men if they resigned their commissions. Information on the incentives was often provided to policemen through a member of the clergy, or, in fewer instances, by a republican sympathising colleague. In the Athlone region, RIC member John Duffy was charged with promoting the initiative along with an Athlone doctor named McDonnell, Roscommon solicitor William Kilmartin and the prominent clergyman Fr O'Flanagan.[132] They hoped to capitalise on growing dissention amongst the RIC rank and file many of whose members had petitioned the IG on the subject of pay

and pensions in late 1917.[133] The IG indicated that there was evidence of
information on the incentives being disseminated, singling out the clergy for
their efforts.[134] There is no real evidence for the success of the initiative[135] and
increasingly, the RIC was identified as part of the enemy cadre. An intelligence
officer for the midlands indicated that as spring 1918 wore on and conscription
again raised its head, 'a bitter and aggressive feeling was gradually and generally
being manifested towards the police in the midlands'.[136]

In early 1918 growth in Athlone's advanced nationalist organisations saw
the continuation of the fall in support for constitutional nationalism. From
the turn of the year, the *Westmeath Independent* wrote of the failure of the IPP
in stark terms:

> … [the] sham constitutional movement prosecuted since the death of
> Parnell … governed and dictated by English Liberals was … bleeding
> Ireland to death. [The IPP] was … politically and morally atrophied
> when Sinn Féin stepped in … Our National life was drugged, and while
> we remained politically insensible the Irish question … dropped back
> to the treacherous days of Keogh and Sadlier.[137]

Efforts made by the IPP at the Irish Convention would have informed some
of the commentary, as Redmond adopted too conciliatory a position for
even his own supporters.[138] J.P. Hayden's *Westmeath Examiner* tried to put a
brave face on Athlone's constitutional nationalist support levels after the loss
of SF to the IPP in the Armagh by-election,[139] describing how Redmond
supporters celebrated joyously after news reached them.[140] The *Westmeath
Independent* stated that the win was influenced by the proportion of pro-union
voters[141] and the influx of 'Belfast thugs'; all it did was provide another 'useless'
IPP man, '[an] attorney on the make'.[142] The increasing distance between
the editorial lines of the county's two largest newspapers had been growing
since late 1916; it was clear now that the pre-Rising homogeneity of much
of the local commentary was broken. March witnessed two additional losses
for SF in East Tyrone and Waterford, where IPP members won seats, though
less joyous scenes were witnessed amongst supporters on the occasion of the
latter win, as the by-election was triggered by the death of John Redmond.

McDermott-Hayes wrote a reasonably balanced piece on Redmond after
his passing, thankful that the man had been 'spared the pitiable spectacle
of the shivering to pieces of the once great Irish movement'.[143] Similarly
when writing of Redmond's legacy, *The Leader* – quite fairly – noted that his
achievements had to be looked at both pre- and post-war, not all through

the lens of March 1918.[144] The occasion of Redmond's death saw both AOH
Division 680 and the local UIL meet, the latter for the final time, as a small
number registered their sadness at his passing.[145] John Dillon assumed control
of the party, though the *Westmeath Independent* saw little to recommend
the Ballaghadereen man, blaming his opposition to the 1903 Land Act for
continued land difficulties in Ireland:

> It is insulting to hear ... Dillon ... challenge Sinn Féin ... and
> endeavour to hold the real national movement responsible for the
> legacy of trouble in which he had so principle a share ... through the
> smashing up of the Wyndham ... Act.[146]

SINN FÉIN, THE LAND, AND FOOD PRODUCTION

It is perhaps elementary to point out that while all of the electoral and organisational efforts made by the various political and politically-interested bodies
during 1917 and 1918 generally make up the bulk of the historiography of
the period under study, some rather more prosaic issues played on the minds
of Irish people. As mentioned in the previous chapter, the demands of war
were not restricted to amassing an army, but to supplying it with the requisite
provisions. The protracted nature of the conflict ensured that the early difficulties encountered in ensuring adequate supplies of reasonably priced food
for the people of Athlone not only continued but were exacerbated. By the
early spring of 1917 the avaricious activities of local farmers, allied with the
still too widespread practice of livestock farming and the poor 1916 harvest,
had reportedly brought some locals to the brink of fatal deprivation.[147]

Though there are numerous reports of Athlone's experience of provisions
shortages throughout the calendar year, it was during the early months of
1917 and 1918 that most problems were encountered. Athlone's markets were
the scene of serious confrontations between working-class purchasers and
farmers, whose arbitrary and opportunistic price increases became national
news. *The Irish Times* and *Irish Independent* dealt with the exceptionally
fractious Athlone markets over a number of weeks detailing the exceptional
prices demanded by farmers, who had reportedly increased the price of
potatoes and turf by 300 and 500 per cent respectively.[148] The reaction of the
purchasers to the increases, which also affected milk, butter and eggs, often
necessitated RIC intervention. Poorer townspeople hectored the farmers,
decrying their actions and reminding them of the assistance rendered by

them in the breaking up of local ranches. The RIC patrolled the markets as if they were political rallies as, on numerous occasions, violent lunges were made by women desperate to secure food.[149]

Many markets were abandoned by farmers, who preferred to leave the tubers 'rotting in the pits' than submit to the directions of the Food Controller, who was charged with setting prices for staples.[150] *The Irish Times* believed that the prices demanded were so high that the average wage of an unskilled worker in Athlone of eighteen shillings per week, minus rent of roughly four to six shillings, meant that the asking price of sixteen shillings per hundred-weight of potatoes valued the sale at almost one week's wage.[151] The situation had deteriorated so much by the end of February 1917 that J.J. Coen, Westmeath County Council chairman, had to intervene. He purchased all of the potatoes at one weekend market, distributing them amongst the poor of the town, many of whom had already been turned away by the Athlone PLG who were unable to deal adequately with the distress.[152]

Similar scenes were witnessed in Ballinasloe and Letterkenny and while some put the lack of potatoes at markets down to simple unavailability, it was more widely reported that around Athlone there were 'immense quantities of potatoes pitted'.[153] Some farmers began trying to forestall outside the town, though again the RIC intervened.[154] There were rumours that the police were to begin potato seizures in districts bordering Athlone in March 1917, and over the following weeks and months a number of prosecutions for overselling were carried through as attempts to assuage local food demand became ever more difficult.[155]

The avaricious actions of Athlone's farmers were extensively covered by D.P. Moran of *The Leader*, who excoriated the 'Potato Shylocks of Athlone … unconscionable profiteers … potato sharks'.[156] He published a poem (of rather poor quality), lambasting those who 'on the stone of hunger grind an axe'.[157] Arthur Griffith, writing in *Nationality*,[158] also criticised the farmers, though pilloried the RIC, who he believed were hypocritically portrayed as 'appearing as a friend of the Poor against the Rancorous Farmer … It is the Paymasters of the RIC who are responsible for the present potato shortage in Ireland'.[159] As 1917 progressed the situation saw no substantial improvement, even with SF efforts; staples were still hard to source or too expensive. Reports emerged of shops closing due to a scarcity of stock.[160] Cecilia H. Daniels, like so many others, believed she knew where the blame lay:

Prices rule very high still in this country, notwithstanding the Food Controllers. The farmers are making fortunes. The living of that class in this country costs them nothing, it is the people in the town who feel the War and the scarcity it has brought ... To go into any shop now is a real gamble.[161]

The local UDC complained about the exportation of Irish food when such hardship was being experienced, the systematic infringement of the Food Controller's orders, which during the summer of 1917 became statutory,[162] as well as the government's disallowance of foreign food, such as American bacon, to enter the Irish market.[163] The council was petitioned by numerous local organisations, SF, the GL and the Roman Catholic clergy, on the need to establish a fund of £3,000 to address the crisis.[164] A local food committee headed by members of SF was set up in an attempt to curb the exportation of local produce, but met with little success,[165] despite taking a hard line, even with those associated with the party.[166] The press laid the blame for the crisis at the feet of the ranchers and complained that locals were never given the chance to purchase much of the food that passed through Athlone.[167] Ranchers were certainly part of the problem, along with some of what *The Leader* referred to as 'Bungs', i.e., shopkeepers or other businessmen with large farms. SF's efforts threatened the business interests of these men and in very few cases gained their co-operation.[168] County Court Judge Wakely, a staunch opponent of land agitation and a figure whom 'nobody can accuse ... of being a Sinn Feiner', helped the food committee by stating that he would not allow anything grown on his lands to be sold outside the region.[169] In some counties attempts were made to assess and retain food stocks for local consumption, but most saw much of the produce leaving, as government policy concentrated on ensuring adequate food supplies for Britain.[170] Irish self-sufficiency in food production was promoted[171] and SF used the food shortage to gain political credit by highlighting the government's unwillingness to deal with the crisis.[172]

Local distress was exacerbated in February 1918 by heavy flooding as 'the early potato crop near Athlone [was] imperilled', while many acres of farmland that were not under water remained unfarmed due to ownership disputes.[173] The *Westmeath Independent* complained bitterly about the situation, lambasting graziers who still controlled a huge proportion of the local agricultural land: 'The Irish landlord at his worst was no greater social sore than the grazier at his best.'[174] The extent of the problem caused the editor to warn of impending mass starvation: 'A journey through Westmeath from Athlone to Mullingar ... showed us in the teeth of oncoming Famine. There was not a field broken up for every mile travelled.'[175] The emotive nature of the term famine turned minds to the gross neglect perpetrated by the governments of the 1840s and could also have motivated the implementation of a compulsory tillage order during 1917.[176] The measure proved ineffective for the most part, given that agitation ensured that disputed lands could not be worked safely. Even if safe conditions were assured, it was contended by Richard Ball in a contemporary article for *Studies: A Quarterly Review* that introducing widespread tillage farming in places like Westmeath would have been counterproductive, given firstly that it would lead to meat shortages, and secondly, that most farmers had not the expertise, nor more importantly, the labour to make it work.[177]

Cattle driving re-emerged in the Athlone region, and allegations of thuggery were levelled at a number of SF activists, who were accused of forcibly seizing disputed lands to sow crops, using the IV as enforcers.[178] This new instalment of agrarian agitation, 'probably as uncongenial to the new national leadership as it had ever been, nonetheless magnified the local position of the Volunteers'.[179] The more direct approach to confronting agrarian issues was a reversion to pre-1912 UIL activities, when the league's raison d'être was still land agitation.[180] Unsurprisingly, such activity was promoted by Laurence Ginnell, who was to spend a period of some months at the king's pleasure for his efforts.[181] His policy was too divisive for Arthur Griffith, whose wish to reduce 'social antagonisms, capable of damaging his inclusive conception of the Irish nation', exercised greater influence over the SF approach to the issue.[182] Irish Chief Secretary H.E. Duke wanted strong action taken against those engaging in driving and seizures, but their number militated against anything other than massive and widespread coercion being effective.[183] Young farmers moved in greater numbers to SF in 1917 and 1918 as it promoted 'a radical agrarian policy … when the IPP was urging its supporters to put their hunger for land on hold'.[184] While there were localised examples of the UIL agitating in contradiction to the IPP edict,[185] activities such as cattle driving and land seizure provided SF with a perfect opportunity to replace the constitutionalists as Ireland's land liberators. SF capitalised on the opportunity the issue provided, displaying their aptitude for administration while showing that they could supplant the IPP in addressing a fundamental national problem.[186] The effective paralysis of the IPP ensured that on the land issue it was rather easily outflanked.[187]

THE CONSCRIPTION THREAT

As if any additional impetus was required to exacerbate the already well-established trend of Athlone nationalists moving to SF, March 1918 saw the British Government again consider implementing a Military Service Act.[188] British opinion on the exclusion of Ireland from a measure of conscription had hardened considerably, especially in light of the fall in voluntary recruit-ment:[189] 'It was difficult to scrape the bottom of the barrel in England, Scotland, and Wales, while Ireland got off scot free', writes D.G. Boyce who noted that Lloyd George went ahead with a scheme to impose conscription despite Duke's opinion that 'we might as well recruit Germans'.[190] The prime minister believed that the army needed 150,000 additional Irishmen given the weakness of the western frontier,[191] but, recognising the enmity that Irish conscription would produce, he again dangled the Home Rule carrot in an attempt to soften Irish opposition.[192] The failure of the Irish Convention meant that most ignored the offer, which was couched in terms of a federal solution.[193] Irish people were instead focussed on efforts to oppose the Military Service Act, which was introduced in the Commons on 9 April.[194]

The reaction of Athlone's nationalists manifested as soon as moves to instigate conscription became clear. Unsurprisingly, the vanguard was led by the *Westmeath Independent*, which utterly condemned the move, printing increasingly vitriolic pieces during March against the government and 'the miserable nondescript of a played out, beaten and discredited faction'[195] that was the Irish Party. J.P. Hayden's furious reaction to the suggestion that Ireland had not played its part in the war effort[196] did little to assuage the editor, who was rapidly becoming one of the most bellicose members of the provincial press. Indeed, his polemics were identified by the Press Censor during March as a violation of DORA, Regulation 5 (causing disaffection), which led the *Westmeath Independent* to join a small number of newspapers that were suppressed in early April.[197] Military forces directed that the publi-cation be withdrawn and the APW, where it and numerous other newspapers were printed, was shut down. The *Irish Independent* covered the occurrence in some detail, describing the *Westmeath Independent* as 'one of the most outspoken critics of the Irish Party in the provincial press':

> The officers … ordered the chief mechanic … to leave, dismantled the machinery, stored the parts in boxes, and had the latter removed in military wagons … people engaged in other industries, assembling at the breakfast time, indulged in hissing and booing [*sic*] as the boxes were removed.[198]

Thomas Chapman, while admitting the strong political line adopted by the newspaper, stated that no warnings had been received, nor had any recent article raised specific objections.[199] The *Irish Independent* printed a letter from a correspondent (citing a similar occurrence in the case of the *Kilkenny People*), who believed that it was the newspaper's support for the

SF candidate in the King's County by-election that had led to its suppression.[200] An editorial supporting the candidacy of Dr Patrick McCartan in the *Westmeath Independent* on 30 March was exceptional in its condemnation of the government. The candidacy of McCartan was highlighted advertisement-like, the first time such prominence was given to an electoral candidate in McDermott-Hayes' eighteen-year tenure.[201]

The closure caused much ill-feeling. The APW employed 100 men, many with dependents estimated at between 250 and 400 people.[202] Pushing them out of work at a time when food was scarce and prices were high was seen as doubly disgraceful. The UDC condemned the move, as did the PLG, the former stating that the paper had 'rendered such valuable assistance … especially … in connection with the … breaking up of the lands'.[203] The Mullingar and Castlerea UDCs followed suit, as did the Manchester Typographical Association. The local Labour party termed it the 'latest evidence of British Militarism in Ireland'.[204] A letter from the Athlone branch of the Typographical Association was read out in the Commons by Alfred Byrne, MP for Dublin Harbour, which queried the ambiguous reasons provided for the closure of the plant, while also questioning: 'Is this the liberty for which men are laying down their lives?', a reference to Irish efforts in the war.[205] The debate on the closure of the Athlone publication occupied more time in the Commons than that of any other provincial newspaper during the second week in April, with T.M. Healy leading the charge.[206] Healy described Athlone as a 'peaceable town' and Thomas Chapman as a Protestant and, incorrectly, a Conservative. He stated sarcastically that the nationalism of the editor may have cancelled out Chapman's leanings and noted that the APW was the largest printing establishment of 'any town in Ireland', with numerous council contracts.[207] He believed that Chapman having a 'fiery editor' should not have led to the entire works closing, and equated the closure with the amputation of a full leg due to the presence of a corn on a foot.[208] In an attempt to allow men back to work, the UDC asked if the military would permit the 'ordinary and commercial contract work' to recommence.[209] Questions were raised in the Commons on the uneven way in which the suppressions were made; all the machinery was seized in Athlone, but not in Belfast, where ancillary commercial work continued.[210] Healy too was more concerned with 'the dislocation of the accompanying business, which had nothing to do with the cause of complaint', than the newspaper itself, with which, he eventually admitted, he was unfamiliar.[211]

The Press Censor was quite happy with the results achieved by the numerous suppressions. This was most especially the case in connection with the *Belfast Evening Telegraph* and *Westmeath Independent*, stating that their 'suppression ... has had an effect of the most salutary nature on the whole Irish Press'.[212] The Competent Military Authority (CMA), based in Athlone Barracks, which was charged with assessing the threat of people, activities and actions under DORA, communicated that the closure of the works in regard to 'general publications' had been lifted just over a week after the seizure. Duke believed their closure unfortunate, but reasonable.[213] However, printing the *Westmeath Independent* was still not sanctioned.[214] Luckily, pressure brought in the Commons appeared to work and the newspaper went back to print after three weeks. However, censorship of tracts became increasingly apparent. McDermott-Hayes complained about it and 'received considerable publicity',[215] as the government tried to exert greater influence over the information and opinions to which the Irish populace were being exposed.

The actions of the government in closing the APW did little to arrest the massive opposition to the Military Service Act, and in the Athlone region it was reported that SF membership virtually doubled during March and April.[216] The PLG and UDC suspended business,[217] the latter denying 'the right of the British Parliament to conscript the people of Ireland', and pledging 'to offer every opposition'.[218] Representatives from virtually all nationalist groups in the country met on 18 April in the Mansion House, Dublin, to agree a pledge of no conscription. These included the IPP (not all members, however[219]), AOH, SF, AFIL, Labour and the trade unions, who organised a strike that closed down factories and crippled public transport all over Ireland.[220] The pledge stated that conscription was to be resisted 'by the most effective means at their disposal'.[221]

Significantly, the Irish Catholic Bishops also issued a statement, which closely followed that sent out from the Mansion House. They stated that the attempt to conscript Irishmen 'must be regarded as a declaration of war on the Irish nation',[222] while counselling that people had to work within God's law to achieve their desired goal.[223] In Athlone, the Mansion House pledge was signed by more than 1,000 local workers and the growth in support for SF, the IV and Cumann na mBan was reflected in an increase in the number of branches and members for each organisation in both Westmeath and Roscommon.[224] The creation of the Athlone Trades Council (ATC) in May gave a strong voice to local supporters of the Labour Party, which made its opposition to conscription clear.[225]

Indeed, the coming together of the disparate supporters of the Labour Party in Athlone was yet another example of how the void created by IPP/UIL inactivity was forcing change in the Irish political landscape. The formation of Trades Councils in Ireland began to spread through the nation's towns from 1917 as labourers and working classes increasingly felt their views were under-represented.[226] The conscription threat and Athlone's first annual Labour Day, or May Day, procession provided the final push required to establish the local council, which gained the affiliation of many of the town's unions, as well as the Athlone branches of national and English unions. The ATC represented local labourers in strike actions (which were much more common during the war), work stoppages and pickets, mainly against industrial concerns such as the AWM and Athlone Sawmills, whose employees (both male and female) began to agitate for wage increases from mid-1918.[227] Its creation was perhaps the first major step in the growth of Labour (with a capital 'L'), in Athlone, a movement that was to expand rapidly over the following two years. The *Voice of Labour*, the most recent in a long line of Labour newspapers, welcomed the ATC, hoping that it would '... lift the workers of Athlone out of the state of helplessness which characterised the past ...' and also deal with local strikebreaking, rendering the town 'Black-leg proof'.[228]

As well as the newly-organised Labour support, the local clergy also came out against conscription; none more so than young curate Fr Michael Keane of Drum.[229] Witness statements note that most RIC men in the town were also against the application of the measure, not an uncommon occurrence, given that the unrest it would cause would have a negative impact on the performance of their duties.[230] Eoin MacNeill gave a lecture in Athlone on the role of Irishmen during the crisis, and the town staged two large anti-conscription meetings, with representatives also attending the national rally in Dublin.[231] At both of the Athlone meetings, large crowds assembled (reportedly 5,000 at St Mary's Square in late April and almost 1,000 at the town hall three weeks later[232]) to hear speeches from local SF representatives, which were loaded with republican rhetoric and anti-imperialist sentiment.[233] Even moderate nationalists such as H.J. Walker spoke strongly against the government, equating Lloyd George with Oliver Cromwell. The anti-conscription pledge was signed at St Mary's Square with many of those making their mark being, at least according to *The Irish Times*, 'strapping young fellows from the rural districts ... accompanied by several priests'.[234] Violence was neither seen nor promoted at either meeting, though it was possibly on the minds of some.[235] As with similar meetings held all over Ireland, 'the emphasis remained on public dissent'.[236] McDermott-Hayes, when commenting on the size and intent of the meeting in St Mary's, asked if Lloyd George was 'foolish enough to think that Irishmen can be rounded up like kaffirs in an African kraal'.[237]

The possibility of such a roundup was on the minds of more militant members of the IV, an organisation which now had a General Headquarters

(GHQ) working on the task of defining brigade areas, amassing arms and assessing the strength of the Crown forces.[238] The move towards conscription 'reinvigorated the strategy of violence, almost quiescent since the Rising',[239] as many IV engaged in raids for weapons and promoted the view that passive resistance would not be sufficient.[240] John Dillon led the IPP out of Westminster on 16 April, unimpressed by 'the vague promise of "a measure of Home Rule"',[241] describing a vote to include Ireland in the Military Service Act as: 'The worst day's work done for England since the War began.'[242] Dillon's move appeared to be an adoption of SF policy and, for some perhaps, validation of the argument against parliamentary involvement.[243] The vicissitudes of the conscription crisis were for Ulster Unionists 'the final confirmation that the aspirations of nationalists and unionists were incompatible'.[244]

As mentioned earlier, not all IPP members toed the party line during the conscription crisis. One of the more prominent dissenters was the representative for South Westmeath, Sir Walter Nugent. As soon as the threat began to take more definite shape, it became apparent that the baronet had his own opinion on the crisis. Nugent neither attended nor supported the Mansion House meeting, for he refused to associate with SF in any fashion.[245] He absented himself from the Commons on 16 April for the vote on the Military Service Act and while his ballot would have made no difference given the large government majority,[246] it had symbolic value. Attendees at a meeting of the Westmeath County Council noted that his name was conspicuously absent from the list of IPP members who had come out against conscription, the implication being that the MP was actually for the measure.[247] Calls for his resignation were made by the *Westmeath Independent*, which asked 'Where is Nugent?', and by some public bodies, including Athlone RDC 1.[248]

As the controversy developed, Nugent set about stating his case, tellingly, through *The Irish Times*. He believed that leaving Parliament was a bad move and that creating a covenant against conscription was not the 'right way to meet the situation'. In a letter to the unionist daily he stated: 'To take the line that, though opposed to conscription, we still want to win the war, and then decline … voluntary enlistment, seems to me an impossible attitude.'[249] *The Leader* rounded on the South Westmeath representative and questioned what John Dillon was to do with Nugent and other IPP dissenters who were striking out on their own.[250] Moran's dislike of the MP led him to reprint part of a letter from Nugent to *The Irish Times*, which gave his view on the compatibility of the IPP and SF:

> The policies of Sinn Féin and Constitutionalism are as wide apart as
> the two Poles, and I am entirely opposed to any … weakening on our
> part … indicating that a union between the two … on any question
> does exist or is desirable.[251]

Nugent's letter reconfirmed his long-held belief in 'a constitutional settlement for the Irish question inside the Empire'.[252] His approach to the crisis,
though consistent, showed him to be divorced from not only most of his
party, but also the bulk of his constituents. He was unable to understand that
the absence of Irish self-government had rendered the 'war effort in the eyes
of many nationalists … de-legitimised'.[253]

   Nugent was not alone in his approach to the threat of conscription.
The Westmeath County Council saw controversy when it was alleged by the
Westmeath SF Executive that J.J. Coen, the chairman, had refused to sign the
anti-conscription covenant. Calls were made for his resignation and fellow
councillor Thomas Chapman unsuccessfully proposed that a delegate from
the executive be allowed to speak at a council meeting to establish the SF case.
Coen, a Roman Catholic, denied that he had not signed the covenant, calling
the accusation a deliberate lie while confirming that he had not subscribed to
the anti-conscription fund as he was not assured that the money would only be
used to pursue that issue. The majority at the council meeting appeared more
concerned about the fashion in which the SF resolution was pursued, and wished
to protect the integrity of the chairman and the local council processes.[254] A few
weeks later Coen faced a fight for the chairmanship, which he won, at a meeting
marked by contradictory statements that highlighted a growing division in the
local authority between SF and established IPP supporters.[255]

   In reaction to the increasing unease in government circles, it was decided
in May to appoint a new Lord Lieutenant for Ireland; Viscount French, a First
World War Commander of the British Expeditionary Force. The *Westmeath
Independent* pulled no punches when it described French as a 'military
dictator', installed to enforce the 'Blood Tax' of conscription.[256] The 'decision
to replace a civilian with a soldier'[257] certainly indicated to observers the
determination of the government to enforce involuntary enlistment, and
with his instatement came draconian measures.[258]

   Initially French targeted the SF leadership, ordering the arrest of virtually
all of the party's main figures, nationally and regionally, on the grounds that
they were conspiring with the Germans. In Athlone Seán O'Hurley was
quickly seized and deported to an unidentified location, along with dozens
of others across Ireland.[259] The arrests were painted by SF as a step towards

implementing conscription,[260] a reasonable deduction given that French believed two-thirds of SF men would have made good soldiers, if they were 'removed from the influence of their leaders'.[261] The *Westmeath Independent* demanded proof of French's allegations, as did numerous other publications and public figures.[262] The 'German Plot' was really nothing more than a propagandist fabrication, designed to lessen SF support at home and abroad (especially in America) by associating the men with the tyrannical Kaiser.[263] When evidence, 'ranging from merely flimsy to diaphanous',[264] was eventually tendered, McDermott-Hayes described it as 'an insult to public intelligence. It can be compared only to an attempt to strangle a bull with a piece of elastic.'[265] Ultimately, French's policies and creation of the German Plot proved counterproductive; SF support was boosted and its progress virtually unimpeded.[266] As stated by David Fitzpatrick, such 'annoyances, clumsily juxtaposed with concessions and attempts at conciliation, allowed public indignation to be maintained'.[267]

The vociferous reaction of the Irish nationalist population to the threat of conscription saw the likelihood of its implementation recede in early May as Lloyd George's hopes for softening its impact with some measure of Home Rule foundered; 'the inherent contradictions of the stillborn dual policy [Conscription plus Home Rule]'[268] being impossible to reconcile.[269] Instead, it was decided to initiate yet another unsuccessful scheme for voluntary recruitment, unsurprisingly backed by Sir Walter Nugent.[270] McDermott-Hayes mockingly drew together a proposed text of French's new offer to those who joined up:

> ... if you return [from the front] we promise you a bog patch in Connaught, dimensioned by your length of service, on which you can – for the remainder of your days – fight against Famine.[271]

The issue of gifting soldiers land 'engendered strong feelings';[272] John Dillon saw the scheme to exchange land for service as a 'swindle' and it was eventually dropped on the basis that it would prove unworkable.[273]

Whatever the opinions held by Athlone's nationalists in relation to French and his stratagem to suppress advanced nationalists, it appeared to be working. By June the tone of reports from Dublin Castle tended towards a degree of optimism, tempered with caution. While noting that SF was still able 'to exercise a widespread and dangerous influence', fewer new members had enrolled in June than during any other month during 1918. IV drilling was down almost two-thirds, though members of Cumann na mBan (still active in anti-recruitment and anti-conscription processions in Athlone[274]) were learning to be 'Green Cross' nurses in the event of conflict. Raids on suspects' houses were conducted in Athlone and south Westmeath and the IG's report for June stated anecdotally that many people actually approved of French's firm stance.[275] In contrast, Patrick Shea recorded that such raids led to himself and his brother being beaten up, for as the sons of a RIC man, they were 'English spies', who were on a side which 'although not yet a minority, was losing support'.[276]

French's firm stance (which tied up 101,000 troops in the country, a four-fold increase in just three months[277]) was soundly backed up in July with the declaration that, under Section 6 of the Criminal Law and Procedures Act 1887, the SF Organisation, SF Clubs, IV, Cumann na mBan and the GL, described as 'an alternative manifestation of republican sympathy' and by now entirely politicised in the eyes of the authorities,[278] were all precluded from holding meetings, assemblies or processions unless authorised by a County Inspector. Additional restrictions came into force locally as Westmeath and Roscommon, along with eleven other counties, were proclaimed under the 1887 Crimes Act.[279] Thankfully, for many enthusiasts, the GAA was not banned. However, it became a requirement that a permit be sought to play games, a restriction which fed annoyance and led the association to become increasingly radical.[280]

The suppression of SF and the IV meant that both groups, if they wished to continue planning and strategising, had to become more clandestine. Secret meetings were held and surreptitious communications methods were developed, with the consequence of increased police ignorance. It was hoped that along with the censorship of the press, the proscription would help stem the flow of republican ideas and impede moves toward armed conflict. 'Sinn Féin propaganda has saturated the minds of the younger generation with revolutionary ambitions and hatred of England', noted the exceptionally wary IG: 'The whole country is … in a state of acute political unrest, rendering the maintenance of a strong military force absolutely necessary.'[281]

Local evidence of efforts to stamp out republican influence was apparent. Celebrations held on the occasion of Arthur Griffith's win (from his jail cell) in the East Cavan by-election in June were muted, especially when compared to earlier examples.[282] There were no reports of SF meetings in Westmeath during the same month and few in August.[283] Some SF activity was witnessed late at night in Athlone on occasion, but appears to have been more a show of bravado as the *Manchester Guardian* reported that 'barricades surmounted by rebel flags had been put up in the principal thoroughfares'.[284] Similar quietude prevailed in Longford, with SF branches in Roscommon during July exhibiting 'little open display since the recent proclamation', though August did see the initial preparations for the December general election directed by Fr O'Flanagan, now SF vice-president.[285]

Seizures of seditious materials continued as the RIC tried to deal with the massive SF propaganda machine.[286] Athlone shops were raided and in one case, that of McManus's, previous forbearance exhibited by the local CMA was replaced by demands for prosecution.[287] Defiance at the imposition of the harsher measures was seen in the UDC chamber in a move to co-opt Seán O'Hurley to the council while he remained interned at Reading prison, one of the many facilities used by the authorities in their attempts to limit rebel interaction.[288]

As the autumn of 1918 wore on, it was becoming apparent that the war on the Continent was turning in the favour of the Entente. The logical inference that was drawn in many quarters was that the fear of conscription would fall off as the Central Powers fell back. Local press reports ensured that Athlone's populace was well informed as to progress on the front and RIC reports indicate that as knowledge of what was transpiring spread, 'the dread of conscription subsided, and with it a good deal of enthusiasm for Sinn Féin'.[289] In Westmeath the CI reported that by October people were 'convinced they will not be conscripted' and that SF and IV activity appeared to have ceased.[290] Numerous witness statements corroborate the inspector's observations, averring that after the threat passed, many left the local IV corps and went back to normal life.[291] However, it quickly became apparent that the end of the war on 11 November would not produce the result many who celebrated the Armistice anticipated.[292] The recently established IV newspaper, *An t-Óglach*, made it clear that while 'an armistice had been signed in France … in Ireland there is no armistice.'[293] A letter to Seán O'Hurley in Reading appeared anything but positive when addressing the question of what Athlone's IV would do now that the war had ended. Thomas Noonan, a colleague of O'Hurley's, attested that the local IV appeared uninterested: 'you said to me once that Athlone was not worth its salt … at the time I had hope, but now I am positive you are right'.[294]

Politically, however, the landscape in Ireland and Athlone had utterly changed. Nationalists, if they were to leave SF, had no alternative party to look to. The IPP had 'manifestly lost its dominating influence over the electorate'[295] and around Athlone it was noted there was not a single operating branch of the UIL,[296] with the town's AOH division basically defunct.[297] As D.G. Boyce has noted, 'the Home Rule-conscription policy had done irreparable damage to the Irish Parliamentary Party, and … constitutionalism in Ireland'.[298] Irish nationalists, so long seeking Home Rule, were now unwilling to accept it when offered; the parameters for settlement had changed.[299] Charles Townshend has written that 'the … government reaped all the political damage [from] the [conscription] threat without achieving any concrete result',[300] an allusion to the often-seen ironic consequences of government policies. Confirmation of the contempt Irish people had for both the government and IPP was to be delivered at the ballot boxes in the general election of December 1918.

GENERAL ELECTION 1918

Athlone's experience of the first general election in eight years was quite varied. The town's voters had to deal with competitors for both constituencies, a situation that the IPP's electoral dominance of the previous twenty years had precluded. They also had to take into account the expansion of the franchise, and, in the case of those voting on the east of the town, the redefinition of the constituency boundaries, which had seen the amalgamation of South and North Westmeath.[301] The election was also the first, be it local or national, in which official SF candidates ran locally; the short life span of Athlone's first SF branch ensured that it had never to adopt an electoral role.

If the eye of a voter unfamiliar with the actions of Walter Nugent and Laurence Ginnell appraised the ballot paper for the new Westmeath constituency, they may have envisaged quite the battle between two incumbents vying for the combined seat. However, it appeared certain, even in the months before the election, that Nugent's view of Ireland's role in the Empire had alienated all but a tiny minority:

> … [Nugent] does not think it worth his while retiring from South Westmeath seeing that the people will in the near future release him … We have heard of the man falling between two stools, but the member for Westmeath does not even allow himself that slender chance. He is now as much on the outside of the Irish Party … as … Sinn Féin … He has left himself no support to grip.[302]

There were rumours that Nugent was to submit to the inevitable and withdraw, but true to his recent form, he ignored the prevailing opinion and signalled his intention to fight.[303] Many of his counterparts bowed out more gracefully. Thirty-two IPP MPs did not seek re-election, gifting, as the RIC put it, SF with at least twenty-five seats. SF put forward 102 candidates for the 105 available posts, many of whom were chosen 'apparently on account of their rebel antecedents'.[304]

Laurence Ginnell, the second of three candidates in the Westmeath constituency, relied only on his own political record, rather than that of deceased relatives, to recommend his candidacy. The 64-year-old barrister, whose political career had up to this point been that of an outsider, was the obvious choice for SF, though he, in common with a number of other candidates, was in Reading prison during the campaign.[305] The final candidate was P.J. Weymes, a Westmeath County Councillor whose considerable business interests made his selection by the IPP anything but surprising.[306]

South Roscommon's ballot paper was more straightforward, as just two candidates contested the seat. The incumbent J.P. Hayden had to fight his first ever contest in his twenty-one-year career as MP against Harry Boland, who was chosen to run against the newspaper proprietor in September.[307]

While both constituencies witnessed contests, it is without doubt that the more vigorous of the two was held in South Roscommon. From the start of campaigning, J.P. Hayden went on the offensive, using his *Roscommon Messenger* to promote his cause and blacken SF and Boland.[308] As early as September he accused Galway SF supporters of burning the American flag and Cork Sinn Féiners of insulting American soldiers and sailors.[309] He stated that parliamentary abstention was 'absolute folly' and would result only in additional taxation, as the government railroaded measures through in the absence of Irish opposition.[310] Hayden invoked, inadvisably, the 'old' Party achievements and policies, stating that he had spent as much time in jail as many SF members, who used their internment as evidence of the sacrifices they were making for Ireland.[311]

At numerous meetings Hayden was shouted down (in at least one case missiles were thrown) by Boland's supporters and in Athlone, where the *Roscommon Messenger* believed he was well supported, IPP canvassers had their houses tarred. In the case of P.V.C. Murtagh, the de facto IPP contact in Athlone, a SF flag was painted on the wall of his house.[312] Hayden believed, incorrectly, he had the support of most of the priests in the constituency and 'calumny and vituperation [and] false charges regarding religion' entered the fray, possibly on the back of Athlone's Archdeacon Keane of St Peter's making his preference for Hayden known.[313] The MP's *Roscommon Messenger* picked up on the poor Roman Catholic clerical support for Hayden, and criticised the inconsistency of senior local clergy, who allowed their curates to promote SF but not the IPP, even if they desired to follow the constitutional party.[314] Hayden did gain support in rural areas of the constituency, though, if Fergus Campbell's study of Galway is representative of Roscommon, most support came from men who had gained under the IPP during the previous two decades; '[those] with something to lose, and who were keen to protect what they held'.[315]

Boland's campaign was equally vigorous. The absence of his own newspaper proved no handicap as both the *Roscommon Herald* and *Westmeath Independent* gave support. McDermott-Hayes published eye-catching 'VOTE FOR IRELAND' banners promoting not only Boland, but most of the midlands' SF candidates.[316] He editorialised that it would be 'a foul crime against Ireland' to vote for the IPP, whose adoption of aspects of the SF manifesto[317] was viewed as confirmation of their inconsequence.[318] Boland himself spoke in Athlone under the pseudonym of 'Henry O'Hanrahan'[319] and stated: 'We are not promising you better labour conditions or better houses or better money for the farmers' produce. We promise you an independent Irish nation.'[320] He was fighting the election, as Fitzpatrick has put it, 'as an outsider preoccupied with national issues rather than local loyalties'.[321] Boland distanced SF from the Germans, decried attempts at partition and lambasted the IPP, though perhaps frustratingly for some, he did not explicitly state how SF intended to achieve the aspiration of Irish independence.[322] Such ambiguity on the methods for gaining independence was intentional and Joe Lee believes that 'the adroitness with which [SF] evaded this question' highlighted the party's political talents.[323] Similarly, Ó Tuathaigh has pointed out that the increasingly broad constituency to which SF spoke required such an approach; voters could be scared away. The party had to appeal to 'a broad spectrum of views and sentiments on both the acceptable form of Irish independence and on the methods appropriate to its achievement'.[324]

The Westmeath contest was less combative and highlighted the virtual absence of IPP allies on the east side of Athlone. Meetings were held to promote Laurence Ginnell, who had to rely on his wife Alice and Athlone's reorganised SF club to speak and canvass on his behalf,[325] with the indefatigable Fr O'Flanagan ensuring that there was much publicity surrounding the upcoming poll.[326] The meeting at which O'Flanagan spoke saw quite a degree of enmity between locals and army men, with a small minority of soldiers singing 'Rule Britannia' upon the commencement of speeches.[327] The *Irish Independent* reported that a 'rush' was made at the soldiers, who returned to the barracks so as to avoid a more serious confrontation.[328] O'Flanagan described the impotency of the IPP at Westminster; Dillon, he stated, was speaking to 'empty benches'.[329] He also made the emotive claim (which was later excised from press reports by the Press Censor) that '… some of the young men laid down their lives in Dublin during Easter Week when they found they could not do it [fight for freedom] any other way'.[330] The IPP candidate P.J. Weymes was criticised for his alleged conscriptionist leanings and while he vigorously disputed the claim,[331] the emotive nature of the term, and the ability to tarnish the reputation of those supposedly supportive of the measure, proved useful for his opponents.

Despite his incarceration, Ginnell made efforts to impart his opinions to constituents.[332] In a letter to Harry Boland,[333] published in expurgated form,

Ginnell stated that he no longer wanted Irish independence viewed as a 'domestic' British issue, but as an Irish issue alone:

> A contest in Westmeath now, would be purely factious … no matter in what guise an opponent would appear, it would be recognised by the people as pro-English and anti-Irish.[334]

Neither Weymes (whose centre of support was Mullingar[335]) nor Sir Walter Nugent staged meetings in Athlone. The latter did canvass,[336] but met with hostility that probably dissuaded him from attempting a large-scale public speech.[337] The baronet's manifesto promoted a solution to the Irish problem: '… on the lines accepted by O'Connell, Parnell and John Redmond … namely Home Rule for Ireland inside the Empire.' He opposed partition and wished, tellingly, to protect the interests of 'the farmers of Great Britain and Ireland.' He stated that his move away from the IPP was precipitated by disagreements 'with them on some issues of National importance'.[338] The *Meath Chronicle* questioned the invocation of Parnell's name by Nugent, quoting the dead leader's desire to destroy 'the last link which keeps Ireland bound to England'. It went further to state that Ginnell was the only IPP member who had actually followed Parnell's policy and was 'the best hated man in England'.[339]

The *Westmeath Examiner* gave much support to Nugent, repeatedly printing his manifesto, though it pushed Weymes' candidacy more prominently. Its editorials during the run up to the election portrayed the IPP as having gained much for Ireland's farmers, associated SF with 'Kaiserism' and questioned the abstentionist policy, asking whether Ireland wished to be represented 'from the most prominent platform in the Universe', Westminster, by Edward Carson.[340] The *Westmeath Independent*'s support for Ginnell was whole-hearted and while it did publish Nugent's and Weymes' manifestos, its editorials left readers in no doubt as to where their duties lay.

On polling day, 14 December, it quickly became clear that SF's support in Athlone greatly outweighed that of the IPP. Both Ginnell and Boland gained seats as Athlone's voters on the east, in the Marist Brothers' school, and the west, in the courthouse, offered them their overwhelming backing. Sixty-seven other SF candidates, many still interned, also won, some taking two seats.[341] In both Westmeath and South Roscommon, more than two-thirds of the votes registered were for SF; the IPP was broken.[342]

In South Roscommon, Boland won by polling more than twice Hayden's total, with Ginnell's victory even more emphatic (some voters reportedly did not even know his name, but went to vote 'for the man in jail'[343]), receiving almost four times the vote of his nearest rival, P.J. Weymes. Walter Nugent received a paltry 603 votes,[344] the lowest of any incumbent MP who contested his seat in the 1918 election. His abject failure was reported upon gleefully by *The Leader*, which recommended that the baronet 'go home and stay there'.[345] Though it has been traditionally written that the IPP gained their best support in urban areas amongst older voters,[346] it appears, if local contemporary estimates can be relied upon, that in the case of the Westmeath seat, their support in Athlone collapsed spectacularly. The *Westmeath Independent* reported that almost 94 per cent, roughly 750 from 800 votes cast, favoured Ginnell, with Thomas Chapman averring a twenty to one ratio in the Delvin man's favour.[347] A letter of congratulations for Ginnell from Lorcan Robbins, a former UIL activist, noted: 'The swing of S. Westmeath to the Republican astonished even the most optimistic amongst us ... tell (Seán O'Hurley) that his pioneer work ... has borne good fruit.'[348] Reports suggest that Ginnell's status as a shoe-in led to the polls on the east of the town being relatively quiescent, Thomas Chapman, who had carried out much promotion for Ginnell,[349] noted that the poll for Ginnell would have been higher, 'were it not that in every part of the county your return was felt to be assured'.[350] Polls on the west side of the town saw greater activity, given that Hayden's political reputation had not suffered the same degree of self-sabotage exhibited by Nugent's.[351]

Historians have attempted to deconstruct the election of December 1918; the results were clear, but how they were arrived at was somewhat less so. Contributing factors in the SF victory were a greatly increased electorate[352] and the decision of 'organised Labour' not to run in the election.[353] The largest such body in Athlone, the ATC, had made clear its neutrality and told people to vote as they pleased, thus keeping the main focus of independence to the fore.[354] The local IV, part of 'the army of the Irish Republic',[355] were said to be instrumental in the victories. Members spent time checking registers, canvassing voters, collecting funds and, perhaps the most pro-active of their methods, providing transport and protection for the SF faithful.[356] Protection was mainly required for those traversing Irishtown, where the separation women (whose reliance on government handouts was well entrenched and continued despite the end of the war[357]) targeted SF voters, throwing glass jars and threatening them with hurleys. Athlone IV member Seamus O'Meara believed that many IPP supporters also engaged in intimidatory acts, something facilitated by the 'RIC ... [who] showed their hostility and blindly allowed disorderly conduct on behalf of the Nationalist Party'.[358]

On the other side of town, Hayden's supporters had engaged in intimi-datory acts, though these people were fewer in number than Boland's and proved unable to sway the vote. The absence of a UIL branch in Athlone stymied Hayden's efforts, and while he gained support from those previously associated with the league, it was without doubt of lesser value without the UIL machine. As Joe Lee has noted, the machinery of the league that was in place throughout Ireland in 1918 lacked what made IPP election successes of 1910 so comprehensive: morale.[359]

Another commonly cited factor also influenced the local vote: personation. Patrick Lennon described it as rife: 'We voted for everyone who was on the register, who was dead or who had left the district, as well as several who were alive also.'[360] The occurrence of Spanish Flu may have prompted some voters to pass their card on to a healthier contemporary; the prevalence of the virus in Athlone (early December saw 300 people diagnosed with fourteen fatalities[361]) was recognised as a difficulty in the South Roscommon constituency, though it still realised a 69 per cent turn out.[362] It should be noted however, that in both constituencies the margin of victory precludes personation from being key to SF success.

Many historians also cite IV intimidation of the electorate as a prominent feature of the election, but in Athlone this does not appear to have manifested to any great extent, at least not overtly. Certainly local Protestant farmer Cecilia Daniels highlighted her fear of SF, whose supporters ('the Catholic Clergy, strangers, adventurers and boys and girls'[363]) were, at least to her mind, generally intimidatory. Others, new to the electoral process, may also have found the overbearing canvassing intimidatory; in some cases they would never have been targeted for their vote and may not have known how to treat the requests made of them. Ms. Daniels believed, possibly due to exposure to SF canvassing methods: 'The democracy in Ireland are a very bad lot … low and uneducated, only a rabble led by … the Catholic Clergy … another form of Kaiserism going for absolute power and a "place in the Sun".'[364] Former Athlone resident Patrick Shea cited the movements 'of the young men in trench coats who were on the move wherever political arguments arose'[365] as a motivation for voter allegiance, while Tom Garvin believes that generally, the chance of a competitive election was stymied by 'considerable intimidation by what was becoming the IRA'.[366] Fergus Campbell alludes to the efficacy of such intimidation in reversing the 'powerful pull that a lifetime of involvement in Home Rule politics exercised on middle-aged Leaguers', in essence implying that if given free choice, many such men and women would not have changed allegiance.[367] James King, a former South Westmeath UIL Executive chairman, communicated to Ginnell that the canvassing had certainly reached a new level:

Words cannot express the enthusiasm of ... the young of both sexes;
the ladies were marvels of electioneering skill and a various stages ...
I felt constrained to admit (to myself of course) that I and others of
some experience in election work, were only handymen, while they
were tradesmen.[368]

Joe Lee disputes claims of widespread intimidation, quoting from the *Freeman's
Journal* ('with few exceptions polling passed off with untoward incidents')
and the *Irish Independent*, which described the election as quite a civilised
affair when contrasted with that seen after the Parnell split.[369] Lee states that
'Sinn Féin won, in short, because of overwhelming support for its policy in
southern Ireland',[370] while the *Hibernian Journal* later wrote that the win was
due to 'the dastardly treachery of the British Government in its dealings with
this country'.[371] Isolated disturbances involving small numbers were seen in
some regions, yet even the *Roscommon Messenger* stated that polling day went off
almost without incident. It appears that creating the impression of widespread
intimidation is misleading, especially if it is presented as being one-sided.[372]

The victory of SF in both local seats was heralded in the weeks after
the results became clear. The *Westmeath Independent* celebrated, stating that
'the obliteration of the Irish Party was essential' to the country moving
forward, for they had sold Ireland 'to the now disrupted Liberals for a mess
of potage, which they didn't get'.[373] Indeed, obliteration was basically what
happened to the constitutional party. The IPP won just six seats in total, a loss
of seventy-three. The political landscape was now radically altered: 'the Irish
question as perceived at Westminster had now entered an entirely new phase.
Home Rule, although few could yet grasp it, was dead'.[374] Those seats the
IPP retained were mainly in the north, where the party had entered into
a voting pact with SF designed to prevent unionist victory in the face of a
split nationalist vote.[375] Indeed, *The Leader* believed that only the West Belfast
seat, that of Joe Devlin, was to be 'genuinely credited' to the IPP[376] (John
Redmond's son also won his seat in Waterford, but Moran saw this as more
a sentimental victory.) The same medium would later refer to the IPP MPs
as a 'remnant, rather than a minority'.[377] Edward Carson stated that the SF
victory had provided clarity to the Irish political situation; the alternatives
had been narrowed to either a republic or a government under the UK
parliament: 'Every other alternative has proven to be a sham'.[378] Archdeacon
Keane, who had supported J.P. Hayden at the election, made it known to his
flock in Athlone that the overwhelming SF victory meant that that party now
represented national policy and should be given the support of all the town's

nationalists.[379] Hayden himself magnanimously described the victory of SF as 'the passing away of a great movement, to be succeeded by another'.[380]

The celebrations that ensued in Athlone were on a large scale and when Boland spoke in the town on the Monday after the election, he was greeted by a large crowd who heard him outline the failings of John Dillon, and the need for an Irish Republic. He pointed people towards the Peace Conference as the next stage in the journey towards Irish independence.[381] The subject of SF prisoners was also highlighted, including the plight of Seán O'Hurley, whose release became the focus of Athlone's SF branch in the New Year.[382] Interestingly, the meeting saw M.J. Lennon reappear on the SF platform.[383]

The SF success at the polls was quickly capitalised on by the party. Despite the handicap of many members being imprisoned, on 21 January 1919 Dáil Éireann was formed and convened in the Mansion House. Those in attendance laid down the rules for the executive, with South Roscommon's Harry Boland's interest in international affairs ensuring he was assigned as an envoy to Clan na Gael in America.[384] Dublin Castle believed that the new body was not taken seriously by the vast majority of the Irish people, rating it more as a gesture than anything else.[385] The local press disagreed, declaring that the opening of the Dáil 'terminated … the ill-fated connection with Britain', and while this was something of an overstatement, it reflected the view amongst SF supporters that they were certainly moving in that direction.[386]

6

Recourse to War:
Politics and Conflict 1919-21

The conditions of this country … are unpleasant and difficult. One could almost wish there was one real 'uprising' and that things would be settled one way or another. Most of the young … are half-cockney, half-yankee – a bad blend … others, the better class of people … cannot stand the changed conditions and … are leaving the country.

Cecilia H. Daniels, 20 January 1919[1]

While the creation of Dáil Éireann was heralded in the *Westmeath Independent* as the severing of the connection with England, it was obvious that the actual achievement of such an outcome required additional efforts. Both Ginnell and Boland had directed people's attention to the Peace Conference in Paris, hoping that international assistance would help in the pursuit of a solution. Other republicans, unconvinced by the efficacy of concentrating on politics alone, began a slowly escalating campaign of violence that intensified as political efforts faltered. In Athlone, repressive government measures fuelled anti-British sentiment and ensured support for the labours of republicans, both political and militant, while changes in local government, the judicial system and policing assured people that a move away from British admin-istration was not merely an aspiration. Government reaction to increased republican activity took an extreme coercive form, motivating Athlone's IV to escalate their campaign. The adoption of guerrilla tactics by republicans ensured that the fight was maintained over a protracted period. The British Government's inability to deal with such tactics effectively eventually obliged it to enter into negotiations with SF, negotiations that eventually resulted in the partitioning of Ireland.

The efforts of the Athlone electorate in ensuring the victories of Ginnell and Boland provided proof of local support for the political aims of SF. However, after the election, militant republicans, liberated from policing the polls, decided that political efforts needed to be supplemented, or indeed driven, by violent opposition to British rule.[2] On the same day that the Dáil first convened, a fatal ambush at Soloheadbeg in County Tipperary[3] appeared to declare the intent of the IV to pursue a military course, and give Ireland the catharsis local septuagenarian Cecilia Daniels believed it needed. Described in the local press as an 'appalling outrage and shocking crime', the ambush appeared to belie the SF manifesto of October 1918, which had not explicitly sought a mandate for rebellion.[4] Regardless, the timing was seen as more than a coincidence, despite it being just that, and gave the impression of republicans adopting a war footing.[5]

The increase in activity demanded that a more definite structure be provided to IV corps around Ireland, and to this end divisional and brigade areas were defined. Athlone Brigade itself was part of the 1st Midland Division and consisted of three battalions: Athlone, Summerhill and Drumraney. Each of the battalions was further subdivided into companies. The companies of the 1st Battalion, Athlone, were Coosan, Mount Temple, Kiltoom, Athlone, Moate, Faheran and Monksland. Drumraney, the 2nd Battalion, hosted the companies of Tang, Drumraney, Tubberclair, Ballymore, Bishopstown, Rosemount and Moyvore. Drum, Summerhill, Bealnamulla, Clonown, Taughmaconnell, Moore and Monksland comprised the 3rd Battalion, Summerhill.[6]

All of the organisational efforts and manoeuvres of the IV had an effect on members of the Crown forces. In Athlone, Patrick Shea's policeman father became 'silent and grim' after news of the Tipperary attack and joined his colleagues in instigating the local instalment of nationwide raids.[7] The anxiety felt by Shea's mother as she saw her husband venture out would not have been lessened by news that the raids unearthed guns, ammunition and bombs.[8] Letters seized from John Harney, a member of the Athlone Brigade of the IV, showed that volunteers had stepped up their search for weapons in 'district [and] private houses, police barracks, small camps, etc'.[9] While the activity gained the commendation of the IV Adjutant General (AG),[10] it also resulted in Harney's arrest, along with that of Thomas Lennon and his brother.[11] During the nationwide raids, plans for an insurrection were discovered, but little had happened since the Tipperary ambush and the authorities were uncertain as to the specifics of republican intentions.[12]

Annoyance precipitated by the arrests was assuaged somewhat in early March, as Lord French 'struck on a surprisingly conciliatory course'[13] by releasing the remaining 1918 prisoners, including O'Hurley[14] and Ginnell.[15] In a letter to the *Westmeath Independent*, O'Hurley outlined some of what he and his fellow internees had to endure during their imprisonment, not least the belief of certain execution and the inspirational contempt for their captors shown by Ginnell.[16] O'Hurley returned to Cork to recuperate, while Ginnell linked up with his Dáil colleagues, who had not yet held a second meeting, something that led observers to question the viability of the assembly.[17] Decisions were still being made by Dáil members, increasingly without reference to SF,[18] and a Ginnell speech alluded to future plans:

> … you will be justified in expecting … pretty strong developments … you
> will be asked to take part in … activities which will … result in the taking
> of the government of this country out of the hands of the foreigner.[19]

The second Dáil, sitting on 1 April, allayed some fears as to the executive's viability and saw the Westmeath TD receive the portfolio of non-Ministerial Director for Propaganda.[20] Differences in opinion on how to best advance the Irish cause did manifest at the meeting, though it is certain that the poor outlook for Ireland at the Peace Conference proved a boost to those espousing a more belligerent approach.[21]

While there was evidence of increased IV activity in Athlone, SF's post-election functions had really been restricted to agitating for the prisoners' release. However, the return of Ginnell ensured that Athlone's SF members were soon provided with a cause to rally around. On 5 May the TD was scheduled to deliver an address in the Fr Mathew Hall. Those who arrived to hear him discovered that the Curragh-based CMA, Brigadier General Burnett, had proscribed the event and directed the Somerset Regiment to seize the premises. Ginnell proposed a change of venue, and, headed by the local Pipers' Band, a crowd paraded east across the river to St Mary's Square, followed by the military. Upon arrival, the RIC Head Constable (HC) made it clear that no meeting would be allowed but, true to form, Ginnell ignored him and, along with Owen Sweeney, addressed the throng. Repeated calls to desist were disregarded, tensions grew and eventually soldiers charged at the crowd, bayonets to the fore.

Chaotic scenes ensued as people, many of them women and children, ran from the soldiers towards the adjacent church. Ginnell climbed atop a wall, from where he shouted denunciations: 'There is English civilisation; there is the British Empire for which Irish men were recruited … to save … Down

Gaelic League Pipers' band, 1917. From left to right back row: Timmy Curley, Gilbert Hughes, Joe Scally, Jack Scally, Tom Keating, Jack Preston, Paddy Kessney (?). Front row: Pat Doran, Bobby Galagher, Thomas Hunt, Dan Sullivan, Jack Sullivan, Christie Miley.

with England, up with the Republic.' His performance did little to defuse the situation and after dismounting, he instigated a march to the train station and began bellowing from a carriage window. RIC intervention was again required as the shouts of local man George Sheffield in support of Ginnell and the Irish Republic caused additional jostling.[22] Eventually Ginnell's train departed, but the tension remained. An army dance in the courthouse was attacked later in the evening and an RIC officer received a 'violent blow' to the head, Athlone's contribution to the national escalation in brutality towards the police.[23] The local press carried much coverage and comment:

> Bayonets ... substituted for ... the knout at St Petersburg in the days of the Czars, against which the world hurled anathemas ... England ... added another laurel to those she has not got as a defender of small nations.[24]

The national and international dailies also picked up on the debacle. The *Irish Independent* printed a telegram sent to Dr McCartan TD in Philadelphia: 'Hun troops celebrate peace by charging Ginnell's constituents with cold steel ... Armoured cars occupy Athlone.'[25] *The New York Times* gave a short description of the occurrence in its 6 May edition, as did the *Manchester Guardian*.[26] The republican publication *New Ireland* criticised the authorities, stating that 'the cruel consequences fall on the shoulders of those who interfere with the rights of the Irish people'.[27] Virtually all local organisations joined in the condemnation, with SF using the publicity to promote the upcoming visit of the American Delegation, which was 'fruitlessly seeking Irish representation at [the] Peace Conference'.[28] McDermott-Hayes highlighted the government's ability to inadvertently promote causes it opposed:

> The Nationality of Athlone was never doubted. It may have been dormant ... but the experiences of last week ... flashed through two Continents ... [and] gathered local National strength as no other thing could.[29]

The reception of the American Delegation in Athlone days later was considered exceptional. As elsewhere, they were greeted as 'conquering heroes'.[30] The bayonet charge was entirely counterproductive:

> As an act of terrorism ... it was a dismal and unmitigated failure. It was angry defiance and protest ... which made the reception of the American Delegates ... the most wonderful National display ... The time will come when whoever originated such an outrage, if not made responsible to public opinion, will find it a hellish memory that will stand a constant accuser long after the excitements of the day have passed into the limbo of forgotten things.[31]

Supplementary to the negative effect of 5 May was the drama of the resultant court cases. Ginnell (already charged in connection with a separate incident[32]), Sweeney and church sacristan Michael Dillon were arraigned on 3 June, with Ginnell refusing to cooperate and referring to the court as 'incompetent' and 'a fraud'.[33] His refusal to sit or remove his hat necessitated police intervention, while his theatrical show of reading aloud highlighted his contempt for proceedings.[34] Sweeney, more prosaically, refused to recognise the court and gained a loud 'Bravo' from Ginnell.[35] H.J. Walker represented Dillon, whose co-operation saw him gain bail; Sweeney and Ginnell were remanded to Mountjoy.[36] Unsurprisingly, a large crowd, with the newly-returned Seán O'Hurley amongst them, cheered them on their way to the station.[37]

The next hearing was on a larger scale. Forty-seven RIC and fifty-seven soldiers escorted the accused to the courthouse.[38] The addition of 100 RIC men to the local force for the day saw the local press joke that the defendants were the town's best employers. In Ginnell's absence, Sweeney took up the reins as master of ceremonies, refusing to sit or remove his hat. When asked to plead, Sweeney stated: 'I ignore this court, I deny its jurisdiction and I refuse to plead.' A considerable amount of testimony was heard, which initially indicated that culpability rested with the Crown forces.[39] The description of a civilised meeting prior to the bayonet charge was countered by RIC HC Feeney, who downplayed the soldiers' charge, instead blaming SF for the incident.[40] The court heard of some minor injuries, with the defence stating: 'It was Prussianism and militarism made in Germany and imported to Athlone'.[41] Both men received a one-month sentence after Dillon too refused to recognise the proceedings.[42] After the verdict, H.J. Walker made it known he believed the wrong people were in the dock, an observation the HC took personally. A 2,000-strong crowd cheered the men off from the station on their way to Mountjoy.[43]

The bayonet charge was not unique to Athlone, and, as in other areas where such occurrences were experienced, its effect was quite wide ranging.[44] Condemnation of the army and police authorities came from the Westmeath County Council and Roman Catholic clergy, while the UDC dealt with divisive resolutions on disallowing the army use of the courthouse for social events[45] and requested that children remained indoors given the 'prevailing state of excitement'.[46] Local republicans burned a large crop of hay used to fodder the horses in Athlone barracks,[47] while other incidents also highlighted the growing dislike for the Crown forces in Athlone, a sentiment that was very apparent to a 'Redmondite soldier', recently returned from the front:

> All our sacrifice was for nothing. We are no longer looked on as men who did a patriotic thing. We are looked at askance by our own people, which we feel most of all. We are simply regarded as discharged British Tommies.[48]

Any hope the authorities had that the release of Sweeney, Dillon and the two Lennon brothers would ease tensions was erased by the imprisonment of Seamus O'Meara, who also refused to recognise the court while declaring that he was a soldier of the Irish Republic.[49] A letter from Laurence Ginnell to the ATC called for continued support: 'the day is coming … when truth can be spoken freely.'[50] The Westmeath CI attested to the enmity of locals and the press towards the RIC, whose nationwide ostracisation 'a crucial precondition to shooting them',[51] was well under way.[52] A leaflet circulated promoting the Dáil's April request for a police boycott: 'Pass On. Boycott the Police and Soldiers. Don't recognise them. They are your enemies. They are traitors.'[53] The HC stated that the request was having an effect, citing the example of a Cumann na mBan member reprimanding a local for greeting

his men.[54] Undoubtedly the heavy-handed approach of the local Crown
forces provided stimulus to the drive to promote antipathy towards the RIC;
quiescent areas, such as Kildare, maintained cordial relations, which even by
late 1920 'could at worst be described as lukewarm'.[55] Patrick Shea wrote that
the 'feeling of an approaching siege grew', as the RIC in Athlone became
'isolated from the townspeople'.[56]

Recognition of the increased opposition informed the approach of
authorities to celebrations for the signing of the Peace Treaty in Versailles.
Plans were scaled back for the 'Peace Day' celebrations of Saturday 19 July,
and even then the 'formidable military display' was described provocatively
in the local press as 'what the entry might have been of Von Bissing into
a small Belgian town'. The army march through Athlone brought soldiers
past a large SF flag 'occupying a … very conspicuous position' over the river,
and numerous republican messages painted on walls. The nationwide anger of
army veterans was reflected in the question painted by local ex-servicemen:
'Ex-Soldiers of Ireland, you fought for Freedom, where is it?'[57] The parade,
greeted with 'curious indifference', terminated early in the morning (a move
which gained the army some kudos), so as not to interfere with markets.
'Disinterested Athlone' wrote the Sunday Independent, noting the absence of a
supportive demonstration from locals. McDermott-Hayes speculated on how
much more impressive the day would have been if not for the 'treachery of
British statesmen'.[58] The persistence of local enmity led the District Inspector
(DI) to recommend that no additional charges in connection with the May
meeting be pursued: 'It would be in the interest of the peace of the town if
the regrettable incident of 5 May … be allowed to sink into obscurity.'[59]

As the furore over the events of May died down in Athlone, the government began to institute measures to deal with the nationwide increase in
republican activity. New press censorship laws were introduced, but did
little to stop the Westmeath Independent from continuing to be 'hostile to the
government and openly sympathetic to Sinn Féin'.[60] The paper celebrated the
'more enlightened and far-reaching basis' of republican efforts, while repeatedly criticising Lloyd George's approach to Ireland.[61] Westmeath's SF activity
continued to centre on Athlone, with the release of Ginnell in September
providing a focus for celebration.[62] His liberation did not see him re-enter
Dáil Éireann however, as one of the 'key suppressive moments' of the period
saw the assembly proscribed.[63] The proscription came too late however; Roy
Foster believes that by September the 'institutions of the visionary republic
were able to take root'.[64] The creation of new departments continued, albeit
in a clandestine manner, and the suppression 'generally … to its [members']

advantage',[65] allowed ministers to roll out plans with even less input from other TDs or the wider SF party.[66]

Supplementary to the suppression of the Dáil was the proclamation under the Jubilee Coercion Act of a number of southern counties and an escalation in local raids.[67] The release of Seamus O'Meara and John Harney did provide reason to celebrate.[68] However, the refusal of the latter to rejoin the IV highlighted the toll that the situation was taking on some volunteers. Indeed, seized documents stated that 120 men had left the Athlone IV, and while the RIC cited the absence of a conscription threat as the main reason, the spreading violence certainly informed the decision of some.[69] Evidence from Knockcroghery, just north of Athlone, shows that IV numbers fell precipitously when it was made clear that they were to pursue Irish independence by military means.[70] The increasing levels of aggression led to local registrations of disgust, some directed at republicans.[71] The *Westmeath Independent*, speaking generally, noted: 'there is an unfortunate tendency amongst some of our own people to credit their own with everything that happened to the national disadvantage.'[72]

Increased British pressure reinvigorated IV operations, both nationally and locally, as documents seized from Seán O'Farrell in October proved.[73] The Athlone Brigade was reassessing Crown forces' strength, increasing the republican weapons cache, acquiring bicycles and planning for attacks on vulnerable rural barracks. Houses were raided for arms by republicans, who stated that most people were happy to hand over weapons upon request, the implication being that they supported the cause. Other avenues pursued for gaining arms included bribing soldiers, a common recourse for individual volunteers, who took advantage of the 'commercial proclivities' of certain army members.[74] Guns pawned by soldiers to local brokers also made it into the hands of the Athlone IV, though the spectre of entrapment did raise its head.[75] Late-night clashes between soldiers and civilians in early November appeared to presage an escalation in local tensions;[76] the Westmeath County Council, amongst others, condemned the escalating campaign of violence, a campaign for which some blamed Dáil Éireann, while others targeted revolutionaries outside of the executive's influence.[77] The increasingly tense atmosphere led Cecilia Daniels, probably in common with others of a similar vintage, to pine for times past: 'the Anglicised, Americanised Ireland of the twentieth-century is not Ireland at all.'[78]

Whatever the support levels offered to republicans by locals, it is certain that the spread in anti-government sentiment was causing much alarm at Westminster. Lloyd George had reneged on the promise to implement Home Rule after the end of the war, and while the measure was in any case unacceptable by late 1919, it was to construct a similar scheme that he established a 'Drafting Committee'.[79] The *Westmeath Independent* stated that the presence of the unfriendly figures of Walter Long, Lord Birkenhead, Ian Macpherson, Lord French and Edward Shortt on the committee was 'absurd … a more reactionary bunch more hateful … to Irishmen could not be assembled to play this ridiculous farce'.[80] Stricter enforcement of press censorship led the newspaper to become 'careful of its utterances' while still calling for 'another solution outside of the influence of the English Parliament'.[81] The committee's plan led to the drafting of the Government of Ireland Bill. Described by Lloyd George as 'Fair, just and right', McDermott-Hayes saw it differently: 'The Nation … split in two, the bleeding of Irish wealth and resources is to continue … in all matters of National importance England is to reign supreme.'[82]

The end of the year saw SF proclaimed, along with the IV, their dispatch carriers Cumann na mBan[83] and the Gaelic League.[84] The move was questioned by some observers, who argued that proclaiming SF was counterproductive given that it 'was a major party … [with] the moral support of the whole population'.[85] Its proclamation could lead to the radicalisation of moderates, who felt they were being targeted unfairly. The measure ensured that the number of affiliated SF branches fell further, exacerbating a trend that had become well established since the establishment of Dáil Éireann, which paid little attention to its grass-roots supporters.[86] It remained to be seen whether the 1920 local elections would reinvigorate a party considered, outside of election time, to have 'ceased to function as a mass organisation'.[87]

LOCAL AUTHORITY ELECTIONS AND LOCAL GOVERNMENT REFORM

The first local authority elections for six years in Athlone were of interest on a number of fronts. It was certain that the political makeup of the UDC was to be radically different. The Labour Party, which had refrained from contesting the 1918 election, was to compete. Increases in the electorate ensured greater participation, while the introduction of proportional representation assisted in guaranteeing a less predictable outcome.[88] The *Westmeath Independent* believed the election to be a 'golden opportunity' to fight 'economic oppression' and deliver a verdict on the Government of Ireland Bill: 'a sham … trotted out late in the day to quell … American hostility.'[89] The newspaper pushed for a SF vote: 'Their programme … should commend itself to every ratepayer who has his own and the country's welfare at heart'.[90]

However, the growth of Labour in Ireland since mid-1918 was to complicate matters.[91] As already noted, the foundation of the ATC heralded the start of a concerted Labour push in Athlone, a push that was greatly bolstered by the unofficial establishment of a local Irish Transport and General Workers Union (ITGWU) branch in October 1918.[92] The union's entry ensured that Athlone's workers had a strong national body to represent them (the ATC was more of a facilitator, with no remit outside of the town), and the large-scale 1919 May Day celebrations in Athlone showed quite clearly the growth in support for Labour.[93] The town's ITGWU branch's official establishment in October 1919, and the immediate enrolment of 560 workers (many of whom deserted English unions), clearly showed that Labour in Athlone was a force to be reckoned with.[94]

In relation to the local elections, it was obvious the many voters were supporters of both SF and Labour, perhaps most prominently Seán O'Hurley, who believed Labour to be 'one of the strongest forces in Irish Nationalism'.[95] Labour's growth had led O'Hurley's confidant Seán O'Farrell to forecast as early as February 1919 that 'they [Labour] will ... make a clean sweep of the UDC'.[96] ATC member J.F. Martin's assertion soon after that 18,000 people in the Athlone district were represented by the Council and affiliated unions showed the pool of voters on which Labour organisers believed they could draw.[97] The local press recognised the membership overlap at a large Labour pre-election meeting, which tellingly saw no attack on SF candidates or policies. The suppression of SF, and consequential small-scale canvassing (as opposed to Labour, which had an active ITGWU body of promoters[98]), meant that SF 'must rely on the discretion of the voters' to distinguish between the respective candidates.[99] So as to not alienate the followers of either camp, the *Westmeath Independent* told people to take advantage of the new system and 'vote for both'.[100]

Logically, the holding of dual membership implied compatibility between the two organisations' aims. The issues that SF intended to tackle in Athlone had much in common with those in which Labour was interested. The promotion of Irish goods, increased access to technical education, building labourers' houses, improved sanitation and lighting and the provision of a municipal library, among numerous other measures, were easily accommodated within the Labour manifesto. Nationally, SF's programme had Labour-friendly aspects, and Labour's supporters were considered quite willing to embrace a republic.[101] While their level of co-operation is difficult to pin down, it was not unusual for local agreement between the two parties to be hammered out,[102] something that was, at least to some extent, shown in Athlone.

Polling day on 15 January saw a higher than average 75 per cent turnout.[103] Results showed that, on the west side of Athlone, one SF, three Labour and five 'Ratepayers Representatives' candidates (mostly middle-aged local businessmen and former IPP supporters) were returned while one SF, four Labour and four Independents gained seats on the east side.[104] A quick overview appears to confirm a sound SF defeat and a good Labour performance; however, matters were more complex than this.

In St Mary's ward two successful 'Independent' candidates, Michael Hogan and Patrick Henry, were proposed by people who performed the same service for SF candidates. Henry, described as 'a very advanced Sinn Féiner' by the RIC,[105] had himself proposed another unsuccessful SF candidate.[106] The *Westmeath Independent* noted: 'Other … members elected were also Sinn Féiners, but … they went forward technically as "independents".'[107] Similar situations were seen elsewhere, as SF candidates had to be circumspect given the party's proscription.[108] Labour's strong result came on the back of securing pay rises for 600 AWM workers, and while there were individual rivalries, the press believed that SF and Labour would work well together.[109] The high-profile Labour organ, the *Watchword of Labour*, stated that there was a 'Red Flag over … Athlone' amongst other midland towns, but decried the selection of J.J. Coen as UDC chairman two weeks later.[110] By May the council had declared its allegiance to Dáil Éireann.[111]

While SF won more seats nationally than any other party, their success – controlling seventy-two of 127 urban councils – was not comprehensive.[112] The tendency for 'urban nationalism to be less efficiently organised and disciplined than rural nationalism'[113] has led to estimates of SF strength in urban councils as low as 30 per cent being promoted.[114] However, if Athlone's experience was not unique, it is probable that SF had greater influence on urban councils than is often stated.

Later in the year, the County and District Council elections, virtually uncontested except in Ulster, provided a clearer picture of local politics in the midland region.[115] The results saw Westmeath County Council dominated by SF and Labour[116] and Athlone RDC1 (Westmeath) and RDC2 (Roscommon) SF controlled,[117] with the Athlone PLG's new chairman, Seán O'Hurley, reflecting that body's republican roster.[118] After predicting a SF sweep in the elections, Thomas Moles, MP for Belfast Ormeau, cited the Westmeath result as proof of the sectarian bias facilitated by the PR system.[119] All of the bodies, following the UDC's lead, declared for Dáil Éireann over the next six weeks.[120]

While it appeared that republicans intended to make a clean break from the British administration by pledging loyalty to the Dáil, it also became apparent that some 'did not clearly grasp the implications of a shift of allegiance from Britain to the Republic'.[121] One of the main problems was that of finance. Both Westmeath County Council and Athlone PLG stated they would continue to deal with the British LGB, given that disassociation in the absence of republican funding would have rendered them unable to carry out their remit.[122] After the elections, widespread declarations for the Dáil led the LGB, in a move designed to impede the spread of further non-co-operation, to state that any body which refused to submit to an audit would not receive funding. The predictably negative reaction of local bodies (the UDC ignored the memo, the county council marked it 'read', while Seán O'Hurley of the PLG called it an 'insolent document') still did not precipitate total disassociation. O'Hurley believed the LGB and the British Government to be separate entities in certain regards; money was needed for ministering to the needy and if that money came from the LGB, so be it. He declared his intention to use LGB grants 'for the good of the people'.[123]

Whatever the logic applied to the situation by O'Hurley, the creation and growth of the Dáil's Department of Local Government (DLG) during the summer of 1920 signalled that ambiguous allegiances were not to be tolerated.[124] Prior to the elections the Dáil had not pushed for separation from the LGB, fearing that such a move would jeopardise the vote. However, post-election, this line was not maintained. Being linked to the LGB was a taint: William Cosgrave, the department's minister, equated acceptance of LGB grants with the taking of a bribe.[125] However, it became apparent that the efforts of 'local voters, ratepayers, vested local interests and entrenched councillors'[126] would complicate the transition.

Slowly, and in a piecemeal fashion, Athlone's local authorities began to distance themselves from LGB money. The UDC stopped communicating with the board in September,[127] refusing the LGB auditor access to its books.[128] The county council followed suit, though it had to shed staff to make ends meet, a common situation which created difficulties between its SF and Labour members who recognised, as Mitchell has noted, that 'essential agreement on the national issue did not necessarily mean agreement on social and economic issues'.[129] Council member Michael McCormack recollected that banks were unwilling to advance loans given the council's uncertain relationship with the LGB, something that also affected rates collections.[130] As in other regions, sureties from 'men of position' on the council sometimes secured loans.[131] Financial difficulties did lead to a wavering in the boycott of the LGB, with small attendances and the arrest of republican members skewing the voting balance in the council; however, one motion to consider reconnecting was struck out,[132] 'probably at pistol point'.[133]

Without doubt, the body with the most controversial approach to changes in local government was the PLG, whose atrocious finances limited its options greatly. Soon after the summer elections, both Roscommon and Westmeath County Councils stopped financing the Athlone Union, with the Guardians' money-saving efforts only delaying the exhaustion of funds until November when moves to petition the LGB began to be seriously considered.[134] Cosgrave saw Westmeath as particularly difficult to convert comprehensively and it appeared that stronger measures had to be deployed.[135] In March 1921 local authorities were informed that maintaining official communications with the LGB, except perhaps to confirm an authority's disassociation, was a treasonous act.[136] While the UDC and, to a lesser extent, county council were relatively safe from such a charge, confusion still existed; one local clerk incorrectly expostulated that his work on behalf of both Athlone RDCs (not in contact with the LGB[137]), and the PLG (which was), did not prejudice the directive.[138]

By the time the directive was passed, Athlone's Guardians, enticed by the dangling of grant cheques, committed themselves to communicating with the LGB,[139] though it should be noted that only three members were present for the vote, which was of dubious legality.[140] Tom Garvin has described the Athlone PLG as 'a doomed body if ever there was one', implying that it had an anti-republican constitution, for it 'remained loyal to the British authorities'.[141] DLG reforms were in the offing to disband the PLGs. however, while Garvin correctly asserts that the body's foreknowledge of its own demise informed its actions, to give the impression that it was stocked with imperialists is misleading. While the developing situation saw members such as O'Hurley disengage from public duties to preserve their liberty, it is unlikely that the SF-dominated post-election roster was changed to the point of adopting an imperialist outlook.[142] Instead it appears that members were fighting for short-term interests that they believed were compatible with the eventual creation of the republic.

DLG reforms envisaged the amalgamation of services to save the new exchequer money. One of the main cost-saving measures proposed was the closure of numerous workhouses and the consolidation of healthcare provision in county hospitals in fewer locations.[143] The Athlone PLG refused to attend the DLG Amalgamation Scheme meeting, justified in their belief (in common with other boards around Ireland[144]) that the amalgamation would result in Athlone losing out to Roscommon town and Mullingar.[145] Their non-attendance was lamented by Cosgrave, who censured them, while making it clear that the measures would be implemented regardless.[146] Letters were sent to Athlone workhouse, terminating the employment of all non-medical staff, and pressure applied by Ballymahon PLG appears to have had some role in convincing the Athlone PLG to attend the Westmeath amalgamation meeting.[147] The confirmation of centralised services in Mullingar and Roscommon led the PLG to issue an impotent resolution condemning both county councils for allowing Athlone Union to descend into financial chaos and, with much pathos apparent, refusing to recognise its own abolition.[148] Their protestations came to nothing. The move away from the British system of local government, an 'augean stable' of corruption, according to J.J. Lee, had a momentum far greater than the Athlone PLG could withstand.[149]

SINN FÉIN COURTS

While efforts to introduce new local government measures in Athlone were hindered, labours to establish the new republican judicial system gained greater support. Since 1917 SF had used 'Parish Courts' to settle land disputes and with the creation of Dáil Éireann, the expansion of that system was envisaged. First tested in west Clare in June 1919, a nationwide system of National Arbitration Courts[150] was drawn up and by May 1920 Athlone's 'increasing disinclination to recognise the administration of justice … under the English government' saw republicans institute initially unofficial efforts to join the move away from the British judicial system.[151] In the Athlone area, the new courts dealt mainly with land disputes linked to increasing agrarian agitation, what *The Irish Times* called a 'little land war in itself'.[152] Congestion due to low war-time emigration increased prices for produce (still reported at local markets[153]) and RIC desertion of rural areas had led to an increase in the number of disputes.[154] Newspaper reports vary as to the level of co-operation garnered in the early days of the courts around Athlone, with pictures of amenable farmers happily dealing with the new system contrasted with others of farmers abandoning lands as intimidation became too great, owners seeing little point in dealing with 'the one-sided legislation of the Republican Land Courts'.[155]

The first official republican court in Westmeath was held in Moate on 3 June 1920.[156] Its convening was proudly proclaimed by McDermott-Hayes as evidence that 'Ireland not only has the ability to govern itself but is … doing so'.[157] The influence of the courts spread quickly and while concerns were raised with regard to the objectivity and regulation of proceedings (some courts arbitrarily expanded their remit[158]), these were allayed as trusted solicitors such as H.J. Walker began to work with the system.[159] By July, local councils and the latest Athlone TTL[160] were using the courts to arbitrate in local disputes, with the *Westmeath Independent* indicating that they were operating well in the town.[161]

The move to the republican courts had an obvious effect on the British equivalent. A quiet July for the Athlone Petty Sessions was followed in August by a virtual absence of cases.[162] Replicated across the country, the move away saw the county council start to close 'British courthouses'.[163] Local magistrates disassociated themselves from the old system, resigning commissions as coercive government policies were condemned.[164] M.J. Lennon communicated to the Lord Chancellor that he could not deal with the 'grossly unfair manner in which the law has been administered in Ireland',[165] while M.J. Hughes was more resolute:

> To be associated, even in the trivial capacity of a magistrate with the present policy of government in Ireland would be a disgrace insufferable to anyone who has any claim to being regarded as an Irishman.[166]

The Westmeath CI recognised that most land disputes were dealt with by the republican courts and that generally 'people appear satisfied with their findings'.[167] Their success was partially ascribed by one unnamed TTL member to the fact that 'To-day the threat to call in the Volunteers is far more potent than the old call "send for the police"'.[168] Nationally the picture was similar, and though it was noted that on occasions IV enforcement led to disputes,[169] the fairness with which the courts generally operated prevented a dangerous land struggle hindering the Dáil.[170] Francis O'Connor noted that in Athlone 'only in a few cases had the Volunteers to enforce the [courts'] decision'.[171]

By September it was recognised by Walter Long that 'everybody is going over to Sinn Féin, not because they believe in it, but because it is the only authority in the country'.[172] Local accounts confirm that in Athlone the republican courts had supplanted the Sessions in the town,[173] with solicitors like Walker, Denis Hannon and Joseph Dixon dealing with them regularly. Athlone's move away from the British system was confirmed by *The Irish Times*, which stated that the RIC had abandoned attending court sittings, as the only people who showed up were the RM and court clerk.[174] One week after *The Irish Times* report, the *Westmeath Independent* confirmed the obsolescence of the Athlone Sessions: 'For the first time in many years not a single case was listed … Even the formality of opening the courthouse was not gone through.'[175] The Sessions continued to be advertised, though not patronised.[176]

Unsurprisingly, the British did instigate measures to counter the republican courts under the August 1920 Restoration of Order in Ireland Act

(ROIA), a rushed, poorly devised replacement for DORA. Operating as part of a nationwide effort, the third week in September witnessed a raid on the Athlone Courthouse where, symbolically, the republican courts had begun to operate.[177] Individuals were searched and those considered less of a threat were allowed to leave. Adjudicators Seán O'Hurley and Owen Sweeney were arrested, along with forty others including three solicitors and a *Westmeath Independent* reporter.[178] After an overnight stay in the army barracks most were released, with the exception of O'Hurley, Sweeney and Stephen McCrann UDC, who were accused of ordering the deportation of two ex-soldiers some weeks previously.[179] While all were eventually released, the raid succeeded in suppressing such courts in Athlone.[180] Seamus O'Meara stated that 'After the arrests ... no further Courts were held in the town; all sittings ... were then held in country areas'.[181] The suppression led to a fall-off in the frequency of their sittings all over Ireland; in many areas they were 'in a state of suspension'.[182] Those that were held operated in a clandestine manner, as British efforts drove the system underground.[183]

RECOURSE TO VIOLENCE

With the proclamation of SF and the IV in November 1919, it was certain that the government was adopting a hard-line approach to dealing with an increasingly disturbed Ireland. After the end of efforts for the 1920 local elections, republicans decided to reciprocate by engaging more frequently in violent acts.[184] Attacks on government installations increased as post office raids were added to those on police barracks, which first manifested around Athlone in February.[185] The cutting of railway lines and roads was carried out frequently, as were train raids, unsurprisingly common around railway hubs such as Athlone.[186] Westmeath received dozens of extra RIC men in March, bringing their local strength to the highest level seen in years. The additional numbers were deployed in the hope that criminal detections and convictions would increase. However, as Peter Hart observed: 'the police often did worst where they were strongest ... [due to] an uncooperative population.'[187] More ominously, Athlone was designated the regional depot for a new arm of the Crown forces, the Black and Tans.[188] Their initial introduction was greeted more with curiosity than fear, as it was reported that: 'Their quaint attire – khaki trousers and RIC tunics – attracted much attention.'[189] The Black and Tans (a name inspired by their uniform) were ex-soldiers who, the government hoped, could be more effective in fighting what was developing into a guerrilla campaign.[190]

Soon after their deployment the Lord Mayor of Cork, Thomas MacCurtain, was killed by members of the ordinary constabulary.[191] Described in the *Westmeath Independent* as 'the foulest murder that ever stilled a patriot heart', his assassination created another martyr and motivated yet more young men to join the republican struggle.[192] In the week following his death, raids were carried out all over the Athlone region,[193] one of which saw Seamus O'Meara rearrested.[194] Laurence Ginnell was also interned; however, as reported by the *Irish Bulletin*, he was 'broken in health' and was released three days later.[195]

Yet another change in the administration of Ireland in April 1920 highlighted the 'incoherence and vacillation'[196] of British policy, 'the failure to establish any unity of command'.[197] Sir Nevil Macready was appointed as Military Governor, with the resignation of Irish Chief Secretary Ian Macpherson, 'the greatest misfit of all the importations',[198] seeing the 'bluff and obdurate' Canadian Hamar Greenwood replace him.[199] Their instatement coincided with the republican campaign of burning abandoned RIC barracks, which were vacated as authorities consolidated their manpower. Athlone's two RIC stations, Brawney on the east and Fry Place on the west, received dozens of additional members from outlying regions,[200] with the *Manchester Guardian* telling of the 'massed police' in the town and the influx of constabulary families from isolated areas.[201] The large numbers meant, however, that houses 'hopelessly vulnerable against organised attack' had to be used to accommodate many of the men, who sandbagged windows in an attempt to provide some protection.[202] Brideswell, Bealnamulla, Lecarrow, Creggan and Corrowrey all saw their empty RIC barracks, 'no more than substantial houses',[203] destroyed, or partially damaged in early April, at Easter.[204] The burnings had the effect of promoting republican activity without much associated risk, boosting morale and allowing Brigade officers to assess their men for future missions.[205] Thomas Costello highlighted the propaganda value, writing 'it was gratifying to read in the daily papers ... the destruction of these enemy posts', while Seamus O'Meara stated that the burnings were 'staged more for propaganda purposes than ... military value'.[206] The 'burnt out shells' provided empirical proof of 'the collapse of Crown authority'.[207]

Unsurprisingly, the destruction led to a reaction from authorities, perhaps the most inconvenient aspect of which was the cordoning off of the town bridge, and interrogation of all who crossed.[208] Carts were searched and locals' social lives were regulated by the closure of the bridge at 10:30 pm. The *Westmeath Independent* sardonically assessed the army's actions:

Where once stood the famous Bridge of Athlone ... soldiers exercised
their bayonets on loads of hay and turf ... Who knows that the
'Rebellion' may not have been inside the hay and turf, and a great
and invisible battle fought without our knowledge which will yet be
handed down in song and story.[209]

The intensification of the republican campaign made members of the police
and army quite nervous, with the *Westmeath Independent* warning local
agrarian agitators (who had increased their efforts hugely as part of a national
'eruption'[210]), specifically cattle drivers, that they were risking their lives:
'Cattle-driving ... is no longer the exhilarating exercise it was, ... conducted
in perfect safety, and generally terminating with a month or six weeks in ...
jail.'[211] Indeed, one large-scale drive in Athlone had led to a Lewis gun (a large
stationary machine gun) being trained on the drivers, who were charged
down by soldiers and police.[212]

In early April, 100 Mountjoy prisoners went on hunger strike and in a
show of solidarity Athlone, and many other towns, observed a two-day
work strike during the middle of the month,[213] while also organising protest
meetings.[214] News of the hunger strike's end led to celebrations, described in
flamboyant terms (and a large font) by McDermott-Hayes:

... the Government ... beaten ... our countrymen ... rescued from
Death ... [a] victory of unparalleled importance ... Athlone went
mad with joy ... The procession again gave physical expression to
the pent-up feeling of the people ... one solid mass of ... humanity.
Athlone was speaking out its heart.[215]

Buoyed by the positive news from Mountjoy, republicans continued their
campaign and gained support in the refusal of rail workers in Dublin to
transport army supplies.[216] Local railway staff supported their colleagues, as did
the local press and political organisations.[217] Athlone's republicans continued
their escalating campaign, stealing £500 worth of petrol and raiding the
Athlone Inland Revenue office on O'Connell Street.[218] Initially targeted for
destruction during the Easter conflagrations when numerous other offices
were destroyed, surveillance delayed its targeting until mid-May.[219] Those who
carried out the attack destroyed specific files (leading to accusations of inside
help) before making a more general sweep. They avoided the neighbouring
Inland Revenue sub-office due to its containing pension information – such
targeting would have led to a loss of support.[220] H.J. Walker, an income tax

collector, resigned after the raid; he had remained taciturn in its aftermath
and wanted to remove himself from the line of fire.[221]

By mid-summer the confidence of local republicans appears to have grown,
despite continued Crown forces' raids and arrests,[222] while the populace
was ever more restive. In June the Westmeath CI stated that 'The spirit of
lawlessness has ... entered into every phase of life', with agrarian agitation
especially common.[223] Poor RIC morale continued, despite the efforts
of the new Chief of Police General Tudor, and the Athlone IV continued
to raid outlying regions with little opposition.[224] Indeed, many policing
duties were actually carried out by the IV, who had to fill the 'yawning gap
in ordinary law enforcement' precipitated by RIC withdrawal from rural
areas.[225] Investigating larceny cases and enforcing licensing laws were among
the many tasks performed by the 'Republican Police', whose efforts gained a
commendation from the Westmeath County Council.[226]

By July, the police noted that robbery, malicious injury, arson, kidnapping,
housebreaking, firing at a person and cattle driving were all on the increase
and of the few outrages reported to them, all were attributable to republicans.
In contrast, the *Westmeath Independent* stated that actual crime was virtually
non-existent; what were reported were breaches of unjust British laws, not
actual transgressions.[227] More RIC barracks were abandoned, even in urban
areas, with Brawney barracks vacated.[228] The CI for Westmeath stated that the
atmosphere was tense:

> Law abiding subjects were alarmed at the further evacuation of police
> barracks, but nobody dared assist the police ... even when outrages
> were committed on their persons and property.[229]

The ATC, which believed Athlone to be 'quiet and uneventful', complained
about the 'indiscriminate firing in the town' and the victimisation of locals
on the basis of military prerogative.[230] The charge of military indiscipline was
rebutted,[231] though the increased incidences of indiscipline on the part of
Crown forces led General MacCready to release a memorandum stating that
disorderly conduct would be punished.[232]

A greater sense of powerlessness began to permeate police reports as the
republican campaign gained momentum.[233] In Westmeath, the CI blamed
the daily newspapers for anti-Crown forces propaganda and noted that
'every effort is being made to destroy their [RIC] morale'.[234] Patrick Shea
ably described the dilemma faced by many RIC men, stating that their
political views often had much in common with those of nationalists (if not

republicans), but that, in his father's case, 'the practical problems of a middle-aged, kindly man with a young family and no alternative occupation' were too great to overcome.[235] The treatment his father received left Shea 'an uncompromising, unapologetic West Briton … to me every Republican was a gunman and the guns were pointed towards those I loved'.[236]

Regardless of the limited options, notices appeared more frequently in the press detailing the early retirement of RIC men.[237] Individual policemen became the target of republican ire as it was 'more potent … than abstract hatred of one's government',[238] and it was inferred in the *Westmeath Independent* that the local members increasingly felt more like part a foreign force, as English recruits replaced Irish retirees.[239] Reports emerged that 'the IV police are doing excellent work' around Athlone, especially in abandoned areas, which had seen an increase in crime.[240] Seán O'Hurley related to Richard Mulcahy that an Athlone RIC insider had made contact, and was quite willing to help persuade his colleagues to retire: 'An offer has come from a few Athlone men, who are still serving … [its] perfectly genuine … They can influence a very big number …'[241] The growing number of locally posted constabulary officers who were contemplating retirement was to grow as opposition to them in Athlone entered a murderous phase.

Up until the late summer of 1920, local republican activity was restricted to intimidatory activities and what were sometimes termed 'small jobs'.[242] The release by republicans of a 'War Map' in *An tÓglách* showed that Westmeath and Roscommon were by far the most active midland counties with regard to IRA[243] operations in July, yet violent encounters were scarce.[244] However, in late August an incident occurred that precipitated an escalation in hostility in the region. At 12:30 a.m. on 22 August Sgt Thomas Craddock was leaving the 'Comrades of the Great War Club'[245] on King St when IRA members James Tormey, Thomas Costello, George Manning and Brian Mulvihill, ambushed him, fatally wounding the sergeant.[246] Craddock's attempt to return fire failed, while a colleague – Constable Mahon – who was in his company, fled, pursued by Tormey, who was unable to apprehend him.[247] The republicans left the scene as members of the Crown forces arrived to render assistance to Craddock, who died of his injuries at one o'clock.[248]

Craddock's death was neither opportunistic nor random; he had been specifically chosen. One witness statement from the Bureau of Military History recorded that Craddock, who had been targeted before, was well known for accosting republicans, often putting a gun to their head to intimidate them.[249] He had received written threats against his life and, according to evidence supplied to his inquest 'entertained an apprehension of such a happening as has occurred'.[250] Seamus O'Meara stated that his murder was ordered by Michael Collins, who wanted to deal a blow to the Crown forces' intelligence network. Collins's main target was local Military Intelligence Officer, Captain Tully.[251] O'Meara believed that Craddock had to be dispatched first, given the sergeant's penchant for like-for-like policing:[252] 'If he was left alive we believed a lot of the town would be burned down.'[253] Craddock's killing, a very bold act (he was shot just 20 yards from the RIC station and fewer than 100 from the army barracks), was part of a more ruthless campaign adopted by the IRA where memos such as 'vicious RIC … to be shot' and 'all Black and Tans are to be shot on sight' were circulated in the hope that 'coercive terror' could be brought into play on the republican side, counterbalancing that already used by the Black and Tans, albeit not yet seen in Athlone.[254] Generally, IRA shootings in urban areas were rare. Augusteijn believes that 'vulnerability to police reaction' due to a higher concentration of RIC militated against urban missions, something with which Tom Garvin concurs: 'police supervision was probably more effective in the small town than in either the cities or the countryside.'[255] Craddock's killing was to be the only IRA assassination within the town's boundaries. His inquest found that his death was caused 'by a bullet wound inflicted by some person or persons unknown',[256] a verdict which further demoralised the local force. The DI appealed to jurors to have 'no sympathy with murder', but was unable to sway them.[257]

The fatal shooting was followed by raids the same morning and the declaration of one of the first curfews in the region on the west side of the town: 10:30 p.m. to 5:30 a.m.[258] Local garrison commander Brigadier General T.S. Lambert instigated the action under the ROIA, which allowed for imprisonment without trial, civilian courts martial, military inquiries into violent deaths and, most controversially, official sanction for reprisals against 'terrorists'.[259] The application of the act, along with the actions of both the Black and Tans and the recently deployed Auxiliary RIC,[260] caused controversy in Britain, where many did not agree with the government's Irish policy: as King George V put it: 'that in punishing the guilty we are inflicting punishment no less severe upon the innocent.'[261] The counterproductive approach saw 'moderate nationalists, initially inclined to condemn republican violence, [fall] silent when confronted with British reprisals'.[262] Counterproductively, ROIA focussed the minds of the IRA, assured them of the malignancy of British governance, and led them to reassess their strategies constantly, thereby creating better revolutionaries.[263]

The curfew led the military to reoccupy the town bridge,[264] with any hope of having it quickly rescinded dashed by the shooting of Constable Potter at

Kiltoom on 26 August.[265] The inquest verdict of 'death from a bullet fired by some person unknown'[266] pushed some of Potter's colleagues to instigate a reactionary hunt for the perpetrators, while it prompted three others to offer their resignations.[267] John Duffy stated that his refusal to partake in reprisals for Potter's death led to a shot being fired at him by a colleague, an incident that galvanised his desire to resign. The intervention of Michael Collins encouraged him to stay.[268] Men such as Duffy, though small in number, provided the IRA with invaluable information and were considered safe in their dual role.[269]

Tensions remained high with the curfew-free east side of Athlone heavily patrolled by soldiers, who conducted random searches.[270] In what *The Irish Times* described as a 'striking sermon', Franciscan friar Fr Columba tried to present the human side of the RIC, telling his congregation of a member who had cried during confession, fearing for his life, while already speaking of forgiveness for whoever might shoot him. Columba, following the line adopted by the majority of clergymen,[271] stated unequivocally that 'We cannot, under God's law, shed blood, even for the freedom of Ireland'.[272] The wider Athlone clergy issued 'earnest exhortations' to people to stay inside after eleven o'clock.[273]

RIC members in the region were so shocked and frightened by the shooting of their colleagues that they wrote a letter of complaint to General Tudor:

> We consider it is almost an impossibility to carry out our functions as a civil police force … The strain … is so great … our comrades … ruthlessly murdered and butchered by the roadside without getting a chance to defend themselves, … the boycotting and threats arraigned against us, … our families, our relatives and our homes … the agony of a suffering force cannot be much further prolonged … every day we are … more alienated … the moderate section of the community are so terrorised or apathetic that not … a voice of sympathy … comes from any side … The dead bodies of our murdered comrades are insulted, kicked and jeered … [274]

The letter also informed Tudor that the Irish members felt they were treated like traitors, while their British colleagues, though not well treated, did not have to deal with a similar level of opprobrium.[275] The letter may provide proof of the effect that, even while republican violence was not particularly common around Athlone at this point, 'individual actions on a comparatively small scale had profound effects on … morale'.[276] Mail stolen by the local IRA in train robberies revealed numerous letters to RIC men from their families, asking them to resign their commissions.[277]

Any hope of a softening in republican sentiment in Athlone receded with the news of Terence MacSwiney's deteriorating health as his hunger strike in Brixton prison continued. The Comrades of the Great War called for his release, while many of the town's shops (by now promoting a boycott of Belfast goods[278]) suspended trading for a period.[279] Masses were held, and MacSwiney's wife was sent letters of solidarity from the UDC, PLG and sympathetic locals.[280] McDermott-Hayes described both Hamar Greenwood and General MacCready as incompetent and bloodthirsty respectively, commenting that: 'A Nation, like an individual, is born in travail. Ireland will step forth from her chains through the labours of her MacSwineys.'[281]

News of MacSwiney's ordeal, allied with an obviously demoralised RIC, '[who had] relinquished ordinary police duty for some time past',[282] assisted the Athlone IRA in its efforts to improve its weapons cache. The houses of local unionists and military men, often seen as good targets for raids, elicited better weapons, with at least one machine gun purloined.[283] Raids on local post offices and postmen continued,[284] though fewer military communications were intercepted as the army began avoiding land-based conveyances altogether, using not only pigeons, but small planes which carried the most important documents.[285] The impunity with which local republicans were acting, allied with the numerous changes in Athlone with regard to courts and local administration, led the *Westmeath Independent* to state that 'England has less hold on Ireland today than … [at] any time since the Norman invasion'.[286]

In response to the IRA raids, the military began counter-raids during the second week in September, even taking weapons that were lawfully held, fearing that they would fall into republican hands.[287] In some cases, people were asked to sign a note averring that the military carried out their duties efficiently and with good conduct; most did without quarrel.[288] However, the efforts of the army to promote good relations were undone by the Black and Tans, who took up active duty in Athlone a week later. Saturday 25 September saw the Auburn Terrace and Arcadia areas of the town terrorised as weapons were seized (even those held by a soldier), windows smashed and a dog beaten.[289] With each incursion the raiders introduced themselves as Black and Tans, stating that they were there to 'give everyone a warning'.[290] In one case reported in the *Sunday Independent*, they assured a man, who was less than enthused by their visit, that they 'would not think a second about putting a bloody bullet through you'. The raids in an area which housed 'high-class industrial workers … many of whom were Protestant'[291] led Revd J.F. Anderson to demand redress.

Such indiscriminate attacks in an area unlikely to support republicanism may not have moved residents' support to the IRA, but it certainly would have moved it further away from Dublin Castle. The officer to whom the complaint was made stated that the raids were unsanctioned. He apologised, giving assurances that damage would be repaired.[292]

The incident was the first in a long list of Black and Tan outrages in the region. The penchant for members to drink excessively ensured that Athlone's public houses saw their fair share of drama as patrons were intimidated by promiscuous gun waving and, on at least one occasion, a grenade was thrown into a pub after two Black and Tans discovered that their bicycles had been stolen.[293] Attacks in south Roscommon saw the SF Hall in Cornafulla vandalised and suspected republicans subjected to mock executions while being forced to recite 'God save the King'.[294]

The deplorable behaviour of most Black and Tans[295] fouled the local atmosphere still further, as did Lambert's extension of the curfew to include the east side of Athlone in the first week of October.[296] Both the Westmeath and Roscommon CIs related that the measures led to a slackening in republican activity,[297] and they ordered the reinstatement of RIC foot patrols.[298] An influx of Auxiliaries into Athlone heralded an escalation in efforts to drive home the perceived advantage,[299] a move, that in combination with other efforts, led the Westmeath CI to state that republicans were 'becoming afraid of their own skins'.[300]

The *Westmeath Independent* continued to be highly critical of the activities of the Crown forces, with McDermott-Hayes consistently criticising their heavy-handed approach. Many within the Crown forces were greatly angered by his editorials and soon after the Auxiliaries were deployed in Athlone, they were assigned their first high profile operation: silencing the *Westmeath Independent*. At midnight on 17 October an attempt was made to close the region's largest newspaper when the APW was damaged. Thomas Chapman's wife, at home alone in the absence of her ill husband, was awoken by the noise of explosives being put 'through the roof and … five large windows', and ran from her adjacent house upon seeing smoke and flames.[301] On the street she encountered Auxiliaries, who impeded her attempts to elicit assistance from neighbours by firing into the air and shouting.[302] Despite the hazards facing those who broke curfew, help was eventually forthcoming and destruction was limited.

The *Freeman's Journal* described the dread of the night, while the *Irish Independent* recounted the 'reign of terror' and 'outbreak[s] of terrorism', detailing the partial destruction of the works. The story made numerous provincial papers and *The New York Times*,[303] while T.P. O'Connor raised the issue in the Commons.[304] McDermott-Hayes, writing the following week, pulled no punches:

> We blame and condemn the administration … which every day is reducing … Ireland to rotten degeneracy … There are so many appalling tragedies occurring … that to refer to such an incident as occurred to the works … appears … insignificant … it is not, [it] is an indication of the terrorism under which we live … [we] denounced the … misrule under which the county has been driven to the verge of madness and will aim at reflecting the opinions held by 90 per cent of the people in the [region]. There is no bravado in this. We know the danger in which our property stands.[305]

The same Saturday night saw Seán O'Hurley evade capture,[306] 'promiscuous rifle firing', the shooting of a terrier dog and numerous raids on local houses where threats were issued that republican family members were being targeted for execution.[307]

The actions of the Crown forces caused serious strain. The *Westmeath Independent* stated that any good feeling between locals and the army was now gone; 'the night … made hideous by the crack of the rifle fire … all felt that life and property was not worth an hour's purchase'.[308] The clergy did what they could to assure people that they were safe and spoke to the military, asking them to ensure that restraint was shown, not only to people, but also to the APW, where many earned a living.[309] General Tudor reassured Chapman's brother that the works would not be targeted again.[310]

Local republicans did not allow the actions of 17 October to go unanswered. The following day, Crown forces investigating rebel activities on some of Lough Ree's islands were attacked on the river at Coosan, leading to a number of injuries, one serious. Up to thirty IRA men took part[311] in the 'rushed, improvised affair',[312] which appeared somewhat peculiarly to have consisted mainly of attempts to sink the boat in which the Crown forces had travelled.[313] The decision not to directly target the soldiers, local army intelligence officer Captain Tully among them, may have indicated an aversion amongst the IRA men involved to such brutality.[314] The boat was brought back to the army barracks and when the injured soldiers alighted, a crowd that had assembled, having heard the gunshots, were rushed by Black and Tans, who had to be restrained by a military officer. Crown forces, RIC included, made for Coosan, where they torched the local temperance hall, fired randomly into houses and warned of later reprisals.[315] Brigadier-General Lambert informed his superiors that he expected more attacks in the Athlone region, but that the nervous tension engendered by the Coosan affair 'may be to [the army's] advantage'.[316]

The association of the RIC with the Black and Tans and Auxiliaries exacerbated the growing dislike for police in Athlone. Three submissions to the Bureau of Military History state that RIC co-operation with the groups in raids such as that in Coosan was unforgivable. The police 'acted as bloodhounds for this force [Black and Tans/Auxiliaries] and led them around to shoot their own kith and kin'; eventually 'there was a distinct barrier between them and the people'.[317] In counterpoint, Patrick Shea contends that most RIC members were honourable men, operating out of their depth, with John Duffy stating that co-operation was seldom whole hearted: 'Black and Tans were badly received by the old RIC … [who] hated the Tans to the end.'[318] Shea stated that the Auxiliaries and the Black and Tans were not 'prepared to be sitting targets' and had 'fewer scruples about seeking out … their enemies than those whose lives had been spent quietly in … small towns'.[319] The fact that the Black and Tans had 'no mental habituation to the methods and restraints of a civil … force, and no affinity with the populace'[320] meant that their role was never going to be conciliatory.[321] Richard Bennett has pointed out that the 'threat of dismissal … had no terror for … men who … joined … in an emergency and … were not embarking on a career for pension rights'.[322] The incidents of the October weekend contributed to the atmosphere of fear:

> … there was … considerable uneasiness … rumours were afloat. People were timorous … and slept in their clothes, fearing … they would be presented with the unusual and … serious. Many … left to take up temporary abode in the country or in … Moate and Roscommon … gloom and uncertainty … seemed to hang over our once quiet and peaceful town.[323]

The increasing number of raids and the violent activities of the Crown forces since the institution of ROIA meant that Athlone's IRA members had to adopt a different approach. Following the October order from GHQ, which had assessed the creation of such bodies for some months, a flying column or Active Service Unit was formed.[324] Usually made up of a dozen to fifteen full-time rebels, columns were designed to engage in guerrilla tactics on an ongoing basis. In Athlone the leader of the column was James Tormey, a 21-year-old farm labourer's son and ex-serviceman who was given the position, despite his lower rank in the IRA, due to his war experience.[325] The Athlone column, which usually consisted of fourteen men,[326] also included other army veterans, whose experience would have been useful in supplementing the efforts of Seamus O'Meara, a butcher, Thomas Costello, a shop assistant, and Dick Bertles, a carpenter.[327] The government had feared that the return of soldiers from the front would swell IRA ranks; however, only a small number joined, and 'most served as drill and ammunition instructors, or as flying columnists',[328] imparting a 'conventional tinge' to republican operations.[329]

From the thirteen who could be located in the 1911 census, it appears that the column's composition follows what Peter Hart has identified in his work on IRA social structure. All were Roman Catholic, with a median age of 23, which meant that most were probably unmarried, a common feature of column members.[330] The census relates that ten of the men came from farming backgrounds (mostly small farms), the most common origin of the IRA rank and file.[331] Of the remaining three, one was the son of a shopkeeper, another the son of a woollen mills operative and the remaining man was a carpenter's son. There were two sets of brothers in the column, which may indicate the powerful effect of familial involvement in republicanism that Hart has identified.[332] Of the twenty in total identified, three were resident in Athlone; seven came from districts bordering the town on the west, with the remaining ten coming from eastern districts.[333] Hart believes that guerrillas were disproportionately 'skilled, trained and urban'[334] and while it is certain that in some cases – Thomas Costello, for example – men left the family farm to take up employment in Athlone, they were not in the majority in the local column. Augusteijn's work in Mayo has shown an urban bias too.[335] However, information from the witness statements, five from column members, indicates a greater emphasis on both rural membership and activity.

Without doubt the most common offensive activity engaged in by the Athlone column was ambushing Crown forces on country roads. The first such engagement saw it attempt to overwhelm troops leaving Athlone on 22 October.[336] However, poor IRA intelligence, allied with their inexperience, ensured that the ambush was a fiasco. The engagement at Parkwood, near Horseleap, saw the IRA kill Constable Henry Briggs before the Crown forces forced them to flee.[337] The return to Athlone of the 'Tans, Auxie's ... generally the worst of drink'[338] saw them fire their weapons indiscriminately (an act which they had a penchant for, even at times injuring their own[339]), fatally wounding local councillor Michael Burke during a 'mad rush down Church St'.[340] Firing continued after Burke fell; it required the intervention of the military to subdue their notoriously ill-disciplined colleagues.[341]

The shooting caused dismay, even more so when Hamar Greenwood, in answer to a question from T.P. O'Connor in the House of Commons, dismissed the incident as a consequence of the situation in Ireland.[342] In what the *Connacht Tribune* called a 'Shock Doctrine', Greenwood stated that the Crown forces were defending themselves and that: 'It is inevitable that in the conditions prevailing in Ireland, the innocent should sometimes suffer for the acts of the wrongdoer.'[343] The contrasting verdicts presented at the inquests for the two men killed on 22 October highlighted where locals believed wrong was perpetrated. Despite entreaties from a HC,[344] no indictment was given in the case of Constable Henry Briggs, while Michael Burke's death was ruled to have been caused by a bullet 'unlawfully fired by one of the armed forces of the Crown'.[345] Members of the constabulary extended their sympathies to Burke's family and joined the 5,000 people who attended the councillor's funeral.[346]

The first incident involving the Athlone flying column led to an escalation in raids and arrests in the days that followed.[347] The raids were carried out against a backdrop of increased anxiety, not only due to Burke's death, but also that of Terence MacSwiney, who had died in Brixton prison three days after the councillor. The heightened tensions after news of MacSwiney's death led to the army being restricted to barracks from 5:30 p.m.,[348] with news six days later of the execution of IRA member Kevin Barry providing additional friction. Both deaths provided motivation to columns all over Ireland, including Athlone, which set about trying to improve its ambush tactics.[349] On 2 November the column wounded two officers and killed Constable Larkin, 'an Englishman in RIC Auxiliary', at Auburn near Athlone.[350] Again, not all went to plan as one their number, 17-year-old James Finn, was fatally wounded, possibly as a result of 'friendly fire'.[351] His body was seized by the Black and Tans and used as an exhibit to entice people in the area to impart information about the incident.[352]

Cllr Michael Burke, Athlone UDC. (*WI*, 11 March 1922)

A second less-than-successful outing soon after reflected the trend of poor column performance experienced in most areas. The ambush was stymied by what was a common difficulty: the failure of home-made bombs to detonate.[353]

The failure to destroy the APW at the first attempt, allied with the increased coverage in the *Westmeath Independent* of Crown forces' outrages and denunciation of the government after the death of MacSwiney, made a second attempt inevitable. One day after the Auburn ambush, an additionally motivated group retargeted the works, this time proving more proficient in the deployment of incendiaries.[354] Described by *The Irish Times* as 'one incident in a night of terrors', and in the *Irish Bulletin* mockingly under the heading 'Restoration of Order', the second conflagration ensured that Ireland's largest provincial printers would remain closed until February 1922.[355] One hundred people lost their jobs and Athlone lost its only weekly newspaper, with knock-on effects for both its readership and historians of the period.[356]

Questions were asked about the arson in the Commons, with Joe Devlin, T.P. O'Connor and a number of British MPs demanding answers from the Chief Secretary.[357] Greenwood gave the impression that he was not particularly interested and issued what was by now a default answer deployed when questions were posed on the disreputable acts of the Crown forces:

> Exhaustive inquiries have been made by the police, who are unable to obtain any information as to the perpetrators … people who are in a position to help the police … will not do so. I can find no grounds whatever for the suggestion that the outrage was committed by the armed forces of the Crown.[358]

O'Connor demanded that the Crown forces, whose actions he called a 'seditious conspiracy', be made accountable for their actions in Athlone: 'the bankrupting of local bodies to bayonetings, bullets and incendiarism in order to create in Ireland … solitude and call it peace.'[359] Much laughter was heard when Greenwood suggested that Ireland was 'the freest country in the world for journalists'.[360] The *Freeman's Journal*, which itself faced much opposition from the British authorities, covered the burning of the works, amongst other attacks on the press, under the editorial banner 'The Sword is Mightier; Militarism abominates a free press'.[361] Numerous questions posed by MPs[362] increasingly concerned over the Irish situation[363] elicited no more detail from Greenwood, with Down South MP Jeremiah MacVeigh sarcastically stating in reply to the Chief Secretary's assertion that no civilians or police were out at the time of the blaze: 'Perhaps it never happened.'[364] Joe Devlin's logical

The remains of the Athlone Printing Works after the second attack by the Crown forces. (AHL)

query on how it could have happened if only the military were out led Greenwood, by now perhaps the only prominent defender of the Black and Tans and Auxiliaries, to state that 'these so-called reprisals [happen] because the community will not denounce murders'.[365] Thomas Chapman's son Ivan issued a strident rebuke to Greenwood's assertion that no civilians attempted to quench the blaze, a reproach that was printed in the *Freeman's Journal* under the heading 'Greenwood Legends – Another Denied'.[366] Harrow MP Oswald Mosley asked why Tudor's previous promise to protect the premises was not carried through. Greenwood replied that it was 'obvious … that it is extremely difficult to protect all persons and all property in Ireland at one and the same time'.[367] The farcical nature of Greenwood's investigations was confirmed when Joe Devlin requested details as to who was conducting them. Greenwood's reply that it was 'Officials responsible to me and this House' led Devlin to retort, 'Are those the same gentlemen who burned the premises down?'; the *Irish Independent* noted that 'no reply was given'.[368] The press contribution to 'stiffening the resistance amongst Irish moderates' led to the suppression and attempted closure of numerous national and provincial newspapers.[369] A number of other printing works in Galway, Tralee and Leitrim were targeted around the same time as the Athlone plant.[370]

The APW was not the only Athlone premises not to survive 1920 as Crown forces tried to flush out IRA members. Laurence Maguire, who had 'no connection with politics', was beaten and robbed by the Black and Tans, who then burned his public house after three IRA men hid there in the aftermath of a skirmish in the centre of the town.[371] Efforts to intimidate locals continued in the run-up to the second anniversary of the Armistice on 11 November. A sign was erected, replete with a 'Cross bones and skull … drawn roughly on the upper left-hand corner',[372] issuing threats against shop-keepers who refused to observe the day:

> Shopkeepers of Athlone are hereby ordered to close their premises on Armistice Day, November 11, in honour of the fallen heroes of the Great War and the police murdered in Ireland. This motion applies to all business houses and factories; any failure to comply … renders destruction of said premises.
>
>   Black and Tans[373]

Such demands were seen elsewhere (Tralee, Longford and Carrick-on-Shannon, for example), and were in stark contrast to the observations scheduled for Britain, where a ten-minute stoppage was envisaged.[374] The threat was heeded by many businesses, including the Athlone Woollen Mills, even though Brigadier General Lambert tried to allay fears by erecting 'official' signs repudiating the threat.[375] His actions were lauded by the *Manchester Guardian*, which stated that 'small towns … have good cause to fear the tyranny of the Auxiliaries'.[376] In the Commons, Hamar Greenwood told T.P. O'Connor that the sign was taken down by the RIC upon its discovery, and Joe Devlin that he, Greenwood, did not believe the sign had been erected by Crown forces.[377] Devlin, exasperated by the Chief Secretary's attitude, asked him 'amidst laughter, if he believed anything'.[378]

The impunity with which the Black and Tans appeared to be acting in Athlone saw numerous robberies on houses, shops and pubs, with an alarming increase in the number of mock executions, house burnings and even evidence of a sexual assault on a teenage girl.[379] British authorities, who believed they were forcing republicans back, were reminded of IRA capabilities with the killing of fourteen of their operatives in Kilmichael, County Cork on 21 November, while the Bloody Sunday reprisal shooting of fourteen civilians in Croke Park escalated tensions to levels previously unseen. Internment became widespread and support for the republican cause was reinforced.[380] In Athlone the absence of a local newspaper and the infrequent delivery of dailies due to rail disruption saw one visitor besieged by locals when they saw him with a copy of the *Freeman's Journal* the day after the Croke Park attack.[381] Increasingly frayed nerves led to the driver of a backfiring train being accused of attempting to shoot an army sentry, while different sections of the Crown forces also exchanged fire on at least one occasion, a sure sign of stress.[382] In November, the town hall was raided and numerous separate arrests were made, while the IRA targeted the Athlone RIC barracks in reply, but were again frustrated by faulty mines.[383]

By the end of the year the Westmeath CI summed up that the 'Sinn Féin movement is very strong beneath the surface', with communications avenues used by Crown forces regularly disrupted.[384] His Roscommon counterpart believed that 'the firmness and resolution of the Crown is commanding the respect of even the IRA', though murders still occurred.[385] Republicans continued to meet in markets and at mass (eventually arrests were made of people leaving services[386]), though consistent British intelligence failures ensured that the details were almost never known to either the enlarged RIC or army, the former increasingly shunned and the latter increasingly isolated in their barracks.[387]

December saw the extension of martial law to parts of the south and south west as violence levels increased. The same month also saw the official sanction of reprisals and the destruction of a large area of Cork city by Crown forces.[388] The demand for a republican arms surrender and Lloyd George's public (as opposed to his earlier private) excusal for Crown forces' outrages accompanied political overtures, namely the Government of Ireland Act.[389] It was rejected by republicans as too little, too late, and in Athlone the efforts of the IRA were directed towards silencing supposed local informers, a group that played an important role in the Crown forces' intelligence operations.

The first known incident of an alleged British informer being executed in the Athlone region occurred in Coosan on 30 December 1920, when James Blagriffe was dragged from his house and shot. The IRA left him with six wounds, attaching a sign which read 'SPY' to his shirt.[390] Blagriffe, an ex-soldier, had previously been on friendly terms with republicans, allowing SF to meet in the room above his lodgings, where the 54-year-old lived with his wife and children.[391] Rumours of a move to join the RIC precipitated his execution.[392] Soon after Blagriffe, another ex-soldier, Martin Heavey from Brideswell, was removed from his home by masked men and not seen again,[393] with a third ex-serviceman named Maher from Irishtown executed and buried some weeks later.[394]

The arrest of seventeen IRA members[395] and the death of James Tormey in an ambush at Cornafulla,[396] west of Athlone, in February cooled the heels of local republicans somewhat. His death saw indiscipline levels rise, as hackles were raised and Seamus O'Meara resigned as OC, fearing that the local IRA would be damaged by the unilateral acts of some members,[397] something often lamented by GHQ and used by historians to question the level of actual control exerted by headquarters on provincial brigades.[398] Few thought that the Dáil controlled the IRA, even after it took responsibility for the republican militants' actions in March, while suggestions that the IRB were directing activities have been generally discounted both locally and nationally.[399] O'Meara's replacement, Thomas Costello, had to deal with Richard Mulcahy's annoyance at their organisation:

> … your recent reports … I found … very disappointing … I should … like to have a report on the work of each particular Battalion in your area; its command; what training they are actually doing; and what definite military work you expect to get out of them within the next two months.[400]

The move of command from O'Meara to Costello came at a time when authorities, tired of ineffective raids,[401] instead instituted large-scale roundups in the region, which 'led to further polarisation', as targeting 'every male who could walk'[402] worsened the sense of persecution.[403] The roundups exacerbated conditions in the barracks as detainees overloaded the jail's capacity, necessitating ad hoc conversions of less secure parts of the complex to compensate.[404] The lull in local IRA activity, during this period at least, has been justified by O'Meara on the basis of creating a false sense of security for Captain Tully[405] and another attempt was made on his life in early April. Yet again he was warned of the ambush and evaded Thomas Costello's efforts: 'Have made several attempts to get Capt Tully … and failed. Attempted ambush in Ballykeeran, Athlone, two lorries expected … didn't arrive. Men withdrawn after day's wait.'[406]

The repeated failures to kill Tully were ascribed to the efficiency of his personal intelligence network, but could easily have been due to the inefficiency of the IRA's 'far from faultless' equivalent.[407] It is probably no coincidence that just one week after Costello's failure, yet another supposed informer was executed. Thirty-five-year-old single farmer (he managed his family's three farms) and Protestant ex-soldier Robert George Johnson (Johnston) was found dead with 'Spies and Traitors beware, IRA' pinned to his shirt.[408] He was considered one of Tully's most important informers and had confirmed his guilt, at least in the eyes of republicans, by never staying at home.[409]

Historians have often questioned the ability of the IRA to identify spies and it is likely that many executions were carried out in the absence of any sort of due process. Peter Hart contends that the targeting of ex-servicemen, especially if they were Protestant, was disproportionately common as they were considered more likely to be loyalists and consequently more likely to inform.[410] However, more recent reanalysis of his work would appear to question his findings, especially those findings which suggest that the religion of those targeted was the primary motivation for their executions.[411] Statistically the shooting of four ex-soldiers in the Athlone district, an area with so few fatalities, perhaps twelve in total), would appear to show an IRA bias towards targeting such men. Religion, it appears, played little or no role in the shootings, as of the four killed, at least three were Roman Catholic. In relation to intelligence gathered on the men, Michael McCormack 'was never satisfied [Blagriffe] was a spy', while his namesake Anthony believed that 'in the real sense [Blagriffe] was not "a spy"'.[412] Local battalion captain Henry O'Brien participated in the execution of Johnson with no knowledge of his guilt and was 'just one of a party ordered to shoot him'.[413] The number of executions caused some republicans concern, with one memorandum to Michael Collins stating that British propagandists, who increased their efforts in late 1920, made 'mendacious, but damaging use' of news of such executions.[414] Richard Mulcahy, somewhat unconcerned by the killings, saw the general activity of the Athlone IRA as a positive step:

> I was glad to see … that you are getting a little work going. The GHQ Inspecting Officer's report indicated that you had much good material … I rely on you to see that all work done … is done in a systematic way … spasmodic work … cannot be of any permanent use … There is a wonderful development of strength and spirit all over … Do not let Athlone Brigade lag behind … [415]

Johnson's assassination was but one of numerous incidents that occurred with greater frequency around the Easter period. A skirmish at Clonown saw four shootings, as well as an 'Extraordinary Fight' (hand-to-hand combat), between members of a RIC cycle patrol and republicans.[416] Another soldier was shot at Kilgarvan, east of the town, and by May even Hamar Greenwood was admitting that rebel activity was rising.[417] The Westmeath CI reported:

> … it is a matter for congratulations that it [the situation] is not worse, as the policy of the IRA is obviously to bring matters to a head … beyond doubt an effort is being made to galvanise to rank and file into greater activity.[418]

The prohibition of markets and fairs, which was first seen nationally in March,[419] reached the east side of Athlone in May. It was hoped that the inconvenience caused would entice the public (whom the Westmeath CI believed to be 'sick', but afraid, of Sinn Féiners[420]) to provide information on republicans who had begun to damage infrastructure ever more frequently in early 1921.[421] The *Freeman's Journal* related news on the repetitive cutting and fixing of roads around Athlone as the 'Comedy of the Trenches'.[422] The most high-profile attack on a military officer came in June, when Brigadier General T. Stanton Lambert, OC of the 13th Brigade, was shot in the neck at Glasson after attending a tennis match at Moydrum Castle, Lord Castlemaine's residence.[423] The *Irish Bulletin*, which was usually reticent about publishing news of IRA violence,[424] stated it was:

> … another instance for the military terrorists to realise the situation they have themselves created. They have declared a state of war and imagine that the war so declared can be confined to one side, their own.[425]

Lambert's death made the front page of *The New York Times*;[426] the reprisal that followed, informed by misinformation, destroyed the village of Knockcroghery County Roscommon, 8 miles north of Athlone.[427]

THE GEOGRAPHY OF REVOLUTION

The killing of Lambert was the last organised fatal attack on a member of the Crown forces during the War of Independence in the Athlone region. While high profile, it was unusual in an area which had seen few fatalities on either side. Attempts were more common certainly, with defective weaponry or poor intelligence often leading to a mission's failure, and it appears that Athlone's situation in Westmeath and Roscommon allowed for a greater experience of violence and its consequences than was seen in other towns, especially outside of Munster. Peter Hart's work on the geographical spread of revolutionary activity from 1920-21 rates Westmeath's IRA violence as second highest in Leinster, behind Longford (which exhibited levels on a par with those of Munster counties) and Roscommon as the most violent in Connacht.[428] Hart shows that work completed by Tom Garvin underestimated IRA violence levels in both counties relative to others further north, an underestimate also seen, albeit more egregiously, in the work of Michael Hopkinson. Hopkinson quotes from the 'historian of the conflict in that area' to substantiate an assertion that there was virtually no IRA activity in Westmeath. The work of the historian in question, Oliver Coogan, makes neither claim nor effort to assess Westmeath's contribution.[429]

There are many reasons posited to explain the varying levels of IRA violence and activity encountered in different regions. Some argue that individual personalities drove the conflict. Dan Breen in Tipperary, Tom Barry in Cork and Seán MacEoin in Longford are three of the most prominent and while David Fitzpatrick discounts the idea of such men being essential to promoting revolutionary activity, Joost Augusteijn's and Marie Coleman's work would indicate otherwise, as would Townshend's observations. In Athlone the absence of such a figure could explain much.[430] Seán O'Hurley participated in no violent activity in the region, as repeated incarcerations had damaged his physical health. His replacement, Seamus O'Meara,[431] was considered an ineffective leader by some under his command,[432] and it is probable that he too doubted his leadership qualities, for when he superseded O'Hurley he asked Michael Collins to reinstate the Corkman.[433] O'Meara's resignation saw Thomas Costello voted in to the position of OC, which showed him to be at least a popular choice amongst his fellow IRA members.[434] He had little time to make his mark however, given that he was OC for less than three months, but if he had serious leadership qualities, it is fair to assume that they would have manifested earlier, perhaps precipitating an earlier submission of O'Meara's resignation, and forcing the conflict in the area along at a faster pace.

Another common reason, or excuse, for a low level of activity offered by Brigade leaders all over Ireland was that the topography was not conducive to guerrilla tactics. Both GHQ organiser Gerald Davis (who believed the local brigade was beset by bad luck[435]) and Seamus O'Meara cited the boggy land and virtual absence of cover in the region as impediments to staging successful ambushes.[436] Work carried out by Peter Hart tends to rebut claims of republicans being handicapped by landscape, and provides statistics from topographically diverse regions that exhibited similar levels of violence, despite republicans from those areas feeling similarly discommoded by either the presence or lack of mountains, bogs or forests.[437] Urban topography probably had little role to play in the virtual absence of republican violence in Athlone itself; the massive military presence covering a land proportion far greater than in other urban areas such as Cork or Dublin, which exhibited high violence levels,[438] undoubtedly helped limit such activity. It is probable that the perception of the rural terrain presenting difficulties limited IRA enthusiasm for staging ambushes; however, tactics could always be altered to take such difficulties into account if motivation was high enough and if other factors, such as community support and good weaponry, were favourable.

It appears that around Athlone the other factors referred to above played varying roles in the promotion of republican violence. Historians often contrast urban enmity towards the IRA with rural support, believing that towns, especially garrison towns such as Athlone, were invariably hostile to militants. Gerald Davis presents a corroborative view, stating his preference for the local rural populace. However, his views should be judged cautiously, given both his rather public socialising with the Black and Tans and the fact that his hotel was quite close to Irishtown, the local Mecca of anti-republican sentiment.[439] Other witness statements make no mention of urban hostility or indeed greater rural support, and if newspaper reports are reliable, it appears that Athlone's populace, if not well disposed towards republicans, were certainly not openly hostile to individuals and were generally supportive of their cause, if not perhaps the methods the IRA deployed.[440]

Weapons were undoubtedly a difficulty, with virtually all the witness statements making repeated references to the absence of good armaments throughout the conflict, with even more frequent references to the scarcity of ammunition.[441] Again Hart believes that, even with more basic weapons, activity could be maintained. Preferences for rifles (which allowed for long-distance shooting) were understandable. However, yet again, if properly motivated the IRA could change tactics to maximise the resources to hand.

TRUCE

Obviously, all wars have a life span, and by June 1921 that between Ireland and Britain was coming to a conclusion. While earlier efforts were made by politicians to seek an accommodation between the two sides, it was not until King George V delivered a motivational speech promoting peace at the opening of the northern parliament on 22 June that the prime minister made more resolute efforts to seek a truce.[442] Militarily the increasingly protracted and expensive conflict seemed destined to escalate upon the almost certain non-convening of the southern parliament. In the absence of a parliament, martial law was to be extended nationwide, a move the authorities recognised as counterproductive.[443] Consequently, negotiations between republicans (who, without any contest, gained 124 of the 128 seats for the southern parliament[444]), and the British Government began in earnest, as it was recognised that the existing stratagem was not effective.[445]

Somewhat ironically, with news of peace overtures came an escalation in the activities of both local republicans and Crown forces; old scores needed to be settled before restrictions were imposed and enforced.[446] On 2 July a final unsuccessful attempt was made on Capt. Tully,[447] while the following day, in answer to the torching of houses in Coosan and Mountemple by the Black and Tans the night before, the IRA targeted Moydrum Castle, the residence of Lord Castlemaine, burning it to the ground.[448] Just hours later Creggan House, home to a retired soldier, Captain Davin, was also robbed and burned.[449] The fact that these actions, amongst others, were perpetrated so close to the start of the truce did not leave the Westmeath CI feeling optimistic:

> … newspapers inaugurated the spirit of the truce some days before it came and military orders inaugurated it two days before … the IRA kept up the attempt to murder 'til the strike of noon on [the] 11 – from this an ill augury is drawn.[450]

The ill augury predicted did not manifest immediately. The lifting of the curfew was, according to the *Freeman's Journal*, greeted with general calm; processions were held, Irish songs were sung and bonfires were lit.[451] *The Irish Times* reported that in Irishtown, those associated with the Crown forces 'danced outside their doors with joy'.[452] In a widely reported occurrence, called a 'remarkable incident' by the *Irish Independent* and a show of 'true bravery' by the *Southern Star*, IRA men saluted British soldiers who were leaving the town in trucks; the soldiers reciprocated, waving handkerchiefs as they drove away.[453] Road and rail lines began to reopen.[454] The appointment of IRA man Fintan Murphy as District Liaison officer[455] marked the beginning of efforts to co-ordinate and monitor the observance of the truce in the region.[456] The Auxiliaries began to leave Athlone in late July and early August, either recalled to England, or let go from their posts.[457] The staging of cultural, sporting, commercial and social events was also slowly reintroduced.[458]

The Westmeath CI maintained his gloomy outlook regardless; the truce had, he believed, pulled the rug out from under his men.[459] He did admit that attacks on the RIC had stopped and news of the police and IRA co-operating presented promise.[460] However, he also felt that 'enemies of the Republic have little security'. The republican court system resurfaced, and the CI stated that non-violent republican activity 'has increased … in spirit the truce is not observed at all', something that numerous articles in the Fintan Murphy Papers bear out.[461] In contrast, his opposite number in Roscommon was more sanguine. Few complaints reached his desk, the truce was adhered to, and, in his opinion, surprise was the most common emotion: 'The general feeling, not admitted by Sinn Féin … is that the government offer exceeds anything expected and will … be accepted'.[462]

Around Athlone IRA membership swelled as the threat of engaging in dangerous manoeuvres disappeared and news of initial treaty negotiations between the Irish and British emerged in August. The Westmeath CI attested to an influx of new recruits,[463] estimating a four- or five-fold increase,[464] with Cumann na mBan also gaining.[465] Its reported five branches at Athlone, Coosan, Summerhill, Drumraney and Tang may have accounted for up to 123 individuals soon after the truce was enacted.[466] The Bureau of Military History witness statements vary as to the state of the Athlone IRA at the time of the truce. Henry O'Brien believed local republicans to be almost overcome, with few weapons and a scattered local presence. Francis O'Connor believed that the long days of summer meant that by the time of the truce, 'the initiative could be said to have passed to the enemy'.[467] He does qualify his remarks to state that morale was high among his comrades; a sentiment similarly mentioned by Patrick Lennon.[468] The number of men still active is difficult to ascertain accurately, but the Miltary Service Pensions Records may provide some indication of improbably high upper estimates of those who maintained their positions at the time of the truce. On 11 July 1921 records contradictorily show that 901 men comprised all ranks of the Athlone Brigade: 359 in the 1st Battalion, Athlone; 184 in the 2nd Battalion, Drumraney; 347 in the 3rd Battalion, Summerhill (a total of 890).[469] It is probable that just a small percentage of this total were truly active participants by the late summer of 1921, with little to indicate that a vigorous organisation still existed in the Athlone region. Nationally the situation appears to have varied from place to place, though 'Collins and Mulcahy took a more pessimistic view than did most of the field commanders'.[470] Hart and Fitzpatrick agree more with Collins and Mulcahy, and while Augusteijn believes somewhat implausibly that an escalation in IRA activities was possible, it is certain that most in Athlone were relieved to see an end to the hostilities that had blighted their lives.[471]

Former Allies, Future Foes: Civil War

While it is certain that change was in the air in the aftermath of the truce, the details of that change were considerably less clear. The post-truce environment had led to a resurgence in republican activity in and around Athlone as many began to view the establishment of a new state as the inevitable outcome of the cessation of hostilities. Many local republicans and quasi-republicans jostled for position, hoping for preferential treatment when the decision on appointments to the new state's bodies came about. However, the negotiations that were undertaken in London to address the Irish question were to result in the signing of a treaty that caused a schism in Irish republicanism, one greater than any witnessed previously. Those who had hoped for a quick return to a life of relative normality were to have their hopes dashed; instead, they were to be subjected to yet another conflict, one that was to divide families and create animosities that were to fester for decades to come.

As the autumn of 1921 wore on, the signs that republicans were asserting themselves in the Athlone region continued to multiply. The Westmeath CI's previously noted pessimistic outlook appeared well founded, as local solicitors abandoned the crown's judicial system and dealt almost exclusively with the proscribed republican equivalent. The republican courts were initially held in St Mary's Hall, though they soon switched to the town courthouse, with the UDC adopting a resolution which stated that no person was to take a case before the 'enemy courts'.[1] The presiding judges were all prominent local Labour Party men and SF members (the local branch had undergone reorganisation in August[2]). Among these judges were James Campbell (butcher and SF branch president), Owen Sweeney, Peter Malynn, Henry Broderick and Patrick Mackin. The court, as in late 1920, ruled mainly on local disputes over debt or land ownership and, when necessary, used the IRA to enforce rulings. In one case where a woman was evicted from a house after she refused to pay rent, the *Irish Independent* described how the 'Irish Volunteer Police' removed her on the orders of the 'Irish Volunteer Court'.[3] Such orders against civilians were breaches of the truce, though no action was taken by the RIC, whose powers of compulsion had been greatly diminished.

It was reported that younger SF members were revelling in their perceived impunity; they believed that the efforts of Irish republicans had ensured that they now had 'England on the run'.[4] The largely groundless optimism of many of these young men, and the egregious arrogance that flowed from this, led them to transgress repeatedly, not only the terms of the truce, but also civil law. In Athlone some stole bicycles and automobiles, engaged in loutish drunken behaviour and intimidated landowners. There were also reports of assaults.[5] Similar conduct was exhibited nationwide and in an attempt to curtail it, republican leaders set up a disciplinary system; IRA members who transgressed first received a warning, followed by a demotion and eventually dismissal if they did not reform.[6] In a speech delivered in the Fr Mathew Hall during October, Seán MacEoin warned that all IRA men needed to maintain discipline in case the fight against the British had not actually been won.[7] The RIC did intervene on occasion in cases of public disorder, most prominently when members of the local IRA (operating as the Republican Police) attempted to arrest people for being drunk. Indeed, in one instance an RIC officer actually threatened IRA men with his pistol demanding that the republicans leave the intoxicated person in their (the RIC's) charge.[8] Generally the constabulary were directed to coexist with the Republican Police and were only to engage them if they overstepped their remit of 'looking after Irish Republican Army personnel only'.[9] The reinterpretation of that remit by IRA members meant that conflict between the two groups was inevitable. In some regions, republicans who had scores to settle and felt assured of their impunity, attempted to get away with murder,[10] and it appears that Athlone's republicans were similarly quite willing to exact revenge on those who had previously been their enemies. Perhaps the most prominent example was the abduction of three former British Army soldiers: Patrick Coffey, Joseph Coffey and John McDonagh. Liaison Officer Fintan Murphy, working on information provided by the RIC, requested that the IRA provide him with assurances that the men were not going to be harmed.[11]

British Army soldiers in Athlone were understandably jittery during this transition phase. A number had gone 'missing' from the local barracks since August 1920, the inference being that they had been killed by the IRA, though desertion could not be ruled out.[12] An attack on an Athlone-based officer, Captain Kane, in late November, confirmed that such men were still considered targets by the IRA and could not afford to let down their guard.[13] The local UDC sent a letter to the Garrison Adjutant when it became clear that increasingly paranoid soldiers were harassing virtually everybody who came close to the Union Workhouse, where many army men were still billeted. In one case they actually fired a shot at a man who was a good distance from the building, engaged in rather unthreatening activities. The Adjutant agreed that the truce should be fully observed and cautioned his men to ensure that this was the case.[14]

Apart from the instances of score-settling, the IRA also engaged in more down-to-earth activities intended to assist the organisation in becoming better established. Members began to seek financial assistance in Athlone, some going door-to-door requesting funds for the nearby Lisanode training camp. On 28 October a meeting called by Thomas Costello, still the OC of the 1st Division of the Athlone Brigade, heard members identify potential sources of funding. Former flying column member George Adamson was present in full IRA uniform when it was announced that publicans were to be taxed, on the basis of their valuation, for the upkeep of the local division. Needless to say, this provoked a negative reaction from some public house owners, who were well represented in the audience.[15] Attempts to garner funds through this type of pressure were not sanctioned by higher authorities within the organisation (indeed, they were explicitly prohibited), though the rush of power that many of the IRA men felt after the truce led them to believe that the inactive civilian populace (who, in their opinion had done little to end British rule) should, by rights, support them, Ireland's heroes.[16] Cecilia H. Daniels highlighted how the intoxicant of victory had greatly inflated the ego of one of the local IRA commanders:

> He is having a high old time round about here. Balls and all kinds of enter-
> tainments given for him, where he makes speeches and tells his audience
> what a hero he is, what he has done and what he is going to do!!![17]

Additionally she spoke critically of those (especially de Valera, whom she described as a 'Yankee-German Jew'), who were trying to create the new government. She termed them 'too low, too ignorant' to do so and stated that:

> The quicker England make a crown province of it [(Ireland)] the better.
> I am tired and sick of it all, and I do so long for rest and cannot help
> feeling the disgrace of living in such uncongenial surroundings.[18]

Despite Ms Daniels' misgivings, the new SF regime did attempt to implement some of the provisions made in their manifesto. Adhering to one of the oldest SF objectives, local members promoted the purchase of Irish goods, and monitored Athlone's shopkeepers' continued boycott of stock from Belfast. The local IRA wanted all shop owners to display a sign stating that no Belfast goods were being sold. However, the low level of co-operation, despite warnings on non-compliance, led to some establishments being subjected to republican hostility. In one instance, John Parson's boot shop at Victoria Place was entered by three men, purportedly IRA members, who pressurised customers to go to the Connaught Boot Shop, 'where you will get Irish goods'.[19] Confusingly for the shop owner, another delegation from the Athlone IRA returned two days later to apologise for the incident, stating that it was an unauthorised intervention. The same shop had earlier drawn the ire of local Labour organisers who '… dragged [the employees] over the counter before'.[20] It is possible that in Athlone, where the *Voice of Labour* believed there were 'a lot of slackers',[21] some Labour supporters were also trying to force their agenda, using the IRA's reputation to their advantage. Other unauthorised interventions were seen in the town, with a rebutted request made by IRA men for the loan of motorbikes from Poole's garage eventually seeing the vehicles purloined.[22] Also, the unpopular local landowner, Lord Castlemaine, had another of his properties set alight (he had been granted £101,359 in compensation for the loss of Moydrum Castle[23]); this time it was his Rent and Estates offices in Athlone. The two-storey structure was reportedly destroyed by IRA men from Tubberclair, an area in which many of his tenants resided.[24]

The increase in lawlessness caused considerable concern. Steps needed to be taken to ensure that a better organised and more disciplined military structure was put in place to regulate IRA activity. National reorganisation of army structures started to roll out, and in the case of Athlone, the most obvious example of the desire to institute reforms was Seán MacEoin's acceptance of command of the local IRA in the first week of December.[25]

MacEoin's instatement came at a time when the negotiations on the Anglo-Irish Treaty were well advanced. Locals had been kept informed about the progress of negotiations by both himself and Harry Boland,[26] yet it was obvious that neither man (nor indeed, Dáil Éireann, SF or the IRA[27]) was conversant with the direction in which negotiations were heading. After the initial round of talks stalled in August, a second round was convened in October, where Irish negotiators (most prominent amongst them Arthur Griffith and Michael Collins[28]) faced a British team that was heavily influenced by Tory opinion and consequently unsupportive of the Irish desire for a republic. By the time of MacEoin's appointment, the provisions of a treaty had been decided, with the Treaty itself signed on 6 December 1921.

The Treaty did nothing to undo the 1920 partition of Ireland, although provision was made for a three-member boundary commission to be presided over by a British Government-appointed chairman. From a republican point of view, the fundamental objection to the Treaty was its failure to deliver an all-island republic, or even one comprised of the twenty-six counties. Two other objections were the maintenance of three British naval bases in Ireland and, perhaps most significant, the requirement that all members of the new Irish parliament take an oath of fidelity to the British monarch.

De Valera expected the Irish delegates to submit a final draft of the Treaty to the Cabinet in Dublin before it would be signed. They failed to do this, submitting to threats from Lloyd George that their immediate assent to the British terms was required if full-scale war with Britain were to be avoided. De Valera, professing surprise and resentment, had to be dissuaded from having the delegates arrested on their return from London. Instead, he and his cabinet colleagues, Cathal Brugha and Austin Stack, publicly disowned the Treaty, making a major political division in the ranks of SF inevitable. Harry Boland initially supported the agreement. However, as he became better acquainted with its contents and the conditions under which it was signed, he too began to campaign against it vigorously.[29]

On the military side, it quickly emerged that there was strong opposition to the Treaty, particularly in Dublin and among IRA units in Munster, which had been the most active and effective region during the War of Independence. The members of the these units saw the Treaty as a betrayal of the republic which they had sworn to defend in 1919. Some saw the signing of the Treaty, given its provisions, as confirmation that Ireland's freedom was a domestic British issue, a cowardly admission that the country was still subordinate to Britain.[30] In other areas divisional commanders led their units in support of the Treaty, hoping that it could facilitate much of what they had fought for. This split in the IRA, to a greater extent than the political schism, was what would eventually bring about the Irish Civil War.

Reaction in Athlone to the signing of the agreement came quickly, most prominently from Seán MacEoin, who issued special orders to his men in regard to their plans for celebrating its signing. On 9 December he reaffirmed a directive that those under his command were '[not to take] part in any jubilations over the reported peace', to maintain strict discipline and not to indulge in alcohol or other energy-wasting activities.[31] MacEoin, a firm supporter of the Treaty, needed to have a reliable cohort of men under his command;

he recognised that tensions precipitated by the signing of the Treaty may have required the new state's army to adopt a different role than that previously envisaged. The Athlone UDC petitioned the constituencies' TDs to vote for the agreement, for in doing so, 'they will be carrying out the wishes of the overwhelming bulk of their constituents'.[32] For the local authority to make such an assertion less than a month after the Treaty was signed may appear like a premature step, yet it has been noted that even anti-Treaty TDs did accept that the next best gauge of Treaty support, the 1922 general election, was likely to confirm this view. Indeed many of them saw little point in appealing to their electors given the strength of the support for the Treaty they encountered over the Christmas recess. Instead, they set about ignoring the democratic process altogether, convinced that the very process which brought about the victory of the republican mandate in 1918 and 1921 had been fundamentally tainted by the signing of the Treaty.[33] The opposition to the Treaty voiced by South Roscommon TD Harry Boland was supplemented in inimitable style by his 1918 election running mate Laurence Ginnell. Ginnell condemned the agreement, stating that it had been negotiated under duress and was therefore not a free choice for the people of Ireland.[34] Local septuagenarian Cecilia H. Daniels may have captured some of the confusion surrounding the fractious reaction to the measure when she noted:

> … it is quite unknown if there will be a Free State as the Republic has the money and all the young men. Affairs are still very unsettled and there is every indication of much misery when the Sinn Féin party breaks in pieces.[35]

Further evidence of the advanced nationalist schism came quite early in the new year, as two important votes were taken. First, the IRB narrowly came out in support of the Treaty after persuasive arguments were made by Michael Collins, Seán MacEoin and others.[36] Second, and most importantly, a slim majority was also seen in the passing of the Treaty in Dáil Éireann on 7 January when just seven votes (sixty-four to fifty-seven) separated the two sides. Athlone UDC may have been pleased by the result, yet the walk-out staged by de Valera and other anti-Treaty TDs must have been of concern. The new editor of the recently reopened *Westmeath Independent*,[37] moderate nationalist and Irish speaker Cathail O'Tuathail, wrote of his support for the Treaty, and struck a pragmatic tone, possibly in the hope that others would adopt a similar viewpoint: 'Though absolute separation has not come as yet, still we can truly say that everything it was possible to wrest from England has been gained.'[38] He gained support from the local Roman Catholic clergy, who not only promoted acceptance of the agreement but, as ever, attempted to mould the opinions of their flock in such as way as to convince churchgoers that acceptance of the Treaty was already assured, despite much evidence of dissention.[39] A provisional government, with Arthur Griffith as president and Michael Collins as chairman, was established on 14 January, and was, despite the refusal of republicans to recognise its legitimacy, seen by many as the representative government of Ireland.[40]

Regardless of the opinion held about the outcome of the Dáil vote, as the provisions of the Treaty came into force, positive developments were witnessed. Locals were relieved to see the Black and Tans leave the barracks in Athlone during February 1922, as preparations for a full-scale British Army withdrawal followed. By Wednesday 1 February, all of the non-Irish regiments had been sent '… for the other side of the Channel'[41] and the 200 ancillary staff in the barracks had been served notice of their redundancy, with the fixtures and fittings inventoried in preparation for an auction.[42] Though bemoaned by *The Irish Times*, which saw the departure of the British from Athlone as economically and socially damaging,[43] the departure of 'small batches' of soldiers who left almost daily during January was not regretted by most townspeople. The *Freeman's Journal* relates that their replacements began to muster in the town later that same month, and greatly impressed all who surveyed their manoeuvres.[44] The transition period saw British Army soldiers stay behind the barrack walls, though reportedly not due to fears of violent encounters:

Of late the occupants seem to have become possessed of that 'holiday feeling', and are to be seen in the barracks, standing in groups … discussing the impending departures … a scene reminiscent of a 'break up' of school holidays.[45]

The impending full evacuation of the barracks led locals to turn their thoughts to the future use of the massive site. Many rumours circulated, one of the most popular being that a large American manufacturer was interested in constructing a factory on the land. While a few possibilities were floated, the car manufacturer Ford being the most prominent, the local press confirmed that there had been no attempt by any concern to purchase the land. Instead, remaining quite conservative (and, it turned out, correct) in its predictions, the *Westmeath Independent* believed that a portion of the land would be earmarked by Dáil Éireann for the construction of new housing schemes, while the greater part would act as a command centre for the new state's army.[46]

Despite such positive developments, it was apparent that tensions surrounding the Treaty were growing. Occasions such as the commemoration of James Tormey's fatal shooting at Cornafulla may have seen the coming together of both pro- and anti-Treaty factions, yet the speech by pro-Treaty George Adamson regarding 'the wonderful change [that] has taken place' may have sounded hollow to many among the 1,000-strong crowd, which not included only local IRA members but those of the anti-Treaty Cumann na mBan and Fianna Éircann.[47] The early stages of the electoral campaign for the new twenty-six-county parliament for which the Treaty allowed began soon after and contributed to the emotive atmosphere, as each side lambasted the other. At a meeting of the ATC, it was decided that the body was to go out of its way not to alienate either side. The Council members wanted a quick transition so that the exceptionally high local unemployment levels and extremely low dole payments could be addressed. The editor of the *Westmeath Independent* warned against moves towards civil war, stating that any military conflict between the two camps would only delay the British departure.[48]

The local SF branch members were also quite worried about the split in the party at national level. Though they did not envisage civil war, speeches delivered at a committee reorganisation meeting in the week before the evacuation of Athlone barracks did highlight their concern. Long-time SF member Owen Sweeney asked both pro- and anti-Treaty members to remember their common heritage and equality of sacrifice over the previous number of years:

> If unfortunately there should be a split in the country let us never forget that we are Irishmen. No matter what we have achieved or can achieve [we] can do more danger to the cause than we can ever hope to accomplish for it by descending to personalities. I say this much: that no man has a right to say that he is a better republican than another … [49]

While it is certain that the branch had members both for and against the Treaty, evidence of a split in the opinion of the local branch members was not reported. The newly elected chairman, Seán O'Hurley, spoke vigorously for the agreement, while the absence of his short-term predecessor, Conor Byrne, may have been indicative of dissent. Most at the meeting agreed that unity of purpose was most important, and it was proposed that the Roscommon side of Athlone should establish a separate SF club to ensure that a comprehensive canvassing campaign could be planned for both sides of the town for the upcoming election.[50]

The last day in February saw the most tangible example thus far of the Treaty's provisions in Athlone. Following on from earlier withdrawals at smaller barracks in Mullingar[51] and Longford, the evacuation of Victoria Barracks in Athlone on Saturday 28 February was a truly impressive occasion.[52] The UDC declared the day a public holiday and requested that all businesses close.[53] Describing the town as *en fête*, the *Irish Independent* celebrated the redesignation of the 'Symbol of Tyranny', describing Seán MacEoin as 'a second Sarsfield'.[54] The local press heralded the changeover as the move from 'Khaki to Green', the removal of 'the buttress of English power in the Midlands and West'. The editor proposed that the occasion was proof of the sense of the Treaty:

> Is this not enough in itself to commend the acceptance of the Treaty to the electorate to know that through its instrumentality the 'mailed fist' has been removed from our country? Yet it is but one thing among many: Finance, Education, Public Services, all are in our hands. Are we going to fling them away? Are we going to invite the English army back again to our Barracks? God help Ireland should it ever come to that.[55]

The event itself was on a considerable scale. Starting at six o'clock in the morning, the remaining British troops began to leave the barracks in formation. Over 120 vehicles removed supplies by road, with much of what remained leaving by rail via the adjoining MGWR station. Later in the morning hundreds of IRA members began to arrive in the town, amassing in Church Street, with brigades representing Beggar's Bush (the new pro-Treaty army headquarters[56]), Longford and the IRA's 3rd Brigade of the 1st Midland division. By eleven o'clock the scene had been set for the formal handover and Commandant General MacEoin TD along with Divisional Quartermaster Colonel Commandant Cooney, went to the barracks to finalise the change. Estimates put the crowds who turned out at 20,000, with pictorial evidence showing throngs of people choking the streets of the town. The Athlone Pipers' Band, accompanied by roughly 100 Marist pupils decked out in skullcaps, badges and green sashes, led a procession of IRA men west across the river towards the barrack entrance, while simultaneously, the remaining British troops left the barracks, marching in the opposite direction. Anthony Lawlor, soon to be MacEoin's second-in-command, stated that the British soldiers did not meet the eyes of the IRA men as they passed, believing them to harbour a bitterness towards the Irish.[57] The *Manchester Guardian's* correspondent, former IPP MP Stephen Gwynn reported otherwise, stating that

the barracks was 'handed over in all friendliness',[58] and as the British passed
the IRA at the Provincial Bank on the eastern end of the bridge, an 'epoch
marking' scene was witnessed by the townspeople, whose cheers echoed
around them.[59]

In the barracks itself, the solemnity of the occasion was observed.
The handover by Colonel Hare of the British Army to MacEoin at twelve
noon allowed for the entry of the marching IRA columns, reportedly 600
men in all, as well as a large number of civilians, to whom the Commandant
General made his first speech as OC of the Athlone barracks:

> Athlone had all our hatred and our joys, and we look on it with pride.
> We had hatred for Athlone because it represented the symbols of British
> rule and the might of Britain's armed battalions … Athlone today for
> Ireland and for the Midlands, from this day forward shall not represent
> the monument of British tyranny, but it will be a guarantee to the
> people of Ireland of their freedom, a guarantee to enable them to live in
> peace and prosperity and progress.[60]

After this address the public were asked to leave and interest shifted to the
castle for a flag-raising ceremony.[61] A problem was encountered when it was
discovered that the British had cut down the flag posts prior to their departure,
though the intervention of a local man, who rigged a pole from the mast of
his fishing vessel, allowed the ceremony to continue and the Irish tricolour to
be raised. *The New York Times* reported that 10,000 people cheered as the flag
made its way up the mast,[62] while afterwards members of SF and the UDC
both addressed MacEoin, congratulating him on his efforts and voicing their
support for the Treaty. MacEoin's 'act of supreme moral courage' evidenced in
his affirmative vote for the agreement was lauded, for it had helped ensure 'the
surrender of this citadel of oppression'.[63] A rather more prosaic scene greeted
the final withdrawal of Crown forces from the town two weeks later when the
RIC handed over their last station at Fry Place.[64]

Soon other Treaty provisions began to manifest in Athlone. The republican
court system began to move from being de facto to de jure,[65] while many
local men made their interest in enlisting in the Civic Guard or the National
Army known to the new authorities. Their clamour for positions disgruntled
anti-Treaty IRA veterans, who believed their eagerness showed that pro-Treaty
supporters were more concerned with gaining employment than with the
profound message of the men of 1916.[66] In an attempt to force their agenda,
the anti-Treaty side, headed (politically at least) by Éamon de Valera, set about

Images of the
British Army
departing
Athlone for
the final
time on 28
February 1922.
(AHL)

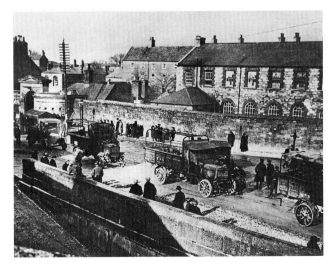

Marist Brothers' School pupils provide Seán MacEoin and the IRA with an honour guard as they pass by Athlone Castle. (AHL)

co-ordinating their opposition. The SF *Ard Fheis* of the 22-23 February saw much expostulating by both sides, and ended in a decision to avoid a vote on the Treaty and postpone the general election for three months.[67] It was hoped that the delay would allow for more negotiation between the two Irish factions, yet it was to become apparent that military activities, rather than discussions of the Treaty or de Valera's alternative, Document No. 2, would prove decisive.

A national convention held on 26 March saw de Valera build on his St Patrick's Day speech, which outlined the impending threat of civil war.[68] The pro-Treaty Minister for Defence, Richard Mulcahy, had given permission for the convention, then prohibited it when his colleagues voiced their unease.[69] It went ahead regardless, and anti-Treaty soldiers and supporters heard resolutions passed demanding that recruitment for both the Beggar's Bush force and the new Civic Guard cease. Seán MacEoin was in Dublin for two days around the time of the convention, discussing its implications with Michael Collins and Mulcahy.[70] He, like his colleagues, must have been concerned by the anti-Treaty side averring that their supporters comprised the vast bulk of recruits in the army, and that it was they who were incontestably the army of the Irish Republic, despite Mulcahy's obvious efforts to form a separate force.[71] The convention additionally saw the IRA (a term henceforth associated with the anti-Treaty side) establish a sixteen-man 'Army Executive', repudiate the authority of the Provisional Government and promise to promote the view that the IRA had won the right to create a republic and that no treaty could undo that. Anti-Treatyites soon established *Cumann na Poblachta* (Republican League), a body charged with organising speaking tours to encourage support for their position and candidates at the impending election, which, if no accommodation between the two sides was reached, promised to be a fractious affair.[72] Their intransigence angered many in Ireland; not just Treaty supporters, but also those who had no desire to see a return to violence. People who had been ambivalent about the Treaty came out in support of it; despite its limitations, they would 'vote for peace rather than for IRA warrior rhetoric.'[73]

The fallout from the convention registered quickly for both Athlone and MacEoin. During MacEoin's absence, two companies of soldiers (one from Athlone, the other from Leitrim) commanded by convention attendee Commandant Patrick Morrisey, attempted to seize the Athlone barracks for the anti-Treaty side. Morrisey supposedly harangued Col. Commandant Anthony Lawlor, MacEoin's Adjutant, for his abandonment of the Republic, while Lawlor's address to Morrisey's men saw him deprecate them and their views. MacEoin's return coincided with an attempt by the anti-Treaty men to seize the barrack armoury, which was being stoutly defended by a small number of pro-Treaty soldiers headed by Lawlor. MacEoin's intervention, a demand delivered vituperatively that the tussle end and the men fall in, appeared to defuse the situation. MacEoin's own testimony shows that he was not at all sure his intercession would have been sufficient to halt the attempted incursion: 'Thank God they fell in, and then I knew I could hold the Barracks in Athlone for the elected Government of Ireland.'[74] Morrisey's refusal to submit to the authority of the Provisional Government saw the general rip 'the Sam Browne from the shoulder of his Brigade Commandant ... [and order] him pushed through the gate'.[75] MacEoin then addressed his men, calling on them to respect their commission, and like so many others before him, called on them to remember Sgt Custume's sacrifice in 1691, a sacrifice MacEoin commemorated in his renaming of Victoria Barracks as Custume Barracks.[76]

Unsurprisingly, the failed attempt to seize the barracks was to be but one of numerous incidents that were to highlight the growing animosity between the two sides. Commandant Morrisey and Capt. Kennedy, another convention attendee, organised an anti-Treaty parade in Athlone for soldiers who wished to show where their loyalties lay, and gained a large degree of support, according to Morrisey's testimony, from 600 local soldiers.[77] Many men departed Custume Barracks to follow Morrisey to the Royal Hotel in the centre of the town, where a small number of anti-Treaty men had been residing since mid-March.[78] When MacEoin heard of the move he set about trying to ascertain their intentions, fearful of having to deal with an entrenched enemy so close to his headquarters.

When questioned, the officers in the hotel iterated that their allegiance lay with the IRA Executive and not with the Provisional Government, which they believed to be masquerading as Dáil Éireann.[79] Somewhat impotently MacEoin suspended those involved, including Col. Morrisey, who quickly issued a statement to the *Westmeath Independent*, affirming the group's allegiance to the Republic and Army Executive:

> I, Col. Commandant Patrick S. Morrisey, appeal to all citizens of Athlone for the same support ... they have hitherto given in carrying out the work of the Brigade and maintaining law and order ... I also wish to inform ... that we are supported in our action by the officers and men of the Athlone Brigade IRA.[80]

MacEoin quickly set about replacing the officers who had departed, appointing George Adamson as Morrisey's replacement at the rank of Acting Brigadier. Col. Commandant Lawlor issued a statement that all officers who refused to obey MacEoin had no authority in the Brigade area, were to be treated as civilians and could not levy charges for goods or services. Morrisey, who incongruously stated that MacEoin was 'a better Republican than he ever hoped to be',[81] called on the breakaway group to continue to respect civil law, not force their views on locals and, perhaps most importantly, not foment bad feeling with the men who remained in the barracks.[82] While Lawlor noted that most of the men who broke away were sincere in their views, he also feared that 'there was a danger of the rough element outside the ranks of the IRA taking advantage of the times by committing provocative acts or victimising the citizens'.[83] This fear played on the minds of many in the Provisional Government too, who recognised they had to quickly reacquaint both soldiers and civilians with what they saw as the duty of a rightful government: to impose law and order.[84]

Michael Collins travelled through Athlone in the same week that Morrisey issued his statement and was greeted by a large crowd at the train station.[85] Seán O'Hurley addressed him and, in common with many others all over Ireland, stated the faith he had in Collins' ability to derail moves towards internecine conflict and push ahead with the implementation of the Treaty:

> We pray you now exert all your great abilities and noble qualities to consummate and crown this magnificent and monumental work for Ireland by bringing all Irishmen together again in a common bond of unity, friendship, and patriotism.[86]

O'Hurley's call was an echo of those heard from members of the local clergy. Canon Crowe of St Peter's allied himself not only with all other Athlone priests in his support, but also with four-fifths of the nation's rank-and-file clergy and the entirety of the Church hierarchy[87] when he asked the anti-Treaty men to respect the Provisional Government, 'who spoke for the people',[88] and for 'bravery in peace'.[89] Fr Chrysostum of the Franciscan Friary warned of the 'greatest of all national dangers from within – the danger of national dissension'.[90] Other clergymen set about assisting in attempts to reinvigorate the Athlone GL (it had fallen away in 1920), believing that the study of the nation's language could be a pacifying influence, moving people away from conflict.[91]

Unfortunately, all of the efforts to deflect both sides from the path of conflict proved ineffective. In Athlone the escalation in tensions between the two camps came quickly when, on Sunday 9 April, General MacEoin ordered that the Royal Hotel (which now also accommodated a number of anti-Treaty soldiers from Kilkenny[92]) be vacated.[93] The order to evacuate was issued by Col. Lawlor to the acting OC of the troops in the hotel, an officer named McGlynn, who refused, stating that the Army Executive was the only authority they recognised. Lawlor arrested McGlynn after he exited the hotel to deliver the demurral, a move that saw Captain Thomas Hughes, the next in command of the hotel troops, refuse to leave the building. At twenty minutes to three that afternoon, soldiers from Custume Barracks massed in front of the hotel, which its residents quickly set about barricading. Nearby houses were evacuated and news of the stand-off quickly reached the nearby Franciscan Friary, from where one of the friars, Fr James, took it upon himself to make his way to the scene to act as mediator, initially telling both sides of the terror permeating the town as a result of their actions. His efforts eventually saw a parley called,[94] with the subsequent negotiations leading to the hotel's evacuation and McGlynn's release. While the *Irish Independent* reported that the IRA men 'marched good-humouredly away',[95] it appears that MacEoin saw the incident as the start of the civil war.[96] This opinion may have been bolstered by news of an influx of additional, heavily armed IRA men the day after the stand-off:

> ... the townspeople were congratulating themselves on having escaped the consequences of a bloody collision between brother-Irishmen, but the arrival ... of ... troops acknowledging the ... Army Executive ... equipped with all the appliances of war again created an atmosphere of uneasiness.[97]

The arrival of the extra IRA men soon saw the Royal Hotel reoccupied, with additional accommodation seized in rooms above the adjacent Sweeney's bakery and Heavey's grocery.[98] All three buildings were barricaded and 'prepared for defending'. In response, the army commandeered Egan's and Boyd's shops, as well as the house of H.J. Walker, all on the opposite side of the street.[99] Again the clergy intervened, and while Michael Hopkinson believes that the Athlone priests did little more than temporise,[100] it appears that the ministrations of Fr James, Fr Chrysostum, Fr Daly and Fr Lennon were of greater substance than that as they, along with Peter Malynn, yet again brought both sides to the table. Seán MacEoin and the newly arrived Comdt. General Fitzpatrick held three hours of talks in Malynn's house, communicating via telegraph with their respective headquarters and eventually an agreement was reached. The clergy spent some time afterwards going to shops and houses requesting that people stayed indoors, while the army set up a checkpoint at Dublin Gate Street, just a few yards west of the Royal Hotel.[101] The standoff was widely reported, with the *Westmeath Examiner*, *Connaught Telegraph* and *Nenagh Guardian* describing it as the first real manifestation of the danger of the Treaty-inspired schism.[102] The *Southern Star* went a step further, stating that the armed conflict that was threatened in Athlone 'may have been the beginning of civil war'.[103]

'Athlone [barracks] stayed uneasily in MacEoin's control'[104] as quiet prevailed for a short period soon after the incident, largely due to the death of APW owner Thomas Chapman. Respected by both sides, Chapman's death may have assisted in providing the time necessary for tension to diffuse somewhat, while his funeral saw a 2,000-person cortège clog the town's streets.[105] Both factions saluted his hearse as it passed them, aware of the great efforts he made to assist SF over the previous five years.[106] However, the lull was short-lived, and any relief that may have been felt amongst locals in the aftermath of the second agreement was probably undone on 13 April, when the IRA occupied the Four Courts in Dublin.[107]

Increasing levels of conflict in Dublin after the taking of the Four Courts were accompanied in Athlone by the shooting of the first high-ranking member of the National Army, the newly promoted Brigadier General George Adamson. On the morning of 25 April, Adamson, along with a number of other officers, had set out to investigate reports of a suspicious car, which they located and removed to the barracks. When they arrived it was noticed that not all of the men had returned and Adamson, along with three others, proceeded back into the town to search for the missing soldiers. After questioning a man they found loitering in the Irishtown area, they were set upon by a number of individuals who had apparently been lying in wait. Adamson and his men were

quickly overpowered and disarmed, with the brigadier general unceremoni-
ously shot before the assailants fled. The commotion led to a crowd gathering,
reportedly first among them Gen. MacEoin. Adamson was carried to a nearby
residence after being examined by a local doctor, who confirmed that the
wound was fatal. The last rites were performed before he was transported to
the barracks, where he died at ten o'clock the same day. His body was placed
on public display and the tricolour that fluttered over the castle was lowered
to half-mast. A few days later, the Athlone Labour Party led a demonstration
through the town against militarism, while soon after that, Athlone hosted yet
another massive funeral procession.[108]

Needless to say, Adamson's death engendered strong emotions amongst
his friends and colleagues. It was reported that MacEoin wasted little time
in marching to the Royal Hotel, where he demanded to know the identity
of the perpetrators. It appeared that the owners of the impounded car, four
men, had indeed visited the hotel and had left just before the incident. When
insufficient information was forthcoming, MacEoin threatened to open fire
on the hotel, a move which saw Col. Fitzpatrick surrender.[109] The name of
one of the men, Commdt. Tom Burke (OC of the Offaly No.2 Brigade), was
provided after much haranguing, and a party was assembled to track him down.
Burke's colleagues in the Offaly brigade, Adjutant Reddan and Quartermaster
Robbins, were targeted additionally, with Burke's quick capture leading to a
heated interrogation involving Michael Collins.[110] The search for the culprits
led MacEoin's troops to Mullingar, where there were two additional fatalities,
one from either side, as resistance was encountered.[111]

The Leader described the Athlone and Mullingar incidents as 'disheartening',
while the *Manchester Guardian* depicted Adamson's assailants as 'mutineers' and
lamented the '… hopeless strain of disease in the rebel morality or mentality',
while detailing how the shooting had 'made a great stir in Dublin … [it
is] the first affair in which … men politically opposed to the Provisional
Government have been arrested on a capital charge.'[112] The editor of the
pro-Treaty *The Separatist* stated that Adamson's shooting proved the 'deadly
ferocity of our civil war',[113] while his counterpart in the *Irish Independent*
called it a 'fiendish crime', with the front page of the *Freeman's Journal* stating
somewhat naively: 'If … Adamson's death brings home to the organisers of
the civil war the ghastliness of their policy, he will not have died in vain.'[114]
The shooting also caused much concern among TDs, with W.T. Cosgrave
greatly annoyed at Harry Boland's initial assertion that Adamson's death was
par for the course. Boland eventually pulled back somewhat from his rather
harsh pronouncement and stated that the shooting was 'unfortunate'.[115]

Accusation, and counter-accusation, were exchanged as each side attempted to blame the other for Adamson's death. MacEoin accused the anti-Treaty men in the Royal Hotel of taking Adamson's life, while the anti-Treaty side pointed the finger at men closer to the Provisional Government.[116] Michael Hopkinson believes that Adamson's death was accidental, a belief that is undermined by a factually incorrect summary of the incident, which states that Adamson was shot while in the seized automobile.[117] Most contemporaries agreed that it was a vindictive act and a commission was convened to enquire into the shooting. Partially informed by a captured report compiled by an anti-Treaty intelligence officer, the commission found that there were 'indiscretions on both sides',[118] that the shooting was probably not premeditated, and that the man who pulled the trigger could not be identified. Needless to say, many disputed the findings, with the anti-Treaty *The Plain People* stating that such inquests were a farce and 'of a kind with the British military "inquiries" ... and ... are of as little value in the eyes of God and man'.[119] Contradictory statements continued to emanate from both the Four Courts and Beggars Bush; the commission did little other than confirm that evidence presented by both sides was 'teeming not only with inconsistencies but with inaccuracies'.[120]

As a result of the shooting, Arthur Griffith paid a short-notice visit to Athlone the following week. In his first public speech since Ireland's failure to gain recognition at the Peace Conference, he spoke of his desire for the Treaty to go before the Irish people to let them decide on its merits.[121] Joined by Seán MacEoin, the local SF branch committee members and Seán Milroy TD, Griffith spoke about those opposing the Treaty:

> These men come to tell the people of Ireland that the occupation of Athlone ... by troops responsible to the Irish Government elected by the Irish people is a sign of surrender to England ... they tell you the way to save the soul of Ireland is to bring back the English troops and hoist the Union Jack again.[122]

Griffith condemned the young men who cowered when the Black and Tans were in Athlone and who now shouted 'Up the Republic'.[123] He lauded George Adamson, who was '... foully murdered ... [and] died for his country as truly as any man ever died'.[124] The reaction of those assembled led the pro-Treaty *Westmeath Independent*, to state:

> It was to him [Griffith] a proof, beyond all question, that here in
> Athlone, the people are at one with him in the policy adopted by him
> and his sterling colleagues in the Dáil for the salvation of Ireland ...
> The people of Athlone know well what the Treaty means for Ireland.
> They have seen the flag of England, floating over the old Castle,
> replaced by the Irish Tricolour. They have witnessed the marching out
> of England's khaki-clad soldiers and her regular and irregular police ...
> They have seen every vestige of English rule disappear from their midst.
> Athlone is now in the hands of Irish people. The Treaty will keep this
> town in Irish hands.[125]

The increasingly serious manifestations of disagreement between the two
sides in Athlone and elsewhere fed fears that the upcoming election contest
would be exceptionally divisive. Recognising this, de Valera and Collins
tried to formulate a system that would allow for a less fractious approach to
canvassing before polling day. In May the two men agreed a seven-point pact,
the purpose of which was to reunite the fragmented SF party, as all candidates,
regardless of their stance on the Treaty, ran on the same ticket and in numbers
equal to their existing strength in Dáil Éireann.[126] The Collins-de Valera Pact
troubled many of Collins' allies, most prominently Arthur Griffith, as well as
the Roman Catholic hierarchy and indeed the British Government, members
of which believed that it could see the Treaty undone if whatever executive
that emerged from the election formulated a separatist, republican constitution for the new state and again pitted the Republic against the Empire.[127]

Indeed, as a consequence of the pact, the British adopted a far more rigid
approach to the formulation of the Irish constitution, not affording leeway
where, prior to the pact, such leeway might have been possible. Recognition
of the strictures that the British imposed on the terms of the constitution
ensured its inability to appease republicans; consequently, Collins made the
politically astute, if somewhat unethical, decision to withhold publication of
the constitution until election day, too late for it to sway the electorate.[128]

The following month saw the election take place against a backdrop of
some confusion. Collins' unease in regard to the pact saw him withdraw
from it, ambiguously, it has to be said, the day before the contest.[129] Collins
could have been looking to capitalise on the advantage growing support
for the Treaty (or at least the extreme aversion of a return to war with the
British) was imparting to his position,[130] or perhaps he may have desired a
more transparent race for all involved, including the nominees in the new
four-seat constituency of Longford-Westmeath. The constituency reworking

meant that for the first time since Athlone had its Borough status rescinded in 1885, the townspeople were all voting for the same candidates, regardless of their being east or west of the River Shannon.[131] As across Ireland, the local press made sure that people recognised which faction candidates represented, despite the political obfuscation, while the pact envisaged that where possible, all incumbent TDs should stand for re-election.[132] In Athlone, three of the four TDs elected in 1921 were on the ballot paper; Longford's Joe McGuinness had passed away in May 1922, and so his brother stepped in to replace him. Local voters therefore had to decide between Seán MacEoin TD, Lorcan Robbins TD and Francis McGuinness, all running on the pro-Treaty ticket, and the only anti-Treaty candidate, the ever-vocal TD, Laurence Ginnell. A vestige of the old constitutional nationalism was also on the ballot paper – Patrick Belton, a Dublin farmer representing the Ratepayers' Association – with the Independent Labour candidate, Seán Lyons, a chair maker from Moate, making six candidates in all.[133]

The contesting of the election by non-SF candidates was a cause of some annoyance to many in SF. They believed that SF was a national movement charged with guiding Ireland's destiny; others were simply being disruptive in forcing contests in constituencies. Annoyance at non-panel candidates standing inevitably led to some of them being intimidated. Patrick Belton's house was attacked as part of a campaign to force his withdrawal; admirably, he was not cowed.[134] In all just fifty-four non-SF candidates stood, a fact that ensured that first, panel candidates took the remaining seventy-four seats without contest and second, that even before the election results were in, the government envisaged under the pact could have been formed.[135] All of the local candidates made their views known in the run-up to polling day, albeit without directly referencing the Treaty or campaigning on its provisions, one of the more important clauses in the May pact. Perhaps most prominent among the six candidates were Laurence Ginnell, who spoke of his disquiet in being opposed to his own countrymen, and Seán MacEoin, who repeatedly stated that 'The law of the gun must cease'.[136]

On election day, 16 June, polling stations were set up at the town hall on the east side of Athlone and the courthouse on the west. Reports state that the election was carried off in a dignified manner, and despite a slow start, a 'fairly heavy poll'[137] was witnessed as almost two-thirds of those eligible to vote cast their ballot. The constituency's quota was set at 5,757 votes after initial calculations, a mark that Seán MacEoin almost doubled on the first count, coming in with 10,162 first preferences. Seán Lyons was also elected on the first count with 7,079 votes, his good showing a local reflection of Labour's strong national performance.[138]

The second count, which was revisited due to discrepancies, did not see either of the remaining two seats filled, though the third count saw Ginnell elected, with the final seat occupied by Francis McGuinness. Patrick Belton gained almost as many first preferences as McGuinness, a total that ensured Lorcan Robbins gained the fewest first preferences. Reports noted that a large number of spoiled votes were discarded; the proportional representation system was still not familiar to some voters, who simply placed an 'X' beside multiple candidates. In the Longford-Westmeath constituency the pro-Treaty faction took 50.1 per cent of the votes, anti-Treaty just 17.5 per cent and 'Third Party' (Independent Labour and Ratepayers Association) support came in at 32.4 per cent.[139] In essence, people were voting for peace, and the result, it has been argued, did much to legitimise the standing of the Provisional Government.[140] It should also be noted, however, that many voters, believing the pact to be in place, may instead have been voting for the coalition the pact had promised; peace was certainly what most who cast their ballot desired; legitimising the Provisional Government should not be seen as a certain corollary.[141] SF undoubtedly won the election, yet, as Michael Gallagher's work has shown, their victory was certainly not evidence that they had the emphatic backing of the Irish electorate.[142]

One aspect of the pact election that is not often adverted to in histo-rigraphies of the period is how votes transferred between the candidates. In Longford-Westmeath, the first transfers were those of Seán MacEoin. The figures show that of his massive surplus, Ginnell received just 582 votes to McGuinness's 2,893, the latter's brother's death ensuring that the sympathy vote was an additional boost to his pro-Treaty credentials.[143] The Independent Labour voters passed the vast majority of their second preference votes to panel candidates, as the only other independent, Patrick Belton, was seen as supporting the business owner, rather than the workers. Lyons' surplus was, however, split far more evenly between the pro- and anti-Treaty camps; Ginnell gained 469 votes to McGuinness's 555.[144] Ginnell's election on the back of Lyons' transfers left him with a 316 vote surplus, fewer than half of which went to McGuinness, who had to compete with Ginnell's erstwhile supporter Lorcan Robbins. McGuinness was eventually elected, after transfers pushed his total past the quota..[145] The local constituency, like many others across Ireland, exhibited greater nuance in the transfer of votes than the general impression often presented of the 1922 election results might lead the casual history reader to believe. Indeed, in the absence of comprehensive data on voter motivations and the absence of contests in so many constituen-cies, it is difficult to say with certainty what exactly people believed their vote would achieve.

Regardless of the way in which the result came about, the effect it had was to ensure certain action on behalf of republicans and the Provisional Government.[146] Many in Athlone believed that more practical expressions of republican anger towards the Treaty were the most likely outcome of the vote, and the rumour mill began to turn. News of imminent incursions was often heard, with the IRA re-initiation of the very effective War of Independence stratagem of destroying communications infrastructure ensuring that actual facts were scarce. Given the information deficit, it was not surprising that many precautions were taken to safeguard against violence in the town,[147] especially after the Provisional Government's decision to begin shelling of the Four Courts on 28 June. This attack on the Courts, an action in which a number of Athlone men were involved,[148] had brought home to many the fact that war had begun in earnest.[149] The assault itself, often presented as the start of the civil war, was planned and executed in just a matter of a day or two. Seán MacEoin, one of the most important commanders, was on his honeymoon in Donegal when the shells started to fall. His ignorance (he was told only after the attack commenced) appears indicative of the rapidity with which the decision to attack was made.[150] The assassination of Field Marshal Sir Henry Wilson in London on 22 June saw the British Government assign blame to associates of the men in the Four Courts and consequently demand that action be taken against the republicans who had made the Courts their headquarters. The most immediate consequence of the demand was the abandonment of moves towards a political accommodation that was being worked on between the two sides after the election.[151]

Despite people voting for peace, war was what the electorate got, and a reinterpretation of the meaning of the election result was adopted by the Provsional Government to help them justify their actions. They now interpreted the result to mean that the people had given their permission for whatever measures were necessary to bring about the implementation of the Treaty. While opinions on what was required varied, it was obvious that Michael Collins took the lead and began to centralise decision making. Quite undemocratically, he refused to convene the newly elected parliament and instead, it appears unilaterally, created a three-man War Council, with himself as leader.[152] His decision to prorogue parliament was criticised by Roscommon County Council among many other councils, trade unions and political figures during July and August.[153] His actions were to see his opponents charge him with attempting to establish a military dictatorship.

The early stages of the war in the Athlone region were dominated by each side assessing the other's capabilities. MacEoin, the only pro-Treaty IRA leader seen as fully committed to the Treaty,[154] conducted a small number of unsuccessful operations against anti-Treaty men in rural areas in late June and early July, poor outings that led him to drop back to the towns of Sligo, Athlone, Birr and Roscommon.[155] Athlone was seen as a safe haven for government troops, with the *Connaught Tribune* relating that the town was generally quiet, while the *Manchester Guardian* observed that 'outlying districts' were the real areas of concern.[156] Ambushes of soldiers in rural areas were initiated by republicans in early July,[157] while rumours of the massing of over 3,000 anti-Treaty men just 3 miles from Athlone soon after[158] saw MacEoin post sentries on all the roads leading to the town. It is certain that some within the IRA believed MacEoin to be averse to civil war, with communiqués between commanders suggesting that he may not have been willing to engage as forcefully as it may have been imagined:

> 1st Midland Area. Arrangements have been made for attacks in this
> area. The Western Division to co-operate in this area. McKeown [*sic*]
> has about 1,000 men at Athlone. It is possible that we may be able
> to keep McKeown [*sic*] neutral. In any case he is now entirely on the
> defensive. We expect to capture a few small posts ... within the next
> week. We will have to keep him busy in any event.[159]

MacEoin's aversion to adopting a bullish approach undoubtedly had much to do with his poor supply of armaments. Athlone had 720 troops in the garrison, yet just 249 rifles, 100 grenades and eighty-seven revolvers.[160] Obviously this was a handicap, but MacEoin had a job to do, and soon after the report of the force of 3,000 (and indeed numerous other stories) was proven false, he set about engaging the IRA in rural areas south of Athlone, taking the barracks at Clara but going no further, a sign of weakness in the eyes of his enemies.[161] MacEoin's men did have some positive returns when fighting in the west, where he believed the greater threat to lie, and where the Athlone Command had primary responsibility.[162] The loss of the armoured car The Ballinalee and the deaths of a number of Athlone-based men when returning from Sligo later in the month were a blow to MacEoin, however; the anti-Treaty *Poblacht na hÉireann War News* celebrated the republican successes.[163]

The tactics employed by the army to deal with the enemy threat in Athlone were redolent of those adopted by the British just months earlier with a considerable number of troops patrolling, erecting checkpoints and limiting the movement of goods. Local cars (especially those of car dealers), were commandeered to facilitate more distant army patrols, often without any compensation forthcoming.[164] Many locals feared for their jobs, as some weeks saw the AWM, which experienced a lot industrial unrest, operate for only two days. Even when

the business received contracts from the new state,[165] transportation of their
stock was stymied by the damage done to local rail infrastructure, something
repeatedly bemoaned by the two local railway companies, whose representatives complained about the danger involved in attempting to carry out their
day-to-day business.[166] Reports of destroyed rail lines increased rapidly, with
repeated attacks leading the GSWR to lay off staff.[167] MacEoin, aware of the
trepidation felt by many who may have used the railways, capitalised on some
western successes in mid-July and took a train from Athlone to Clare later the
same month. The longest journey on the line since early June was undertaken to
suggest, not without justification, that the Provisional Government was having
success in dealing with those who were targeting the country's infrastructure.[168]

Even though the success of MacEoin's early efforts was restricted, a large
number of supposed IRA members were arrested and had to be detained securely,
especially as Collins had, in yet another example of his desire to centralise
authority, pushed for the law that established the Irish courts to be rescinded.[169]
Custume Barracks was deigned to be the most suitable location for large-scale,
longer-term detentions, and, over time, hundreds from the midlands and west
were imprisoned there. The fact that the numbers far outstripped the capacity
of the purpose-built prison in the barracks meant that makeshift facilities, often
little more than guarded camps, had to be erected, facilities that were inadequate
to the task of detaining those averse to having their freedom curtailed. Even
before the war began in earnest, reports of an IRA memo from early spring in
the *Irish Independent* detailed how poor conditions were and that the treatment
meted out to those arrested for anti-Treaty activities was 'not what ought to be
expected from comrade officers at a recent date'. It went further, condemning
the rehiring of civilian workers who had previously worked for the British, while
also criticising the enlisting of at least thirty new recruits 'who were never in the
Volunteers, and [were] always hostile to the Republic ...' Such men, it was alleged,
were abusing some of the inmates, who had to sleep on makeshift beds and be
content with a very restricted diet.[170] The authorities in the barracks denied all
of these assertions, including additional allegations made by Commdt. Morrisey,
who stated that men were being refused medical treatment and visitation rights;
interestingly however, he did state that the guards were 'kind and considerate'.[171]
With the escalation in hostilities from late June, conditions were to deteriorate.

The prevalence of poor conditions led to many escape attempts during
the war. One such endeavour in mid-August 1922 saw IRA detainees gain
possession of a large explosive device, which they ignited and positioned near a
boundary wall. The loud explosion that accompanied its detonation was heard
throughout the town and, given the ease with which rumours were generated

and spread, many readily believed that the explosion was the beginning of a full-scale assault on the barracks.[172] The *Westmeath Independent*, while questioning how the device fell into the hands of the would-be escapees, related how only a small breach was made, one inadequate to the task of funnelling men out.[173] Evidence of outside help was noted by *The Irish Times*, which detailed how the nearby Concannon's shop had been set ablaze as a distraction.[174] The abortive attempt at liberation was perhaps the most overt action taken by the IRA in Athlone, as the region continued to exhibit evidence of generally small-scale activity. The local anti-treaty men were keeping a very low profile, something that greatly annoyed organiser Ernie O'Malley, who complained to the military leader of the IRA, Liam Lynch, that he could not contact anyone in the area, and instead was looking to Longford for more active participants.[175]

Any hopes that anti-Treaty forces in the Athlone region were to gain additional support were dealt two serious blows in August. Whatever sympathy they may have garnered from the death of Harry Boland in Skerries on the second of the month was overshadowed by the sudden death of Arthur Griffith on the twelfth,[176] and more comprehensively by the killing of Michael Collins at Beál na mBláth in Cork ten days later. The Athlone UDC declared that Ireland had lost 'her Commander-in-Chief … through whose transcendent courage and brilliant and heroic services she has achieved a large measure of liberty … '[177] Athlone-born American Archbishop Curley lamented Collins' loss in a speech given in the town, declaring that it would have been better if the English had shot him, rather than 'brother Irishmen'.[178] Shops and factories closed for most of the morning and early afternoon on the day of Collins' funeral, with the Roman Catholic churches in the area all holding masses. The local garrison also remembered Collins with a gun salute. His death saw the increasingly sidelined IRB effectively collapse, with his SF faction critically compromised in his absence.[179]

In the months immediately after Collins' death, the army capitalised on the anger it provoked and redoubled its efforts to achieve comprehensive control of the Athlone district. MacEoin again sent men out into the countryside in an effort to arrest IRA activists, and some success was seen, albeit not without casualties.[180] MacEoin harried the enemy, losing a young soldier at Glasson, 16-year-old John McCormack, in the process.[181] The arrest of a Dr Roland, one of the medics used by the anti-Treaty men in the Athlone region, resulted in a memorandum being sent to the OC of the 'Free' State troops in Custume Barracks, one which complained of MacEoin's recourse to ignoring the rules of warfare:

> Dr Roland, who is an Officer of our Medical Service, has been arrested
> by men of your command and imprisoned in Athlone. This is a breach

of Red Cross regulations. If he is not released and returned to his area forthwith, we will be reluctantly forced to treat all officers and men of your Medical Service as combatants.[182]

The increasing trend of pro-treaty forces to gloss over such conventions (be it incarcerating medics or not extending prisoner-of-war status to captured enemy troops) led Liam Lynch to state that 'drastic' measures would be taken to protect his men.[183] Roscommon County Council, ever more disturbed by the war's continuance, set forth proposals for the convening of a peace conference, which gained good support from many areas across Ireland but not from the recently convened parliament, which granted retrospective permission for all the acts carried out by its operatives since the war began.[184] Such overtures from councils were often resented by members of the government, whose desire to crush their opponents greatly inhibited the deployment of whatever political pragmatism would have been necessary to lead them to negotiate.[185] Local TD Laurence Ginnell, described in *Freedom* as the 'member for all Ireland', sent a letter to the Archbishop of Dublin in the hope that he might have been able to exert his 'moral authority' in regard to the actions of Ginnell's adversaries:

[There is in] existence in Dublin … a salaried Murder Gang, having headquarters at Oriel House, paid and maintained with Irish money by William Cosgrave and operating under the supreme command of Richard Mulcahy …

Ginnell went on to state that the machinations of the two men and their supporters had rendered every coroners' verdict a fait accompli, that government censorship had excised virtually all negative information about the pro-Treaty side in mainstream local and national newspapers and that the overthrow of the court system had rendered both men virtually immune from prosecution.[186] His entreaty appears to have done little to sway the archbishop, who continued to show his support for the Treaty and those who wished to implement its provisions.

As tensions increased, Seán MacEoin (who was also occupied with furnishing his new barracks residence[187]) communicated to his superiors his distress at the vulnerability of Custume Barracks. He noted that enemies could easily enter from the MGWR station using 'a few planks', that barbed wire was scarce around the perimeter walls and that the sentries posted at the Watergate were vulnerable to being 'sniped at' by anti-Treaty forces.[188] MacEoin complained bitterly about the conditions within the barracks and the grossly inadequate level of supplies and provisions. He noted that he had just 600 blankets for 756 prisoners, a situation that was causing tension within the overcrowded prison camp. Reports on the conditions in the camp provided numerous anti-Treaty publications with material for their propaganda[189] (government media censorship ensured that mainstream titles were unlikely to print such accounts), with *Poblacht na hÉireann – War News* publishing a letter, purportedly from a detainee, which detailed how MacEoin was facilitiating the degradation of his fellow countrymen:

> The prison is filthy; bedding dirty and verminous; cells overcrowded; no soap, towels, knives, spoons, forks or plates. Hardly any exercise. Ex-British soldiers, recently enlisted, are allowed to domineer over the prisoners.[190]

Such articles deeply annoyed MacEoin, who appears to have felt under siege, as those under his command also gave him cause for concern. By September, some of his men had not been paid in four months, many had no uniform or underwear and the general believed that his influence over them was in danger if '… GHQ carry on as at present':

> We have very much to complain about in the way in which our requisitions are being treated, such as bicycles, transport, Verey Lights …, etc. These are specially mentioned in nearly every weekly and daily report we make and still we appear to be no nearer securing them.[191]

He noted that the appointment of 'insolent pay officers' and transport officials, without reference to the chain of command, were causing internal tensions, as was the appointment of Dr McDonnell (a former rebel who worked with Seán O'Hurley), to the position of inspector/medical officer. It was noted that a number of medics had left well-paid jobs to join the army, only to be given posts below their station and a promise of employment for the duration of the war only. MacEoin reminded his superiors that such men would not work for an army that had no respect for them and that soldiers would be similarly disposed. He stated additionally that the number of incidences of insubordination reported from outlying barracks was increasing, while former informants cooperated with him less frequently given that he could no longer pay them for their intelligence.[192] His inability to glean the most up-to-date information on the movement of his enemies further fed his unease.

It appears, however, that if MacEoin was aware of the actual state of the local IRA, he might not have been so concerned. Ernie O'Malley, who had eventually made contact, recommended comprehensive reorganisation of the region, one which he believed to be susceptible to attack:

> Since my last report I got in touch with a man in Athlone Bde. The spirit is good there but they are very poorly armed, as an instance, one good company there has 28 men 20 of whom I know myself would form a very good flying column; there is not a single gun in the whole area. I have asked acting O/C 1st Eastern [Mick Price] to take charge of Athlone and Longford areas. The areas in the 1st Midland are weakly held by the enemy. If some of the Western Divs. crossed the Shannon now and again they could help to make things rather hot for the enemy there. The local F.S. troops are of very poor material and would be easy to beat.[193]

Liam Lynch believed that the introduction of Price was a good move and noted, 'Athlone of course is one of the enemy's most important bases, which it is necessary should be harassed'.[194] Even with O'Malley's reorganisation, the 'practically hopeless' region was still considered ineffective,[195] but the importance of Athlone ensured that it could not be ignored, and efforts were made to supply the locally active participants with weapons:

> Athlone area: there is a flying column of eight men operating in this area. There is certainly manpower available here – not to any great extent, though certainly more numerous than in any other area in the 1st Eastern Div. This Bde is very short of arms, especially rifles. If we had rifles we could have good flying column of about 35 men. I asked Offaly 2 to lend them six rifles, as the men in this area are very eager and willing to fight.[196]

By the end of September, O'Malley reported that the officers in the Athlone region had improved and were on their way to becoming well organised, but that 'it will be a considerable time before they are effective'.[197] Similar assessments for brigades across the more inactive parts of Ireland ensured that any attempt by the IRA to engage in a conventional war was abandoned around this time; guerrilla tactics had to be adopted.[198] In the case of Athlone, Liam Lynch counselled against the creation of a local column, instead voicing his preference for 'sniping parties' and the introduction of more explosives for clandestine operations. He believed that '… the great strength [of the National Army], [and] the hostility of civilian population' required a surreptitious approach, though he did note that '… columns could be mobilised for specific jobs sometimes'.[199] It was also reported that Athlone had received a machine gun and Mick Price believed 'if somebody is not hit, it will be a sad job'.[200]

The very low level of IRA activity around Athlone fed into a Westmeath-wide fall in IRA violence during the war. Counties such as Longford, Offaly and Laois all saw their activity levels rise to surpass those seen in the previously more active Westmeath.[201] Many reasons can be posited for this, with Ernie O'Malley iterating Lynch's impression of a hostile local populace, while also stating that the hostility was not immutable:

> In the Athlone Bde area in some Coy areas the people are very friendly but in the greater part of the Bde area they are hostile. Generally speaking, the people here are turning round very, very slowly but surely.[202]

All throughout the summer period of hostilities, political disagreement also continued to manifest. By September 1922 politicians were still attempting to put in place the political structures provided for under the Treaty; they believed that as the new state's mechanisms began to operate, the enthusiasm for anti-Treaty activity would wane. On the ninth of the month the 'New Dáil' met for the first time since the beginning of hostilities, and while it was intended to reflect the results of the June election, it was instead seen as affirming the role of the Provisional Government and moving forward with a Treaty-compliant constitution under William Cosgrave. This view was reflected in the comments of Laurence Ginnell (the only anti-Treaty TD in attendance; as yet, there was no 'Republican Government' in place[203]), who accused the assembled deputies of 'illegally, at the bidding of a foreign government [starting] a civil war … overthrowing Dáil Éireann and substituting their own government'. Maintaining his reputation as a belligerent, Ginnell demanded to know whether the current Dáil was 'for the whole of Ireland or … a partition Parliament'. His bellicosity led to his being ejected,[204] a fact that makes him a unique figure in Irish political history; he is the only sitting member to have been forcibly removed from both the House of Commons and Dáil Éireann.[205] Interestingly, as had happened some years previously, Ginnell's efforts were lauded in the anti-establishment press, with *The Fenian* stating, 'Those who seek a symbol, have it here'.[206] *Poblacht na hÉireann – War News* was similarly supportive, detailing how Ginnell was 'forcibly expelled from Churchill's Partition Parliament … for carrying on the protest of Pearse'.[207] Other republicans, in common with Ginnell, consistently spoke of the legitimacy of the 'Second Dáil', that of 1921, but could do little to halt the new executive from drafting a Constitution for Ireland, one over which the Treaty held primacy.[208] The government redoubled efforts to reinforce its legitimacy, with circulars demanding that it now be referred to as the 'National Government', while also seeking to additionally delegitimise anti-Treaty personnel, who it directed the media to refer to as 'Irregulars'.[209]

One of the first and most controversial bills passed by the new Executive was the Public Safety Bill, which, while having much in common with earlier repressive British legislation, also allowed for the execution of captured enemy combatants.[210] The killing of prisoners had been demanded by Richard Mulcahy, now both Minister for Defence and Commander-in-Chief, and was to see both prominent IRA men such as Rory O'Connor and Liam Mellows join their subordinates in front of the firing squad in December, despite the fact that the law was introduced after their arrests, no trial was ever staged, or charges laid against them.[211] Soon after, military courts were introduced, but did little to foster an impression of the fair application of law, intended as they were to allow for additional executions under the sanction of local commanders.[212] Unsurprisingly, the IRA threatened to execute those opposing the Republic in retaliation, most significantly TDs who had voted for the Bill.[213] The threat of a premature, state-sponsored demise for captured republicans introduced a darker tinge to the war and demoralised many on the anti-Treaty side.[214] Further demoralisation came with the Roman Catholic Church's coincident release of an exceptionally partisan pastoral letter that restated the legitimacy of the Provisional Government and the immorality of the IRA's guerrilla campaign.[215]

The bishops' pastoral may have provided much of the impetus for the anti-Treaty side to create a republican government.[216] De Valera, with the agreement of the Army Executive, established an emergency government in late October and portfolios were assigned to a number of prominent republican leaders such as Austin Stack (finance) and the imprisoned Liam Mellows (defence). De Valera believed that the establishment of the government would help republicans persuade the Vatican to look more favourably upon their cause, and, as well as this, allow them to exercise a more convincing claim to funds still held in America.[217] To assist in the latter cause, Laurence Ginnell was dispatched to Washington to progress the Republic's claim to the money and promote the republican belief that the Second Dáil had never been dissolved and that the Provisional Government was an illegal assembly.[218] Unfortunately for republicans, that 'illegal assembly' had been doing far more to assert its governmental credentials than they had. In tandem with contesting the conflict, Cosgrave's government better established the machinery, institutions and processes of a democratic state, and while they were hardly convincing when they claimed that they were protecting people's liberty and property from a destructive insurgency, they were planning for managing Ireland after the conflict had concluded, something republicans could not have claimed.

The harsher measures introduced by the government appeared to spur local republicans in their efforts to force their agenda. Around Athlone it was reported that the IRA were burning properties and carrying out raids on 'country residences', post offices and banks, presumably for weapons, money and other valuables. The goods purloined, though intended ostensibly to assist in building up republican coffers, sometimes made their way into the personal possession of certain members, whose aims were rather more selfish.[219] At times such avaricious actions led to the identification of the thieves, yet even when, on one occasion, four men were arrested, the fear of reprisals ensured that witnesses were exceptionally slow to come forward and even then non-committal in their testimony.[220] The caution exhibited was justified, for the IRA did at times remind people of their willingness to use force. On 20 October Commandant General Thomas Maguire of the 2nd Western Division of the Athlone IRA put his name to a notice prohibiting people from rendering assistance to the Executive's enemy: 'On or after above date any person or persons found in any way removing barricades or road blockages or repairing bridges will be fired on.'[221] Both sides disputed the number of attacks made by the IRA with, for example, the government's assertion that Westmeath experienced just four attacks in July rebutted in the republican press, which stated that the true figure was actually thirteen.[222]

The increase in IRA activity brought about a concomitant response from MacEoin, whose inability to comprehensively retake the west of Ireland had exposed him and the Athlone Command to censure.[223] The local republicans' ASU was disbanded to lessen the likelihood of capture as over 100 troops from Athlone began regular forays into regions considered likely to harbour enemy combatants. The cache of rifles held by the local IRA (just ten and one Lewis gun) forced them to adopt an evasive, guerilla strategy and it was reported that most avoided capture. National Army successes in October were followed by a lull until late November, when Lough Ree's islands were targeted.[224] MacEoin, it was reported, intended to maintain robust searches until 1923 came around, and, given his greater (albeit unimpressive) cache of weaponry, the evasive methodology adopted by the local republicans had, perforce, to continue. This ongoing strategy ensured that the IRA was limited in its range of actions, and it appears that outside of an abortive attempt on the Athlone barracks,[225] the local members restricted themselves to damaging communications infrastructure, something recommended by their superiors in the event that other activities were beyond them.[226] It was obvious that

Athlone's republicans felt under pressure, as IRA GHQ complained about the virtual absence of Athlone officers from Divisional Council meetings,[227] the incompetence of the Athlone 3rd Brigade, 1st Eastern Division intelligence officer and the need to repeatedly move the district's IRA headquarters.[228]

Outside of the efforts of the army to subdue the IRA, the new state required a more comprehensive civil policing policy to lend credence to its claim that it was capable of maintaining law and order. In late February 1922 a Civic Guard was created to assume the functions of the RIC, but a generally incompetent approach during the early months of its existence meant that Athlone did not receive the twenty-five men assigned to the town until after the force had been reconstituted.[229] September saw the newly appointed men set about patrolling the district, making themselves known to the inhabitants.[230] Following the RIC's lead, the new force tried to ensure that members were not posted in their home districts (pre-existing relationships could easily compromise an officer), a fact that disgruntled some local men who had assumed policing responsibilities since the truce.[231] Few former RIC men were recruited, with the duties of the new force restricted to civil disturbances only; they were 'systematically urged to hold to the ideal of the unarmed peace officer'.[232]

These civil duties became more important with the suspension of the district and parish courts, for it meant that often the Civic Guard had to hold suspects until a local justice could hear the case or until the new court system was established.[233] Detaining such men often led to Civic Guard barracks becoming the target of IRA forces and soon after the guards' deployment their Kiltoom barracks was attacked, albeit in a half-hearted manner. The raiders, despite being armed in the face of an unarmed enemy, made away empty-handed.[234] Indeed, Tom Garvin describes the 'tacit bargain' between the two sides that ensured that in most cases members of the Civic Guard, or their barracks, were not targeted. Republicans accepted that the force was necessary, and by extension, though they may have been loathe to admit it, some of the Provisional Government's policies.[235]

The continued fighting was widely lamented, and while condemnation of republicans was common, there were others, such as Cecilia H. Daniels, who continued to believe that the blame actually lay with Britain and its duplicitous ministers:

> Loyd [sic] George and W. Churchill finished Ireland … it was they
> who set the people fighting with themselves, supplied them with arms,
> ammunition and all the motor cars … Some are Republicans some are
> 'Free Staters' but all alike are 'dancing' to the tune which the coalition

government has called … they [the government in Britain] wronged the poor country grievously.[236]

As winter approached, the district's IRA members began to become more active in their targeting of Free State supporters. In Moate and Glasson, their actions led to a number of deaths and the fear of their influence leading to similar problems in Athlone led the army to deploy 121 soldiers on the streets at all time; 100 from the newly named Adamson Castle and the balance from the barracks.[237] The army maintained its inconsistent record in achieving some success with the shooting of former pro-Treaty officer turned prominent republican Commandant Christopher 'Kit' MacEoin,[238] while failing in its attempt to defend 'The Batteries', army land, west of Custume Barracks, when it was attacked in retaliation.[239]

The inconsistency displayed in the approach of the army was of concern to many within the defence forces hierarchy, and was usually attributed to the as yet poorly trained soldiers and officers. From its inception the army had to deal with high levels of indiscipline, immature enlistees, desertion, poorly trained soldiers and officers (guerrillas do not easily transform into soldiers), and an active enemy. The rank structures of a normal army had not been efficiently established or enforced, a situation which led to unsuitable egalitarian relationships between officers and their subordinates.[240] In relation to Athlone, Richard Mulcahy was specifically concerned about the competency of Custume Barracks' Commandant Lawlor; amongst other issues, his progress reports were apparently deplorably poor:

> If it were that I had to regard it that Lawlor was just a bit touched it would be serious enough to think that important operations were left in his hands … I feel that the matter is very … serious and that Lawlor is not the only person without a clear solder-like mind on the important details of his work.[241]

The fact that that army was attempting to put in place command structures and training systems when involved in a conflict undoubtedly impacted on its ability to concentrate on dealing with IRA activity in the Athlone region. However, the new army had to be professionalised and haltingly the new structures and systems began to emerge from the early confusion of the army's establishment.

MacEoin's winter raids had the desired effect of limiting republican attempts to harm his troops. Yet, admittedly, engaging MacEoin on his own terms was not something in which the region's IRA men had much

interest. Instead they decided to direct their efforts at more vulnerable targets.
Some landowners began to feel the pressure of IRA demands that they divest
themselves of their landholdings, while raids on trains were also resumed.[242]
The deployment of landmines damaged large sections of track in and around
Athlone and by January 1923, the MGWR reported that sabotage was endan-
gering their business and had already cost them over £50,000 in lost trains and
carriages.[243] The Westmeath Executive of the Farmers' Union, greatly annoyed
at the dislocation caused by the ongoing hostilities, called for an immediate
truce and a general election using a new voters' register but – like so many
similar calls and peace proposals from other organisations, including the Neutral
IRA – it was unable to influence the intransigent protagonists.[244] The army's
counter raids did see a number of arrests and weapons seizures, yet only exacerbated the problems already quite apparent in the overcrowded prison camp.[245]
The number of inmates during the winter months of 1922/23 reached 950,[246]
as dozens of additional republicans joined their comrades and a number of
TDs behind the barrack wall. Anti-Treaty publications continued to report on
the worsening conditions, with *Freedom* detailing the foul smells, multiplying
vermin, terrible food, extreme cold and exceptional overcrowding.[247] *Poblacht
na hÉireann – War News*, playing its part in exposing what was an undoubtedly
horrific existence in the facility, wrote that prisoners had themselves offered to
purchase Jeyes Fluid, fearful that the conditions would lead to the proliferation
of filth diseases.[248] Ladies, generally IRA message carriers,[249] were also arrested
in small numbers and, for reasons of propriety, were detained separately in
Adamson Castle, where conditions were not as repugnant. Escape attempts by
members of both sexes increased in frequency with the introduction of exercise
time for the inmates (ironically intended to allay unrest) as many, some after
stealing a soldier's uniform, attempted to bluff their way to freedom.[250] Tunnels
were frequently uncovered by soldiers, with knotted blankets and missing table
legs also indicating the probability of multiple attempts by prisoners to liberate
themselves.[251] The prison's reputation was further damaged by the confinement of all inmates after the fatal shooting of Patrick Mulrennan, a republican
prisoner, whose killing led to a hunger strike among 600 of the interned.[252]

Mulrennan's death was one of the most controversial incidents in the Athlone
region during the civil war. Army sources confirm that he died as a result of
being shot by Commandant Anthony Lawlor, whose senseless behaviour
was to embarrass the army and prove 'of marvellous propaganda value to the
republicans'.[253] Numerous anti-Treaty publications leapt upon the chance to
discredit the army authorities as a result of the incident. *Freedom*, in a special
edition, described how the young man 'who had survived the English Terror'

was brutally slain by Lawlor in the presence of Seán MacEoin.[254] The same newspaper published a captured letter purportedly from Lawlor to his mother, in which he boasted of the 'wonderful shot' which felled Mulrennan, while also detailing MacEoin's support for the killing and threat of further shootings.[255] The Scottish edition of *An Phoblacht* wrote similarly, describing how Lawlor shot into a crowd of men who were doing little more than 'sitting on bins'. It additionally related Lawlor's belief in the salutary effect the killing had on discipline among the internees, while also stating in a later issue that officers were allowed to take 'potshots' at the prisoners, something the paper, amongst others, averred Seán MacEoin did frequently.[256] The *Republican War Bulletin* also published a letter, reportedly from internee Peter Shortall, which detailed Mulrennan's shooting and noted how many prisoners had 'narrow escapes' due to MacEoin's proclivity for firing his weapon.[257] *Poblacht na hÉireann – War News* wrote that the Mulcahys and MacEoins were happy to engage in such offences simply to 'earn the contemptuous thanks of their Imperial masters'.[258]

However angered the anti-Treatyites must have been at incidents such as Mulrennan's, it was becoming increasingly certain that they were losing the war. The Irish Constitution came into effect on 6 December 1922, after the act that confirmed its existence passed through the House of Commons. The establishment of the Irish Free State was confirmed, as was the partition of Ireland, when the northern government quickly exercised its right to answer to London rather than Dublin.[259]

The official creation of the new state added yet more weight to the Free State government's assertion of its legitimacy. It desperately wanted to end the internecine strife and brought in a conciliatory measure primarily intended to alleviate the pressure at the country's barracks. A declaration was drawn up which stated that if released, the signatory would promise not to thwart the Free State in its efforts to normalise conditions and create the structures required in a modern democracy. Most who were offered the option in Athlone demurred, with their disgust at the conditions in the barracks outweighed by their hatred for those who maintained them.[260] The poor reaction to the measure increased the pressure on the local soldiers, who began to injure their comrades more frequently in cases of friendly fire.[261]

The recognition that some of the men were wholly ill-suited to the army life led the defence forces to begin to actively seek more suitable candidates to bolster its numbers. Advertisements were carried in the local press stating that those interested in joining the 'National Army' would, if posted in Athlone, be inducted into the 5th Infantry Battalion and serve for a period of at least twelve months. All applicants had to provide a character reference from a former employer or clergyman, a criterion of the application that it was hoped would assist in ensuring a higher calibre of recruit.[262] Early 1923 saw the finalisation of training and command structures as well as the confirmation of appointments in Custume Barracks.[263] Athlone was designated as the headquarters for all soldiers in Athlone, Longford, Boyle, Maryboro and Roscrea, with Seán MacEoin in command and the much-maligned Anthony Lawlor retained as his second-in-command.

At the same time as the army was recruiting, the anti-Treaty side were also advertising, albeit with rather more ominous intentions. Two notices appeared on the town bridge; the first, later declared a hoax, stated that: 'Any person or persons found speaking to 'Bolshies'[264] shall be shot at sight – signed Military Headquarters, Athlone',[265] while the second, the authenticity of which MacEoin disputed, read: 'All officers in uniforms to be shot at sight. All persons found talking to men or officers will be treated as spies [sic].'[266] Early 1923, when resistance to the Free State was becoming increasingly futile, saw the staging of executions in Athlone, executions that caused much concern to many in the locality, including local TD Seán Lyons. In Athlone, on 20 January, five men were shot for being in possession of weapons. One was a local man, Captain Thomas Hughes of Bogganfin, while the other four were from Galway. The executions took place at eight a.m., before the families concerned had been notified.[267] Lyons stated that in at least one instance, a mother was told about her son's death while she was returning from the town market, and that the body of the executed man was retained by the army, despite his mother requesting it for burial.[268] In all, seventy-seven republicans were 'officially' put to death during the war. It is certain, however, that many more died at the hands of the National Army as a result of unofficial executions.[269]

The damaging psychological effect that the executions had on local republicans was something of which Seán MacEoin undoubtedly took advantage. He redoubled his efforts in areas bordering Athlone, with the regions of Kiltoom and Coosan repeatedly raided, and even occupied for short periods as the army tried to flush out the local guerrillas.[270] Temporary, poor-quality shelters were set up at all bridges approaching the town and the soldiers within carried out searches of those who wished to cross. The level of activity on the part of the army, the fear of execution and IRA commander Liam Deasy's call for surrender[271] may all have influenced twenty-seven members of the Athlone IRA from Fahereen to accept the reality of the situation and hand in their weapons to the military at Moate in February. They signed a declaration of their submission, which stated that they wished to give the government a chance and return to their jobs.[272] The anti-Treaty press rejected the reports of the surrender,

Funeral cortege for the executed Capt. Thomas Hughes, January 1923. (AHL)

stating that the OC, David Daly, had resigned due to ill health, while ten others, 'who were never anxious to help our cause', joined sixteen additional men who had already left the IRA and had no weapons or ammunition.[273] Hopes that locals may have harboured for the end of republican resistance on the back of the Fahereen surrender may have faltered somewhat later the same month as Athlone hosted a number of IRA men who made Saturday night, 27 February 'hideous for a short while'. The absence of solid information forced the local newspaper to remain vague in its description: 'there was marked activity, regular and otherwise, which didn't cease until long after dawn appeared.'[274]

The prolongation of the civil war, as with the War of Independence, began to see more and more of people's day-to-day lives impacted upon negatively. Perhaps the most inconvenient of the many attacks on local infrastructure was the republicans' destruction of the town's waterworks in retaliation for the executions in the barracks.[275] The Athlone UDC, already experiencing severe financial diffi- culties given the number of unforeseen events, moved towards bankruptcy after the attack. The thoroughfares of the town were so badly neglected that people had difficulty moving their carts and cars through them, with one description equating them with the streets of Flanders after the Great War. The exception- ally poor level of rate collection ensured that little could be done to address the problem; even what was collected was widely considered an exorbitant levy,

despite accounting for just one third of the council's expenditure.[276] The slow
pace at which the army honoured bills for vehicles commandeered, damage
done or goods acquired from local merchants ensured that it was not only the
council that faced bankruptcy.[277] Very often businesses' claims were refused,
as in the case of Peter Malynn, whose request was dismissed on the basis that
'in general our line must be to refuse claims for losses which are, in the main,
consequential'.[278] Labour Party efforts to exert pressure on the government to
negotiate a peace and refocus on the economy proved ineffective and unemployment increased dramatically as the disruption caused to some businesses
rendered them insolvent.[279] The most striking example locally was the closure of
the Athlone Sawmills with the loss of over 100 jobs,[280] while news of the army
exporting contracts that the AWM could have fulfilled led to many expressions
of annoyance.[281] The town was, if reports were to be believed, becoming infested
with 'Knights of the Road',[282] while military reports from March noted:

> Unemployment is appalling, and towns are severely hit in this respect.
> Trade is dislocated and practically at a standstill. Enterprising people
> cannot afford to expend money in business through fear of depredation
> by Irregulars or their accomplices.[283]

On the positive side, trains began to enter Athlone on the western and eastern
lines on a more frequent basis during the spring of 1923. However, hopes
that the southern line was to reopen were dashed by the destruction of an
additional bridge at Kilgarvan on the main Athlone–Tullamore route.[284]

Casualties continued to add up on both sides, with the local press noting
that the Westmeath County Coroner had surpassed his usual yearly total of
five or six inquests in just ten days, as the county's civil war dead, in common
with most regions in Ireland, outstripped those of the War of Independence.[285]
The UDC's increasing dismay led it to pass an amended version of a March
resolution passed on to the council by the Birr RDC 1:

> That we pledge our support to members of the IRA in their effort to
> bring peace to the country, and that we ask for a stay to be put to all execu-
> tions that are at present carried on in Ireland, and a stay upon the shooting
> of National Soldiers and the destruction and burning of property.[286]

It appeared however that the Free State army, recognising the momentum it
had built up, was more inclined to escalate rather than moderate its campaign.
Saturday nights, which 'it would seem [are] specially set apart for the outbreak

of firing'[287] saw the most violent incidents, as the two or three IRA cells Seán MacEoin believed were operating in the region became more active. The first cell at Kiltoom was headed by Michael Pender, one of the many escapees from the barracks, who had about fifteen men under his command. The cell had access to fifteen rifles, fifteen revolvers, four bombs, three landmines and a couple of motorbikes. A supplementary second group may also have been active in Brideswell nearby, with a man surnamed Martin in command. It appears that both groups used the same resources. A third group was run from Ballymore on the Athlone-Mullingar road by Thomas McGiff, a former Fianna Éireann leader from Tang.[288] This twenty-man cell had similar arsenal to Pender's, though they relied more heavily on pushbikes for mobility, something they had in common with the military, who were attempting to arrest them.[289] In total the army believed that in Athlone by March:

> … there is an Irregular Force of forty men operating on both sides of the Shannon. Their activities … have lessened considerably due to the vigilance of troops in the various garrisons [despite the fact that] the civil population in this district are sympathetic to the Irregulars … [290]

Very often the perception of an unco-operative rural populace led the army to restrict its activities until after dark. The element of surprise assisted them in capturing a number of 'sleeping opponents', including some prominent IRA officers, whose ability to unleash their firearms was curtailed by their somnolence.[291] The fact that the army believed that, 'Irregulars are harboured and fed by the country people' ensured that most arrests were witnessed outside Athlone's urban boundaries, with the influence 'of the female element'[292] prominent among the reasons posited for the rural support. There were also accusations that the army was deliberately shooting supposed 'Irregulars' they encountered in the field, with the option of arrest not even entertained.[293]

The celebration of Easter 1923 was a low-key affair given the prevailing conditions, with most people remaining indoors for the duration of the weekend, Mass attendance excluded. The week after the festival saw more republican activity in the area, first at Waterstown House near Glasson, which had been commandeered by the army. It was attacked by over fifty IRA men armed with rifles and machine guns, and while it was obvious that the twelve soldiers were outnumbered and outgunned, they still succeeded in repelling the attack.[294] Soon after this incident, a Sgt Stapleton from Custume Barracks in Athlone was kidnapped and pressed for information. His unco-operative approach led to an unsuccessful execution attempt and also saw his house set alight after his wife and child were removed.[295] The impression of repeated IRA failures may have induced additional members to sign the pledge at Custume Barracks, which by March 1923 held 600 inmates, over three hundred fewer than in late 1922. Certainly executions had a small effect on pushing the number down, as did the almost constant escape attempts, some of which were later linked to civilians working in the barracks, as well as a complicit governor and deputy-governor.[296]

From the sources studied, it is obvious that by the late spring of 1923, Athlone was generally quiescent. On most occasions soldiers' daily rounds of the town led to reports relating that the situation was 'all correct'.[297] Some republicans had begun to engage more frequently in theft against innocent citizens, yet internal 'special disciplinary action' dealt with such transgressions in many cases.[298] The army too had internal problems to deal with as friendly fire incidents and desertions continued.[299] The more tranquil atmosphere was still punctuated by a small number of arrests and raids (most prominently at Bogganfin[300]), yet instances of firearms being discharged were considerably fewer and the local rail lines began to host trains on a more frequent basis.[301] By mid-April Seán MacEoin went as far as to state:

> The morale of the Irregulars is very low. Their organisation is completely broken. They are now absolutely smashed up, keeping in very small numbers, breaking up to as small as two. The inclination to ambush or fight is finished.[302]

Political support for the republican cause also suffered in the region. In April Laurence Ginnell passed away in America; he had never fully recovered from his last period of incarceration and it appears his trip to Washington D.C. to act as de Valera's envoy asked too much of him.[303] Soon after, indeed by May, it is certain that republicans' military efforts were almost non-existent. The town patrols of the 5th and 22nd battalions were shortened as IRA activity virtually disappeared, while inmates in the barracks' prison were afforded greater freedom as many began to sense an end to the hostilities.[304] Searches of suspected republican hideouts in regions considered to be opposed to the Free State such as The Berries, Bogginfin, Bealnamulla, Brideswell, Baylough and Monksland produced nothing.[305] It appears that the only seizures made were at a shop called Tighe's, where some ammunition and one revolver were found after a tip-off from a local boy.[306] While a short report from the Office of the Director of Intelligence in Portobello Barracks from June 1923 noted that the army's local Intelligence Officer had been remiss in his duties (indeed, his department was described as 'deplorable'), it appears unlikely that his inability to compile or maintain comprehensive, valuable reports, his penchant for hiring 'decidedly undesirable' informants, or his general unsuitability for the job would have been entirely responsible for the army finding little.[307] It appears they found little and arrested few, largely due to a general absence of an active IRA cohort in the Athlone district.

The death of Liam Lynch, the intransigent military leader of the IRA,[308] in April was to assist in the move towards peace, and soon after his passing de Valera, who for some time had worked towards ending the fighting, publicly called for the cessation of hostilities.[309] Believed to be the unofficial end of the civil war, the call was basically an admission of defeat. Republicans began to decamp and initiated a campaign of arms dumping all over the country; surrendering their weapons would have been too ignominious a move for a side that had not actually conceded on its demands.[310] On occasion guns were handed over to priests, with the signing of a simple declaration averring to the signatory's promise not to engage in further violence against the Free State often ensuring their liberty.[311] Such compromises were not favoured by Cosgrave, who stuck doggedly to his demands that republicans decommission their arms and operate under the terms of the Treaty: 'Peace talks … boiled down to two issues, arms and the oath'.[312] The inability of the two sides to reconcile these issues was to ensure that even when the war ended, their ideologies were to continue stoking animosity for quite some time. Officially the war 'ended with a whimper' on 24 May 1923, after over ten months of fighting that was costly in both human and monetary terms.[313] The IRA had lost a war that in the initial phases looked like theirs to lose. However, their poor organisation and planning largely proved their undoing as the army, hardly a good model in itself, capitalised on their failings.[314]

The manner in which the civil war ended ensured that the following months were to be exceptionally trying. No large-scale prison releases occurred as IRA arms remained operational, while a new Public Order Bill was introduced in June to force home the authority of the Free State.[315] The comprehensive victory of the pro-Treaty side in the 1922 election was not to be reflected in the general election of 1923,[316] which saw fifteen candidates compete for the five seats in Longford-Westmeath. Cosgrave's election pitch for his newly-formed Cumann na nGaedheal party was quite simply presented as a choice between his government's stability and republicans' anarchy, while those opposed to the Treaty asked people to remain true to the Republic.[317] Counterproductively for those in favour of the pro-Treaty parties, eleven candidates were supporting the Free State, something that ensured a split in the vote. Seán MacEoin's 1922 majority was not to be repeated, as he withdrew from electoral politics to concentrate on his army career; his absence from the ballot ensured that fewer transfers were spread out amongst the greater number of candidates. The constituency saw short-term Athlone SF president and Republican Conor Byrne top the poll, followed by Cumann na nGaedheal's Patrick Shaw, Independent Labour incumbent Seán Lyons, Republican James Killane and Farmer's Party member and previous IPP candidate Patrick McKenna.[318] The poor canvassing strategy of Cumann na nGaedheal ensured that de Valera's SF won a large number of seats in the expanded executive: forty-four against Cosgrave's total of sixty-three. It was only SF's abstentionist policy that allowed Cosgrave to govern without too much opposition from within the chamber.[319]

After mid-summer the IRA appeared to disintegrate as a group in the Athlone region. Their inclusion in military reports was due invariably to the arrest of the few members who were still at large, with virtually no reports of any activity on their part. Indeed, by October a summary report produced by the army noted that there was no question of an increase in their number, with just a handful of 'wholetime' local IRA men still at large, men who did little to 'hamper civil administration' or foment agrarian unrest. Their morale was described as indifferent at best over the summer months, though by October 1923 the newly instated local army Intelligence Officer believed that it had been broken,[320] as hunger strikes became widespread across the prison population.[321] Over the period of June to October 1923 there were no reports under the headings 'Rail Destruction', 'Destruction of Property (by mines, fire, etc)', 'Road Destruction', 'Telegraph and Telephone wire cutting', 'Raiding of houses' or 'Commandeering'.[322] The IRA's own communiqués reinforce the view of republican structures falling asunder with a July letter from Thomas McGiff to a fellow OC highlighting the breakdown in the region's IRA communications network, and the collapse of the command framework:

> I am writing to you to ask you what you mean by your constantly ignoring my communications to you for the past month. You have not even acknowledged any of my communications or neither have you let me know if you are prepared to carry on as Comdt of 1st battalion as asked to do ... Will you at once acknowledge all my communications to date and send me all the reports asked for to date?
>
> You will also call a Battalion Council for Tuesday night next, 24th Inst. for Mount Temple and have all Staff Officers (Battn) and Coy

OCs and Lieuts summonsed to attend. I will attend and try and put
your Battalion in working order and improve the personell [*sic*] of your
Battn Officers. Let me know the time and house. You will hold the
council by 23rd.

Mise
T. McGiff, Brig O.C.[323]

It is certain that by the end of 1923, local republicans had stopped engaging
in virtually all activity. Undoubtedly some members maintained their dislike
for the Free State, yet the overwhelming desire for peace evoked by the civil
populace ensured that republicans could not maintain active militant opposition as funds dried up and in-kind support disappeared. Individual members
did attempt to sustain their efforts, yet in total, Athlone, Coosan, Kiltoom and
Ballymore anti-Treaty men numbered at most sixty, whose level of commitment varied.[324] The effects of war had been a blot on the lives of Athlone's
citizens for almost a decade. Most of them, like the majority of their fellow
countrymen, wanted the differences still extant between the two side to be
addressed using non-violent means.

Conclusion

Undoubtedly, much of what Athlone experienced during the period 1900-23 represents in microcosm that which was seen contemporaneously elsewhere in Ireland. However, while in the broad brushstrokes of general historiographies Athlone's story can find accommodation, some of the trends, occurrences and personalities studied in this publication may justify the reassessment of some hitherto mostly unchallenged generalisations, assertions and assumptions.

It cannot be denied that in Athlone throughout the period under study, the efforts of just a few individuals were pivotal in defining the town's political development. The growth of movements such as the UIL, GL and SF, while often drawing on the energy of national personalities such as William O'Brien, Douglas Hyde or Arthur Griffith, required the backing of provincial figures, whose efforts, when aggregated, could ensure the success or failure of such ventures. Without the backing of men such as Michael McDermott-Hayes, Dean J.J. Kelly and Thomas Chapman, the UIL would have charted an even less impressive course in Athlone during the first decade of the twentieth century, as it was largely their energy which led to its repeated reinvigoration, with the inability of the IPP to make the organisation truly relevant to urbanites quite a handicap to those men's local efforts. The fact that none of the three was a native of Athlone is also worthy of note and, as was later seen in advanced nationalist circles, appears to have been a unifying characteristic amongst the most prominent activists in Athlone, a town whose indigenous inhabitants were difficult to rouse. Be it the UIL, which was too concerned by rural affairs, the GL, which, in relation to the Irish language at least, was too cerebral, or even the TTL, whose association with the UIL was disliked by many urban landlords, sustained support for each organisation's efforts was never achieved. The adrenaline shot that an election contest or rally administered to the body of supporters for these organisations often provided a misleading impression of their vitality; outside of a small number of individuals, the majority were indifferent.

Such apathy, especially among constitutional nationalists, would perhaps, in a different environment, be an indicator that there was an opening to be exploited by those holding different or unconventional political views. However, it was abundantly apparent that even when IPP failures such as the Irish Council Bill promoted disillusionment with John Redmond, few locals were inclined towards a radical reappraisal of their political allegiances; their indifference to political activism appeared too strongly ingrained. Certainly evidence of inchoate advanced nationalism was apparent, most prominently in the person of M.J. Lennon, yet as his later exploits showed, he was more a self-promoting political opportunist than an archetypal SF political ideologue. It can be convincingly argued that constitutional nationalism was an intrinsic part of the townspeople's political outlook in the first decade of the twentieth century; they were aware of advanced nationalist alternatives, but their passive relationship with political movements generally and cosy familiarity with the IPP ensured that they saw little to recommend these alternatives during the first decade of the twentieth century.

The political homogeneity seen in Athlone during the first decade of the twentieth century was carried forward into the first years of the second. The establishment of the Athlone AOH did little more than ensure that the town had the full complement of IPP-linked organisations, while the short-lived move of the local GL into the political field during its association with Clan Uisneach saw it promote Home Rule, rather than anything more radical, something identified with the GL elsewhere. Undoubtedly, the parliamentary strength of the IPP in 1910 and the subsequent move towards Home Rule in 1912 would have made abandoning the constitutional course an asinine move, with the local reaction to the opposition tactics of Ulster unionists appearing to further reinforce Athlone's loyalty to Redmond's party. It could be viewed as ironic that in evincing a more definite show of support for Home Rule and the IPP with the creation of the MVF in October 1913, McDermott-Hayes and his associates were pursuing a course to which Redmond's party was generally opposed. Additionally, it cannot be denied that the creation of the MVF was quite a departure from Athlone's established attitude of indifference to political activism. While admittedly the MVF's exploits were greatly exaggerated in the *Westmeath Independent*, it appears that its raison d'etre of opposing unionist militancy was the most popularly promoted use for the later Irish Volunteers, despite the conciliatory overtones in Eoin MacNeill's 'The North Began', the article most commonly promoted as that which inspired the Volunteers' inception.

As has been explored in detail, Athlone played a pivotal role in the propaganda campaign adopted by IPP-supportive media outlets (very much in the majority, it should be remembered), in justifying both Redmond's adoption of the IV in May 1914, and his right to call for its members to fight for the British Empire on the battlefields of Europe four months later. The fact that the IV split saw original members of the MVF take opposing sides has to be assessed as a factor in qualifying the MVF's contribution to the creation and early development of the IV and its legacy. Certainly dissenters such as Seán O'Mullany and James Gough were in the minority, yet of course so were those who went with MacNeill after Redmond's Woodenbridge speech and those who later participated in the Easter Rising. It is without doubt that the significance of the MVF has been ignored by most historians writing on this period, and significantly misrepresented or underplayed by those who have briefly turned their attention to the issue.

The advent of the Great War was perhaps the most pivotal event in defining the future fortunes of constitutional nationalism in Ireland. While it initially brought significant economic benefits to Athlone, the conflict's continuation ensured that the early, steady flow of local recruits abated, casualties mounted and advanced nationalist propaganda, in part spread from the training camp in Coosan, began to achieve greater purchase with the local people. J.P. Hayden's call for citizens to stifle their grievances until the war's end became increasingly difficult for people to comply with; the IPP strategy of promoting political stasis undermined Redmond's authority, allowing those opposing the constitutional nationalist agenda to move towards implementing their own.

When it came, the move from constitutional nationalism to advanced nationalism in Athlone was a relatively rapid process, one that was undeniably bolstered by the British Government's reaction to the activities of Easter week 1916. The widespread application of draconian measures, allied with the IPP's anaemic approach to addressing Irish peoples' concerns about those measures, ensured that Athlone's previously moderate nationalists began to see greater profundity in the arguments of their advanced nationalist contemporaries. Slowly, the profile of men such as Seán O'Hurley and Peter Malynn began to grow as others like Michael McDermott-Hayes and Thomas Chapman agitated for their release. As previously experienced with constitutional nationalism, the *Westmeath Independent* began to provide much of the drive for the promotion of political ideology locally, energising the swing towards SF. The IPP's excessive reliance on, and obviously poor knowledge of, Athlone's provincial promoters ensured that when such promoters shifted allegiance or were no longer present, the party's efforts for the South Longford by-election were hugely weakened. For too long the IPP had dealt with Athlone's grass roots by proxy; the distance they maintained was little more than political negligence, something for which constitutional nationalists paid dearly. The consolidation in SF and IV circles that followed in Athlone yet again evinced the prominence of non-natives in forcing along the local nationalist agenda, as the perennially active Dubliner Thomas Chapman and Limerick man Michael McDermott-Hayes joined Cork man Seán O'Hurley at the vanguard of Athlone's advanced nationalism.

Confirmation of the electorate's political realignment at the polls in December 1918 showed that the emotive threat of conscription was essential in boosting SF fortunes in Athlone. The crushing defeat of the perceived conscription advocate Sir Walter Nugent by Laurence Ginnell (a much neglected figure in Irish historiography, more than deserving of a comprehensive biography) illustrated this clearly, while J.P. Hayden's less comprehensive loss to Harry Boland showed that SF had the numbers to thwart the remnants of the IPP old guard, who backed Hayden strongly. Both the local and national manifestations of coercive policies by the British administration in 1919 after the election ensured the continued growth in the local support for SF, the IV, and the newly created Dáil Éireann, as generally well-supported changes in local government and the judicial system brought about by advanced nationalist representatives and bodies came on stream.

The eventual recourse to violence by Athlone's republicans in 1920, while never reaching the levels experienced in Cork or Longford, was obviously a significant step up from anything seen previously. Apart from the killing of Sgt Craddock, the town itself saw few instances of extreme republican violence within its boundaries, yet operations in bordering regions assured locals that the IRA was operational, albeit not consistently active. Local election results strengthened the grip that republicans had on local bodies and authorities that had been formerly loyal to the Crown, with dissention only arising in the Athlone region as a result of the exigencies of providing for the needy. The efforts of the Black and Tans and Auxiliaries assisted republicans greatly in promoting the legitimacy of their efforts, with the deaths of men such as Terence MacSwiney and Athlone UDC member Michael Burke stimulating local resentment towards British policy. The reaction to the eventual declaration of the truce in July 1921 evinced not only local relief at the cessation of hostilities, but belief that republicans were about to achieve – with just over five years' worth of efforts – what constitutional nationalists had failed to deliver in thirty.

Undoubtedly, as news of the detail of the Treaty spread, Athlone's citizens' feeling of elation was replaced by one of trepidation. Locals certainly saw the consequences of the pro- and anti-Treaty ideological fracture quite early in 1922 with the occupation of the Royal Hotel by the anti-Treaty side in March and, more shockingly, with the killing of George Adamson in April. The Irish Civil War, though often given the commencement date of 28 June when The Four Courts were shelled, may have already been at least two months old in the minds of Athlone's citizens by the time historians, as so often happens, looked towards Dublin before starting their stopwatches. The strong civil, political and military support for the pro-Treaty side in Athlone ensured that levels of violence never reached the heights seen further south, yet the damage to local infrastructure, the movement of Seán MacEoin's troops and the sporadic attempts of republicans to exert their influence would never have left a contemporary with the sense that the conflict was passing them by. Attempting to assess the specifics of the political allegiance of Athlone's electorate during the conflict is difficult, and while a facile overview of the general elections of 1922 and 1923 may appear to offer clarity, it performs no such service, given the unique circumstances under which the first election was conducted and the effect that the prosecution of the conflict must have had on many electors' views by the time August 1923 came about.

The truce that ended the Irish Civil War did little to provide political certainty to Athlone's electorate. Undoubtedly Ireland had gained a degree of separation from Britain, yet the powerful voice of republican dissenters was to ensure that decades were to pass before civil war-inspired divisions were to be worn away.

Bibliography

PRIMARY SOURCES

Private papers

DUBLIN
National Library of Ireland
John Redmond Papers
Francis Sheehy Skeffington Papers
Florence O'Donoghue Papers
George Noble Count Plunkett Papers
Piaras Béaslaí Papers

Military Archives of Ireland, Cathal Brugha Barracks
Captured Documents
Michael Collins Papers
Fintan Murphy Papers
Military Service Pensions Records

Bureau of Military History Witness Statements
No. 89: Michael Ó Cuill
No. 114: Éamon O'Connor
No. 161: Donal O'Halligan
No. 170: Peter Paul Galligan
No. 239: Frank Necy
No. 331: Diarmuid (Dermot) Murtagh
No. 348: Capt. E. Gerrard
No. 361: Peadar Bracken
No. 400: Richard Walsh

No. 480: Mrs Martin Murphy (Eileen Walsh)
No. 500: Seán O Cuill
No. 563: Michael Cremin
No. 580: John Duffy
No. 701: Thomas Kelly
No. 845: Tomás Ó Maoileoin
No. 954: Seán Leavy
No. 955: Patrick Mullooly★
No. 982: Mrs Alice Ginnell
No. 1,046: Patrick J. Ramsbottom
No. 1,086: Patrick Mullooly★
No. 1,087: Patrick Mullooly★
No. 1,296: Thomas Costello
No. 1,308: Henry O'Brien
No. 1,309: Francis O'Connor
No. 1,336: Patrick Lennon
No. 1,337: David Daly
No. 1,361: Commandant Gerald Davis
No. 1,439: James Maguire
No. 1,498: Michael Murray
No. 1,500: Anthony McCormack
No. 1,503: Michael McCormack
No. 1,504: Seamus O'Meara
No. 1,610: Michael McCoy
No. 1,698: Liam de Róiste
No. 1,716: Seán MacEoin
(★ same contributor)

University College Dublin Archives
Eoin MacNeill Papers
Terence MacSwiney Papers
Seán MacEoin Papers
Richard Mulcahy Papers
George Noble Count Plunkett Papers
Ernie O'Malley Papers
The O'Rahilly Papers
Moss Twomey Papers

BELFAST
Public Records Office for Northern Ireland
T/2782, Cecilia H. Daniel Letters 1911–1922

Government records and official publications
ATHLONE
Aidan Heavey Library

Minute Book of Athlone Urban District Council, 1900-1923
Minute Book of Athlone Poor Law Guardians, 1900-1920

DUBLIN
National Library of Ireland
MS 708, Minute Book of the National Directory of the UIL,
    10 August 1904-30 April 1918

National Archives of Ireland
RIC Reports 1903-1908
NA IG + CI/1-15

British in Ireland microfilm series
RIC County Inspector's Monthly Reports, 1900-1903, 1909-1921, CO 904/69-116
RIC Inspector General's Monthly Reports, 1900-1903, 1909-1921, CO 904/69-116
Postal Censorship, CO 904/164
Precís of Information (Crime Special Branch) CO 904/117-121
Press Censorship, CO 904/166
Sinn Féin and Republican Suspects, 1899-1922, Laurence Ginnell, CO 904/202/162
Sinn Féin and Republican Suspects, 1899-1922, Arthur Griffith, CO 904/202/175
Sinn Féin and Republican Suspects, 1899-1922, Revd M. O'Flanagan, CO
    904/202/334
UIL Quarterly Returns 1898-1921, CO/904/20

Department of Environment and Local Government:
DELG 30/11

Department of Finance:
Fin 1/1028; Fin 1/2571; Fin 1/2988

Ancient Order of Hibernian Records 1907-81:
Ancient Order of Hibernian Biennial Convention Agendas 1913-1919.
    LOU 13/2/1-2
Ancient Order of Hibernians Agenda Book 1912-81 LOU 13/2/1-2

Dáil Éireann
Dáil debates: Vol. 1, 20 August 1919

PRINTED SOURCES

Parliamentary and other official publications
House of Commons, London
Agricultural Statistics of Ireland, with detailed report on Agriculture for 1903
    (Agriculture (Ireland): Statistics), 1904 [Cd. 2196], CV.333

Agricultural Statistics of Ireland, with detailed report on Agriculture for 1904
    (Agriculture (Ireland): Statistics), 1906 [Cd. 2722], CXXXIII
Agricultural Statistics of Ireland, with detailed report on Agriculture for 1908
    (Agriculture (Ireland): Statistics), 1909 [Cd. 4940], CII.355
Agricultural Statistics of Ireland; with Detailed Report for the year 1909
    (Agriculture (Ireland): Acreage, Crops, Live Stock, Prices, Produce, &c), 1910
    [Cd. 5382], CVIII.489
Agricultural Statistics of Ireland; with Detailed Report for 1910 (Agriculture
    (Ireland): Acreage, Crops, Live Stock, Prices, Produce, &c), 1911 [Cd. 594], C.517
Annual report of the Local Government Board for Ireland, for the year ended 31st
    March, 1919, being the forty-seventh report under the Local Government Board
    (Ireland) Act, 1872, 35 & 36 Vic., c. 69, 1920 [Cmd. 578]
Annual report of the Local Government Board for Ireland, for the year ended 31st
    March, 1920, being the forty-eighth report under the Local Government Board
    (Ireland) Act, 1872, 35 & 36 Vic., c. 69, 1921 [Cmd. 1432]
Army Report on Recruiting in Ireland, H.C., 1914-16 [Cd. 8168], XXXIX.525
Census Returns of Ireland for 1901; giving details of the Area, Houses,
    and Population, also Ages, Civil or Conjugal Condition, Occupations,
    Birth-places, Religion and Education of the People, in each County,
    and Summary Tables for each Province, Vol. I. Province of Leinster (Population
    (Ireland): Census Returns, 1901), 1902 [Cd. 847], CXXII, CXXIII
Census Returns of Ireland for 1901; giving details of the Area, Houses,
    and Population, also Ages, Civil or Conjugal Condition, Occupations,
    Birth-places, Religion and Education of the People, in each County,
    and Summary Tables for each Province, Vol. IV. Province of Connaught
    (Population (Ireland): Census Returns, 1901), 1902 [Cd. 1059], CXXVIII
Census returns for Ireland, 1911, showing Area, Houses, and Population; also the
    ages, civil or conjugal condition, occupations, birthplaces, religions, and education
    of the people Province of Connaught (Population (Ireland): Census Returns,
    1911), 1912-13 [Cd. 6052], CXVII.1
Census returns for Ireland, 1911, showing Area, Houses, and Population; also
    the ages, civil or conjugal condition, occupations, birthplaces, religions,
    and education of the people Province of Leinster (Population (Ireland): Census
    Returns, 1911), 1912-13 [Cd. 6049], CXIV.1
Documents relative to the Sinn Féin movement, 1921 [Cmd. 1108]
Emigration Statistics of Ireland 1915, HC [Cd.8230], xxxii
House of Commons Parliamentary Debates 1900-21
Government of Ireland. A bill to amend the provision for the government of
    Ireland, HC, 1912-13, Bills [347]
Report and Tables showing the number, ages, conjugal conditions, and destinations
    of the Emigrants from each County and Province in Ireland during the year
    for 1915; also the occupations of the Emigrants, and the number of Emigrants
    who left each port in each month of the year (Emigration (Ireland): Emigration
    Statistics (Ireland)), HC, 1916 [Cd. 8230], xxxii
Report of the Irish Land Commissioners for the period from 1st April, 1919 to 31st
    March, 1920 [Cmd. 1064]

Return of charges made to Candidates at the General Election of January, 1910,
    in Great Britain and Ireland by Returning Officers, specifying the Total
    Expenses of each Candidate and the number of votes polled for each Candidate
    (in continuation of No. 302 of 1906) (Electors and Representation of the People:
    Election Expenses (January, 1910), 1910 [299], LXXIII.705
Royal Commission on the Rebellion in Ireland, HC, 1916 [Cd. 8279]
Statement giving particulars of men of military age in Ireland, HC, 1916 [Cd. 8390],
    XVII.581

Newspapers and periodicals

An Claidheamh Soluis agus Fáinne an Lae
Anglo Celt
Athlone Times
Church of Ireland Gazette
Connaught Tribune
Derry Journal
East Galway Democrat
Éire
Freeman's Journal
Hibernian
Hibernian Journal
Honesty
Iris an Airm
Irish Bulletin
Irish Freedom
Irish Independent
Irish Life
Irish Nation
Irish National Volunteer
Irish Opinion
Irish Peasant
Irish People
Irish Volunteer
Irishman
Leitrim Observer
Manchester Guardian
Midland Reporter and Westmeath Nationalist
Nationality
Nationist
New Ireland
New Leader
Observer
Offaly Independent
Old Ireland
Peasant
Poblacht na h-Éireann (Scottish ed.)

Poblacht na h-Éireann (Southern ed.)
Poblacht na h-Éireann – War News
Republican War Bulletin
Roscommon Herald
Roscommon Journal Roscommon Messenger
Sinn Féin (Daily)
Sinn Féin (Weekly)
Sinn Féiner
Southern Bulletin
Southern Star
Straight Talk
The Fenian
The Harp
The Irish Times
The Irish Worker
The Leader
The New York Times
The Plain People
The United Irishman
The Separatist
The Toiler
The Voice of Labour
The Workers' Republic
Tullamore and King's County Advertiser
Truth – War Issue
United Irishman
Watchword of Labour
Westmeath Examiner
Westmeath Guardian
Westmeath Independent
Young Ireland

Contemporary periodicals

The Irish Catholic Directory and Almanac for 1900 with complete directory in English
The Irish Catholic Directory and Almanac for 1905 with complete directory in English
The Irish Catholic Directory and Almanac for 1910 with complete directory in English
Thom's Official Directory of the United Kingdom of Great Britain and Ireland 1900–21
   (Dublin, 1900-1921)

MEMOIRS AND OTHER WORKS BY CONTEMPORARIES

Bulfin, William, *Rambles in Eirinn* (Dublin, 1907)
Clery, Arthur E., 'The Gaelic League, 1893-1919', in *Studies* 8 (1919), pp. 398-408
Hobson, Bulmer, *A Short History of the Irish Volunteers*, with a preface by Eoin
   MacNeill, Vol. 1 (Dublin, 1918)

Ginnell, Laurence, *Land and Liberty* (Dublin, 1908)

Ginnell, Laurence, *DORA at Westminster: Being selections from Mr. Ginnell's parliamentary activities* (Reprint from Hansard) *Before Easter week. After Easter week* (Dublin, 1918)

Ginnell, Laurence, *The Irish Republic, Why? Official Statement Prepared for Submission to the Peace Conference* (New York, 1919)

Ginnell, Laurence, *Ireland's case for freedom: Written in Mountjoy Prison, Dublin, in the summer of 1918* (New York, 1921)

Healy, T.M., *Letters and Leaders of my Day*, Vol. 1 (London, 1928)

Lysaght, Edward E., Westropp Bennett, T.W. and Ball, Richard, 'The Farmers and the Food Problem', in *Studies: An Irish Quarterly Review*, Vol. 6, No. 21 (March, 1917), pp. 21-34

Magan, William, *An Irish Boyhood* (Durham, 1996)

Mannion, Vergil OFM, *A life Recalled: Experiences of an Irish Franciscan* (Dublin, 1984)

Mitchell, Maud, *The Man With the Long Hair: I am Eighty; My life is at an end. What I write is the Truth. Do nothing about it until I am Dead* (Belfast, 1993)

Ó Rahilly, Michael Joseph, *The secret history of the Irish Volunteers* (Dublin, 1915)

Shea, Patrick, *Voices and the Sound of Drums: An Irish Autobiography* (Belfast, 1981)

Twohig, Patrick J., *Blood on the Flag: Autobiography of a Freedom Fighter* (Cork, 1996)

SECONDARY SOURCES

Books

aan De Wiel, Jérôme, *The Catholic Church in Ireland: 1914-1918: War and Politics* (Dublin, 2003)

Abbott, Richard, *Police Casualties in Ireland: 1919-1922* (Cork, 2000)

Augusteijn, Joost, *From Public Defiance to Guerrilla Warfare: The Experience of Ordinary Volunteers in the Irish War of Independence 1916-1921* (Dublin, 1996)

Augusteijn, Joost (ed.), *The Irish Revolution: 1913-1923* (New York, 2002)

Bairner, Alan (ed.), *Sport and the Irish: Histories, Identities, Issues* (Dublin, 2005)

Bartlett, Thomas and Jeffery, Keith (eds), *A Military History of Ireland* (Cambridge, 1996)

Barton, Brian, *From Behind a Closed Door: Secret Courts Martial Records of the 1916 Rising* (Belfast, 2002)

Beckett, F.W. (ed.), *The Army and the Curragh Incident 1914* (London, 1986)

Beckett, J.C., *Confrontations: Studies in Irish History* (London, 1972)

Beckett, J.C., *The Making of Modern Ireland: 1603-1923* (London, 1989)

Bennett, Martyn, *The Civil Wars Experienced: Britain and Ireland, 1638-1661* (London, 2000)

Bennett, Richard, *The Black and Tans* (New York, 1995)

Bew, Paul, *Conflict and Conciliation in Ireland: 1890-1910, Parnellites and Radical Agrarians* (Oxford, 1987)

Bew, Paul, *Ideology and the Irish Question: Ulster Unionism and Irish Nationalism 1912-1916* (Oxford, 1994)

Bew, Paul, *Ireland: The Politics of Enmity 1789-2006* (Oxford, 2007)

Bourke, Angela (ed.), *The Irish Field Day Anthology of Irish Writing, Vol. 5, Irish Women's Writings and Traditions* (New York, 2002)

Boyce, D.G., *Englishmen and Irish Troubles: British Public Opinion and the Making of Irish Policy 1918-22* (London, 1972)

Boyce, D.G. (ed.), *The Revolution in Ireland: 1879-1923* (London, 1988)

Boyce, D.G., *Nineteenth-Century Ireland: The Search for Stability* (Dublin, 1990)

Boyce, D.G., *Nationalism in Ireland* (Oxford, 1995)

Boyce, D.G., *The Irish Question and British Politics: 1868-1996* (London, 1996)

Boyce, D.G. and O'Day, Alan (eds), *Ireland in Transition: 1867-1921* (Oxford, 2004)

Boyce, D.G. and O'Day, Alan (eds), *The Ulster Crisis: 1885-1921* (New York, 2006)

Breathnach, Diarmuid agus Ní Mhurcú, *Máire, Beathaisnéis a Cúig* (Baile Átha Cliath, 1997)

Brown, Stewart J. and Miller, Daniel W., *Piety and Power in Ireland: 1760-1960* (Belfast, 2000)

Buckland, Pat, *Irish Unionism: One: The Anglo Irish and the New Ireland: 1885-1922* (Dublin, 1972)

Bull, Philip, *Land, Politics and Nationalism: A Study of the Irish Land Question* (Dublin, 1996)

Buttimer, Neil, Rynne, Colin and Guerin, Helen (eds), *The Heritage of Ireland* (Cork, 2000)

Campbell, Colm, *Emergency Law in Ireland: 1918-1925* (New York, 1994)

Campbell, Fergus, *Land and Revolution: Nationalist Politics in the West of Ireland 1891-1921* (Oxford, 2005)

Campbell, Fergus, *The Irish Establishment, 1879-1914* (Oxford, 2009)

Cannon, John (ed.), *The Oxford Companion to British History* (Oxford, 1997)

Carroll, Denis, *They have Fooled you Again: Michael O'Flanagan (1876-1942): Priest, Republican, Social Critic* (Dublin, 1993)

Clark, Samuel and Donnelly, James S. (eds), *Irish Peasants: Violence and Political Unrest, 1780-1914* (Wisconsin, 1986)

Coleman, Marie, *County Longford and the Irish Revolution: 1910-1923* (Dublin, 2003)

Collins, Peter (ed.), *Nationalism and Unionism: Conflict in Ireland, 1885-1921* (Belfast, 1994)

Connolly, S.J. (ed.), *The Oxford Companion to Irish History* (Oxford, 2007)

Coogan, Oliver, *Politics and War in Meath: 1913-23* (Dublin, 1983)

Corkery, Daniel, *The Fortunes of the Irish Language* (Cork, 1968)

Costello, Francis J., *Enduring the Most: The Life and Death of Terence MacSwiney* (Kerry, 1995)

Costello, Francis, *The Irish Revolution and its Aftermath: 1916-1923: Years of Revolt* (Dublin, 2003)

Cronin, Mike and Adair, Daryl, *The Wearing of the Green: A History of St Patrick's Day* (London, 2002)

Crowley, Tony, *The Politics of Language in Ireland: 1366-1922: A Sourcebook* (Oxford, 2000)

Cullen, Louis M., *An Economic History of Ireland Since 1660* (London, 1972)

Curtis, T.B. and McDowell, R.B., *Irish Historical Documents: 1172-1922* (London, 1977)

Daly, Leo, *Titles* (Mullingar, 1981)

Daly, Mary E., *The Buffer State: the Historical Roots of the Department of the Environment* (Dublin, 1997)

Dangerfield, George, *The Damnable Question: a Study of Anglo-Irish Relations* (London, 1977)

Davis, Richard P., *Arthur Griffith and Non-Violent Sinn Féin* (Dublin, 1974)

Deane, Seamus (ed.), *The Field Day Anthology of Irish Writing, Vol. 2* (Derry, 1991)

Doerries, Reinhard R., *Prelude to the Easter Rising: Sir Roger Casement in Imperial Germany* (London, 2000)

Doherty, Gabriel and Keogh, Dermot, *1916: The Long Revolution* (Cork, 2007)

Dooley, Terence, *'The Land for the People': The Land Question in Independent Ireland* (Dublin, 2004)

Drudy, P.J., *Irish Studies 2: Ireland: Land, Politics and People* (Cambridge, 1982)

Dudley Edwards, R., *A New History of Ireland* (Dublin, 1972)

English, Richard and Walker, Graham, *Unionism in Modern Ireland: New Perspectives on Politics and Culture* (London, 1996)

English, Richard, *Armed Struggle: the History of the IRA* (New York, 2003)

English, Richard, *Irish Freedom: The History of Nationalism in Ireland* (London, 2006)

Evans, Martin and Lunn, Kenneth (eds), *War and Memory in the Twentieth Century* (Oxford, 1997)

Fanning, Ronan, *Fatal Path: British Government and Irish Revolution, 1910–1922* (London, 2013)

Farrell, Brian (ed.), *The Creation of the Dáil: a Volume of Essays from the Thomas Davis Lectures* (Dublin, 1994)

Farry, Michael, *Sligo 1914-1921: A Chronicle of Conflict* (Trim, 1992)

Farry, Michael, *The Aftermath of Revolution: Sligo 1921-23* (Dublin, 2000)

Ferguson, Sir James, *The Curragh Incident* (London, 1964)

Ferriter, Diarmuid, *The Transformation of Ireland: 1900-2000* (London, 2004)

Finnan, Joseph P., *John Redmond and Irish Unity: 1912-1918* (New York, 2004)

Fitzpatrick, David, *Harry Boland's Irish Revolution* (Cork, 2003)

Fitzpatrick, David, *Politics and Irish Life 1913-1921: Provincial Experience of War and Revolution* (2nd ed., Cork, 1998)

Fitzpatrick, David (ed.), *Revolution? Ireland: 1917-1923* (Dublin, 1990)

Fitzpatrick, David, *The Two Irelands: 1912-1939* (New York, 1998)

Flynn, M.K., *Ideology, Mobilization and the Nation: the rise of Irish, Basque and Carlist Nationalist Movements in the Nineteenth and Early Twentieth Centuries* (London, 2000)

Foster, R.F., *Modern Ireland: 1600-1972* (London, 1988)

Foster, R.F. (ed.), *The Oxford Illustrated History of Ireland* (Oxford, 1989)

Foy, Michael and Barton, Brian, *The Easter Rising* (Gloucestershire, 2004)

Fraser, Murray, *John Bull's Other Homes: State Housing and British Policy in Ireland 1883-1922* (Liverpool, 1996)

Garvin, Tom, *1922: The Birth of Irish Democracy* (Dublin, 1996)

Garvin, Tom, *The Evolution of Irish Nationalist Politics* (New York, 1981)

Garvin, Tom, *Nationalist revolutionaries in Ireland: 1858-1928* (Oxford, 1987)

Glandon, Virginia E., *Arthur Griffith and the Advanced Nationalist Press in Ireland 1900-1922* (New York, 1985)

Goldstrom, J.M. and Clarkson, L.A. (eds), *Irish Population, Economy and Society. Essays in Honour of K.H. Connell* (Oxford, 1981)

Grayzel, Susan R., *Women and the First World War* (Essex, 2002)

Greaves, Desmond C., *Liam Mellows and the Irish Revolution* (Belfast, 2004)

Gregory, Adrian and Pašeta, Senia (eds), *Ireland and the Great War: 'A war to unite us all?'* (Manchester, 2002)

Griffith, Kenneth and O'Grady, Timothy E., *Curious Journey: An Oral History of Ireland's Unfinished Revolution* (London, 1982)

Hanley, Lt Col. M.K., *The Story of Custume Barracks Athlone* (Athlone, 1974)

Hardach, Gerd, *The First World War: 1914-1918* (Berkeley, 1977)

Harkness, David, *Ireland in the Twentieth Century: Divided Island* (London, 1996)

Hart, Peter, *The IRA and its Enemies: Violence and Community in Cork 1916-1923* (Oxford, 1998)

Hart, Peter, *British Intelligence in Ireland, 1920-21: the final reports* (Cork, 2002)

Hart, Peter, *The IRA at War: 1916-1923* (Oxford, 2003)

Hay, Marnie, *Bulmer Hobson and the Nationalist Movement in Twentieth-Century Ireland* (Manchester, 2009)

Hegarty Thorne, Kathleen, *'They put the Flag a-Flyin': The Roscommon Volunteers: 1916-1923* (Oregon, 2007)

Hennessey, Thomas, *Dividing Ireland: World War One and Partition* (Oxford, 1998)

Hepburn, A.C., *The Conflict of Nationality in Modern Ireland* (London, 1980)

Hepburn, Anthony C., *A Past Apart: Studies in the History of Catholic Belfast, 1850-1950* (Belfast, 1996)

Hepburn, A.C., *Catholic Belfast and Nationalist Ireland in the era of Joe Devlin: 1872-1934* (Oxford, 2008)

Hindley, Reg, *The Death of the Irish Language: a Qualified Obituary* (London, 1990)

Hobson, Bulmer, *Ireland Yesterday and Tomorrow* (Tralee, 1968)

Hopkinson, Michael, *Green against Green: Ireland's Civil War* (Dublin, 1988)

Hopkinson, Michael, *The Irish War of Independence* (Dublin, 2002)

Hoppen, K. Theodore, *Ireland Since 1800: Conflict and Conformity* (New York, 1999)

Horne, John (ed.), *Our War: Ireland and the Great War* (Dublin, 2008)

Hutchinson, John, *The Dynamics of Cultural Nationalism: The Gaelic Revival and the Creation of the Irish Nation State* (London, 1987)

Jackson, Alvin, *Ireland: 1798-1998* (Oxford, 1999)

Jackson, Alvin, *Home Rule, An Irish History: 1800-2000* (Oxford, 2003)

Jeffery, Keith, *Ireland and the Great War* (Cambridge, 2000)

Johnson, Nuala C., *Ireland, The Great War and the Geography of Remembrance* (Cambridge, 2003)

Johnstone, Tom, *Orange, Green and Khaki: The Story of the Irish Regiments in the Great War, 1914-18* (Dublin, 1992)

Jones, David Seth, *Graziers, Land Reform, and Political Conflict in Ireland* (Washington DC, 1995)

Jordan, Anthony J., *Boer War to Easter Rising: The Writings of John McBride* (Dublin, 2006)

Kautt, W.H., *Ambushes and Armour: The Irish Rebellion, 1919-1921* (Dublin, 2011)

Keaney, M. and O'Brien, G., *Athlone: Bridging the Centuries* (Mullingar, 1991)

Kee, Robert, *The Green Flag: A History of Irish Nationalism* (London, 1972)

Kelly, M.J., *The Fenian Ideal and Irish Nationalism 1882-1916* (Suffolk, 2006)

Kenneally, Ian, *The Paper Wall: Newspapers and Propaganda in Ireland 1919-1921* (Cork, 2008)

Kennedy, Kieran A., *From Famine to Feast: Economic and Social Change in Ireland 1847-1997* (Dublin, 1998)

Kenny, Kevin, *Making Sense of the Molly Maguires* (Oxford, 1998)

Kenny, Kevin, *Ireland and the British Empire* (Oxford, 2004)

Kenny, Michael, *The Road to Freedom: Photographs and Memorabilia from the 1916 Rising and Afterwards* (Dublin, 1993)

Keogh, Dermot, *Twentieth-Century Ireland: Nation and State* (Dublin, 1994)

Kissane, Bill, *The Politics of the Irish Civil War* (New York, 2007)

Kostick, Conor, *Revolution in Ireland: Popular Military 1917-1923* (London, 1996)

Laffan, Michael, *The Resurrection of Ireland: The Sinn Féin Party, 1916-1923* (Cambridge, 1999)

Lafflin, John, *Tommy Atkins: The Story of a British Soldier* (London, 1966)

Laird, Heather, *Subversive Law in Ireland, 1879-1920: From 'Unwritten Law' to the Dáil courts* (Dublin, 2005)

Lee, J.J., *Ireland 1912-1985: Politics and Society* (Cambridge, 1989)

Lee, Joseph, *The Modernisation of Irish Society: 1848-1918* (Dublin, 1973)

Leeson, D.M., *The Black and Tans: British Police and Auxiliaries in the Irish War of Independence, 1920-1921* (Oxford, 2011)

Longford, The Earl of and O'Neill, T.P., *Éamon de Valera* (Dublin, 1970)

Luddy, Maria, *Women in Ireland, 1800-1922: A Documentary History* (Cork, 1995)

Lyons, F.S.L., *Ireland Since the Famine* (London, 1973)

Lyons, F.S.L., *John Dillon: A Biography* (London, 1968)

Lyons, F.S.L., *The Irish Parliamentary Party, 1890-1910* (Westport, 1975)

Macardle, Dorothy, *The Irish Republic* (5th edition, London, 1968)

MacEoin, Uinseann (ed.), *Survivors* (Dublin, 1980)

Mac Finn, Pádraig Eric, *An tAthair Mícheál P. Ó hIceadha* (Baile Átha Cliath, 1974)

Mac Giolla Choille, Breandán, *Intelligence Notes: 1913-1916, preserved in the State Paper Office* (Dublin, 1966)

Mac Giolla Chriost, Diarmait, *The Irish Language in Ireland: From Goidel to Globalisation* (Oxford, 2005)

Maher, Jim, *Harry Boland, A Biography* (Cork, 1998)

Malcolm, Elizabeth and Jones, Greta, *Medicine, Disease and the State in Ireland 1650–1940* (Cork, 1999)

Malcolm, Elizabeth, *The Irish Policeman, 1822-1922: A Life* (Dublin, 2006)

Martin, F.X., *Sources for the Irish Volunteers: 1913-1916* (Dublin, 1963)

Martin, F.X. (ed.), *The Howth Gun-Running and the Kilcoole Gun-Running 1914* (Dublin, 1964)

Martin, F.X. and Byrne, F.J. (eds), *The Scholar Revolutionary: Eoin MacNeill, 1867-1945, and the Making of the New Ireland* (Dublin, 1973)

Mathews, P.J., *Revival: The Abbey Theatre, Sinn Féin, the Gaelic League and the Co-operative Movement* (Cork, 2003)

Maume, Patrick, *The Long Gestation: Irish Nationalist Life 1891-1918* (Dublin, 1999)

Maye, Brian, *Arthur Griffith* (Dublin, 1997)

Mays, Michael, *Nation States: The Cultures of Irish Nationalism* (Maryland, 2007)

McCaffrey, Lawrence John, *The Irish Question: Two Centuries of Conflict* (Kentucky, 1995)

McCarthy, Cal, *Cumann na mBan and the Irish Revolution* (Cork, 2007)

McConville, Seán, *Irish Political Prisoners, 1848-1922: Theatres of War* (Oxon, 2005)

McCoole, Sinéad, *Guns and Chiffon* (Dublin, 1997)

McDowell, R.B., *Crisis and Decline: The Fate of Southern Unionists* (Dublin, 1997)

McDowell, R.B., *The Irish Convention, 1917-1918* (London, 1970)

McGarry, Fearghal and McConnel, James (eds), *The Black Hand of Republicanism: Fenianism in Modern Ireland* (Dublin, 2009).

McGee, Owen, *The IRB: The Irish Republican Brotherhood from the Land War to Sinn Féin* (Dublin, 2005)

McGrath, Conor and O'Malley, Eoin (eds), *Irish Political Studies Reader: Key Contributions* (London, 2007)

McGuire, James and Quinn, James, *Dictionary of Irish Biography: 9 Volume Set* (Dublin, 2009)

McMahon, Timothy G., *The Gaelic Revival and Irish Society: 1893-1910* (New York, 2008)

Miller, David W., *Church, State and Nation in Ireland: 1898-1921* (Dublin, 1971)

Mitchell, Arthur, *Labour in Irish Politics, 1890-1930: the Irish Labour Movement in an Age of Revolution* (Dublin, 1974)

Mitchell, Arthur, *Revolutionary Government in Ireland: Dáil Éireann 1919-22* (Dublin, 1995)

Mulcahy, Risteárd, *My Father, The General: Richard Mulcahy and the Military History of the Revolution* (Dublin, 2009)

Murphy, John A., *Ireland in the Twentieth Century* (Dublin, 1989)

Murray, Patrick, *Oracles of God: The Roman Catholic Church and Irish Politics, 1922-37* (Dublin, 2000)

Murtagh, H., *Irish Historic Towns Atlas Volume VI: Athlone* (Dublin, 1994)

Neeson, Eoin, *Birth of a Republic* (Dublin, 1998)

Neeson, Eoin, *The Civil War: 1922-23* (Dublin, 1989)

Nolan, William and McGrath, Thomas (eds), *Kildare: History and Society: Interdisciplinary Essays on the History of an Irish County* (Dublin, 2006)

Novick, Ben, *Conceiving Revolution: Irish Nationalist Propaganda during the First World War* (Dublin, 2001)

Nowlan, Kevin B. (ed.), *The Making of 1916* (Dublin, 1969)

O'Brien, Gearóid, *Athlone in Old Photographs* (Dublin, 2002)

O'Brien, Gearóid, *Athlone in Old Picture Postcards* (Zaltbommel, 1996)

O'Brien, Gerard (ed.), *Derry and Londonderry, History and Society: Interdisciplinary Essays on the History of an Irish County* (Dublin, 1999)

O'Brien, Gearóid, *St Mary's Parish, Athlone: a History* (Longford, 1989)

O'Brien, Joseph V., *William O'Brien and the Course of Irish Politics: 1881-1918* (Berkeley, 1976)

O'Brien, Seamus (ed.), *A Town in Transition: Post Famine Mullingar* (Mullingar, 2007)

O'Callaghan, Micheál, *For Ireland and Freedom: Roscommon's Contribution to the Fight for Independence, 1917-1921* (3rd Ed.: Cork, 2012)

O'Connor, Emmet, *Syndicalism in Ireland, 1917-1923* (Cork, 1988)

Ó Croidheáin, Caoimhghin, *Language from Below: The Irish Language, Ideology and*

Power in 20th Century Ireland (Bern, 2006)

O'Day, Alan (ed.), *Reactions to Irish Nationalism: 1865-1914* (London, 1987)

O'Day, Alan, *Irish Home Rule: 1867-1921* (Manchester, 1998)

O'Halpin, Eunan, *Defending Ireland: The Irish State and its Enemies Since 1922* (Oxford, 1999)

O'Leary, Cornelius and Maume, Patrick, *Controversial Issues in Anglo-Irish Relations: 1910-1921* (Dublin, 2004)

O'Leary, Philip, *The Prose Literature of the Gaelic Revival, 1881-1921: Ideology and Innovation* (Pennsylvania, 1994)

O'Mahony, Seán, *Frongoch: University of Revolution* (Dublin, 1987)

O'Rahilly, Aodogán, *Winding the Clock: O'Rahilly and the 1916 Rising* (Dublin, 1991)

Ó Snodaigh, Pádraig, *Comhghuaillithe na Réabhlóide 1913-1916* (Dublin, 1966)

Ó Tuama, Seán (ed.), *The Gaelic League Idea* (Cork, 1972)

Philpin, C.H.E., *Nationalism and Popular Protest in Ireland* (Cambridge, 1987)

Pollard, H.B.C., *Secret Societies of Ireland: Their Rise and Progress* (originally published 1922, reprinted Massachusetts, 2003)

Price, Dominic, *The Flame and the Candle: War in Mayo 1919-1924* (Dublin, 2012)

Pugh, Martin, *The Making of Modern British Politics, 1867-1945* (Oxford, 2002)

Ranelagh, John O'Beirne, *A Short History of Ireland* (Cambridge, 1999)

Regan, John M., *Myth and the Irish State* (Sallins, 2013)

Regan, John M., *The Irish Counter-Revolution* (Dublin, 1999)

Reilly, George R., *Hibernians on the March: An examination of the origins and history of the Ancient Order of Hibernians with a programme for the future* (San Francisco, 1948)

Rumpf, E., and Hepburn, A.C., *Nationalism and Socialism in Twentieth-Century Ireland* (Liverpool, 1977)

Ryan, Meda, *Tom Barry: IRA Freedom Fighter* (Cork, 2003)

Scanlan, Margaret, *Culture and Customs of Ireland* (Connecticut, 2006)

Sheehan, Jeremiah, *South Westmeath: Farm and Folk* (Dublin, 1978)

Sheehan, William, *Hearts and Mines: The British 5th Division, Ireland, 1920-1922* (Dublin, 2009)

Sterns, Peter N., *The Encyclopaedia of World History* (New York, 2001)

Stewart, A.T.Q., *The Shape of Irish History* (Belfast, 2001)

Stewart, A.T.Q., *The Ulster Crisis* (London, 1979)

Stockton, Lewis, *Marriage considered From Legal and Ecclesiastical Viewpoints, in Connection with the Recent Ne Temere Decree of the Roman Catholic Church* (originally published 1912, reprinted Massachusetts, 2008)

Strachan, Hew, *The Politics of the British Army* (Oxford, 1997)

Tierney, Michael, *Eoin MacNeill: Scholar and Man of Action, 1867-1945* (Oxford, 1980)

Tompkins, Phil, *Twice a Hero. From the Trenches of the Great War to the Ditches of the Irish Midlands, 1915-1922* (Cirencester, 2012)

Townshend, Charles, *Easter 1916: The Irish Rebellion* (London, 2006)

Townshend, Charles, *Political Violence in Ireland: Government and Resistance since 1848* (Oxford, 1984)

Townshend, Charles, *The British Campaign in Ireland 1919-1921: The Development of Political and Military Policies* (London, 1975)

Townshend, Charles, *The Republic: The Fight for Irish Independence* (London, 2013)

Valiulis, Maryann Gialanella, *Portrait of a Revolutionary: General Richard Mulcahy*

(Kentucky, 1992)

Vaughan, W.E. (ed.), *A New History of Ireland VI: Ireland 1870-1920* (Oxford, 2000)

Vaughan, W.E. (ed.), *A New History of Ireland VII: Ireland 1921-1984* (Oxford, 2003)

Walker, B.M. (ed.), *Parliamentary Election Results in Ireland: 1801-1922* (Dublin, 1978)

Walker, Brian M. (ed.), *Parliamentary Election Results in Ireland: 1918-92* (Dublin, 1992)

Walsh, Oonagh, *Ireland's Independence, 1880-1923* (London, 2002)

Wheatley, Michael, *Nationalism and the Irish Party: Provincial Ireland 1910-1916* (Oxford, 2005)

Wright, Sue, *Language and the State: Revitalisation and Revival in Israel and Eire* (Bristol, 1996)

Wulff, Helena, *Dancing at the Crossroads: Memory and Mobility in Ireland* (Oxford, 2007)

Younger, Calton, *Arthur Griffith* (Dublin, 1981)

Younger, Calton, *Ireland's Civil War* (London, 1968)

Articles

Aalen, F.H.A., 'Homes for Irish heroes: housing under the Irish Land (Provision for Soldiers and Sailors) Act 1919, and the Irish Sailors' and Soldiers' Land Trust', in *The Town Planning Review*, Vol. 59, No. 3 (July, 1988), pp. 305-323

Augusteijn, Joost, 'Motivation: why did they fight for Ireland? The motivation of volunteers in the Revolution' in Augusteijn, Joost (ed.), *The Irish Revolution: 1913-1923* (New York, 2002), pp. 87-102

Augusteijn, Joost, 'The importance of being Irish. Ideas and the volunteers in Mayo and Tipperary', in Fitzpatrick, David (ed.), *Revolution? Ireland: 1917-1923* (Dublin, 1990), pp. 25-42

Augusteijn, Joost, 'Radical nationalist activities in County Derry 1900-1921', in O'Brien, Gerard (ed.), *Derry and Londonderry, History and Society: Interdisciplinary Essays on the History of an Irish County* (Dublin, 1999), pp. 573-600

Bew, Paul, 'Moderate nationalism and the Irish revolution, 1916-1923', in *The Historical Journal*, Vol. 42, No. 3 (1999), pp. 729-749

Bew, Paul, 'The politics of war', in Horne, John (ed.), *Our War: Ireland and the Great War* (Dublin, 2008), pp. 95-107

Bowden, Tom, 'The Irish Underground and the War of Independence 1919-21', in *Journal of Contemporary History*, Vol. 8, No. 2 (April, 1973), pp. 3-23

Bowman, Timothy, 'The Ulster Volunteer Force and the formation of the 36th (Ulster) Division', in *Irish Historical Studies*, Vol. 32, No. 128 (November, 2001), pp. 498-518

Bowman, Timothy, 'The Ulster Volunteer Force, 1910-1920: new perspectives', in Boyce, D. George and O'Day, Alan (eds), *The Ulster Crisis: 1885-1921* (New York, 2006), pp. 247-258

Boyce, D.G., 'British Conservative opinion, the Ulster question, and the partition of Ireland, 1912-21', in *Irish Historical Studies*, Vol. 17, No. 65 (March, 1970), pp. 89-112

Boyce, David G., 'British opinion, Ireland, and the War, 1916-1918', in *The Historical Journal*, Vol. 17, No. 3 (September, 1974), pp. 575-593

Boyce, D.G. and Hazelhurst, Cameron, 'The unknown Chief Secretary: H.E. Duke and Ireland, 1916-18', in *Irish Historical Studies*, Vol. 20, No. 79 (March, 1977), pp. 286-311

Boyce, D.G., "That party politics should divide our tents': nationalism, unionism and the First World War', in Gregory, Adrian and Pašeta, Senia (eds), *Ireland and the Great War: 'A War to Unite us All?'* (Manchester, 2002), pp. 190-216

Boyce, D. George and O'Day Alan, 'A time of transitions', in Boyce, D. George and O'Day, Alan (eds.), *Ireland in Transition: 1867-1921* (London, 2004), pp. 1-14

Boyce, D. George, 'A First World War transition. State and citizen in Ireland, 1914-1919', in Boyce, D. George and O'Day, Alan (eds), *Ireland in Transition: 1867-1921* (London, 2004), pp. 92-112

Boyce, D.G., 'The Ulster crisis: prelude to 1916?', in Doherty, Gabriel and Keogh, Dermot, *1916: The Long Revolution* (Cork, 2007), pp. 45-60

Boyce, George, 'British politics and the Irish Question, 1912-1922', in Collins, Peter (ed.), *Nationalism and Unionism: Conflict in Ireland, 1885-1921* (Belfast, 1994), pp. 91-106

Breathnach, Diarmuid and Ní Mhuirchú, Máire, 'The early Gaelic League: A Bansha connection', in *Tipperary Historical Journal* (2006), pp. 174-178

Brown, Terence, 'Cultural nationalism 1880-1930', in Deane, Seamus (ed.), *The Field Day Anthology of Irish Writing, Vol. 2* (Derry, 1991), pp. 516-562

Brown, Terence, 'Writing the war', in Horne, John (ed.), *Our War: Ireland and the Great War* (Dublin, 2008), pp. 233-246

Buckland, Patrick, 'Carson, Craig and the partition of Ireland', in Collins, Peter (ed.), *Nationalism and Unionism: Conflict in Ireland, 1885-1921* (Belfast, 1994), pp. 75-90

Buckland, P.J., 'The southern Irish unionists, the Irish Question and British politics, 1906-1914', in O'Day, Alan (ed.), *Reactions to Irish Nationalism: 1865-1914* (London, 1987), pp. 365-392

Bull, Philip, 'Land and politics, 1879-1903', in Boyce, D.G. (ed.), *The Revolution in Ireland: 1879-1923* (London, 1988), pp. 23-46

Bull, Philip, 'The formation of the United Irish League, 1898-1900: The dynamics of Irish agrarian agitation', in *Irish Historical Studies, Vol. 33, No. 132 (November, 2003), pp. 404-423

Bull, Philip, 'The significance of the nationalist response to the Irish Land Act of 1903', in *Irish Historical Studies, Vol. 28, No. 111 (May, 1993), pp. 283-305

Bull, Philip, 'The United Irish League and the reunion of the Irish Parliamentary Party, 1898-1900', in *Irish Historical Studies, Vol. 26, No. 101 (May, 1988), pp. 51-78

Buttimer, Neil, 'The Irish Language', in Buttimer, Neil, Rynne, Colin and Guerin, Helen (eds.), *The Heritage of Ireland* (Cork, 2000), pp. 92-106

Callan, Patrick, 'Recruiting for the British Army in Ireland during the First World War', in *Irish Sword, Vol. 17, No. 6 (1987-90), pp. 42-56

Campbell, Fergus, 'Irish popular politics and the making of the Wyndham Act, 1901-1903', in *The Historical Journal, Vol. 45, No. 4 (2002), pp. 755-773

Campbell, Fergus, 'The social dynamics of nationalist politics in the west of Ireland 1898-1918', in *Past and Present*, No. 182 (February, 2004), pp. 175-209

Campbell, Fergus, 'Who ruled Ireland? The Irish Administration, 1879-1914', in *The Historical Journal, Vol. 50, No. 3 (2007), pp. 623-644

Campbell, Fergus and O'Shiel, Kevin, 'The last land war? Kevin O'Shiel's memoir of the Irish revolution (1916-21)', in *Archivium Hibernicum, Vol. 57 (2003), pp. 155-200

Casey, Patrick, 'Irish casualties in the First World War', in *Irish Sword*, Vol. 20, No. 8 (Summer, 1997), pp. 193-206

Clark, Marie, 'The appeal of the United Irish League in County Roscommon 1903-7', in *Roscommon Historical and Archaeological Journal*, Vol. 5 (1994), pp. 72-75

Clear, Caitriona, 'Fewer ladies, more women', in Horne, John (ed.), *Our War: Ireland and the Great War* (Dublin, 2008), pp. 157-170

Coleman, Marie, 'Mobilisation: The South Longford by-election and its impact on political mobilisation', in Augusteijn, Joost (ed.), *The Irish Revolution: 1913-1923* (New York, 2002), pp. 53-69

Coleman, Marie, 'Nugent, Sir Walter Richard', in McGuire, James and Quinn, James, *Dictionary of Irish Biography*, Vol. VI (Dublin, 2009), p. 987

Collins, Peter, 'Irish Labour and politics in the late nineteenth and early twentieth centuries', in Collins, Peter (ed.), *Nationalism and Unionism: Conflict in Ireland, 1885-1921* (Belfast, 1994), pp. 123-154

Comstock Weston, Corinne, 'The Liberal leadership and the Lords' veto, 1907-1910', in *The Historical Journal*, Vol. 11, No. 3 (1968), pp. 508-537

Conlon, P., 'The outlaw friars of Athlone: 1916', in *Journal of the Old Athlone Society*, Vol. 1, No. 2 (1971), pp. 55-60

Connell, Gretta, 'Westmeath County Council and the struggle for independence, 1916-1922', in O'Brien, Seamus (ed.), *A Town in Transition: Post Famine Mullingar* (Mullingar, 2007), pp. 55-74

Corley, Fintan, 'Ambush at Auburn: 1920', in *Journal of the Old Athlone Society*, Vol. 2, No. 7 (2003), pp. 189-190

Costello, Francis, 'Lloyd George and Ireland, 1919-1921: an uncertain policy', in *The Canadian Journal of Irish Studies*, Vol. 14, No. 1 (July, 1988), pp. 5-16

Costello, Francis J., 'The role of propaganda in the Anglo-Irish War 1919-1921', in *The Canadian Journal of Irish Studies*, Vol. 14, No. 2 (January, 1989), pp. 5-24

Costello, Francis, 'The Republican Courts and the decline of British rule in Ireland, 1919-1921', in *Éire-Ireland*, Vol. 25, No. 2 (1990), pp. 36-55

Costello, Francis, 'Labour, Irish republicanism, and the social order during the Anglo-Irish War', in *The Canadian Journal of Irish Studies*, Vol. 17, No. 2 (December, 1991), pp. 1-22

Curtis, L. Perry Jr, 'Moral and physical force: The language of violence in Irish nationalism', in *The Journal of British Studies*, Vol. 27, No. 2 (April, 1988), pp. 150-189

Curtis, L.P. Jr, 'Ireland in 1914', in Vaughan, W.E. (ed.), *A New History of Ireland VI: Ireland 1870-1920* (Oxford, 2000), pp. 145-188

Daly, Mary, 'Local government and the First Dáil', in Farrell, Brian (ed.), *The Creation of the Dáil: a Volume of Essays from the Thomas Davis Lectures* (Dublin, 1994), pp. 123-136

Davis, Eoghan, 'The guerrilla mind', in Fitzpatrick, David (ed.), *Revolution? Ireland: 1917-1923* (Dublin, 1990), pp. 43-59

Dempsey, Pauric J. and Boylan, Seán, 'Ginnell, Laurence', in McGuire, James and Quinn, James, *Dictionary of Irish Biography, Vol. IV* (Dublin, 2009), pp. 102-103

Denman, Terence, 'The Catholic Irish Soldier in the First World War: 'The Racial Environment", in *Irish Historical Studies*, Vol. 27, No. 108 (November, 1991), pp. 352-365

Denman, Terence, '"The red livery of shame": the campaign against recruitment in

Ireland 1899-1914', in *Irish Historical Studies*, Vol. 29, No. 114 (November, 1994), pp. 208-233

Doherty, Gabriel and Borgonovo, John, 'Smoking gun? RIC reprisals, Summer 1920', in *History Ireland*, Vol. 17, No. 2 (March/April, 2009), pp. 36-39

Doherty, M.A., 'Kevin Barry and the Anglo-Irish propaganda war', *Irish Historical Studies*, Vol. 32, No. 126 (November, 2000), pp. 217-231

Dooley, Terence, 'IRA activity in Kildare during the War of Independence', in Nolan, William & McGrath, Thomas (eds), *Kildare: History and Society: Interdisciplinary Essays on the History of an Irish County* (Dublin, 2006), pp. 625-656

Douglas, Roy, 'Voluntary enlistment in the First World War and the work of the Parliamentary Recruiting Committee', *in The Journal of Modern History*, Vol. 42, No. 4 (December, 1970), pp. 564-585

Ferriter, Diarmuid, 'In such deadly earnest', in *Dublin Review 12* (2003)

Fitzpatrick, David, 'Home front and everyday life', in Horne, John (ed.), *Our War: Ireland and the Great War* (Dublin, 2008), pp. 131-142

Fitzpatrick, David, 'Ireland since 1870', in Foster, R.F. (ed.), *The Oxford Illustrated History of Ireland* (Oxford, 1989), pp. 213-274

Fitzpatrick, David, 'Irish farming families before the First World War', in *Comparative Studies in Society and History*, Vol. 25, No. 2 (April, 1983), pp. 339-374

Fitzpatrick, David, 'Militarism in Ireland, 1900-22', in Bartlett, Thomas and Jeffery, Keith (eds.), *A Military History of Ireland* (Cambridge, 1996), pp. 379-406

Fitzpatrick, David, 'The geography of Irish nationalism, 1910-1921', in *Past and Present*, No. 78 (February, 1978), pp. 113-144

Fitzpatrick, David, 'The logic of collective sacrifice: Ireland and the British Army, 1914-1918', in *The Historical Journal*, Vol. 38, No. 4 (December, 1995), pp. 1017-1030

Foster, R.F., 'History and the Irish Question', in Transactions of the Royal Historical Society, *Fifth Series*, Vol. 33 (1983), pp. 169-192

Fox, Catherine, 'John P. Hayden and the *Westmeath Examiner*', in O'Brien, Seamus (ed.), *A Town in Transition: Post Famine Mullingar* (Mullingar, 2007), pp. 29-54

Gallagher, Michael, 'The pact general election of 1922', in *Irish Historical Studies*, Vol. 21, No. 84 (1981), pp. 404-421.

Garvin, Tom, 'Priests and patriots: Irish separatism and fear of the modern, 1890-1914', in *Irish Historical Studies*, Vol. 25, No. 97 (May, 1986), pp. 67-81

Garvin, Tom, 'The anatomy of a nationalist revolution: Ireland, 1858-1922', in *Comparative Studies in Society and History*, Vol. 28, No. 3 (July, 1986), pp. 468-501

Garvin, Tom, 'The politics of language and literature in pre-independence Ireland', in McGrath, Conor and O'Malley, Eoin (eds), *Irish Political Studies Reader: Key Contributions* (Oxford, 2007), pp. 176-194

Graham, B. and Hood, S., "Every creed and party': town tenant protest in late nineteenth and early twentieth-century Ireland', in *Journal of Historical Geography*, Vol. 24, Is. 2 (April, 1998), pp. 170-187

Greene, David, 'The founding of the Gaelic League', in Ó Tuama, Seán (ed.), *The Gaelic League Idea* (Cork, 1972), pp. 9-19

Gregory, Adrian, "You might as well recruit Germans': British public opinion and the decision to conscript the Irish in 1918', in Gregory, Adrian and Pašeta, Senia, *Ireland and the Great War: 'A War to Unite us All?'* (Manchester, 2002), pp. 113-132

Haddick Flynn, Kevin, 'Soloheadbeg: what really happened?' *History Ireland*, Vol. 5, No. 1 (Spring, 1997), pp. 43-46

Hardiman, Adrian, "Shot in cold blood': military law and Irish perceptions in the suppression of the 1916 Rebellion', in Doherty, Gabriel and Keogh, Dermot (eds), *1916: The Long Revolution* (Cork, 2007), pp. 225-249

Hart, Peter, 'The Protestant experience of revolution in southern Ireland', in English, Richard and Walker, Graham, *Unionism in Modern Ireland: New Perspectives on Politics and Culture* (London, 1996), pp. 81-98

Hart, Peter, 'The geography of revolution in Ireland, 1917-1923', in *Past and Present*, No. 155 (May, 1997), pp. 142-176

Hart, Peter, 'The social structure of the Irish Republican Army, 1916-1923' in *The Historical Journal*, Vol. 42, No. 1 (1999), pp. 207-231

Hart, Peter, 'Definition: defining the Irish revolution', in Augusteijn, Joost (ed.), *The Irish Revolution: 1913-1923* (New York, 2002), pp. 17-33

Harvey, A.D., 'Who were the Auxiliaries?', in *The Historical Journal*, Vol. 35, No. 3 (September, 1992), pp. 665-669

Hepburn, A.C., 'Catholic Ulster and Irish politics: the Ancient Order of Hibernians, 1905-14', in Hepburn, Anthony C., *A Past Apart: Studies in the History of Catholic Belfast, 1850-1950* (Belfast, 1996), pp. 157-173

Hepburn, A.C., 'Language, religion and national identity in Ireland since 1880', in *Perspectives on European Politics and Society*, Vol. 2, No. 2 (2001), pp. 197-220

Hepburn, A.C., 'The Irish Council Bill and the fall of Sir Anthony MacDonnell, 1906', in *Irish Historical Studies*, Vol. 17, No. 68 (September, 1971), pp. 470-498

Hopkinson, Michael, 'Negotiation: The Anglo-Irish War and revolution', in Augusteijn, Joost (ed.), *The Irish Revolution: 1913-1923* (New York, 2002), pp. 121-134

Horne, John, 'Our war, our history', in Horne, John (ed.), *Our War: Ireland and the Great War* (Dublin, 2008), pp. 1-14

Hughes, E.W., 'Republican Courts 1918-1923: a unique experience', in *Old Kilkenny Review*, Vol. 4, No. 2 (1990), pp. 731-744

Huttman, John P., 'Fenians and farmers: The merger of the Home Rule and owner-occupier movements in Ireland, 1850-1915', in *Albion: A Quarterly Journal Concerned with British Studies*, Vol. 3, No. 4 (Winter, 1971), pp. 182-197.

Inoue, Keiko, 'Propaganda II: propaganda of Dáil Éireann, 1919-21', in Augusteijn, Joost (ed.), *The Irish Revolution: 1913-1923* (New York, 2002), pp. 87-102

Jackson, Alvin, 'Irish unionism, 1905-21', in Collins, Peter (ed.), *Nationalism and Unionism: Conflict in Ireland, 1885-1921* (Belfast, 1994), pp. 35-46

Jeffery, Keith, 'British security policy in Ireland, 1919-21', in Collins, Peter (ed.), *Nationalism and Unionism: Conflict in Ireland, 1885-1921* (Belfast, 1994), pp. 163-176

Jeffery, Keith, 'Echoes of war', in Horne, John (ed.), *Our War: Ireland and the Great War* (Dublin, 2008), pp. 261-275

Jeffery, Keith, 'The First World War and the Rising: mode, moment and memory', in Doherty, Gabriel and Keogh, Dermot (eds), *1916: The Long Revolution* (Cork, 2007), pp. 86-101

Johnson, D.S., 'The Belfast Boycott, 1920-22', in Goldstrom, J.M. and Clarkson, L.A. (eds), *Irish Population, Economy and Society: Essays in Honour of K.H. Connell* (Oxford, 1981), pp. 287-308

Jones, David S., 'The cleavage between graziers and peasants in the land struggle, 1890-1910', in Clark, Samuel and Donnelly, James S. (eds), *Irish Peasants: Violence and Political Unrest, 1780-1914* (Wisconsin, 1986), pp. 374-417

Karsten, Peter, 'Irish soldiers in the British Army, 1792-1922: suborned or subordinate?', in *Journal of Social History*, Vol. 17, No. 1 (Autumn, 1983), pp. 31-64

Kelly, Matthew, 'The Irish Volunteers: A Machiavellian moment?', in Boyce, D. George and O'Day, Alan (eds), *The Ulster Crisis: 1885-1921* (New York, 2006), pp. 64-85

Kennedy, Liam, 'Farmers, traders and agricultural politics in pre-independence Ireland', in Clark, Samuel and Donnelly, James S. (eds), *Irish Peasants: Violence and Political Unrest, 1780-1914* (Wisconsin, 1986), pp. 339-373

Kennedy, Liam, 'Traders in the Irish rural economy', in *The Economic History Review*, Vol. 32, No. 2 (May, 1979), pp. 201-210

Kenny, Liam, 'Kildare County Council, 1919-1921', in Nolan, William and McGrath, Thomas (eds), *Kildare: History and Society: Interdisciplinary Essays on the History of an Irish County* (Dublin, 2006), pp. 657-672

Keogh, Dermot, 'The Catholic Church, the Holy See and the 1916 Rising', in Doherty, Gabriel and Keogh, Dermot (eds), *1916: The Long Revolution* (Cork, 2007), pp. 250-309

Kielty, Francis, 'Jasper Tully', in *Roscommon Historical and Archaeological Society Journal*, Vol. 3 (1990), pp. 59-62

Kotsonouris, Mary, 'The Courts of Dáil Éireann', in Farrell, Brian (ed.), *The Creation of the Dáil: A Volume of Essays from the Thomas Davis Lectures* (Dublin, 1994), pp. 91-105

Laffan, Michael, 'The unification of Sinn Féin in 1917', in *Irish Historical Studies*, Vol. 17, No. 67 (March, 1971), pp. 353-379

Larkin, Emmet, 'Church, state and nation in modern Ireland', in *The American Historical Review*, Vol. 80, No. 5 (December, 1975), pp. 1244-1276

Lawrence, Jon, 'Forging a peaceable kingdom: war, violence, and fear of brutalization in post-First World War Britain', in *The Journal of Modern History*, Vol. 75, No. 3 (September, 2003), pp. 557-589

Leonard, Jane, 'Facing the "finger of scorn": veterans' memories of Ireland after the Great War', in Evans, Martin and Lunn, Kenneth (eds), *War and Memory in the Twentieth-Century* (Oxford, 1997), pp. 59-72

Leonard, Jane, 'Getting them at last. The IRA and ex-servicemen', in Fitzpatrick, David (ed.), *Revolution? Ireland: 1917-1923* (Dublin, 1990), pp. 118-129

Leonard, Jane, 'Survivors', in Horne, John (ed.), *Our War: Ireland and the Great War* (Dublin, 2008), pp. 209-223

Leonard, Jane, 'The twinge of memory: Armistice Day and Remembrance Sunday in Dublin since 1919', in English, Richard and Walker, Graham (eds), *Unionism in Modern Ireland: New Perspectives on Politics and Culture* (London, 1996), pp. 99-114

Loughlin, James, 'The Irish Protestant Home Rule Association and nationalist politics, 1886-93', in *Irish Historical Studies*, Vol. 25, No. 95 (May, 1985), pp. 345-360

Lowe, W.J., 'Who were the Black-and-Tans?', in *History Ireland*, Vol. 12, No. 3 (Autumn, 2004), pp. 47-51

Lyons, F.S.L., 'The developing crisis, 1907-14', in Vaughan, W.E. (ed.), *A New History of Ireland VI: Ireland 1870-1920* (Oxford, 2000), pp. 123-144

Lyons, F.S.L., 'The new Nationalism, 1916-18', in Vaughan, W.E. (ed.), *A New History of Ireland VI: Ireland 1870-1920* (Oxford, 2000), pp. 224-239

Lyons, F.S.L., 'The revolution in train', in Vaughan, W.E. (ed.), *A New History of Ireland VI: Ireland 1870-1920* (Oxford, 2000), pp. 189-205

Lyons, F.S.L., 'The Rising and after', in Vaughan, W.E. (ed.), *A New History of Ireland VI: Ireland 1870-1920* (Oxford, 2000), pp. 207-223

Lyons, F.S.L., 'The War of Independence', in Vaughan, W.E. (ed.), *A New History of Ireland VI: Ireland 1870-1920* (Oxford, 2000), pp. 240-259

Lyons, F.S.L., 'The watershed 1903-7', in Vaughan, W.E. (ed.), *A New History of Ireland VI: Ireland 1870-1920* (Oxford, 2000), pp. 111-122

Mac Aodha, Breandán S., 'Was this a social revolution?', in Ó Tuama, Seán (ed.), *The Gaelic League Idea* (Cork, 1972), pp. 20-30

MacEoin, Seán, 'The lone patriot', in *Comoru na Casca Digest*, Vol. 8 (1966), pp. 189-190

MacCartney, Donal, 'The political use of history in the work of Arthur Griffith', in *Journal of Contemporary History*, Vol. 8, No. 1 (January, 1973), pp. 3-19

MacCready, H.W., 'Home Rule and the Liberal Party, 1899-1906', in *Irish Historical Studies*, Vol. 13, No. 52 (September, 1963), pp. 316-348

Martin, F.X. and MacNeill, Eoin, 'Eoin MacNeill on the 1916 Rising', in *Irish Historical Studies*, Vol. 12, No. 47 (March, 1961), pp. 226-271

Martin, F.X., 'MacNeill and the foundation of the Irish Volunteers', in Martin, F.X. and Byrne, F.J. (eds), *The Scholar Revolutionary: Eoin MacNeill, 1867-1945, and the Making of the New Ireland* (Dublin, 1973), pp. 99-180

McCaffrey, Lawrence J., 'Irish nationalism and Irish Catholicism: A study in cultural identity', in *Church History*, Vol. 42, No. 4 (December, 1973), pp. 524-534

McConnel, James, "Jobbing with the Tory and Liberal' Irish nationalists and the politics of patronage, 1880-1914', in *Past and Present*, No. 188 (Aug, 2005), pp. 105-131

McConnel, James, 'The franchise factor in the defeat of the Irish Parliamentary Party, 1885-1918', in *The Historical Journal*, Vol. 47, No. 2 (2004), pp. 355-377

McDevitt, Patrick F., 'Muscular Catholicism: nationalism, masculinity and Gaelic team sports, 1884-1916', in *Gender and History*, Vol. 9 (1997), pp. 262-284

McEwan, John M., 'The Liberal Party and the Irish Question during the First World War', in *The Journal of British Studies*, Vol. 12, No.1 (November 1972), pp. 109-131

McGee, Owen, 'Who were the "Fenian Dead"? The IRB and the background to the 1916 Rising', in Doherty, Gabriel and Keogh, Dermot (eds), *1916: The Long Revolution* (Cork, 2007), pp. 102-120

McManus, Ruth, 'Blue Collars, "Red Forts", and Green Fields: working-class housing in Ireland in the twentieth-century', in *International Labour and Working Class History*, Autumn 2003 (2003), pp. 38-54

Mitchell, Arthur, 'Alternative government: "exit Britannia" – the formation of the Irish national state, 1918-21', in Augusteijn, Joost (ed.), *The Irish Revolution: 1913-1923* (New York, 2002), pp. 70-86

Moriarty, Theresa, 'Work, warfare and wages: industrial controls and Irish trade unionism in the First World War', in Gregory, Adrian and Pašeta, Senia, *Ireland and the Great War: 'A War to Unite us All?'* (Manchester, 2002), pp. 73-93

Murphy, Cliona, 'Suffragists and nationalism in twentieth-century Ireland', in *History of European Ideas*, Vol. 1, No. 4-6 (London, 1993), pp. 1009-1015

Murphy, Richard, 'Walter Long and the making of the Government of Ireland Act, 1919-20', in *Irish Historical Studies*, Vol. 25, No. 97 (May, 1986), pp. 82-96

Murray, A.C., 'Nationality and local politics in late nineteenth-century Ireland: the case of County Westmeath', in *Irish Historical Studies*, Vol. 25, No. 98 (November, 1986), pp. 144-158

Murray, Peter, 'Irish cultural nationalism in the United Kingdom state: politics and the Gaelic League 1900-18', in *Irish Political Studies*, Vol. 8 (1993), pp. 55-72

Newsinger, John, '"I bring not peace but a sword": The religious motif in the Irish War of Independence', in *Journal of Contemporary History*, Vol. 13, No. 3 (1978), pp. 609-628

Novick, Benjamin Z., 'DORA, suppression and nationalist propaganda in Ireland, 1914-1915', in *New Hibernian Review*, Vol. 1, No. 4 (Winter, 1997), pp. 41-57

Novick, Ben, 'Postal censorship in Ireland 1914-1916', in *Irish Historical Studies*, Vol. 31, No. 123 (May, 1999), pp. 343-356

Novick, Ben, 'Propaganda 1: advanced nationalist propaganda and moralistic revolution, 1914-18' in Augusteijn, Joost (ed.), *The Irish Revolution: 1913-1923* (New York, 2002), pp. 34-52

Novick, Ben, 'The arming of Ireland: gun-running and the Great War, 1914-16', in Gregory, Adrian and Pašeta, Senia, *Ireland and the Great War: 'A War to Unite us All?'* (Manchester, 2002), pp. 94-112

O Bolguidher, Liam, 'The early years of the Gaelic League in Kilkenny', in *Old Kilkenny Review*, Vol. 4, No. 4 (1992), pp. 1014-1026

Ó Fiaich, Tomás, 'The great controversy', in Ó Tuama, Seán (ed.), *The Gaelic League Idea* (Cork, 1972), pp. 63-75

Ó Ríordáin, Traolach, 'Conradh na Gaeilge i gCorcaigh i dtosach a ré', in *Journal of the Cork Historical and Archaeological Society*, Vol. 98 (1993), pp. 1-26

Ó Snodaigh, Pádraig, 'Fórsa Óglach Lár na Tíre 1913', in *Studia Hibernica*, No. 5 (1965), pp. 113-122

Ó Tuathaigh, M.A.G., 'The land question, politics and Irish society, 1922-1960', in Drudy, P.J., *Irish Studies 2: Ireland: Land, Politics and People* (Cambridge, 1982), p. 167-190

Ó Tuathaigh, Gearóid, 'Nationalist Ireland, 1912-1922: aspects of continuity and change', in Collins, Peter (ed.), *Nationalism and Unionism: Conflict in Ireland, 1885-1921* (Belfast:, 1994), pp. 47-74

O'Beirne-Ranelagh, John, 'The IRB from the Treaty to 1924', in *Irish Historical Studies*, Vol. 20, No. 77 (1976), pp. 26-39

O'Beirne Ranelagh, John, 'The Irish Republican Brotherhood in the revolutionary period, 1879-1923', in Boyce, D.G. (ed.), *The Revolution in Ireland: 1879-1923* (London, 1988), pp. 137-156

O'Halpin, Eunan, 'Historical revision XX: H.E. Duke and the Irish Administration 1916-18', in *Irish Historical Studies*, Vol. 22, No. 88 (September, 1981), pp. 362-376

O'Halpin, Eunan, 'British Intelligence in Ireland 1914-1921', in Andrew, Christopher and Dilks, David (eds), *The Missing Dimension: Governments and Intelligence in the Twentieth-Century* (London, 1984), pp. 54-77

O'Laoire, Muiris, 'An historical perspective of the revival of Irish outside of the Gaeltacht, 1880-1930, with reference to the revitalisation of Hebrew', in Wright, Sue, *Language and the State: Revitalisation and Revival in Israel and Eire* (Bristol, 1996), pp. 51-63

O'Meara, Seamus, 'Some activities in Westmeath: 1920', in *Capuchin Annual 1970* (1970), pp. 548-553

O'Mullany, Seán, 'Athlone started the volunteer movement', in *The Athlone Annual 1963* (1963), pp. 23-5

Orr, Philip, '200,000 volunteer soldiers', in Horne, John (ed.), *Our War: Ireland and the Great War* (Dublin, 2008), pp. 63-77

Pašeta, Senia, 'Nationalist responses to two royal visits, 1900 and 1903', in *Irish Historical Studies*, Vol. 34, No. 124 (November, 1999), pp. 488-504

Pennell, Caitriona, 'Going to war', in Horne, John (ed.), *Our War: Ireland and the Great War* (Dublin, 2008), pp. 35-48

Phoenix, Éamonn, 'Northern nationalists, Ulster unionists and the development of partition, 1900-21', in Collins, Peter (ed.), *Nationalism and Unionism: Conflict in Ireland, 1885-1921* (Belfast, 1994), pp. 107-122

Puirséil, Niamh, 'War, work and labour', in Horne, John (ed.), *Our War: Ireland and the Great War* (Dublin, 2008), pp. 181-194

Regan, John M., 'Michael Collins, General Commanding-in-Chief, as a historiographical problem', in *History*, Vol. 92, No. 307 (July, 2007), pp. 318-346

Regan, John M., 'Southern Irish nationalism as a historical problem', in *The Historical Journal*, Vol. 50, No. 1 (2007), pp. 197-223

Rouse, Paul, 'Hayden, John Patrick', in McGuire, James and Quinn, James (eds), *Dictionary of Irish Biography*, Vol. IV (Dublin, 2009), pp. 530-531

Ryan, Louise, "Drunken Tans': representations of sex and violence in the Anglo-Irish War (1919-21)', in *Feminist Review*, No. 66 (Autumn, 2000), pp. 73-94

Schneider, Fred D., 'British Labour and Ireland, 1918-1921: the retreat to Houndsditch', in *The Review of Politics*, Vol. 40, No. 3 (July, 1978), pp. 368-391

Shortt, Russell, 'IRA activity in Westmeath during the War of Independence, 1918-21: Part One', in *Ríocht na Midhe – Records of Meath Archaeological and Historical Society*, Vol. 16 (2005), pp. 170-188

Shortt, Russell, 'IRA activity in Westmeath during the War of Independence, 1918-21: Part Two', in *Ríocht na Midhe – Records of Meath Archaeological and Historical Society*, Vol. 17 (2006), pp. 254-265

Snoddy, Oliver, 'The Midland Volunteer Force of 1913', in *Journal of the Old Athlone Society*, Vol. 1, No. 1 (1969), pp. 39-44

Snoddy, Oliver, '1916 government propaganda', in *Journal of the Old Athlone Society*, Vol. 1, No. 3 (1973), pp. 204-205

Snoddy, Oliver, 'Decline of the Redmondite Volunteers in Athlone', in *Journal of the Old Athlone Society*, Vol. 1, No. 2 (1971), pp. 116-7

Stubbs, John O., 'The unionists and Ireland, 1914-18', in *The Historical Journal*, Vol. 33, No. 4 (December, 1990), pp. 867-893

Taaffe, Frank, 'Athy and the Great War', in Nolan, William and McGrath, Thomas (eds), *Kildare: History and Society: Interdisciplinary Essays on the History of an Irish County* (Dublin, 2006), pp. 585-624

Taillon, Ruth and Urquhart, Diane (eds), 'Ladies Auxiliary', in Bourke, Angela (ed.), *The Irish Field Day Anthology of Irish Writing, Vol. 5, Irish Women's Writings and Traditions* (New York, 2002), p. 359

Townshend, Charles, 'Historiography: telling the Irish revolution', in Augusteijn, Joost (ed.), *The Irish Revolution: 1913-1923* (New York, 2002), pp. 1-16

Townshend, Charles, 'Military force and civil authority in the United Kingdom, 1914-1921', in *The Journal of British Studies*, Vol. 28, No. 3 (July, 1989), pp. 262-292

Townshend, Charles, 'The Irish railway strike of 1920: industrial action and civil resistance in the struggle for independence', in *Irish Historical Studies*, Vol. 22, No. 83 (March, 1979), pp. 265-282

Townshend, Charles, 'The Irish Republican Army and the development of guerrilla warfare, 1916-21', in *The English Historical Review*, Vol. 94, No. 371 (1979), pp. 318-345

Varley, Tony. 'A region of sturdy smallholders? Western nationalists and agrarian politics during the First World War', in *Journal of the Galway Archaeological and Historical Society*, Vol. 55 (2003), pp. 127-150

Walsh, Oonagh, 'Testimony from imprisoned women', in Fitzpatrick, David (ed.), *Revolution? Ireland: 1917-1923* (Dublin, 1990), pp. 69-86

Ward, Alan J., 'Lloyd George and the 1918 conscription crisis' in *Irish Historical Studies*, Vol. 17, No. 1 (March, 1974), pp. 107-129

Wheatley, Michael, "Ireland is out for blood and murder': nationalist opinion and the Ulster crisis in provincial Ireland, 1913-1914', in Boyce, D. George and O'Day, Alan (eds), *The Ulster Crisis: 1885-1921* (New York, 2006), pp. 182-201

Wheatley, Michael, "Irreconcilable enemies' or 'flesh and blood'? The Irish Party and the Easter rebels, 1914-16', in Doherty, Gabriel and Keogh, Dermot, *1916: The Long Revolution* (Cork, 2007), pp. 61-85

Wheatley, Michael, 'John Redmond and federalism in 1910', in *Irish Historical Studies*, Vol. 32, No. 127 (May, 2001), pp. 343-364

Wheatley, Michael, "These quiet days of peace": Nationalist opinion before the Home Rule crisis, 1909-13', in Boyce, D. George and O'Day, Alan (eds), *Ireland in Transition: 1867-1921* (London, 2004), pp. 57-75

Theses

Ashe, Brendan, 'The development of the IRA's concepts of guerilla warfare, 1917-1921' (Unpublished MA thesis, UCC, 1999)

Coplen, Richard D., 'The burning of Moydrum Castle, 3 July 1921' (Unpublished MA thesis, NUI Maynooth, 2005)

Foy, Michael Thomas, 'The Ancient Order of Hibernians: an Irish political-religious pressure group, 1884-1975' (Unpublished MA thesis, Q.U.B., 1976)

Hall, Donal, 'World War One and its impact on nationalist politics in County Louth, 1914-1920' (Unpublished MA thesis, NUI Maynooth, 2004)

Hannon, Charles, 'The Irish Volunteers and the concepts of military service and defence 1913-1924' (Unpublished PhD thesis, UCD, 1989)

Hughes, Paul Michael, 'The role of King's County (Offaly) in the Irish revolution, 1913-21' (Unpublished MA thesis, NUI Maynooth, 2005)

Kennedy, Christopher, 'Genesis of the Rising 1912-1916: A transformation of nationalist opinion?' (Unpublished PhD thesis, UCC, 2003)

McCarthy, Cal, 'The 1918 general election – The swing to Sinn Féin' (Unpublished MA thesis, UCC, 2005)

McEvoy, John Noel, 'A study of the United Irish League in the King's County: 1899-1918' (Unpublished MA thesis, NUI Maynooth, 1992)

Moran, Mary Denise, 'A force beleaguered: the Royal Irish Constabulary, 1900-1922' (Unpublished MA thesis, NUI Galway, 1989)

Murphy, William, 'The tower of hunger: political imprisonment and the Irish, 1910-21' (Unpublished PhD thesis, UCD, 2006)

Rasuol, Shireen, 'The rise of nationalist activity in Tullamore 1914-20: was Tullamore, Co Offaly, greatly affected by the Irish War of Independence and did it mirror events that took place in other localities around the country during this period?' (Unpublished MA Thesis, NUI Galway, 2008)

Shortt, Russell W., 'IRA activity in Westmeath during the War of Independence, 1918-21' (Unpublished MA thesis, NUI Maynooth, 2001)

Wylie, John, 'Laurence Ginnell 1852-1923: Westmeath's radical agrarian' (Unpublished MA thesis, NUI Maynooth, 1999)

Websites and other media

'Eoin MacNeill', in The 1916 Rising: Personalities and Perspectives, www.nli. ie/1916/pdf/3.1.5.pdf, accessed 29 September 2009

'Carson and the Ulster Unionists', in The 1916 Rising: Personalities and Perspectives, www.nli.ie/1916/pdf/3.1.4.pdf, accessed 29 September 2009

Dáil Éireann Debates 1919-23: http://historical-debates.oireachtas.ie, accessed 6 January 2010

Dáil Éireann Members Database: www.oireachtas.ie/members-hist/default.asp, accessed 10 January 2011

Census of Ireland 1911, Westmeath: www.census.nationalarchives.ie/pages/1911/ Westmeath/, accessed 22-25 January 2010

Census of Ireland 1911, Roscommon: www.census.nationalarchives.ie/pages/1911/Roscommon/, accessed 22-25 January 2010

Commonwealth War Graves Commission: www.cwgc.org/, accessed 15 January 2010

Public Record Office of Northern Ireland: www.proni.gov.uk/index/search_the_ archives/ulster_covenant.htm, accessed 12 January 2010

Election results for the constituency of Longford-Westmeath, 1922 General Election: http://electionsireland.org, accessed 10 November 2013

Soldiers who Died in the Great War, CD-ROM Version 2 (East Sussex, 2004)

Notes

INTRODUCTION

1   John Burke, *Athlone in the Victorian Era* (Athlone, 2007), pp. 184-200.

CHAPTER 1

1   Philip Bull, *Land, Politics and Nationalism: A Study of the Irish Land Question* (Dublin, 1996), p. 162.

2   Burke, *Athlone*, pp. 22-34; Ruth McManus, 'Blue Collars, "Red Forts", and Green Fields: working-class housing in Ireland in the twentieth-century', in *International Labour and Working Class History* (2003), pp. 38-41.

3   B. Graham and S. Hood, '"Every creed and party": town tenant protest in late nineteenth and early twentieth-century Ireland', in *Journal of Historical Geography*, Vol. 24, No. 2 (April, 1998), pp. 173-4.

4   Large holdings were set at 200 acres, and south Roscommon had seen a fall of just 4 per cent. (David Seth Jones, *Graziers, Land Reform, and Political Conflict in Ireland* (Washington DC, 1995), pp. 54, 97-99, 242; David S. Jones, 'The cleavage between graziers and peasants in the land struggle, 1890-1910', in Samuel Clark and James S. Donnelly (eds), *Irish Peasants: Violence and Political Unrest, 1780-1914* (Wisconsin, 1986), p. 392; David Fitzpatrick, 'Irish farming families before the First World War', in *Comparative Studies in Society and History*, Vol. 25, No. 2 (April, 1983), p. 345).

5   Census Returns of Ireland for 1901; giving details of the Area, Houses, and Population, also Ages, Civil or Conjugal Condition, Occupations, Birth-places, Religion and Education of the People, in each County, and Summary Tables for each Province Vol. I. *Province of Leinster* (Population (Ireland): Census Returns, 1901), 1902 [Cd. 847], CXXII, CXXIII, p. 1271;

Census Returns of Ireland for 1901; giving details of the Area, Houses, and Population, also Ages, Civil or Conjugal Condition, Occupations, Birth-places, Religion and Education of the People, in each County, and Summary Tables for each Province Vol. IV. Province of Connaught (Population (Ireland): Census Returns, 1901), 1902 [Cd. 1059], CXXVIII, p. 671.

6   Burke, *Athlone*, pp. 191-192.

7   Jones, *Graziers*, pp. 142, 146, 148.

8   R.F. Foster, *Modern Ireland: 1600-1972* (London, 1988), p. 431.

9   Patrick Maume, *The Long Gestation: Irish Nationalist Life 1891-1918* (Dublin, 1999), p. 31.

10 Philip Bull, 'The United Irish League and the reunion of the Irish Parliamentary Party, 1898-1900', in *Irish Historical Studies*, Vol. 26, No. 101 (May, 1988), pp. 51-78.

11 *The Irish Times*, 31 July 1897; Paul Rouse, 'Hayden, John Patrick', in James McGuire and James Quinn, *Dictionary of Irish Biography, Vol. IV* (Dublin, 2009), pp. 530-531.

12 *IT*, 9 August 1900; Burke, *Athlone*, pp. 199-201.

13 A.C. Murray, 'Nationality and local politics in late nineteenth-century Ireland: the case of County Westmeath', in *Irish Historical Studies*, Vol. 25, No. 98 (November, 1986), p. 151; Alan O'Day, *Irish Home Rule, 1867-1921* (Manchester, 1998), p. 35.

14 NLI, CO/904/20, UIL Quarterly Returns, p. 452.

15 County Inspector's Report, Roscommon, March 1900, CO/904/69.

16 Philip Bull, 'The formation of the United Irish League, 1898-1900: the dynamics of Irish agrarian agitation', in *Irish Historical Studies*, Vol. 33, No. 132 (November, 2003), p. 417.

17 CI Report, Westmeath, March 1900, CO/904/69; UIL Quarterly Returns, p. 452.

18 *Westmeath Independent*, 7 July 1900; *WI*, 14 July 1900; *WI*, 11 August 1900.

19 UIL Quarterly Returns, pp. 433-4.

20 Sullivan was not fully behind Healy. He did not attend a conference held before the National Convention, even though it was thought that his vote at the conference would have been crucial in securing a more Healyite focus to the convention (*IT*, 19 June 1900).

21 *IP*, 7 July 1900.

22 *IP*, 28 July 1900; *WI*, 4 August 1900.

23 D. George Boyce, *Nationalism in Ireland* (Oxford, 1995), p. 266.

24 Burke, *Athlone*, pp. 193, 199.

25 *WI*, 4 August 1900.

26 *FJ*, 8 August 1900.

27 *FJ*, 8 August 1900.

28 *FJ*, 9 August 1900.

29 *WI*, 22 September 1900; *WI*, 29 September 1900.

30 *WI*, 21 July 1900.

31 *FJ*, 2 October 1900.

32 *FJ*, 3 October 1900; *WI*, 6 October 1900; *IP*, 13 October 1900.

33 *WI*, 13 October 1900.

34   *WI*, 17 November 1900.

35   *WI*, 17 November 1900; *Westmeath Examiner*, 17 November 1900.

36   *IP*, 24 November 1900.

37   *IP*, 24 November 1900.

38   *WI*, 24 November 1900; *IP*, 1 December 1900; *WI*, 8 December 1900.

39   *WI*, 29 December 1900.

40   *WI*, 29 December 1900; *IP*, 29 December 1900; *WI*, 5 January 1901;
      IP, 5 January 1901; *WI*, 12 January 1901.

41   *IP*, 13 April 1901.

42   *WI,* 20 April 1901.

43   *IP*, 2 February 1901.

44   CI Report, Roscommon, May 1901, CO/904/73; CI Report, Westmeath,
      May 1901, CO/904/73; *WI*, 11 May 1901; *WI*, 18 May 1901.

45   Liam Kennedy, 'Farmers, traders and agricultural politics in pre-independence
      Ireland', in Clark and Donnelly, *Irish Peasants*, pp. 342-344; Tony Varley,
      'A region of sturdy smallholders? Western nationalists and agrarian politics
      during the First World War', in *Journal of the Galway Archaeological and
      Historical Society*, Vol. 55 (2003), p. 129.

46   CI Report, Roscommon, June 1901, CO/904/73; IG Report, June 1901,
      CO/904/73.

47   L. Perry Curtis Jr, 'Moral and physical force: the language of violence in
      Irish nationalism', in *The Journal of British Studies*, Vol. 27, No. 2 (April 1988),
      pp. 150-189.

48   Westmeath County Council; Athlone Poor Law Guardians; Athlone Rural District
      Council 1; South Westmeath UIL Executive (*IT*, 7 June 1900; *IT*, 15 July 1901).

49   O'Donoghue sold land in December 1901. Tenants who lived and worked on
      a plot (for agricultural purposes only) valued at £40 or less could buy the
      land at a rate of twenty years' purchase, though in many cases depreciation
      made the figure eighteen years. Larger plots were generally excluded, as were
      those leased in perpetuity. Interested parties were given one month to sign
      up (*WI*, 8 June 1901; *WI*, 15 June 1901; *WI*, 3 August 1901;
      WI, 14 December 1901; *IT*, 14 December 1901).

50   *WI*, 2 November 1901; *WI*, 7 December 1901.

51   Dean Kelly's involvement with the Athlone UIL did not satisfy Sullivan
      in his search for a clergyman in the league in south Westmeath. Kelly was
      based in St Peter's parish and was represented by J.P. Hayden. Sullivan was
      even reticent about joining the Ballinahown branch due to Canon Columb's
      proximity to King's County (*WI*, 7 September 1901).

52   IG Report, November 1901, CO/904/74; Bull, *Land, Politics and Nationalism*, p. 111.

53   CI Report, Westmeath, October 1901, CO/904/73; CI Report, Westmeath,
      November 1901, CO/904/74; CI Report, Roscommon, October 1901,
      CO/904/74; CI Report, Roscommon, November 1901, CO/904/74.

54   *IT*, 14 October 1901; *WI*, 19 October 1901; *IP*, 19 October 1901.

55   *WI*, 11 November 1901; *WI*, 7 December 1901.

56   Heather Laird, *Subversive Law in Ireland, 1879-1920: From 'Unwritten Law' to the
      Dáil Courts* (Dublin, 2005), p. 122.

57   IG Report, January 1902, CO/904/75.
58   Fergus Campbell, 'Irish popular politics and the making of the Wyndham Act, 1901–1903', in *The Historical Journal*, Vol. 45, No. 4 (2002), p. 762.
59   UIL Quarterly Returns, p. 427.
60   *WI*, 4 January 1902.
61   He was arrested for intimidation, inciting to intimidate and inciting not to pay rent. He was sentenced to twenty-one days' imprisonment without hard labour; unfavourable medical reports saw him gain early release (*IT*, 12 December 1901; *IP*, 21 December 1901; *IT*, 28 December 1901; *IT*, 11 January 1902; *IT*, 22 January 1902; *IT*, 24 January 1902; *IT*, 28 February 1902; *IT*, 1 March 1902).
62   *WI*, 15 February 1902; *WI*, 22 February 1902.
63   Foster, *Modern Ireland*, p. 432.
64   CI Report, Westmeath, March 1902, CO/904/74; *WI*, 22 March 1902.
65   CI Report, Roscommon, March 1902, CO/904/74; CI Report, Westmeath, March 1902, CO/904/74.
66   *WI*, 29 March 1902.
67   CI Report, Westmeath, April 1902, CO/904/75; *WI*, 3 May 1902.
68   The first chairman of the Westmeath County Council after the introduction of the 1898 Local Government Act, Greville had promoted himself as a Home Rule nationalist for the purposes of gaining the position, but according to the *Westmeath Independent*: 'His popularity has not been lasting and the bubble has long since burst' (*WI*, 31 May 1902).
69   Marie Coleman, 'Nugent, Sir Walter Richard', in McGuire and Quinn, *Irish Biography*, p. 987.
70   *WI*, 3 May 1902; *WI*, 10 May 1902; *WI*, 17 May 1902; *WI*, 24 May 1902; *WI*, 31 May 1902. O'Donoghue remained in the position for just seven months. He died in January 1903, aged 42 (*WI*, 31 January 1903; *IT*, 31 January 1903, *IP*, 31 January 1903).
71   Campbell, 'Irish popular politics', p. 762.
72   Bull, *Land, Politics and Nationalism*, p. 134.
73   *WI*, 21 June 1902.
74   CI Report, Westmeath, August 1902, CO/904/75.
75   CI Report, Roscommon, July 1902, CO/904/75; CI Report, Roscommon, August 1902, CO/904/75; CI Report, Westmeath, August 1902, CO/904/76; CI Report, Roscommon, September 1902, CO/904/76; CI Report, Westmeath, September 1902, CO/904/76; *IT*, 18 September 1902.
76   CI Report, Roscommon, April 1902, CO/904/75; *WI*, 12 July 1902; CI Report, Westmeath, September 1902, CO/904/76.
77   *IP*, 15 November 1902.
78   *WI*, 20 September 1902; *WI*, 25 October 1902; *WI*, 8 November 1902.
79   *WI*, 26 July 1902.
80   Paul Bew, *Ireland, The Politics of Enmity: 1789-2006* (Oxford, 2007), p. 362.
81   *IT*, 8 January 1903; *IP*, 17 January 1903; NAI, IG + CI Reports, Box 3, CI Report, Westmeath, January 1903.
82   *IP*, 24 January 1903; *IT*, 31 January 1903.

83   NAI, IG + CI Reports, Box 3, CI Report, Westmeath, January 1903;
     WI, 24 January 1903; *IP*, 24 January 1903.

84   *IP*, 24 January 1903. O'Brien, never a political ally of Sullivan, wrote
     sarcastically of his pain in opposing the MP for South Westmeath.
     He inferred that Sullivan was an absentee MP, whose opinions on the bill
     were informed by reading a resolution passed by Athlone RDC1, a body
     that was ignorant of the report's actual recommendations. A later edition
     of the *Irish People* stated that the resolution of the RDC was 'silly' (*IP*,
     14 February 1903). Sullivan had the best attendance record at Parliament of
     any IPP MP; the consequence being that he rarely visited his constituency
     when Parliament was in session (*IP*, 23 August 1902).

85   *WI*, 24 January 1903.

86   Bull, *Land, Politics and Nationalism*, pp. 111, 147.

87   R.V. Comerford, 'Land Commission', in S.J. Connolly (ed.), *The Oxford
     Companion to Irish History* (Oxford, 2007), p. 296; Terence Dooley,
     'The Land for the People': The Land Question in Independent Ireland
     (Dublin, 2004), p. 29.

88   Alan O'Day, 'Max Weber and leadership, Butt, Parnell and Dillon: nationalism
     in transition', in D. George Boyce, and Alan O'Day (eds), *Ireland in Transition,
     1867-1921* (London, 2004), pp. 30-1.

89   D.G. Boyce, *The Irish Question and British Politics, 1868-1996* (London, 1996), p. 45.

90   Joseph V. O'Brien, *William O'Brien and the Course of Irish Politics, 1881-1918*
     (Berkeley, 1976), pp. 155-156.

91   *WI*, 7 March 1903; *WI*, 28 March 1903.

92   *WI*, 18 April 1903; *WI*, 25 April 1903.

93   Some delegates, such as Michael Kilkelly UDC, were unwilling to join (his
     reasoning was unclear, dealing with supporting the League, while not to
     be seen supporting it). Others believed that the co-operative movement
     (which dealt with the sale of seeds and manure between landlords and tenant
     farmers) would stymie the growth of the UIL (*WI*, 13 June 1903).

94   *WI*, 13 June 1903; *IP*, 13 June 1903.

95   NAI, IG + CI Reports, Box 3, CI Report, Westmeath, May 1903.

96   Members of the UDC defeated a resolution of welcome for the king upon
     his arrival in Ireland, as Home Rule had not been granted (*WI*, 18 July 1903).

97   *WI*, 27 June 1903; *WI*, 4 July 1903; *WI*, 18 July 1903.

98   *IP*, 23 May 1903; *IP*, 20 June 1903.

99   *WI*, 1 August 1903.

100 The *Freeman's Journal* was not fully supportive; neither were Michael Davitt
     or John Dillon. William O'Brien closed the *Irish People* and resigned from
     the IPP (much to the annoyance of the as yet pro-O'Brien editor of the
     Westmeath Independent (*WI*, 7 November 1903; *WI*, 14 November 1903;
     WI, 21 November 1903)), due to the disagreement amongst members
     as to the efficacy of the politics of conciliation (Paul Bew, *Conflict and
     Conciliation in Ireland: 1890-1910, Parnellites and Radical Agrarians* (Oxford, 1987),
     pp. 102-106, 111; O'Brien, *William O'Brien*, p. 159; F.S.L. Lyons, *Ireland Since
     the Famine* (Dublin, 1992), pp. 218-219).

101   Bull, *Land, Politics and Nationalism*, p. 155.

102   John P. Huttman, 'Fenians and farmers: The merger of the Home Rule and owner-occupier movements in Ireland, 1850-1915', in *Albion: A Quarterly Journal Concerned with British Studies*, Vol. 3, No. 4 (Winter, 1971), pp. 182-197.

103   K.T. Hoppen, *Ireland Since 1800: Conflict and Conformity* (London, 1999), p. 104; Dooley, *'The Land for the People'*, p. 9.

104   Dooley, *'The Land for the People'*, p. 29.

105   *WI*, 26 September 1903.

106   *WI*, 17 October 1903.

107   *WI*, 20 June 1903.

108   *WI*, 24 October 1903.

109   Bull, *Land, Politics and Nationalism*, p. 162.

110   *WI*, 21 November 1903; *WI*, 2 January 1904.

111   Murray Fraser, *John Bull's Other Homes: State Housing and British Policy in Ireland, 1883-1922* (Liverpool, 1996), p. 36; *WI*, 19 March 1904.

112   *WI*, 28 November 1903; *WI*, 5 December 1903; *WI*, 12 December 1903.

113   NLI, MS 15,191/2, Redmond Papers, Laurence Ginnell to John Redmond, 11 January 1904.

114   Bew, *Conflict and Conciliation*, p. 77.

115   *WI*, 28 November 1903; *WI*, 9 January 1904; *WI*, 23 January 1904.

116   AHL, Minute Book of Athlone Urban District Council, 28 September 1904; *WI*, 1 October 1904.

117   Hayden spent much time in North Westmeath due to his editorial role in the Mullingar-based *Westmeath Examiner* and the inactivity of the incumbent MP, P.J. Kennedy. Hayden's approach to solving local land issues conflicted with those of Ginnell (*WI*, 2 July 1904; *WI*, 16 July 1904; *WI*, 23 July 1904; *WI*, 30 July 1904; *WI*, 6 August 1904; *WI*, 13 August 1904; NAI, IG + CI Reports, Box 6, IG Report, August 1904).

118   *WI*, 15 October 1904.

119   Graham and Hood, 'Every creed and party', p. 177.

120   *WI*, 12 March 1904; *WI*, 5 November 1904; *WI*, 10 December 1904.

121   *WI*, 10 December 1904.

122   *WI*, 22 October 1904; *WI*, 29 October 1904.

123   *WI*, 5 November 1904.

124   *WI*, 12 November 1904.

125   The 'district' encompassed Bealnamulla, Cloongowna, Bogginfin, the Batteries, Duvogue, Newtownflood and Carricknaughton.

126   *WI*, 3 December 1904.

127   *WI*, 3 December 1904; *WI*, 17 December 1904.

128   *WI*, 1 October 1904; *WI*, 22 October 1904; *WI*, 5 November 1904; *WI*, 10 December 1904.

129   Graham and Hood, 'Every creed and party', pp. 179-181; Fraser, *Other Homes*, pp. 83-4.

130   *WI*, 7 January 1905; *WI*, 14 January 1905; *WI*, 11 February 1905; *WI*, 25 February 1905.

131   Graham and Hood, 'Every creed and party', p. 177.

132 Michael Wheatley, *Nationalism and the Irish Party: Provincial Ireland 1910-1916* (Oxford, 2005), p. 54; Graham and Hood, 'Every creed and party', p. 183.

133 *WI*, 4 February 1905; *WI*, 11 March 1905; *WI*, 18 March 1905; *WI*, 1 April 1905; *WI*, 15 April 1905; *WI*, 6 May 1905.

134 *WI*, 13 May 1905.

135 *WI*, 13 May 1905; *WI*, 20 May 1905; *WI*, 10 June 1905.

136 *WI*, 10 June 1905; *WI*, 17 June 1905.

137 Fergus Campbell, *Land and Revolution: Nationalist Politics in the West of Ireland, 1891-1921* (Oxford, 2005), pp. 88, 90; Dooley, *'The Land for the People'*, p. 31.

138 *WE*, 24 June 1905; *WI*, 12 August 1905; *WI*, 26 August 1905; *WI*, 16 September 1905; *WI*, 2 December 1905.

139 *WI*, 8 July 1905; *WI*, 7 October 1905; *WI*, 14 October 1905; *WI*, 28 October 1905; *WI*, 4 November 1905.

140 F.S.L. Lyons, 'The watershed 1903-7', in W.E. Vaughan (ed.), *A New History of Ireland VI – Ireland 1870-1920* (Oxford, 2000), p. 111.

141 Francis Costello, *The Irish Revolution and its Aftermath, 1916-1923: Years of Revolt* (Dublin, 2003), p. 3; *WI*, 4 February 1905.

142 *WI*, 6 January 1906; *IP*, 6 January 1906; *WI*, 13 January 1906; *WI*, 20 January 1906; *Irish Independent*, 3 January 1906; *IT*, 3 January 1906; *IT*, 6 January 1906; *IT*, 19 January 1906; *IT*, 20 January 1906; *II*, 20 January 1906; Bureau of Military History Witness Statement No. 982, Mrs. Alice Ginnell, p. 3.

143 Meetings were held in either Castlerea or Roscommon. John Fitzgibbon, Chairman of the Executive, had promised to introduce a rotation system that included Athlone (*WI*, 31 March 1906).

144 *WI*, 10 February 1906.

145 See Chapter 2.

146 *WI*, 10 February 1906.

147 *WI*, 28 April 1906.

148 *WI*, 8 September 1906; *WI*, 22 September 1906; *WI*, 29 September 1906; *WI*, 6 October 1906; *WI*, 13 October 1906.

149 *IP*, 13 October 1906.

150 *IT*, 8 October 1906.

151 There is some variance in the actual quote ascribed to Redmond. The *Westmeath Independent* (as above, *WI*, 13 October 1906), the *Westmeath Examiner* ('cramped, crooked and impractical' (*WE*, 13 October 1906)), *The Irish Times* and *Irish People* ('cramped, crooked and unworkable' (*IT*, 8 October 1906; *IP*, 13 October 1906)) and the *Freeman's Journal* ('cramped and halting' (*FJ*, 13 October 1906)), though all share the same sentiment.

152 *Manchester Guardian*, 8 October 1906.

153 A.C. Hepburn, 'The Irish Council Bill and the fall of Sir Anthony MacDonnell, 1906', in *Irish Historical Studies*, Vol. 17, No. 68 (September, 1971), p. 476.

154 Graham and Hood, 'Every creed and party', pp. 177-178.

155 Fraser, *Other Homes*, p. 86; Graham and Hood, 'Every creed and party', pp. 184-5.

156 *IP*, 16 June 1906.

157 *WI*, 3 October 1906; *WI*, 10 November 1906; *WI*, 1 December 1906; *WI*, 15 December 1906.

158 *WI*, 9 February 1907.

159 *WI*, 9 February 1907.

160 David Fitzpatrick, *Politics and Irish Life 1913-1921: Provincial Experience of War and Revolution* (2nd ed., Cork, 1998), p. 93.

161 *II*, 28 February 1907; *II*, 2 March 1907; *II*, 5 March 1907; *IT*, 5 March 1907; *II*, 6 March 1907; *II*, 7 March 1907; *IT*, 7 March 1907; *IT*, 9 March 1907.

162 *WI*, 12 January 1907; *WI*, 2 March 1907; *WI*, 9 March 1907; *WI*, 16 March 1907.

163 Healy was referring to the 'Smoke Room' at Westminster when he noted that Sullivan never spoke (T.M. Healy, *Letters and Leaders of my Day*: Vol. 1 (London, 1928), p. 262).

164 The *Irish People* blamed his death on his compulsive attendance, which he maintained despite deteriorating health (*IP*, 9 March 1907).

165 *WI*, 21 January 1901; *WI*, 19 October 1901; *WI*, 18 October 1902; *WI*, 17 October 1903; *WI*, 15 October 1904; *WI*, 28 January 1905; *WI*, 2 March 1907.

166 *II*, 9 March 1907.

167 *WI*, 16 March 1907.

168 *WI*, 6 May 1905; *II*, 19 May 1905; *II*, 22 May 1905; *WI*, 27 May 1905; *II*, 3 January 1906; *WI*, 6 January 1906; *IT*, 19 January 1906; *II*, 19 January 1906.

169 *II*, 3 April 1906; *II*, 29 June 1906; *II*, 14 September 1906; *II*, 5 October 1906; *II*, 19 February 1906; *II*, 9 March 1907; *Return of Advances made under the Irish Land Act, 1903, during the period from 1st November 1903 to 31st December 1905*: Vol. I, Part IV (Land - Landlord and Tenant (Ireland): Advances: Advances under the Land Act of 1903), 1906 [Cd. 328] c.625, pp. 259-260; *Return of Advances made under the Irish Land Act, 1903, during the period from 1st January to 31s t December 1906*: Vol. I, Part V (Land – Landlord and Tenant (Ireland): Advances: Advances under the Land Act of 1903), 1907, [Cd. 3815, 3921, 4012, 4035, 4048, 4113, 4159, 4163, 4172, 4273, 4296], xc.131, p. 149.

170 *IT*, 16 March 1907; *WI*, 23 March 1907.

171 *IT*, 8 March 1907.

172 *WI*, 23 March 1907; *WI*, 30 March 1907; *II*, 2 April 1907.

173 *WI*, 30 March 1907.

174 *II*, 4 April 1907; *II*, 5 April 1907; *WI*, 6 April 1907; *IT*, 20 April 1907.

175 *IT*, 4 April 1907; *WI*, 6 April 1907.

176 *IT*, 4 April 1907.

177 *Peasant*, 13 April 1907.

178 *II*, 9 April 1907; *II*, 15 April 1907; *IT*, 15 April 1907; *II*, 16 April 1907; *IT*, 20 April 1907; *II*, 20 April 1907; *IP*, 27 April 1907; NAI, IG + CI Reports, Box 11, CI Report, Westmeath, April 1907; *WI*, 6 April 1907.

179 A.C. Hepburn, 'Irish Council Bill', in Connolly, *Oxford Companion*, p. 267.

180 Hepburn, 'Irish Council Bill', pp. 489-490; Bew, *Ireland*, p. 365.

181 Campbell, *Land and Revolution*, p. 111.

182 Boyce, *Irish Question*, p. 46.

183 NAI, IG + CI Reports, Box 11, IG Report, June 1907; *WI*, 8 June 1907; *IP*, 15 June 1907.

184   *WI*, 11 May 1907.

185   *WI*, 18 May 1907.

186   *WI*, 25 May 1907.

187   William Bulfin, *Rambles in Eirinn* (Dublin, 1907), p. 88.

188   A meeting at The Downs in north Westmeath chaired by J.P. Hayden heard a
      vitriolic speech from Ginnell, who desired to 'smash and finish ranching and
      land monopoly.' A more confrontational approach to solving land redistribution
      called 'The Downs Policy' resulted (*IT*, 10 October 1906; *IT*, 15 October 1906;
      Jones, *Graziers,* pp. 185-6; Jones, 'Graziers and Peasants', pp. 382-3).

189   Bew, *Conflict and Conciliation*, p. 139; Campbell, *Land and Revolution*, pp. 85-86.

190   Pauric J. Dempsey and Seán Boylan, 'Ginnell, Laurence', in McGuire and
      Quinn, *Irish Biography*, p. 103; Dooley, *'Land for the People'*, pp. 18, 28, 29; *WI*,
      19 October 1907; Maume, *Long Gestation*, p. 229; Bew, *Conflict and Conciliation*,
      p. 138; Laird, *Subversive Law*, p. 115.

191   Agricultural Statistics of Ireland, with detailed report on Agriculture for 1903
      (Agriculture (Ireland): Statistics), 1904 [Cd. 2196], CV.333, p. 60.

192   Jones, *Graziers*, pp. 116-118.

193   *Agricultural Statistics of Ireland, with detailed report on Agriculture for 1904*
      (Agriculture (Ireland): Statistics), 1906 [Cd. 2722], CXXXIII.459, p. 66.

194   *The Leader*, 10 February 1906.

195   Campbell, *Land and Revolution*, p. 103.

196   Varley, 'Sturdy smallholders?', p. 128.

197   NAI, IG + CI Reports, Box 11, IG Report, June 1907; Campbell, *Land and
      Revolution*, pp. 105-106, 118-119.

198   Diarmuid Ferriter, *The Transformation of Ireland: 1900-2000* (London, 2004),
      p. 69; O'Day, *Irish Home Rule*, p. 219; Alvin Jackson, *Home Rule, An Irish
      History: 1800-2000* (Oxford, 2003), p. 97.

199   Jones, *Graziers*, pp. 116-118

200   *IT*, 19 August 1907; *II*, 19 August 1907.

201   *WI*, 17 August 1907; *IP*, 24 August 1907.

202   *WI*, 7 September 1907; *WI*, 21 September 1907; *IP*, 14 September 1907; *IP*,
      28 September 1907; *IP*, 2 November 1907.

203   NAI, IG + CI Reports, Box 12, CI Report, Roscommon, November 1907;
      IG + CI Reports, Box 12, CI Report, Westmeath, November 1907; *WI*,
      2 November 1907; *WI*, 9 November 1907; *WI*, 16 November 1907; *WI*,
      30 November 1907.

204   *WI*, 14 December 1907.

205   Bew, *Conflict and Conciliation*, p. 142; Jones, *Graziers*, p. 189.

206   Wheatley, *Nationalism and the Irish Party*, p. 24.

207   NLI, MS 15,191-3, Redmond Papers, 12 January 1907. Ginnell wrote that
      'the grazing interest is wealthy and has command of several engines of
      attack and defence, the chief of which … has been the *Westmeath Examiner*',
      Hayden's publication (MS 15,191-3, Redmond Papers, Laurence Ginnell to
      John Redmond, 14 October 1907).

208   *WI*, 31 August 1907; *IT*, 21 June 1907; *IT*, 3 January 1908

209   *II*, 1 November 1907; *IT*, 16 December 1907.

210   Jones, *Graziers*, p. 198.

211   Ginnell believed Birrell to be a 'trickster and a fraud', while Birrell referred
       to Ginnell as 'a pestilent ass' (*IT*, 16 December 1907; Bew, *Ireland*, p. 366;
       Jones, *Graziers*, p. 206).

212   NLI, MS 15,191-3, Florence O'Donoghue Papers, Laurence Ginnell,
       14 October 1907; *WI*, 21 December 1907; Bew, *Conflict and Conciliation*, p. 162.

213   *WI*, 14 December 1907; *IP*, 28 December 1907.

214   *II*, 16 December 1907; *WI*, 21 December 1907; *IP*, 21 December 1907.

215   Bew, *Conflict and Conciliation*, pp. 158, 179, 79.

216   NAI, IG + CI Reports, Box 13, IG Report, January 1908; Bew, *Conflict and
       Conciliation*, p. 168.

217   NAI, IG + CI Reports, Box 13, IG Report, January 1908; Bew, *Conflict and
       Conciliation*, p. 168.

218   Westmeath was to achieve the highest levels of boycotting for the whole of
       Leinster during the period 1905-1909. Roscommon's levels were slightly less
       than half those of Westmeath during the same time (Jones, *Graziers*, p. 191).
       NAI, IG + CI Reports, Box 13, CI Report, Westmeath, January 1908; *WI*,
       4 January 1908; *WI*, 11 January 1908; *WI*, 18 January 1908; *WI*, 25 January 1908.

219   NAI, IG + CI Reports, Box 13, CI Report, Westmeath, February 1908.

220   *WI*, 1 February 1908.

221   *WI*, 14 March 1908; NAI, IG + CI Reports, Box 13, CI Report, Westmeath,
       March 1908.

222   *WI*, 15 February 1908; *WI*, 29 February 1908; *WI*, 7 March 1908; *WI*,
       14 March 1908.

223   *WI*, 18 April 1908; *WI*, 25 April 1908; *WI*, 2 May 1908.

224   *WI*, 4 April 1908. A large tract of the *Westmeath Independent*'s editorial was
       republished in the *Irish People*, which backed the views expressed in the
       Athlone newspaper (*IP*, 11 April 1908).

225   *II*, 1 April 1908; Boyce, *Irish Question*, p. 44.

226   *WI*, 11 April 1908; *WI*, 18 April 1908; *WI*, 2 May 1908; *WI*, 16 May 1908.

227   *WI*, 18 April 1908. This piece was also reproduced in the *Irish People*
       (*IP*, 25 April 1908).

228   A minority of UIL branches remained supportive of the Ginnell. One branch at
       Rochfortbridge was suspended by the UIL Standing Committee after making a
       number of unwelcome resolutions, supposedly inspired by the Ginnell. The *Irish
       People* believed the North Westmeath MP was being made a scapegoat by the
       IPP and was hung out to dry by John Dillon. By September, the RIC had
       begun to identify the two groups separately; those who supported Ginnell
       and 'official UIL' (NAI, IG + CI Reports, Box 13, CI Report, Westmeath,
       June 1908; IG + CI Reports, Box 14, CI Report, Westmeath, July 1908; IG +
       CI Reports, Box 14, CI Report, Westmeath, August 1908; IG + CI Reports,
       Box 14, CI Report, Westmeath, September 1908; IG + CI Reports, Box 13, IG
       Report, June 1908; IG + CI Reports, Box 14, IG Report, July 1908; IG + CI
       Reports, Box 14, IG Report August 1908; IG + CI Reports, Box 14, IG Report,
       September 1908; *II*, 18 June 1908; *IT*, 10 July 1908; *WI*, 1 August 1908; *IP*,
       8 August 1908; *IT*, 8 August 1908; *IP*, 29 August 1908; *IP*, 19 December 1908).

229 NAI, IG + CI Reports, Box 13, IG Report, May 1908.

230 *IP*, 9 May 1908; *IP*, 16 May 1908.

231 *II*, 8 May 1908; *WI*, 9 May 1908.

232 *WI*, 2 May 1908; *WI*, 9 May 1908; *WI*, 30 May 1908.

233 Campbell, *Land and Revolution*, p. 97; Bew, *Conflict and Conciliation*, p. 168.

234 Jones, 'Graziers and peasants', p. 383; Jackson, *Home Rule*, p. 95.

235 *IP*, 18 July 1908; *IP*, 25 July 1908.

236 NAI, IG + CI Reports, Box 13, IG Report, June 1908; IG + CI Reports, Box 13, CI Report, Westmeath, June 1908; IG + CI Reports, Box 14, IG Report, July 1908; *WI*, 6 June 1908; *WI*, 13 June 1908.

237 *WI*, 12 September 1908.

238 *WI*, 13 June 1908; *WI*, 20 June 1908; *IP*, 27 June 1908.

239 *IP*, 19 September 1908.

240 *WI*, 12 September 1908.

241 *WI*, 26 September 1908.

242 *II*, 24 September 1908; *FJ*, 24 September 1908.

243 *FJ*, 28 September 1908. The Clara UIL was angered by one 'of the most important Urban Councils in Ireland' having such a debate (*IP*, 19 September 1908).

244 *IT*, 3 October 1908; *WI*, 3 October 1908. The UDC discussion made the columns of *The Leader* the following week. Councillor J.H. Rafferty defended the UIL, detailing how years of attending meetings gave him the sense to recognise a useful political movement when he saw one. *The Leader* was more interested, however, in the threat from John Smith, a labour man, to throw M.J. Hughes out of a window over his hiring practices (*TL*, 10 October 1908).

245 *FJ*, 8 October 1908; *WI*, 10 October 1908; *II*, 12 October 1908; *FJ*, 12 October 1908; *FJ*, 14 October 1908.

246 NAI, IG + CI Reports, Box 14, CI Report, Roscommon, September 1908.

247 *WI*, 17 October 1908.

248 *FJ*, 20 October 1908; *WI*, 24 October 1908; *WE*, 24 October 1908.

249 *WI*, 31 October 1908; *WI*, 7 November 1908; *WI*, 21 November 1908.

250 *WI*, 14 November 1908; *WI*, 21 November 1908.

251 David Fitzpatrick, 'The geography of Irish nationalism, 1910-1921', in *Past and Present*, No. 78 (February, 1978), p. 131.

252 *WI*, 5 December 1908.

253 Tom Garvin, *The Evolution of Irish Nationalist Politics* (New York, 1981), p. 93.

254 NAI, IG + CI Reports, Box 15, IG Report, November 1908; IG + CI Reports, Box 15, CI Report, Roscommon, November 1908; IG + CI Reports, Box 15, IG Report, December 1908.

255 NAI, IG + CI Reports, Box 15, CI Report, Westmeath, November 1908. Chapman told the visiting officer that the newspaper generally did not print reports from UIL courts, while facetiously adding that the editor could have done with some time in a prison regardless. He added that editorial decisions would not be decided on the basis of RIC threats or government decree (*WI*, 7 November 1908).

256   Bew, *Conflict and Conciliation*, p. 186; Jackson, *Home Rule*, p. 97; O'Brien, *William O'Brien*, p. 187. The convention heard Laurence Ginnell air his views on parliamentary arrangements, views very much of a Sinn Féin variety, that led to his being ejected (*WI*, 13 February 1909; *IP*, 13 February 1909; *WI*, 20 February 1909; *WI*, 17 April 1909; *TL*, 20 February 1909; *IP*, 20 February 1909).

257   *IT*, 10 February 1909; *MG*, 10 February 1909; *II*, 10 February 1909; *FJ*, 10 February 1909; *FJ*, 11 February 1909; *Anglo Celt*, 13 February 1909; *IP*, 13 February 1909.

258   Jones, *Graziers*, p. 189.

259   *WI*, 3 April 1909; *WI*, 10 April 1909; *WI*, 17 April 1909; *WI*, 24 April 1909; *WI*, 8 May 1909; *FJ*, 26 May 1909; *WI*, 10 July 1909; *WI*, 17 July 1909; *WI*, 24 July 1909; *WI*, 31 July 1909; *WI*, 7 August 1909; *WI*, 4 September 1909; *WI*, 11 September 1909; *WI*, 18 September 1909; *WI*, 25 September 1909; *WI*, 2 October 1909; *WI*, 23 October 1909; *WI*, 13 November 1909; *WI*, 27 November 1909; *WI*, 11 December 1909; *WI*, 18 December 1909.

260   *WI*, 31 July 1909.

261   *WI*, 31 July 1909; CI Report, Westmeath, April 1909, CO/904/77; CI Report, Westmeath, May 1909, CO/904/78; CI Report, Roscommon, May 1909, CO/904/78; CI Report, Westmeath, June 1909, CO/904/78; *FJ*, 8 July 1909.

262   CI Report, Roscommon, May 1909, CO/904/78.

263   *II*, 9 April 1909; *FJ*, 9 April 1909.

264   *WI*, 3 April 1909.

265   *Agricultural Statistics of Ireland, with detailed report on Agriculture for 1908 (Agriculture (Ireland): Statistics)*, 1909 [Cd. 4940] CII.355, p. 60; *Agricultural Statistics of Ireland; with Detailed Report for the year 1909 (Agriculture (Ireland): Acreage, Crops, Live Stock, Prices, Produce, &c)*, 1910 [Cd. 5382], CVIII.489, p. 62.

266   CI Report, Westmeath, August 1909, CO/904/78; CI Report, Westmeath, September 1909, CO/904/79; CI Report, Roscommon, August 1909, CO/904/78; CI Report, Roscommon, September 1909, CO/904/79; IG Report, August 1909, CO/904/78.

267   Dooley, *Land for the People*, p. 26; R.V. Comerford, 'Land Acts', in Connolly, *Oxford Companion*, p. 295; Jones, *Graziers*, pp. 209–213; Huttman, 'Fenians and farmers', p. 191.

268   Alvin Jackson, *Ireland: 1798-1998* (Oxford, 1999), p. 161; *WI*, 27 November 1909.

269   *Agricultural Statistics of Ireland; with Detailed Report for 1910 (Agriculture (Ireland): Acreage, Crops, Live Stock, Prices, Produce, &c)*, 1911 [Cd. 594], C.517, p. 62.

270   *MG*, 4 May 1909.

271   Boyce, *The Irish Question*, p. 53; Hoppen, *Ireland Since 1800*, p. 141; Marie Coleman, *County Longford and the Irish Revolution: 1910-1923* (Dublin, 2003), p. 21.

272   *FJ*, 16 November 1909.

273   RIC Report, Precís of Information, Westmeath, November, 1909, CO/904/118; *WI*, 13 November 1909; AHL, Minute Book of the Athlone Poor Law Guardians, 13 November 1909; Minute Book of Athlone UDC, 14 November 1909; *MG*, 22 November 1909.

274   Foster, *Modern Ireland*, p. 462; Boyce, *Irish Question*, p. 50.

275 *Return of charges made to Candidates at the General Election of January, 1910,*
    in Great Britain and Ireland by Returning Officers, specifying the Total Expenses of
    each Candidate and the number of votes polled for each Candidate (in continuation
    of No. 302 of 1906) (Electors and Representation of the People: Election Expenses
    (January, 1910), 1910 [299], LXXIII.705, p. 73; *FJ,* 7 January 1910; *FJ,*
    8 January 1910; *IT,* 18 January 1910; *IT,* 22 January 1910.

276 *WI,* 1 January 1910; *WI,* 8 January 1910; *FJ,* 10 January 1910; *FJ,*
    11 January 1910; *WI,* 15 January 1910; *FJ,* 24 January 1910; BMHWS No. 982,
    Mrs. Alice Ginnell, p. 6; David Fitzpatrick, 'Ireland since 1870', in R.F. Foster
    (ed.), *The Oxford Illustrated History of Ireland* (Oxford, 1989), p. 228

277 NLI, MS 15,191/3, Redmond Papers, Walter Nugent to John Redmond,
    16 February 1910; John Redmond to Walter Nugent 19 February 1910.
    His exclusion left him in a somewhat anomalous position in Westminster, for
    although he stated that he would 'sit and vote with the Irish Party', it was
    obvious that his actions had made him a pariah (*Irish Nation,* 22 January 1910).

278 The IPP had seventy-one seats with independents, including eight members
    of William O'Brien's All-for-Ireland League (AFIL), making up the balance.
    Labour MPs accounted for an additional forty seats.

279 F.S.L. Lyons, 'The developing crisis, 1907-14', in Vaughan, *A New History of*
    Ireland VI, p. 129; Maume, *Long Gestation,* p. 103.

280 D. George Boyce, *Nineteenth-Century Ireland: The Search for Stability*
    (Dublin, 1990), p. 233.

281 Boyce, *Irish Question,* p. 51.

282 *WI,* 5 February 1910; *WI,* 12 February 1910; *WI,* 19 February 1910;
    WI, 26 February 1910. Advanced nationalist newspaper the *Irish Nation*
    dealt with the *Westmeath Independent's* election forecast on two occasions,
    initially believing it to be 'ridiculous', but then changed its mind (*IN,*
    12 February 1910; *IN,* 26 February 1910).

283 The *Freeman's Journal* had stated that news of an historic announcement was
    unfounded and that the proposed meeting had been set weeks previously.
    This was disputed by M.J. Hughes, secretary of the Athlone UIL, who
    showed that the first intimation of such a meeting had only surfaced on
    22 March. T.M. Healy stated that the 'important pronouncement' term
    came from Walter Nugent (*WI,* 19 March 1910; *IT,* 25 March 1910; *WI,*
    26 March 1910; *FJ,* 1 April 1910; *IT,* 4 April 1910; *FJ,* 4 April 1910; *II,*
    4 April 1910; *MG,* 14 April 1910; *II,* 14 April 1910.

284 *WI,* 26 March 1910; *II,* 29 March 1910; *FJ,* 29 March 1910; *FJ,* 2 April 1910;
    WI, 2 April 1910; *IT,* 2 April 1910.

285 William O'Brien dismissed the meetings, calling Redmond and Dillon
    hypocrites (*MG,* 4 April 1910).

286 *WI,* 9 April 1910.

287 AHL, Minute Book of Athlone UDC, 24 April 1910.

288 *II,* 4 April 1910; *FJ,* 4 April 1910; *WI,* 9 April 1910; *MG,* 14 April 1910.

289 H.W. MacCready, 'Home Rule and the Liberal Party, 1899-1906', in *Irish*
    Historical Studies, Vol. 13, No. 52 (September, 1963), p. 316; Boyce, *Irish*
    Question, p. 53.

290   CI Report, Westmeath, April 1910, CO/904/80.

291   *WI*, 16 April 1910; *WI*, 30 April 1910.

292   Michael Wheatley, '"These quiet days of peace": nationalist opinion before the
      Home Rule crisis, 1909-13', in D. George Boyce and Alan O'Day (eds), *Ireland
      in Transition: 1867-1921* (London, 2004), p. 61.

293   Lyons, 'The developing crisis', p. 128.

294   IG Report, December 1910, CO/904/82.

295   *WI*, 8 October 1910; *WI*, 15 October 1910; *WI*, 22 October 1910; *WI*,
      5 November 1910; *WI*, 19 November 1910; *FJ*, 9 January 1911; Michael
      Wheatley, 'John Redmond and federalism in 1910', in *Irish Historical Studies*,
      Vol. 32, No. 127 (May, 2001), pp. 343-364.

296   CI Report, Westmeath, September 1910, CO/904/82; CI Report, Westmeath,
      October 1910, CO/904/82; *WI*, 3 September 1910; *WI*, 8 October 1910.

297   *WI*, 3 December 1910; *WI*, 24 December 1910.

298   *FJ*, 12 December 1910.

299   IG Report, December 1910, CO/904/82; CI Report, Westmeath,
      December 1910, CO/904/82; CI Report, Roscommon, December 1910,
      CO/904/82; *FJ*, 7 December 1910; *WI*, 10 December 1910; *WI*,
      17 December 1910; *IT*, 17 December 1910; *IT*, 6 December 1910.

300   *WI*, 10 December 1910; 'Sinn Féin and Republican Suspects, 1899-1922',
      Laurence Ginnell, CO 904/202/162; Wheatley, '"These quiet days of peace", p. 61.

301   *WI*, 17 December 1910; *WI*, 31 December 1910. The IPP secured seventy-four
      seats, including T.P. O'Connor's (an Athlone native) Liverpool constituency.
      Independent Irish MPs numbered ten, while the Liberals secured 272
      seats, with the Tories and 'Liberal Unionists' also taking 272 (Martin Pugh,
      The Making of Modern British Politics: 1867-1945 (Oxford, 2002), p. 132).

302   Lyons, 'The developing crisis', p. 128.

303   The same meeting also heard from failed electoral candidate Patrick
      McKenna, who stated that if Home Rule was not introduced within three
      years, there would be moves towards a republic (*IT*, 9 January 1911; *WI*,
      14 January 1911).

304   CI Report, Westmeath, January 1911, CO/904/83; *WI*, 15 April 1911.
      The *Irish Nation* referred to Ginnell's group as the 'Westmeath Independent
      League' (*IN*, 12 November 1910).

305   NLI, MS 708, Minute Book of the National Directory of the UIL,
      10 August 1904 – 30 April 1918, pp. 406-416. See John Noel McEvoy, 'A study
      of the United Irish League in the King's County: 1899-1918' (Unpublished
      MA thesis, NUI Maynooth, 1992).

306   CI Report, Westmeath, January 1911, CO/904/83; CI Report, Roscommon,
      January 1911, CO/904/83; CI Report, Westmeath, February 1911,
      CO/904/83; CI Report, Roscommon, February 1911, CO/904/83; CI
      Report, Westmeath, March 1911, CO/904/83; CI Report, Roscommon,
      March 1911, CO/904/83.

307   *WI*, 21 January 1911. Prime Minister Herbert Asquith had stated that an Irish
      parliament would operate under an imperial one, something Redmond had
      accepted in principle (*WI*, 18 February 1911).

308 *WI*, 13 May 1911.

309 In a Manchester speech, Nugent stated that unionist 'irreconcilables'…
professions of loyalty were all a sham and that their vaunted devotion to the
Empire was a brazen lie.' He cited their propensity for attacking the crown
and inciting their followers to engage in violence when events went against
them. He unrealistically opined that most unionists were secretly hoping for
Home Rule (*II*, 19 September 1911).

310 *WI*, 13 May 1911.

311 *WI*, 11 February 1911; *WI*, 20 May 1911.

312 Christopher Kennedy, 'Genesis of the Rising, 1912-1916: A transformation of
nationalist opinion?' (Unpublished PhD thesis, UCC, 2003), pp. 13-18; James
McConnel, "Jobbing with the Tory and Liberal': Irish nationalists and the politics
of patronage, 1880-1914', in *Past and Present*, No. 188 (August, 2005), pp. 108-9.

313 CI Report, Westmeath, May 1911, CO/904/84; *WI*, 3 June 1911. See Chapter 2.

314 *MG*, 12 August 1911; *IT*, 19 September 1911; *MG*, 22 September 1911;
TL, 23 September 1911; *WI*, 23 September 1911; *WI*, 30 September 1911.
The *MG* published a review of the visit, noting that 'a prominent
nationalist at Athlone … told me that one of the first results of a Home
Rule Parliament … would be the displacement of many Nationalist MPs
by the election of the gentry who had sold out to their tenants' (*MG*,
6 October 1911).

315 CI Report, Westmeath, August 1911, CO/904/84; CI Report, Roscommon,
August 1911, CO/904/84; CI Report, Westmeath, September 1911,
CO/904/85; CI Report, Roscommon, September 1911, CO/904/85.

316 *WI*, 7 October 1911.

317 Wheatley, 'These quiet days of peace', p. 61.

318 Since the failure of the 1904/5 branch, repeated calls had been made to
reorganise. 'Athlone has the reputation for doing many things in turn
and doing none of them for very long', noted McDermott-Hayes in
connection with the TTL debate. While wishing the new branch every
success, he questioned the need for it, in a reversal of his previous advocation.
The branch was headed by H.J. Walker and included urban councillors.
It met irregularly over the next twelve months (*WI*, 4 August 1906;
WI, 19 October 1907; *WI*, 22 February 1909; *WI*, 23 April 1910; *WI*,
9 September 1911; *WI*, 18 November 1911; *WI*, 2 December 1911; CI
Report, Westmeath, December 1911 CO/904/86; *WI*, 3 February 1912; *WI*,
9 March 1912; *WI*, 16 March 1912; *WI*, 23 March 1912; *IT*, 23 March 1912; *II*,
23 March 1912; *S.I.*, 24 March 1912; *II*, 27 April 1912; *WI*, 2 November 1912;
WI, 30 November 1912).

319 *WI*, 23 December 1911.

320 *II*, 2 January 1912; *WI*, 6 January 1912.

321 *IT*, 20 December 1911.

322 *WI*, 13 January 1912.

323 Established in Dublin in 1907, the Young Ireland UIL offered conditional
support to the IPP (Lyons, 'The watershed', pp. 114-115).

324 CI Report, Westmeath, January 1912, CO/904/86.

CHAPTER 2

1   Burke, *Athlone*, pp. 249-267.
2   A.C. Hepburn, 'Language, religion and national identity in Ireland since 1880', in *Perspectives on European Politics and Society*, Vol. 2, No. 2 (2001), p. 203.
3   P.J. Mathews, *Revival: The Abbey Theatre, Sinn Féin, the Gaelic League and the Co-operative Movement* (Cork, 2003), p. 23.
4   Tony Crowley, *The Politics of Language in Ireland 1366-1922: A Sourcebook* (London, 2000), p. 176; Reg Hindley, *The Death of the Irish Language: A Qualified Obituary* (London, 1990), p. 24; Breandán S. Mac Aodha, 'Was this a social revolution?', in Seán Ó Tuama (ed.), *The Gaelic League Idea* (Cork, 1972), p. 21.
5   *WI*, 27 April 1901; *WI*, 4 May 1901; *WI*, 11 May 1901; *WI*, 21 September 1901.
6   Timothy G. McMahon, *Gaelic Revival and Irish Society: 1893-1910* (New York, 2008), p. 88.
7   Burke, *Athlone*, p. 75.
8   Mullingar had, in contrast with Athlone, a massive ratio of male Irish speakers to female, coming in at almost 3:1. The obvious reason for the disparity is that Mullingar had more boys schools teaching Irish (Census Returns of Ireland for 1901, Province of Leinster, p. 1308).
9   Census Returns of Ireland for 1901, Province of Connaught, p. 712.
10 Mike Cronin and Daryl Adair, *The Wearing of the Green: A History of St Patrick's Day* (London, 2002), p. 63.
11 *WI*, 14 September 1901.
12 *WI*, 21 September 1901.
13 Fr Forde had presented a paper, 'The language movement: its philosophy', in 1900, which detailed his view of the Catholic, Gaelic nature of Irish. He stated that it was not for 'the Marchmen of the Pale', or those of a similar background (Diarmuid Breathnach agus Máire Ní Mhurcú, *Beathaisnéis a Cúig* (Baile Átha Cliath, 1997), p. 62). *An Claidheamh Soluis agus Fáinne an Lae* (The Sword of Light and the Dawning of the Day), the GL newspaper, championed Forde's work on occasion, albeit with qualifications (Crowley, *Politics of Language*, pp. 197-199).
14 Crowley, *Politics of Language*, p. 177; McMahon, *Gaelic Revival*, pp. 9-12, 35, 41-51; Mathews, *Revival*, p. 24; *WI*, 28 September 1901.
15 Almost 70 per cent of branch presidents in 1901 were priests (McMahon, *Gaelic Revival*, p. 48).
16 *WI*, 19 October 1901.
17 Caoimhghin Ó Croidheáin, *Language from Below: The Irish Language, Ideology and Power in Twentieth-Century Ireland* (Bern, 2006), p. 140.
18 *ACS*, 19 October 1901; *ACS*, 26 October 1901.
19 *WI*, 21 September 1901; *WI*, 28 September 1901.
20 Tom Garvin, *Nationalist Revolutionaries in Ireland: 1858-1928* (Oxford, 1987), pp. 79-80; Diarmait Mac Giolla Chriost, *The Irish Language in Ireland: From Goídel to Globalisation* (London, 2005), p. 103. Two articles on the GL, one from Kilkenny and another from Cork, show that the middle classes and clergy dominated their local committees (Liam O Bolguidher, 'The early years of the Gaelic League in Kilkenny', in *Old Kilkenny Review*, Vol. 4, No. 4 (1992),

pp. 1015-1016; Traolach O Ríordáin, 'Conradh na Gaeilge i gCorcaigh i dtosach a
ré', in Journal of the Cork Historical and Archaeological Society, Vol. 98 (1993), p. 1).

21 Arthur E. Clery, 'The Gaelic League, 1893-1919', in Studies 8 (1919), p. 404;
Peter Murray, 'Irish cultural nationalism in the United Kingdom state: politics
and the Gaelic League, 1900-18', in Irish Political Studies, Vol. 8 (1993), pp. 57-8.

22 McMahon, Gaelic Revival, pp. 85-87; WI, 23 November 1901; WI,
30 November 1901; ACS, 14 December 1901; WI, 5 April 1902.

23 Muiris Ó Laoire, 'An historical perspective of the revival of Irish outside of
the Gaeltacht, 1880-1930, with reference to the revitalisation of Hebrew',
in Sue Wright, Language and the State: Revitalisation and Revival in Israel and
Eire (Bristol, 1996), p. 56.

24 McMahon, Gaelic Revival, pp. 90-91, 111-113; WI, 23 November 1901; WI,
30 November 1901; ACS, 14 December 1901; WI, 5 April 1902; Maria Luddy,
Women in Ireland, 1800-1922: A Documentary History (Cork, 1995), p. 299.

25 Protestants maintained a minority membership in the league, and while in its
early years the GL could 'accommodate both political separatists and unionists'
(Michael Mays, Nation States: The Cultures of Irish Nationalism (Maryland, 2007)
p. 56), as time went by 'the increasingly tense sectarian context … meant … it
became … difficult to uphold the pluralist ideal' (Jackson, Ireland, p. 178).

26 Ó Croidheáin, Language from Below, pp. 133-5; WI, 18 January 1902.

27 ACS, 1 February 1902.

28 Mathews, Revival, p. 25; Bew, Ireland, p. 361; Margaret Scanlan, Culture and
Customs of Ireland (Connecticut, 2006), p. 19; Crowley, Politics of Language,
p. 176; Terence Brown, 'Cultural nationalism 1880-1930', in Seamus Deane
(ed.), The Field Day Anthology of Irish Writing, Vol. 2 (Derry, 1991), p. 516;
Garvin, 'Priests and patriots', p. 73; Daniel Corkery, The Fortunes of the
Irish Language (Cork, 1968), p. 127; John Hutchinson, The Dynamics of
Cultural Nationalism: Gaelic Revival and the Creation of the Irish Nation State
(London, 1987), p. 152.

29 Hebrew had been reintroduced as the first language of Israel, and was one of
many examples language enthusiasts used to try and stimulate interest in Irish
(Philip O'Leary, The Prose Literature of Gaelic Revival, 1881-1921 – Ideology and
Innovation (Pennsylvania, 1994), p. 72; O Laoire, 'Historical perspective', p. 55).

30 Garvin, 'Priests and patriots', p. 74.

31 WI, 15 February 1902.

32 United Irishman, 22 February 1902.

33 WI, 1 February 1902; WI, 15 February 1902; WI, 1 March 1902; WI,
15 March 1902; WI, 28 June 1902.

34 ACS, 3 May 1902.

35 WI, 20 September 1902; WI, 27 December 1902.

36 WI, 18 October 1902.

37 WI, 29 November 1902. Tommy Atkins was a nineteenth-century generic
term for a British solider (John Lafflin, Tommy Atkins: The Story of a British
Soldier (London, 1966), p. xi).

38 WI, 27 December 1902; WI, 31 January 1903; WI, 4 April 1903; WI,
30 May 1903; WI, 6 June 1903.

39   *WI*, 30 May 1903. The same observation was made in Kilkenny
      (O Bolguidher, 'Gaelic League in Kilkenny', p. 1016).

40   *WI*, 13 February 1904.

41   McMahon, *Gaelic Revival*, pp. 90-91.

42   *WI*, 19 March 1904.

43   McMahon, *Gaelic Revival*, pp. 160-161, 166; Helena Wulff, *Dancing at the
      Crossroads: Memory and Mobility in Ireland* (Oxford, 2007), p. 92; Hutchinson,
      Cultural Nationalism, p. 165.

44   *WI*, 16 April 1904.

45   *WI*, 16 April 1904. The battle between the Jacobites and Williamites at
      Athlone in 1691 was the most frequently employed historical parable in
      speeches intended to inspire local nationalists.

46   *WI*, 21 May 1904; *ACS*, 11 June 1904; *ACS*, 18 June 1904; *ACS*, 25 June 1904.

47   *WI*, 21 May 1904.

48   *WI*, 7 May 1904; *WI*, 14 May 1904; *WI*, 21 May 1904; *WI*, 28 May 1904; *WI*,
      4 June 1904, *WI*, 11 June 1904; *WI*, 18 June 1904; *WI*, 25 June 1904.

49   *WI*, 2 July 1904.

50   *WI*, 9 July 1904.

51   *ACS*, 9 July 1904.

52   *UI*, 9 July 1904.

53   The term 'shoneen' referred to Irish people who preferred English society
      to their own. Unfortunately, no illustration or description of the postcard
      accompanied the article.

54   *TL*, 9 July 1904.

55   McMahon, *Gaelic Revival*, p. 129.

56   *WI*, 27 August 1904.

57   McMahon, *Gaelic Revival*, pp. 185-186.

58   Forde had been sent to Summerhill College in Sligo (*WI*, 3 September 1904).

59   *UI*, 10 September 1904.

60   *WI*, 3 September 1904; *WI*, 10 September 1904; *WI*, 17 September 1904.
      The advertisement requested a native Irish speaker who could also teach
      Irish dance classes (*ACS*, 3 September 1904; *ACS*, 10 September 1904; *ACS*,
      17 September 1904; *ACS*, 24 September 1904; *ACS*, 1 October 1904; *ACS*,
      8 October 1904; *ACS*, 15 October 1904).

61   Clery, 'Gaelic League', p. 403; Wulff, *Dancing at the Crossroads*, p. 92; Neil
      Buttimer, 'The Irish language', in Neil Buttimer, Colin Rynne and Helen
      Guerin (eds), *The Heritage of Ireland* (Cork, 2000), p. 96; Mac Aodha, 'Was this
      a social revolution?', p. 22.

62   Mathews, *Revival*, p. 25.

63   O'Leary, *Prose Literature*, p. 24.

64   Questions were asked by the Portarlington clergy with regard to the actual
      motivations of some people attending the mixed classes; lasciviousness
      was assumed (Mathews, *Revival*, p. 26; McMahon, *Gaelic Revival*, pp. 61-68;
      Murray, 'Irish cultural nationalism', p. 63; O'Leary, *Prose Literature*, p. 24).

65   *WI*, 1 October 1904.

66 Both firms later advertised in the columns of *An Claidheamh Soluis* for protracted periods – for examples see *ACS*, 10 June 1905; *ACS*, 17 February 1912.

67 *WI*, 15 October 1904.

68 *WI*, 15 October 1904; *ACS*, 19 November 1904; Mathews, *Revival*, pp. 27-28.

69 *UI*, 1 October 1904; *UI*, 22 October 1904.

70 *WI*, 22 October 1904; *WI*, 29 October 1904; *WI*, 12 November 1904; *WI*, 19 November 1904; *ACS*, 19 November 1904; *WI*, 26 November 1904; *WI*, 10 December 1904; *WI*, 31 December 1904.

71 *WI*, 7 January 1905; *WI*, 21 January 1905; *WI*, 28 January 1905.

72 *WI*, 28 January 1905

73 McMahon, *Gaelic Revival*, pp. 91-2

74 McMahon, *Gaelic Revival*, p. 137.

75 *WI*, 18 March 1905.

76 Burke, *Athlone*, pp. 242-258.

77 *WI*, 20 May 1905; *WI*, 3 June 1905; *WI*, 10 June 1905; *WI*, 24 June 1905; *ACS*, 18 March 1905; *ACS*, 29 March 1905; *ACS*, 8 April 1905; *ACS*, 22 April 1905; *ACS*, 29 April 1905; *UI*, 3 June 1905.

78 *WI*, 1 July 1905.

79 *ACS*, 1 July 1905.

80 *UI*, 8 July 1905; *ACS*, 8 July 1905.

81 *WI*, 26 August 1905; *WI*, 30 September 1905; *WI*, 21 October 1905; *WI*, 2 December 1905; *WI*, 16 December 1905.

82 *WI*, 6 January 1906.

83 *UI*, 24 June 1905; *Irish Peasant*, 16 December 1905.

84 *WI*, 6 January 1906.

85 *TL*, 10 February 1906.

86 *TIP*, 3 February 1906; *TIP*, 10 February 1906.

87 *Nationist*, 1 March 1906.

88 *WI*, 26 May 1906; *TIP*, 26 May 1906; *WI*, 2 June 1906; *TIP*, 2 June 1906; *WI*, 9 June 1906; *TIP*, 9 June 1906; *WI*, 16 June 1906; *ACS*, 16 June 1906; *WI*, 23 June 1906; *TIP*, 23 June 1906; *WI*, 30 June 1906; *II*, 30 June 1906; *WE*, 7 July 1906; *TIP*, 7 July 1906; *ACS*, 7 July 1906.

89 *TIP*, 12 May 1906.

90 McMahon, *Gaelic Revival*, pp. 127-128.

91 McMahon, *Gaelic Revival*, pp. 173-175; *WI*, 8 September 1906; *WI*, 6 October 1906; *WI*, 1 December 1906.

92 *WI*, 27 April 1907.

93 *TP*, 11 May 1907.

94 *WI*, 22 June 1907; *TP*, 22 June 1907.

95 *TIP*, 21 April 1906; *TIP*, 28 April 1906.

96 *WI*, 13 April 1907; *WI*, 20 April 1907; *WI*, 27 April 1907; *WI*, 4 May 1907; *WI*, 11 May 1907; *WE*, 11 May 1907; *WI*, 18 May 1907.

97 *WI*, 6 July 1907; *WI*, 21 September 1907.

98 *WI*, 5 October 1907; *WI*, 12 October 1907; *WI*, 19 October 1907; *WI*, 21 December 1907.

99 His four-year absence ended in March 1908 (*WI*, 28 March 1908).

100   *WI*, 11 January 1908; *WI*, 22 February 1908; *WI*, 25 April 1908; *WI*,
       2 May 1908; *WI*, 13 June 1908; *WI*, 20 June 1908; *WI*, 4 July 1908;
       WI, 11 July 1908; *TP*, 10 October 1908; *WI*, 17 October 1908; *WI*,
       24 October 1908; *WI*, 5 December 1908; *WI*, 9 January 1909.

101   *WI*, 3 October 1908.

102   Ó Croidheáin, *Language from Below*, p. 141; Hindley, *Death of the Irish Language*,
       pp. 23-4; Gabriel Doherty, 'National identity and the study of Irish history',
       in *The English Historical Review*, Vol. 111, No. 441 (April, 1996), p. 331; Tomás
       Ó Fiaich, 'The great controversy', in Ó Tuama, *Gaelic League Idea*, p. 70.

103   This was a moniker that identified Douglas Hyde alone.

104   *TL*, 30 January 1909.

105   *II*, 22 January 1909.

106   *IN*, 30 January 1909.

107   Pádraig Eric Mac Finn, *An tAthair Mícheál P. Ó hIceadha* (Baile Átha Cliath,
       1974), p. 128. O'Hickey had earlier sent a letter to Forde with his thoughts
       on the controversy. In it he congratulated Athlone for rallying to the 'Irish
       standard', calling upon the often quoted 'spirit of the men who held Athlone
       Bridge' (Mac Finn, *Mícheál P. Ó hIceadha*, pp. 141-146).

108   *II*, 22 January 1909. The letter was later reproduced in *An Claidheamh Soluis*
       (*ACS*, 14 August 1909).

109   Mac Finn, *Mícheál P. Ó hIceadha*, p. 146.

110   *II*, 22 January 1909.

111   *TL*, 30 January 1909; *IN*, 30 January 1909.

112   *ACS*, 9 January 1909.

113   *ACS*, 30 January 1909. Fr Forde stated that Irish needed to be made
       compulsory in educational institutions because, 'If the heads of...schools
       left the study of Irish to the...pleasure of the students...very little progress
       would have been made' (*TL*, 30 January 1909).

114   Clancy had supported the introduction of Irish at primary and secondary
       level (*TL*, 8 August 1908). He was against the hasty implementation of
       the new scheme (a lead-in of four to five years was his preference) for he
       believed that the poor knowledge of Irish would lead to many would-be
       students being excluded from the National University (*IT*, 2 January 1909; *IP*,
       2 January 1909; David W. Miller, *Church State and Nation in Ireland: 1898-1921*
       (Dublin, 1971), p. 235).

115   Ó Fiaich, 'Great controversy', p. 73.

116   He continued to maintain a low profile and left Athlone for Castlerea in
       1910. He was eventually posted to Nebraska in the USA (Breathnach agus Ní
       Mhurcú, *Beathaisnéis a Cúig*, p. 62).

117   Mac Finn, *Mícheál P. Ó hIceadha*, p. 220.

118   *ACS*, 10 July 1909

119   McMahon, *Gaelic Revival*, pp. 76-77.

120   *II*, 20 September 1909.

121   *WI*, 13 March 1909; *WI*, 24 April 1909; *WI*, 12 June 1909; *WI*, 3 July 1909;
       WI, 17 July 1909; *FJ*, 21 July 1909; *WI*, 24 July 1909; *WI*, 9 October 1909; *WI*,
       8 January 1910.

122   *WI*, 13 November 1909.

123   *IN*, 31 July 1909.

124   *WI*, 3 July 1909; *ACS*, 18 September 1909; *WI*, 29 January 1910; *WI*,
      19 March 1910; *II*, 12 February 1912.

125   *WE*, 7 May 1910; *WI*, 28 May 1910; *II*, 13 June 1910; *TL*, 4 June 1910.

126   *WI*, 11 February 1911.

127   *WI*, 22 October 1910; *WI*, 4 February 1911; *WI*, 11 February 1911; *WI*,
      8 April 1911.

128   *IN*, 29 October 1910; *WI*, 4 February 1911.

129   *WI*, 16 July 1910; *IN*, 23 July 1910; CI Report, Westmeath, July 1910,
      CO/904/82; Bew, *Ireland*, p. 366; Hutchinson, *Cultural Nationalism*, p. 186.

130   The Manchester Martyrs – William Philip Allen, Michael Larkin and Michael
      O'Brien – were three Irishmen who were hanged in the aftermath of the
      failed Fenian insurrection of 1867 (Seán McConville, *Irish Political Prisoners,
      1848-1922: Theatres of War* (Oxford, 2005), pp. 132-133).

131   *WI*, 23 July 1910; *WI*, 20 August 1910; *WI*, 10 September 1910; *WI*,
      8 October 1910; *WI*, 22 October 1910; *WI*, 29 October 1910; *WI*,
      3 December 1910; *WI*, 21 January 1911.

132   *WI*, 21 January 1911. Previous Uisneach Feiseanna had been held at Togherstown
      House, near the Hill of Uisneach (*ACS*, 13 November 1909; *TL*, 4 June 1910; *II*,
      13 June 1910; *WE*, 18 June 1910; *WE*, 25 June 1910; *WI*, 29 April 1911).

133   *FJ*, 11 April 1911.

134   *ACS*, 27 May 1911.

135   *WI*, 13 May 1911.

136   *WI*, 13 May 1911.

137   *WI*, 20 May 1911.

138   This time the letter writer signed off just as 'A Gaelic Leaguer' (*WI*,
      27 May 1911).

139   This referred to an English court system, abolished in 1641, where a small
      number of judges would sit in closed session and adjudicate privately on
      issues of national importance.

140   *WI*, 27 May 1911.

141   *WI*, 27 May 1911.

142   *II*, 12 February 1912.

143   *WI*, 21 January 1911; *WI*, 11 February 1911; *WI*, 4 March 1911; *WI*,
      1 April 1911; *WI*, 8 April 1911; *WI*, 15 April 1911; *WI*, 6 May 1911; *WI*,
      3 June 1911; *WI*, 10 June 1911; *WI*, 24 June 1911.

144   *ACS*, 22 April 1911.

145   *WI*, 22 July 1911.

146   *WI*, 15 July 1911; *WI*, 22 July 1911.

147   Founded by Maud Gonne and Bulmer Hobson in 1909 (Richard Davis,
      Arthur Griffith and Non-Violent Sinn Féin (Dublin, 1974), p. 68). The Athlone
      branch, established on St Stephen's Day 1911, was one of eight in Ireland
      whose aims included training 'Irish boys to work for the independence
      of Ireland and to combat the anglicising influence of the Baden-Powell
      Scouts' (CI Report, Westmeath, December 1911, CO/904/85; IG Report,

December 1911, CO/904/85). The Athlone branch, *Sluagh* (troop) Leo
Casey, engaged in drilling in the Pipers' Club under seventeen-year-old
Seán O'Mullany, with the RIC ensuring they were 'kept under observation.'
They marched, without weapons, and had just over two dozen members
on the books by the spring of 1912 (IG Report, January 1912, CO/904/86;
CI Report, Westmeath, January 1912, CO/904/86; CI Report, Westmeath,
February 1912, CO/904/86; *WI*, 23 March 1912).

148   *Connaught Tribune*, 12 August 1911; *WI*, 30 September 1911; *WI*,
22 October 1911; *WI*, 14 November 1911; *WI*, 9 December 1911; *II*,
9 December 1911; *WI*, 18 May 1912; *WI*, 1 March 1913.

149   *WI*, 4 November 1911.

150   Athlone's population gains of almost 13 per cent were accounted for by
a number of factors: the employment offered at one of the largest tweed
mills in Ireland or Britain, the Athlone Woollen Mills (*IT*, 2 March 1912;
IT, 18 April 1912; *IT*, 28 April 1913), changes in personnel stationed in the
garrison and migration to the town from rural areas (Census returns for
Ireland, 1911, showing Area, Houses, and Population; also the ages, civil or
conjugal condition, occupations, birthplaces, religions, and education of the
people Province of Leinster (Population (Ireland): Census Returns, 1911)
1912-13 [Cd. 6049], CXIV.1, p. 1044).

151   Murray, 'Irish cultural nationalism', p. 59.

152   Census returns for Ireland, 1911, Province of Leinster, p. 1152.

153   Census returns for Ireland, 1911, showing Area, Houses, and Population;
also the ages, civil or conjugal condition, occupations, birthplaces, religions,
and education of the people Province of Connaught (Population (Ireland):
Census Returns, 1911) 1912-13 [Cd. 6052], CXVII.1, p. 653.

154   *WI*, 13 January 1912.

155   *WE*, 27 January 1912.

156   *WE*, 27 January 1912.

157   *WE*, 20 January 1912.

158   *WI*, 24 February 1912.

159   *IT*, 12 February 1912; *IT*, 17 February 1912; *AC*, 17 February 1912; *II*,
19 February 1912.

160   *WI*, 9 March 1912.

161   *WI*, 2 March 1912.

162   *IT*, 12 February 1912; *WI*, 24 February 1912; *IT*, 24 February 1912; *II*,
4 March 1912.

163   *IT*, 12 March 1912.

164   *WI*, 23 March 1912; *ACS*, 13 April 1912; *ACS*, 4 May 1912; *WI*, 1 June 1912;
WI, 8 June 1912; *WI*, 15 June 1912; *WI*, 7 June 1913.

165   *WI*, 11 January 1913; *ACS*, 26 October 1912.

166   *WI*, 22 June 1912; *ACS*, 31 August 1912; *ACS*, 21 September 1912.

167   *WI*, 15 March 1913; *WI*, 22 March 1913. Michael McCormack, in his
submission to the Bureau of Military History, stated that Ballymore's
Fr Casey 'was a very enthusiastic Gaelic Leaguer, one might say an extremist'
(BMHWS No. 1,503, Michael McCormack, p. 2).

168   *WI*, 12 April 1913.

169   *ACS*, 30 August 1913. From the middle of 1913, *An Claidheamh Soluis* published numerous pieces on the internal wrangling.

170   Mac Giolla Chriost, *Irish Language*, p. 103.

171   *WI*, 12 July 1913.

172   *WI*, 7 June 1913; *WI*, 28 June 1913; *WI*, 20 September 1913; *ACS*, 27 September 1913; *WI*, 27 September 1913.

173   *WI*, 4 October 1913; *WE*, 11 October 1913.

174   A report in the *Westmeath Independent* from June 1914 noted an Athlone Coiste Ceanntair receiving assistance from the Uisneach Coiste Ceanntair in ensuring the active participation of outlying regions. On the day of its staging Dean Kelly referred to the event as 'Feis Mór Áth Luain', while *An Claidheamh Soluis* referred to it as 'Feis Uisneach' (*WI*, 23 May 1914; *WI*, 6 June 1914; *WI*, 13 June 1914; *ACS*, 13 June 1914; *WI*, 27 September 1913).

175   *WI*, 4 October 1913; *ACS*, 11 October 1913.

176   Donal MacCartney, 'The political use of history in the work of Arthur Griffith', in *Journal of Contemporary History*, Vol. 8, No. 1 (January, 1973), pp. 8-9.

177   R.F. Foster, 'History and the Irish Question', in *Transactions of the Royal Historical Society*, Fifth Series, Vol. 33 (1983), p. 184.

178   Whereby one monarch is head of state for two countries, but both states are equal to, and independent of, each other (M.J. Kelly, *The Fenian Ideal and Irish Nationalism: 1882-1916* (Suffolk, 2006), p. 202).

179   Associated with Henry Grattan, the 1782 legislation redefined the constitutional relationship between Ireland and Britain. 'Legislative Independence', as it was termed, allowed the Irish Parliament greater, though not total, control over the passing and implementation of laws (James Kelly, 'Henry Gratten', in Connolly, *Oxford Companion*, pp. 227-8).

180   MacCartney, 'Work of Arthur Griffith', p. 7; Owen McGee, *The IRB: The Irish Republican Brotherhood from the Land War to Sinn Féin* (Dublin, 2005), pp. 311-313.

181   Maume, *Long Gestation*, p. 57; Foster, *Modern Ireland*, p. 450.

182   *WI*, 3 December 1904.

183   McGee, *The IRB*, pp. 309-311. For an overview of the people, parties and politics involved see Laffan, *Resurrection of Ireland*, p. 21; Kelly, *Fenian Ideal*, pp. 22-40; Davis, *Arthur Griffith*, pp. 26, 74; NAI, IG + CI Reports, Box 8, IG Report, December 1905.

184   RIC Report, Precís of Information, Westmeath, December 1905, CO/904/116.

185   *WI*, 10 February 1906; *WI*, 17 February 1906.

186   *WI*, 24 February 1906.

187   Davis, *Arthur Griffith*, p. 79.

188   *WI*, 24 November 1906. The INF, GL and GAA organised the event (NAI, IG + CI Reports, Box 10, CI Report, Westmeath, November 1906).

189   *WI*, 1 December 1906.

190   NAI, IG + CI Reports, Box 10, CI Report, Westmeath, December 1906.

191   *WI*, 8 December 1906; *WI*, 23 March 1907.

192 *WI*, 9 March 1907; *WI*, 6 April 1907.

193 *WI*, 18 May 1907.

194 *WI*, 1 June 1907.

195 NAI, IG + CI Reports, Box 11, IG Report, June 1907; Kelly, *Fenian Ideal*, pp. 141, 173; Calton Younger, *Arthur Griffith* (Dublin, 1981), p. 27. Laffan, *Resurrection of Ireland*, pp. 24-5; Davis, *Arthur Griffith*, p. 33.

196 *WI*, 1 June 1907; *WI*, 8 June 1907.

197 NAI, IG + CI Reports, Box 12, CI Report, Westmeath, July 1907.

198 *WI*, 10 August 1907; Davis, *Arthur Griffith*, p. 34.

199 Myles O'Reilly died in 1644 at the bridge at Finea while fighting against English and Scottish troops during the Confederate Wars (Martyn Bennett, *The Civil Wars Experienced: Britain and Ireland: 1638-1661* (London, 2000), p. 53).

200 RIC Report, Précis of Information, Westmeath, August 1907, CO/904/117; Wheatley, *Nationalism and the Irish Party*, p. 125. Richard Davis described Ginnell as 'almost converted by Hobson' (Davis, *Arthur Griffith*, p. 68).

201 *II*, 4 April 1907; Coleman, *Longford*, pp. 18-21.

202 *II*, 8 August 1907; NAI, IG + CI Reports, Box 12, CI Report, Roscommon, October 1907.

203 McEvoy, 'King's County', pp. 89-91.

204 NAI, I.G + CI Reports, Box 12, CI Report, Westmeath, September 1907; IG + CI Reports, Box 12, IG Report, September 1907.

205 For the full speech see Anthony J. Jordan, *Boer War to Easter Rising: The Writings of John MacBride* (Dublin, 2006), pp. 132-3.

206 Cronin and Adair, *Wearing of the Green*, p. 93; McGee, *The IRB*, p. 303.

207 RIC Report, Précis of Information, Westmeath, November 1907, CO/904/117; *WI*, 30 November 1907.

208 NAI, IG + CI Reports, Box 12, CI Report, Westmeath, November 1907; *WI*, 2 November 1907.

209 Russell Shortt, 'IRA activity in Westmeath during the War of Independence, 1918-21: Part One', in *Ríocht na Midhe: Records of Meath Archaeological and Historical Society*, Vol. 26 (2005), p. 171.

210 Davis, *Arthur Griffith*, pp. 44-48; Brian Maye, *Arthur Griffith* (Dublin, 1997), p. 104.

211 NAI, IG + CI Reports Box 11, IG Report, June 1907.

212 *WI*, 5 October 1907.

213 *WI*, 30 November 1907; *WI*, 28 December 1907.

214 Lennon was awarded the position on the basis of rotation and his willingness to assume the role. He ran a divisive campaign against fellow incumbent John O'Meara after they disagreed over the appointment of a rate collector. Lennon supported two INF members, the previously mentioned O.J. Dolan, and J.H. Rafferty. Both won along with O'Meara (*WI*, 11 January 1908; *WI*, 18 January 1908; *WI*, 25 January 1908).

215 *WI*, 1 February 1908.

216 *WI*, 1 February 1908.

217 *WI*, 15 February 1908; *WI*, 7 March 1908; *WI*, 14 March 1908.

218 *WI*, 28 March 1908.

219 C.J. Dolan was beaten by a margin of three to one, but did secure over 1,100 votes, which surprised observers in SF, the IPP and the media. McDermott-Hayes put the loss down to SF's unfamiliarity with the electorate (*WI*, 29 February 1908; NAI, I.G + CI Reports, Box 13, IG Report, February 1908; Jackson, *Ireland*, pp. 186-7; Laffan, *Resurrection of Ireland*, p. 29).

220 Bew, *Ireland*, p. 366.

221 *TP*, 29 February 1908; Davis, *Arthur Griffith*, p. 50.

222 *II*, 1 April 1908.

223 RIC Report, Precís of Information, Westmeath, April 1908, CO/904/118. MacBride met with Dr Sheridan and others in August at a GAA match. The RIC noted that many known IRB men were in attendance though, unsurprisingly, what was discussed was not known (RIC Report, Precís of Information, Westmeath, August 1908, CO/904/118). September witnessed another unsuccessful foundation attempt (RIC Report, Precís of Information, Westmeath, September 1908, CO/904/118).

224 *WI*, 26 September 1908

225 *WI*, 12 September 1908; *WI*, 26 September 1908; *WI*, 3 October 1908; *TP*, 10 October 1908.

226 *TP*, 7 November 1908.

227 The Renunciation Act recognised the exclusive right of the Irish Parliament to legislate for Ireland.

228 *IN*, 30 January 1909.

229 *IT*, 22 January 1909; *IP*, 30 January 1909.

230 *WI*, 23 January 1909.

231 Younger, *Arthur Griffith*, p. 35.

232 RIC Report, Precis of Information, Westmeath, February, 1909, CO/904/118; Virginia E. Glandon, *Arthur Griffith and the Advanced Nationalist Press in Ireland 1900-1922* (New York, 1985), p. 45.

233 *WI*, 6 February 1909.

234 *WI*, 20 February 1909.

235 *SF*, 3 April 1909; *WI*, 10 April 1909; *SF*, 10 April 1909.

236 RIC Report, Precís of Information, Westmeath, March 1909, CO/904/118.

237 *SF*, 27 March 1909.

238 CI Report, Westmeath, March 1909, CO/904/78; RIC Report, Precís of Information, Westmeath, March 1909, CO/904/118; *WI*, 27 March 1909.

239 *WI*, 5 January 1907; *SF*, 27 March 1909.

240 CI Report, Westmeath, March 1909, CO/904/77; *SF*, 10 April 1909.

241 *WI*, 3 April 1909.

242 *SF*, 10 April 1909.

243 *WI*, 3 April 1909.

244 *WI*, 3 April 1909.

245 Campbell, *Land and Revolution*, pp. 170-171.

246 RIC Report, Precís of Information, Westmeath, May 1909, CO/904/118; *WI*, 8 May 1909; *WI*, 22 May 1909.

247 *IT*, 5 May 1909; *WI*, 8 May 1909.

248 *IN*, 8 May 1909; *WI*, 22 May 1909; *WI*, 29 May 1909; *IN*, 29 May 1909; *WI*, 12 June 1909; *FJ*, 15 June 1909; *IN*, 19 June 1909; *WI*, 3 July 1909; *IN*, 21 July 1909.

249 *WI*, 3 July 1909; *WI*, 28 August 1909; *WI*, 4 September 1909; *WI*, 9 October 1909; *WI*, 16 October 1909.

250 AHL, Minute Book of Athlone UDC, 10 September 1909; RIC Report, Precís of Information, Westmeath, November 1909, CO/904/118; CI Report, Westmeath, November 1909, CO/904/79; IG Report, November 1909, CO/904/79.

251 RIC Report, Precís of Information, Westmeath, November 1909, CO/904/118.

252 Athlone's branch had paid the 10s affiliation fee, but nothing additional (*SF*, 28 August 1909).

253 Owen Sweeney spoke of Nugent's attempts to fight for the British with Lord Longford's yeomanry corps in the Boer War. After he was rejected for service, Sweeney stated that Nugent made a £5 donation and 'became a Nationalist' (*FJ*, 9 November 1909; *IT*, 9 November 1909).

254 *FJ*, 9 November 1909.

255 *IT*, 10 September 1909.

256 *WI*, 13 November 1909.

257 *TL*, 20 November 1909.

258 RIC Report, Precís of Information, Westmeath, November 1909, CO/904/118; *WI*, 20 November 1909.

259 *WI*, 4 December 1909.

260 Davis, *Arthur Griffith*, p. 82.

261 *FJ*, 12 November 1909; *IT*, 22 November 1909; *WI*, 12 March 1910.

262 Laffan, *Resurrection of Ireland*, pp. 23-4.

263 Davis, *Arthur Griffith*, p. 76; Tom Garvin, 'The politics of language and literature in pre-independence Ireland', in Conor McGrath and Eoin O'Malley (eds), *Irish Political Studies Reader: Key Contributions* (London, 2007), p. 185; Kelly, *Fenian Ideal*, p. 189.

264 Wheatley, *Nationalism and the Irish Party*, pp. 58-59.

265 Kelly, *Fenian Ideal*, p. 189; Maye, *Arthur Griffith*, p. 105.

266 Jackson, *Ireland*, p. 187.

267 Terence Denman, '"The red livery of shame": the campaign against recruitment in Ireland 1899-1914', in *Irish Historical Studies*, Vol. 29, No. 114 (November, 1994), p. 229.

268 SF assisted in organising the 1911 St Patrick's Day celebrations (*WI*, 11 March 1911; CI Report, Westmeath, December 1911, CO/904/85).

269 David Fitzpatrick, *The Two Irelands: 1912-1939* (Oxford, 1998), p. 14.

270 Anthony C. Hepburn, 'Catholic Ulster and Irish politics: the Ancient Order of Hibernians, 1905-14', in Anthony C. Hepburn, *A Past Apart: Studies in the History of Catholic Belfast, 1850-1950* (Belfast, 1996), p. 159.

271 Joost Augusteijn, 'Radical nationalist activities in County Derry 1900-1921', in Gerard O'Brien (ed.), *Derry and Londonderry, History and Society: Interdisciplinary Essays on the History of an Irish County* (Dublin, 1999), p. 574; Hepburn, 'Catholic Ulster and Irish politics', p. 159; Maume, *Long Gestation*, p. 45; Bew, *Conflict and Conciliation*, p. 186.

272 Miller, *Church State and Nation*, pp. 211-213.

273   NAI, IG + CI Reports, Box 6, CI Report, Roscommon, July 1904; IG + CI
      Reports, Box 6, CI Report, Roscommon, August 1904; IG + CI Reports,
      Box 6, CI Report, Roscommon, October 1904; IG + CI Reports, Box 6, CI
      Report, Roscommon, November 1904; IG + CI Reports, Box 7, CI Report,
      Roscommon, January 1905.

274   Foster, *Modern Ireland*, p. 610; NAI, IG + CI Reports, Box 7, IG Report,
      February 1905; IG + CI Reports, Box 7, CI Report, Roscommon,
      February 1905; IG + CI Reports, Box 7, CI Report, Roscommon,
      March 1905; IG + CI Reports, Box 8, CI Report, Roscommon, July 1905;
      IG + CI Reports, Box 8, CI Report, Roscommon, August 1905; IG + CI
      Reports, Box 8, CI Report, Roscommon, December 1905; RIC Report,
      Precís of Information, Roscommon, April 1905, CO/904/116.

275   *WI*, 28 January 1905; A.C. Hepburn, *Catholic Belfast and Nationalist Ireland
      in the era of Joe Devlin: 1872-1934* (Oxford, 2008), pp. 90-91; Kevin Kenny,
      Making Sense of the Molly Maguires (Oxford, 1998), p. 13; *Hibernian Journal*,
      November 1907.

276   Fitzpatrick, *Politics and Irish Life*, p. 82; Miller, *Church State and Nation*, p. 210.

277   A.C. Hepburn, 'Ancient Order of Hibernians', in Connolly, *Oxford
      Companion*, p. 14.

278   Michael Thomas Foy, 'The Ancient Order of Hibernians: An Irish political-
      religious pressure group, 1884-1975' (Unpublished MA thesis, Q.U.B., 1976),
      p. 88-89; Hepburn, 'Catholic Ulster and Irish politics', p. 159.

279   NAI, IG + CI Reports, Box 8, IG Report, August 1905; IG + CI Reports, Box
      9, IG Report, March 1906; IG + CI Reports, Box 9, IG Report, April 1906;
      IG + CI Reports, Box 9, CI Report, Roscommon, April 1906; CI Report, IG
      + CI Reports, Box 9, Roscommon, June 1906; IG + CI Reports, Box 10, CI
      Report, Roscommon, December 1906; IG + CI Reports, Box 12, IG Report,
      July 1907; Hepburn, 'Ancient Order of Hibernians', pp. 13-14.

280   NAI, IG + CI Reports, Box 10, CI Report, Westmeath, October 1906; IG +
      CI Reports, Box 11, CI Report, Westmeath, January 1907; IG + CI Reports,
      Box 13, IG Report, January 1908; IG + CI Reports, Box 13, CI Report,
      Westmeath, May 1908.

281   CI Report, Westmeath, May 1909, CO/904/78.

282   *WI*, 10 April 1909.

283   *WI*, 3 April 1909.

284   McKenna was a member of the South Westmeath UIL. He was the local
      organiser for the AOH and signed off using the title 'Divisional Director for
      South Westmeath' (*WI*, 3 April 1909).

285   *WI*, 3 April 1909.

286   Hepburn, *Catholic Belfast*, p. 92; NAI, IG + CI Reports, Box 14, CI Report,
      Roscommon, July 1908.

287   *IP*, 14 April 1906.

288   Miller, *Church State and Nation*, pp. 210-1.

289   IG Report, July 1909, CO/904/78; IG Report, August 1909, CO/904/78; CI
      Report, Roscommon, August 1909, CO/904/78; IG Report, September 1909,
      CO/904/79.

290 Hepburn, 'Catholic Ulster and Irish politics', p. 161.

291 Hepburn, 'Ancient Order of Hibernians', p. 14.

292 IG Report, January 1910, CO/904/80.

293 McGee, *The IRB*, p. 324.

294 Foy, 'Ancient Order of Hibernians', pp. 88-89.

295 See H.B.C. Pollard, *Secret Societies of Ireland: Their Rise and Progress* (1922) (Massachusetts, 2003), p. 110.

296 *HJ*, February 1912; J.J. Lee, *Ireland, 1912-1985: Politics and Society* (Cambridge, 1989), p. 10.

297 *WI*, 3 June 1911; *HJ*, June 1911.

298 McEvoy, 'King's County', p. 89; *HJ*, December 1908.

299 *HJ*, June 1911.

300 CI Report, Westmeath, June 1911, CO/904/84; *WI*, 24 June 1911.

301 *WI*, 10 June 1911; *WI*, 17 June 1911.

302 IG Report, July 1911, CO/904/84; CI Report, Westmeath, July 1911, CO/904/84; CI Report, Roscommon, July 1911, CO/904/84.

303 *WI*, 24 June 1911; *WI*, 15 July 1911; *WI*, 5 August 1911; *WI*, 7 September 1911; *WI*, 7 October 1911; *WI*, 14 October 1911.

304 *WI*, 15 July 1911; *WI*, 14 October 1911.

305 *WI*, 28 October 1911.

306 *WI*, 18 November 1911.

307 *WI*, 25 November 1911.

308 Rafferty was a member of the INF and an active UIL member for at least seven years. He gained a UDC seat in 1908, but did not retain it in 1911 (*WI*, 21 January 1911). Waterston had little or no reported activity in local bodies, be they political or quasi-political, over the previous decade, but may have been on the fringes of the short-lived SF branch.

309 *WI*, 25 November 1911; *WI*, 16 December 1911; *WI*, 13 January 1912; *S.I.*, 3 December 1911.

310 *WI*, 2 December 1911.

311 Maume, *Long Gestation*, p.130.

312 See *HJ*, January 1908.

313 O'Leary, *Prose Literature*, pp. 39-40.

314 O'Leary, *Prose Literature*, p. 62.

315 The hall was unofficially opened on November 20 (*CT*, 25 November 1911).

316 *IT*, 19 December 1911.

317 *WI*, 16 December 1911; *IT*, 19 December 1911; *WI*, 23 December 1911.

318 There was one division noted for south Roscommon and while this may have been Athlone, all later notes in reference to the local division dealt with it in the context of Westmeath (*HJ*, January 1912).

319 *WI*, 13 January 1912; *WI*, 6 April 1911.

320 CI Report, Roscommon, May 1912, CO/904/88.

321 *WI*, 4 May 1912. The Ladies, Auxiliary AOH had been formed in 1908, as 'social workers' (*HJ*, August 1908). See Ruth Taillon and Diane Urquhart (eds), 'Ladies Auxiliary', in Angela Bourke (ed.), *The Irish Field Day Anthology of Irish Writing, Vol. 5: Irish Women's Writings and Traditions* (New York, 2002), p. 359).

322 *WI*, 22 June 1912; *WI*, 29 June 1912; *WI*, 14 September 1912; *WI*,
4 January 1913; *WI*, 8 March 1913; *WI*, 29 March 1913; *WI*, 5 July 1913.

323 Maume, *Long Gestation*, p. 122.

324 Nugent, a confirmed conservative, said he was against female suffrage because
women themselves did not want to vote! (*II*, 13 July 1910; *FJ*, 16 July 1910;
II, 25 July 1910; *Hansard 5 Commons*, xix, 233-236 (12 July 1910); Cliona
Murphy, 'Suffragists and nationalism in twentieth-century Ireland', in *History
of European Ideas*, Vol. 1, No. 4-6 (1993), pp. 1011-1012).

325 IG Report, June 1912, CO/904/87.

326 *HJ*, June 1912; *WI*, 15 June 1912; *WI*, 29 June 1912; CI Report, Westmeath,
June 1912, CO/904/87; CI Report, Westmeath, July 1912, CO/904/87.

327 Jackson, *Ireland*, p. 201.

328 D. George Boyce and Alan O'Day, 'A time of transitions', in Boyce and
O'Day, *Ireland in Transition*, p. 12.

329 *WI*, 15 June 1912.

330 The hall was now on Grattan Row (*WI*, 6 July 1912; *WI*, 30 March 1912).

331 *WI*, 20 July 1912; *WI*, 17 August 1912; *WI*, 24 August 1912; *WI*,
31 August 1912; *WI*, 14 September 1912; *WI*, 19 October 1912; *WI*,
2 November 1912; *WI*, 30 November 1912; *WI*, 14 December 1912;
WI, 21 December 1912; *WI*, 4 January 1913; *WI*, 11 January 1913; *WI*,
25 January 1913; *WI*, 1 February 1913; *WI*, 1 March 1913; *WI*, 8 March 1913;
WI, 29 March 1913; *WI*, 19 April 1913; *WI*, 3 May 1913; *WI*, 31 May 1913;
WI, 5 July 1913; *WI*, 19 July 1913; *WI*, 2 August 1913; *WI*, 30 August 1913.

332 NAI, LOU 13/2/1-2, Ancient Order of Hibernians Agenda Book, 1912-81,
13 August 1912.

333 *WI*, 5 May 1913.

334 *WI*, 13 January 1912; *WI*, 27 March 1912; *WI*, 23 April 1912; *WI*,
30 November 1912.

335 *HJ*, April 1913; *HJ*, June 1913.

336 *HJ*, April 1913; *HJ*, June 1913.

337 Fitzpatrick, *Politics and Irish Life*, p. 82

CHAPTER 3

1 *WI*, 13 January 1912; *WI*, 3 February 1912; *WI*, 10 February 1912;
II, 13 February 1912; *WI*, 17 February 1912; *WI*, 24 February 1912; *WI*,
2 March 1912; *WI*, 16 March 1912.

2 *WI*, 23 March 1912.

3 *WI*, 23 March 1912.

4 Joseph P. Finnan, *John Redmond and Irish Unity: 1912-1918* (New York, 2004), p. 32.

5 *IT*, 17 February 1912

6 A Vatican directive extensively promulgated from 1908 which, most controversially, decreed that all mixed marriage ceremonies had to be carried out by a
Roman Catholic priest who would seek a commitment that all children born to
the couple be brought up as Catholics. Marriages celebrated without a Catholic

priest were not recognised by the Vatican (Lewis Stockton, *Marriage considered From Legal and Ecclesiastical Viewpoints, in Connection with the Recent Ne Temere Decree of the Roman Catholic Church (1912)* (Massachusetts, 2008), pp. 29-36, 73-83).

7   *IT*, 2 January 1912.

8   *IT*, 6 February 1912.

9   D.G. Boyce, 'The Ulster crisis: prelude to 1916?', in Gabriel Doherty and Dermot Keogh, *1916: The Long Revolution* (Cork, 2007), p. 48.

10   IG Report, December 1911, CO/904/85; Jackson, *Home Rule*, p. 116.

11   A.T.Q. Stewart, *The Ulster Crisis* (London, 1979), pp. 69-70.

12   IG Report, February 1912, CO/904/86.

13   Charles Townshend, *Easter 1916: The Irish Rebellion* (London, 2006), p. 31.

14   Boyce, 'The Ulster crisis', p. 48.

15   *Government of Ireland. A Bill to Amend the Provision for the Government of Ireland*, HC, 1912-13, Bills [347].

16   Finnan, *John Redmond*, p. 21. America was an important fundraising area for the IPP and, like Britain, hosted a UIL presence (Finnan, *John Redmond*, pp. 154-164).

17   Finnan, *John Redmond*, p. 34; Cornelius O'Leary and Patrick Maume, *Controversial Issues in Anglo-Irish Relations: 1910-1921* (Dublin, 2004), p. 18.

18   *WI*, 13 April 1912.

19   O'Day, *Irish Home Rule*, pp. 247-8.

20   *WI*, 13 April 1912.

21   *II*, 13 April 1912; *WI*, 20 April 1912.

22   *II*, 13 April 1912.

23   O'Day, *Irish Home Rule*, pp. 248-250.

24   *II*, 29 March 1912; *WI*, 30 March 1912.

25   James Loughlin, 'The Irish Protestant Home Rule Association and nationalist politics, 1886-93', in *Irish Historical Studies*, Vol. 25, No. 95 (May, 1985), p. 348.

26   *II*, 29 March 1912; *WI*, 30 March 1912.

27   Stewart, *Ulster Crisis*, p. 58; Boyce, 'The Ulster crisis', p. 47; Bew, *Ireland*, p. 367; Finnan, *John Redmond*, p. 36; D.G. Boyce, *Englishmen and Irish Troubles: British Public Opinion and the Making of Irish Policy 1918-22* (London, 1972), p. 28.

28   *IT*, 16 August 1912.

29   *WI*, 20 July 1912.

30   CI Report, Westmeath, August 1912, CO/904/87; CI Report, Roscommon, August 1912, CO/904/87; CI Report, Westmeath, September 1912, CO/904/88; CI Report, Roscommon, September 1912, CO/904/88; CI Report, Westmeath, October 1912, CO/904/88; CI Report, Roscommon, October 1912, CO/904/88; *WI*, 5 October 1912; *WI*, 12 October 1912; AHL, Minute Book of Athlone UDC, 13 November 1912; Minute Book of Athlone PLG, 9 November 1912.

31   *WI*, 6 July 1912.

32   *WI*, 19 October 1912.

33   Finnan, *John Redmond*, pp. 37, 159.

34   Gearóid Ó Tuathaigh, 'Nationalist Ireland, 1912-1922: aspects of continuity and change', in Peter Collins (ed.), *Nationalism and Unionism: Conflict in Ireland, 1885-1921* (Belfast, 1994), p. 49.

35 Finnan, *John Redmond*, p. 40; O'Leary and Maume, *Controversial Issues*, pp. 23-4. The expulsions were triggered by an incident on 29 June at Castledawson, County Derry, where Protestant children were attacked by AOH members, who took exception to the waving of Union flags (Stewart, *Ulster Crisis*, pp. 59-60).

36 *WI*, 10 August 1912; D.G. Boyce, 'British Conservative opinion, the Ulster question, and the partition of Ireland, 1912-21', in *Irish Historical Studies,* Vol. 17, No. 65 (March, 1970), p. 91; Ó Tuathaigh, 'Nationalist Ireland', pp. 52-53.

37 *WI*, 3 August 1912; *WI*, 10 August 1912.

38 *WI*, 7 September 1912; *WI*, 5 October 1912; *WI*, 26 October 1912; O'Day, *Irish Home Rule*, p. 253; Stewart, *Ulster Crisis*, p. 62.

39 Boyce, 'The Ulster crisis', p. 52; Patrick Buckland, 'Carson, Craig and the partition of Ireland', in Collins, *Nationalism and Unionism*, pp. 83-85.

40 A.T.Q. Stewart, *The Shape of Irish History* (Belfast, 2001), p. 166.

41 *WI*, 28 September 1912.

42 Foster, *Modern Ireland*, p. 466; O'Leary and Maume, *Controversial Issues*, p. 24.

43 *WI*, 17 August 1912.

44 *WI*, 24 August 1912.

45 *WI*, 12 October 1912.

46 *IT*, 19 October 1912.

47 *MG*, 18 November 1912.

48 Stewart, *Ulster Crisis*, p. 67; *WI*, 30 November 1912; *WI*, 14 December 1912; *WI*, 21 December 1912; *WI*, 11 January 1913.

49 Jackson, *Home Rule*, p. 123.

50 Stewart, *Ulster Crisis*, p. 70; Alvin Jackson, 'Irish unionism, 1905-21', in Collins, *Nationalism and Unionism*, p. 43.

51 O'Leary and Maume, *Controversial Issues*, p. 26.

52 *WI*, 25 January 1913.

53 AHL, Minute Book of Athlone PLG, 18 January 1913.

54 *II*, 4 February 1913.

55 *WI*, 25 January 1913.

56 *WI*, 11 January 1913.

57 *WI*, 1 February 1913.

58 O'Day, *Irish Home Rule*, p. 254.

59 *WI*, 8 February 1913.

60 *WI*, 18 January 1913.

61 AHL, Minute Book of Athlone PLG, 1 February 1913.

62 *II*, 10 February 1913.

63 *II*, 13 February 1913; *WI*, 15 February 1913.

64 *II*, 17 March 1913; *WI*, 22 March 1913; *WI*, 5 April 1913; *II*, 11 April 1913.

65 *WI*, 24 May 1913.

66 *WI*, 1 February 1913.

67 Finnan, *John Redmond*, p. 48; *WI*, 8 March 1913; IG Report, January 1913, CO/904/89.

68 *WI*, 22 February 1913; *WI*, 12 April 1913.

69 *WI*, 3 May 1913.

70   Jackson, *Home Rule*, p. 111.

71   Boyce, 'Ulster crisis', p. 47.

72   *WI*, 3 May 1913.

73   *WI*, 5 July 1913; *WI*, 19 July 1913.

74   *WI*, 19 July 1913.

75   *WI*, 23 August 1913.

76   *WI*, 23 August 1913.

77   *WI*, 7 June 1913.

78   The bill was again rejected by the Lords on the fifteenth (O'Day, *Irish Home Rule*, p. 255).

79   *WI*, 2 August 1913.

80   *WI*, 13 September 1913.

81   IG Report, September 1913, CO/904/91; Lyons, 'The developing crisis', p. 136.

82   Kennedy, 'Genesis of the Rising', pp. 64-65; Fitzpatrick, *Politics and Irish Life*, p. 52.

83   Fitzpatrick, *Two Irelands*, p. 155.

84   Stewart, *Ulster Crisis*, p. 106.

85   Bulmer Hobson, *A Short History of the Irish Volunteers by Bulmer Hobson, with a preface by Eoin MacNeill, Vol. 1* (Dublin, 1918), p. 17. See Marnie Hay, *Bulmer Hobson and the Nationalist Movement in Twentieth-Century Ireland* (Manchester, 2009), pp. 109-110.

86   Charles Townshend, *Political Violence in Ireland: Government and Resistance since 1848* (Oxford, 1984), p. 239.

87   Lyons, 'The developing crisis', p. 136.

88   Townshend, *Easter 1916*, p. 36.

89   *IT*, 29 September 1913.

90   *IT*, 7 January 1914.

91   P.J. Buckland, 'The southern Irish unionists, the Irish Question and British politics, 1906-1914', in Alan O'Day (ed.), *Reactions to Irish Nationalism: 1865-1914* (London, 1987), pp. 375-381.

92   *WI*, 3 January 1914; *WI*, 17 January 1914.

93   There is a biography that dates the idea for a force to an earlier period; however, it is unreliable, containing information at odds with that already established. Written in the 1980s when the author, Maud Mitchell, was an octogenarian, it contains numerous inaccuracies. Mitchell was a member of the Clan Uisneach-linked GL in Athlone and stated that it was in that organisation in the spring of 1912 that the idea for 'men scouts', along the lines of FÉ, was first mooted (Maud Mitchell, *The Man With the Long Hair* (Belfast, 1993), pp. 21-22).

94   SF was not active in Athlone in 1913. The meeting was connected with another event, perhaps a GAA match. The ascendant trajectory of the SF in August 1917 may explain why this erroneous addition was made to the article.

95   *WI*, 25 August 1917.

96   Oliver Snoddy, 'The Midland Volunteer Force of 1913', in *Journal of the Old Athlone Society*, Vol. 1, No. 1 (1969), pp. 40-42.

97   The tree was felled in 1949, despite local opposition (*WI*, 12 February 1949).

98 By this time *Irish Freedom* reported that the Athlone FÉ branch had become 'practically *non est*'. Many of the adult workers in the National movement in Athlone have apparently become luke warm. They have handed in their guns and retired from the light … this *nil deperandum* is perhaps too out-of-date for the people of Athlone' (*IF*, October 1913).

99 O'Brien had been a member of the Athlone SF branch (*WI*, 3 April 1909).

100 *WI*, 25 August 1917; Snoddy, 'Midland Volunteer Force', p. 38.

101 The UVF's Colonel Beresford threatened, entirely unrealistically, that Ulster would put 'an armed force of a quarter of a million into the field' if Home Rule was enforced. This assertion was ridiculed by McDermott-Hayes, who stated that Carson had quoted a figure of one million two years previously (*WI*, 11 October 1913).

102 *WI*, 11 October 1913.

103 *WI*, 18 October 1913.

104 *WI*, 18 October 1913.

105 *WI*, 18 October 1913.

106 *WI*, 25 August 1917.

107 *WI*, 25 August 1917.

108 *WI*, 25 October 1913.

109 *National Volunteer*, 17 October 1914; *WI*, 25 August 1917.

110 Moate, Kilbeggan, Horseleap and Mullingar in Westmeath. Ballycumber, Clara and Tullamore in King's County (*WI*, 25 October 1913).

111 *WI*, 25 October 1914.

112 CI Report, Westmeath, October 1913, CO/904/91.

113 RIC Report, Precís of Information, Westmeath, October 1913, CO/904/120.

114 BMHWS No. 331, Diarmuid Murtagh, pp. 1-2.

115 BMHWS No. 331, Diarmuid Murtagh, pp. 1-2.

116 *WI*, 25 August 1917; Seán O'Mullany, 'Athlone started the volunteer movement', in *The Athlone Annual, 1963* (Athlone, 1963), p. 23.

117 *IT*, 4 October 1913.

118 *Evening Herald*, 14 October 1913; *FJ*, 15 October 1913. 'The Midland Volunteer Force was recently raised in the Athlone district to meet hostility with hostility if the Ulster people make themselves disagreeable after the passing of Home Rule' (*IT*, 15 October 1913).

119 *II*, 25 October 1913; *FJ*, 25 October 1913.

120 *TL*, 25 October 1913.

121 *Derry Journal*, 27 October 1913.

122 *IF*, November 1913.

123 George Dangerfield, *The Damnable Question: a Study of Anglo-Irish Relations* (London, 1977), p. 97; Michael Wheatley, "Ireland is out for blood and murder': nationalist opinion and the Ulster crisis in provincial Ireland, 1913-1914', in D. George Boyce and Alan O'Day (eds), *The Ulster Crisis: 1885-1921* (New York, 2006), pp. 186-187.

124 Wheatley, *Nationalism and the Irish Party*, p. 181.

125 F.X. Martin, 'MacNeill and the foundation of the Irish Volunteers', in F.X. Martin and F.J. Byrne (eds), *The Scholar Revolutionary: Eoin MacNeill, 1867-1945,*

and the Making of the New Ireland (Dublin, 1973), p. 125; Townshend, Easter 1916, p. 38.

126   ACS, 1 November 1913.

127   ACS, 1 November 1913.

128   Townshend, Easter 1916, p. 38.

129   Snoddy, 'Midland Volunteer Force', pp. 40-42. This article is basically, with some additions, an anglicised version of Pádraig O Snodaigh, 'Fórsa Óglách Lár na Tíre 1913', in Studia Hibernica, No. 5 (1965), pp. 113-122 and a section from Pádraig O Snodaigh, Comhghuaillithe na Réabhlóide: 1913-1916 (Dublin, 1966), pp. 7-9, 20.

130   Martin, 'MacNeill', p. 128.

131   A number of pieces penned by Eoin MacNeill, Bulmer Hobson and The O'Rahilly either discount Athlone's contribution or do not mention it at all (F.X. Martin, Sources for the Irish Volunteers, 1913-1916 (Dublin, 1963)).

132   Michael Joseph O'Rahilly, The Secret History of the Irish Volunteers (Dublin, 1915), p. 3.

133   Martin, 'MacNeill', p. 126.

134   Liam de Róiste Diary, 11 November 1914, cited in Kennedy, 'Genesis of the Rising', p. 68

135   Kennedy, 'Genesis of the Rising', p. 68. See also BMHWS No. 1,698, Liam de Róiste, p. 116; BMHWS No. 500, Seán O Cuill, p. 2.

136   Michael McDermott-Hayes had a long journalistic career, working for the Limerick Leader, Kilkenny Journal and Midland Tribune before joining the Daily Express in Dublin, where he was a Chief Ranger with the INF (WI, 17 February 1912). He moved from Dublin to Athlone upon his appointment as editor of the Westmeath Independent in 1900 and during his tenure increased its size, coverage and distribution, on a number of occasions laying claim to editing the largest provincial newspaper in Ireland (WI, 15 December 1900; WI, 12 July 1902; WI, 31 March 1906; TL, 7 April 1906). The paper was praised by The Leader's D.P. Moran for its commitment to Irish industry, 'excellent' reports and was used by Moran to provide information for his own publication (TL, 18 November 1905; TL, 10 February 1905; TL, 7 April 1904; TL, 12 May 1906; TL, 19 January 1907; TL, 23 March 1907; TL, 11 July 1908). Dermot Murtagh states that MacDermott-Hayes 'was a drunken fellow, and foul-mouthed to his subordinates', a rather damning assessment of the man, seemingly informed by Murtagh's father, P.V.C., whose position as Town Clerk probably brought him into conflict with the newspaper editor (BMHWS No. 331, Dermot Murtagh, p. 1). Maud Mitchell was similarly unimpressed by MacDermott-Hayes, whom she described, entirely unreasonably, as 'Pro-British', anti-nationalist and entirely unsupportive of efforts to raise a local volunteer militia (Mitchell, The Man With the Long Hair, p. 21). However, it appears that others held him in higher regard. Soon after the MVF was formed, some members of the PLG requested his co-option to that body given that, in the words of one member, 'he informs' their decisions (WI, 15 November 1913). He was voted in as the chairman of the Central Ireland Branch of the Irish Journalists' Association in 1919 (II,

17 June 1919). After the destruction of the *Westmeath Independent* offices in
1920 he attempted to set up a new paper in Tullamore, though he found the
logistics involved too great at a time when money was scarce. In 1921 he
was hired by the *Irish News* in Belfast, initially as a journalist but was quickly
promoted to sub-editor at the international desk, a position he held until his
death in 1924. Joe Devlin MP and president of the AOH attended his funeral;
the *Freeman's Journal* ran an obituary reminding readers of his founding
role in the National Volunteers, as did the *Irish Independent* (*FJ*, 4 April 1924,
II, 4 April 1924, *WI*, 5 April 1924, *WI*, 12 April 1924, *Leitrim Observer*,
26 April 1924). Seán Mac Eoin (stationed as the Free State Army OC in
Athlone in 1921) in a 1966 article for *Comorú na Cásca Digest* described
McDermott-Hayes as 'very energetic [and] deeply interested in Irish affairs'
(Seán Mac Eoin, 'The Lone Patriot' in *Comorú na Cásca Digest*, Vol. 8 (1966),
pp. 189-190). Additionally, as this publication has shown, and will continue
to show, the tone of the editorials and articles in the *Westmeath Independent*
during his tenure show a man whose nationalist views were, like many
others during that period, changing and evolving as different situations
arose. He presented up-to-date information on most aspects of the national
struggle and his involvement at committee level with organisations other
than the MVF, such as the UIL and TTL and, from 1917 onwards, SF, show
him to be not just a 'barstool patriot.'

137   Hobson, in his semi-autobiographical work *Ireland Yesterday and Tomorrow*
      (1968), ignores the force altogether, having called them a fabrication in his
      earlier tome *A Short History of the Irish Volunteers* (1918) (Bulmer Hobson,
      Ireland Yesterday and Tomorrow (Tralee, 1968), pp. 43-45). For a description of
      the events that led up to the creation of the IV from Hobson's point of view
      see Hay, *Bulmer Hobson*, pp. 109-113.

138   *IT*, 8 June 1914.

139   Eoin Neeson, *Birth of a Republic* (Dublin, 1998), pp. 93-94.

140   *WI*, 25 August 1917.

141   The preface of the second edition of *The Secret History of the Irish Volunteers*
      (1915) noted that the work was to impart O'Rahilly's 'view of the facts'
      (Snoddy, 'Midland Volunteer Force', p. 39).

142   O'Rahilly stated, in what may have been a side swipe at the Athlone
      movement, that those at the Rotunda had founded the IV 'solely to further
      the Irish cause and…acknowledged no Queen but Dark Rosaleen' (*IT*,
      8 June 1914).

143   See Robert Kee, *The Green Flag: A History of Irish Nationalism* (London, 1972),
      pp. 498-499; John O'Beirne Ranelagh, *A Short History of Ireland* (Cambridge,
      1999), p. 176; Lyons, 'The developing crisis', p. 136; Maume, *Long Gestation*,
      p. 140; Foster, *Modern Ireland*, p. 468; Townshend, *Easter 1916*, p. 38;
      Townshend, *Political Violence*, p. 259; David Fitzpatrick, 'Militarism in Ireland,
      1900-22', in Thomas Bartlett and Keith Jeffery (eds), *A Military History of
      Ireland* (Cambridge, 1996), p. 384; Matthew Kelly, 'The Irish Volunteers: A
      Machiavellian moment?', in Boyce and O'Day, *The Ulster Crisis*, p. 67.

144   Wheatley, *Nationalism and the Irish Party*, pp. 19, 133, 258.

145   Wheatley believes that McDermott-Hayes was trying to position himself as a
      political 'boss' akin to J.P. Farrell in Longford or Jasper Tully in Roscommon,
      both newspaper men and MPs for a time (Wheatley, *Nationalism and the
      Irish Party*, p. 33). There is no evidence for this. McDermott-Hayes tended to
      occupy lower committee positions and even refused a seat in the local PLG
      when offered (*WI*, 20 December 1913). When it came to the MVF, Seán
      O'Mullany stated that McDermott-Hayes was 'in the background' for the
      foundation meeting and Martin's assessment led to a similar accusation of
      modesty on McDermott-Hayes' behalf (Martin, 'MacNeill', p. 123).

146   Wheatley, *Nationalism and the Irish Party*, p. 61.

147   Wheatley, 'Ireland is out for blood', p. 187.

148   BMHWS No. 239, Frank Necy, p. 1; BMHWS No. 89, Michael Ó Cuill, p. 2.

149   *TL*, 8 November 1913.

150   *FJ*, 8 November 1913. One author signed off as 'A Volunteer', Derry'
      (*II*, 11 November 1913). Another signed off as just 'Volunteer' (*II*,
      17 November 1913).

151   The author signed off as 'Miles Hibernicus' and recommended that northern
      AOH members should look towards creating a force (*II*, 14 November 1913).

152   O'Connor said he received a reply, which was not particularly detailed,
      regarding the MVF's intentions (BMHWS No. 114, Éamon O'Connor, p. 1).

153   The note was written in Irish and is contained in UDCA, The O'Rahilly
      Papers, P102/302. Translation taken from Aodogán O'Rahilly, *Winding the
      Clock: O'Rahilly and the 1916 Rising* (Dublin, 1991), p. 96.

154   Martin, 'MacNeill', pp. 146–147.

155   Nuala C. Johnson, *Ireland, the Great War and the Geography of Remembrance*
      (Cambridge, 2003), p. 21.

156   *East Galway Democrat*, 22 November 1913.

157   *MG*, 24 November 1913. The newspaper's belief that it was the Athlone AOH that
      had formed the MVF is understandable given the manifesto's sectarian undertones.

158   The IRB had twelve members; the UIL and AOH four apiece, with
      unaffiliated members such as MacNeill, O'Rahilly, Pearse and Roger Casement
      accounting for the remaining ten positions (Martin, 'MacNeill', p. 149).

159   Hay, *Bulmer Hobson*, p. 124.

160   At this juncture, 'MacNeill, The O'Rahilly and Pearse were neither
      republicans nor revolutionaries, but Catholic intellectuals who…were
      sympathisers with both the Irish Party and Sinn Féin' (Owen McGee, 'Who
      were the 'Fenian Dead'? The IRB and the background to the 1916 Rising',
      in Doherty and Keogh, *1916*, pp. 110–111).

161   Costello, *Irish Revolution*, p. 15; Martin, 'MacNeill', pp. 164–169.

162   Martin, 'MacNeill', pp. 170–171; Townshend, *Easter 1916*, p. 41.

163   *WI*, 29 November 1913; *WI*, 6 December 1913; *WI*, 13 December 1913.
      The local coverage of the meeting was not particularly detailed. Indeed,
      the meeting was virtually ignored by the Irish dailies, with the exception of
      the *Freeman's Journal*, which printed just a brief summary (Martin, 'MacNeill',
      p. 178).

164   *IF*, December 1913.

165   *IF*, December 1913. Reportedly a crowd of 1,000 joined in the march, a move that led to the soldiers being ordered back to the barracks where, outside of the entrance, the Pipers' Club band played 'A Nation Once Again.' The *Irish Volunteer* used the same story in its edition of 7 February 1914 (*IV*, 7 February 1914). The RIC averred that the press reports were exaggerated (Denman, 'The red livery of shame', p. 231). Upon being asked about the incident, Augustine Birrell stated that the Leinster Regiment had been received favourably in Athlone, and that the soldiers had been followed only by 'a small band of Irish pipers' (*Hansard 5 Commons,* lviii, 1928-9 (26 February 1914)). Bonar Law used the incident to show nationalist antipathy towards enlistment (MG, 22 November 1913). The episode also made the columns of *The New York Times* (*NYT* 23 November 1913).

166   *WI*, 8 November 1913; *FJ*, 8 November 1913; *MG*, 8 November 1913; CI Report, Westmeath, November 1913, CO/904/91; AHL, Minute Book of Athlone UDC, 12 November 1913.

167   *WI*, 13 December 1913.

168   *TL*, 20 December 1913. It appears that Moran was alluding to the ability of Irishmen on opposing sides of an internal debate to threaten military force while both claiming to represent the Empire.

169   *WI*, 6 December 1913.

170   Townshend, *Easter 1916*, p. 35.

171   Stewart, *Ulster Crisis*, p. 107; Ben Novick, 'The arming of Ireland: gun-running and the Great War, 1914-16', in Adrian Gregory and Senia Pašeta, *Ireland and the Great War: 'A War to Unite us All?'* (Manchester, 2002), p. 96.

172   *WI*, 13 December 1913.

173   Snoddy, 'Midland Volunteer Force', p. 42.

174   *WI*, 20 May 1916.

175   *WI*, 8 August 1914; *WI*, 5 February 1916; *WI*, 25 August 1917.

176   *WI*, 13 December 1913.

177   *WI*, 3 January 1914; BMHWS No. 1,503, Michael McCormack, p. 1.

178   *WI*, 3 January 1914.

179   *CT*, 27 December 1913; *FJ*, 31 December 1913.

180   BMHWS No. 1,046, Patrick J. Ramsbottom, p. 2.

181   O'Mullany stated that the merger happened as 'not all of the Committee could be relied on in a national emergency' (O'Mullany, 'Athlone started the volunteer movement', p. 23).

182   Michael Kenny, *The Road to Freedom: Photographs and Memorabilia from the 1916 Rising and Afterwards* (Dublin, 1993), p. 11.

183   The local press referred inconsistently to the local volunteers as the 'Midland Volunteers' until May 1914 (*WI*, 30 May 1914). Both *Sinn Féin* and the RIC stated that the Athlone IV corp. was established in January (*SF*, 10 January 1914; CI Report, Westmeath, January 1914, CO/904/92).

184   *IV*, 7 February 1914; *IV*, 21 February 1914.

185   *FJ*, 20 January 1914. Figures compiled by its National Directory confirmed the organisation's inexorable move towards obsolescence; only four branches

in Westmeath were affiliated (the lowest figure in Leinster), while nationally, almost 300 had disappeared since 1912 (NAI, Minute Book of the National Directory of the UIL, February 1913; Minute Book of the National Directory of the UIL, February 1916, pp. 447-452).

186 *FJ*, 8 January 1912; *II*, 8 January 1912; *FJ*, 9 January 1914; *WI*, 10 January 1914; *II*, 12 January 1914; *FJ*, 12 January 1914.

187 Moate hosted 10,000 nationalists as Joe Devlin, flanked by Nugent and Hayden, spoke of Carson's civil war 'bluff' and ironic claim, given the Act of Union, that the 'whole foundation of government must be the consent of the governed' (*IT*, 2 February 1914; *WI*, 7 February 1914; *WE*, 7 February 1914; *WE*, 14 February 1914).

188 *FJ*, 26 January 1914.

189 Paul Bew, *Ideology and the Irish Question: Ulster Unionism and Irish Nationalism 1912-1916* (Oxford, 1994), p. 151.

190 Ó Tuathaigh, 'Nationalist Ireland', p. 54.

191 *II*, 16 March 1914; *FJ*, 16 March 1914.

192 The UDC had begun to present a more uniform opinion on the bill since the resignation of Robert Baile in January 1914. He died two months later (*IT*, 30 January 1914; *WI*, 31 January 1914; *II*, 27 March 1914; *WI*, 28 March 1914; *FJ*, 1 April 1914).

193 *II*, 18 March 1914; *II*, 21 March 1914; *IT*, 21 March 1914; *FJ*, 25 March 1914.

194 *FJ*, 18 March 1914.

195 *FJ*, 21 March 1914; *II*, 21 March 1914; *WI*, 28 March 1914.

196 *FJ*, 28 March 1914.

197 Bew, *Irish Question*, pp. 77-78.

198 *IT*, 27 February 1914.

199 *WI*, 7 March 1914.

200 Hew Strachan, *The Politics of the British Army* (Oxford, 1997), pp. 112-117.

201 O'Leary and Maume, *Controversial Issues*, p. 38.

202 Lee, *Ireland*, p. 18; Finnan, *John Redmond*, pp. 68-9; Jackson, *Home Rule*, pp. 129-130; Stewart, *Ulster Crisis*, pp. 145-146; Neeson, *Birth of a Republic*, pp. 86-91.

203 *NYT*, 22 March 1914.

204 Boyce, 'The Ulster crisis', p. 54.

205 *WI*, 28 March 1914.

206 Bew, *Ireland*, p. 370.

207 M.K. Flynn, *Ideology, Mobilization and the Nation: the Rise of Irish, Basque and Carlist Nationalist Movements in the Nineteenth and Early Twentieth Centuries* (London, 2000), p. 79.

208 Ó Tuathaigh, 'Nationalist Ireland', p. 62.

209 *WI*, 3 January 1914; IG Report, January 1914, CO/904/92; CI Report, Westmeath, January 1914, CO/904/92.

210 CI Report, Westmeath, March 1914 CO/904/92.

211 CI Report, Westmeath, March 1914 CO/904/92; Bodleian Library, Birrell MSS, Dep. 301, Oxford, Cabinet paper April 1914, 'Irish Volunteers', cited in Wheatley, *Nationalism and the Irish Party*, p. 184.

212 *WI*, 31 January 1914; *WI*, 28 February 1914.

213   Townshend, *Easter 1916*, pp. 44-45.

214   At times quite emotive pieces were published: 'The representatives of Unionist Ulster tell us that as soon as Home Rule is passed the fiery cross will be raised, and Ireland, and not Ireland alone, but England, Scotland and Wales be involved in a civil war compared with which the outbreak in America was only a painted fire' (*WI*, 3 January 1914).

215   *WI*, 28 March 1914.

216   CI Report, Westmeath, April 1914, CO/904/93.

217   CI Report, Roscommon, April 1914, CO/904/93; CI Report, Roscommon, May 1914 CO/904/93.

218   *IV*, 18 April 1914.

219   *IV*, 4 April 1914.

220   *II*, 18 April 1914; *FJ*, 18 April 1914; *MG*, 18 April 1914; *II*, 29 April 1914; *FJ*, 29 April 1914; *II*, 30 April 1914.

221   F.X. Martin, *The Howth Gun-Running and the Kilcoole Gun-Running 1914* (Dublin, 1964), p. xiii; Townshend, *Easter 1916*, p. 51.

222   Stewart, *Ulster Crisis*, pp. 196-212.

223   Bew, *Ireland*, p. 370.

224   Lee, *Ireland*, p. 18; Boyce, 'The Ulster crisis', p. 52.

225   The *Westmeath Independent* reported that: 'The scenes in Athlone all during Tuesday night were memorable … in the immense numbers … assembled …in the National Pride they evoked … to mark the … greater coming of the Nation.' The event was organised by the AOH and INF; the UIL was moribund (*WI*, 30 May 1914; CI Report, Westmeath, May 1914, CO/904/93). Numerous local groups attended the celebratory meeting, where Dean Kelly told them that a 'grievous wrong [had been] undone.' H.J. Walker soothed locals' fears on partition, while M.J. Lennon criticised the unionist press. The description of the festivities in the *Freeman's Journal* paints a picture of great joy and relief (*FJ*, 28 May 1914; *II*, 28 May 1914; *FJ*, 29 May 1914; *II*, 29 May 1914). Local publicans defied directions from the RIC to remove green flags from their pub fronts; instead additions were made (*IT*, 1 June 1914). For a personal account of the celebrations see Patrick Shea, *Voices and the Sound of Drums: An Irish Autobiography* (Belfast, 1981), pp. 4-6.

226   Neeson, *Birth of a Republic*, pp. 92-93, 97-98; O'Leary and Maume, *Controversial Issues*, p. 41.

227   IG Report, March 1914, CO/904/92; IG Report, May 1914, CO/904/93.

228   *MG*, 22 May 1914; *MG*, 25 May 1914.

229   Lee, *Ireland*, p. 20; Hay, *Bulmer Hobson*, pp. 128-134.

230   O'Leary and Maume, *Controversial Issues*, p. 42.

231   Michael Tierney, *Eoin MacNeill: Scholar and Man of Action, 1867-1945* (Oxford, 1980), p. 132.

232   Jackson, *Home Rule*, p. 135.

233   IG Report, June 1914, CO/904/93; Ó Tuathaigh, 'Nationalist Ireland', p. 61.

234   CI Report, Westmeath, May 1914, CO/904/93; CI Report, Westmeath, June 1914, CO/904/93.

235   IG Report, June 1914, CI Report, Westmeath, June 1914, CO/904/93; CI

Report, Roscommon, June 1914, CO/904/93.

236   Charles Hannon, 'The Irish Volunteers and the concepts of military service and defence 1913-1924', (Unpublished PhD thesis, UCD, 1989), pp. 27-28.

237   *Hansard 5 Commons,* lxiv, 1214-6 (09 July 1914).

238   *MG,* 1 June 1914; *MG,* 17 July 1914.

239   *WI,* 23 May 1914; *FJ,* 27 May 1914.

240   *The Irish Worker,* 9 May 1914; *TIW,* 30 May 1914.

241   *IT,* 13 June 1914; A.H.L, Minute Book of Athlone UDC, 27 May 1914. This call came after the mobilisation of a large number of RIC from the region. 'Practically all the forces of the county', were to descend on Derry; the especial drilling in April was a preliminary for such a deployment (*II,* 25 May 1914).

242   *WI,* 20 June 1914.

243   Referred to as William O'Frehill in *The Irish Times* and both Shaun O'Frighail and C. O'Freehill in the *Freeman's Journal.*

244   He quoted a figure of seventy-five as the total Athlone enrolment in SF, a considerably higher number than was ever quoted by the RIC (*II,* 16 June 1914).

245   *IT,* 16 June 1914; *WI,* 20 June 1914; The *Irish Independent* reported that 'the Roscommon Volunteers…passed a resolution declaring the Irish Party's interference very much uncalled for' (*II,* 12 June 1914).

246   CI Report, Westmeath, April 1914, CO/904/93.

247   *WI,* 20 June 1914.

248   *IT,* 16 June 1914; *II,* 16 June 1914.

249   He believed that a letter Redmond wrote explaining his endorsement brought 'the Provisional Committee into public contempt, a thing which they in no way deserved' (*II,* 17 June 1914).

250   *WI,* 20 June 1914.

251   *II,* 20 June 1914; *FJ,* 20 June 1914.

252   *CT,* 6 June 1914.

253   *Southern Star,* 6 June 1914; *S.S.,* 13 June 1914.

254   'The National Volunteer Movement originated, it is well known, in Athlone, the birthplace of T.P. O'Connor and a town in the ambit of Ballaghadereen. These two influences have permeated it and when, two months ago, the Curragh mutiny broke out, Athlone showed that the spirit of T.P. O'Connor and John Dillon exalted its people. It founded the movement, but owing to the fact that a number of persons, including some who never subscribed in their lives to the support of the Party, had founded it seven months beforehand and chosen a Provisional Committee, Athlone was deprived of the fruits of its patriotic enterprise' (*FJ,* 8 June 1914).

255   *SF,* 13 June 1914.

256   *FJ,* 10 June 1914.

257   *FJ,* 16 June 1914.

258   *TL,* 20 June 1914.

259   *TL,* 20 June 1914.

260   *FJ,* 14 July 1914.

261 *FJ*, 21 July 1914.

262 Fitzpatrick, *Politics and Irish Life*, p. 107.

263 *Thom's Official Directory of the United Kingdom of Great Britain and Ireland* (Dublin, 1914), p. 1280.

264 *FJ*, 3 July 1914; *WI*, 4 July 1914; *WI*, 25 July 1914.

265 *FJ*, 3 July 1914; *FJ*, 11 July 1914; *WI*, 11 July 1914.

266 *FJ*, 15 July 1914; *FJ*, 21 July 1914.

267 *FJ*, 23 July 1914; *IT*, 27 July 1914; *FJ*, 27 July 1914; *II*, 31 July 1914.

268 George Boyce, 'British politics and the Irish Question, 1912-1922', in Collins, *Nationalism and Unionism*, p. 95.

269 *II*, 31 July 1914.

270 *Hansard 5 Commons*, lxiv, 527-8 (02 July 1914).

271 Martin, *Howth Gun-Running*, p. xxi.

272 Jackson, *Home Rule*, p. 135. 1,500 guns and 45,000 rounds of ammunition were landed in total; another drop was made at Kilcoole the following week (Townshend, *Easter 1916*, p. 56).

273 Townshend, *Easter 1916*, p. 55.

274 Lee, *Ireland*, p. 22; O'Leary and Maume, *Controversial Issues*, pp. 43-4; D. George Boyce, 'A First World War transition: state and citizen in Ireland, 1914-1919', in Boyce and O'Day, *Ireland in Transition*, p. 95.

275 *WI*, 1 August 1914. Initially, it was intended to prosecute Carson, but fears of creating a martyr informed the eventual decision not to so do (O'Leary and Maume, *Controversial Issues*, p. 41).

276 Finnan, *John Redmond*, p. 76.

277 Hansard 5 Commons, lxv, 1022-30 (27 July 1914).

278 Foster, *Modern Ireland*, p. 469; Novick, 'The arming of Ireland', p. 96; Flynn, *Ideology, Mobilization and the Nation*, p. 79; Townshend, *Easter 1916*, p. 55.

279 Maume, *Long Gestation*, p. 146; Joseph Lee, *The Modernisation of Irish Society: 1848-1918* (Dublin, 1973), p. 153.

280 AHL, Minute Book of Athlone UDC, 17 June 1914; *IV*, 1 August 1914.

281 CI Report, Westmeath, August 1914, CO/904/94; CI Report, Roscommon, August 1914, CO/904/94.

282 *MG*, 29 July 1914; *IT*, 1 August 1914; *WI*, 8 August 1914.

283 Stewart, *Ulster Crisis*, p. 231.

284 Townshend, *Easter 1916*, p. 59.

285 *FJ*, 3 August 1914.

286 John O. Stubbs, 'The unionists and Ireland, 1914-18', in *The Historical Journal*, Vol. 33, No. 4 (December, 1990), p. 869.

287 A.C. Hepburn, *The Conflict of Nationality in Modern Ireland* (London, 1980), pp. 83-84; Rouse, 'Hayden, John Patrick', p. 531.

288 Finnan, *John Redmond*, p. 141; *II*, 4 August 1914.

289 Jackson, *Home Rule*, p. 144.

290 Stubbs, 'Unionists and Ireland', p. 870.

291 F.S.L. Lyons, 'The revolution in train, 1914-16', in Vaughan, *A New History of Ireland VI*, p. 189; *WI*, 8 August 1914.

292 *WI*, 8 August 1914.

293   *IV*, 8 August 1914.

294   *IT*, 5 August 1914; *II*, 5 August 1914.

295   *IT*, 6 August 1914; *II*, 6 August 1914.

296   *IT*, 6 August 1914.

297   *IT*, 6 August 1914; *IT*, 15 August 1914.

298   *II*, 6 August 1914; *WI*, 8 August 1914.

299   *II*, 8 August 1914; *LO*, 15 August 1914.

300   *WI*, 22 August 1914; *WE*, 22 August 1914.

301   Fitzpatrick, *Politics and Irish Life*, p. 63; Michael Farry, *Sligo 1914-1921:
      A Chronicle of Conflict* (Trim, 1992), p. 35.

302   Stubbs, 'Unionists and Ireland', pp. 872-873.

303   *WI*, 29 August 1914.

304   Boyce, 'British politics and the Irish Question', p. 95.

305   Some people lit bonfires at the Batteries on the western edge of the town in
      celebration. The additional work required for providing goods and services to
      the army ensured that most curtailed their revelry (*WI*, 26 September 1914;
      WE, 26 September 1914; Shea, *Voices*, p. 7).

306   CI Report, Westmeath, August 1914, CO/904/94; CI Report, Westmeath,
      September 1914, CO/904/94.

307   Boyce, 'The Ulster crisis', pp. 57-58; Stubbs, 'Unionists and Ireland', p. 872.

308   O'Day, *Irish Home Rule*, p. 261; Boyce, 'The Ulster crisis', p. 56.

309   Lee, *Ireland*, p. 21; Lyons, 'The developing crisis', p.144; O'Day, *Irish Home
      Rule*, p. 261.

310   *WI*, 26 September 1914; Finnan, *John Redmond*, p. 87.

311   Lyons, 'The revolution in train', p. 190.

312   Finnan, *John Redmond*, p. 88.

313   D. George Boyce, 'A First World War transition. State and citizen in Ireland,
      1914-1919', in Boyce and O'Day, *Ireland in Transition*, p. 96.

314   *WI*, 26 September 1914; *WI*, 3 October 1914.

315   John Horne, 'Our war, our history', in John Horne (ed.), *Our War: Ireland
      and the Great War* (Dublin, 2008), p. 8. See: D.G. Boyce, "That party politics
      should divide our tents': nationalism, unionism and the First World War',
      in Gregory and Pašeta, *Ireland and the Great War*, pp. 190-216.

316   Asquith had given Redmond hope that such a situation could arise at a
      recruiting meeting at the Mansion House on 25 September (Tierney, *Eoin
      MacNeill*, pp. 151-152).

317   Jackson, *Home Rule*, p. 146.

318   O'Day, *Irish Home Rule*, p. 268.

319   Lee, *Ireland*, p. 21.

320   Tierney, *Eoin MacNeill*, pp. 152-154.

321   Breandán Mac Giolla Choille, *Intelligence Notes: 1913-1916, Preserved in the State
      Paper Office* (Dublin, 1966), pp. 175-176; *IV*, 3 October 1914.

322   *WI*, 3 October 1914; *FJ*, 5 October 1914.

323   Lee, *Ireland*, pp. 22-3.

324   Novick, 'The arming of Ireland', p. 98; Hobson, *Irish Volunteers*, pp. 192-205.

325   *TIW*, 5 Sep 1914; *TIW*, 10 October 1914.

326   *FJ*, 26 September 1914.

327   *TL*, 3 October 1914.

328   *IV*, 10 October 1914.

329   McDermott-Hayes described himself as: 'Chairman of the First Organising Committee' (*NV*, 17 October 1914).

330   *The Toiler*, 17 October 1914.

331   *NV*, 6 November 1914.

332   *FJ*, 19 November 1914.

333   *WI*, 3 October 1914; *WI*, 17 October 1914.

334   *WI*, 24 October 1914.

335   *II*, 20 October 1914.

336   *WI*, 24 October 1914; *WI*, 31 October 1914.

337   *WI*, 10 October 1914; *WI*, 17 October 1914.

338   *NV*, 17 October 1914; *IT*, 24 October 1914; *NV*, 12 December 1914.

339   CI Report, Westmeath, October 1914, CO/904/95.

340   Bew, *Irish Question*, p. 123; *IV*, 17 October 1914. The Tang corps was initially neutral, but then went with MacNeill. Drumraney saw a vote of seventeen to sixteen in favour of MacNeill (BMHWS No. 1,503, Michael McCormack, p. 3). Ballykeeran saw the majority go with Redmond (BMHWS No. 1,308, Henry O'Brien, p. 2).

341   Tierney, *Eoin MacNeill*, p. 154.

342   *Éire*, 26 October 1914.

343   IG Report, November 1914, CO/904/95; Lyons, 'The revolution in train', p. 191.

344   Glandon, *Arthur Griffith*, p. 81.

345   Kennedy, *Genesis of the Rising*, pp. 105-109.

346   *IV*, 24 October 1914. This quotation was taken from a speech delivered at the annual C.S. Parnell Anniversary in Dublin. Ginnell offered to co-ordinate an anti-recruitment campaign for Eoin MacNeill, if his expenses were paid (BMHWS No. 982, Mrs. Alice Ginnell, p. 8).

CHAPTER 4

1   *Army Report on Recruiting in Ireland*, 1914-16 [Cd. 8168], p. 2.

2   Philip Orr, '200,000 volunteer soldiers', in Horne, *Our War*, p. 65. 17,804 were 'Reservists' and 12,462 were 'Special Reservists' (*Report on Recruiting*, p. 2).

3   John M. McEwan, 'The Liberal Party and the Irish Question during the First World War', in *The Journal of British Studies*, Vol. 12 (1972), p. 112.

4   AHL, Minute Book of Athlone UDC, 2 December 1914. The PLG agreed to the same inducement (*FJ*, 16 November 1914).

5   AHL, Minute Book of Athlone UDC, 9 December 1914; Minute Book of Athlone UDC, 16 December 1914. It was assumed that the War Office criticism related to recruitment. P.V.C. Murtagh believed the comments actually called into question the claim of having paid half-wages (*IT*, 12 December 1914; *II*, 12 December 1914; *FJ*, 12 December 1914; *S.S.*,

19 December 1914; *WE*, 19 December 1914).

6   *FJ*, 15 December 1914.

7   *IT*, 12 December 1914; *IT*, 19 December 1914.

8   David Fitzpatrick, 'The logic of collective sacrifice: Ireland and the British Army, 1914-1918', in *The Historical Journal*, Vol. 38, No. 4 (December, 1995), p. 1028; Boyce, 'That party politics should divide our tents', p. 203.

9   IG Report, November 1914, CO/904/95; *NV*, 12 December 1914; L.P. Curtis Jr, 'Ireland in 1914', in Vaughan, *A New History of Ireland VI*, p. 184; Fitzpatrick, 'collective sacrifice', p. 1028.

10 *IT*, 12 December 1914; *IT*, 19 December 1914.

11 Keith Jeffery, 'The First World War and the Rising: mode, moment and memory', in Doherty and Keogh, *1916*, pp. 88-89.

12 *II*, 2 December 1914.

13 *II*, 2 December 1914. Additional depots for the Rangers were in Boyle, Ballinasloe and Castlerea, with Mullingar, Longford, Drogheda and Maryboro hosting offices for the Leinsters (*Irish Life*, 1 October 1915).

14 *WI*, 10 April 1915.

15 Patrick Callan, 'Recruiting for the British Army in Ireland during the First World War', in *Irish Sword*, Vol. 17 (1987-90), p. 43.

16 *WI*, 17 April 1915. Rumours of the imposition of the Militia Ballot Act 1882 gave rural men ample excuse to emigrate (*IV*, 24 October 1914; *IV*, 31 October 1914). The Act allowed for compulsory 'balloting' of recruits under certain conditions (Wheatley, *Nationalism and the Irish Party*, pp. 221-222). Described as a 'bogey' in the local press, McDermott-Hayes condemned the 'craven-hearted curs in Connaught', who left for foreign lands when the rumours abounded (*WI*, 24 October 1914).

17 *IT*, 25 March 1915; *FJ*, 26 March 1915; *NV*, 3 April 1915.

18 *IT*, 8 April 1915; *FJ*, 9 April 1915. Similar movements were seen in the busy ship factories of Belfast (Theresa Moriarty, 'Work, warfare and wages: industrial controls and Irish trade unionism in the First World War', in Gregory and Pašeta, *Ireland and the Great War*, p. 75).

19 *IT*, 8 April 1915. The workload in the mills had increased to such an extent that the working day started at six in the morning and continued 'to a late hour at night'. Support for the war effort was evinced, at least according to *The Irish Times*, by the fact that drinking was almost unknown and the men had 'thrown themselves entirely into the work' (*IT*, 8 May 1915).

20 *IT*, 8 April 1915.

21 Hoppen, *Ireland Since 1800*, p. 147; Fitzpatrick, 'Militarism in Ireland', p. 389; David Fitzpatrick, 'Home front and everyday life', in Horne, *Our War*, p. 134. See Fitzpatrick, 'collective sacrifice', pp. 1017-1030; Orr, '200,000 volunteer soldiers', p. 67; Keith Jeffery, *Ireland and the Great War* (Cambridge, 2000), pp. 8-10; Peter Karsten, 'Irish soldiers in the British Army, 1792-1922: suborned or subordinate?', in *Journal of Social History*, Vol. 17, No. 1 (1983), pp. 38-41; Jeffery, 'The First World War', p. 89.

22 Johnson, *Ireland, the Great War*, p. 28.

23 *Report on Recruiting*, p. 2.

24   *IT*, 23 April 1915; *FJ*, 23 April 1915; *II*, 23 April 1915; *IT*, 17 July 1915.

25   *IT*, 23 March 1915; *WI*, 17 April 1915; *WI*, 24 April 1915; *WI*, 8 May 1915;
      WI, 15 May 1915; *WI*, 22 May 1915; *WI*, 29 May 1915; Orr, '200,000 volunteer
      soldiers', pp. 69-70; William Magan, *An Irish Boyhood* (Durham, 1996), p. 61.

26   *IT*, 3 August 1915.

27   *WI*, 3 July 1915; *WI*, 10 July 1915; *WI*, 17 July 1915.

28   Michael Burke, PLG, was unsupportive: 'I don't believe in men volunteering
      their services too freely for those who never did anything for them' (*WI*,
      4 September 1915; *WI*, 18 September 1915).

29   *II*, 7 June 1915; *WI*, 12 June 1915; *IT*, 24 June 1915; *II*, 5 August 1915.

30   'Republican Suspects', Laurence Ginnell, CO 904/202/162, p. 199.

31   *WE*, 7 August 1915. Westmeath was part of a 'midland belt', which, outside of
      Dublin and the northeast, gave the greatest proportion of recruits (Fitzpatrick,
      'Militarism in Ireland', p. 389).

32   *WI*, 31 July 1915.

33   *WI*, 4 September 1915.

34   Separation allowances, based on a soldier's rank, marital status, etc. funded the
      household in the man's absence (Susan R. Grayzel, *Women and the First World
      War* (Essex, 2002), p. 22). Women in receipt were often portrayed as drunken
      harridans, a generalisation which, though it had some merit, was greatly
      overplayed (Caitríona Clear, 'Fewer ladies, more women', in Horne, *Our War*,
      p. 168). In Athlone, some of their homes were described by police as 'flooded
      with porter' (*IT*, 19 August 1915; *II*, 19 August 1915).

35   *WI*, 31 July 1915; *WI*, 25 September 1915; *WI*, 2 October 1915.

36   *II*, 14 August 1915.

37   The Westmeath CI noted in October 1914 that few INV members had
      enlisted, while the *Freeman's Journal* stated that the Athlone INV had
      proved a fecund recruiting pool (CI Report, Westmeath, October 1914,
      CO/904/95; *FJ*, 26 November 1914). Similarly, the *National Volunteer* spoke
      of 'brisk' recruiting in Roscommon in January 1915, while the CI stated that
      virtually no-one had enlisted (*NV*, 30 January 1915; CI Report, Roscommon,
      January 1915, CO/904/96).

38   Callan, 'Recruiting', p. 50.

39   Callan, 'Recruiting', p. 50.

40   *IT*, 1 January 1916; *II*, 1 January 1916; *WI*, 1 January 1916.

41   Athlone Union was comprised of parts of south Westmeath and south
      Roscommon. Pop.: 20,254 (Census returns for Ireland, 1911, Province of
      Leinster, p. 1052; Census returns for Ireland, 1911, Province of Connaught,
      p. 544).

42   New recruits were referred to as 'post-war enlistments' (*Report on Recruiting*, p. 2).

43   The majority of the balance would have come from Westmeath.
      Roscommon's proportionate contribution was almost exactly half that of
      its neighbour; roughly 6 per cent of men of 'military age' to Westmeath's
      12 per cent (*Statement giving Particulars of Men of Military Age in Ireland*, HC,
      1916 [Cd.8390] XVII.581, p. 583).

44   The estimate uses the number of males between fifteen and forty enumerated

for the 1911 census. It does not discount those between fifteen and nineteen who were ineligible (19 to 41 was the official range for the military), nor does it discount those with disabilities or essential occupations (Census returns for Ireland, 1911, Province of Leinster, p. 1096).

45   *Hansard 5 Commons,* lxxiii, 1092-1093 (15 July 1915).

46   *Statement giving particulars,* p. 583. In Westmeath, a general ratio of 90 per cent Catholic, 10 per cent Protestant was observed. The INV accounted for roughly 55 per cent of the county's recruits to the end of 1915 (Mac Giolla Choille, *Intelligence Notes,* p. 176).

47   Fitzpatrick, 'Militarism in Ireland', p. 392.

48   *WI,* 2 October 1915.

49   *WI,* 2 October 1915; *WI,* 1 January 1916; *II,* 7 January 1916; *II,* 17 January 1916.

50   *WI,* 21 August 1915.

51   After the war, a figure of 800 recruits from Athlone town was cited (*WI,* 5 April 1919).

52   *WI,* 2 October 1915; *WI,* 9 October 1915.

53   *WI,* 2 October 1915; *WI,* 9 October 1915; *WI,* 23 October 1915; *WI,* 30 October 1915; CI Report, Roscommon, October 1915, CO/904/98.

54   Johnson, *Ireland, the Great War,* p. 28.

55   *Report on Recruiting,* p. 2.

56   Fitzpatrick, 'collective sacrifice', p. 1021.

57   *Report on Recruiting,* p. 2; NAI, CSO Registered Papers, 5622/25973/1916.

58   *WI,* 2 October 1915; *WI,* 9 October 1915; *WI,* 23 October 1915; *WI,* 30 October 1915; CI Report, Roscommon, October 1915, CO/904/98.

59   *IT,* 3 November 1915.

60   *IT,* 3 November 1915.

61   *IT,* 8 November 1915; *II,* 8 November 1915.

62   *WI,* 12 February 1916; *WI,* 19 February 1916.

63   Garvin, *Irish Nationalist Politics,* p. 110.

64   *IT,* 13 November 1915.

65   Fitzpatrick, 'Home front', p. 136.

66   *Emigration Statistics of Ireland 1915,* HC [Cd.8230], xxxii, p. 4.

67   *Report on Recruiting,* p. 2.

68   The friars' persecution gained much exposure (*WI,* 9 January 1915; *TL,* 22 January 1916; *WI,* 13 February 1916; *TL,* 4 March 1916; *TL,* 25 March 1916; *HJ,* March 1916, *HJ,* April 1916; P. Conlon, 'The outlaw friars of Athlone: 1916', in *Journal of the Old Athlone Society,* Vol. 1, No. 2 (1971), pp. 55-60).

69   *WI,* 13 November 1915.

70   CI Report, Westmeath, November 1915, CO/904/98.

71   PRONI, T/2782/21, Cecilia H. Daniels to Mrs. Flett, Australia, 8 November 1915.

72   *II,* 26 November 1915; IG Report, December 1915, CO/904/98.

73   *WI,* 20 November 1915.

74   *HJ,* December 1915.

75   Finnan, *John Redmond*, p. 146.

76   Stubbs, 'Unionists and Ireland', pp. 875-876.

77   Finnan, *John Redmond*, pp. 110, 232.

78   *Report on Recruiting*, p. 2; Clear, 'Fewer ladies', pp. 165-166.

79   *Report on Recruiting*, p. 2.

80   *Report on Recruiting*, p. 4; NAI, CSO Registered Papers, 5622/25887/1916.

81   Caitriona Pennell, 'Going to war', in Horne, *Our War*, p. 44.

82   Garvin, *Irish Nationalist Politics*, p. 110.

83   *WI*, 8 January 1916; *WI*, 15 January 1916; *WI*, 22 January 1916;
      WI, 29 January 1916; *WI*, 5 February 1916; *WI*, 12 February 1916;
      WI, 19 February 1916; *WI*, 26 February 1916; *WI*, 4 March 1916; *WI*,
      11 March 1916; *WI*, 18 March 1916.

84   Horne, 'Our war', p. 12.

85   Fitzpatrick, 'Militarism in Ireland', p. 388.

86   *WI*, 7 November 1914; *WI*, 14 November 1914; *WI*, 21 November 1914.

87   *WI*, 20 March 1915.

88   *IT*, 21 April 1915.

89   *WI*, 5 September 1914.

90   *WI*, 20 November 1915.

91   *WI*, 20 November 1915.

92   AHL, Minute book of Athlone UDC, 23 September 1914; *IT*,
      25 September 1914.

93   Vergil Mannion O.F.M., *A life Recalled – Experiences of an Irish Franciscan*
      (Dublin, 1984), pp. 9-10.

94   The allegation was made in a letter sent from the artillery depot in Athlone to a
      Mr O'Grady in London. O'Grady sent it to Athlone UDC (*NV*, 10 April 1915).

95   *IT*, 2 April 1915; *FJ*, 2 April 1915.

96   *NV*, 10 April 1915.

97   *WI*, 10 October 1914; Fitzpatrick, *Politics and Irish Life*, p. 26.

98   Lt Col. M.K. Hanley, *The Story of Custume Barracks Athlone* (Athlone, 1974), p. 10.

99   *WI*, 20 November 1915.

100   *WI*, 20 November 1915.

101   CI Report, Westmeath, June 1914, CO/904/93; *WI*, 22 August 1914; *WI*,
      5 September 1914; *WI*, 12 September 1914; *WI*, 26 September 1914; *WI*,
      3 October 1914; *WI*, 17 October 1914.

102   *IT*, 15 February 1915.

103   *WI*, 8 January 1916; *II*, 16 February 1916; Pennell, 'Going to war', p. 40;
      Moriarty, 'Work, warfare and wages', p. 75.

104   *II*, 7 April 1916.

105   Niamh Puirséil, 'War, work and labour', in Horne, *Our War*, p. 184; Moriarty,
      'Work, warfare and wages', p. 78.

106   Fitzpatrick, 'Home front', p. 137.

107   *WI*, 8 August 1914; *WI*, 15 August 1914; *WI*, 12 September 1914.

108   PRONI, T/2782/20, Cecilia H. Daniels to Mrs. Flett, Australia, Late Autumn
      1915; *WI*, 20 November 1915; Moriarty, 'Work, warfare and wages', p. 76.

109   *WE*, 26 September 1914; *WI*, 8 January 1916; Pennell, 'Going to war', p. 40;

Moriarty, 'Work, warfare and wages', p. 79.

110   Foster, *Modern Ireland*, p. 471.

111   Horne, 'Our war', p. 8.

112   Farry, *Sligo*, p. 66; Hoppen, *Ireland Since 1800*, p. 113; Fitzpatrick, 'Home front', p. 137.

113   CI Report, Westmeath, November 1914, CO/904/95.

114   Snoddy, 'Midland Volunteer Force', pp. 43-4.

115   Shea, *Voices*, p. 21.

116   Paul Bew, 'The politics of war', in Horne, *Our War*, p. 98.

117   Glandon, *Arthur Griffith*, pp. 147-148; *Irish Volunteer* and its UVF equivalent were allowed to go to print (Glandon, *Arthur Griffith*, pp. 82, 89).

118   For information on DORA see Adrian Hardiman, "Shot in cold blood': military law and Irish perceptions in the suppression of the 1916 rebellion', in Doherty and Keogh, *1916*, pp. 227-237.

119   Michael Wheatley, "Irreconcilable enemies' or 'flesh and blood'? – The Irish Party and the Easter rebels, 1914-16', in Doherty and Keogh, *1916*, p. 66.

120   IG Report, October 1914, CO/904/95.

121   Pennell, 'Going to war', pp. 46-47.

122   CI Report, Westmeath, December 1914, CO/904/95.

123   Mac Giolla Choille, *Intelligence Notes*, p. 211.

124   CI Report, Westmeath, December 1914, CO/904/95; CI Report, Roscommon, December 1914, CO/904/95. Police reports do not note a branch at Tang but the *Irish Volunteer* carried a report on the branch's progress from this time (*IV*, 16 January 1915).

125   *IV*, 16 January 1915.

126   *IV*, 16 January 1915.

127   *NV*, 21 November 1914.

128   Farry, *Sligo*, p. 50.

129   CI Report, Westmeath, August 1914, CO/904/94; CI Report, Westmeath, September 1914, CO/904/94; CI Report, Westmeath, October 1914, CO/904/95; CI Report, Westmeath, November 1914, CO/904/95; CI Report, Westmeath, December 1914, CO/904/94.

130   CI Report, Roscommon, August 1914, CO/904/94; CI Report, Roscommon, September 1914, CO/904/94; CI Report, Roscommon, October 1914, CO/904/95; CI Report, Roscommon, November 1914, CO/904/95; CI Report, Roscommon, December 1914, CO/904/94.

131   *WI*, 24 October 1914.

132   *FJ*, 7 December 1914.

133   *FJ*, 27 January 1915; *WI*, 30 January 1915.

134   *WI*, 30 January 1915. Post-split, the INV had 9,000 rifles; the IV retained 2,000 (Novick, 'The arming of Ireland', pp. 94-95).

135   Joe Devlin had asked all branches to begin reorganisation in January as affiliations plummeted (Coleman, *Longford*, p. 39).

136   *FJ*, 27 January 1915; *WE*, 30 January 1915; *NV*, 30 January 1915.

137   *WI*, 30 January 1915.

138   *WI*, 12 February 1915.

139 *WI*, 13 March 1915; *WI*, 20 March 1915; *WI*, 3 April 1915.

140 Finnan, *John Redmond*, p. 148; Bew, 'The politics of war', p. 99.

141 CI Report, Westmeath, March 1915, CO/904/96.

142 *IV*, 13 March 1915; *IV*, 3 April 1915; CI Report, Westmeath, May 1915, CO/904/96.

143 McEwan, 'The Liberal Party and the Irish Question', pp. 112-113.

144 Jackson, *Home Rule*, p. 149.

145 O'Day, *Irish Home Rule*, p. 268; Bew, 'The politics of war', p. 100.

146 Bew, 'The politics of war', p. 100.

147 F.S.L. Lyons, *John Dillon: a Biography* (London, 1968), p. 366.

148 IG Report, June 1915, CO/904/97; IG Report, July 1915, CO/904/97.

149 *WI*, 29 May 1915; *WI*, 5 June 1915.

150 Nugent had promoted the creation of the War Loan, a bond system where citizens would buy government bonds that could be redeemed after the war concluded (*IV*, 31 July 1915).

151 Moran criticised the baronet's membership of the Reform Club in London and the United Service Club in Dublin; neither were 'truly national'. He additionally criticised Nugent's ignorance of the INV, and questioned his ability as an orator (*TL*, 31 July 1915).

152 CI Report, Westmeath, July 1915, CO/904/97; *WI*, 17 July 1915; *WI*, 24 July 1915; *II*, 24 July 1915; *WE*, 31 July 1915; *NV*, 24 July 1915; *NV*, 31 July 1915.

153 Maume, *Long Gestation*, p. 160; Oliver Coogan, *Politics and War in Meath: 1913-23* (Dublin, 1983), pp. 32-34.

154 NAI, Minute Book of the National Directory of the UIL, pp. 447-452.

155 *FJ*, 22 November 1915.

156 Hundreds of companies had folded and many shops de-listed the *National Volunteer* due to poor sales (Finnan, *John Redmond*, p. 151).

157 *NV*, 25 September 1915; *NV*, 13 November 1915

158 *Royal Commission on the Rebellion in Ireland*, HC, 1916 [Cd.8279], p. 7.

159 Fitzpatrick, *Politics and Irish Life*, pp. 112-114.

160 *WI*, 7 August 1915; *II*, 7 August 1915.

161 F.S.L. Lyons, 'The two faces of Home Rule', in Kevin B. Nowlan (ed.), *The Making of 1916* (Dublin, 1969), p. 120; Garvin, *Irish Nationalist Politics*, p. 89.

162 Bew, 'The politics of war', p. 106.

163 The *National Volunteer* used the vote of confidence to outline how it believed the *Irish Independent* was determined to 'stab the Irish Party in the back'. The latter only published the speech of the one dissident at the meeting, ignoring the majority verdict (*NV*, 19 June 1915).

164 By June, Westmeath had an additional IV corps at Tyrellspass, yet still only 100 members in total (CI Report, Westmeath, June 1915, CO/904/97; *WI*, 31 July 1915; IG Report, August 1915, CO/904/97; CI Report, Westmeath, August 1915, CO/904/97; IG Report, September 1915, CO/904/97; CI Report, Westmeath, September 1915, CO/904/97).

165 BMHWS No. 563, Michael Cremin, p. 2; BMHWS No. 170, Peter Paul Galligan, p. 4; Maryann Gialanella Valiulis, *Portrait of a Revolutionary: General*

Richard Mulcahy (Kentucky, 1992), p. 10.

166 IV, 26 September 1915; IV, 2 October 1915.

167 IV, 26 September 1915; IV, 2 October 1915.

168 Other prominent trainees at Athlone included Austin Stack and Pierce McCann (Risteárd Mulcahy, My Father, the General. Richard Mulcahy and the Military History of the Revolution (Dublin, 2009), pp. 8, 27).

169 Valiulis, Portrait, pp. 10-11.

170 IV strength in December 1915 was 6,355, up from 3,911 in October when the recruitment drive started and the conscription threat loomed (IG Report, October 1915, CO/904/98; IG Report, November 1915, CO/904/98; IG Report, December 1915, CO/904/98).

171 'Postal Censorship', 30 May 1915, CO 904/164, p. 144.

172 Cumann na mBan was first established in April 1914 (Sinéad McCoole, Guns and Chiffon (Dublin, 1997), pp. 13-14). The organisation predated the Volunteer split and witnessed a similar schism on a smaller scale (Cal McCarthy, Cumann na mBan and the Irish Revolution (Cork, 2007), pp. 34-40).

173 WI, 11 December 1915.

174 McCarthy, Cumann na mBan, pp. 32-3.

175 IV, 18 December 1915; IV, 25 December 1915; IV, 12 February 1916; CI Report, Westmeath, March 1916 CO/904/99.

176 McCarthy, Cumann na mBan, p. 14.

177 IV, 12 February 1916. Athlone's IV continued to maintain a core membership of around twenty men, drilling regularly (CI Report, Westmeath, February 1916, CO/904/99).

178 Coleman, Longford, p. 37; CI Report, Roscommon, February 1916, CO/904/99; CI Report, Roscommon, March 1916, CO/904/99.

179 IG Report, February 1916, CO/904/99; Ireland was excluded yet again from the act that was passed in April (Fitzpatrick, 'Militarism in Ireland', p. 397).

180 Finnan, John Redmond, p. 142.

181 WI, 25 March 1916. The charges were later downgraded, much to McDermott-Hayes' satisfaction (WI, 24 June 1916).

182 Wheatley, 'Irreconcilable enemies', p. 70.

183 CI Report, Westmeath, January 1916, CO/904/99; CI Report, Westmeath, February 1916, CO/904/99; CI Report, Roscommon, March 1916, CO/904/99.

184 IG Report, February 1916, CO/904/99.

185 McGee, The IRB, p. 315.

186 Fitzpatrick, Politics and Irish Life, p. 134.

187 TL, 22 January 1916. The support was sustained for a period (TL, 5 February 1916; TL, 4 March 1916; TL, 11 March 1916). The previous year, the same newspaper had stated that while it had admiration for Ginnell's 'moral courage', it did not 'place much confidence in [his] judgement or tact' (TL, 8 May 1915).

188 Nationality outlined the antipathy of the mainstream media to Ginnell (the Freeman's Journal and National Volunteer both denounced him) and promoted the Westmeath man as the only MP who thought of Ireland and not of 'looking after the … British Empire' (Nationality, 10 July 1915).

See *Nationality*, 31 July 1915; *Nationality*, 25 September 1915; *Nationality*, 27 November 1915; *Nationality*, 8 January 1916; *Nationality*, 22 January 1916; *Nationality*, 12 February 1915; *Nationality*, 26 February 1916; *Nationality*, 18 March 1916; *Nationality*, 1 April 1916; *Nationality*, 8 April 1916).

189   Ó Tuathaigh, 'Nationalist Ireland', p. 63.

190   The IG stated that 'the Irish Volunteer leaders are a pack of rebels who would revolt and proclaim their independence in the event of any favourable opportunity' (IG Report, March 1916, CO/904/99).

191   Pennell, 'Going to war', p. 45.

192   Bew, 'The politics of war', p. 102.

193   In his account of the plan, Tomás Ó Maoileóin stated that IV forces were to rendezvous at Shannon Harbour (Uinseann MacEoin (ed.), *Survivors* (Dublin, 1980), p. 78). A similar claim was made by Séamus Ó Maoileóin in his biography (Patrick J. Twohig, *Blood on the Flag – Autobiography of a Freedom Fighter* (Cork, 1996), p. 27).

194   MacEoin, *Survivors*, p. 200; MA, A/0102, 'The general plan of campaign', in *The Kerryman*, 11 March 1939. The Rising's planners believed that controlling the line from Athlone to Limerick was essential for taking the west and portions of the south of Ireland (Michael Foy and Brian Barton, *The Easter Rising* (Gloucestershire, 2004), p. 24.

195   BMHWS No. 348, Capt. E. Gerrard, pp. 2-3.

196   Thomas Hennessey, *Dividing Ireland: World War One and Partition* (Oxford, 1998), p. 131; Foy and Barton, *Easter Rising*, p. 26; BMHWS No. 161, Donal O'Halligan, pp. 10-11.

197   BMHWS No. 1,503, Michael McCormack, pp. 5-7; BMHWS No. 1,308, Henry O'Brien, p. 2; BMHWS No. 1,309, Francis O'Connor p. 2; Mitchell, *Man With the Long Hair*, p. 25.

198   BMHWS No. 480, Mrs. Martin Murphy (Eileen Walsh), pp. 3-4.

199   BMHWS No. 1,503, Michael McCormack, p. 6. See also BMHWS No. 1,337, David Daly, p. 1; BMHWS No. 1,309, Francis O'Connor p. 3; BMHWS No. 845, Tomás Ó Maoileoin, pp. 3-5; BMHWS No. 343, James Barrett, p. 3; BMHWS No. 361, Peadar Bracken, pp. 6-7.

200   BMHWS No. 1,500, Anthony McCormack, pp. 1-2.

201   UCDA, Mulcahy Papers, P7/A&B/182.

202   Joost Augusteijn, 'The importance of being Irish. Ideas and the volunteers in Mayo and Tipperary', in David Fitzpatrick (ed.), *Revolution? Ireland, 1917-1923* (Dublin, 1990), p. 31.

203   This was a purportedly official plan drawn up by Dublin Castle authorities to arrest Irish nationalists in Dublin and seize their weapons. The authenticity of the document has often been questioned, but Charles Townshend believes that in essence it was an official paper, smuggled out by a republican sympathiser, which was then 'sexed up' by republicans in an attempt to motivate moderates such as Eoin MacNeill to take up arms (Townshend, *Easter 1916*, pp. 131-133; Dermot Keogh, 'The Catholic Church, the Holy See and the 1916 Rising', in Doherty and Keogh, *1916*, pp. 273-276).

204   Reinhard R. Doerries, *Prelude to the Easter Rising. Sir Roger Casement in*

Imperial Germany (London, 2000), pp. 14-24.

205   MacNeill had learned of the Rising despite IRB efforts to keep him in the
      dark. The release of the Castle Document had put him on something of a
      battle footing, and he greeted news of Casement's efforts positively. When
      told that the document was a fake and that Casement had failed, MacNeill
      issued a countermand, primarily through the *Sunday Independent* (Townshend,
      Easter 1916, pp. 134-137; Finnan, *John Redmond*, p. 195; Keogh, 'Catholic
      Church', pp. 276-278).

206   Shortt, 'IRA activity in Westmeath…part one', p. 173.

207   Townshend, *Easter 1916*, p. 227.

208   Foy and Barton, *Easter Rising*, pp. 336.

209   Troops were also sent to Athlone from Dublin, to limit the chances of
      artillery seizures (Brian Barton, *From Behind a Closed Door: Secret Courts
      Martial Records of the 1916 Rising* (Belfast, 2002), p. 42; Foy and Barton, *Easter
      Rising*, p. 337).

210   *WE*, 6 May 1916; Townshend, *Easter 1916*, pp. 169-170, 186, 191.
      Lord Wimborne had called for troops from Athlone to be posted in Dublin
      on the Sunday, but 'it was decided to postpone action' (*MG*, 27 May 1916).
      For a description of the Rising see Townshend, *Easter 1916*, pp. 152-242.

211   Wheatley, 'Irreconcilable enemies', p. 63; Ó Tuathaigh, 'Nationalist Ireland', p. 64.

212   Oliver Snoddy, '1916 government propaganda', in *Journal of the Old Athlone
      Society*, Vol. 1, No. 3 (1973), pp. 204-205.

213   *WI*, 29 April 1916.

214   *WI*, 6 September 1913; *WI*, 13 September 1913; *WI*, 20 September 1913; *WI*,
      27 September 1913; *WI*, 4 October 1913; *WI*, 13 December 1913.

215   *WI*, 29 April 1916. The *Royal Commission on the Rebellion in Ireland*
      pinpointed ICA militancy in 1913 as the first step towards the events of
      Easter 1916 (*Commission on the Rebellion*, p. 5).

216   *WI*, 29 April 1916.

217   Finnan, *John Redmond*, p. 196.

218   *WI*, 29 April 1916; Joost Augusteijn, *From Public Defiance to Guerilla Warfare:
      The Experience of Ordinary Volunteers in the Irish War of Independence 1916-1921*
      (Dublin, 1996), p. 252.

219   Orr, '200,000 volunteer soldiers', p. 71.

220   *II*, 5 May 1916.

221   Augusteijn, *Public Defiance*, p. 255.

222   *TL*, 27 May 1916. Laurence Ginnell informed the Commons of the error
      (*Hansard 5 Commons*, lxxxii, 966-967 (11 May 1916)).

223   Kelly, *Fenian Ideal*, p. 234.

224   Lee, *Ireland*, p. 38.

225   McConville, *Irish Political Prisoners*, p. 442. Ginnell stated that he was
      addressing 'an assembly stained with the blood of some of my dearest
      friends, for no crime but that of attempting to do for Ireland what you
      urge the Belgians to do for Belgium' (*Hansard 5 Commons*, lxxxii, 966-967
      (11 May 1916)).

226   F.S.L. Lyons, 'The Rising and after', in Vaughan, *A New History of Ireland VI*,

pp. 218-219; Townshend, *Easter 1916*, pp. 278-280.

227   Fitzpatrick, 'Militarism in Ireland', p. 395. The declaration of martial law originally covered Dublin only. Reports of rebellion in Galway and rumours of a large column marching on Athlone, amongst other rumours, led to its extension countrywide (Foy and Barton, *Easter Rising*, p. 342). In reality, it was DORA whose provisions were really used across Ireland, rather than martial law. However, the inability of people, quite understandably, to recognise the difference between the two fed the impression that the Irish were being grossly suppressed (Charles Townshend, 'Military force and civil authority in the United Kingdom, 1914-1921', in *The Journal of British Studies*, Vol. 28, No. 3 (July, 1989), pp. 283-284). Maxwell used DORA regulations 'in such a way as to approximate martial law' (Hardiman, 'Shot in cold blood', p. 225).

228   Orr, '200,000 volunteer soldiers', p. 71.

229   *WI*, 6 May 1916.

230   Townshend, *Easter 1916*, p. 273; Barton, *From behind a closed door*, pp. 54-55.

231   Townshend, *Easter 1916*, pp. 273-274.

232   Foy and Barton, *Easter Rising*, p. 346.

233   RIC Report, Précis of Information, Westmeath in 1916, CO/904/122. This was written in January 1917.

234   CI Report, Westmeath, May 1916, CO/904/100.

235   CI Report, Westmeath, April 1916, CO/904/100.

236   BMHWS No. 1,503, Michael McCormack, p. 6.

237   *WI*, 6 May 1916.

238   Hardiman, 'Shot in cold blood' p. 226; McConville, *Irish Political Prisoners*, p. 451.

239   *WI*, 13 May 1916.

240   Nationally, almost half of those arrested were released. 1,841 were interned (Hardiman, 'Shot in cold blood' p. 226). Townshend, *Easter 1916*, p. 316; BMHWS No. 1,503, Michael McCormack, p. 7.

241   *WI*, 13 May 1916.

242   Reports contradict each other regarding the total number of men who were actually sent to Dublin. The names of those reportedly sent to the capital were John O'Brien, Peter Murray, George Severs, Gilbert Hughes, John Blayney, Seamus O'Brien, Owen Sweeney, Michael McCormack, Peter Malynn, Seán O'Hurley, Seán O'Mullany and Edward Martin (*WI*, 13 May 1916). It should be noted that a George Amos was also reportedly arrested. It appears that the press was unsure whether it was George Amos or George Severs that was taken to Dublin (*WI*, 20 May 1916).

243   *Hansard 5 Commons*, lxxxii, 940-941 (11 May 1916).

244   *WI*, 13 May 1916.

245   Townshend, 'Military force', p. 283.

246   Wheatley, 'Irreconcilable enemies', p. 72.

247   *WI*, 20 May 1916.

248   AHL, Minute Book of Athlone PLG, 20 May 1916.

249   AHL, Minute Book of Athlone PLG, 20 May 1916; BMHWS No. 1,503, Michael McCormack, p. 7; *WI*, 20 May 1916.

250   Fitzpatrick, *Politics and Irish Life*, p. 116.

251   Wheatley, 'Irreconcilable enemies', p. 73-74.

252   Paul Bew, 'Moderate nationalism and the Irish revolution, 1916-1923',
      in *The Historical Journal*, Vol. 42, No. 3 (1999), p. 730.

253   Garvin, *Irish Nationalist Politics*, p. 99.

254   Fitzpatrick, *Politics and Irish Life*, p. 112.

255   *WI*, 13 May 1916; *Meath Chronicle*, 20 May 1916.

256   It was noted that the low attendance had an impact on the vote (*WI*,
      20 May 1916). General Botha, Maxwell's equivalent in South Africa, had
      executed just one man after the Boer War (Finnan, *John Redmond*, p. 170).

257   *WI*, 20 May 1916.

258   NAI, CSO Registered Papers, 5622/25887/1916.

259   *WI*, 3 June 1916.

260   CI Report, Roscommon, May 1916, CO/904/100.

261   *WI*, 20 May 1916; *WI*, 27 May 1916; BMHWS No. 1308, Henry O'Brien, p. 3.

262   *WI*, 27 May 1916.

263   CI Report, Westmeath, June 1916, CO/904/100.

264   AHL, Minute Book of Athlone UDC, 31 May 1916; *WI*, 3 June 1916. John
      Burgess objected to accusations that the prisoners were being starved or
      held in solitary confinement. His protestations led to the description of the
      conditions as 'inhumane' being removed (*WI*, 17 June 1916).

265   *II*, 29 May 1916; AHL, Minute Book of Athlone UDC, 31 May 1916.

266   Keogh, 'Catholic Church', pp. 291, 295, 307. See also Jérôme aan de Wiel,
      The Catholic Church in Ireland, 1914-1918: War and Politics (Dublin, 2003),
      pp. 157-163.

267   Townshend, *Easter 1916*, p. 276.

268   *WI*, 10 June 1916.

269   Fitzpatrick, 'Militarism in Ireland', p. 395.

270   *WI*, 10 June 1916.

271   *II*, 12 June 1916; *LO*, 17 June 1916. Michael McCormack stated that they
      remained in solitary at Wakefield for three weeks 'lying on boards', with
      'little food' (BMHWS No. 1,503, Michael McCormack, p. 7).

272   Martin was honorary secretary of the General Council in the prison, which
      was designed to organise the prisoners (Seán O'Mahony, *Frongoch, University
      of Revolution* (Dublin, 1987), pp. 47, 212).

273   *II*, 5 June 1916; *WI*, 17 June 1916.

274   Townshend, *Easter 1916*, p. 317. For a description of the conditions see
      McConville, *Political Prisoners*, pp. 466-469.

275   Augusteijn, *Public Defiance*, pp. 190-191.

276   McConville, *Political Prisoners*, pp. 459; Maume, *Long Gestation*, p. 182;
      Dempsey and Boylan, 'Ginnell, Laurence', p. 103.

277   Ginnell secreted letters in cigarette cases (William Murphy, 'The tower of
      hunger: political imprisonment and the Irish, 1910-21' (Unpublished PhD
      thesis, UCD, 2006), p. 121).

278   *WI*, 17 June 1916; *WI*, 24 June 1916.

279   *II*, 12 May 1916; *WI*, 27 May 1916; BMHWS No. 1308, Henry O'Brien, p. 3;
      CI Report, Westmeath, June 1916, CO/904/100.

280 *WI*, 1 July 1916.

281 *WI*, 17 June 1916; *WI*, 24 June 1916; *WI*, 1 July 1916. See David G. Boyce, 'British Opinion, Ireland, and the War, 1916-1918', in *The Historical Journal*, Vol. 17, No. 3 (September, 1974), pp. 579-583; McEwan, 'The Liberal Party and the Irish Question', pp. 116-119; Stubbs, 'Unionists and Ireland', pp. 876-883; Boyce, 'British politics and the Irish Question', pp. 97-99.

282 Fitzpatrick, 'Home front', p. 141.

283 Wheatley, 'Irreconcilable enemies', p. 80.

284 Ginnell's demanding manner saw him suspended at the end of July. He was readmitted in mid-October (*Hansard 5 Commons,* lxxxiv, 1859-62 (27 July 1916); *Hansard 5 Commons,* lxxxvi, 435 (17 October 1916)).

285 *WI*, 8 July 1916; CI Report, Westmeath, June 1916, CO/904/100.

286 *WI*, 15 July 1916.

287 Fitzpatrick, *Politics and Irish Life*, p. 117.

288 CI Report, Westmeath, July 1916, CO/904/100.

289 F.S.L. Lyons, 'The new nationalism, 1916-18', in Vaughan, *A New History of Ireland VI*, p. 225.

290 Shea, *Voices*, p. 21.

291 *WI*, 8 July 1916; *WI*, 29 July 1916.

292 *WI*, 22 July 1916.

293 *WI*, 22 July 1916; *II*, 24 July 1916; *II*, 26 July 1916; *IT*, 29 July 1916; *CT*, 29 July 1916.

294 Keogh, 'Catholic Church', pp. 296.

295 *WI*, 5 August 1916.

296 CI Report, Westmeath, August 1916, CO/904/100; *WI*, 5 August 1916; *WI*, 26 August 1916.

297 *WI*, 12 August 1916; NAI, 15564/16, CSO, Easter Rising 1916, Index of Internees.

298 CI Report, Westmeath, September 1916, CO/904/101; CI Report, Westmeath, October 1916, CO/904/101.

299 Lyons, 'The new nationalism', p. 226.

300 Augusteijn, *Public Defiance*, p. 57.

301 CI Report, Westmeath, September 1916, CO/904/101; CI Report, Westmeath, November 1916, CO/904/101.

302 IG Report, September 1916, CO/904/101.

303 Ms Daniels' experience of the Land War and political manoeuvres up to 1916 had left her somewhat cynical about Irish nationalism: 'National Ireland is the only country that will not 'go forward'. It is always looking back trying to 'arrange' what does not now concern them (PRONI, T/2782/23, Cecilia H. Daniels to Mrs. Flett, Australia, 22 September 1916).

304 *WI*, 5 August 1916.

305 *WI*, 10 June 1916.

306 *WI*, 9 September 1916; *WI*, 16 September 1916.

307 Lyons, *John Dillon*, p. 402.

308 O'Leary and Maume, *Controversial Issues*, p. 56.

309 Fitzpatrick, *Politics and Irish Life*, p. 91.

310 *WI*, 23 September 1916.

311   *WI*, 30 September 1916.

312   Wheatley, 'Irreconcilable enemies', p. 83.

313   Townshend, *Easter 1916*, p. 314.

314   *WI*, 2 September 1916.

315   IG Report, October 1916, CO/904/101.

316   Fitzpatrick, *Politics and Irish Life*, p. 129.

317   CI Report, Westmeath, October 1916, CO/904/101; *II*, 21 October 1916;
      IT, 21 October 1916. The government had stopped the running of 'special
      excursion trains' earlier in the year. Most were used to get to GAA matches,
      events which were often used as cover for advanced nationalist meetings
      (Fitzpatrick, *Politics and Irish Life*, p. 129).

318   AHL, Minute Book of Athlone UDC, 25 October 1916. J.P. Hayden, in reply
      to a UDC complaint, noted that it was a continuation of a situation
      described by the Secretary of State for War as 'stupid and malignant' (*II*,
      10 November 1916; NAI, 5622/25633/1916, CSO Registered Papers).

319   *WI*, 28 October 1916; *WI*, 4 November 1916; *WI*, 18 November 1916.

320   *WI*, 18 November 1916.

321   Townshend, 'Military force', p. 285.

322   *WI*, 4 November 1916.

323   Augusteijn, *Public Defiance*, p. 254.

324   PRONI, T/2782/23, Cecilia H. Daniels to Mrs Flett, Australia,
      22 September 1916.

325   AHL, Minute Book of Athlone UDC, 18 October 1916.

326   Charles Townshend, *The British Campaign in Ireland 1919-1921: The Development
      of Political and Military Policies* (London, 1975), p. 6.

327   D.G. Boyce and Cameron Hazelhurst, 'The unknown Chief Secretary:
      H.E. Duke and Ireland, 1916-18', in *Irish Historical Studies*, 20 (1977), p. 286.
      Also see - Eunan O'Halpin, 'Historical revision XX: H.E. Duke and the
      Irish Administration 1916-18', in *Irish Historical Studies*, Vol. 22, No. 88 (1981),
      pp. 362-376.

328   Finnan, *John Redmond*, pp. 110-111.

329   *Hansard 5 Commons,* lxxxviii, 1354-1355 (19 December 1916).

330   Augusteijn, *Public Defiance*, p. 57; Fitzpatrick, 'Militarism in Ireland', p. 396.
      The deterioration in prison conditions informed the eventual decision to
      release the men (Murphy, 'The tower of hunger', p. 141).

331   Townshend, *Easter 1916*, p. 327.

CHAPTER 5

1   CI Report, Roscommon, January 1917, CO/904/102; BMHWS No. 1,336,
      Patrick Lennon, p. 1.

2   For additional biographical information see Michael Laffan, 'The unification
      of Sinn Féin in 1917', in Irish Historical Studies, Vol. 17, No. 67 (March, 1971),
      p. 358.

3   Lyons, 'The new nationalism', p. 226.

4 *TL*, 6 January 1917; CI Report, Roscommon, January 1917, CO/904/102.

5 *WI*, 27 January 1917; Micheál O'Callaghan, *For Ireland and Freedom: Roscommon's Contribution to the Fight for Independence, 1917-1921* (3rd Ed.: Cork, 2012), pp. 19-20.

6 Denis Carroll, *They have Fooled you Again – Michael O'Flanagan (1876-1942): Priest, Republican, Social Critic* (Dublin, 1993), p. 55.

7 O'Leary and Maume, *Controversial Issues*, p. 57. Ginnell had walked for four hours through heavy snow to support the count at a rally in Elphin (*TL*, 17 February 1917). Heavy snowfall plagued the by-election and led to huge efforts to clear roads for voters (Carroll, *Fooled you Again*, p. 55).

8 Laffan, 'Unification of Sinn Féin', p. 358. Laffan describes Plunkett's arrival as 'fortunate … too late … to do any damage to his own cause' (Laffan, *Resurrection of Ireland*, p. 84).

9 *TL*, 3 February 1917.

10 Francis Kielty, 'Jasper Tully', in *Roscommon Historical and Archaeological Society Journal*, Vol. 3 (1990), p. 60.

11 O'Callaghan, *For Ireland and Freedom*, pp. 27-34.

12 CI Report, Roscommon, February 1917, CO/904/102.

13 *II*, 7 February 1917.

14 *WI*, 10 February 1917.

15 Laffan, *Resurrection of Ireland*, p. 82.

16 Foster, *Modern Ireland*, p. 488.

17 Carroll, *Fooled you Again*, p. 58.

18 Coleman, *Longford*, pp. 82-83.

19 *II*, 12 February 1917.

20 *WI*, 17 February 1917.

21 Townshend, *Easter 1916*, p. 328.

22 Finnan, *John Redmond*, p. 212; O'Leary and Maume, *Controversial Issues*, p. 57.

23 *TL*, 10 February 1917; *TL*, 3 March 1917.

24 *WI*, 17 March 1917. McDermott-Hayes was reacting to the efforts of T.P. O'Connor (who the editor referred to as the 'Prime Minister's Henchman' (*WI*, 17 February 1917)) to have Home Rule tackled by the war-occupied cabinet (*Hansard 5 Commons*, lxxxxi, 440-443 (7 March 1917)).

25 *WI*, 24 March 1917.

26 Athlone, 'where the majority … sympathise with Sinn Féin' (CI Report, Westmeath, February 1917, CO/904/102), saw SF members plan a St Patrick's Day parade despite the prohibition of such events. The RIC stated that if any 'Sinn Féin Display' occurred, prosecutions under DORA would follow. Consequently, the clergy refused to associate with the parade. *The Leader* questioned the prohibition, asking whether the authorities were 'certain people [are] looking for trouble', or if they had 'clean gone mad?' The *Westmeath Independent* opined that such actions 'brought us back to the days when … they were hanging men and women for the wearing of the green' (CI Report, Westmeath, March 1917, CO/904/102; *IT*, 19 March 1917; *TL*, 24 March 1917; *WI*, 24 March 1917).

27 *TL*, 14 April 1917; Laffan, *Resurrection of Ireland*, pp. 96-97.

28 IG Report, April 1917, CO/904/102.

29 Fr O'Flanagan did not canvass as his political orations had led to him being censured by Bishop Coyne of Elphin. O'Flanagan did however send a letter of support (Carroll, *Fooled you Again*, pp. 62, 67, 95).

30 BMHWS No. 1,504, Seamus O'Meara, p. 6.

31 Townshend, *Easter 1916*, p. 328.

32 Marie Coleman, 'Mobilisation: The South Longford by-election and its impact on political mobilisation', in Joost Augusteijn (ed.), *The Irish Revolution: 1913-1923* (New York, 2002), p. 61. The loyalty of the local bishop and the majority of priests lay with the IPP (Jackson, *Ireland*, p. 209).

33 BMHWS No. 1,503, Michael McCormack, p. 8; Coleman, *Longford*, p. 62.

34 *WI*, 5 May 1917. *The Leader* was not impressed by the support shown to McGuinness by the *Westmeath Independent*. It noted that the Athlone paper was quite happy to run recruitment advertisements for the army, and was unlikely to be supporting a republic (*TL*, 12 May 1917).

35 Fitzpatrick, 'Geography of Irish nationalism', p. 125; James McConnel, 'The franchise factor in the defeat of the Irish Parliamentary Party, 1885-1918', in *The Historical Journal*, Vol. 47, No. 2 (2004), p. 368.

36 *WI*, 12 May 1917. The *Westmeath Independent* reported that the AOH was experiencing a revolt in many areas as members moved to SF (*WI*, 19 May 1917).

37 IG Report, May 1917, CO/904/102; CI Report, Longford, May 1917, CO/904/102; *WI*, 12 May 1917; Coleman, *Longford*, pp. 51-67.

38 *TL*, 19 May 1917; aan de Wiel, *Catholic Church*, pp. 174-175.

39 O'Leary and Maume, *Controversial Issues*, p. 59.

40 Coleman, 'Mobilisation', pp. 54-5. McKenna was the same man who had directed the activities of the UIL and AOH in South Westmeath at the start of the decade.

41 For a detailed account of the by-election see Coleman, *Longford*, pp. 45-67.

42 Maume, *Long Gestation*, p. 196.

43 *II*, 19 June 1917; *II*, 21 June 1917; *WE*, 23 June 1917.

44 *II*, 12 May 1917; *WI*, 12 May 1917; CI Report, Westmeath, May 1917, CO/904/102; CI Report, Roscommon, May 1917, CO/904/102.

45 *WI*, 12 May 1917.

46 CI Report, Roscommon, May 1917, CO/904/102.

47 PRONI, T/2782/26, Cecilia H. Daniels to Mrs Flett, Australia, 9 May 1917.

48 BMHWS No. 1,504, Seamus O'Meara, p. 7; CI Report, Westmeath, May 1917, CO/904/10.

49 *WI*, 2 June 1917; *WI*, 23 June 1917; *WI*, 30 June 1917.

50 *IT*, 8 May 1917.

51 *IT*, 24 May 1917.

52 *WI*, 23 June 1917.

53 Coleman, *Longford*, pp. 68-72; Farry, *Sligo*, pp. 98-100.

54 IG Report, June 1917, CO/904/103.

55 IG Report, June 1917, CO/904/103; *IT*, 10 July 1917; Fitzpatrick, *Two Irelands*, pp. 66-67.

56 *II*, 13 July 1917; *WI*, 14 July 1917; *WI*, 28 July 1917. Fines were levied on a

number of the attackers (*WE*, 28 July 1917; *AC*, 28 July 1917).

57 Orr, '200,000 volunteer soldiers', p. 73; Townshend, *Easter 1916*, p. 335.

58 Lyons, 'The new nationalism', p. 228.

59 Augusteijn, 'County Derry', p. 579.

60 David Fitzpatrick, *Harry Boland's Irish Revolution* (Cork, 2003), pp. vii, 18, 31.

61 *WI*, 7 July 1917; Dempsey and Boylan, 'Ginnell, Laurence', p. 103; Laffan, *Resurrection of Ireland*, p. 81. Ginnell's abstention had been agreed in early June, when it was noted that he would 'withdraw when requested by Republicans, and his constituency will endorse his action' (*Documents Relative to the Sinn Féin Movement 1921* [Cmd.1108], p. 32).

62 BMHWS No. 1,336, Patrick Lennon, p. 2; *WI*, 21 July 1917.

63 The team was established towards the end of 1916 (*WI*, 9 December 1916; *WI*, 19 May 1917; *WI*, 16 June 1917; *WI*, 29 September 1917; BMHWS No. 1,504, Seamus O'Meara, p. 7)

64 Townshend, *Easter 1916*, p. 331.

65 BMHWS No. 701, Thomas Kelly, p. 2; BMHWS No. 1,296, Thomas Costello, p. 2; BMHWS No. 1,336, Patrick Lennon, p. 2.

66 AHL, Minute Book of Athlone UDC, 25 July 1917.

67 *WI*, 2 June 1917.

68 See Laffan, *Resurrection of Ireland*, pp. 103-106; Carroll, *Fooled you Again*, pp. 64-67; Laffan, 'Unification of Sinn Féin', pp. 358-375. Plunkett's activities led to registrations of annoyance at meetings of Athlone UDC and PLG (AHL, Minute Book of Athlone UDC, 28 March 1917; *II*, 30 March 1917; *IT*, 31 March 1917; *WI*, 7 April 1917), and Westmeath County Council (*WI*, 21 April 1917; *WI*, 28 April 1917). The *Westmeath Independent* questioned the capacity of local authority representatives to represent their electorate truthfully: 'it is a serious mistake to assume that the public generally approve of all that is said or acted by local representatives.' The newspaper clarified that whatever councillors said, being anti-Plunkett did not make one anti-SF, or pro-IPP (*WI*, 7 April 1917; *WI*, 21 April 1917).

69 CI Report, Westmeath, July 1917, CO/904/103; CI Report, Roscommon, July 1917, CO/904/103.

70 NAI, Ancient Order of Hibernians Agenda Book 1912-81, 14 June 1917, LOU 13/2/1-2.

71 *FJ*, 8 June 1917. See Alan J. Ward, 'America and the Irish problem, 1899-1921', in *Irish Historical Studies*, Vol. 16, No. 61 (1968), pp. 80-83.

72 O'Leary and Maume, *Controversial Issues*, p. 58.

73 Finnan, *John Redmond*, p. 191.

74 R.B. McDowell, *The Irish Convention, 1917-1918* (London, 1970), p. 219; *WI*, 7 July 1917.

75 Hennessey, *Dividing Ireland*, pp. 205-206.

76 Peter Collins, 'Irish Labour and politics in the late nineteenth and early twentieth centuries', in Collins, *Nationalism and Unionism*, p. 142.

77 Boyce, 'British Conservative Opinion', pp. 95-97; Hennessey, *Dividing Ireland*, pp. 206-220.

78 O'Leary and Maume, *Controversial Issues*, p. 60.

79   *Hansard 5 Commons*, lxxxxiii, 2029 (21 May 1917).

80   Foster, *Modern Ireland*, p. 486.

81   *IT*, 13 August 1917. *WE*, 25 August 1917; 'Press Censorship', 13 August 1917, Athlone, CO 904/166, p. 119.

82   *II*, 13 August 1917; *WI*, 18 August 1917. The number of Westmeath Hibernians had more than halved to just 316; Roscommon's fell to 896, and numerous county boards disappeared (*HJ*, September 1917; *HJ*, January 1918). The Ballymahon AOH erected a banner at the meeting, 'ostentatiously emphasising their severance from the body [the Board of Erin]' ('Press Censorship', 13 August 1917, Athlone, CO 904/166, p. 120).

83   *II*, 13 August 1917; *WI*, 18 August 1917.

84   Augusteijn, *Public Defiance*, p. 192.

85   'Press Censorship', 16 August 1917, Athlone, CO 904/166, p. 124.

86   Laffan, *Resurrection of Ireland*, p. 196.

87   BMHWS No. 1,503, Michael McCormack, p. 9; BMHWS No. 1308, Henry O'Brien, p. 4.

88   Sweeney was also instrumental in ensuring the viability of the Drumraney SF, which was headed by local priest Fr Clarke ('Press Censorship', 22 September 1917, Drumraney Hill, CO 904/166, p. 153).

89   *WI*, 18 August 1917.

90   Fitzpatrick, *Politics and Irish Life*, pp. 128, 138, 283.

91   Coleman, *Longford*, pp. 74-76; Farry, *Sligo*, p. 102.

92   Fergus Campbell, 'The social dynamics of nationalist politics in the west of Ireland 1898-1918', in *Past and Present*, No. 182 (February, 2004), pp. 180-182; Campbell, *Land and Revolution*, pp. 224-225.

93   The assessment was arrived at by comparing the incomplete list of names that accompanied the report of the meeting with information on political activism in Athlone from the previous decade-and-a-half and the 1911 Census Returns. www.census.nationalarchives.ie/pages/1911/Westmeath/; www.census.nationalarchives.ie/pages/1911/Roscommon/: accessed 18-22 January 2010).

94   CI Report, Westmeath, September 1917, CO/904/104; CI Report, Roscommon, September 1917, CO/904/104.

95   *TL*, 6 October 1917.

96   IG Report, September 1917, CO/904/104.

97   See McConville, *Political Prisoners,* pp. 610-619.

98   AHL, Minute Book of Athlone UDC, 10 October 1917.

99   *WI*, 29 September 1917.

100   *II*, 1 October 1918.

101   Peter Hart, 'The social structure of the Irish Republican Army, 1916-1923' in *The Historical Journal*, Vol. 42, No. 1 (1999), p. 219.

102   CI Report, Westmeath, September 1917, CO/904/104; BMHWS No. 1,504, Seamus O'Meara, p. 8.

103   Townshend, *Easter 1916*, p. 336.

104   Augusteijn, *Public Defiance*, p. 65.

105   CI Report, Westmeath, October 1917, CO/904/104; *WI*, 6 October 1917; *AC*,

6 October 1917.

106 *WI*, 10 November 1917.

107 *WI*, 27 October 1917; *IT*, 1 November 1917; *WI*, 3 November 1917; *II*, 5 November 1917.

108 *WI*, 6 October 1917.

109 *WI*, 22 September 1917; *WI*, 29 September 1917.

110 *WI*, 6 October 1917.

111 AHL, Minute Book of Athlone UDC, 31 October 1917.

112 *WI*, 22 September 1917; *WI*, 13 October 1917.

113 CI Report, Westmeath, November 1917, CO/904/104; CI Report, Roscommon, November 1917, CO/904/104; CI Report, Westmeath, December 1917, CO/904/104; CI Report, Westmeath, December 1917, CO/904/104.

114 Townshend, *British Campaign*, p. 7.

115 Lyons, 'The new nationalism', p. 233. Laurence Ginnell was elected as treasurer (Carroll, *Fooled you Again*, p. 77).

116 Townshend, *British Campaign*, p. 7.

117 Townshend, *Easter 1916*, p. 334.

118 O'Leary and Maume, *Controversial Issues*, p. 62.

119 Costello, *Irish Revolution*, p. 26.

120 Augusteijn, *Public Defiance*, p. 64.

121 Hennessey, *Dividing Ireland*, p. 231.

122 BMHWS No. 1,336, Patrick Lennon, p. 1.

123 BMHWS No. 701, Thomas Kelly, p. 1.

124 'Press Censorship', CO 904/166, 9 December 1917, Lecarrow, p. 266.

125 *TL*, 6 October 1917; Finnan, *John Redmond*, p. 152.

126 Augusteijn, *Public Defiance*, pp. 63, 67.

127 Orr, '200,000 volunteer soldiers', p. 75.

128 IG Report, January 1918, CO/904/105.

129 IG Report, March 1918, CO/904/105.

130 CI Report, Westmeath, January 1918, CO/904/105; CI Report, Roscommon, January 1918, CO/904/105; *WI*, 23 March 1918; BMHWS No. 1,504, Seamus O'Meara, p. 8.

131 Fitzpatrick, 'Geography of Irish nationalism', p. 115.

132 BMHWS No. 580, John Duffy, pp. 1-4.

133 *WI*, 13 October 1917.

134 Fitzpatrick, *Politics and Irish Life*, p. 34.

135 Fitzpatrick, *Politics and Irish Life*, pp. 35-37.

136 Townshend, *British Campaign*, p. 7; Augusteijn, *Public Defiance*, p. 196.

137 *WI*, 5 January 1918. William Keogh and John Sadlier were nineteenth-century Irish MPs who had abandoned their interest in Irish affairs upon being gifted prominent posts by the British administration; Keogh as Irish Solicitor General and Sadlier as Junior Lord of the Treasury. Keogh (a former Athlone MP) and Sadlier were by 1918, 'Long established among Irish nationalists as the archetypal modern traitors to the national cause' (Kelly, *Fenian Ideal*, p. 64).

138   Finnan, *John Redmond*, pp. 220-1; Stubbs, 'Unionists and Ireland', pp. 887-888.

139   IG Report, February 1918, CO/904/105. Seán O'Hurley, now also SF
      South Westmeath Executive chairman, had sent funds to Armagh (*WI*,
      26 January 1918).

140   *WE*, 9 February 1918.

141   Éamonn Phoenix, 'Northern Nationalists, Ulster Unionists and the
      Development of Partition, 1900-21', in Collins, *Nationalism and Unionism*, p. 118.

142   *WI*, 9 February 1918.

143   *WI*, 9 March 1918.

144   *TL*, 16 March 1918.

145   *II*, 11 March 1918; *WI*, 16 March 1918.

146   *WI*, 20 March 1918.

147   PRONI, T/2782/24, Cecilia H. Daniels to Mrs Flett, Australia,
      24 November 1916; T/2782/25, Cecilia H. Daniels to Mrs Flett, Australia,
      14 January 1917; T/2782/26 Cecilia H. Daniels to Mrs Flett, Australia, 9 May 1917.

148   *II*, 31 January 1917; *IT*, 31 January 1917; *II*, 12 February 1917; *IT*,
      12 February 1917; *IT*, 14 February 1917; *IT*, 19 February 1917; *WI*,
      24 February 1917; *IT*, 5 January 1918; *II*, 8 January 1918; *LO*, 12 January 1918;
      AC, 12 January 1918; *IT*, 14 January 1918; *IT*, 19 January 1918.

149   *II*, 31 January 1917; *IT*, 31 January 1917; *II*, 12 February 1917; *IT*,
      12 February 1917; *WI*, 17 February 1917.

150   *II*, 5 February 1917, *AC*, 10 February 1917; *II*, 26 February 1917. Gerd
      Hardach, *The First World War, 1914-1918* (Berkeley, 1977), p. 128.

151   *IT*, 12 February 1917.

152   *IT*, 19 February 1917; *WI*, 24 February 1917; *WI*, 3 March 1917; *WI*,
      24 March 1917; *II*, 26 March 1917.

153   *IT*, 1 March 1917; *IT*, 10 March 1917.

154   *II*, 5 March 1917.

155   *WI*, 31 March 1917; *WI*, 14 April 1917; *WI*, 21 April 1917; *WI*, 28 April 1917.

156   *TL*, 10 February 1917; *TL*, 24 February 1917.

157   *TL*, 3 March 1917.

158   This was the newspaper's second incarnation (Glandon, *Arthur Griffith*,
      pp. 159, 165-166).

159   *Nationality*, 31 March 1917.

160   *IT*, 25 May 1917; *IT*, 5 July 1917; *IT*, 10 September 1917; *IT*, 4 February 1918.

161   PRONI, T/2782/27, Cecilia H. Daniels to Mrs Flett, Australia, 6 January 1918.

162   Hardach, *First World War*, p. 128.

163   *II*, 21 January 1918; *IT*, 26 January 1918.

164   AHL, Minute Book of Athlone UDC, 18 February 1918; *IT*, 12 February 1918.

165   *WI*, 16 February, 1918; *II*, 21 February 1918; *WI*, 23 February 1918; *AC*,
      23 February 1918; *WI*, 9 March 1918.

166   Peter Malynn, SF South Westmeath Executive secretary, was called before
      the committee after it was reported that he had exported turkeys to England.
      He was exonerated when he proved that he had done all he could to sell them
      locally, and that they were not a 'staple' foodstuff (*WI*, 19 January 1918; *WI*,
      9 February 1918).

167 *WI*, 9 February 1918.

168 Fitzpatrick, *Two Irelands*, p. 69.

169 Varley, 'Sturdy smallholders', p. 138; *II*, 4 March 1918.

170 Fitzpatrick, *Politics and Irish Life*, pp. 59-61; Maume, *Long Gestation*, p. 194.

171 Edward E. Lysaght, T.W. Westropp Bennett and Richard Ball, 'The farmers and the food problem', in *Studies: An Irish Quarterly Review*, Vol. 6, No. 21 (March, 1917), pp. 21-34.

172 Fitzpatrick, *Politics and Irish Life*, p. 140.

173 *II*, 4 February 1918.

174 *WI*, 5 January 1918; *WI*, 30 March 1918.

175 *WI*, 12 January 1918; *WI*, 16 February 1918.

176 Moriarty, 'Work, warfare and wages', p. 83.

177 Lysaght, Westropp Bennett and Ball, 'Farmers and the food problem', pp. 31-34.

178 CI Report, Westmeath, February 1918, CO/904/105; CI Report, Roscommon, February 1918, CO/904/105.

179 Townshend, *Easter 1916*, p. 340.

180 Fitzpatrick, 'Geography of Irish Nationalism', p. 136.

181 Ginnell travelled all over Ireland promoting agrarian agitation. His work rate was such that the RIC in twelve counties was asked to assess whether he could be charged with incitement. His arrest was initially postponed as it was believed he would go on hunger strike, something he duly did when eventually interned ('Republican Suspects', Laurence Ginnell, CO 904/202/162; *IT*, 30 March 1918; BMHWS No. 982, Mrs Alice Ginnell, p. 20).

182 Varley, 'Sturdy smallholders', p. 139.

183 O'Halpin, 'H.E. Duke', p. 371.

184 Campbell, 'Social dynamics', p. 182; Augusteijn, *Public Defiance*, p. 256.

185 Varley, 'Sturdy smallholders', pp. 131-132.

186 Townshend, *Easter 1916*, p. 340.

187 Fitzpatrick, 'Geography of Irish nationalism', p. 136; Townshend, *Easter 1916*, p. 341; Campbell, 'Social dynamics', p. 183.

188 Townshend, *Easter 1916*, p. 337.

189 Boyce, 'British Opinion', pp. 586-587; Alan J. Ward, 'Lloyd George and the 1918 conscription crisis', in *Irish Historical Studies*, Vol. 17, No. 1 (1974), p. 108.

190 Boyce and Hazelhurst, 'Unknown Chief Secretary', pp. 307-308; Boyce, 'British opinion', p. 587; McEwan, 'Liberal Party', p. 125.

191 It was the 'very severe jolt' of German gains in March 1918 that precipitated the move towards conscription (Ward, 'Lloyd George', pp. 109-110).

192 Foster, *Modern Ireland*, p. 487.

193 Boyce, 'British Opinion', pp. 589-590; Stubbs, 'Unionists and Ireland', pp. 889-890.

194 Lyons, 'The new nationalism', p. 235.

195 *WI*, 30 March 1918.

196 *Hansard 5 Commons*, civ, 1374 (9 April 1918).

197 'Press Censorship', March 1918, CO 904/166, p. 386. Others included the *Clare Champion*, *Kilkenny People* and the unionist *Belfast Evening Telegraph*

(*Hansard 5 Commons*, civ, 1439-1440 (9 April 1918)).

198   *II*, 6 April 1918.

199   *IT*, 6 April 1918; *IT*, 13 April 1918. The editor had received a warning
in January for surreptitiously adding an editorial that blamed Ireland's
poverty and subjugation on the union with Britain ('Press Censorship',
5 January 1918, *Westmeath Independent*, CO 904/166, pp. 292-293). Another
piece in the *Westmeath's* sister paper the *King's County Independent* in February
had also caught the censor's eye ('Press Censorship', 2 February 1918, *King's
Co. Independent*, CO 904/166, p. 317).

200   *II*, 6 April 1918.

201   *WI*, 30 March 1918.

202   *II*, 6 April 1918; *Hansard 5 Commons*, civ, 1813-1814 (11 April 1918); *WE*,
13 April 1918.

203   *WI*, 20 April 1918.

204   *WI*, 20 April 1918.

205   *Hansard 5 Commons*, civ, 1449-56 (9 April 1918). Two of Chapman's three
sons were serving with the British Army in Europe (*Hansard 5 Commons*, 104,
1643-45 (11 April 1918)).

206   *Hansard 5 Commons*, civ, 1327 (9 April 1918).

207   *Hansard 5 Commons*, civ, 1439 (9 April 1918); *II*, 10 April 1918.

208   *Hansard 5 Commons*, civ, 1456 (9 April 1918).

209   AHL, Minute Book of Athlone UDC, 5 April 1918.

210   *Hansard 5 Commons*, civ, 1813-1814 (11 April 1918).

211   *Hansard 5 Commons*, civ, 1813-1815 (11 April 1918).

212   'Press Censorship', April 1918, CO 904/166, p. 425.

213   *Hansard 5 Commons*, civ, 1452-1453 (9 April 1918); *Hansard 5 Commons*,
civ, 1643-1645 (11 April 1918). Duke received a letter of protest which
outlined that 85 per cent of those put out of work were not employed
by the offending publication. The English Labour Party was informed
of the suppression in the hope that pressure could be brought to bear
(*II*, 12 April 1918).

214   *II*, 15 April 1918.

215   'Press Censorship', April 1918, CO 904/166, p. 430.

216   *WI*, 20 April 1918.

217   *II*, 15 April 1918; *IT*, 15 April 1918. Some members of the PLG spoke about
forsaking their JP commissions in protest at the threat (*II*, 22 April 1918).

218   AHL, Minute Book of Athlone UDC, 24 April 1918.

219   Maume, *Long Gestation*, p. 206.

220   Foster, *Modern Ireland*, p. 490; O'Leary and Maume, *Controversial Issues*, pp. 66-67.

221   Lyons, 'The new nationalism', p. 235.

222   Costello, *Irish Revolution*, pp. 31-32.

223   Lyons, 'The new nationalism', p. 235. See aan de Wiel, *The Catholic Church*,
pp. 157-163.

224   CI Report, Westmeath, April 1918, CO/904/105; CI Report, Roscommon,
April 1918, CO/904/106. By September 1918 Westmeath had three branches
with sixty-three members and Roscommon had 130 members in its three

branches (McCarthy, *Cumann na mBan*, p.111). FÉ added an extra branch in
Westmeath, bringing it back up to two (CI Report, Westmeath, May 1918,
CO/904/106). Thomas Costello, in disagreement with the majority of local
witness statements, noted that the threat of conscription did *not* lead to an
influx of new recruits (BMHWS No. 1,296, Thomas Costello, p. 2).

225 *WI*, 27 April 1918; CI Report, Westmeath, May 1918, CO/904/106;
       WI, 8 June 1918; *IT*, 13 July 1918; *WI*, 3 August 1918; *IT*, 7 August 1918;
       WI, 17 August 1918; *IT*, 24 August 1918; *WI*, 31 August 1918; CI Report,
       Westmeath, September 1918, CO/904/107; *IT*, 4 September 1918; *WI*,
       14 September 1918.

226 Emmet O'Connor, *Syndicalism in Ireland, 1917-1923* (Cork, 1988), pp. 22-23.

227 *WI*, 8 June 1918; *WI*, 3 August 1918; *WI*, 17 August 1918; *WI*, 31 Aug 1918;
       WI, 25 January 1919.

228 *The Voice of Labour*, 24 Aug, 1918.

229 BMHWS No. 1,336, Patrick Lennon, p. 2; BMHWS No. 1,309, Francis
       O'Connor p. 6.

230 BMHWS No. 1,309, Francis O'Connor p. 5; Augusteijn, *Public Defiance*, p. 203.

231 *WI*, 20 April 1918; *II*, 29 April 1918.

232 *IT*, 23 April 1918; *II*, 24 April 1918.

233 *WI*, 27 April 1918; *WI*, 18 May 1918.

234 *IT*, 22 April 1918.

235 There had been violent encounters at some meetings (IG Report, April 1918,
       CO/904/105).

236 Augusteijn, *Public Defiance*, p. 77.

237 *WI*, 27 April 1918.

238 Hennessey, *Dividing Ireland*, p. 231; Augusteijn, *Public Defiance*, p. 75.

239 Fitzpatrick, *Two Irelands*, p. 72.

240 Laffan, *Resurrection of Ireland*, p. 136; Augusteijn, *Public Defiance*, p. 257.

241 Ward, 'Lloyd George', p. 114.

242 *Hansard 5 Commons*, cv, 363 (16 April 1918).

243 Townshend, *Easter 1916*, p. 339.

244 Hennessey, *Dividing Ireland,* p. 228.

245 Fergus Campbell, *The Irish Establishment, 1879-1914* (Oxford, 2009), p. 179.

246 *Hansard 5 Commons*, cv, 363 (16 April 1918). J.P. Hayden was in attendance,
       voting with Dillon.

247 *II*, 22 April 1918.

248 *WI*, 4 May 1918; *WI*, 18 May 1918.

249 *IT*, 10 June 1918.

250 *TL*, 15 June 1918. Moran believed that Dillon did not ask for his resignation,
       or that of Stephen Gwynn, due to the recognition that he would not be able
       to find anyone to fill the seats (*TL*, 3 August 1918). Gwynn held opinions
       similar to Nugent on army recruitment, naively believing that neither he
       nor Nugent 'would lose for having spoken out their minds to Ireland' (*WE*,
       5 October 1918).

251 *IT*, 20 July 1918; *TL*, 3 August 1918.

252 *IT*, 20 July 1918.

253   Horne, 'Our war', p. 12.

254   *WI*, 25 May 1918; *WE*, 25 May 1918.

255   *WI*, 22 June 1918. The contest saw Coen compete against SF's Hugh O'Neill.
      Coen dealt with the 'false' allegations levelled against him, while O'Neill
      attempted to interrupt Coen's rebuttal so as to, at least according to the
      J.P. Hayden-controlled *Westmeath Examiner*, not allow the chairman to air the
      truth. Coen produced much to back up his claims of having signed the pledge
      and offered a cash reward to anyone who could prove otherwise. The editor of
      the *Westmeath Examiner* observed that O'Neill must not have been a 'persona
      grata', as his ownership of 1,000 acres in the county should have disqualified
      him as being a good SF candidate. In a rather partisan statement, O'Neill
      was described as a 'demagogue, who was now stretching out his hand to
      grasp the chair of the Council in the name of Sinn Féin' (*WE*, 22 June 1918).
      The *Westmeath Independent* also highlighted O'Neill's weakness as a candidate,
      while making clear its opposition to Coen (*WI*, 22 June 1918). Coen won
      by eleven votes to eight, with a rather important six abstentions, including
      Thomas Chapman, who may not have wished to drive the wedge any further
      into the council (*WI*, 22 June 1918; *WE*, 22 June 1918). Similar, if less dramatic,
      scenes had been witnessed at the Athlone PLG upon Robert Smyth's refusal to
      sign the pledge (*WI*, 4 May 1918).

256   *WI*, 11 May 1918; *WI*, 25 May 1918.

257   McConville, *Political Prisoners*, p. 624.

258   *WI*, 11 May 1918.

259   Bew, 'Moderate Nationalism', p. 735; *II*, 20 May 1918; *LO*, 25 May 1918; *WI*,
      25 May 1918; BMHWS No. 1,309, Francis O'Connor, p. 9.

260   Hennessey, *Dividing Ireland*, pp. 225-226.

261   Ward, 'Lloyd George', p. 110.

262   *WI*, 25 May 1918.

263   Lyons, 'The new nationalism', p. 236; Costello, *Irish Revolution*, pp. 33-34; Lee,
      Modernisation, p. 158.

264   Murphy, 'The tower of hunger', p. 232.

265   *WI*, 1 June 1918. Athlone PLG also thought the accusations absurd (*IT*,
      29 January 1919).

266   Costello, *Irish Revolution*, pp. 33-34; Townshend, *Easter 1916*, p. 338-339;
      O'Leary and Maume, *Controversial Issues*, p. 70.

267   Fitzpatrick, *Two Irelands*, p. 70.

268   Stubbs, 'Unionists and Ireland', pp. 890-891.

269   O'Leary and Maume, *Controversial Issues*, pp. 67-72; Ward, 'Lloyd George',
      pp. 112-114, 116-117.

270   Athlone was designated a centre under the 'Irish Voluntary Recruitment Scheme'
      (*AC*, 17 August 1918). Nugent chaired meetings of the Westmeath committee
      that sought an additional 500 recruits (*WE*, 31 August 1918; *WE*, 5 October 1918).

271   *WI*, 15 June 1918.

272   Joost Augusteijn, 'Motivation: why did they fight for Ireland? The motivation
      of volunteers in the revolution' in Augusteijn, *Irish Revolution*, p. 114.

273   See F.H.A. Aalen, 'Homes for Irish heroes: Housing under the Irish Land

(Provision for Soldiers and Sailors) Act 1919, and the Irish Sailors' and Soldiers' Land Trust', in *The Town Planning Review*, Vol. 59, No. 3 (July, 1988), pp. 305-323.

274   *WI*, 15 June 1918.

275   *MG*, 3 June 1918; IG Report, June 1918, CO/904/106.

276   Shea, *Voices*, pp. 18-25.

277   Ward, 'Lloyd George', p. 122.

278   Murray, 'Irish cultural nationalism', p. 70.

279   Townshend, *British Campaign*, p. 10; Ward, 'Lloyd George', p. 119-120.

280   O'Leary and Maume, *Controversial Issues*, p. 74. Fitzpatrick, *Politics and Irish Life*, p. 130.

281   IG Report, July 1918, CO/904/106.

282   *II*, 24 June 1918; *WI*, 29 June 1918.

283   CI Report, Westmeath, July 1918, CO/904/106; CI Report, Westmeath, August 1918, CO/904/106.

284   *MG*, 20 August 1918; *II*, 20 August 1918; *WE*, 24 August 1918; *AC*, 24 August 1918; *IT*, 24 August 1918.

285   Coleman, *Longford*, p. 83; CI Report, Roscommon, July 1918, CO/904/106; CI Report Roscommon, August 1918, CO/904/106; IG Report, August 1918, CO/904/106.

286   *II*, 27 July 1918.

287   McManus' had been raided on at least three occasions over the previous nine months with the third raid eliciting a £5 fine for carrying seditious ballads and rebel pictures. The owner refused to pay (CI Report, Westmeath, October 1917, CO/904/104; CI Report, Westmeath, February 1918, CO/904/105; *WI*, 2 February 1918; CI Report, Westmeath, July 1918, CO/904/106; CI Report, Westmeath, August 1918, CO/904/106; *II*, 21 August 1918; *WI*, 24 August 1918).

288   *WI*, 20 July 1918; *WI*, 24 August 1918; McConville, *Political Prisoners*, pp. 630-631. O'Hurley later sent a letter to the UDC thanking them, but declined the position as he could achieve little from prison (*AC*, 31 August 1918; *WI*, 7 September 1918; *II*, 7 September 1918; *IT*, 14 September 1918).

289   IG Report, October 1918, CO/904/107.

290   CI Report, Westmeath, October 1918 CO/904/107.

291   BMHWS No. 1,336, Patrick Lennon, p. 2; BMHWS No. 1,503, Michael McCormack, p. 9; BMHWS No. 1,337, David Daly, p. 6; BMHWS No. 1308, Henry O'Brien, p. 4; BMHWS No. 1,309, Francis O'Connor, p. 6.

292   In Athlone *The Irish Times* described the town as 'beflagged', with revelry throughout the day assisted by music from the Somerset Regiment (*IT*, 12 November 1918). The *Westmeath Independent* described the day's activities as 'good humoured' (*WI*, 16 November 1918).

293   *An tÓglách*, 30 November 1918.

294   'Postal Censorship', Thomas Nunin [sic. Noonan] to Seán O'Hurley, 13 November 1918, CO 904/164, p. 987.

295   IG Report, October 1918, CO/904/107.

296   *WI*, 3 August 1918.

297   The Division had not paid fees for the first time since its inception (*HJ*, October 1918). Athlone's division was still operational in 1919, and the County Board paid affiliation fees, but little activity was seen (4 March 1919, NAI, Ancient Order of Hibernian Biennial Convention Agendas 1913-1919. LOU 13/2/1-2). This situation persisted for the remainder of the period under study (*HJ*, April 1919; *HJ*, June 1919; *HJ*, October 1919; *HJ*, November 1919).

298   Boyce, 'British opinion', p. 591.

299   Boyce, 'British opinion', p. 592.

300   Townshend, *Easter 1916*, p. 342.

301   The numbers entitled to vote increased to two million in 1918, more than twice that of 1910. Men not in property ownership and women over 30 with property were now included (Garvin, *Irish Nationalist Politics*, p. 119).

302   *WI*, 27 July 1918.

303   *WI*, 28 September 1918.

304   IG Report, November 1918, CO/904/107.

305   He had been moved there in early September after being rearrested upon release from Mountjoy in August (BMHWS No. 982, Mrs Alice Ginnell, p. 20; *II*, 3 September 1918). His health suffered and by the time of his official candidacy his captors believed him not to be 'in a normal state of mind' ('Postal Censorship', September 1918, CO 904/164, p. 824). Ginnell was one of just two candidates with Westminster credentials. The other was James O'Meara of South Kilkenny.

306   Weymes was chosen as the IPP candidate by the Westmeath UIL Executive, which was constituted almost entirely of men from the North Westmeath Executive, still chaired by J.P. Hayden. Athlone had no representatives on the committee (or reportedly at the meeting), with Patrick McKenna the only remnant of the South Westmeath Executive. The *Westmeath Independent* noted that no priests were in attendance when the choice was made, but some had sent letters of support (*WE*, 23 November 1918; *WE*, 30 November 1918; *WI*, 30 November 1918).

307   *LO*, 14 September 1918. Boland was a good choice as his grandfather was from Roscommon (Fitzpatrick, *Harry Boland's Irish Revolution*, p. 109).

308   *II*, 30 November 1918.

309   *II*, 26 September 1918.

310   *II*, 29 November 1918.

311   *II*, 4 December 1918; Fitzpatrick, *Harry Boland's Irish Revolution*, p. 111; Jim Maher, *Harry Boland, A Biography* (Cork, 1998), p. 70.

312   Fitzpatrick, *Harry Boland's Irish Revolution*, p. 111; *II*, 2 December 1918; *AC*, 7 December 1918; *Roscommon Messenger*, 7 December 1918. Unsurprisingly, SF did not admit responsibility for the acts. Indeed, some members said they were falsified to blacken their reputation. Ginnell advocated the promotion of SF by decorating prominent walls with their symbols ('Postal Censorship', Laurence Ginnell to Patrick Brett, 13 November 1918, CO 904/164, p. 730).

313   *CT*, 7 December 1918; *II*, 11 December 1918; Fitzpatrick, *Harry Boland's Irish Revolution*, p. 110.

314   *RM*, 14 December 1918.

315   Campbell, 'Social dynamics', p. 195.

316   *WI*, 30 November 1918.

317   The manifesto outlined, amongst other things, the party's plans for abstention
      from Westminster, the creation of a separate assembly and an appeal to the Peace
      Conference to recognise Ireland's independence (Carroll, *Fooled you Again*, p. 89).

318   *WI*, 14 December 1918.

319   Boland had a friend in Lewes prison called Henry O'Hanrahan (Fitzpatrick,
      Harry Boland's Irish Revolution, p. 79).

320   *II*, 25 November 1918. His short speech was followed by a quick getaway
      before the RIC recognised him. In general, a relaxation of the order
      prohibiting meetings made such getaways unnecessary and in most cases,
      orders to arrest wanted men were rescinded if the men were speaking as
      candidates in their own constituency (Maher, *Harry Boland*, p. 69).

321   Fitzpatrick, *Harry Boland's Irish Revolution*, p. 109.

322   Boland's speeches did not vary, regardless of where he canvassed (Maher,
      Harry Boland, p. 69).

323   Lee, *Modernisation*, p. 161.

324   Ó Tuathaigh, 'Nationalist Ireland', pp. 66, 71.

325   'Postal Censorship', Bessie Doyle to Seán O'Hurley, 28 October 1918, CO
      904/164, p. 736; *AC*, 7 December 1918. Mrs Ginnell acted as his election
      agent, by her account the first time a woman had carried out such duties
      (BMHWS No. 982, Mrs Alice Ginnell, p. 21).

326   *II*, 3 December 1918; *II*, 11 December 1918; BMHWS No. 1,296, Thomas
      Costello, p. 4.

327   *WI*, 7 December 1918.

328   *II*, 3 December 1918; *IT*, 3 December 1918.

329   *II*, 3 December 1918.

330   'Press Censorship', 5 December 1918, *Westmeath Independent*, CO 904/166,
      pp. 379-380.

331   *II*, 2 December 1918; *WI*, 7 December 1918; *AC*, 7 December 1918.
      The allegation arose from Weymes' support for J.J. Coen during the
      earlier controversy. Weymes strongly denied the charge, stating that he had
      subscribed £35 to the anti-conscription fund and gifted the use of one of his
      stores to the local defence committee (*AC*, 14 December 1918).

332   His warders believed that 'he is making every effort to direct the ... campaign
      from the prison' ('Postal Censorship', November 1918, CO 904/164, p. 728).

333   Ginnell complained that his post was not reaching him in jail and that
      letters sent by him to Boland were intercepted (*II*, 29 November 1918).
      He sarcastically noted that letters asking Boland to send on his thanks to
      his constituents 'were dangerous to small nations and to the great cause of
      making the world safe for democracy.' He signed off, for the benefit of his
      captors: 'Yours in the unconquerable cause, Laurence Ginnell, Poisonous
      Insect' ('Postal Censorship', Laurence Ginnell to 6 Harcourt St (SF offices),
      18 November 1918, CO 904/164, p. 978).

334   *II*, 19 November 1918; 'Republican Suspects', Arthur Griffith, CO
      904/202/175, p. 69. For a complete transcript see ('Postal Censorship',

November 1918, CO 904/164, p. 729).

335   *AC*, 7 December 1918.

336   Nugent had stated that he did not intend to 'make a personal canvas'
given the absence of supportive machinery (*WE*, 23 November 1918).
The declaration led some to believe that he was pulling out from the race; to
allay such fears, he toured the constituency by car ('Postal Censorship', James
King to Laurence Ginnell, 17 November 1918, CO 904/164, p. 979; 'Postal
Censorship', Alice Ginnell to Laurence Ginnell, 23 November 1918 CO
904/164, p. 981; *AC*, 14 December 1918).

337   *WI*, 30 November 1918; *WI*, 12 December 1918.

338   *WE*, 23 November 1918; *II*, 23 November 1918; *WE*, 30 November 1918; *WE*,
7 December 1918; *WE*, 14 December 1918.

339   *MC*, 14 December 1918.

340   *WE*, 23 November 1918.

341   IG Report, December 1918, CO/904/107.

342   Laffan, *Resurrection of Ireland*, p. 167.

343   *WI*, 21 December 1918. Thomas Chapman believed that the men's
imprisonment was instrumental in ensuring a positive outcome and that
their 'hearts would be full of gladness' if they had witnessed the support
(Thomas Chapman to Seán O'Hurley, 17 December 1918, CO 904/164,
p. 1028). Chapman was attempting to raise O'Hurley's spirits as it had
become clear that continued imprisonment was increasingly psychologically
debilitating. His captors referred to O'Hurley as 'rather a morose character'
('Postal Censorship', October 1918, CO 904/164, p. 837). O'Hurley relayed
to Chapman that 'whatever prospect we may have had of getting out has
receded into the limbs of uncertainty … instead … the advisability of
taking some steps that may terminate either in our release from here or
from the sphere of mundane things altogether [must be considered]' ('Postal
Censorship', Seán O'Hurley to Thomas Chapman, 11 December 1918,
CO 904/164, p. 914). He had previously written that: 'I believe it would
be best for Ireland if we were kept here for the next 20 years, and I for
one am prepared to stay' ('Postal Censorship', Seán O'Hurley to T. Harris,
18 November 1918, CO 904/164, p. 986).

344   *WI*, 4 January 1919. Roscommon results: Boland 10,685; Hayden 4,233.
Westmeath results: Ginnell 12,435; Weymes 3,458; Nugent 603 (Brian M. Walker
(ed.), *Parliamentary Election Results in Ireland 1801-1922* (Dublin, 1978), pp. 396, 398).

345   *TL*, 4 January 1919.

346   Fitzpatrick, *Politics and Irish Life*, p. 101; McConnel, 'The Franchise Factor',
p. 372; Augusteijn, *Public Defiance*, p. 259.

347   *WI*, 21 December 1918; 'Postal Censorship', Thomas Chapman to Seán
O'Hurley, 17 December 1918, CO 904/164, p. 1028.

348   Lorcan Robins to L. Ginnell 4 February 1919, CO 904/164, p. 1183.
Mullingar (North Westmeath) was considered less supportive; Patrick Brett,
SF's local organiser, was not rated highly by Ginnell. Ginnell derogatorily
referred to Mullingar as, 'What a town!' ('Postal Censorship', Laurence
Ginnell to Alice Ginnell, 5 February 1919, CO 904/164, p. 1184). Brett had

provided positive reports on the north of the county and poor reports on Athlone; however, it is clear that he knew very little of Athlone's actual SF support, instead recommending, somewhat oddly, that Ginnell talk to the imprisoned O'Hurley about it ('Postal Censorship', Patrick Brett to Laurence Ginnell, 14 November 1918, CO 904/164, p. 980).

349 Jasper Tully refused to do work for Ginnell due to the latter's desertion of Tully during the 1917 North Roscommon by-election. The APW carried out Ginnell's election work ('Postal Censorship', Laurence Ginnell (nephew) to Laurence Ginnell, 17 November 1918, CO 904/164, p. 979).

350 'Postal Censorship', Thomas Chapman to L. Ginnell, 11 January 1919, CO 904/164, p. 1076.

351 *WI*, 21 December 1918.

352 See McConnel, 'The franchise factor', pp. 368-377.

353 Collins, 'Irish Labour', pp. 144-145.

354 Lyons, 'The new nationalism', p. 239; *WI*, 14 December 1918.

355 *AtÓ*, 15 August 1918.

356 BMHWS No. 1,296, Thomas Costello, p. 4; BMHWS No. 1,336, Patrick Lennon p. 3.

357 In Athlone the weekly payout totalled £502 during 1918 (*AC*, 5 January 1918, *IT*, 5 January 1918). The end of the war had not meant that Irishmen in the army returned home. Given the political climate, 'the Cabinet had recognised the danger involved in expecting Irish soldiers to aid the civil power against their fellow countrymen' (Fitzpatrick, *Politics and Irish Life*, p. 23).

358 BMHWS No. 1,504, Seamus O'Meara, p. 14.

359 Lee, *Modernisation*, p. 160.

360 BMHWS No. 1,336, Patrick Lennon, p. 3; BMHWS No. 1,503, Michael McCormack, p. 9.

361 The flu had spread to Ireland during 1918 via traders from French ports (Stewart, *The Shape of Irish History*, pp. 170-1). The first reports of the virus in Athlone came in June 1918, when the *Irish Independent* reported that 200 AWM workers were afflicted (*II*, 27 June 1918; *IT*, 29 June 1918). The spread slowed for a time but by late October the virus had become' widespread (*II*, 28 October 1918; *IT*, 28 October 1918; *II*, 30 October 1918; *IT*, 31 October 1918). Its contagious nature led to dances being cancelled, with children, the clergy and shopkeepers badly affected due to their regular interaction with others (*IT*, 5 November 1918; *IT*, 7 November 1918; *II*, 27 November 1918; *II*, 2 December 1918; *II*, 6 December 1918; *II*, 7 December 1918; *IT*, 7 December 1918).

362 Maher, *Harry Boland*, p. 70.

363 PRONI, T/2782/29 Cecilia H. Daniels to Mrs Flett, Australia, 21 September 1918.

364 PRONI, T/2782/31 Cecilia H. Daniels to Mrs Flett, Australia, 3 December 1918.

365 Shea, *Voices*, p. 24.

366 Tom Garvin, *1922: The Birth of Irish Democracy* (Dublin, 1996), p. 39. There had been a move to redefine the IV/IRA after the First World War ended;

they now had to fight for Irish liberty (Peter Hart, *The IRA at War: 1916-1923* (Oxford, 2003), pp. 95, 103).

367   Campbell, *Land and Revolution*, p. 236.

368   'Postal Censorship', James King to Laurence Ginnell, December 1918, CO 904/164, p. 1027.

369   Lee, *Modernisation*, p. 160.

370   Lee, *Modernisation*, p. 161.

371   *HJ*, October 1919.

372   *RM*, 21 December 1918; Augusteijn, *Public Defiance*, pp. 82-83. Skirmishes were witnessed at polling centres in South Roscommon. SF flags and bunting were torn down and trampled upon by Hayden's supporters, and a contingent of IV men 'put the Party men to flight.' Boland's supporters demanded the right to secure the boxes (with RIC supervision) in which voting cards were deposited, and were granted the concession by The O'Connor Don, Roscommon sub-sheriff (*LO*, 21 December 1918).

373   *WI*, 4 January 1919.

374   Stubbs, 'Unionists and Ireland', p. 891.

375   Lee, *Modernisation*, p. 162; Hennessey, *Dividing Ireland*, pp. 228-229.

376   *TL*, 4 January 1919.

377   *New Leader*, 15 November 1921.

378   *IT*, 30 December 1918.

379   *II*, 6 January 1919; *IT*, 6 January 1919.

380   Fitzpatrick, *Harry Boland's Irish Revolution*, p. 112.

381   *II*, 31 December 1918; *WI*, 4 January 1919.

382   Numerous meetings were held nationwide promoting the men's release. The Athlone meeting on 5 January saw IPP and SF supporters march side-by-side, while recently installed SF branch president Owen Sweeney spoke of the prisoners' plight. He noted that O'Hurley had done much for the cause and despite ill health (Alice Ginnell believed that O'Hurley was in terminal decline), he had never asked for mercy from the British (*WI*, 4 January 1919; *WI*, 11 January 1919). Workers in the APW and the UDC petitioned for his release (*II*, 3 January 1919; AHL, Minute Book of Athlone UDC, 8 January 1919).

383   *II*, 31 December 1918; *WI*, 4 January 1919.

384   Boland did not remain in Ireland. He criticised the League of Nations and President Woodrow Wilson (Ginnell counselled against censuring Wilson until it was apparent what would come out of the Peace Conference), and at Dáil level mostly 'confined himself to insisting that all documents be issued in English as well as Irish, attending to the interests of prisoners ... and seconding the nomination of Collins as Secretary for Finance' (Fitzpatrick, *Harry Boland's Irish Revolution*, p. 118-121).

385   IG Report, January 1919, CO/904/108.

386   *WI*, 25 January 1919.

CHAPTER 6

1   PRONI, T/2782/33, Cecilia H. Daniels to Mrs Flett, Australia, 20 January 1919.

2   Costello, *Irish Revolution*, p. 41; Arthur Mitchell, *Revolutionary Government in Ireland: Dáil Éireann 1919-22* (Dublin, 1995), pp. 18, 66-67.

3   Two RIC men providing security for a gelignite shipment were killed by IV, who stole the explosive (Kevin Haddick Flynn, 'Soloheadbeg: What really happened?' *History Ireland*, Vol. 5, No. 1 (Spring, 1997), pp. 43-46).

4   *WI*, 25 January 1919; Townshend, *Easter 1916*, p. 343.

5   Charles Townshend, 'The Irish Republican Army and the development of guerrilla warfare, 1916-21', in *The English Historical Review*, Vol. 94, No. 371 (1979), p. 321; Valiulis, *Portrait*, pp. 38-40; Hart, *IRA at War*, p. 63; Bew, 'Moderate nationalism', pp. 737-739.

6   MA, RO/563-566, Athlone Brigade, Miltary Service Pensions Records.

7   Shea, *Voices*, p. 27; IG Report, January 1919, CO/904/108.

8   *IT*, 4 February 1919; CI Report, Westmeath, February 1919, CO/904/108; *NG*, 8 February 1919.

9   *IT*, 9 April 1919; *WI*, 12 April 1919.

10   Seamus O'Meara, acting OC of the Athlone Brigade during Seán O'Hurley's imprisonment, was also requested to ensure 'some of your officers will put a little more work into it than they usually do' (MA, Collins' Papers, A files, AG to OC Athlone Brigade, 19 February 1919).

11   CI Report, Westmeath, March 1919, CO/904/108; *II*, 28 March 1919; *WI*, 29 March 1919.

12   IG Report, March 1919, CO/904/108.

13   Bew, 'Moderate nationalism', p. 739.

14   O'Hurley was reportedly the only prisoner in Reading doing very poorly (NLI, MS 35,262, Walter Cole to Henry Dixon, 3 January 1919). He was transferred to Birmingham Prison on 27 January as his health deteriorated. He was 'promptly introduced by the other internees to their methods of evading censorship' after initially refusing to pen any notes, and soon sent a letter to Alice Ginnell, via his uncle ('Postal Censorship', February 1919, CO 904/164, p. 1153). She released it to the *Irish Independent*. It detailed that he was 'living under worse conditions than … in Reading. I am confined to a miserable dirty cell, on a hard bed, with nothing to eat but rice and milk. As far as I can make out I was sent here as a sort of punishment. The first day I was locked in an evil smelling box. I broke it open with a stool. I was brought before the governor, who, with some warders, rough-handled me … I do not know what is yet in store for me. I am in very delicate health. If my conditions are not improved immediately, I have threatened to break up everything and anything' (*II*, 7 February 1919; *WI*, 8 February 1919; *II*, 14 February 1919; *WI*, 15 February 1919).

15   *WI*, 8 March 1919; IG Report, March 1919, CO/904/108.

16   O'Hurley wrote that internees crossed the Irish Sea in a gunboat, manned by 'poorly dressed and antiquely armed soldiers', who warned of the possibility

of a German attack. After a night in Holyhead they went to Gloucester, where they were howled at by protestors. Upon imprisonment they were informed that a committee was to hear each man's case. The prevailing belief was that it was a *fait accompli*, and executions were certain. O'Hurley was sent to Reading with sixteen others including Ginnell who, despite his age, inspired 'the youngest amongst us in spirit and daring'. The belief that they were suffering for a great cause helped them endure poor conditions. An escape plan was in its final stages when the death of TD Pierce McCann precipitated their release (*WI*, 29 March 1919; O'Leary and Maume, *Controversial Issues*, p. 80).

17   Mitchell, *Revolutionary Government*, p. 21.

18   Laffan, *Resurrection of Ireland*, p. 307.

19   *IT*, 19 March 1919; 'Press Censorship', CO 904/167, pp. 544-545.

20   F.S.L. Lyons, 'The War of Independence', in Vaughan, *A New History of Ireland VI*, p. 242; Mitchell, *Revolutionary Government*, pp. 32-33, 100-101.

21   Ranelagh, *Short History of Ireland*, p. 191.

22   *WI*, 10 May 1919; *NG*, 10 May 1919; *IT*, 10 May 1919; *The Irishman*, 10 May 1919; CI Report, Westmeath, May 1919, CO/904/109; BMHWS No. 982, Mrs Alice Ginnell, p. 22; 'Republican Suspects', Laurence Ginnell, 11 May 1919, CO 904/202/162, p. 156.

23   'Republican Suspects', Laurence Ginnell, 6 May 1919, CO 904/202/162, p. 185; Mitchell, *Revolutionary Government*, p. 74.

24   *WI*, 10 May 1919.

25   *II*, 10 May 1919.

26   *NYT*, 6 May 1919; *MG*, 6 May 1919; *NYT*, 31 May 1919.

27   *New Ireland*, 10 May 1919.

28   Fitzpatrick, *Harry Boland's Irish Revolution*, p. 426.

29   *WI*, 17 May 1919.

30   They visited Athlone twice; once while heading west and again when returning east. The delegation provided a report on the bayonet charge (*II*, 13 May 1919; *CT*, 17 May 1919; *WI*, 17 May 1919; Mitchell, *Revolutionary Government*, p. 40). One member, Michael J. Ryan, referred to Athlone specifically when he stated that in Ireland 'two thirds of the men, five-sixths of the women … are in favour of the Republic' (*II*, 22 June 1919). IV efforts in connection with the visit saw a warrant issued for Seamus O'Meara, who absconded (BMHWS No. 1,504, Seamus O'Meara, pp. 15-16).

31   *WI*, 17 May 1919.

32   *WI*, 14 June 1919. A speech delivered at Delvin, County Westmeath, saw him receive a four-month sentence (*WI*, 7 June 1919; *TI*, 7 June 1919; *NYT*, 8 June 1919; *Nationality*, 14 June 1919; BMHWS No. 982, Mrs. Alice Ginnell, p. 22; *Hansard 5 Commons,* cxvii, 1401 (7 July 1919)).

33   A warrant for George Sheffield could not be served as he had fled (*WI*, 7 June 1919; 'Republican Suspects', Laurence Ginnell, CO 904/202/162, 2 July 1919, p. 79).

34   His hat was removed for him and his book was seized (*TI*, 7 June 1919).

35   *II*, 4 June 1919.

36   *II*, 6 June 1919; *WI*, 7 June 1919; 'Republican Suspects', Laurence Ginnell,
       CO 904/202/162, 8-11 June 1919, p. 119-121.

37   O'Hurley returned on 19 May (*WI*, 24 May 1919; *WI*, 7 June 1919).

38   Only Sweeney and Dillon appeared; Ginnell's case had been adjourned.
       The case against the TD was eventually dropped. The Solicitor General
       believed that the four months he was serving were adequate punishment
       ('Republican Suspects', Laurence Ginnell, 2 July 1919, CO 904/202/162, p. 79).

39   Burnett's late proscription was repeatedly cited as an aggravating factor.
       The RIC knew of the meeting two weeks before it was held ('Republican
       Suspects', Laurence Ginnell, CO 904/202/162).

40   *II*, 11 June 1919; 'Republican Suspects', Laurence Ginnell, 6 May 1919, CO
       904/202/162, pp. 185-188.

41   *WI*, 14 June 1919.

42   *II*, 11 June 1919.

43   CI Report, Westmeath, June 1919, CO/904/109; *IT*, 11 June 1919; *WI*,
       14 June 1919; *LO*, 14 June 1919; *WE*, 14 June 1919.

44   Similar rushes were made in Mullingar, Castlepollard, Kilbeggan and Delvin
       (*WI*, 14 June 1919; *Irish Bulletin*, 12 August 1919; Shortt, 'IRA activity in
       Westmeath – part one', p. 177).

45   *WI*, 7 June 1919; *TI*, 21 June 1919. Fr Keane, Drum, asked the UDC to close
       the courthouse. J.J. Coen was unsupportive given the £1,000 contribution
       the army gave in lieu of rates (*II*, 6 June 1919; *IT*, 6 June 1919). When a vote
       was held, the acrimonious meeting (which heard Patrick Henry call for a
       boycott of the RIC and their families) saw Keane's request passed by six votes
       to five (AHL, Minute Book of Athlone UDC, 18 June 1919; *II*, 20 June 1919;
       IT, 20 June 1919). The RIC believed Keane was not representative of local
       clergymen and spent much time spreading 'spite … and vindictiveness against
       all connected with the government … particularly the police' ('Republican
       Suspects', Laurence Ginnell, 9 June 1919, CO 904/202/162, p. 138).

46   AHL, Minute Book of Athlone UDC, 4 June 1919.

47   *IT*, 10 May 1919; *II*, 12 June 1919; *IT*, 12 June 1919; *II*, 13 June 1919; *WE*,
       14 June 1919; 'Republican Suspects', Laurence Ginnell, 14 May 1919, CO
       904/202/162, p. 115. RIC evidence stated that those responsible came
       from 'Athlone Urban' and Coosan (*IT*, 24 May 1919; *IT*, 10 July 1919; *IT*,
       11 July 1919; *LO*, 12 July 1919; *WE*, 12 July 1919; *IT*, 22 August 1919).

48   *WI*, 28 June 1919. Earlier reports noted that local war veterans felt
       ill-treated by the government, but were warmly received in Athlone (*WI*,
       11 January 1919; *WI*, 18 January 1919).

49   CI Report, Westmeath, July 1919, CO/904/109; *II*, 16 July 1919; *WI*,
       19 July 1919; BMHWS No. 1,504, Seamus O'Meara, p. 16.

50   *II*, 5 July 1919; *II*, 19 July 1919; *WI*, 19 July 1919.

51   Richard English, *Armed Struggle: the History of the IRA* (New York, 2003), p. 21.

52   CI Report, Westmeath, July 1919, CO/904/109.

53   English, *Armed Struggle*, p. 21; Augusteijn, *Public Defiance*, pp. 203-209;
       'Republican Suspects', Laurence Ginnell, CO 904/202/162, p. 145.

54   'Republican Suspects', Laurence Ginnell, 8 June 1919, CO 904/202/162, p. 144.

55   Terence Dooley, 'IRA Activity in Kildare during the War of Independence',
      in William Nolan and Thomas McGrath (eds), *Kildare: History and Society:
      Interdisciplinary Essays on the History of an Irish County* (Dublin, 2006), p. 628.

56   Shea, *Voices*, p. 34.

57   *II*, 21 July 1919; Jane Leonard, 'Survivors', in Horne, *Our War*, p. 214.

58   *SI*, 20 July 1919; *WI*, 26 July 1919.

59   'Republican Suspects', Laurence Ginnell, 14 July 1919, CO 904/202/162, p. 128.

60   CI Report, Westmeath, September 1919, CO/904/110.

61   *WI*, 12 July 1919; *WI*, 19 July 1919; *WI*, 26 July 1919; *WI*, 2 August 1919;
      WI, 9 August 1919; *WI*, 16 August 1919; *WI*, 30 August 1919; *WI*,
      6 September 1919.

62   *IT*, 5 September 1919; *II*, 5 September 1919; *WI*, 6 September 1919; *LO*,
      13 September 1919; CI Report, Westmeath, October 1919, CO/904/110.
      Ginnell, when writing to friend and solicitor Henry Dixon, related that his
      latest imprisonment was 'more severe on my nervous system then any before'
      (NLI, MS 35,262/1, Laurence Ginnell to Henry Dixon, 15 August 1919; MS
      35,262/1, Laurence Ginnell to Henry Dixon, 26 August 1919).

63   Hart, *IRA at War*, p. 84; *WI*, 20 September 1919.

64   Foster, *Modern Ireland*, p. 495

65   Arthur Mitchell, 'Alternative government: "exit Britannia" – the formation of
      the Irish national state. 1918-21', in Augusteijn, *Irish Revolution*, p. 75.

66   Lyons, 'The War of Independence', p. 243; Mitchell, *Revolutionary Government*, p. 47.

67   *WI*, 13 September 1919; *IT*, 13 September 1919; *MG*, 13 September 1919.

68   O'Meara was released in the second week of October. He had demanded
      political status, went on hunger strike and smashed his cell furniture (*MG*,
      15 October 1919; *IT*, 15 October 1919; *WI*, 18 October 1919; BMHWS No. 1,504,
      Seamus O'Meara, p. 16). Harney was released a week later (*WI*, 25 October 1919).

69   CI Report, Westmeath, September 1919, CO/904/110; IG Report,
      October 1919, CO/904/110.

70   BMHWS No. 701, Thomas Kelly, p. 2.

71   Michael Hopkinson, 'Negotiation: The Anglo-Irish War and revolution',
      in Augusteijn, *Irish Revolution*, p. 122.

72   *WI*, 13 September 1919. McDermott-Hayes believed that such dissent played
      into Unionist hands.

73   Valiulis, *Portrait*, p. 41; *IT*, 30 October 1919. O'Farrell, who refused to
      recognise the court, was acquitted when the police were unable to prove
      the documents were his property – his lodgings had numerous boarders
      (*IB*, 18 October 1919; *WI*, 25 October 1919; *II*, 30 October 1919; *WI*,
      1 November 1919; *IB*, 1 November 1919).

74   Townshend, 'Irish Republican Army', pp. 324-325; BMHWS No. 1,336,
      Patrick Lennon, p. 5; BMHWS No. 1,500, Anthony McCormack, p. 6;
      BMHWS No. 701, Thomas Kelly, p. 7; BMHWS No. 1,296, Thomas Costello,
      p. 5; BMHWS No. 1,503, Michael McCormack, p. 12. Rifles were difficult to
      source, with revolvers and shotguns more easily procured. Good ammunition
      was scarce. Some fashioned their own buckshot (which was susceptible
      to damp), and incendiaries (BMHWS No. 1,296, Thomas Costello, p. 28).

Seamus O'Meara stated that regular weapons purchases with soldiers were not countenanced: 'It was felt that a dribble of arms ... would not be noticed' (BMHWS No. 1,504, Seamus O'Meara, pp. 12-13).

75   BMHWS No. 1,503, Michael McCormack, pp. 12-13; BMHWS No. 580, John Duffy, p. 14; BMHWS No. 1,296, Thomas Costello, p. 13. Both McCormack and Duffy specifically mention Thomas Keaveney, who was indicted, though found innocent, of buying weapons from soldiers (*II*, 13 January 1920; *IT*, 13 January 1920; *FJ*, 23 January 1920; *II*, 23 January 1920; *IT*, 23 January 1920).

76   The Gordon Highlanders clashed with residents on 8 November. The *Irish Bulletin* reported that the soldiers 'demolished premises', while it appears that the damage was actually limited to broken windows. The incident made the pages of the *Manchester Guardian*, which stated that the soldiers were chased into their barracks by people wielding 'tongs, pokers and sticks' (*MG*, 10 November 1919; *II*, 10 November 1919; *IT*, 10 November 1919; *IB*, 14 November 1919; *NG*, 15 November 1919).

77   Mitchell, *Revolutionary Government*, p. 72.

78   PRONI, T/2782/34, Cecilia H. Daniels to Mrs Flett, Australia, 20 November 1919.

79   O'Leary and Maume, *Controversial Issues*, pp. 86-90; Richard Murphy, 'Walter Long and the making of the Government of Ireland Act, 1919-20', in *Irish Historical Studies*, Vol. 25, No. 97 (May, 1986), p. 83.

80   *WI*, 18 October 1919.

81   CI Report, Westmeath, November 1919, CO/904/110; *WI*, 1 November 1919.

82   *WI*, 27 December 1919.

83   The members' sex meant they were unlikely to be subjected to searches by Crown forces, while their familial links meant they were trusted by republicans (McCarthy, *Cumann na mBan*, p. 121). Local members were used for carrying memos and organising fundraisers (BMHWS No. 1,503, Michael McCormack, p. 33; BMHWS No. 1,336, Patrick Lennon, p. 12).

84   Townshend, *British Campaign*, pp. 24-27.

85   Townshend, *British Campaign*, p. 24.

86   Laffan, *Resurrection of Ireland*, p. 309.

87   Fitzpatrick, *Politics and Irish Life*, p. 137.

88   *WI*, 1 November 1919. Information on the new system was published in the *Westmeath Independent*, and public information sessions were held in Longworth Hall.

89   *WI*, 3 January 1920.

90   *WI*, 10 January 1920.

91   O'Connor, *Syndicalism*, p. 23.

92   NLI, MS 7282, ITGWU, List of Branches in Chronological Order. Westmeath was one of the slowest counties to form branches and was part of an unenthusiastic north Leinster belt (ITGWU, List of Branches; Foster, *Modern Ireland*, pp. 442-443; Fitzpatrick, 'Geography of Irish nationalism', pp. 128-130).

93   *WI*, 3 May 1919.

94   NLI, ITGWU, List of Branches; *WI*, 8 March 1919; *WI*, 3 May 1919; *WI*, 18 October 1919; *WI*, 8 November 1919.

95   *WI*, 8 March 1919; *WI*, 7 June 1919. See Francis Costello, 'Labour,
      Irish republicanism, and the social order during the Anglo-Irish War',
      in *The Canadian Journal of Irish Studies*, Vol. 17, No. 2 (December, 1991), pp. 1–22.

96   O'Farrell appeared unconcerned by the prospect of a Labour win.
      He wanted to see the 'end of [M.J.] Hughes and Co. … any change there
      [the UDC] would be a change for the better' ('Postal Censorship', Seán
      O'Farrell to Seán O'Hurley, 7 February 1919, CO 904/164, p. 1154).

97   *TVL*, 1 May 1919.

98   CI Report, Westmeath, January 1920, CO/904/111.

99   *WI*, 10 January 1920; *WI*, 17 January 1920.

100   *WI*, 29 November 1919.

101   Costello, *Irish Revolution*, p. 151.

102   Arthur Mitchell, *Labour in Irish Politics, 1890-1930; the Irish Labour Movement in
      an Age of Revolution* (Dublin, 1974), pp. 122–123.

103   The national average was 72 per cent (Mitchell, *Revolutionary Government*, p. 123).

104   The Ratepayers Representatives were former IPP supporters such as
      J.J. Coen and O.J. Dolan (*WI*, 10 January 1920; *FJ*, 17 January 1920; *II*,
      17 January 1920; *IT*, 17 January 1920; *FJ*, 19 January 1920; *II*, 19 January 1920;
      IT, 19 January 1920).

105   'Republican Suspects', Laurence Ginnell, CO 904/202/162, p. 139.

106   *WI*, 10 January 1920.

107   *WI*, 24 January 1920.

108   Laffan, *Resurrection of Ireland*, p. 325.

109   *Watchword of Labour*, 20 December 1919; *The Watchword*, 17 January 1920; *WI*,
      7 February 1920; Mitchell, *Labour*, p. 123.

110   *TW*, 24 January 1920; *TW*, 31 January 1920. The *Watchword* detailed the
      cowardice of the two SF members in not putting themselves forward and
      then abstaining from the vote which saw a Labour candidate take on Coen.
      'Soviet wanted for Athlone', ran the headline for a piece which decried Coen
      as 'one of the worst pro-Imperialists in Ireland' (*TW*, 7 February 1920).

111   AHL, Minute Book of Athlone UDC, 5 May 1920.

112   Townshend, *British Campaign*, p. 67; Foster, *Modern Ireland*, p. 497; *WI*,
      24 January 1920.

113   Fitzpatrick, 'Geography of Irish nationalism', p. 125.

114   Hart, *IRA at War*, p. 53.

115   Fitzpatrick, 'Geography of Irish nationalism', p. 123.

116   *II*, 3 June 1920; *AC*, 5 June 1920; BMHWS No. 1,503, Michael McCormack,
      p. 20. The council elected its 'first Republican chairman', while the vice
      chairman, SF's Henry O'Brien, gave 'honour to Labour' in his acceptance
      speech. As a symbolic act (seen elsewhere - Coleman, *Longford*, p. 92; *IB*,
      9 February 1920) the 1916 Minute Book had the resolution condemning
      the Rising excised and burned. The Council also co-opted Seán O'Hurley
      (*II*, 18 June 1920). The *Irish Bulletin* believed that most Labour candidates in
      Westmeath were 'Republican Labour' (Mitchell, *Revolutionary Government*, p. 126).

117   *FJ*, 8 June 1920; *WI*, 12 June 1920. Labour was poorly organised in rural areas
      and invariably supported SF outside of the towns and cities (Mitchell, *Labour*,

pp. 127-128). Owen Sweeney was elected vice-chairman of RDC1. There were reports that 'masked men' had forced one RDC incumbent not to run (*IT*, 15 May 1920; *II*, 20 May 1920).

118 Only two members of the thirty-seven-strong board had previously been Guardians. All claimed to be SF supporters. The board elected Cumann na mBan member Bridget Reynolds as Vice-Chair (*IT*, 8 June 1920; *WI*, 19 June 1920; *WI*, 3 July 1920; *IB*, 19 July 1920).

119 O'Leary and Maume, *Controversial Issues*, p. 85. Moles stated: 'Of the 31 members of the Westmeath County Council, 19 are Sinn Feiners and there is not one Nationalist. Athlone No. 1 is Sinn Fein, and so is Athlone No. 2' (*Hansard 5 Commons*, cxxx, 1186-1187 (15 June 1920)).

120 In the case of the County Council, P.J. Weymes was a prominent, solitary dissenter. The PLG declared in mid-June while RDC1 declared by mid-July (*WI*, 19 June 1920; *WI*, 17 July 1920).

121 Mitchell, *Revolutionary Government*, p. 160.

122 *WI*, 19 June 1920; *WI*, 3 July 1920.

123 *WI*, 7 August 1920; *WI*, 21 August 1920; *WI*, 4 September 1920.

124 Fitzpatrick, *Politics and Irish Life*, p. 141.

125 Townshend, *British Campaign*, p. 68; Mitchell, *Revolutionary Government*, p. 159.

126 Garvin, *1922*, p. 68.

127 AHL, Minute Book of Athlone UDC, 22 September 1920; *WI*, 2 October 1920.

128 Athlone RDC1 had acted similarly (*WI*, 18 September 1920).

129 *WI*, 16 October 1920; Mitchell, *Labour*, p. 129.

130 Mary E. Daly, *The Buffer State: the Historical Roots of the Department of the Environment* (Dublin, 1997), pp. 58-60. For a local example see UCDA, Mulcahy Papers, P7/A/17, 30 March 1921.

131 BMHWS No. 1,503, Michael McCormack, pp. 20-21; Coleman, *Longford*, p. 95; *WG*, 17 December 1920.

132 *WE*, 4 December 1920; *FJ*, 7 December 1920; *WG*, 10 December 1920; *WE*, 11 December 1920.

133 Mitchell, *Revolutionary Government*, p. 231. The DLG blamed the financial difficulties on the Westmeath rate collectors. It told the council to appoint the National Bank as treasurer (*WG*, 21 January 1921).

134 *WI*, 16 October 1920; *IT*, 15 November 1920; *II*, 16 November 1920. Guardians' efforts to secure £6,000 from the National Bank failed (*FJ*, 14 March 1921; *II*, 26 May 1921; *FJ*, 26 May 1921).

135 Garvin, *1922*, p. 72.

136 UCDA, Mulcahy Papers, P7/A/17, 11 March 1921.

137 An LGB auditor had, with Crown forces' assistance, seized the accounts of both Athlone RDCs and the PLG. His work was carried out under armed guard and the books were kept in the army barracks (*II*, 13 January 1921; *II*, 15 January 1921; Mitchell, *Revolutionary Government*, p. 235).

138 *II*, 4 March 1921; *II*, 26 March 1921; *Midland Reporter and Westmeath Nationalist*, 14 April 1921; *WG*, 13 April 1920).

139 Daly, *Buffer State*, p. 54.

140   It was noted that members did not rescind a previous motion severing ties with the LGB, but were assured by the clerk that their new resolution was valid (*WG*, 13 April 1920).

141   Garvin, *1922*, p. 84.

142   It had been requested that republicans who were unable to attend would resign their seats. This could then allow others who were better able to meet the obligations of the post maintain the SF line. This happened in just a few cases (NAI, DELG 30/11, Department of Environment and Local Government Files, 15 June 1921).

143   Daly, *Buffer State*, p. 75; Mitchell, *Revolutionary Government*, p. 159.

144   Daly, *Buffer State*, p. 75.

145   Garvin, *1922*, pp. 77-81.

146   NAI, DELG 30/11, Department of Environment and Local Government Files, 15 June 1921.

147   NAI, DELG 30/11; *IT*, 25 June 1921; *II*, 25 May 1921; *FJ*, 15 June 1921; *II*, 20 June 1921. Ballymahon Union threatened to send away 'tramps' that were referred to it by the Athlone PLG, which owed £2,000 to its Longford equivalent (*FJ*, 27 July 1921).

148   *II*, 16 August 1921; *AC*, 20 August 1921; *NG*, 20 August 1921.

149   Lee, *Modernisation*, p. 128.

150   Fergus Campbell and Kevin O'Shiel, 'The last land war? Kevin O'Shiel's memoir of the Irish revolution (1916-21)', in *Archivium Hibernicum*, Vol. 57 (2003), pp. 160-161. Contemporary articles label the courts variously as 'Parish Courts', 'Sinn Féin courts' or 'Dáil courts', a fact that highlights the 'carelessness with which the terms Sinn Féin and Dáil Éireann were applied' during the period (Fitzpatrick, *Politics and Irish Life*, p. 165).

151   *WI*, 29 May 1920. 'People's Land Courts' were seen during May and it was related that the courts' 'judgement[s] [are] as binding and irrevocable as the laws of the Church ... decision[s] made can be enforced with an authority there is no escaping' (*WI*, 22 May 1920).

152   *IT*, 22 May 1920.

153   *WI*, 12 June 1920.

154   Campbell and O'Shiel, 'The last land war?', p. 161; Laird, *Subversive Law*, p. 114.

155   Mitchell, *Revolutionary Government*, p. 131; *IT*, 22 May 1920.

156   *WI*, 5 June 1920.

157   *WI*, 5 June 1920; *IB*, 17 June 1920.

158   Mitchell, *Revolutionary Government*, p. 140. Generally the courts were administered by local republicans and clergy without legal training, while claimants were often represented by solicitors. Minor grievances were heard by the three-man parish court, appeals by the five-man district court, and intractable cases were dealt with by a qualified lawyer who operated a circuit court (Oonagh Walsh, *Ireland's Independence, 1880-1923* (London, 2002), pp. 60-61).

159   *WI*, 26 June 1920.

160   As ever, it was hoped that the 'fleeting existence and uneventful eclipse' of previous branches would not be replicated. Over 200 people joined the

branch, which declared its allegiance to Dáil Éireann (*WI*, 26 June 1920; *WI*, 3 July 1920; *WI*, 10 July 1920; *WI*, 24 July 1920).

161   *WI*, 3 July 1920.

162   *IB*, 14 July 1920; *WI*, 31 July 1920; *LO*, 7 August 1920.

163   *IB*, 27 August 1920; Mitchell, *Revolutionary Government*, p. 144.

164   *WI*, 7 August 1920; *WI*, 11 September 1920. The *Irish Bulletin* listed the names of JPs that had forsaken the post (*IB*, 4 August 1920). By the end of October 1920, over one-fifth had resigned (*Hansard 5 Commons*, cxxxiii, 1380W (25 October 1920)).

165   *FJ*, 5 August 1920.

166   *FJ*, 6 August 1920; *WI*, 7 August 1920.

167   CI Report, Westmeath, August 1920, PRO/CO/904.

168   *WI*, 10 July 1920.

169   Laffan, *Resurrection of Ireland*, p. 317-318; Walsh, *Ireland's Independence*, p. 61.

170   Townshend, *British Campaign*, p. 68; Campbell, *Land and Revolution*, pp. 255-256.

171   BMHWS No. 1,309, Francis O'Connor, p. 16.

172   Townshend, *British Campaign*, p. 69.

173   BMHWS No. 701, Thomas Kelly, p. 4; BMHWS No. 1,296, Thomas Costello, p. 7; BMHWS No. 1,336, Patrick Lennon, p. 6; BMHWS No. 1,503, Michael McCormack, p. 11; BMHWS No. 1,337, David Daly, p. 9; BMHWS No. 1,504, Seamus O'Meara, p. 27.

174   *IT*, 8 September 1920.

175   *WI*, 18 September 1920.

176   *AC*, 6 November 1920. Local assizes carried on as 'police cases' kept them busy, nothing unusual for a garrison town (Costello, *Irish Revolution*, p. 62; Fitzpatrick, *Politics and Irish Life*, p. 12).

177   *IT*, 20 September 1920; *II*, 20 September 1920; *MG*, 20 September 1920.

178   *Observer*, 19 September 1920; *MC*, 25 September 1920.

179   Deportations had been ordered in the case of two ex-soldiers accused of robbery (*WI*, 18 September 1920). Seamus O'Meara described IV court work as 'carrying out … decisions, arresting some men and deporting those who needed it' (Seamus O'Meara, 'Some activities in Westmeath: 1920', in *Capuchin Annual 1970* (1970), p. 550).

180   *II*, 20 September 1920; *WI*, 25 September 1920; *AC*, 25 September 1920; *LO*, 25 September 1920; *IB*, 25 September 1920.

181   BMHWS No. 1,504, Seamus O'Meara, p. 27.

182   Mitchell, 'Alternative government', p. 82.

183   Francis Costello, 'The Republican Courts and the decline of British rule in Ireland, 1919-1921', in *Éire-Ireland*, Vol. 25, No. 2 (1990), pp. 36-37, 52-54; Mary Kotsonouris, 'The Courts of Dáil Éireann', in Brian Farrell (ed.), *The Creation of the Dáil: A volume of essays from the Thomas Davis lectures* (Dublin, 1994), pp. 96-98.

184   Peter Hart, 'The Geography of revolution in Ireland, 1917-1923', in *Past and Present*, No. 155 (May, 1997), p. 146.

185   O'Meara, 'Some activities in Westmeath', p. 548.

186 IG Report, February 1920, CO/904/111. Numerous press reports cover the cutting of communications infrastructure and train raids around Athlone during 1920 and 1921, with June 1920 to July 1921 being the most active time for such activity nationally (Fitzpatrick, *Politics and Irish Life*, p. 229).

187 Hart, 'Geography of revolution', p. 165.

188 *WI*, 6 March 1920.

189 *WI*, 6 March 1920.

190 Black and Tan recruitment began in late 1919. The majority were British; Irish representation equalled 16 per cent (W.J. Lowe, 'Who were the Black-and-Tans?', in *History Ireland*, Vol. 12, No. 3 (Autumn, 2004), pp. 47-51).

191 Peter Hart, *The IRA and its Enemies: Violence and Community in Cork 1916-1923* (Oxford, 1998), p. 78.

192 *WI*, 27 March 1920.

193 *WI*, 3 April 1920; *IB*, 3 April 1920.

194 *WI*, 27 March 1920. O'Meara was released after going on hunger strike; 'the prison authorities ... thought that ... I ... [was] going to crack up and they decided to release [me]' (O'Meara, 'Some Activities in Westmeath', p. 549; BMHWS No. 1,504, Seamus O'Meara, pp. 20-23; *CT*, 24 April 1920).

195 *WI*, 16 March 1920; *IB*, 29 March 1920; *NYT*, 30 March 1920; *WI*, 3 April 1920; BMHWS No. 982, Mrs Alice Ginnell, p. 24; *Hansard 5 Commons*, cxxvii, 1388-1389 (12 April 1920). The seemingly indefatigable 67-year-old took twelve months paid leave, moving to Chicago to head up the Labour Bureau for Irish Independence (Dempsey and Boylan, 'Ginnell, Laurence', p. 103; BMHWS No. 982, Mrs Alice Ginnell, pp. 24-25).

196 Bew, 'Moderate nationalism', p. 743.

197 Hopkinson, 'Negotiation', p. 127.

198 *WI*, 3 April 1920.

199 Mitchell, *Revolutionary Government*, pp. 201-202.

200 *FJ*, 20 March 1920. Athlone was also made Divisional HQ for Connacht (*II*, 27 March 1920).

201 *MG*, 20 March 1920.

202 Shea, *Voices*, p. 32.

203 Townshend, 'Irish Republican Army', p. 329.

204 A letter from IV GHQ to Seamus O'Meara queried the reported success of the Athlone Brigade's burning spree; 'you say the barracks were burned to the ground. Could you be more definite and let me know the exact number that were burned?' (MA, Collins' Papers, AG to OC Athlone Brigade, May 1920). Additional efforts were made to ensure the absolute destruction of Creggan barracks (*WI*, 1 May 1920; BMHWS No. 1,504, Seamus O'Meara, p. 19).

205 Augusteijn, *Public Defiance*, p. 97.

206 BMHWS No. 1,296, Thomas Costello, p. 6; BMHWS No. 1,504, Seamus O'Meara, p. 20; Francis J. Costello, 'The Role of Propaganda in the Anglo-Irish War 1919-1921', in *The Canadian Journal of Irish Studies*, Vol. 14, No. 2 (January, 1989), p. 7; Townshend, 'Irish Republican Army', pp. 329-330.

207 Brendan Ashe, 'The development of the IRA's concepts of guerrilla warfare, 1917-1921' (Unpublished PhD thesis, UCC, 1999), p. 64.

208 *II*, 5 April 1920; *FJ*, 6 April 1920; *MG*, 6 April 1920; *IT*, 6 April 1920; *WI*,
10 April 1920; *IT*, 10 April 1920.

209 *WI*, 10 April 1920.

210 Mitchell, *Revolutionary Government*, p. 131; Hart, 'Geography of revolution', p. 164.

211 *WI*, 10 April 1920.

212 *II*, 8 April 1920; *IT*, 8 April 1920; *MG*, 9 April 1920; *FJ*, 9 April 1920.

213 Mitchell, *Labour*, p. 119.

214 It was noted that all shops closed, bar one run by a local unionist. That also
closed after the employees walked out (*II*, 14 April 1920).

215 *WI*, 17 April 1920.

216 Charles Townshend, 'The Irish railway strike of 1920: Industrial action
and civil resistance in the struggle for independence', in *Irish Historical
Studies*, Vol. 22, No. 83 (March, 1979), pp. 265-282; Costello, 'Labour, Irish
republicanism, and the social order', pp. 2-7.

217 SF, ITWGU, ATC, PLG, Westmeath County Council, and the TTL all
supported the railway men. Seán O'Hurley and McDermott-Hayes called
for the separation of Irish and English Labour; the latter, especially the
NUR, had deserted the men (*WI*, 12 June 1920; *WI*, 19 June 1920; *WI*,
26 June 1920; *WI*, 3 July 1920; Townshend, 'Irish railway strike', pp. 267-268;
Fred D. Schneider, 'British Labour and Ireland, 1918-1921: The retreat to
Houndsditch', in *The Review of Politics*, Vol. 40, No. 3 (July, 1978), pp. 378-379).
The railway impasse continued for some months. In Athlone numerous rail
workers were arrested or dismissed, with the general public (except farmers)
giving generously to the support fund (*WI*, 5 June 1920; *II*, 22 June 1920;
IT, 23 June 1920; *II*, 28 June 1920; *IT*, 28 June 1920; *FJ*, 28 June 1920;
MG, 28 June 1920; *II*, 29 June 1920; *FJ*, 30 June 1920; *MG*, 30 June 1920;
WI, 3 July 1920; *TNL*, 10 July 1920; *WI*, 10 July 1920; *WI*, 31 July 1920; *FJ*,
2 August 1920; *II*, 7 August 1920). By October a boycott of military men
using the trains saw daily closures and staffing levels fall (*FJ*, 12 October 1920;
II, 12 October 1920; *IT*, 12 October 1920; *II*, 16 October 1920;
II, 19 October 1920; *II*, 20 October 1920; *II*, 21 October 1920; *FJ*,
1 November 1920; *II*, 2 November 1920). Almost daily refusals continued until
the end of the year, when the workers backed down (*FJ*, 2 December 1920;
Costello, 'Labour, Irish republicanism, and the social order', pp. 7-11).

218 *NYT*, 24 May 1920.

219 Fitzpatrick, *Politics and Irish Life*, p. 143. O'Meara, 'Some activities in
Westmeath', p. 549; BMHWS No. 1,504, Seamus O'Meara, pp. 7, 23;
BMHWS No. 1309, Francis O'Connor, p. 13. Tax offices in Meath were also
targeted in mid-May (Coogan, *Meath*, pp. 118-119).

220 *IT*, 14 May 1920; *II*, 14 May 1920; *MG*, 14 May 1920; *II*, 15 May 1920; *WI*,
15 May 1920. The Athlone office dealt with tax information for Westmeath,
Longford, Roscommon and King's County. The same night saw a small
number of sub-offices raided in each of the four counties.

221 *WI*, 29 May 1920.

222 *IB*, 1 May 1920; *IB*, 15 May 1920; *IB*, 5 June 1920; *IB*, 19 June 1920. John Duffy
reported that on occasion, word of an impending raid was sent to the intended

target (BMHWS No. 580, John Duffy, pp. 4–5). Other occasions saw RIC members misdirected by colleagues with republican sympathies (BMHWS No. 1,296, Thomas Costello, p. 29), or carts allowed to pass checkpoints manned by supportive policemen (BMHWS No. 1,500, Anthony McCormack, p. 6).

223 CI Report, Westmeath, June 1920, CO/904/112.

224 It was noted that raiders acted courteously, even promising to return weapons (*WI*, 10 July 1920).

225 Mitchell, *Revolutionary Government*, p. 151.

226 *WI*, 10 July 1920; *IB*, 13 July 1920; *WI*, 17 July 1920; BMHWS No. 1,336, Patrick Lennon, p. 4; BMHWS No. 1308, Henry O'Brien, p. 9. The RIC had abandoned both Lecarrow and Knockcroghery in south Roscommon, leaving the policing in the hands of the IV (*WI*, 26 June 1920). The Athlone IV forcibly ejected RIC members from public houses after hours (O'Meara, 'Some Activities in Westmeath', p. 550; BMHWS No. 1,504, Seamus O'Meara, p. 27). Abandoned houses in rural areas, referred to as 'unknown destinations', were used to detain suspected transgressors (BMHWS No. 1,503, Michael McCormack, p. 11; BMHWS No. 1,296, Thomas Costello, p. 7).

227 *WI*, 10 July 1920.

228 It was also destroyed along with barracks in Streamstown, Glasson and Littleton (CI Report, Westmeath, July 1920, CO/904/112; *WI*, 10 July 1920; CI Report, Westmeath, August 1920, CO/904/112; BMHWS No. 1,500, Anthony McCormack, p. 6; BMHWS No. 1,337, David Daly, p. 13.

229 CI Report, Westmeath, July 1920, CO/904/112.

230 *FJ*, 18 August 1920; *FJ*, 20 August 1920; *WI*, 21 August 1920.

231 The ATC received a letter from Colonel Challoner, which stated that the incidents referred to had occurred after midnight and were highly suspicious. Law-abiding people, he reasoned, conducted business during the day and did not act 'stealthily' near army installations (*IT*, 1 September 1920; *WI*, 4 September 1920).

232 *WI*, 21 August 1920; Francis Costello, 'Lloyd George and Ireland, 1919–1921: An uncertain policy', in *The Canadian Journal of Irish Studies*, Vol. 14, No. 1 (July, 1988), p. 11.

233 Mitchell, *Revolutionary Government*, p. 76.

234 CI Report, Westmeath, August 1920, CO/904/112.

235 Shea, *Voices*, pp. 30–31.

236 Shea, *Voices*, p. 37.

237 The *Irish Bulletin* printed lists of retiring RIC men to foster the impression of a trend towards leaving the force (*IB*, 10 July 1920; *IB*, 4 August 1920).

238 Fitzpatrick, *Politics and Irish Life*, p. 3.

239 *WI*, 24 July 1920; *WI*, 31 July 1920; *WI*, 7 August 1920.

240 *WI*, 17 July 1920; *WI*, 14 August 1920.

241 UCDA, Mulcahy Papers, P7/A/17, 20 July 1920. Seamus O'Meara stated that there were two RIC men in Athlone who 'were in touch with Michael Collins as intelligence agents' (O'Meara, 'Some activities in Westmeath', p. 553).

242 This was a term used in *An tÓglách* to describe raids, road cutting and similar, usually non-fatal activities (*AtÓ*, 1 May 1920).

243 The acronym now more commonly used after IV members were requested to swear an oath to the Republic. Some in Athlone refused the oath: 'These were generally the old men … It was not that they were not loyally disposed … but rather that they did not like taking an oath in a secret organisation.' Those who refused generally stood down (BMHWS No. 1,336, Patrick Lennon, p. 4; BMHWS No. 1,503, Michael McCormack, p. 10; BMHWS No. 1,296, Thomas Costello, p. 5; BMHWS No. 1,504, Seamus O'Meara, p. 14).

244 Both had seven operations under headings such as 'Outpost and Patrol Encounters', 'Raids on Buildings, Stores, etc.' and 'Evacuated Posts Destroyed'. In contrast, Meath and Laois had one operation each, Offaly two, and Longford none whatsoever (*AtÓ*, 15 August 1920).

245 A government-funded club for war veterans established in April 1919 (*WI*, 5 April 1919).

246 *WI*, 28 August 1920; BMHWS No. 1,504, Seamus O'Meara, p. 30.

247 Craddock's shots went off randomly, lodging in nearby walls, while Mahon's escape was helped by Tormey's misfiring gun (BMHWS No. 1,504, Seamus O'Meara, p. 30). Mahon, who 'made many converts to Sinn Féin by beating people to bolster his own courage', retired less than a month later (O'Meara, 'Some activities in Westmeath', pp. 550-551; *WI*, 18 September 1920).

248 CI Report, Westmeath, August 1920, CO/904/112; *FJ*, 23 August 1920; *IT*, 23 August 1920; *NYT*, 23 August 1920; *MG*, 23 August 1920; *II*, 24 August 1920; *FJ*, 24 August 1920; *WI*, 28 August 1920; *WG*, 27 August 1920; *RM*, 28 August 1920; Richard Abbott, *Police Casualties in Ireland, 1919-1922* (Cork, 2000), p. 113.

249 BMHWS No. 1,296, Thomas Costello, p. 12; BMHWS No. 1,504, Seamus O'Meara, pp. 27-28.

250 *FJ*, 23 August 1920.

251 Tully drove a motorbike, wore body armour and carried two revolvers with him at all times (BMHWS No. 1,337, David Daly, p. 18; BMHWS No. 1,296, Thomas Costello, p. 23; BMHWS No. 1,309, Francis O'Connor, p. 20).

252 BMHWS No. 1,504, Seamus O'Meara, p. 28.

253 O'Meara, 'Some activities in Westmeath', p. 550.

254 Ashe, 'Guerrilla warfare', p. 105. The *Westmeath Independent* of 7 August noted that no Black and Tans had yet been deployed in the town (*WI*, 7 August 1920).

255 Augusteijn, *Public Defiance*, p. 112-114; Tom Garvin, 'The anatomy of a nationalist revolution: Ireland, 1858-1922', in *Comparative Studies in Society and History*, Vol. 28, No. 3 (July, 1986), p. 483; Hart, *IRA at War*, pp. 47-48.

256 *II*, 24 August 1920; *IT*, 24 August 1920.

257 *LO*, 28 August 1920; *IT*, 24 August 1920.

258 *FJ*, 24 August 1920; *AC*, 28 August 1920; *IB*, 28 August 1920.

259 Colm Campbell, *Emergency Law in Ireland, 1918-1925* (New York, 1994), pp. 27-29.

260 A.D. Harvey, 'Who were the Auxiliaries?', in *The Historical Journal*, Vol. 35, No. 3 (September, 1992), pp. 665-669.

261 Boyce, *Englishmen and Irish Troubles*, p. 51; Carroll, *Fooled you Again*, p. 118.

262 Bew, 'Moderate nationalism', p. 741.

263 Fitzpatrick, *Politics and Irish Life*, p. 179.

264 CI Report, Westmeath, August 1920, CO/904/112; *WI*, 28 August 1920.

265 CI Report, Roscommon, August 1920, CO/904/112; *II*, 28 August 1920.

266 *FJ*, 28 August 1920; *CT*, 4 September 1920; *IT*, 4 September 1920.

267 BMHWS No. 701, Thomas Kelly, pp. 7-8; *WI*, 11 September 1920.

268 Collins told Duffy that resigning would have been cowardly (BMHWS No. 580, John Duffy, pp. 6-7).

269 Eunan O'Halpin, 'British Intelligence in Ireland, 1914-1921', in Christopher Andrew and David Dilks (eds), *The Missing Dimension: Governments and Intelligence in the Twentieth Century* (London, 1984), p. 75.

270 *WI*, 4 September 1920.

271 John Newsinger, '"I bring not peace but a sword": The religious motif in the Irish War of Independence', in *Journal of Contemporary History*, Vol. 13, No. 3 (July, 1978), pp. 623-624.

272 *II*, 31 August 1920. Fr Columba's full homily was printed in *The Irish Times* (*IT*, 30 August 1920).

273 *WI*, 4 September 1920.

274 RIC members at Athlone RIC Station to General Tudor, Executive Officer for Police in Ireland, August 1920, CO 904, in Costello, *Irish Revolution*, p. 81.

275 RIC members at Athlone RIC Station to General Tudor, Executive Officer for Police in Ireland, August 1920, C.O. 904, in Costello, *Irish Revolution*, p. 81.

276 Michael Hopkinson, *The Irish War of Independence* (Dublin, 2002), p. 201.

277 BMHWS No. 1,309, Francis O'Connor, p. 11.

278 D.S. Johnson, 'The Belfast Boycott, 1920-22', in J.M. Goldstrom and L.A. Clarkson (eds), *Irish Population, Economy and Society* (Oxford, 1981), pp. 291-294. Regulated by the ATC, the boycott was comprehensive and protracted. Permits to sell existing Belfast stock were granted, while some stock was destroyed. Complaints were heard (mostly from unhappy northern firms), and it appears that the town's Protestant shopkeepers held ambiguous views, which were highlighted by D.P. Moran in the *The Leader*. By the end of September, the Athlone Boycott Committee declared that there was not a single Belfast account in the town. The boycott continued into the summer of 1922 (*IT*, 16 August 1920; *FJ*, 17 August 1920; *AC*, 21 August 1920; *IT*, 27 August 1920; *FJ*, 3 September 1920; *II*, 3 September 1920; *WI*, 4 September 1920; *IT*, 7 September 1920; *II*, 10 September 1920; *FJ*, 10 September 1920; *WE*, 11 September 1920; *WI*, 11 September 1920; *II*, 13 September 1920; *AC*, 18 September 1920; *TL*, 18 September 1920; *FJ*, 21 September 1920; *II*, 21 September 1920; *FJ*, 24 September 1920; *FJ*, 9 October 1920; *TL*, 16 October 1920; *II*, 9 May 1921).

279 *FJ*, 6 September 1920.

280 *II*, 3 September 1920; *FJ*, 3 September 1920; *FJ*, 8 September 1920; *II*, 13 September 1920; *FJ*, 21 September 1920.

281 *WI*, 4 September 1920; *WI*, 25 September 1920.

282 *WI*, 18 September 1920.

283 Augusteijn, *Public Defiance*, p. 94; *II*, 8 September 1920; *FJ*, 8 September 1920; *II*, 9 September 1920; *IT*, 9 September 1920; *WE*, 11 September 1920. Arms were hidden in Coosan (BMHWS No. 1,504, Seamus O'Meara, p. 32).

284 BMHWS No. 580, John Duffy, p. 11; BMHWS No. 1,361, Commandant Gerald Davis, p. 19; Townshend, *British Campaign*, p. 187.

285 An aerodrome was opened at Fardrum, east of Athlone. Correspondences were dropped into the garrison from low-flying aircraft (*II*, 7 September 1920; *FJ*, 7 September 1920; *WI*, 11 September 1920). On one occasion, a soldier dropped the mailbag too soon, and instead of entering the barracks it rested on the roof of the Palace Bar, where it was later retrieved by the army (*WI*, 2 October 1920).

286 *WI*, 18 September 1920.

287 *II*, 14 September 1920; *FJ*, 17 September 1920.

288 *WI*, 25 September 1920; *IT*, 25 September 1920.

289 The soldier, Edward Hewitt, noted that the raiders 'had drink taken' (*II*, 27 September 1920).

290 *II*, 27 September 1920; *MG*, 27 September 1920. Patrick Lennon stated that the Black and Tans were 'dressed to terrorise and … went around with a rifle, bandolier of ammunition and a revolver or two strapped to their legs, and a few hand grenades hanging out of their belts' (BMHWS No. 1,336, Patrick Lennon, p. 7).

291 *SI*, 26 September 1920.

292 The assurances gave 'much satisfaction locally' (*II*, 29 September 1920; *IT*, 29 September 1920; *WI*, 2 October 1920). Hamar Greenwood stated that those who perpetrated the offences were never identified (*Hansard 5 Commons,* cxxxxii, col. 1219 (2 June 1921)).

293 Richard Bennett, *The Black and Tans* (New York, 1995), p. 56; *WI*, 9 October 1920; *Sinn Féiner*, 13 November 1920. The grenade was inert. They were later arrested by police.

294 *II*, 12 October 1920; *WI*, 16 October 1920; *AC*, 16 October 1920.

295 Michael McCormack wrote that he met one member who confessed his shame at the way Irish people were being treated (BMHWS No. 1,503, Michael McCormack, p. 25). Gerald Davis associated with the Black and Tans in Athlone upon his arrival (they socialised in the hotel in which he was staying); 'they were not such a bad crowd at all and I got on alright with them.' Needless to say, the company he kept handicapped his ability to work with local republicans, though he believed it to be a useful policy (BMHWS No. 1,361, Commandant Gerald Davis, p. 11).

296 *FJ*, 6 October 1920; *IT*, 6 October 1920; *WI*, 9 October 1920.

297 Kiltoom RIC barracks was burned, and four policemen were killed, facts that make for incongruous reading in the case of the Roscommon report (*IT*, 11 October 1920; *CT*, 16 October 1920; CI Report, Roscommon, October 1920, CO/904/113).

298 *IT*, 2 October 1920; *IT*, 7 October 1920.

299 *IT*, 7 October 1920; *IT*, 14 October 1920; *WI*, 23 October 1920.

300 CI Report, Westmeath, October 1920 CO/904/113; *II*, 7 October 1920.

301 *MRWN*, 21 October 1920.

302 *FJ*, 18 October 1920; *IT*, 18 October 1920. Some reports state that it was Auxiliaries, others the Black and Tans. The *Westmeath Independent* described the attackers as 'the armed forces of the Crown, no matter

what they be called, Black and Tans, auxiliary police, it is all the one' (*WI*, 23 October 1920).

303   *FJ*, 18 October 1920; *II*, 18 October 1920; *NYT*, 18 October 1920; *LO*, 23 October 1920; *AC*, 23 October 1920.

304   *Hansard 5 Commons,* cxxxiii, 1478 (25 October 1920); *Hansard 5 Commons,* cxxxiv, 1533 (26 October 1920).

305   *WI*, 23 October 1920.

306   The commotion that preceded the men notified him of their arrival and he hid on the roof of his house (*II*, 18 October 1920; *IT*, 18 October 1920; *WE*, 23 October 1920; O'Meara, 'Some activities in Westmeath', p. 551).

307   BMHWS No. 1,504, Seamus O'Meara, pp. 30-31; *WI*, 23 October 1920; *FJ*, 18 October 1920.

308   *WI*, 23 October 1920.

309   *II*, 19 October 1920.

310   *Hansard 5 Commons,* cxxxiv, 1382-1383 W (11 November 1920); *FJ*, 26 November 1920.

311   An army report states unrealistically that up to 150 were involved (W.H. Kautt, *Ambushes and Armour: The Irish Rebellion, 1919-1921* (Dublin, 2011), pp. 268-272).

312   BMHWS No. 1,504, Seamus O'Meara, p. 34.

313   *FJ*, 18 October 1920; *IT*, 18 October 1920; *NYT*, 19 October 1920; *WI*, 23 October 1920; *LO*, 23 October 1920; *MG*, 23 October 1920; O'Meara, 'Some activities in Westmeath', p. 551; BMHWS No. 1,504, Seamus O'Meara, p. 31. The *Freeman's Journal* and *Westmeath Independent* reported that good wishes were passed on to the injured by some locals (*FJ*, 19 October 1920; *WI*, 23 October 1920).

314   BMHWS No. 1,504, Seamus O'Meara, p. 31; BMHWS No. 1,309, Francis O'Connor, p. 17; *MRWN*, 21 October 1920.

315   *II*, 19 October 1920; *WI*, 23 October 1920; *AC*, 6 November 1920; CI Report, Westmeath, October 1920, CO/904/113.

316   Kautt, *Ambushes and Armour*, p. 269.

317   *WI*, 23 October 1920; BMHWS No. 1,296, Thomas Costello, p. 6; BMHWS No. 1,309, Francis O'Connor, p. 15; BMHWS No. 1,336, Patrick Lennon, p. 7.

318   Shea, *Voices*, p. 81. Duffy states that the RIC often went with other Crown forces to ensure that raids were conducted civilly (BMHWS No. 580, John Duffy, pp. 5, 22, 24).

319   Shea, *Voices*, p. 35.

320   Townshend, *British Campaign*, pp. 50-51.

321   Townshend, *British Campaign*, p. 95.

322   Bennett, *Black and Tans*, p. 38.

323   *WI*, 23 October 1920.

324   Townshend, 'Irish Republican Army', p. 330; Augusteijn, *Public Defiance*, pp. 124-126. Most witness statements attest that the local column was formed in September/October (BMHWS No. 1,503, Michael McCormack, p. 16; BMHWS No. 1,500, Anthony McCormack, p. 8; BMHWS No. 1,337, David Daly, p. 13; BMHWS No. 1308, Henry O'Brien, p. 10).

325 O'Meara, 'Some activities in Westmeath', p. 551; BMHWS No. 1,337, David Daly, p. 16. Thomas Costello stated that senior IRA members needed more time to plan and allowed those lower down to take the lead in full-time rebel activities (BMHWS No. 1,296, Thomas Costello, p. 15).

326 Additions were made as time passed and it appears that in total, twenty men participated in the column between October 1920 and July 1921.

327 O'Meara, 'Some activities in Westmeath', p. 551; UCDA, O'Malley Papers, P17b/106, Gerry Davis, p. 65.

328 Leonard, 'Survivors', p. 218.

329 Townshend, 'Irish Republican Army', p. 322.

330 Hart, 'Social structure', p. 217.

331 Hart, 'Social structure', p. 211.

332 Hart, *IRA and its Enemies*, p. 208.

333 Kiltoom, Carricknaughton and Summerhill west of Athlone; Moate, Coosan, Rosemount, Walderstown and Castlepollard east of the town (www.census. nationalarchives.ie/pages/1911/Westmeath/; www.census.nationalarchives. ie/pages/1911/Roscommon/: accessed 18-22 February 2010; *Westmeath Independent* 1911-1920. The Miltary Service Pensions Records note a improbably high number of sixty-four men in total working with the column during its existence (MA, RO/567A, Athlone Brigade, Miltary Service Pensions Records).

334 Hart, 'Social structure', p. 212.

335 Augusteijn, 'The importance of being Irish', p. 37.

336 *II*, 23 October 1923; *FJ*, 23 October 1923; *IT*, 23 October 1920; *WE*, 30 October 1920; *LO*, 30 October 1920; *AC*, 30 October 1920. The same day saw the first IRA ambush in King's County, which was also carried out by the Athlone Brigade.

337 BMHWS No. 1,504, Seamus O'Meara, p. 35; BMHWS No. 1308, Henry O'Brien, pp. 11-12; BMHWS No. 1,500, Anthony McCormack, p. 9.

338 BMHWS No. 1,337, David Daly, p. 17.

339 Townshend, *British Campaign*, p. 112; *S.I.*, 24 October 1920; *WE*, 23 October 1920.

340 *II*, 26 October 1920; *FJ*, 26 October 1920; *II*, 27 October 1920; *IT*, 28 October 1920; *WI*, 30 October 1920.

341 *SI*, 24 October 1920; *NYT*, 24 October 1920; *FJ*, 25 October 1920; *II*, 25 October 1920; *IT*, 25 October 1920.

342 *MG*, 30 October 1920; *MG*, 2 November 1920; *Hansard 5 Commons*, cxxxiii, 1326 (25 October 1920); *Hansard 5 Commons*, cxxxiv, 702-703 (4 November 1920); *Hansard 5 Commons*, cxxxiv, 27 (1 November 1920).

343 *Hansard 5 Commons*, cxxxiii, 1534-1536 (26 October 1920); *II*, 27 October 1920; *FJ*, 27 October 1920; *WI*, 30 October 1920. McDermott-Hayes described the Commons as a 'University of Lies'. A question about the incident later posed by Louth MP Thomas Wintringham led Greenwood to answer that 'every effort to trace the culprits has failed' (*Hansard 5 Commons*, cxxxiii, 627-628W (16 June 1921)).

344 Head Constable Storey asked that 'For the good of Athlone ... Westmeath ...

King's County and ... Ireland, return a verdict of wilful murder.' The verdict
was 'died of shock and haemorrhage caused by ... wounds inflicted by
some person or persons unknown' (*WI*, 30 October 1920). Storey stated
that he would have rather lost his right hand than see Burke killed (*II*,
30 October 1920).

345 *IT*, 30 October 1920.

346 *II*, 1 November 1920; *FJ*, 1 November 1920; *IT*, 1 November 1920; *WE*,
6 November 1920; *CT*, 6 November 1920.

347 *IT*, 1 November 1920. Coosan, Ballykeeran and Cornamagh were targeted,
and in a minority of cases (most of the raids were carried out by the regular
'courteous' military), property was damaged (*WI*, 30 October 1920; *IT*,
2 November 1920; *CT*, 6 November 1920). Seán O'Hurley, amongst others,
continued to evade capture (*II*, 2 November 1920; *FJ*, 2 November 1920).

348 *II*, 27 October 1920.

349 BMHWS No. 1,504, Seamus O'Meara, p. 49; BMHWS No. 1,503, Michael
McCormack, p. 17; Augusteijn, *Public Defiance*, pp. 135-136; M.A. Doherty,
'Kevin Barry and the Anglo-Irish propaganda war', *Irish Historical Studies*, Vol. 32,
No. 126 (November, 2000), pp. 217-231.

350 *FJ*, 3 November 1920; *II*, 3 November 1920; *IT*, 4 November 1920; *WG*,
5 November 1920; *LO*, 6 November 1920; *AC*, 6 November 1920; Abbott,
Police Casualties, p. 147.

351 BMHWS No. 1,296, Thomas Costello, p. 18.

352 Three houses were burned in reprisal (*FJ*, 3 November 1920; *II*,
3 November 1920; *II*, 4 November 1920; *IT*, 3 November 1920; *MRWN*,
4 November 1920; *WE*, 6 November 1920; *LO*, 6 November 1920; CI
Report, Westmeath, November 1920, CO/904/113; BMHWS No. 1,296,
Thomas Costello, p. 18; BMHWS No. 1,498, Michael Murray, p. 6; O'Meara,
'Some activities in Westmeath', p. 552; Fintan Corley, 'Ambush at Auburn:
1920', in *Journal of the Old Athlone Society*, Vol. 2, No. 7 (2003), pp. 189-190).

353 Townshend, 'Irish Republican Army', p. 330; BMHWS No. 1,500, Anthony
McCormack, p. 11; BMHWS No. 1,503, Michael McCormack, p. 19;
Townshend, 'Irish Republican Army', pp. 325-326.

354 *II*, 4 November 1920; *IT*, 4 November 1920; *MG*, 4 November 1920; *II*,
6 November 1920.

355 *II*, 4 November 1920; *IT*, 4 November 1920; *FJ*, 4 November 1920; *IB*,
4 November 1920; *CT*, 6 November 1920; *WI*, 4 February 1922.

356 *MRWN*, 3 February 1921.

357 *Hansard 5 Commons*, cxxxiv, 702-703 (4 November 1920); *Hansard 5 Commons*,
cxxxiv, 768-769 (5 November 1920).

358 *Hansard 5 Commons*, cxxxiii, 1952W (28 October 1920). George Roberts, MP
for Norwich, and Lt. Com. Joseph Kenworthy, MP for Kingston upon Hull
Upper, posed the question.

359 *Hansard 5 Commons*, cxxxiv, 772-773 (5 November 1920).

360 *Hansard 5 Commons*, cxxxiv, 360 (3 November 1920); *FJ*, 5 November 1920; *II*,
5 November 1920; *IT*, 5 November 1920; *WE*, 13 November 1920.

361 *FJ*, 9 November 1920.

362 West Bromwich MP Frederick Roberts called Greenwood's attention to the Athlone conflagration in the Commons on 4 November (*Hansard 5 Commons,* cxxxiv, 548 (4 November 1920)). Fife MP William Adamson asked about efforts to provide maintenance for those rendered jobless (*Hansard 5 Commons,* cxxxiv, 548 (4 November 1920)), as did Roberts and Barnard Castle MP John Swan (*Hansard 5 Commons,* cxxxiv, 1198-1199W (10 November 1920); *Hansard 5 Commons,* cxxxiv, 1383W (11 November 1920)). Both men tried to gain clearer answers from Greenwood (*Hansard 5 Commons,* cxxxiv, 853-854 (8 November 1920)).

363 See Jon Lawrence, 'Forging a peaceable kingdom: war, violence, and fear of brutalization in post-First World War Britain', in *The Journal of Modern History,* Vol. 75, No. 3 (September, 2003), pp. 575-587.

364 *Hansard 5 Commons,* cxxxiv, 548-549 (4 November 1920). MacVeigh asked repeatedly about the 'police or military excesses' at Athlone, among other places (*Hansard 5 Commons,* cxxxiv, 1345-1347 (11 November 1920); *Hansard 5 Commons,* cxxxiv, 2056 (18 November 1920)).

365 Lawrence, 'Forging a peaceable kingdom', pp. 578-579; *Hansard 5 Commons,* cxxxiv, 549 (4 November 1920); *Hansard 5 Commons,* cxxxiv, 702-703 (4 November 1920).

366 *Hansard 5 Commons,* cxxxiv, 853-854 (8 November 1920); *FJ,* 11 November 1920; *II,* 11 November 1920.

367 *Hansard 5 Commons,* cxxxiv 34, 617 (25 November 1920).

368 *Hansard 5 Commons,* cxxxiv 34, 617 (25 November 1920); *FJ,* 26 November 1920; *IT,* 26 November 1920; *II,* 26 November 1920.

369 Townshend, *British Campaign,* p. 159.

370 *II,* 5 November 1920. The Chapmans lodged claims for losses totalling £55,650 (AHL, Minute Book of Athlone UDC, 20 November 1920).

371 *II,* 6 November 1920; *FJ,* 6 November 1920; *IB,* 13 November 1920; BMHWS No. 1,296, Thomas Costello, p. 27; BMHWS No. 1,504, Seamus O'Meara, pp. 38-39; BMHWS No. 1308, Henry O'Brien, pp. 13-14; BMHWS No. 1,309, Francis O'Connor, p. 24; O'Meara, 'Some activities in Westmeath', p. 552; *FJ,* 5 April 1921.

372 *FJ,* 10 November 1920.

373 *II,* 10 November 1920; *IT,* 10 November 1920; *MRWN,* 11 November 1920; *WE,* 13 November 1920; *IB,* 13 November 1920.

374 *II,* 10 November 1920; *II,* 11 November 1920; Jane Leonard, 'The twinge of memory: Armistice Day and Remembrance Sunday in Dublin since 1919', in Richard English and Graham Walker, *Unionism in Modern Ireland: New Perspectives on Politics and Culture* (London, 1996), p. 103.

375 *II,* 11 November 1920; *FJ,* 11 November 1920; *MG,* 12 November 1920. The military parade lasted from 10:45 to 11:45, and went off without incident (*FJ,* 12 November 1920).

376 *MG,* 11 November 1920.

377 *Hansard 5 Commons,* cxxxiv, 1190 (10 November 1920).

378 *II,* 11 November 1920; *IT,* 11 November 1920.

379 CI Report, Westmeath, November 1920, CO/904/113; CI Report, Westmeath, December 1920, CO/904/113; *FJ,* 8 November 1920; *II,* 9 November 1920.

One witness stated at a later inquest that the men had their faces blackened, wore their coats inside out and were foul mouthed (*II*, 1 February 1921). The assault on the girl was investigated after the truce. She was found to 'be in a state of nervous excitement almost bordering on imbecility' (*IB*, 27 November 1920; NAI, DE 2/248, Dáil Éireann Files, Duffy Case, Ballykeeran, Athlone, August 1921).

380   Mitchell, *Revolutionary Government*, pp. 216, 271; Augusteijn, *Public Defiance*, pp. 212-213, 274; Tom Bowden, 'The Irish Underground and the War of Independence 1919-21', in *Journal of Contemporary History*, Vol. 8, No. 2 (April, 1973), p. 4.

381   *FJ*, 24 November 1920.

382   *FJ*, 9 November 1920; *IT*, 4 November 1920; Augusteijn, *Public Defiance*, p. 227.

383   CI Report, Westmeath, November 1920, CO/904/113; *MG*, 23 November 1920; *NYT*, 24 November 1920.

384   Rail travel was virtually non-existent, with roads and telegraph wires regularly cut. The MGWR halted all traffic in November, letting its staff go (AHL, Minute Book of Athlone UDC, 20 November 1920; Mitchell, *Revolutionary Government*, p. 182).

385   CI Report, Roscommon, December 1920, CO/904/113.

386   *IB*, 15 January 1921.

387   CI Report, Westmeath, November 1920, CO/904/113; CI Report, Westmeath, December 1920, CO/904/113; Fitzpatrick, *Politics and Irish Life*, p. 27; O'Halpin, 'British Intelligence in Ireland', p. 75.

388   Gabriel Doherty and John Borgonovo, 'Smoking gun? RIC reprisals, summer 1920', in *History Ireland*, Vol. 17, No. 2 (March/April, 2009), p. 37.

389   Hopkinson, 'Negotiation', p. 126; Costello, 'Lloyd George', p. 10.

390   CI Report, Westmeath, January 1921, CO/904/114; *IT*, 1 January 1921; *FJ*, 1 January 1921; *MRWN*, 6 January 1921; *WG*, 7 January 1921; *Roscommon Journal*, 8 January 1921; *WG*, 14 January 1921.

391   *II*, 3 January 1921; *IT*, 13 January 1921.

392   BMHWS No. 1,500, Anthony McCormack, p. 13; BMHWS No. 1,504, Seamus O'Meara, p. 50; *II*, 4 January 1921; CI Report, Westmeath, January 1921, CO/904/114; *IB*, 8 January 1921.

393   *II*, 6 January 1921; *II*, 8 January 1921. Ten local men were later sentenced to eighteen months for his kidnap (*II*, 28 May 1921; *RJ*, 28 May 1921; *II*, 8 June 1921). Heavey was still missing at the time of their trial.

394   BMHWS No. 1,504, Seamus O'Meara, p. 50; BMHWS No. 1,336, Patrick Lennon, p. 11.

395   CI Report, Westmeath, February 1921, CO/904/114.

396   An ambush laid for the RIC resulted in a shoot-out that saw Tormey fatally wounded. The recent death of his brother in Ballykinlar prison camp informed his staging of the ambush (BMHWS No. 1,337, David Daly, p. 21; BMHWS No. 1,296, Thomas Costello, p. 17; BMHWS No. 1,504, Seamus O'Meara, pp. 44-45). His body was later recovered by the IRA and brought to Clonmacnoise, where it was buried in a shallow grave. Crown forces recovered it, and had his father identify the remains in Athlone (*FJ*,

3 February 1921; *IT*, 3 February 1921; *IT*, 4 February 1921; *II*, 4 February 1921; *II*, 8 February 1921; *AC*, 12 February 1921; BMHWS No. 1,296, Thomas Costello, p. 17; BMHWS No. 1,336, Patrick Lennon, p. 10; BMHWS No. 1,504, Seamus O'Meara, p. 45; O'Callaghan, *For Ireland and Freedom*, pp. 180-185).

397 BMHWS No. 1,504, Seamus O'Meara, pp. 46-47.

398 Townshend, 'Irish Republican Army', pp. 335-337; Hart, *IRA at War*, p. 85.

399 Townshend, 'Irish Republican Army', p. 341; John O'Beirne Ranelagh, 'The Irish Republican Brotherhood in the revolutionary period, 1879-1923', in D.G. Boyce (ed.), *The Revolution in Ireland: 1879-1923* (London, 1988), p. 147. In Athlone Seamus O'Meara is emphatic that: 'There never was ... any attempt to direct Volunteer activities by the IRB' (BMHWS No. 1,504, Seamus O'Meara, p. 52). Five other statements attest to IRB circles in the region. All local IRB members gained membership before 1919, with observations made that as the war wore on, the Brotherhood appeared to serve little purpose (BMHWS No. 1,296, Thomas Costello, p. 30; BMHWS No. 1,337, David Daly, pp. 26-27; BMHWS No. 1,503, Michael McCormack, pp. 1-2; BMHWS No.1309, Francis O'Connor, p. 27; BMHWS No.1308, Henry O'Brien p. 22).

400 UCDA, Mulcahy Papers, P7/A/17, 4 March 1921.

401 CI Report, Westmeath, January 1921, CO/904/114; CI Report, Westmeath, February 1921, CO/904/114; CI Report, Westmeath, March 1921, CO/904/114).

402 BMHWS No. 1,337, David Daly, p. 24.

403 Augusteijn, *Public Defiance*, p. 275; *II*, 7 March 1921; *FJ*, 12 March 1921; *II*, 18 March 1921; *IT*, 17 June 1921; *II*, 17 June 1921; *FJ*, 21 June 1921; *II*, 21 June 1921; *IB*, 23 June 1921; *II*, 2 July 1921. Hundreds of men were interrogated; most were released after a member of the RIC attested to their good character. A DI and numerous soldiers in civilian clothes were also held until they were identified (*RH*, 18 June 1921).

404 *FJ*, 3 December 1920; *MRWN*, 2 June 1921. Escape attempts, sometimes assisted by soldiers, were frequent and, at times, successful. Tunnelling, bribes and feigned illnesses were popularly employed (BMHWS No. 580, John Duffy, p. 18; BMHWS No. 1,610, Michael McCoy, p. 33-37). Restricted visiting rights were brought in after a series of escapes in May, with the interaction between inmates curtailed as much as was practicable (UCDA, Mulcahy Papers, P7/A/16, 26 May 1921; 27 May 1921; 30 May 1921; *FJ*, 26 May 1921; *MC*, 28 May 1921; *AC*, 28 May 1921; *MRWN*, 2 June 1921). Athlone barracks was the holding centre for women caught in the west of Ireland. Their detention led to controversy, as they were monitored solely by male attendants (*MG*, 4 February 1921; *FJ*, 19 March 1921; *MG*, 18 April 1921).

405 BMHWS No. 1,308, Henry O'Brien p. 24; BMHWS No. 1,504, Seamus O'Meara, p. 47; O'Meara, 'Some activities in Westmeath', p. 552.

406 UCDA, Mulcahy Papers, P7/A/17, Thomas Costello to Richard Mulcahy, 5 April 1921.

407 See Townshend, 'Irish Republican Army', pp. 326-329. The BMHWS for the Athlone Brigade present a general ignorance of intelligence collection; most assumed it happened, perhaps through the relaying of information by

a sympathetic postal worker or soldier. It appears not to have risen above the level of general observation, with statements from the two OCs rating it as basic (BMHWS No. 1,504, Seamus O'Meara, p. 51; BMHWS No. 1,296, Thomas Costello, p. 28).

408   *IT*, 13 April 1921; *NYT*, 13 April 1921; *FJ*, 14 April 1921; *AC*, 16 April 1921; *WG*, 18 July 1921. All of the articles cited refer to Johnson as a Protestant, while the 1911 Census appears to identify an individual, almost certainly the same man, as Roman Catholic.

409   BMHWS No. 1,504, Seamus O'Meara, p. 50; BMHWS No. 1,308, Henry O'Brien, p. 20; BMHWS No. 1,500, Anthony McCormack, p. 13; UCDA, Mulcahy Papers, P7/A/16, 13 April 1921.

410   Hart, *IRA at War*, pp. 223-234; Peter Hart, 'The Protestant experience of revolution in southern Ireland', in English and Walker, *Unionism in Modern Ireland*, pp. 81-98

411   John M. Regan, *Myth and the Irish State* (Sallins, 2013), pp. 45-47; 56-86, 176-205; Jane Leonard, 'Getting them at last. The IRA and ex-servicemen', in Fitzpatrick, *Revolution?*, pp. 118-129; Augusteijn, *Public Defiance*, pp. 294-299.

412   BMHWS No. 1,503, Michael McCormack, p. 33; BMHWS No. 1,500, Anthony McCormack, p. 14.

413   BMHWS No. 1,308, Henry O'Brien, p. 20. Francis O'Connor stated that it was just 'accepted without question … that he was a spy … the principal enemy agent in the county' (BMHWS No. 1,309, Francis O'Connor p. 25).

414   'Postal Censorship', CO 904/168, p. 427; Costello, 'Role of propaganda', p. 13; Keiko Inoue, 'Propaganda II: propaganda of Dáil Éireann, 1919-21', in Augusteijn, *Irish Revolution*, p. 96.

415   UCDA, Mulcahy Papers, P7/A/17, 11 April 1921.

416   *II*, 12 April 1921; *MG*, 12 April 1921; *II*, 13 April 1921; *MRWN*, 14 April 1921; *RJ*, 16 April 1921.

417   CI Report, Westmeath, April 1921, CO/904/115; Costello, 'Lloyd George', p. 10.

418   CI Report, Westmeath, May 1921, CO/904/115.

419   IG Report, March 1921, CO 904/114.

420   CI Report, Westmeath, January 1921, CO/904/114; CI Report, Westmeath, February 1921, CO/904/114; CI Report, Westmeath, March 1921, CO/904/114.

421   *IT*, 28 May 1921; *II*, 11 June 1921; *Hansard 5 Commons*, cxxxiii, 1569W (23 June 1921); Townshend, 'Irish Republican Army', pp. 330-331. Police rounded up 'about 100 young men … in Athlone and district and compelled them to fill in Crannagh Bridge' (*IT*, 3 June 1921; *II*, 3 June 1921).

422   *FJ*, 14 April 1921; *II*, 14 April 1921.

423   CI Report, Westmeath, June 1921, CO/904/115; *II*, 21 June 1921; *FJ*, 21 June 1921; *II*, 22 June 1921; *MRWN*, 23 June 1921; *WG*, 24 June 1921; BMHWS No. 1,296, Thomas Costello, p. 20; UCDA, Mulcahy Papers, P7/A/16, 21 June 1921.

424   Inoue, 'Propaganda II', p. 92.

425   *IB*, 30 June 1921.

426   *NYT*, 21 June 1921.

427   The village was targeted after information received from an informant

named Heary. He was later killed by republicans (CI Report, Roscommon, June 1921, CO/904/115; BMHWS No. 1,336, Patrick Lennon, p. 12; *II*, 22 June 1921; O'Callaghan, *For Ireland and Freedom*, pp. 186-187). The army closed all shops and factories in Athlone for two days until Lambert's remains left for England (*FJ*, 22 June 1921; *IT*, 23 June 1921; *II*, 24 June 1921). Many Glasson residents moved away for a number of days (*II*, 25 June 1921).

428 Hart, 'Geography of revolution', p. 147.

429 Hopkinson, *War of Independence*, p. 144-145.

430 Fitzpatrick, 'Geography of Irish Nationalism', p. 117; Augusteijn, *Public Defiance*, pp. 95, 150-151; Coleman, *Longford*, p. 162; Townshend, 'Irish Republican Army', pp. 334-335.

431 O'Meara went from Acting OC in O'Hurley's absence to OC after the two men disagreed over an unauthorised raid carried out at a local quarry. O'Meara states that he censured the men, while O'Hurley criticised him for attempting to curtail efforts to gain gelignite. In a chronologically muddled paragraph, O'Meara states that he was exonerated by GHQ and O'Hurley resigned, demoting himself to the rank and file (BMHWS No. 1,504, Seamus O'Meara, pp. 10-11, 15).

432 BMHWS No. 1,337, David Daly, p. 22; BMHWS No. 1,308, Henry O'Brien, p. 23. Accusations were made that he promoted inactivity in the town to protect his family business (BMHWS No. 1,504, Seamus O'Meara, p. 46).

433 O'Meara wanted O'Hurley reinstated purportedly because he felt that O'Hurley's work over the previous three years merited it (BMHWS No. 1,504, Seamus O'Meara, p. 15).

434 BMHWS No. 1,504, Seamus O'Meara, p. 47. See Augusteijn, *Public Defiance*, pp. 105-108.

435 UCDA, O'Malley Papers, P17b/106, Gerry Davis, p. 65.

436 BMHWS No. 1,361, Commandant Gerald Davis, p. 12; O'Meara, 'Some activities in Westmeath', p. 552.

437 Hart, 'Geography of revolution', p. 159.

438 Hart, 'Geography of revolution', p. 160.

439 BMHWS No. 1,361, Commandant Gerald Davis, p. 12.

440 The *Irish Independent* reported that on the occasion of a prisoner transfer between Athlone and Ballykinlar, 'crowds on the streets responded lustily' to the prisoners' rendition of the 'Soldier's Song' (*II*, 11 January 1921; *IB*, 15 January 1921).

441 Augusteijn, *Public Defiance*, p. 145; BMHWS No. 1,503, Michael McCormack, pp. 12-13; BMHWS No. 580, John Duffy, p. 14; BMHWS No. 1,296, Thomas Costello, pp. 5, 13, 28; BMHWS No. 1,336, Patrick Lennon, p. 5; BMHWS No. 1,500, Anthony McCormack, p. 6; BMHWS No. 701, Thomas Kelly, p. 7; BMHWS No. 1,504, Seamus O'Meara, pp. 12-13.

442 Costello, 'Lloyd George', p. 14.

443 Townshend, *British Campaign*, pp. 189-192.

444 O'Leary and Maume, *Controversial Issues*, pp. 112-115. The four TDs returned unopposed were Laurence Ginnell, Seán MacEoin, Lorcan Robbins and Joe McGuinness (*RH*, 28 May 1921).

445   Mitchell, *Revolutionary Government*, p. 295; Townshend, *British Campaign*,
      pp. 191–192.

446   The truce 'provided for a ceasefire and no provocative actions by either side'
      (Mitchell, *Revolutionary Government*, p. 298).

447   'On July 2, three Volunteers attacked Capt. Tully and four RIC men who
      were in a private car near Drumraney Chapel. After a fight lasting fifteen
      minutes the enemy retreated into the chapel yard and the men had to cease
      firing for fear of the bullets entering the chapel or parochial house. "Another
      obstacle in the way … was that the enemy had two hostages … so that they
      had to fire with great caution and judgement". It is believed that two of
      the enemy were seriously wounded.' Michael McCormack noted that Tully
      was hit, though gained his feet quickly, thanks to his protective plating (NLI,
      MS 33,913 (2), Piaras Béaslaí Papers, July 1921; BMHWS No. 1,503, Michael
      McCormack, p. 31).

448   *FJ*, 4 July 1921; *II*, 5 July 1921; *FJ*, 5 July 1921; *IT*, 5 July 1921; *WG*,
      8 July 1921. Five houses were burned in Coosan (BMHWS No. 1,308, Henry
      O'Brien, p. 16; BMHWS, No. 1,309, Francis O'Connor, p. 21; *IB*, 5 July 1921;
      FJ, 9 July 1921). Lady Castlemaine was given five minutes to retrieve her
      most valued possessions before the house was doused with inflammables
      and set alight. The RIC reported that 'everything was burned, save the walls'
      (CI Report, Westmeath, July 1921, CO/904/116; *IT*, 9 July 1921; *MRWN*,
      20 October 1921; BMHWS No. 1,296, Thomas Costello, p. 20; BMHWS
      No. 1309, Francis O'Connor, pp. 22–23; UCDA, Mulcahy Papers, P7/A/17,
      5 July 1921).

449   CI Report, Westmeath, July 1921, CO/904/116; BMHWS No. 1,309, Francis
      O'Connor, p. 23; MA, Fintan Murphy Papers, C.D. 227/21/A.13.

450   CI Report, Westmeath, July 1921, CO/904/116.

451   *FJ*, 12 July 1921. Bonfires held later in the week were extinguished by the
      IRA, who ordered people home (*FJ*, 16 July 1921).

452   *IT*, 11 July 1921.

453   300 IRA men arrived in small, unarmed groups and did not adopt military
      formation while travelling through Athlone (*FJ*, 14 July 1921; *II*, 14 July 1921;
      WG, 15 July 1921; *NG*, 16 July 1921; *S.S.*, 16 July 1921; *AC*, 16 July 1921).

454   Some lines and roads needed to be repaired, with co-ordination efforts
      carried out by the IRA (*FJ*, 19 July 1921; *FJ*, 22 July 1921). Telegraph wires
      were also reinstated; the repetitive cutting of them prior to the truce had led
      to them being abandoned (*FJ*, 25 June 1921; *II*, 25 June 1921).

455   Murphy's area was that of the 13th Infantry Division, which was comprised
      of Westmeath, Roscommon, Sligo, Leitrim and Longford. He took up
      residence at Prince of Wales Hotel in Athlone (*SI*, 17 July 1921; *FJ*,
      18 July 1921; *FJ*, 22 July 1921; MA, CD 227/21, Fintan Murphy Papers).

456   *IT*, 19 July 1921; *RJ*, 23 July 1921.

457   *MRWN*, 5 August 1921.

458   The first GAA match in twelve months was played between Athlone and
      Drumraney on Sunday 24 July (*FJ*, 27 July 1921).

459   CI Report, Westmeath, July 1921, CO/904/116. In his June report he had

asked that concessions not be granted to the IRA (C.I Report, Westmeath, June 1921, CO/904/115).

460 A fire at Lyster's Sawmills saw the RIC, IRA and army all work together in a futile attempt to save the premises (*II*, 24 August 1921; *FJ*, 24 August 1921; *IT*, 24 August 1921; *MRWN*, 25 August 1921).

461 CI Report, Westmeath, August 1921, CO/904/116; MA, CD 227/21/A, Athlone Brigade, Fintan Murphy Papers; MA, CD 227/21/G, South Roscommon Brigade, Fintan Murphy Papers.

462 CI Report, Roscommon, August 1921, CO/904/116.

463 Sometimes referred to as 'flagwaggers', 'Trucileers' or 'sunshine soldiers', post-truce recruits were resented by many in the IRA, who believed them to be misappropriating glory. The tension between the two groups later fed into the civil war (Fitzpatrick, *Irish Life and Politics*, p. 191).

464 There were two camps; one trained sixty men, the other 100. Many of those who joined did so in the hope of landing a police job whenever the new force was established (CI Report, Westmeath, August 1921, CO/904/116; CI Report, Westmeath, September 1921, CO/904/116; BMHWS No. 1,296, Thomas Costello, p. 28; Garvin, *1922*, p. 52).

465 Branches in Westmeath had grown to five (112 members) while in Roscommon the number had also reached five (187 members) (McCarthy, *Cumann na mBan*, pp. 155-158, 163-4).

466 MA, CMB/150, Athlone District Council, Miltary Service Pensions Records.

467 BMHWS No. 1,308, Henry O'Brien, p. 21; BMHWS No. 1,309, Francis O'Connor, p. 26.

468 BMHWS No. 1,336, Patrick Lennon, p. 5.

469 MA, RO/563-566, Athlone Brigade, Miltary Service Pensions Records.

470 Mitchell, *Revolutionary Government*, p. 278; Townshend, 'Irish Republican Army', pp. 342-343.

471 Hart, *IRA and its Enemies*, p. 124; Fitzpatrick, *Politics and Irish Life*, p. 230; Augusteijn, *Public Defiance*, p. 352.

CHAPTER 7

1 AHL, Minute Book of Athlone UDC, 5 October 1921.

2 *WI*, 25 February 1922; Laffan, *Resurrection of Ireland*, p. 344.

3 *II*, 18 October 1921.

4 CI Report, Westmeath, September 1921, CO/904/116; UCDA, MacEoin Papers, P151/110, 29 September 1921; BMHWS No. 1,296, Thomas Costello, p. 27; BMHWS No.1308, Henry O'Brien, p. 22, BMHWS No.1309, Francis O'Connor, p. 25; Laffan, *Resurrection of Ireland*, p. 343.

5 MA, C.D. 227/21/A, Fintan Murphy Papers; C.D. 227/21/G, Fintan Murphy Papers.

6 UCDA, Mulcahy Papers, P7/A/17, 4 November 1921.

7 *IT*, 24 October 1921; *FJ*, 24 October 1921.

8 RIC Report, Précis of Information, December 1921, CO/904/124.

9 Fitzpatrick, *Politics and Irish Life*, p. 38.

10   Garvin, *1922*, p. 47.

11   RIC Report, Précis of Information, December 1921, CO/904/124.

12   It was noted that at least four soldiers had disappeared and were unaccounted for (UCDA, Mulcahy Papers, P7/B/22, 23 July 1922).

13   *FJ*, 1 December 1921; *II*, 1 December 1921.

14   AHL, Minute Book of Athlone UDC, 2 November 1921; Minute Book of Athlone UDC, 16 November 1921.

15   RIC Report, Précis of Information, December 1921, CO/904/124.

16   Laffan, *Resurrection of Ireland*, p. 299.

17   PRONI, T/2782/36, Cecilia H. Daniels to Mrs Flett, Australia, 3 November 1921.

18   PRONI, T/2782/36, Cecilia H. Daniels to Mrs Flett, Australia, 3 November 1921.

19   RIC Report, Précis of Information, December 1921, CO/904/124.

20   *The Voice of Labour*, 5 November 1921.

21   *TVL*, 19 November 1921.

22   Apparently some of Poole's staff members were complicit in the theft (RIC Report, Précis of Information, December 1921, CO/904/124).

23   *FJ*, 17 October 1921; *MRWN*, 20 October 1921.

24   RIC Report, Précis of Information, December 1921, PRO CO/904/124.

25   UCDA, Mulcahy Papers, P7/A/37, 3 December 1921, *IT*, 9 December 1921.

26   Boland had revisited Athlone with MacEoin in September, a few weeks after his return from the USA. An estimated 2,000 people besieged the Prince of Wales Hotel, where they were staying. It was even reported that two British Army soldiers requested MacEoin's autograph (Fitzpatrick, *Harry Boland's Irish Revolution*, pp. 223, 230-231).

27   Michael Hopkinson, *Green against Green* (2nd ed., Dublin, 2004), pp. 32-40.

28   De Valera stayed in Dublin. He had attended the first round of negotiations and his motivation for staying behind on the second occasion is still questioned by historians.

29   Fitzpatrick, *Harry Boland's Irish Revolution*, p. 264.

30   Bill Kissane, *The Politics of the Irish Civil War* (New York, 2007), pp. 55-56.

31   UCDA, MacEoin Papers, P151/110, 9 December 1921.

32   AHL, Minute Book of Athlone UDC, 2 January 1922.

33   Kissane, *Civil War*, pp. 59-60.

34   *MRWN*, 26 January 1922.

35   PRONI, T/2782/37, Cecilia H. Daniels to Mrs Flett, Australia, 17 February 1922.

36   Charles Townshend, *The Republic. The Fight for Irish Independence* (London, 2013), pp. 367-369.

37   The newspaper's return to print was described by one UDC member as '… absolute proof that the tyranny is over' (*WI*, 18 February 1922). It appears from anecdotal evidence that Ivan Chapman, manager of the APW due to the decline in his father's (Thomas') health, did not entertain the notion of rehiring Michael McDermott-Hayes.

38   *WI*, 4 February 1922.

39   Patrick Murray, *Oracles of God: The Roman Catholic Church and Irish Politics,*
      1922-37 (Dublin, 2000), p. 44.

40   Kissane, *Civil War*, p. 67.

41   *WI*, 4 February 1922.

42   *IT*, 26 January 1922.

43   *IT*, 3 January 1922.

44   *FJ*, 30 January 1922; *WE*, 4 February 1922.

45   *WI*, 4 February 1922.

46   *WI*, 4 February 1922.

47   *II*, 7 February 1922; *WI*, 11 February 1922.

48   *WI*, 11 February 1922; *WI*, 18 February 1922

49   *WI*, 25 February 1922.

50   *WI*, 25 February 1922. Interestingly, (and in common with the earlier attempts to
      create a comprehensive UIL presence in Athlone), members at the SF meeting
      noted how earlier SF clubs on the west side of the town had fallen away.

51   At Mullingar anti-Treaty IRA members refused to allow Free State troops
      access after the British had withdrawn (*NYT*, 4 April 1922; *MG*, 4 April 1922).

52   Mullingar had been handed over on the thirteenth and Longford on the
      seventeenth – all three barracks were combined to become the 1st Midland
      Division (UCDA, Mulcahy Papers, P7/B/102, pp. 36-38).

53   AHL, Minute Book of Athlone UDC, 15 February 1922.

54   *II*, 1 March 1922.

55   *WI*, 25 February 1922.

56   Eoin Neeson, *The Civil War 1922-23* (Dublin, 1989), p. 90.

57   Calton Younger, *Ireland's Civil War* (London, 1968), p. 241.

58   *MG*, 16 April 1922.

59   *FJ*, 1 March 1922.

60   *WI*, 4 March 1922.

61   In all the barracks, castle, military gas works and firing range were handed
      over (UCDA, Mulcahy Papers, P7/B/103).

62   *NYT*, 2 March 1922.

63   *WI*, 4 March 1922; *WE*, 4 March 1922; *SI*, 5 March 1922. MacEoin ended
      the day with a meal hosted by the UDC, an event which caused some
      tension in local authority circles when it transpired that none of the Labour
      councillors had been invited. The Sinn Féin chairman had organised the
      meal after the end of the previous UDC meeting, purposely keeping
      its staging a secret from the Labour members, as well as selected others.
      Henry Broderick, a Labour councillor, outlined his disgust at the snub at
      a subsequent meeting and noted that his party colleagues had supported
      the release of the prisoners in Mountjoy, would have happily welcomed
      MacEoin and were fully entitled to attend the event as good Irishmen (*WI*,
      11 March 1922; *WI*, 18 March 1922; AHL, Minute Book of Athlone UDC,
      10 March 1922).

64   *II*, 15 March 1922.

65   *WI*, 25 March 1922. In Athlone elections were held in the second last week in
      March to decide on the five magistrates for the area. Initially ten candidates

were proposed, though two clergymen pulled out on the grounds that they believed the court should consist only of members of the laity. Confusingly, they also stated that they would not vote on the same grounds, though local Anglican Rector Revd Anderson did take up the chairmanship of the meeting, thus wielding a deciding vote. Luckily he did not have to use it and the five elected magistrates were Henry Broderick (Labour and UDC), Thomas Malone (Irish Postal Union), Stephen McCrann (Sinn Féin and UDC), Peter Mulvihill (ITGWU) and Patrick Macken (Athlone No.1 Council). Malone was elected as president of the court, a position he had held in the previous 'illegal' setup (*WI*, 1 April 1922).

66 Garvin, *1922*, pp. 133, 153.
67 Hopkinson, *Green against Green*, pp. 56–57.
68 Costello, *Irish Revolution*, p. 288; Younger, *Ireland's Civil War*, pp. 253–4.
69 Kissane, *Civil War*, p. 69; Hopkinson, *Green against Green*, pp. 59–60.
70 Younger, *Ireland's Civil War*, p. 255.
71 Neeson, *Civil War*, pp. 95–96; Garvin, *Irish Nationalist Politics*, p. 132; Hopkinson, *Green against Green*, pp. 66–68.
72 The Earl of Longford and T.P. O'Neill, *Éamon de Valera* (Dublin, 1970), p. 184.
73 Garvin, *1922*, pp. 47, 124, 158.
74 UCDA, MacEoin Papers, P151/1809.
75 Younger, *Ireland's Civil War*, pp. 255–6.
76 Younger, *Ireland's Civil War*, pp. 256–7.
77 *IT*, 4 April 1922; *II*, 4 April 1922.
78 *II*, 15 March 1922; *FJ*, 28 March 1922.
79 *IT*, 11 April 1922.
80 *WI*, 8 April 1922.
81 *II*, 31 March 1922.
82 *II*, 29 March 1922.
83 *WI*, 8 April 1922.
84 Eunan O'Halpin, *Defending Ireland: The Irish State and its Enemies Since 1922* (Oxford, 1999), p. 2.
85 *II*, 3 April 1922.
86 *WI*, 8 April 1922.
87 See Murray, *Oracles*, pp. 35–67; 443–444.
88 *IT*, 4 April 1922.
89 *II*, 4 April 1922.
90 *WI*, 8 April 1922.
91 *WI*, 8 April 1922; *WI*, 15 April 1922.
92 *II*, 1 April 1922.
93 *II*, 11 April 1922.
94 *II*, 11 April 1922.
95 *II*, 11 April 1922; *IT*, 12 April 1922.
96 Younger, *Ireland's Civil War*, p. 257.
97 *WI*, 15 April 1922.
98 *II*, 12 April 1922.
99 *II*, 12 April 1922.

100   Hopkinson, *Green against Green*, p. 75.

101   *WI*, 15 April 1922.

102   *WE*, 15 April 1922; *CT*, 15 April 1922; *NG*, 15 April 1922.

103   *SS*, 15 April 1922.

104   Hopkinson, *Green against Green*, p. 75.

105   *SI*, 16 April 1922; *II*, 17 April 1922.

106   *IT*, 17 April 1922.

107   Kissane, *Civil War*, p. 69.

108   *IT*, 26 April 1922; *IT*, 27 April 1922; *FJ*, 28 April 1922.

109   *II*, 26 April 1922; *FJ*, 26 April 1922.

110   *WI*, 29 April 1922. '"After the arrest of Commdt. [Tom] Bourke, he was interrogated in Maryborough Prison by the late CIC. Free State Army, Michael Collins, RIP. During this interrogation Collins charged him with being responsible for the death of Adamson and struck him with his fist; Bourke retaliated. Collins called in the Guard and ordered him to be kept in solitary confinement. Commdt Bourke is still in solitary confinement and our information is that the charge is being proceeded with." I expect the charge means the 'Murder of Adamson' in Athlone. This is the point we want cleared up. It seems very unlikely that enemy will proceed with the charge in view of Athlone Enquiry' (UCDA, Ernie O'Malley Papers, P69/77, Con Maloney to Ernie O'Malley, 3 October 1922; P17A/56, Ernie O'Malley to Liam Lynch, 3 September 1922).

111   *FJ*, 28 April 1922; *FJ*, 5 Jun 1922.

112   *TNL*, 6 May 1922; *MG*, 27 April 1922.

113   *The Separatist*, 6 May 1922.

114   *II*, 26 April 1922; *FJ*, 26 April 1922.

115   *MG*, 27 April 1922; *FJ*, 27 April 1922.

116   MacEoin, *Survivors*, pp. 269-270. Interestingly, in UinSeánn MacEoin's *Survivors* it was noted by Liam Carroll, an IRA man from Roscrea, that he and five other IRA men were in Athlone on that night and had abandoned a car in the town. This was not the car impounded by Adamson, as Carroll stated that their car was untouched when they collected it the next day. He noted that the anti-Treaty IRA condemned the murder of Adamson and instead pointed the finger at one of Seán MacEoin's 'bodyguards'.

117   Hopkinson, *Green against Green*, p. 74.

118   *IT*, 2 June 1922.

119   *Plain People*, 14 May 1922.

120   *S.I.*, 28 May 1922. The shooting and investigation were covered extensively (*FJ*, 27 April 1922; *II*, 27 April 1922; *II*, 28 April 1922; *FJ*, 29 April 1922; *II*, 29 April 1922; *FJ*, 1 May 1922; *II*, 1 May 1922; *II*, 2 May 1922; *II*, 3 May 1922; *IT*, 8 May 1922; *II*, 8 May 1922; *FJ*, 8 May 1922; *IT*, 26 May 1922; *FJ*, 26 May 1922; *II*, 26 May 1922; *II*, 27 May 1922; *FJ*, 27 May 1922; *IT*, 27 May 1922; *IT*, 29 May 1922 *FJ*, 29 May 1922; *II*, 29 May 1922; *FJ*, 2 June 1922). See also Phil Tompkins, *Twice a Hero. From the trenches of the Great War to the ditches of the Irish Midlands, 1915-1922* (Cirencester, 2012).

121   *WE*, 6 May 1922.

122 *WI*, 6 May 1922.

123 *FJ*, 1 May 1922.

124 *FJ*, 27 April 1922.

125 *WI*, 6 May 1922.

126 Michael Gallagher, 'The pact general election of 1922', in *Irish Historical Studies*, Vol. 21, No. 84 (1981), pp. 405-406.

127 Townshend, *The Republic*, pp. 398-400; Murray, *Oracles*, pp. 62-63; Hopkinson, *Green against Green*, pp. 105-108.

128 Kissane, *Civil War*, p. 73.

129 Gallagher, 'The pact general election', pp. 412-413.

130 Costello, *Irish Revolution*, pp. 300-301.

131 No vote would have been necessary in the South Roscommon constituency, now redefined as Mayo South-Roscommon South, as the four candidates who stood faced no opposition. Republicans Harry Boland and Thomas Maguire took seats alongside the pro-Treaty Daniel O'Rourke and William Sears.

132 Gallagher, 'The pact general election', p. 406.

133 *WI*, 3 June 1922; *TVL*, 10 June 1922; *WI*, 17 June 1922.

134 *II*, 31 May 1922.

135 Gallagher, 'The pact general election', p. 408.

136 *II*, 13 June 1922; *S.S.*, 17 June 1922; *AC*, 17 June 1922.

137 *IT*, 17 June 1922.

138 Gallagher, 'The pact general election', pp. 415-416.

139 Brian M. Walker (ed.), *Parliamentary Election Results in Ireland, 1918-92* (Dublin, 1992), pp. 104-108.

140 *The Irish Times* and *Freeman's Journal* were supportive of the new government, with the *Irish Independent* considered to require 'much pressure and persuasion' to be of a similar mind (Glandon, *Arthur Griffith*, p. 229).

141 Kissane, *Civil War*, p. 73; Regan, *Myth*, pp. 40-41.

142 Gallagher, 'The pact general election', pp. 414-416.

143 MacEoin's total surplus was 4,395. Lorcan Robbins accounted for the bulk of transfers not apportioned to McGuinness and Ginnell.

144 Lyons' total surplus was 1,396.

145 www.electionsireland.org; Ginnell achieved a total of 6,073 votes, and McGuinness, 5,873 (*WI*, 24 June 1922).

146 Kissane, *Civil War*, pp. 72-73.

147 *II*, 1 July 1922.

148 *FJ*, 22 July 1922.

149 Hopkinson, *Green against Green*, pp. 115-122.

150 Kenneth Griffith and Timothy E. O'Grady, *Curious Journey: An Oral History of Ireland's Unfinished Revolution* (London, 1982), p. 287.

151 Kissane, *Civil War*, pp. 154-155.

152 See John M. Regan, 'Michael Collins, General Commanding-in-Chief, as a Historiographical Problem', in *History*, Vol. 92, No. 307 (July, 2007), pp. 318-346.

153 Kissane, *Civil War*, p. 133.

154 Kissane, *Civil War*, p. 77.

155 UCDA, O'Malley Papers, P17A/15.

156   *CT*, 1 July 1922; *MG*, 8 July 1922.

157   *IT*, 7 July 1922; *IT*, 11 July 1922.

158   *WI* , 8 July 1922.

159   UCDA, O'Malley Papers, P17A/15, Con Maloney AG to Oscar Traynor, OC
      Dublin Brigade, 9 July 1922; Hopkinson, *Green against Green*, p. 156.

160   UCDA, Mulcahy Papers, P7/B/22, 23 July 1922.

161   UCDA, O'Malley Papers, P17A/60, Con Maloney to Ernie O'Malley,
      13 July 1922.

162   Hopkinson, *Green against Green*, p. 156, 158; *FJ*, 13 July 1922.

163   *Poblacht na hÉireann – War News*, 16 July 1922; *Observer,* 16 July 1922; *NYT*,
      16 July 1922; *AC*, 22 July 1922; Younger, *Ireland's Civil War*, p. 361-3.

164   UCDA, Mulcahy Papers, P7/B/22, 23 July 1922.

165   NAI, Department of Finance, Fin 1/1886.

166   *TVL*, 29 October 1921; *TVL*, 21 January 1922; *WI*, 8 July 1922.

167   *CT*, 1 July 1922; *II*, 18 July 1922; *II*, 21 July 1922.

168   *II*, 28 July 1922.

169   Kissane, *Civil War*, pp. 80-81.

170   *II*, 29 April 1922.

171   *II*, 2 May 1922.

172   Shots which accompanied the escape attempt appeared to give credence to
      the rumour of an assault (UCDA, Mulcahy Papers, P7/B/74, p. 62).

173   *WI*, 26 August 1922.

174   UCDA, O'Malley Papers, P17A/55, Ernie O'Malley to Liam Lynch,
      24 August 1922; O'Malley Papers, P17A/56, Ernie O'Malley to Liam Lynch,
      3 September 1922.

175   *IT*, 23 August 1922.

176   Laffan, *Resurrection of Ireland*, p. 417.

177   AHL, Minute Book of Athlone UDC, 6 September 1922.

178   *NYT*, 27 August 1922.

179   Laffan, *Resurrection of Ireland*, p. 417.

180   *WI*, 2 September 1922.

181   *IT*, 11 September 1922.

182   MA Captured Documents, Lot 184, 2nd and 4th Western Division IRA
      Documents, 14 September 1922.

183   Neeson, *Civil War*, p. 277.

184   *IT*, 1 September 1922; *IT*, 12 September 1922. The same council later called
      for republicans to disarm and respect a Treaty-compliant constitution (*IT*,
      6 November 1922).

185   Kissane, *Civil War*, pp. 143-144.

186   *Freedom*, 24 September 1922; NLI, Ginnell Papers, Laurence Ginnell TDE
      to Archbishop of Dublin 'Government by Assassination', 14 September 1922.
      In a separate letter in response to an enquiry from a supposed constituent,
      Ginnell went into great detail as to why he opposed the Treaty and the
      current state of Irish politics. He explained that he could not sit in an
      'English-made Partition Parliament, which has enacted the torture, murder
      and transportation of Irish Republican prisoners and which calls for fewer

prisoners and more corpses'. He accused the Irish Government of being 'fools or knaves, who have fallen victim … to English wiles'. He stated that the Irish delegates accepted the treaty '… in a weak moment … under threats of a terrible and immediate war of extermination … under duress they disobeyed their instructions and violated their oaths'. On the topic of the IRA's apparently ineffective opposition to the Treaty, Ginnell believed that many had lost their faith and could not continue to fight, though remained loyal to the 'legitimate authority only'. Ginnell also complained about the failure of the pre-election pact that had been drawn up between Collins and de Valera and how the English government forced it down '… and their Irish creatures obeyed'. Describing the Treaty as '… more deadly than the Act of Union', Ginnell stated that acceptance of the Treaty confirmed '… the definite consummation of the subjugation of Ireland by England'. This letter was printed independently by Ginnell and distributed in his constituency; he had no faith in the local press printing it, or indeed any of his views on the Treaty, given the hold the pro-Treaty forces had over the Irish media (NLI, Ginnell Papers, Laurence Ginnell, 'Where Lies the Blame?').

187   MacEoin had ordered '£1,191 odd' to be spent on furnishing his new abode. Apparently greatly influenced by his new wife, he had requested many imported goods such as Windsor chairs and Axminster carpets as well as Chesterfield presses (NAI, Dept. of Finance, Fin 1/612, 12 September 1922).

188   UCDA, MacEoin Papers, P151/163, 15 September 1922.

189   *The Fenian*, 13 September 1922; *Republican War Bulletin*, 15 October 1922; *PhÉWN*, 7 November 1922; *An Phoblacht* (Scot. Ed.), 6 January 1923.

190   *PhÉWN*, 3 August 1922.

191   UCDA, Mulcahy Papers, P7/B/75, pp. 36-38.

192   UCDA, Mulcahy Papers, P7/B/74, pp. 154-156, 163, 22 September 1922; UCDA, Mulcahy Papers, P7/B/75, p. 38.

193   UCDA, O'Malley Papers, P17A/56, Ernie O'Malley to Liam Lynch, 9 September 1922.

194   UCDA, O'Malley Papers, P17A/56, Liam Lynch to Ernie O'Malley, 18 September 1922.

195   Coleman, *Longford*, pp. 144-145.

196   UCDA, O'Malley Papers, P17A/57, Ernie O'Malley to Liam Lynch, 24 September 1922.

197   UCDA, O'Malley Papers, P17A/57, Ernie O'Malley to Con Moloney, 30 September 1922.

198   Kissane, *Civil War*, p. 99.

199   UCDA, O'Malley Papers, P17A/64, Liam Lynch to Ernie O'Malley, 5 October 1922.

200   UCDA, O'Malley Papers, P17A/64, Mick Price to Ernie O'Malley, 5 October 1922.

201   Hart, *IRA at War*, p. 41.

202   UCDA, P17A/56 O'Malley Papers, Ernie O'Malley to Liam Deasy (OC 1st Southern Division), 9 September 1922.

203   Hopkinson, *Green against Green*, p. 180, 185-188.

204 Laurence Ginnell, *Dáil Debates 1, cols 8-13, 9 September 1922*; *TNL*, 16 September 1922; *Freedom*, 17 September 1922.

205 Neeson, *Civil War*, p. 267.

206 *TF*, 11 September 1922.

207 *PhÉWN*, 14 September 1922.

208 Garvin, *1922*, p. 39.

209 Hopkinson, *Green against Green*, p. 180.

210 Costello, *Irish Revolution*, pp. 315-316; Garvin, *1922*, pp. 140, 163.

211 Neeson, *Civil War*, p. 272-274; Younger, *Ireland's Civil War*, pp. 476-478.

212 Kissane, *Civil War*, p. 87.

213 Garvin, *1922*, p. 53; Kissane, *Civil War*, pp. 88, 91.

214 O'Halpin, *Defending Ireland*, p. 31.

215 Murray, *Oracles*, pp. 75-78.

216 Murray, *Oracles*, p. 88.

217 Kissane, *Civil War*, pp. 89-90.

218 See Dorothy Macardle, *The Irish Republic* (5th edition, London, 1968), pp. 705-738.

219 NAI, Dept. of Finance Records, Fin1/788, Fin 1/793, Fin 1/815, Fin 1/816; Garvin*, 1922*, p. 101.

220 *WI*, 9 September 1922.

221 MA, Captured Documents, Lot 184, 2nd and 4th Western Division IRA Documents.

222 *PhÉWN*, 21 September 1922.

223 Hopkinson, *Green against Green*, p. 212.

224 *IT*, 30 October 1922; *IT*, 1 December 1922; *II*, 1 December 1922; *Iris an Airm*, 4 December 1922.

225 *IT*, 7 December 1922.

226 UCDA, Twomey Papers, P69/30, p.202.

227 UCDA, Twomey Papers, P69/30, p. 81.

228 UCDA, O'Malley Papers, P17A/65, OC 3rd Brigade 1st Eastern Division Athlone to Ernie O'Malley, 30 October 1922.

229 Hopkinson, *Green against Green*, pp. 91-92;,140.

230 *II*, 30 September 1922.

231 Garvin, *1922*, p. 109. Two local men enlisted the assistance of the UDC in an attempt to stake their claim to a local berth in the Guard (AHL, Minute Book of Athlone UDC, 20 September 1922).

232 Garvin, *1922*, pp. 108, 113.

233 *WI*, 21 October 1922.

234 MA, Military Operations Report (MOR), Athlone, 5 November 1922.

235 Garvin, *1922*, pp. 110-111; Younger, *Ireland's Civil War*, pp. 482-484.

236 PRONI, T/2782/38, Cecilia H. Daniels to Mrs. Flett, Australia, 21 October 1922.

237 PRONI, T/2782/38, Cecilia H. Daniels to Mrs. Flett, Australia, 21 October 1922.; MA, MOR, Athlone, 9 November 1922; MA, MOR, Athlone, 10 November 1922.

238 *FJ*, 7 November 1922; *II*, 7 November 1922; *WI*, 11 November 1922; *WE*,

11 November 1922; *IA*, 14 November 1922.

239   *CT*, 25 November 1922.

240   Hopkinson, *Green against Green*, pp. 63-64, 136-138.

241   UCDA, Mulcahy Papers, P7/B/75, 22 November 1922, p. 6. One of the reports that Lawlor submitted attempted to quantify the support for the Free State Army on the basis on some local men shouting supportive slogans for MacEoin. Mulcahy, it seems, required something rather more substantial (Mulcahy Papers, P7/B/75, 22 November 1922, p. 8).

242   *II*, 23 November 1922; *FJ*, 23 November 1922; *WI*, 25 November 1922.

243   UCDA, Mulcahy Papers, P7/B/23; Mulcahy Papers, P7/B/74; *WI*, 11 November 1922; *WI*, 2 December 1922; *WI*, 20 January 1923, *WI*, 27 January 1923.

244   *IT*, 6 November 1922; Kissane, *Civil War*, pp. 146-148.

245   *WI*, 11 November 1922; *WI*, 2 December 1922.

246   UCDA, Mulcahy Papers, P7/B/74, p. 126; *II*, 9 December 1922.

247   *Freedom* 29 November 1922.

248   *PhÉWN*, 7 November 1922.

249   Of the girls used, many had never been members of Athlone's Cumann na mBan, which was said to be very disorganised. The Moss Twomey Papers relate that the activity of the organisation's midland branches '… has been confined to scrapping among [themselves] for positions and notoriety with the result that many good workers left the organisation, preferring to assist the army as individuals. It is these people the IRA use at present (UCDA, Twomey Papers, P69/56, p.42-3). The 'few irresponsible girls' that worked for the IRA were able to exploit the aversion soldiers maintained to searching women.

250   UCDA, MacEoin Papers, P151/220/22.

251   *II*, 9 December 1922; *FJ*, 23 December 1922; *II*, 23 December 1922.

252   *II*, 9 December 1922; *FJ*, 9 December 1922; *WI*, 20 December 1922.

253   Hopkinson, *Green against Green*, p. 216.

254   *Freedom*, 1 November 1922.

255   *Freedom*, 22 November 1922.

256   *AP* (S.ed.), 18 November 1922; *AP* (S.ed.), 6 January 1923; *RWB.*, 15 October 1922; *RWB*, 19 October 1922; Hopkinson, *Green against Green*, p. 216.

257   *RWB*, 19 October 1922. A number of publications would later accuse MacEoin of shooting a man dead at the Longford races in a fit of pique (*Straight Talk*, 28 Dec 1922; *PhÉWN*, 21 December 1922; *AP* (S.ed.), 6 January 1923).

258   *PhÉWN*, 11 November 1922.

259   Younger, *Ireland's Civil War*, pp. 492-493; Hopkinson, *Green against Green*, p. 192.

260   NAI, 1369/20, Dept. of the Taoiseach, 20 March 1923.

261   *FJ*, 30 December 1922; *WI*, 6 January 1923; UCDA, Mulcahy Papers, P7/B/214, p.12; *IT*, 29 March 1923; *IT*, 4 April 1923.

262   *WI,* 27 January 1923.

263   *IT*, 12 March 1923.

264   A reference to Bolsheviks, i.e., in this context, pro-Treaty Labour supporters.

265   *WI*, 3 February 1923.

266   UCDA, MacEoin Papers, P151/194.

267 *SI*, 21 January 1923; *MG*, 22 January 1923; *FJ*, 22 Jan 1923; *IT*, 27 January 1923; *II*, 31 January 1923.

268 *II*, 31 March 1923; *WI*, 3 February 1923.

269 Kissane, *Civil War*, pp. 92-93.

270 *WI*, 3 February 1923.

271 Kissane, *Civil War*, p. 112.

272 *IT*, 8 February 1923; *II*, 8 February 1922; *WI*, 10 February 1923; *MG*, 10 February 1923; *SS*, 10 February 1923.

273 *PhÉWN*, 7 March 1923.

274 *WI*, 3 March 1923.

275 UCDA, Mulcahy Papers, P7/B/216, pp. 18-19. The UDC set up a temporary water supply soon after and the army provided a guard to ensure no interference. The cost of the damage to the original waterworks was estimated at £3,000 (*FJ*, 9 February, 1923; *II*, 9 February 1923; *WI*, 10 February 1923; *WI*, 17 February 1923; *WE*, 17 February 1922; MA, MOR, Athlone, 7 February 1923; AHL, Minute Book of Athlone UDC, 9 February 1923).

276 *LO*, 3 March 1923.

277 NAI, Fin 1/2571, Dept. of Finance; Fin 1/2988, Dept. of Finance.

278 NAI, Fin 1/1028, Dept. of Finance.

279 Kissane, *Civil War*, pp. 147-148.

280 *IT*, 22 March 1923.

281 *IT*, 5 May 1923.

282 *WI*, 31 March 1923.

283 MA, MOR, Athlone, 8 March 1923.

284 *WI*, 17 March 1923; *WI*, 17 February 1923; MA, MOR, Athlone, 12 March 1923. An additional bridge was also targeted on the Athlone/ Longford line (UCDA, Twomey Papers, P69/30, 22 March 1923, p. 154).

285 Laffan, *Resurrection of Ireland*, pp. 414-415.

286 AHL, Minute Book of Athlone UDC, 21 March 1923.

287 *WI*, 17 March 1923; *WI*, 31 March 1923.

288 BMHWS No. 1,500, Anthony McCormack, p. 14.

289 MA, MOR, Athlone, 6 March 1923; MOR, Athlone, 23 March 1923.

290 MA, MOR, Athlone, 8 March 1923.

291 *IT*, 29 March 1923; *WI*, 31 March 1923.

292 MA, MOR, Athlone, 23 March 1923.

293 *IT*, 23 March 1923.

294 *WI*, 7 April 1923.

295 UCDA, Mulcahy Papers, P7/B/216, 7 April 1923; *IT*, 7 April 1923; *FJ*, 7 April 1923; *SI*, 8 April 1923.

296 *IT*, 10 May 1923; UCDA, MacEoin Papers, P155/228/1, 19 June-13 July 1923.

297 MA, MOR, Athlone, 11 April 1923.

298 UCDA, Twomey Papers, P69/30, p. 85, 9 May 1923.

299 MA, MOR, Athlone, 2 April 1923; MA, MOR, Athlone, 9 April 1923.

300 *FJ*, 23 March 1923.

301 MA, MOR, Athlone, 12 April 1923; MOR, Athlone, 17 April 1923; MOR,

Athlone, 19 April 1923; MOR, Athlone, 23 April 1923.

302 UCDA, MacEoin Papers, P151/220/53, 19 April 1923.

303 *WI*, 21 April 1923.

304 *WI,* 12 May 1923; *WI,* 26 May 1923.

305 MA, MOR, Athlone, 12 May 1923; MOR, Athlone, 18 May 1923; UCDA, MacEoin Papers, P151/220/53, 19 April 1923.

306 MA, MOR, Athlone, 2 May 1923.

307 Unsurprisingly, it was recommended that he be removed (UCDA, MacEoin Papers, P155/220/23, 5 June 1923).

308 *II*, 24 April 1923.

309 Kissane, *Civil War*, pp. 116-122; Neeson, *Civil War*, p. 265.

310 Hopkinson, *Green against Green*, pp. 237-238.

311 Costello, *Irish Revolution*, p. 317, Garvin, *1922*, p. 165.

312 Kissane, *Civil War*, p. 121.

313 Garvin, *1922*, pp. 121, 164.

314 Neeson, *Civil War*, p. 88.

315' Hopkinson, *Green against Green*, p. 263.

316 Garvin, *1922*, p. 135.

317 *IT*, 25 August 1923.

318 www.oireachtas.ie/members-hist.

319 Costello, *Irish Revolution*, p. 318.

320 One incongruous report from August stated that morale was good and 'going on apace' (UCDA, MacEoin Papers, p151/220/35, 30 August 1923).

321 Hopkinson, *Green against Green*, pp. 268-271.

322 MA, MOR, Athlone, 26 October 1923.

323 MA, Captured Documents, Lot 66, Seán Costello Papers.

324 UCDA, Twomey Papers, P.69/88, 23 March 1924, p. 4; p. 10; P.69/90, 9 April 1924, p. 30; P.69/90, 9 April 1924, p. 31.

Index